ECONOMY, DIFFERENCE, EMPIRE

Columbia Series on Religion and Politics

The Columbia Series on Religion and Politics, edited by Gastón Espinosa (Clare-mont McKenna College) and Chester Gillis (Georgetown University), addresses the growing demand for scholarship on the intersection of religion and politics in a world in which religion attempts to influence politics and politics regularly must consider the effects of religion. The series examines the influence religion exercises in public life on areas including politics, environmental policy, social policy, law, church-state relations, foreign policy, race, class, gender, and culture. Written by experts in a variety of fields, the series explores the historical and contemporary intersection of religion and politics in the United States and globally.

Mark Hulsether, *Religion, Culture, and Politics in the Twentieth-Century United States*

Gastón Espinosa, editor, *Religion and the American Presidency: George Washington to George W. Bush with Commentary and Primary Sources*

Richard B. Miller, *Terror, Religion, and Liberal Social Criticism*

Economy, Difference, Empire

Social Ethics for Social Justice

GARY DORRIEN

Columbia University Press
New York

Columbia University Press
Publishers Since 1893
New York   Chichester, West Sussex
Copyright © 2010 Columbia University Press
All rights reserved
Library of Congress Cataloging-in-Publication Data
Dorrien, Gary J.
Economy, difference, empire : social ethics for social justice / Gary Dorrien.
p.   cm.—(The Columbia series on religion and politics)
Includes bibliographical references and index.
ISBN 978-0-231-14984-6 (cloth : alk. paper) — ISBN 978-0-231-52629-6 (ebook)
1. United States—Social conditions—21st century.   2. Social ethics—United
States.   3. Social justice—United States.   I. Title   II. Series.
HN59.2.D67 2010
303.3'72097309045—dc22
2010006605
∞
References to Internet Web sites (URLs) were accurate at the time of writing. Neither
the author nor Columbia University Press is responsible for URLs that may have
expired or changed since the manuscript was prepared.

For James F. Jones, Jr.

Cherished friend and educational leader

CONTENTS

INTRODUCTION

This book is a four-pronged collection of lectures and essays on social justice and progressive Christian social ethics. As the title suggests, it has three main subjects—economic democracy, racial and gender justice, and U.S. American empire—plus a fourth subject, the tradition of social ethical discourse out of which I approach the other subjects.

The ethical injunctions to lift the yoke of oppression and build a just order are stated emphatically in the Bible, although much of historic Christianity managed not to notice. Modern social ethics has done better at taking seriously the injunctions, but not without disagreeing about how to relate ethical values to the social order and which ones to favor. This book makes arguments about where modern Christianity has been and where it should go in addressing these issues.

The book is organized by two sets of threes, plus a fourth component. Just as the subject matter features three social ethical topics, plus social ethics itself, the book's social ethical frame features the three major traditions of U.S. American social ethics, plus the neoconservative challenge to them. The major traditions are social gospel progressivism, Niebuhrian realism, and liberationism. My method is to tie together the descriptive "about" and the normative "should," fusing historical analysis with arguments about the social ethical necessity of social justice politics and why the history matters. In the book's opening section on the social gospel and Niebuhrian foundations of social Christianity, the featured subjects are economic justice, war and militarism, and racial justice. The rest of book builds on this trinity of concerns, featuring discussions of economic democracy as a social justice strategy, neoconservatism and American empire, and racial and gender justice.

The idea that Christianity has a mission to transform the structures of society in the direction of social justice is distinctly modern, as it is a product of the social gospel movement described in chapter 1. Since Reinhold Niebuhr is by far the most influential social ethicist of the past hundred years, this book contains two chapters dealing with his thought and legacy and a third comparing Niebuhr and evangelist Billy Graham on racial justice. The third major tradition of social ethics, liberationist social criticism, is discussed briefly in section 2 and extensively in section 4. American social ethics in its three major traditions and in numerous offshoots has been known for taking up political issues at the level of theory, practice, and sometimes both mixed together, often hazarding judgments about specific policies and politicians. Niebuhr's books were notable examples of social ethical mixing, while his articles for *Christianity and Society* and *Christianity and Crisis* got very specific about policies and politicians.

This book is similarly immersed in politics and hazardous judgments. Chapters 8 and 9 are the centerpiece of the volume, reflecting my longtime engagement with economic globalization and economic democracy, now in the context of a global economic meltdown and the challenges facing Barack Obama's administration. Nearly as central to the book's framework and constructive perspective are my chapters on foreign policy anti-imperialism, especially chapters 12 and 13, and my articles on Obama's historic presidential candidacy and election, most of which are collected in chapter 18, though some of my campaign speaking and writing is folded into chapter 8. The book's final chapter, my inaugural lecture as the Reinhold Niebuhr Professor at Union Theological Seminary, ties together the book's main arguments and themes.

A book featuring the words "social justice" in the title needs to say something about it as a category. "Justice," the idea of each getting what she or he is due, had a rich history in Western philosophy and theology long b   modern socialists gave currency to the term "social justice."
          ce is procedural, having to do with the impartial and con-
          ation of principles. Retributive justice is housed mainly in
          nd deals with the justification of punishment. Commutative
          ined mainly in civil law and deals with the relationships
          society to one another. Distributive justice considers the

whole in relation to its parts, dealing principally with the fairness of the distribution of resources. The Protestant social gospelers who embraced the term "social justice" in the late nineteenth century had distributive justice chiefly in mind, as did subsequent Catholic social ethicists. Social justice was principally about the fair distribution of social goods, which could be conceived either through a theory of rights or of right order, and which could be in accordance with needs (as in socialism), or the greatest good for the greatest number (utilitarianism), or the common good (the usual social gospel option).

The socialist background of social justice rhetoric showed through even among mainstream social gospel thinkers who rejected socialism, such as Shailer Mathews and Francis Greenwood Peabody. Surely, they believed, modernity had a stage beyond capitalism. If modernity was a good thing, which they emphatically believed, it *had* to have a stage beyond capitalism. Virtually all social gospelers, not just the radical socialist ones, took for granted that capitalism was too predatory and selfish to be compatible with social justice. Reinhold Niebuhr assumed the same thing even as he blasted the social gospel for its liberal idealism and rationalism. In his early realist phase Niebuhr treated equality as the sole regulative principle of justice, an echo of the command to love thy neighbor as thyself. In his later career he added freedom and order as regulative principles of justice, conceiving justice as right ordering. Social justice is an application of the law of love to the sociopolitical sphere, Niebuhr argued, and love is the motivating energy of the struggle for justice. But love is not the goal or highest good in politics, nor can the meaning of social justice be taken directly from the regulative principles. For Niebuhrian realism, the meaning of justice was determined only in the interaction of love and situation, through the mediation of the principles of freedom, equality, and order (or balance of power), and politics was fundamentally a struggle for power.

The third major tradition of social ethics, liberationism, shares the social gospel concern with just distribution and the Niebuhrian emphasis on power politics, but not the social gospel idealism about the common good or Niebuhr's conservative and American nationalist tendencies. In liberation theology, social justice has to do with giving voice to oppressed communities and being liberated from structures of oppression and dependency. Oppression is multifaceted, concrete, and particular. It does not reduce to concerns about the fair distribution of things, nor is it best approached or understood within a universal theory of justice. Racism, sexism, exploitation, cultural imperialism, violence, and exclusion all involve social structures and relations that include, but also transcend, problems of distributive justice. Thus, in liberationist forms of social ethics and social criticism, social justice is fundamentally about overthrowing domination and oppression.

Each of these discourse traditions features something crucial to my understanding of social justice. I do not give up the social gospel emphasis on the common good, which has centuries of Christian moral theology behind it and is indispensable on environmental issues, and I do not give up the social ethical idealism that fired the social gospel activism of Walter Rauschenbusch, Jane Addams, and Reverdy Ransom. For these reasons I side with the right order tradition in justice theory, which is more relational and solidaristic than the justice-as-rights view, but I share the social gospel conviction that the way beyond liberalism is through it, taking as foundational the rights of individuals to freedom of speech, association, preference, and the like, and the liberal emphasis on equality of opportunity.

For me the principle of equality is central, and there is no equality of individual opportunity without approximate equality of condition. When your zip code is a highly reliable indicator of your life chances, as it is in the USA, your society is short on equal opportunity. The early Niebuhr took this truism more seriously than the later one, which is the main reason I prefer the early Niebuhr. But I accept Niebuhr's later stress on freedom and order as regulative concepts, his critique of rationalism and idealistic moralism, and his profound emphasis on the limiting realities of human selfishness and the will-to-power of organizations.

Niebuhr's realism was too dispositional to yield a general theory of justice, a point in his favor from a liberationist perspective. But liberationist criticism rightly judges that the social gospel and Christian realism were too white, male-dominated, socially privileged, and nationalistic to produce anything more than a provincial politics of social justice, including its account of the "realities" of politics and society. With the rise of black liberationist and feminist forms of social criticism in the 1970s, business as usual ended in social ethics. Social justice did not reduce to distributional issues; race, gender, and sexuality were fundamental sites of oppression; and social ethics was not about "speaking for those who cannot speak for themselves," the standard progressive aspiration. For me, liberationist criticism does not negate the social gospel and realist traditions, but it does adjudicate what I take from these traditions and it transforms fundamental assumptions about what social ethics should be was discredited by the neo-orthodox reaction, especially Karl Barth and Reinhold Niebuhr. Reading Rauschenbusch, I could see various problems; he loved idealistic rhetoric, said nothing about racial justice, and seemed to regard his anti-Catholic prejudice as a virtue. But for grasping and expressing the prophetic core of the gospel, Rauschenbusch soared above everyone except King. *Christianity and the Social Crisis* settled the question of what I would do with my life, though I waited six years to join a church.

In the meantime I befriended the closest thing to a mentor or role model I have ever had, socialist intellectual and activist Michael Harrington. In college I wrote a senior thesis on Marxist social theory, which prompted my adviser, Dave Lemmon, to remark that I sounded like Michael Harrington, a Democratic Socialist and lapsed Catholic. Had Harrington influenced me? No, I had never heard of Harrington, but within two weeks I had read all five of his books and found a political lodestar.

The following fall I was a graduate student at Harvard, where Harrington gave a speech urging students to launch a chapter of his new organization, the Democratic Socialist Organizing Committee (DSOC). A handful of us founded Harvard DSOC; three years later, in 1977, I launched a chapter at Union Theological Seminary; and in subsequent years I joined a highly intellectual chapter at Princeton University and co-founded a thriving one in Albany, New York. I also served on national boards of DSOC and its successor organization, Democratic Socialists of America.

Like his great predecessor, Norman Thomas, Harrington was a buoyant activist and captivating speaker who poured himself out for all manner of social justice causes and tried to make socialism speak American. Like Thomas, he was anti-utopian, freedom-loving, ethical, humanistic, and democratic. Unlike Thomas, Harrington considered himself a Marxist, which sometimes got in the way of communicating that he was anti-utopian, freedom-loving, ethical, and the rest. For an old left Social Democrat like Harrington, having Marx on your side was an existential and ideological necessity; you didn't let your left-totalitarian foes lay claim to Marx wrongly or let your right-wing foes smear him with distortions. So Harrington spent many pages trying to convince readers that Marx agreed with him, and in one of my early books I spent many pages showing that some of these arguments were sound, some were ambiguous, some were dubious, and others were flat wrong. This book revisits some of that terrain and also includes a chapter on Thomas.

Harrington was steeped in the visceral anticommunism of old left social democracy, but by the late 1960s he had cut loose from the militantly
cold war side of that tradition and joined the anti-Vietnam War movement. In the early 1970s he coined the term "neoconservative" as an act
of dissociation from former allies that hated the antiwar movement. A bit
later, while the neocons streamed into the Republican Party, he tried to
build up the social democratic wing of the Democratic Party. Harrington
realized that his strategy of working in the Democratic Party was frustrating and demoralizing to many progressives, especially those who longed
for purity in their politics. He replied that it was pointless to wait for a
third party; zero successes since 1860 was a chastening record. He accepted that his main public role was to provide lecture-touring inspiration
for demoralized progressives, which he provided dutifully. But after the
lecture was over and Heineken time had commenced at a hotel bar, Mike
could be bleak about the fate of social justice in his country.

Often when we were together in a relaxed setting he picked an argument with me about religion or Marx or both. By then I was an Episcopal
priest serving a parish and teaching at an ecumenical school in Albany,
and I did a great deal of speaking for Latin American solidarity organizations, in addition to Mike's organization. Mike liked having religious types
like Cornel West, Rosemary Radford Ruether, Harvey Cox, Joe Holland,
Maxine Phillips, Michael Eric Dyson, John C. Cort, Juanita Webster,
Norm Faramelli, and me in his organization, yet it gnawed at him that
we stuck with Christianity. Many times he would get started on the subject, almost get into it, and then shut down; we were done with religion
for that day. Marx and Freud had set Mike straight about religion, and
he wasn't really interested in rethinking that business, much as it gnawed
at him. More important, it depressed him to think, as I assured him, that
religion had a stronger future than socialism.

In the early 1970s the social ethics position at the University of Chicago Divinity School became available, and the faculty discussed offering
it to Harrington. His book *The Accidental Century* was a gem of social
criticism, they noted; his book *Socialism* was a major scholarly work; and
his book *The Other America* was famous for "launching the war on poverty." Mike's atheism gave them only slight pause, but the question arose
whether he could teach social ethics or would even know what it was. A
pro-Harrington faction argued that he would be asked to teach the sort of
thing he wrote. Surely that was social ethics, whatever social ethics was.

But this argument was too unsettling to prevail, and Harrington ended up teaching at Queens College in New York. A year before Mike's death, I spoke at Chicago, heard the story from Divinity School dean Franklin Gamwell, and relayed it to Mike. He lit up with delight: "Can you imagine me as a divinity professor?" Actually I could.

I have spent much of my career writing and speaking about economic democracy, so my debt to Michael Harrington is rather large, though it was Rauschenbusch that started me on this path. As Harrington is also the one that tagged the neoconservative phenomenon, my debt is larger yet. But I noticed neoconservatism before I met Mike, at just about the time that he named it, when I was a college student. *Commentary* magazine, in particular, got my attention, especially its extensive letters section.

Every month I anticipated the next issue with appalled fascination. I was immersed in progressive theology and politics, which prized ecumenical dialogue and inclusiveness. *Commentary* was nothing like that. It blasted feminism, the antiwar movement, Black Power, political liberalism, and the ecumenical churches ferociously. It did not say that some feminists went too far; it said that all feminists were pathetic and ridiculous. The magazine was about demolishing opponents, not dialoguing with them. Most fascinating was that nearly everybody who wrote for *Commentary* was a former leftist or still claimed to be one.

How had that happened? Who were these people that wrote such fiercely knowing polemics against people I admired? Without the conversion story, I would not have been hooked by the new conservatism. As it was, I was already something of an expert on it when the neocons streamed out of the Democratic Party to become Ronald Reagan's foreign policy braintrust. My first book on neoconservatism, which was published just after the Soviet Union imploded, analyzed where neoconservatism had come from, how it had succeeded politically, why it was fading, and why its imperial ambitions were the key to its future as a political movement. Ten years later, after George W. Bush and the neocons invaded Iraq, I wrote a book on the wreckage caused by the movement's imperial ambitions. Part 3 of this book contains capsule versions of both stories, plus two lectures on the consequences of the Iraq War and the way beyond it.

My commitment to feminism runs deeper in my personal experience than the other subjects mentioned here, because I had a mother whose conflicted puzzlement and occasional rage at her circumstances made a profound impact on me. My earliest memories of understanding anything have to do with grasping her disappointment at missing her chance not to be poor, dependent, and lacking a college education. The imprint of this experience on my psyche made me ripe for feminism as soon as it arose.

In college I had a simple understanding of it as the imperative of equal rights for women and the liberalization of gender roles. Feminism was political and cultural, having to do with the Equal Rights Amendment, sexist attitudes in American society, and social policies on child care and parental leave. To the extent that feminism applied to religion, it was about the right of women to be ordained and accepted as church leaders. The idea of feminist theology—applying feminist criticism to Christian doctrine—was just beginning to germinate.

I entered divinity school just as feminist theology became a movement. Feminism was not merely a liberal reform, it turned out, but a revolution of consciousness. In my first week of divinity school I read Mary Daly's *Beyond God the Father* (1973) in one sitting, stunned by the book's apocalyptic ferocity. Two days later I read it again, this time catching more of its scathing Nietzschean humor. A month later I knew much of it by memory.[1]

The parallels between Daly's radical feminist vision and the Black Power theology of James Cone were obvious, but Daly's book hit me harder emotionally. In college I had studied Cone intently, memorizing sections of *Black Theology and Black Power* (1969) and *A Black Theology of Liberation* (1970); I also persuaded Alma College to bring Cone to campus for a day of lecturing and discussion. But I had spent years preparing for Cone's blistering attack on racism. I understood American history primarily through the lens of slavery and racism before Cone taught me to interrogate the racist history of theology.[2]

Daly's book and the radical feminists I met in Boston struck a similar chord for which I was less prepared. Daly called radical feminism "the ultimate revolution" and the "cause of causes." She argued that until radical feminists had enough physical and psychic separation from males to think out of their own existence, it was not even possible to say what a radical feminist ethic would be like.[3]

Beyond God the Father stopped just short of claiming that Christianity was inherently oppressive or that male evil was hopelessly unredeemable. Daly's feminism was not yet explicitly post-Christian. Her case for women's-space seemed right to me as a situational necessity, but the book teetered on the edge of three disastrous moves, strongly suggesting she would not stop there. Ethically, it raised the question of dehumanizing males as a class; politically, it seemed to promote antipolitical separatism as a way of life, not a survival tactic; religiously, it conjured a new species of Gnostic dualism and otherworldliness.

Daly's subsequent writings dispensed with teetering on these points. *Gyn/Ecology: The Metaethics of Radical Feminism* (1978) described patriarchy as the homeland of the male sex, civilization as a misogynistic conspiracy of the male sex, culture as the male regime of rape and genocide that supported male civilization, and radical feminism as "absolutely Anti-androcrat, A-mazingly Anti-male, Furiously and Finally Female." Patriarchy, "the prevailing religion of the entire planet," was the same everywhere, she contended; the various world religions and ideologies were merely variations of the universal patriarchal drive to extinguish women's original surge of life. Her subsequent books ventured deeply into what she called "Cronespace" or "The Realm of the Wild," citing occult literature for support, contending that the aim of Christianity was to annihilate female power and spirit.[4] Since the feminist awakening was too powerful for liberal denominations to ignore, they placated it by ordaining female ministers and priests, which retarded the awakening. Daly exhorted women not to join "the processions of priestly predators."[5]

Daly was the first major feminist theologian, though she eventually spurned the word "feminism" as hopelessly ruined. To her the biblical story of the fall was fundamentally a myth of feminine evil, an example of cosmic false naming that metamorphosed the viewpoint of women-hating men into God's viewpoint. Truly liberating feminism indwelt the metamorphic power of words and female energy, she urged; it imagined ultimate reality as verb, the original surge of life, reclaiming women's elemental powers.

For my generation of divinity students, sorting out one's relationship to Daly-style feminism was a personal necessity, and often a vocational one. For many readers Daly's blend of scathing critique, imaginative wordplay, and leaps into cronespace were intensely exciting; she possessed an inspired capacity to open new worlds of experience. For many others it was imperative to identify the point at which a bracing critique of Christian myth veered into anti-intellectual sectarianism and witchcraft.

My beloved partner, Brenda Biggs, a Presbyterian pastor, was in the latter group. Brenda loved Daly's first book, *The Church and the Second Sex*; she liked half of *Beyond God the Father*; and when she saw me poring over any of the others, she had a tendency to erupt. Brenda roared for Christian feminism through the sixteen years of church ministry that were given to her. Though she never read my books, she was always eager to assess a gestating sermon or lecture, shredding trade jargon mercilessly. This book contains sections she would have recognized, as some of these chapters had to pass through her before being heard by anyone.

As most of these chapters began as lectures, and some morphed into more than a dozen versions continuously updated on the lecture trail, my acknowledgments could go on for several pages. Here I will limit myself to a handful of friends and occasions that launched a maiden voyage or a major revision of one. Parts of this book were first heard as the D. R. Sharpe Lecture at the University of Chicago Divinity School, with thanks to Franklin Gamwell; the Paul E. Rather Distinguished Scholar Lectures at Trinity College, with thanks to James F. Jones Jr.; the Earl Lectures at Pacific School of Religion, with thanks to Bill McKinney and Delwin Brown; the Lucasse Award Lecture at Kalamazoo College, with thanks to Lawrence Bryan and the college faculty; the Southwest Michigan Phi Beta Kappa Lecture, with thanks to Joe Fugate and the Southwest Michigan Chapter of Phi Beta Kappa; the William Frederick Allen Lectures of the Bayview Chautauqua Society, with thanks to David Scarrow; the Transatlantic Dialogue of the Protestant Academies in Germany Lectures at the Evangelische Akademie Arnoldshain, Germany, with thanks to Franz Grubauer and Gotlind Ulshöfer; the Reinhold Niebuhr Society Lecture at the American Academy of Religion Convention, with thanks to Robin Lovin and Max Stackhouse; the Walter and Mary Brueggeman Lectures at Eden Theological Seminary, with thanks to David Greenhaw; the Summer Lectures of the Highlands Institute for Religious and Philosophical Thought, with thanks to Creighton Peden and E. J. Tarbox; the Afternoon Lecture Series of the Chautauqua Institution, with thanks to Joan Brown Campbell; the General Assembly of the National Council of Churches Keynote Address, with thanks to Michael Kinnamon; the Winslow Lecture at Allegheny College, with thanks to Richard Cook; the Council of Centers on Jewish-Christian Relations Keynote Address, with thanks to Elena Procario-Foley; and the Reinhold Niebuhr Inaugural Lecture at Union Theological Seminary, with thanks to my treasured colleagues at Union Seminary, especially former president Joseph Hough.

Moving to New York gradually recomposed my group of closest friends, though not entirely. In this category I am grateful to the late Forrest Church, James Cone, Esther Hamori, Peter Heltzel, Christian Iosso, James F. Jones, Jr., Serene Jones, Catherine Keller, Becca Kutz-Marks, Chuck Kutz-Marks, Christopher Latiolais, Laura-Packard Latiolais, Carolyn Buck Luce, Eris McClure, Christopher Morse, Donald Shriver, Peggy Shriver, and Cynthia Stravers. I am deeply grateful for the friendship and collegiality of my current doctoral students Lisa Anderson, Malinda Berry, Chloe Breyer, Ian Doescher, Babydoll Kennedy, Jeremy Kirk, Eboni Marshall, David Orr, Dan Rohrer, Gabriel Salguero, Charlene Sinclair, Joe Strife, Rima Vesely-Flad, Colleen Wessel-McCoy, Demian Wheeler, and Michael Wissa, plus a recently graduated doctoral student, Christine Pae. Special thanks go to Jeremy Kirk and Jennifer Heckart for their friendship and exemplary work as teaching assistants, plus Jeremy's generous work in organizing a proofreading team including Nkosi Anderson, Joel Berning, Preston Davis, Jennifer Heckart, Peter Herman, Sara Jane Muratori, David Orr, Elijah Prewitt-Davis, Tracy Riggle, Dan Rohrer, and Charlene Sinclair.

Above all I am grateful to my friends Cornel West and Serene Jones, with whom I co-taught a course and public forum titled "Christianity and the U.S. Crisis" in the spring of 2009 at Union Theological Seminary. Serene, as the new president of Union, and Cornel, as a renowned public intellectual who loves Union, cooked up the idea of what came to be called, locally, "the mega-course," where they engaged in a sparkling discussion of the meaning of it all and I struggled to keep up. Parts of this book were aired throughout the semester.

At Columbia University Press I am grateful to senior executive editor Wendy Lochner, assistant editor Christine Mortlock, series editors Gastón Espinosa and Chester Gillis, and copy editor Rita Bernhard. And once again I am grateful to Diana Witt for a superb index.

ACKNOWLEDGMENTS

Grateful acknowledgment is made to Fortress Press for the right to adapt previously published material from Gary Dorrien, *Soul in Society: The Making and Renewal of Social Christianity* (1995); Temple University Press, for material from Dorrien, *The Neoconservative Mind: Politics, Culture and the War of Ideology* (1993); Routledge, for material from Dorrien, *Imperial Designs: Neoconservatism and the New Pax Americana* (2004); Orbis Books, for material from Dorrien, "The Golden Years of Welfare Capitalism," in *The Twentieth Century: A Theological Overview*, ed. Gregory Baum (1999); Westminster John Knox Press, for material from Dorrien, *The Making of American Liberal Theology: Imagining Progressive Religion* (2001); Westminster John Knox Press, for material from Dorrien, *The Making of American Liberal Theology: Idealism, Realism, and Modernity* (2003); Westminster John Knox Press, for material from Dorrien, *The Making of American Liberal Theology: Crisis, Irony, and Postmodernity* (2006); Westminster John Knox Press, for material from Dorrien, "Social Salvation: The Social Gospel as Theology and Economics," in *The Social Gospel Today*, ed. Christopher H. Evans (2001); Westminster John Knox Press, for material from Dorrien, "Niebuhr and Graham: Modernity, White Supremacism, Justice, Ambiguity," in *The Legacy of Billy Graham*, ed. Michael G. Long (2008); *Religion & Ethics Newsweekly*, a PBS production of Thirteen/WNET New York, for material from Dorrien, "Yes We Can . . . Change the Subject?" (August 26, 2008), "Visible Man Rising" (September 2, 2008), "Impulsive Distractions" (September 3, 2008), "Back to the Subject" (September 9, 2008), and "Taking Social Investment Seriously" (December 12, 2008); Wiley-Blackwell, for material from Dorrien, *Social Ethics in the Making* (2009); Rowman & Littlefield, for material from Dorrien, *The Democratic Socialist Vision* (1986); *Tikkun: A Bimonthly Interfaith Critique of Politics, Culture, and Society*, for material from Dorrien, "A Case for Economic Democracy" (May/June 2009); and the *Christian Century*, for material from Dorrien, "The Other American" (October 11, 2000), "Grand Illusion: Costs of War and Empire" (December 26, 2006), "Hope or Hype?" (May 29, 2007), "Financial Collapse" (December 28, 2008), and "Health Care Fix: The Role of a Public Option" (July 14, 2009).

ECONOMY, DIFFERENCE, EMPIRE

Part I

The Social Gospel and Niebuhrian Realism

Chapter 1

Society as the Subject of Redemption

WASHINGTON GLADDEN, WALTER RAUSCHENBUSCH, AND THE SOCIAL GOSPEL

The idea that Christianity has a regenerative social mission is rooted in the biblical message of letting justice flow like a river, pouring yourself out for the poor and vulnerable, and attending to what Jesus called the "weightier matters of the law," justice and mercy. But the idea that Christianity has a social mission to transform the structures of society in the direction of social justice is distinctly modern.

Early Christianity had a regenerative social ethic, but the early church was a marginalized eschatological community. The medieval church had a social ethic of the common good, but it was an ethic of authority and social control. Calvinism had a covenantal social ethic with transformational potential, but it was turned into an apologetic for commercial society. The Anabaptist churches had a radical-conservative social ethic of (usually pacifist) dissent, but the Anabaptists were ascetic or apocalyptic or both. Evangelical pietism had a postmillennial social ethic that fought against slavery and alcohol, but it fixated on personal conversion.

Only with the Christian Socialist movements that arose in England, Germany, France, and elsewhere in the late nineteenth century did the Christian church seek to transform society in the direction of freedom and equality. The North American version of this phenomenon was called the Social Gospel. In it, society became the subject of redemption. Social justice was intrinsic to salvation. If there were such a thing as social structure, redemption had to be reconceptualized to take account of it; salvation had to be personal *and* social to be saving. The nineteenth-century evangelical forerunners of the social gospel were rich in abolitionist and temperance convictions, but they had no theology of social salvation. Until the social gospel, no Christian movement did.

Notoriously, the social gospel movement had many faults and limitations. Much of it was sentimental, moralistic, idealistic, and politically naïve. Most of it preached a gospel of cultural optimism and a Jesus of middle-class idealism. It spoke the language of triumphal missionary religion, sometimes baptized the Anglo-Saxon ideology of Manifest Destiny, and usually claimed that American imperialism was not really imperialism because it had good intentions. The social gospel helped to build colleges and universities for African Americans, but only rarely did it demand justice for blacks. It supported suffrage for women, but that was the extent of its feminism. It created the ecumenical movement in the U.S., but it had a strongly Protestant, anti-Catholic idea of ecumenism, and the greatest social gospeler, Walter Rauschenbusch, was especially harsh on this topic.

Most social gospel leaders opposed World War I until a liberal Protestant president took the U.S. into the war, whereupon they promptly ditched their opposition to war, with the notable exceptions of Rauschenbusch and Jane Addams. After the war they overreacted by reducing the social gospel to pacifist idealism. In the 1930s, faced with a generation that did not believe the world was getting better, the social gospelers tried to make adjustments, but not very convincingly.

By then some of the movement's key leaders had been erased from memory, out of embarrassment; later there were more embarrassments to forget. Josiah Strong was an irrepressible movement founder and activist, but his ardent defense of Anglo-American superiority belatedly embarrassed American liberal Protestants. George Herron preached a sensational gospel of national salvation by class, but American capitalists did not repent of being capitalists, and Herron's scandalous divorce in 1901 put an embarrassing stop to his social gospel career. Harry F. Ward, the movement's successor to Rauschenbusch, sought to renew the social gospel after it plunged into the ditch of World War I, but he became infatuated with Soviet Communism, the ultimate embarrassment.[1]

For decades the social gospel was ridiculed for all these factors, beginning with Reinhold Niebuhr's frosty proto-Marxist polemic of 1932, *Moral Man and Immoral Society*. Two generations of seminarians learned about the social gospel by reading its Niebuhrian critics, not Rauschenbusch or Washington Gladden. Niebuhr taught, wrongly, that the social gospel had no doctrine of sin and, more justly, that it was too middle-class and idealistic to be a serious force in power politics. After Niebuhr's generation had passed, liberationists judged that the social gospel *and* Christian realism were too middle-class, white, male-dominated, nationalistic, and socially privileged to be agents of liberation.

Yet the social gospel, for all its faults, had a greater progressive religious legacy than any other North American movement. Christian realism inspired no hymns and built no lasting institutions. It was not even a movement but rather a reaction to the social gospel centered on one person, Reinhold Niebuhr. The social gospel, by contrast, was a half-century movement and enduring perspective that paved the way for modern ecumenism, social Christianity, the Civil Rights movement, and the field of social ethics. It had a tradition in the black churches that was the wellspring of the Civil Rights movement through the ministries of Reverdy Ransom, Ida B. Wells-Barnett, Benjamin E. Mays, Mordecai Johnson, and Howard Thurman. It had anti-imperialist, socialist, and feminist advocates in addition to its liberal reformers. It created the ecumenical and social justice ministries that remain the heart of American social Christianity. And it espoused a vision of economic democracy that is as relevant today as it was a hundred years ago.[2]

For the movement's two greatest figures, Washington Gladden and Walter Rauschenbusch, the social gospel was unapologetically political, with a progressive ideology, and vibrantly evangelical, in a theologically liberal fashion. Gladden developed the theology of social salvation and epitomized the progressive idealism of the social gospel movement. Rauschenbusch converted to social salvation theology and provided the movement's most powerful case for it.

Good Theology and the Social Good: Washington Gladden

For nearly thirty years the social gospelers called their movement "applied Christianity" or "social Christianity." Gladden, Strong, Herron, Richard Ely, Shailer Mathews, Francis Greenwood Peabody, and Graham Taylor were prominent among them; Rauschenbusch suddenly became prominent in 1907. By 1910 they usually called it the Social Gospel, though Rauschenbusch considered the name redundant; justly, Gladden was tagged as its father.

Born in 1833, Gladden began his career as an ill-prepared evangelical preacher. Barely a few months into his first pastorate in Brooklyn, New

York, at the outset of the Civil War, he suffered a nervous breakdown. In a healing mode, in the quieter climes of Morrisania, New York, he read Horace Bushnell and converted to theological liberalism. Gladden ministered to several churches, took a journalistic stint at a major Congregational newspaper, the *Independent*, and acquired social ideas. In the mid-1870s he started writing books that expressed his theologically liberal and mildly social approach to Christianity. In 1885, while serving as a pastor in Columbus, Ohio, he worked with Strong and Ely to launch the founding social gospel organizations, the Inter-Denominational Congress and the American Economic Association.[3]

The social gospel began as a gloss on the Golden Rule. If all are commanded to love their neighbors as themselves, Gladden reasoned, employers and employees should practice cooperation, disagreements should be negotiated in a spirit of other-regarding fellowship, and society should be organized to serve human welfare rather than profits. In his early social gospel career Gladden opposed business corporations and corporate unionism, urging that the virtues of other-regarding cooperation were practicable only for individuals and small groups. All individuals combined traits of egotism and altruism, he judged, and both were essential to the creation of a good society. Moreover, there was such a thing as self-regarding virtue, for a society lacking competitive vigor would have no dynamism. The problem with American society was that its economy was based on competitive vigor alone. Gladden was a bit slow to see that this was a structural problem, not merely a moral one, but he was among the first to say that it mattered.[4]

The social gospel was a product of Home Missions evangelicalism, Gilded Age reformism, the rise of sociological consciousness, urbanization, the spectacle of Christian Socialist movements in England, and other causal factors that impacted one another. But above all it was a response to the clash between a rising corporate capitalism and a rising workers' movement that demanded economic justice, not charity. Workers insisted on being treated as citizens with rights to decent wages and working conditions. For Gladden, the year 1886 was a watershed that revealed the structural essence of the social problem.

By that year the Knights of Labor, founded in 1869, had one million members. In March 1886 the Knights struck against Jay Gould's Missouri-Pacific railroad system, tying up five thousand miles of track. In April President Grover Cleveland gave the first presidential address dealing with trade union and labor issues, suggesting that government serve as an arbitrator in labor-capital disputes. On May 1 the Knights joined with the Black International anarchists, the socialist unions, and other trade unions in massive demonstrations for an eight-hour day. This march, the first "May Day" demonstration, sent eighty thousand protesters down Michigan Avenue in Chicago. Two days later an attack on strikebreaking workers at the McCormick Reaper Manufacturing Company in Chicago led to a deadly police reaction that sparked a riot in Haymarket Square. On May 10 the Supreme Court ruled that a corporation was a legal person under the Fourteenth Amendment, giving corporations the privileges of citizenship. On June 8 anarchists were convicted of conspiracy to murder in the Haymarket riot, despite a weak case against them. Later that month Congress passed legal authorization for the incorporation of trade unions. In October the Supreme Court ruled that states could not regulate interstate commerce passing through their borders, annulling the legal power of states over numerous trusts, railroads, and holding companies. In December the American Federation of Labor was organized out of the former Federation of Trades and Labor Unions, comprising a major new force in unionism.[5]

These events inspired, goaded, and frightened middle-class Protestants to take the social gospelers seriously. Ely's *The Labor Movement in America* (1886) counseled Americans not to dread the rising of the working class; his best-selling *Aspects of Social Christianity* (1889) encouraged readers to send money to the American Economic Association, "a real legitimate Christian institution." Gladden charged that American capitalism amounted to a form of warfare, "a war in which the strongest will win," which was the heart of the social problem. In Gladden's view, the wage system was antisocial, immoral, and anti-Christian. There were three fundamental choices in political economy: relations of labor and capital could be based on slavery, wages, or cooperation. The wage system marked a sizable improvement over slavery, Gladden allowed, but it fell short of anything acceptable to Christian morality. The first stage of industrial progress featured the subjugation of labor by capital; the second stage was essentially a war between labor and capital; the third stage was the social and moral ideal, the cooperative commonwealth in which labor and capital shared a common interest and spirit.[6]

For a while Gladden tried to combine a structural view of the problem with an optimistic ethical solution to it. In the late 1880s he assured that the ideal was immanently attainable. "It is not a difficult problem," he claimed, speaking of the class struggle. "The solution of it is quite within

the power of the Christian employer. All he has to do is admit his laborers to an *industrial partnership* with himself *by giving them a fixed share
in the profits of production*, to be divided among them, in proportion
to their earnings, at the end of the year." Profit sharing was the key to
making the economy serve the cause of a good society. It rewarded productivity and cooperative action, channeled the virtues of self-regard and
self-sacrifice, socialized the profit motive, abolished the wage system, and
promoted mutuality, equality, and community. To the "Christian man,"
Gladden contended, the strongest argument for cooperative economics
was its simple justice:

> Experience has shown him that the wage-receiving class is getting no fair
> share of the enormous increase of wealth; reason teaches that they never
> will receive an equitable proportion of it under a wage-system that is based
> on sheer competition; equity demands, therefore, that some modification
> of the wage-system be made in the interest of the laborer. If it is made, the
> employer must make it.[7]

To the respected Protestant pastor who preached every Sunday to the
business class and very few workers, the crucial hearts and minds belonged
to the employers. The ideal solution was to convince the capitalist class to
set up profit-sharing enterprises, not to abolish capitalism from above or
below. Gladden stressed that most employers were no less moral than the
laborers they employed. It was not too late to create a decentralized, cooperative alternative to the wage system. Socialism was a poor alternative
because it required an over-reaching bureaucracy that placed important
freedoms in jeopardy. Socialists wanted to pull down the existing order.
Gladden judged they were right to condemn the greed and predatory competitiveness of capitalism, but foolish to suppose that humanity would
flourish "under a system which discards or cripples these self-regarding
forces." A better system would mobilize goodwill and channel self-interest
to good ends. The reform that was needed was "the Christianization of
the present order," not its destruction. The principal remedy for the evils
of the prevailing system was "the application by individuals of Christian
principles and methods to the solution of the social problem."[8]

Gladden appealed to the rationality and moral feelings of a capitalist
class confronted by embittered workers; only gradually did he perceive
the irony of his assurance that business executives were at least as moral

as their employees. If that was true, the remedy had to deal with more than the morality of individuals. In 1893 he still focused on the moral feelings of the business class, arguing, in *Tools and the Man*, that the ideal was to create "industrial partnerships" based on profit sharing: "I would seek to commend this scheme to the captains of industry by appealing to their humanity and their justice; by asking them to consider the welfare of their workmen as well as their own. I believe that these leaders of business are not devoid of chivalry; that they are ready to respond to the summons of good-will."[9]

But by then Gladden was struggling to believe it. He liked cooperative ownership, but doubted it would make much headway in individualistic America. He believed in profit sharing but realized, increasingly, that it had little chance without strong unions. The latter recognition pulled him gradually to the left in the 1890s, even as he deplored union violence and featherbedding and prized his capacity to mediate between labor and capital. Gladden's insistent optimism on other subjects and his delight at the ascension of the social gospel did not prevent him from recognizing that his vision of a nonsocialist, decentralized economic democracy had less and less of a material basis in a society increasingly divided along class lines.

His critique of state socialism was sensible and prescient. Gladden charged that socialism, which he identified with centralized state ownership and control, denigrated the spirit of individual creativity and invention: "It ignores or depreciates the function of mind in production—the organizing mind and the inventive mind." He rejected the Marxist dogma that labor creates all value: "It is not true that labor is the sole cause of value or wealth. Many substances and possessions have great value on which no labor has ever been expended." He spurned the socialist promise to provide meaningful work for everyone: "Socialism takes away the burdens that are necessary for the development of strength. It undertakes too much. It removes from the individual the responsibilities and cares by which his mind is awakened and his will invigorated."[10]

Above all, socialism was too grandiose and bureaucratic to work. It required enormous governmental power and virtually infinite bureaucratic wisdom. Gladden urged: "The theory that it proposes is too vast for human power. It requires the state to take possession of all the lands, the mines, the houses, the stores, the railroads, the furnaces, the factories, the ships—all the capital of the country of every description." Under a socialist order, American government bureaucrats would be vested with the power to set wages, prices, and production quotas for a sprawling continent of consumers and producers:

"What an enormous undertaking it must be to discover all the multiform, the infinite variety of wants of sixty millions of people, and to supply all these wants, by governmental machinery! What a tremendous machine a government must be which undertakes, in a country like ours, to perform such a service as this!" Americans were not accustomed to viewing government as an agent of redemption. Gladden linked arms with the socialists in seeking to make American society less stratified and antisocial, but he kept his distance from socialist promises to make centralized government "the medium and minister of all social good."[11]

Gladden-style social Christianity was essentially moralistic, cooperative, and predisposed to make peace. It was allergic to Marxist rhetoric about smashing the capitalist state. It was skeptical even toward the milder state socialism of European social democracy. The social gospelers sought to Christianize society through further progress, reforms, and evangelization, not through revolutionary schemes to collectivize the economic order.

Yet the founder and symbol of the social gospel mainstream, for all his determination to stand for a mediating third way, found himself in the political Left, protesting that corporate capitalism demolished better possibilities. Confronted with a burgeoning capitalist order, Gladden counseled that socialists should be respected, and respectfully corrected, as long as they refrained from unnecessary violence. He called himself "enough of a Socialist" to embrace a foreign policy opposed to war and committed to international treaties. Since working people were losing the class struggle, he defended the union movement most of the time, urging that the right to property was subordinate to the rights of life and freedom. On that ground he also qualified his opposition to nationalized state ownership, making exceptions for the entire class of economic monopolies, which included (in the early 1890s) the railroad, telegraph, gas, and electric companies. Later he judged that mines, watercourses, water suppliers, and telephone services also belonged to this category. The railroad companies in particular were "gigantic instruments of oppression," Gladden argued. In any industry where no effective competition existed, the only just recourse was state control. The railroad and electric companies did not operate under the law of supply and demand, nor offer their commodities or services in an open market; in effect, they closed the market. Gladden urged: "This is not, in any proper sense, trade; this is essentially taxation. And, therefore, I think that all virtual monopolies must eventually belong to the state."[12]

To call for the nationalization of monopolies and decentralized economic democracy everywhere else was certainly to advocate a type of socialism, though Gladden preferred, like the social gospel generally, to call it something else. His deepening realism about the class struggle even made him less inclined to censure hardball union tactics. The goal of trade unionism must be human solidarity, he urged in 1897, not proletarian solidarity, but unionists had legitimate reasons to intimidate scab laborers. In his memoir, *Recollections* (1909), Gladden judged that America was probably heading "into a Socialistic experiment," though he preferred cooperative strategies and worried that American society was too selfish and uneducated for either approach. Two years later, in *The Labor Question*, he did not share Rauschenbusch's faith that the last un-Christianized sector of American society—the economy—was being Christianized. The clash between a triumphant corporate capitalism and a rising tide of aggressive labor organizations such as the National Association of Manufacturers and the revolutionary Industrial Workers of the World ended Gladden's fantasy of a paternalistic share-economy. Giving up on profit sharing and cooperatives, he took his stand with a flawed labor movement. Unorganized labor was "steadily forced down toward starvation and misery," he observed. Elsewhere he lamented that corporate capitalism was becoming utterly predatory and vengeful toward unions, "maintaining toward them an attitude of almost vindictive opposition." In this context, unionism was the only serious force of resistance against the corporate degradation of labor. If the dream of economic democracy was to be redeemed, Gladden argued, it would have to be as a form of union-gained industrial democracy.[13]

Social Salvation: The Social Gospel Difference

The social gospelers were products of the evangelical reform movements they extended. Raised in evangelical traditions, they converted to theological liberalism and gave mainline Protestantism an energizing social mission through their desire to Christianize America. Their movement gained much of its missionary impulse from its connections to the Home Missions movement. The social gospel theology of social salvation was a product of these influences; in 1893 Gladden gave classic expression to it, with no glimmer of how a later generation would cringe at its sexism and perfectionism.

In his rendering the social gospel was a progressive twist on postmillennialism. "The end of Christianity is twofold, a perfect man in a perfect society," he declared. "These purposes are never separated; they cannot be separated. No man can be redeemed and saved alone; no community can be reformed and elevated save as the individuals of which it is composed are regenerated." The gospel addressed individuals, but it addressed each individual as a member of a social organism that created the medium through which one responded to the gospel message: "This vital and necessary relation of the individual to society lies at the basis of the Christian conception of life. Christianity would create a perfect society, and to this end it must produce perfect men; it would bring forth perfect men, and to this end it must construct a perfect society." To Gladden the themes of modern social Christianity were the themes of Christ: repentance, regeneration, and the presence of the kingdom. Christ taught, "Be ye perfect as your Father in heaven is perfect" and "Repent, for the kingdom of heaven is at hand." Gladden admonished against breaking the copula in the latter statement, for repentance was intrinsically connected to the presence of God's kingdom: "The opportunity, the motive, the condition of repentance is the presence of a divine society, of which the penitent, by virtue of his penitence, at once becomes a member."[14]

The social gospel thus claimed to recover the meaning of Christ's petition, "Thy kingdom come." For Jesus, as for genuine Christianity, the purpose of God's inbreaking kingdom was to regenerate individuals and society as coordinate interests. Gladden urged that neither form of regeneration was possible without the other: "Whatever the order of logic may be, there can be no difference in time between the two kinds of work; that we are to labor as constantly and as diligently for the improvement of the social order as for the conversion of man." Since American Protestantism overstressed personal salvation, it needed to emphasize "the social side of our Christian work," seeking to Christianize American society. The church's social mission was to claim the kingdoms of this world for the kingdom of Christ, including "the kingdom of commerce, and the kingdom of industry, and the kingdom of fashion, and the kingdom of learning, and the kingdom of amusement; every great department of society is to be pervaded by the Christian spirit and governed by Christian law."[15]

That was the essential idea of social salvation. Gladden assured his congregation that applied Christianity contained ample room for personal religion. Every Sunday morning he preached on personal religion, and every Sunday evening he preached on social Christianity. Implicitly in that practice, the old dichotomy still obtained. But the burgeoning movement for applied Christianity put into practice Gladden's assurance that personal and social religion were inseparably linked in the gospel of Christ. Salvation brought the personal and social dimensions together or it was not saving. Gladden and Rauschenbusch kept the faith that this was the religion of Jesus. Shailer Mathews, influenced by German history of religions scholarship, judged that Jesus was too apocalyptical to see it that way, but he agreed that in the modern age the best expression of the spirit of Jesus was the gospel of social salvation. Near the end of his career, Gladden's ministerial successor in Columbus told him that he had two absorbing interests—liberal theology and the social gospel. Gladden looked at the pastor quizzically and asked, "Well, what else IS there?"[16]

That was a plausible question in 1912; Rauschenbusch might well have asked it. Then the Great War overwhelmed and deformed the social gospel. Most social gospelers urged Americans to stay out of the war, except to help England on the side; Rauschenbusch bitterly perceived that the war was a catastrophe for the movement, but he was accused of merely favoring Germany; Gladden championed and reflected the social gospel mainstream, fervently opposing intervention right up to the moment that America entered the war in April 1917, whereupon he made a convincing reversal of conviction. The call of country and President Wilson's soaring rhetoric about saving the world for democracy were irresistible to him and the movement. Liberal Protestant leader Lyman Abbott, who converted early, called the war "a crusade to make this world a home in which God's children can live in peace and safety, a crusade far more in harmony with the spirit and will of Christ than the crusade to recover from the pagans the tomb in which the body of Christ was buried." Mathews, who traveled the same path as Gladden, exulted that America at war was proving to be "a glorious super-person, possessed of virtues, power, ideals, daring, and sacrifice."[17]

Gladden was never as jingoistic as Abbott, but he matched Mathews for wartime mythmaking. As soon as Wilson called on America to make the world safe for democracy, Gladden preached a sermon titled, "Making the World Safe for Democracy." He looked forward to a League of

Nations and proclaimed that this was, indeed, the war to end all wars. He never doubted that the United States was fighting for democracy or that his country sought to create a world order based on the Golden Rule. To the end of his life he preached, "All that is needed to bring permanent peace to earth is that every nation trust all other nations just as it wishes to be trusted by them." Gladden accepted and preached Wilson's vision of the war as a social gospel cause. He understood that World War I was an imperial tragedy, but he could not think of America as an empire. America was the redeemer nation, the world's great experiment in democracy. America went to war to advance the cause of democratic civilization; he seemed to forget having preached that war belonged to the jungle phase of human existence: "This war needn't be a curse; it may be the greatest blessing that has ever befallen this land."[18]

The war certainly dramatized his capacity for optimism. Gladden and Rauschenbusch died in the same year, 1918, but very differently. For all they shared as founders and champions of American social Christianity, they were different kinds of social gospelers. Rauschenbusch was a socialist and high-voltage prose stylist who condemned capitalism as unregenerate, supported the union movement, and blasted his opponents. Gladden supported trade unionism selectively but dreaded socialism; he tried to be realistic about the class struggle but could never say with Rauschenbusch that idealism was too weak and sentimental to effect any great social change.[19]

Rauschenbusch was inspiring and challenging to pastors, but he was also dangerous. He called for a radical extension of democracy and a socialist transformation of the economy, and he was devastated by the war, which he saw as the death of social gospel progress. Gladden was never dangerous. In every way he epitomized the movement's mainstream. He spoke the language of moral progress, cooperation, and peace to the end of his life and claimed to see a renewal of social Christian hope in America's burst of wartime pride. Asked near the end of his life if he knew of any reason not to be hopeful, Gladden replied, "Not one." His entire life had been a miracle, lived through eighty-three years of transforming American progress.[20]

In 1912 he declared in a sermon: "I have never doubted that the Kingdom I have always prayed for is coming; that the gospel I have always preached is true." Six years later he published the sermon: "I believe that the democracy is getting a new heart, and a new spirit, that the nation is being saved. It is not yet saved and its salvation depends on you and me, but it is being saved. There are signs that a *new way of thinking, a new social consciousness*, are taking possession of the nation." To Gladden, cooperation, democracy, and progress were god-terms; he never lost faith that the kingdom of God was an ongoing American project.[21]

Walter Rauschenbusch and Christian Socialism

Rauschenbusch blended the same faith with a more radical politics and a grittier sense of evil. He began his ministerial career in 1886 as a Baptist pastor in the Hell's Kitchen district of New York, where he served a poor, hurting, immigrant congregation, and where he converted to the Social Gospel. Rauschenbusch's searing encounter with urban poverty, especially the funerals he performed for children, drove him to social activism. If people suffered because of politics and economics, the church had to deal with politics and economics. He later recalled that during his early ministry he had six books in his head: five were scholarly, one was dangerous. Three times he tried to write the dangerous one but had to put it aside; each time he returned to it, he found that he had outgrown the manuscript and had to start over.

In 1891 Rauschenbusch decided, with deep sadness, that he had to resign from the ministry, because he was going deaf. A surf-like roar in his ears made it very difficult to do pastoral tasks; he called it "physical loneliness." He was offered a teaching position at Rochester Seminary but doubted that teaching would work any better than ministry for a deaf person. His idea was to resign his position, go abroad for a year, write the dangerous book, and launch a literary career. His congregation insisted, instead, that he take a paid sabbatical, which he gratefully took in Germany.

There he labored on a book titled *Revolutionary Christianity*, which argued that Christianity should be essentially revolutionary, in the manner of Jesus. During his seminary days Rauschenbusch had taken a mildly liberal turn theologically by reading Horace Bushnell and Frederick Robertson on the side, and in his early ministry he preached the trademark liberal Ritschlian school idea of Christianity as an ellipse with two centers: eternal life as the goal of individual existence and the kingdom of God as the goal of humanity. The old pietism and the social-ethical Jesus of modern theology folded together. But in Germany it occurred to him that Jesus had one center, the kingdom of God. Jesus proclaimed and launched a postmillennial idea of the coming reign of God, and the church was supposed to be a new kind of community that transformed the world by the power of Christ's kingdom-bringing Spirit. Rauschenbusch later recalled: "Here was a concept that embraced everything. Here was something so big that absolutely nothing that interested me was excluded from it . . . Wherever I touched, there was the kingdom of God . . . It carries God into everything that you do."[22]

Revolutionary Christianity contended that the kingdom of God is always at work toward the realized life of God. Rauschenbusch stressed that this idea was beautiful, comprehensive, filled with justice-making ethical content, *and* evangelical: the authority of the Lord Jesus was behind it. But the year passed, the book never quite came together, Rauschenbusch returned to his congregation, and the following year he married a schoolteacher, Pauline Rother, who helped him cope with his worsening deafness. They made pastoral calls together, and their marriage was a sustained love affair, mutually supportive and affectionate, which pulled him out of his depressive spiral. The next time Rochester Seminary called, in 1897, Rauschenbusch felt he was ready for an academic career. His father had directed the German Department at Rochester Seminary for many years. For five years Rauschenbusch carried on his father's work, teaching English and American literature, physiology, physics, civil government, political economy, astronomy, zoology, and New Testament, all in German, in addition to raising money for the German Department.

This exhausting regimen left no time for his own work, and the German-American community that he served was mostly hostile to the social gospel. Finally, in 1902, the seminary's position in church history opened up, which is why the greatest works of the social gospel have a strong historical bent. Walter Rauschenbusch made his living as a professor of church history. While learning a new field, he spoke at civic groups and churches about the social gospel, helped to organize the Federal Council of Churches, and wrote pamphlets for an outfit called the Brotherhood of the Kingdom (which, after a brief debate, admitted sister members). And he started thinking again about that big, dangerous book.

He went back to his sprawling manuscript to see what he could salvage from it, and he found a few things, especially the starting point: Jesus and his kingdom. That was the basis for a mostly new book that he finished in 1907: *Christianity and the Social Crisis*. The first part described the essential purpose of prophetic biblical religion as the transformation of human society into the kingdom of God. The second part explained why the church had never carried out this mission. The third part urged that it was not too late for the church to follow Jesus.

Rauschenbusch realized that the key to the book was the second part, but he feared that the third part would get him fired. It had a blazing manifesto for socialism in a closing eighty-page chapter titled, "What to Do." For his second part analysis of what happened to Christianity, he leaned on Adolf von Harnack but argued that no one had given a satisfactory answer. Rauschenbusch implied, but was too modest to say, "No one until now." In his view, every chapter of church history could be titled, "How the Kingdom of God Was Misconstrued in This Era, or Replaced by Something Else."

Revolutionary Christianity had patches of labored writing and clumsy connections, but all was smooth and sparkling in *Christianity and the Social Crisis*. The book enthralled a huge audience with its graceful flow of short, clear sentences, its charming metaphors, and its vigorous pace. Its basic argument was that prophetic religion is the "beating heart" of scripture, the prophetic spirit "rose from the dead" in Jesus and the early church, and Christianity is supposed to be a prophetic Christ-following religion of the divine commonwealth.

To be really serious about standing for the ethical-justice content of the gospel, Rauschenbusch argued, the modern church needed to stand for democratic socialism. "The modern socialist movement is really the first intelligent, concerted, and continuous effort to reshape society in accordance with the laws of social development," he claimed, adding that Christianity was moving in a socialist direction: "The current of modern religion does not run away from the world, but toward it . . . To us salvation means victory over sin rather than escape from hell." For Rauschenbusch, social salvation depended on making Christianity socialist and socialism Christian. In the social sphere, to live in sin was to live by the law of predatory competition; to be saved was to live by the law and spirit of cooperation: "Every joint-stock company, trust, or labor union organized, every extension of government interference or government ownership, is a surrender of the competitive principle and a halting step toward cooperation." Cooperative and public ownership were economically viable, he assured; more important, they did not militate against community and personal virtue: "If money dominates, the ideal cannot dominate. If we serve mammon, we cannot serve the Christ."[23]

For Rauschenbusch, the crisis of capitalist civilization was an opportunity to recover the lost kingdom ideal of Jesus. If production could be organized on a cooperative basis, if distribution could be organized by principles of justice, if workers could be treated as valuable ends and not as dispensable means to a commercial end, if parasitic wealth and predatory commerce could be abolished . . . His fantasy of "ifs" went on for a half-page. If all these things could be accomplished, Rauschenbusch dreamed, "then there might be a chance to live such a life of gentleness and brotherly kindness and tranquility of heart as Jesus desired for men. It may be that the cooperative Commonwealth would give us the first chance in history to live a really Christian life without retiring from the world, and would make the Sermon on the Mount a philosophy of life feasible for all who care to try."[24]

Individualism is neither warm nor saving, he admonished. Ordinary Americans rightly cherished the home, school, and church, which were socialist institutions. Life is redeemed and made good by the social impulse. But Rauschenbusch was not naïve about the force of ethical idealism: "We must not blink the fact that the idealists alone have never carried through any great social change. In vain they dash their fair ideas against the solid granite of human selfishness." The possessing classes ruled by force and cunning and long-standing monopoly of power, he observed: "They control nearly all property. The law is on their side, for they have made it. They control the machinery of government and can use force under the form of law." Thus the capitalist and aristocratic classes were nearly impervious to moral truth. It was a good thing to be on the side of moral truth, Rauschenbusch assured, but being morally right was not enough: "For a definite historical victory a given truth must depend on the class which makes that truth its own and fights for it."[25]

The German Peasant Revolt of 1525 was, for him, a chastening reminder on this theme. The Anabaptist peasants, despite their deep Christianity and just cause, were crushed in streams of blood, lacking the organized power to win their rights. There is no substitute for organized power, Rauschenbusch implored: "If there is no such army to fight its cause, the truth will drive individuals to a comparatively fruitless martyrdom and will continue to hover over humanity as a disembodied ideal." The class struggle had to be taken seriously on its own terms. Essentially it was a "war of conflicting interests." No ruling class ever gave up its privileges out of altruism, and no proletarian class ever made social gains without fighting for them: "Christian idealists must not make the mistake of trying to hold the working class down to the use of moral suasion only, or be repelled when they hear the brute note of selfishness and anger.

The class struggle is bound to be transferred to the field of politics in our country in some form. It would be folly if the working class failed to use the leverage which their political power gives them." A generation later, that is exactly what Reinhold Niebuhr maintained in bidding farewell to an idealistic Social Gospel movement.[26]

So when Niebuhr and three generations of imitators blasted Rauschenbusch and the social gospel for naïve ethical idealism, somehow they missed Rauschenbusch's discussion of the class struggle in *Christianity and the Social Crisis* and his six chapters on sin culminating with "the kingdom of evil" in *A Theology for the Social Gospel*. Moreover, Rauschenbusch never said that the divine commonwealth was attainable; he said that one cannot find out how much of it is attainable without struggling for it: "We shall never have a perfect social life, yet we must seek it with faith. At best there is always an approximation to a perfect social order. The kingdom of God is always but coming. But every approximation to it is worth while."[27]

The Social Gospel Ascending

Christianity and the Social Crisis was skillfully fashioned and perfectly timed. It sold fifty thousand copies, went through thirteen printings in five years, and was a supercharger for the social gospel movement. It stood on the shoulders of Gladden's *Applied Christianity*, Josiah Strong's *Our Country*, George Herron's *The Larger Christ*, Shailer Mathews's *The Social Teaching of Jesus*, and Francis G. Peabody's *Jesus Christ and the Social Question*, but it set a new standard for political theology.[28] The book had a huge impact at liberal seminaries and inspired social gospel leaders to be more daring. To a churchly religious establishment Rauschenbusch warned: "If the Church tries to confine itself to theology and the Bible, and refuses its larger mission to humanity, its theology will gradually become mythology and its Bible a closed book."[29]

He thought he was done with this subject, having crammed everything he knew into the book. Instead he returned from a sabbatical in Germany to find he was famous, which required new lectures: "The social awakening of our nation had set in like an equinoctial gale in March, and when I came home, I found myself caught in the tail of the storm. *Christianity and the Social Crisis* had won popular approval far beyond my boldest hopes, and the friends of the book drew me, in spite of myself, into the public discussion of social questions." Rauschenbusch's lecture touring produced a large sequel in 1912, *Christianizing the Social Order*, which appeared in the same month that Theodore Roosevelt, Woodrow Wilson, and Eugene Debs competed for the left vote in the U.S. presidential election. Incredibly for a Socialist, Debs won twelve million votes—nearly 6 percent of the electorate. Veteran social gospelers declined to vote Republican for the first time in their lives; the party of Lincoln had become alien to them by opting for big business conservatism. Progressives debated whether progressivism should be a political party or the ideology permeating every party. Many social gospelers saw the kingdom coming.[30]

Rauschenbusch was one of them. Posing as a reluctant movement leader, he apologized for burdening the public with another large tome on social Christianity, then took it back: "The subject of the book needs no such apology as is implied in the foregoing statements. If there is any bigger or more pressing subject for the mind of a Christian man to handle, I do not know of it." The world was getting better; who could deny it? It astonished him that premillennialists found a large following by denying it. Rauschenbusch wrote *Christianizing the Social Order* at the high point of his optimism that America could be won for Christ, democracy, and the cooperative commonwealth. He recalled that before 1900 he belonged to a handful of socially concerned ministers who shouted in the wilderness: "It was always a happy surprise when we found a new man who had seen the light. We used to form a kind of flying wedge to support a man who was preparing to attack a ministers' conference with the social Gospel." But now the social gospel was sweeping the ministers' conferences. A third great Awakening was occurring in American life, one that recovered the social spirit and kingdom goal of Jesus.[31]

Christianizing the Social Order reworked familiar Rauschenbusch themes, sometimes with heightened claims. The kingdom of God was not only "the lost social ideal of Christendom" but also "the first and the most essential dogma of the Christian faith." The sixteenth-century Reformation was a revival of Pauline theology, but "the present-day Reformation is a revival of the spirit and aims of Jesus himself." Rauschenbusch allowed that Jesus retained some unfortunate thought-forms of his background. But most crucial was the spirit and trajectory of Jesus' religion, not the dogmas he retained from his religious inheritance. We should not ask, "What did Jesus think?" but rather: "In what direction were his thoughts working?" To follow Jesus had nothing to do with embracing every aspect of his worldview. On that basis Rauschenbusch brushed off the problem of apocalypticism: "I know that this charge will pain some devout Christian minds whom I would not willingly hurt, but in the interest of the very hope for which they stand I have to say that the idea of the Kingdom of God must slough off apocalypticism if it is to become the religious property of the modern world." Those who vested their hope in "salvation by catastrophe" needed to historicize the kingdom hope of the early church and update their own. Religiously, they needed to grow up: "They must outgrow the diabolism and demonism with which Judaism was infected in Persia and face the stern facts of racial sin. They must break with the artificial schemes and the determinism of an unhistorical age and use modern resources to understand the way God works out retribution and salvation in human affairs."[32]

The Reformation recovered Paul's doctrinal system but not the theology and spirit of Jesus: "It was a discussion of old Catholic problems from new points of view." Luther and Calvin had little feeling for the kingdom and they possessed precious little democratic spirit. The Reformation broke the Catholic Church's imprisonment of the kingdom idea, but not for the sake of the kingdom's true meaning. It took modern social idealism and historical criticism to recover Jesus and his kingdom, Rauschenbusch declared: "The eclipse of the Kingdom idea was an eclipse of Jesus. We had listened too much to voices talking about him, and not enough to his own voice. Now his own thoughts in their lifelike simplicity and open-air fragrance have become a fresh religious possession, and when we listen to Jesus, we cannot help thinking about the Kingdom of God."[33]

The evangelical and modernist impulses were equally crucial. The Reformation worked back to Paul; modern theology worked back to Jesus *and* it adopted the master concept of modern thought, evolution. The modern rethinking of the kingdom was rooted in evolutionary theory, Rauschenbusch observed. Evolution prepared Christians to understand the world as the reign of God toward which all creation is moving: "Translate the evolutionary theories into religious faith, and you have the doctrine of the Kingdom of God." History is God's workshop, the unfolding of an immanent divine purpose that works "toward the commonwealth of spiritual liberty and righteousness."[34]

Even at the high tide of the social gospel, *Christianizing the Social Order* was a provocative title. Rauschenbusch recognized that his rhetoric about "Christianizing" society was unsettling to many. He assured that he had no theocratic hankerings. The social gospel was not about putting

Christ's name in the U.S. Constitution or breaching the American wall between church and state. To Christianize society was to bring it into harmony with the ethical values of Christ. They were universal, shared by all people of goodwill.[35]

Then why insist on the off-putting language of Christianization? Rauschenbusch had two reasons. One, Jesus was the ultimate teacher and exemplar of the values of freedom, sacrificial love, compassion, justice, fellowship, and equality, and he deserved to be recognized as such. Two, any Christian movement that avoided Christ's name would lose whatever spiritual and social power it possessed: "To say that we want to moralize the social order would be both vague and powerless to most men. To say that we want to Christianize it is both concrete and compelling."[36]

Rauschenbusch used "Christianize," "moralize," "humanize," and "democratize" as interchangeable terms: "Christianizing means humanizing in the highest sense." Most of American society was already Christianized, he judged, but the unregenerate part threatened everything else. A bad society made good people do bad things; a good society compelled even bad people to be cooperative and democratic. In his telling, American society in 1912 was semi-Christian. Its families, churches, politics, and educational systems were Christian for the most part, but these sectors were threatened by an economic system that militated against America's democratizing Christian spirit.[37]

Until the modern age, Rauschenbusch argued, most families and churches were decidedly bad, as they were reactionary and coercive. Both were despotic in ways that influenced each other, condemning women to subservience. The democratizing spirit of the modern age changed this picture, raising the legal status of women nearly to the point of equality with men. Rauschenbusch looked forward to the next stage of women's progress: "The suffrage will abolish one of the last remnants of patriarchal autocracy by giving woman a direct relation to the political organism of society, instead of allowing man to exercise her political rights for her." He stressed that the churches did not welcome their salvation; they had to be converted to the good against their will. Christianized by their loss of temporal authority and unearned wealth, the churches learned belatedly that coercion has the same relation to true religion that rape has to love. Rauschenbusch noted with embarrassment that many churches were still determined to oppress women.[38]

He was a good enough Victorian to be deeply conflicted on this issue. Rauschenbusch supported the right of women to equal rights in society, but he wanted wives and mothers to stay home and take care of their families. He supported the right of women to higher education, but he shuddered that most college-educated women remained unmarried. Repeatedly he urged his audiences not to erode the (late Victorian) middle-class ideal of family life in the name of individual progress for women. What made the middle-class family *ideal* was precisely that it allowed women not to work outside the home. On the lecture circuit he could be florid on the cult of true womanhood; *Christianity and the Social Crisis* had a typical warning: "The health of society rests on the welfare of the home. What, then, will be the outcome if the unmarried multiply; if homes remain childless; if families are homeless; if girls do not know housework; and if men come to distrust the purity of women?"[39]

That was a vision of barbarism to Rauschenbusch. Capitalism emptied the home of its nurturing wives and mothers. Christian socialism was the wholesome alternative, lifting women to the equality they deserved, while supporting the family as the key to a healthy society. Just as modern Christianity needed the socialist passion for justice to fulfill the social ideals of the gospel, the socialist movement needed the spiritual and moral conscience of Christianity to be saved from crude materialism, especially on the subject of family values. Though most social gospelers stopped short of wrapping socialism in the banner of family values, they shared Rauschenbusch's conflicted and qualified support of the women's movement. Like him, they were anxious to be counted as advocates of women's rights and worried that feminism eroded family values. As long as the suffrage movement cherished Victorian womanhood and resisted cultural barbarism, it was a product of the same redemptive impulse that brought American churches into the orbit of the spirit of Jesus.

Rauschenbusch understood why his anti-clerical friends hated the church, but he assured them that modern democracy and the spirit of Jesus were converting it. The church was becoming Christian—"unlearning despotism and exploitation, and coming under the law of love and service"—in the same way that the family was unlearning patriarchal domination. He applied similar arguments to education and politics. In a pre-democratic society, education was the privilege of the few; in a democracy it was the right of all. Though democracy was not quite the same entity as Christianity, he allowed, "in politics democracy is the expression and method of the Christian spirit." By this criterion America was nearly Christianized.[40]

The exception was the economic system, "the unregenerate section of our social order." To Rauschenbusch the problem was systemic, not personal. He doubted that capitalists as individuals were less moral than others. What made capitalism evil was that it made even good people do bad things. Capitalism had a predatory, antisocial spirit that was inimical to Christianity, he judged, yet Christian moralists timidly avoided the subject. By his account this neglect was an especially Protestant problem. In Catholicism the dominant power was the dogmatic mythology of a priestly class; in Protestantism it was the financial and cultural power of a ruling capitalist class. But the tests of Christian morality applied to every sphere, including economics: Does a given system reward cooperation and the common good, or selfishness and will to power? Does it call people to the good or tempt them downward?[41]

Rauschenbusch answered that capitalism was essentially corrupting. Anticipating Daniel Bell's "cultural contradictions of capitalism" thesis by sixty years, Rauschenbusch argued that capitalism sapped its own foundations by degrading the cultural capital on which America's economic success depended.[42] Capitalism commodified everything it touched, turned impressionable people into small-minded consumers, and extended to every sector of society. The learned professions were not as commercialized as the rest of American society, he judged, but they, too, were being corrupted, especially the legal profession: "'Commercializing a profession' always means degrading it. Of the learned professions the Law is farthest gone. The most lucrative practice is the service of corporations, and they need the lawyer to protect their interests against the claims of the public." Wherever capitalism intruded it brought about "a surrender of the human point of view, a relaxing of the sense of duty, and a willingness to betray the public—if it pays."[43]

Liberal reformism would never solve this problem, he urged, because the problem was structural. Reform movements made the capitalist beast more tolerable "by pulling a few of the teeth and shortening the tether of greed." But that turned capitalism against the Christianized sectors of American society, "invading the regenerate portions of the social order, paralyzing their activities, breaking down the respect for the higher values, desecrating the holy, and invading God's country." Pulling a few more teeth was not the answer. The answer was to break the autocratic power "unrestrained by democratic checks" that capitalism gave to owners and managers. Rauschenbusch believed that profit had a sound moral basis to the extent that it represented a fair return on one's useful labor and service. Even the wage system could be justified where free land was available, or a certain kind of labor was scarce, or an employer was especially generous. But, most of the time, crowded labor markets and the capitalist control of the instruments of production allowed capitalists to make unearned profits off the exploited labors of the weak. Rauschenbusch called it "a tribute collected by power."[44]

The root problem was that workers had no property rights under capitalism. In the political sphere an American worker was a rights-bearing citizen, but in the economic sphere the same worker "has only himself." One could give forty years of labor to a factory and still possess no more rights over property than a medieval serf. Workers labored on industrial property that was too expensive for them to own, but which was financed by the savings of working people through their banks and insurance companies: "But therewith the money passes out of the control of the owners. What a man deposits today may be used next week to pay Pinkertons who will do things he abominates." The solution was to democratize the process of investment: "Political democracy without economic democracy is an uncashed promissory note, a pot without the roast, a form without substance. But in so far as democracy has become effective, it has quickened everything it has touched." Democracy was needed in the economic sphere for the same reasons it was needed everywhere else. It promoted freedom and equality, legitimated the necessary exercise of authority, and served as a brake on domination of privileged classes.[45]

Economic democracy was not about the elimination of property rights, Rauschenbusch cautioned; it was about the expansion of property rights under new forms. He took for granted that economic power led to political power. Under capitalism, the capitalist class wrote its interests into the law; under a fully realized democracy, property laws would serve the interests of the public as a whole. Rauschenbusch's concept of a fully realized economic democracy was a patchwork of socialist and reformist themes that did not always fit together. He could be sloppy in failing to distinguish between direct workers' ownership, mixed forms of cooperative ownership, and public ownership of production. He offered no help in delineating between various schools of socialism, and he had a tendency to adopt utopian fancies, for example, that prices would be based entirely on services rendered in a socialist society. Economic democracy ran straight from the farm to the kitchen, he promised: "It means the power to cut all monopoly prices out of business and to base prices solely on service rendered." He thus retained the utopian Marxist vision of a cooperative society while grasping—as Marx did not—that markets cannot be abolished in a free society.[46]

Rauschenbusch's weakness for idealistic rhetoric caused him to exaggerate the extent to which economic democracy could replace economic competition. While he rejected Marx's materialistic determinism and his contempt for liberal democracy, he accepted the Marxist theories of surplus value and the class struggle. He argued that extending the democratizing logic of liberal democracy into the economic sphere would save the good parts of Marxism. For all his idealistic rhetoric and unassimilated borrowings from Marx, however, Rauschenbusch wisely urged that the mix of ownership modes in a democracy must always be a matter of contextual judgment. The blueprint dogmatism of the Marxist tradition was alien to him. John Stuart Mill's vision of decentralized socialism fit Rauschenbusch better, as did Mill's claim that the logic of liberal democracy led to democratic socialism. Mill's *Principles of Political Economy* envisioned workers "collectively owning the capital with which they carry on their operations, and working under managers elected and removable by themselves." *Christianizing the Social Order* embraced this vision of pluralistic democratic socialism, claiming that only socialism could compete with militarism as a unifying social force in American life.[47]

Rauschenbusch tried to be optimistic that Americans were up to it. He knew that liberalism was too weak to compete with the spirit of capitalism or the spirit of nationalistic militarism. He tried to believe that Christianity linked with socialism could overcome America's assiduously cultivated egocentrism. "Capitalism has overdeveloped the selfish instincts in us all and left the capacity of devotion to larger ends shrunken and atrophied," he lamented. He worried that Americans lifted themselves to a sense of common purpose only when they went to war. He feared that the habits of cooperation would be hardest to learn in a culture that celebrated isolation, self-preoccupation, acquisitiveness, and will to power. He was concerned that reformers would settle for liberalism: "We fritter away precious time by dallying at the half-way house of mere public supervision and control. We must come to public ownership some time, and anyone whose thinking parts are in order ought to see it by this time."[48]

But in 1912 Rauschenbusch had faith that a new epoch was beginning in American life. The human race took centuries to consolidate the patriarchal family, the village commune, and the modern state, he recalled. The task of building a cooperative commonwealth would be considerably more daunting, especially in a country that prized its individualism: "But if anyone thinks it is beyond the possibilities of human nature, let him rub his eyes and look around him." The cultural problem was less daunting if one did not conceive socialism as one specific thing. There were many kinds of democracy, and democratic socialism needed to be no less pluralistic, he urged. True democracies were inclusive, pluralistic, and non-chauvinist; thus democracy adapted well to cultural diversity: "There is unity of movement, and yet endless diversity of life." If democratic socialism was to get a hearing in the United States, it had to become American.[49]

Rauschenbusch held the same hope for socialism that he held for Christianity: that it would become more truly itself. He was well aware, he told Francis G. Peabody, that most Socialists wanted nothing to do with Christianity. But if modern Christians could hope for the Christianization of China, why was it ridiculous to hope for the Christianization of a Western political movement that got its inspiration from Christianity? "The Socialists are hopeless about the social regeneration of the Church. Yet it has come faster than I dared to hope. At any rate I am not going to tell the Socialists that I expect them to remain atheists. I shall tell them that they are now religious in spite of themselves and that an increased approach to religion is inevitable as they emerge from the age of polemics and dogmatism."[50]

In that mood he dispensed with the cautionary words about the class struggle that ended *Christianity and the Social Crisis*. The social gospel movement was soaring, churches were scrambling to get on the right side of the social question, and politicians were competing for the mantle of progressivism. In *Christianizing the Social Order*, Rauschenbusch dared to hope that idealism might prevail without a class war after all. He counseled liberals and progressives to own up to the socialism in their creed: "Every reformer is charged with socialism, because no constructive reform is possible without taking a leaf from the book of socialism." It was better to wear the label as a badge of honor than to cower from it. The social gospel was primarily a call for a revival of religion and a Christian transformation of society:

> We do not want less religion; we want more; but it must be a religion that gets its orientation from the Kingdom of God. To concentrate our efforts on personal salvation, as orthodoxy has done, or on soul culture, as liberalism has done, comes close to refined selfishness. All of us who have been trained in egotistic religion need a conversion to Christian Christianity, even if we are bishops or theological professors. Seek ye first the Kingdom

of God and God's righteousness, and the salvation of your souls will be added to you.[51]

That was the social gospel at its best during its prewar heyday. To most social gospel leaders, opposing World War I was imperative before America intervened and unthinkable afterward. Rauschenbusch, as a son of Germany and by then a near-pacifist, held out against a patriotic tidal wave, and paid dearly for it. He could not combine Christianity and the war spirit, he explained to friends. It amazed him that his social gospel colleagues believed there could be such a thing as an idealistic victory. By the time most social gospelers wished that they had opposed the war, too, Rauschenbusch was gone. The social gospel did not die with him, contrary to conventional renderings. It had its greatest impact on the churches in the 1920s and early 1930s, as nearly every mainline denomination vowed never to support another war. But the fact that two generations of American church leaders had actually expected to create a cooperative commonwealth became hard to imagine.[52]

Chapter 2

Reinhold Niebuhr, Karl Barth, and the Crises of War and Capitalism

Reinhold Niebuhr, the greatest American theologian of the twentieth century, had the same intellectual trajectory as the other giant theologians of his generation—Karl Barth, Emil Brunner, Rudolf Bultmann, and Paul Tillich. He was trained in liberal theology, turned against it with mighty polemical force, was tagged as neo-orthodox, and retained crucial aspects of liberalism despite the polemics. In Europe, where the antiliberal revolt was first called "crisis theology," the leading figure was Barth. In the U.S., where the crisis occurred a decade later, Niebuhr had the Barth role.

European crisis theology was a reaction against the slaughter and destruction of World War I, the pro-war boosterism of prominent liberal German theologians, and the conceits of bourgeois liberal culture. It was about shattered illusions and the experience of emptiness before a hidden God. Since the United States did not experience the war as a devastating calamity, there was no American version of crisis theology in the 1920s. It took the Great Depression to create one, a time when social ethics overtook theology. In a normal age Niebuhr might not have been a great theologian, since he had little theological training and did not do what theologians normally do. But for the American generation that endured World War I, the Great Depression, World War II, and the Cold War, Niebuhr defined what it meant for Christianity to be realistic and relevant.[1]

He spent the 1920s trying to shore up liberal theology, just as Barth inveighed against it. Niebuhr preached an idealistic religion of pacifism, political reform, and liberal theology, and served as president of the liberal pacifist Fellowship of Reconciliation. But Niebuhr's attempt at pacifist idealism was always a strained affair. Often he complained that liberal Protestantism was too soft to confront the evils of the world. Never tempted by isolationism or sentimentality, he warned that moral idealism had little power, even as he called for moral efforts to redeem American society.

These awkwardly mixed feelings intensified after Niebuhr joined the faculty of Union Theological Seminary in 1928, teaching in a field— social ethics—that had no history apart from the social gospel. By the early 1930s the terrible wreckage of the Great Depression drove him to a sterner creed. What did it mean to be a social ethicist if one did not believe in redeemed institutions, the progressive character of history, or an idealistic theology of social salvation? Niebuhr's answer launched a new era in American theology and social ethics.

In 1932 he ran for Congress as a Socialist Party candidate, telling New Yorkers that only socialism could save Western civilization. Niebuhr warned in *Harper's* magazine: "It will be practically impossible to secure social change in America without the use of very considerable violence." He won 4 percent of the vote; a month later Niebuhr published the blockbuster book that changed American theology, *Moral Man and Immoral Society*.[2]

The book had an icy and aggressive tone, with an eerie sense of omniscience that partly reflected Niebuhr's debt to Marxism. Politics was about struggling for power, he admonished. Liberal denials of this truism were stupid, especially the moral idealism of liberal Christianity. Niebuhr argued that human groups never willingly subordinated their interests to the interests of others. Morality belonged to the sphere of individual action. On occasion, individuals rose above self-interest, motivated by compassion or love, but groups never overcame the power of self-interest and collective egotism that sustained their existence. Thus the liberal Christian attempt to moralize society was not only futile but was desperately lacking intelligence.[3]

With this book, "stupid" became Niebuhr's favorite epithet. Liberal idealists failed to recognize the brutal character of human groups and the resistance of all groups to moral suasion, he argued; thus they succumbed to "unrealistic and confused political thought." Secular liberals like John Dewey appealed to reason; Christian liberals appealed to love; both strategies were maddeningly stupid. *Moral Man and Immoral Society* seethed with Niebuhr's anger at the human ravages of the Depression and his frustration at America's aversion to socialism. It featured a prediction: "The full maturity of American capitalism will inevitably be followed by the emergence of the American Marxian proletarian. Marxian socialism is a true enough interpretation of what the industrial worker feels about society and history to have become the accepted social and political philosophy of all self-conscious and politically intelligent industrial workers."[4]

Like Christianity at its best, Niebuhr reasoned, Marxism was both realistic and utopian; it had a tragic view of history that was tempered by its hope for the transformation of history. Modern Christianity needed to regain a realistic sense of the tragedy of life: "The perennial tragedy of human history is that those who cultivate the spiritual elements usually do so by divorcing themselves from or misunderstanding the problems of collective man, where the brutal elements are most obvious. These problems remain unsolved, and force clashes with force, with nothing to mitigate the brutalities or eliminate the futilities of the social struggle." Niebuhr stressed that the historical sweep of human life always reflected the predatory world of nature. Thus he gave up his vow to follow Jesus as a pacifist. For the sake of justice *and* peace, modern Christianity had to renounce its sentimental idealism: "If the mind and the spirit of man does not attempt the impossible, if it does not seek to conquer or to eliminate nature but tries only to make the forces of nature the servants of the human spirit and the instruments of the moral ideal, a progressively higher justice and more stable peace can be achieved."[5]

Liberal Protestant leaders howled that Niebuhr ignored the teachings of Jesus, he had no theology of the church or the kingdom, and he treated his lack of faith in God's regenerative power as a virtue. Niebuhr replied that they were too comfortable in their moralistic idealism and humanism to understand him; he had moved to the right theologically and to the left politically: "If such a position seems unduly cynical and pessimistic to the American mind my own feeling is that this judgment is due to the fact that the American mind is still pretty deeply immersed in the sentimentalities of a dying culture." The right combination was Marxist radicalism and the biblical doctrine of sin. If politics was about struggling for power and radical politics was about struggling for a just redistribution of power, religion served the cause of justice only if it took a realistic attitude toward power, interest, and evil.[6]

Niebuhr's explanation of the crisis of capitalism was a page from Marx on the inevitability of overproduction. The problem was the system itself, not a defect in it or the egotism of individuals who profited from it: "The sickness from which modern civilization suffers is organic and constitutional. It is not due to an incidental defect in the mechanism of production or distribution but to the very character of the social system . . . Private ownership means social power; and the unequal distribution of social power leads automatically to inequality and injustice."[7]

Capitalism was great at mass production but also prodigious at generating injustice. Mass production needed mass consumption, Niebuhr explained, but capitalism was too predatory and class-stratified to sustain mass consumption. Thus capitalist society was disintegrating on the contradictions of a system that required, but could not accommodate, continually expanding markets.[8]

Liberalism and capitalism were finished. Niebuhr admonished that no amount of reformist tinkering would stop the world historical drift toward fascism. The ravages of capitalism would never be removed by moral effort, political reformism, or even the recognition that capitalism was destroying modern civilization. The only way to avert a fascist takeover of the entire Western world was for the West to embrace radical state socialism.[9]

In 1934 Niebuhr resigned from the Fellowship of Reconciliation, dramatically declaring that liberal Christian pacifism was too consumed with its pretense of virtue to make gains toward justice: "Recognizing, as liberal Christianity does not, that the world of politics is full of demonic forces, we have chosen on the whole to support the devil of vengeance against the devil of hypocrisy." He chose to support Marxist vengeance, knowing there was a devil in it, rather then allow the devil of hypocrisy to avoid conflict and preserve the status quo. To avoid any traffic with devils was simply to make oneself an accomplice to injustice and perhaps genocide; moral purity was an illusion.[10]

These were political arguments, however, with very hard edges. Liberal Protestant leaders did not talk about preferring Marxist vengeance to the devil of hypocrisy. They thought that ethical idealism applied everywhere, including international politics. In their revulsion against the vengeful outcome of World War I they had turned against war. Pacifism was ascending in the mainline denominations; it spoke mostly in religious terms; and its leaders included popular religious writers such as Harry Emerson Fosdick, Georgia Harkness, Vida Scudder, Kirby Page, John Haynes Holmes, Walter Russell Bowie, Edmund Chaffee, Richard Roberts, and John Nevin Sayre. They appealed to the nonviolent way of Jesus as the normative way of Christian discipleship. In the mid-1930s nearly every mainline

Protestant denomination vowed never to support another war. Niebuhr had played a role in bringing about this outcome; now he sought to undo it. To challenge the pacifist ethos of American liberal Protestantism, he had to deal with Jesus, not rest with politics.

That was the burden of his signature work, *An Interpretation of Christian Ethics* (1935), which argued that Jesus taught an ethic of love perfectionism, which was not socially relevant. Niebuhr put it starkly: "The ethic of Jesus does not deal at all with the immediate moral problem of every human life—the problem of attempting some kind of armistice between various contending factions and forces. It has nothing to say about the relativities of politics and economics, nor of the necessary balances of power which exist and must exist in even the most intimate social relationships."[11]

The teachings of Jesus were counsels of perfection; they were not prescriptions for social order or justice. Jesus had nothing to say about how a good society should be organized. In Niebuhr's rendering, Jesus lacked any horizontal point of reference and any hint of prudential calculation. His points of reference were always vertical, defining the moral ideal for individuals in their relationship to God. Jesus called his followers to forgive because God forgives; he called them to love their enemies because God's love is impartial. He did not teach that enmity could be transmuted into friendship by returning evil with love. He did not teach his followers to redeem the world through their care or moral effort. These Ghandian sentiments were commonplace in liberal sermons, but Jesus-style love perfectionism was not a social ethic.

In Niebuhr's view, the teaching of Jesus had social relevance in only one sense: it affirmed that a moral ideal existed, which judged all forms of social order or rule. It was a good thing to have an ideal, but the ethic of Jesus, being impossible, offered no guidance on how to hold the world in check.

The central problem of politics—justice—was about gaining and defending a relative balance of power. Jesus was no help with that. Niebuhr explained: "The very essence of politics is the achievement of justice through equilibria of power. A balance of power is not conflict; but a tension between opposing forces underlies it. Where there is tension there is potential conflict, and where there is conflict there is potential violence." Since the highest good in the political sphere was to establish justice, justice-making politics could not disavow resorting to violence. Liberal Christian leaders refused to accept this elementary truism; Niebuhr blasted them repeatedly, especially Shailer Mathews, who claimed that Christianity was committed to a "moral process" of regeneration and cooperation. Niebuhr acidly replied: "Christianity, in other words, is interpreted as the preaching of a moral ideal, which men do not follow, but which they ought to."[12]

There was such a thing as legitimate Christian pacifism, Niebuhr allowed, but it was not what liberal pastors in mainline denominations preached, and the Quakers fell short of it, too. The real thing was the pacifism of the Franciscans, Mennonites, Amish, and Brethren, which accepted the love perfectionism of Jesus' ethic in a literal way, and thus withdrew from active involvement in politics. These communities grasped the vertical orientation of Jesus' teaching and tried to organize their entire lives in accord with its literal meaning.

Niebuhr allowed that under sectarian circumstances, some practical teaching might be derived from the teaching of Jesus, though he was skeptical. Resistance to violence would be forbidden. Rewards for work or service would be eschewed. Resentment against wrongdoers would be forbidden. Love of enemies would be commanded. That was a tall order even for sectarian communities, Niebuhr cautioned. Everywhere else, the love perfectionism of Jesus was a relevant impossibility only for individuals in their lives before God. No part of Jesus' ethic could be applied seriously to the problems of social relationships in a fallen world outside the confines of countercultural sects.[13]

The peace of the world in a fallen world could not be gained by following the way of Christ. Neither could it be gained by turning the perfectionism of Jesus into a social ethic. Peace movements did not bring peace. Niebuhr stressed that middle-class professionals led the peace movements—people whose social and economic privileges were made possible by the unacknowledged struggles and violence of others. To inject a perfectionist ethic into public discussion was to imperil the interests of justice. Realism rested on the Augustinian maxim that the peace of the world is gained by strife.[14]

Niebuhr implored that liberal idealism was no match for the cynical evils of fascism or the enormous savageries of Stalinism and capitalism. Terrible things were happening in the world, yet liberals like Mathews and Dewey claimed to believe that reason and goodwill could solve the world's problems. In 1936, in exasperation, Niebuhr summarized the tenets of the liberal faith. Liberals apparently believed, he wrote:

a. That injustice is caused by ignorance and will yield to education and greater intelligence.

b. That civilization is becoming gradually more moral and that it is a sin to challenge either the inevitability or the efficacy of gradualness.

c. That the character of individuals rather than social systems and arrangements is the guarantee of justice in society.

d. That appeals to love, justice, good-will and brotherhood are bound to be efficacious in the end. If they have not been so to date we must have more appeals to love, justice, good-will and brotherhood.

e. That goodness makes for happiness and that the increasing knowledge of this fact will overcome human selfishness and greed.

f. That wars are stupid and can therefore only be caused by people who are more stupid than those who recognize the stupidity of war.[15]

To Niebuhr it was astonishing that such a faith had survived the terrors of the past half-century. He poured out a torrent of words to refute it, charging that liberalism was blind to "the inevitable tragedy of human existence, the irreducible irrationality of human behavior and the tortuous character of human history." Repeatedly he blasted Dewey for purveying liberal nonsense, notwithstanding that he and Dewey had nearly the same politics. Both believed that authentic democracy required democratic socialism. Both believed that to secure existing democratic gains, democracy had to be extended into the economic system. Both believed that only democratic socialism could achieve social justice, which Niebuhr defined as "a tolerable equilibrium of economic power." Both used the rhetoric of progress in claiming that socialism was the next step for history to take. In 1936 Niebuhr explained: "Socialism is the logical next step in a technical society, just as certainly as capitalism was a logical first step. First private enterprise developed vast social progress. Then history proved that the private possession of these social processes is incompatible with the necessities of a technical age." For Niebuhr, as for Dewey, modern civilization had to choose between retrogression and progress.[16]

By this reckoning, fascism was not a genuine historical alternative but rather "a frantic effort to escape the logic of history by returning to the primitive." Whatever victories it won, it would produce only "pathological perversities" with no staying power. The real choice was between retrogression and socialism, Niebuhr urged: "Socialism means the next step forward. That next step is the elimination of the specific causes of anarchy in our present society. The basic specific cause of anarchy and injustice is the disproportion of social power which arises from the private possession of social process."[17] For Niebuhr, as for Dewey, social ownership of the means of production was "a minimal requirement of social health in a technical age."[18]

Since socialism was "a primary requisite of social health," the half-hearted measures of the New Deal to save a dying patient were ridiculous. Capitalism was obviously destroying itself, Niebuhr urged; more important, capitalism had to be destroyed before it reduced the Western democracies to barbarism. Niebuhr stuck to that line through the 1930s, denying that the New Deal changed the equation. Nothing short of government ownership and control of the economy would save Western civilization; Niebuhr seemed not to notice that his own penetrating analysis of ruling group egotism applied to his solution. Instead of questioning the immense power state socialism placed in a self-interested, technocratic planning elite, he invoked a dogma: history would move forward to radical state socialism or backward to a barbaric, unregulated capitalism.[19]

This dogma secured another one, that Roosevelt's budget deficits ruined any chance of an economic recovery, contrary evidence notwithstanding. In Roosevelt's first term, the New Deal reduced national unemployment from 25 to 14 percent, and only once, in 1936, did his budget deficit exceed $4 billion. To Niebuhr, however, the serious choice was between nationalizing the means of production and balancing the federal budget. Tragically Roosevelt failed to manage either one; he refused to nationalize the economy and mortgaged the future with budget deficits. Niebuhr urged Roosevelt to raise taxes during the recession of 1937–38, which would have exacerbated the recession and unemployment.[20]

To Niebuhr, Roosevelt's cautious economic interventionism was futile and dangerous; capitalism had to be accepted on its own terms or abolished. By the end of the 1930s he was willing to say that radicals had to defend the New Deal against its "reactionary critics," but he persisted that Roosevelt's deficit spending was a form of insulin "which wards off dissolution without giving the patient health." The New Dealers were quacks who pretended not to realize that their cure worked only for a little while: "This quackery must be recognized and exposed."[21] Sometimes he called it "whirligig reform." In 1938 Niebuhr exclaimed: "If that man could only make up his mind to cross the Rubicon! A better metaphor is that he is like Lot's wife. Let him beware lest he turn into a pillar of salt." Arthur

Schlesinger Jr. later replied aptly that Roosevelt's task was to navigate his nation's way up the Rubicon, not to cross it.[22]

Despite believing that Roosevelt wasted his opportunity to save America, Niebuhr began voting for him in 1936. Since the Socialists were nowhere politically, and Roosevelt carried out much of the socialist platform, pragmatism called for holding one's nose and voting Democrat. In 1940 Niebuhr remarked, "Socialism must come in America through some other instrument than the Socialist Party." With an eye on the British Labour Party he assured that the emergence of a genuine farmer-labor party was one of the "inevitabilities of American politics," but it would take at least four to eight years.[23]

In the meantime, realistic radicals were stuck with the party that prolonged a dying capitalism. In 1939 Niebuhr urged Christian Socialists to support the better parts of the New Deal, especially the Wagner Act, while demanding something better, state socialism. Two years later he began to concede that Roosevelt's reforms were more than palliatives and that social justice would depend "increasingly upon taxation schedules in the coming years." A few months later he retreated further from the Marxist either/or, declaring that taxation schedules "will have more to do with the kind of justice we achieve in our society than any other single factor." In 1943 he retreated even further, noting that he had given up much of his Marxism; on the other hand, it remained "quite obvious that these forms of 'private' property which represent primarily social power, and the most potent social power of our day at that, cannot remain in private hands. The socialization of such power is a *sine qua non* of social justice."[24]

The semi-Keynesian policies of the New Deal had their place but merely as a holding action on inexorable social forces. Niebuhr still believed in the Marxist either/or. Not until 1944, after World War II had taken care of America's unemployment problem, did he give it up.

The dialectic that replaced it in Niebuhr's lexicon was the title of his book, *The Children of Light and the Children of Darkness* (1944). American liberals were "children of light," he judged. They recognized the existence of a moral law beyond themselves but failed to recognize the centrality of will-to-power in politics and history. Modern totalitarians of both fascist and Stalinist varieties, on the other hand, were "children of darkness." Cunning and immoral in their pursuit of power, they recognized no moral law beyond their collective struggle to dominate. This dialectic yielded Niebuhr's most famous epigram: "Man's capacity for justice makes democracy possible; but man's inclination to injustice makes democracy necessary."[25]

To Niebuhr, the chief value of democracy was not the one routinely invoked by political leaders overfed on Jeffersonian and progressive idealism. Liberal democracy was worth defending as the best way to restrain human evil and will-to-power, not because it fulfilled an ideal that people deserved by virtue of their moral worth. *The Children of Light and the Children of Darkness* pressed this argument as a brief for democratic socialism. Just as democracy was needed in the political sphere as a brake on political tyranny, Niebuhr argued, democracy was needed in the economic sphere as a brake on the overweening will-to-domination of the capitalist class. As late as 1944 he could write that "since economic power, as every other form of social power, is a defensive force when possessed in moderation and a temptation to injustice when it is great enough to give the agent power over others, it would seem that its widest and most equitable distribution would make for the highest degree of justice."[26]

"It would seem" was a signal, however. By the mid-1940s Niebuhr still believed in economic democracy as an ideal, even that it was essential to social justice. But he no longer believed it was happening or even possible in his country. Having ridiculed the New Deal in its time, he reconciled himself to it after Roosevelt was gone. Liberal reformism was a viable politics after all; most of his friends were in the Democratic Party; Niebuhr joined them there and stopped calling himself a Socialist. In 1947 his religious group, the Fellowship of Socialist Christians, changed its name to Frontier Fellowship. The same year he folded his chief political vehicle, the Union for Democratic Action, into a new organization dominated by establishment liberals, Americans for Democratic Action. Niebuhr and his Christian realist comrades entered the mainstream of U.S. politics and devoted themselves to the question of how a triumphant American democracy should exercise its international and domestic power in a morally responsible way. In 1949 he remarked that there was "a bare possibility that the kind of pragmatic political program which has been elaborated under the 'New Deal' and the 'Fair Deal' may prove to be a better answer to the problems of justice in a technical age than its critics of either right or left had assumed."[27]

This "possibility" became Niebuhr's guiding political truism in the 1950s. On economic issues his rhetoric cooled and diminished. Following his lead, Frontier Fellowship changed its name in 1951 to Christian Action and reduced its economic plank to a vague political exhortation "to maintain a high and stable level of economic activity, avoiding inflation and depression."[28] Even Republicans could have signed on for that. The following year, Niebuhr explained that he no longer thought in terms of general positions about capitalism and socialism. He had become a good liberal Democrat, embracing the militant anticommunism of his party's "vital center" and its pragmatic managerial approach to economics. The American Right and Left still thought about economics in ideological terms, he observed, opposing the New Deal for opposite reasons, but the New Dealers established a basically just order by thinking and acting pragmatically.[29]

"We have equilibrated power," Niebuhr enthused in 1952. "We have attained a certain equilibrium in economic society by setting organized power against organized power."[30] Against the grain of hyper-capitalist ideology, the U.S. built up a threefold order of countervailing trade union, capitalist, and governmental power. Welfare state capitalism attained as much of the socialist vision as appeared to be possible under American democracy. It created a just society by restraining human egotism through a balance-of-power politics, not by appealing to goodwill or moral ideals.[31]

The Niebuhr later invoked by neoconservatives was the Niebuhr of this period, the late 1940s to the mid-1950s, who provided much of the rationale for cold war ideology by describing Soviet communism as a perverted messianic religion with global ambitions. The next chapter explores some of this terrain. But Niebuhr had caveats about the cold war from its outset. He warned that every struggle for justice and against tyranny was inevitably corrupted by collective self-interest and the sinful human desire to dominate others. He opposed the witch-hunting anticommunism of the McCarthy movement and the fervently ideological, militaristic anticommunism of James Burnham and John Foster Dulles. And in the late 1950s Niebuhr began to demythologize parts of the cold war ideology that he had helped fashion, contending that Soviet communism was not an immutable monolith, an overpowering enemy, a world-threatening conspiracy, or an enemy with which the U.S. could not coexist. A decade later his nation's debacle in Vietnam forced him to rethink his idea of anticommunist containment.[32]

Niebuhr was always more pragmatic and discriminating in his anticommunism than the stereotype of him as a cold war ideologue, and he was a sharp critic of American presumptions to superiority and goodness. But he epitomized the conformism of a theological generation that trimmed its sails on economic justice and made its peace with the political establishment. Niebuhrian realists streamed into the Democratic establishment celebrated by Arthur Schlesinger's book, *The Vital Center*. Many other theologians swung toward apolitical existentialism in the 1950s, retreating from social justice concerns. Paul Tillich remained a religious socialist in theory but stopped writing about it, turning to depth psychology and his massive *Systematic Theology*. Emil Brunner concentrated on dogmatic theology and confined his statements on political economics to vague endorsements of the welfare state. Rudolf Bultmann reduced Christianity to privatized I-and-Thou experiences of the eternal in time in the moment. Karl Barth scorned the cold war consensus in theology, but he wrote little about politics.[33]

The defining crisis of the dialectical theology generation had passed. The losers of World War II and most of the victors worked together to build a new capitalist order with new international institutions devoted to economic development and security. Prophetic urges were stifled by the mood of the times and the sense of threat engendered by an expansionist Soviet enemy. The communist threat deterred theologians from criticizing Western inequality or imperialism. Postwar debates about how theology should relate to sociopolitical issues were pervaded by the politics of the cold war. Niebuhr's line prevailed, though not without a sharp protest from Barth.

In 1948 Barth gave the opening address at the inaugural assembly of the World Council of Churches in Amsterdam. The theme of the conference was "The Disorder of the World and God's Design." To Barth, that was putting it backward. The World Council was terribly wrong to begin by speaking of the world's disorder, he admonished, for the church did not exist to prescribe solutions for the world's social problems. Christian discourse, even about the world, rightly began with God's kingdom, "which has already come, is already victorious, and is already set up in all its majesty." The Council needed to begin "with our Lord Jesus Christ, who has already robbed sin and death, the devil and hell of their power."[34]

Much of the Council's pre-conference literature was secular and politicized by comparison. It gave Barth "the same strange impression as garments of deep mourning." Barth implored the World Council of Churches to come out of its mourning. Christians were called to be God's witnesses, not God's lawyers, managers, or engineers. The conference literature featured Christian plans to rebuild and reform the postwar world; Barth countered that "God's design" was not "something like a Christian Marshall Plan." Instead of straightening out the world or presuming to be its caretaker, the churches were called to confess and preach that the world belonged to God. The church was the body of God's children called to trust in God and proclaim God's victory over sin and live according to God's way.[35]

Niebuhr shook his head, as usual, at Barth's otherworldliness. In 1928 he had rendered a judgment on Barth that he never took back, contending that Barth's revelationist dogmatism amounted to "a new kind of fundamentalism or an old kind of orthodoxy." Barth replaced the liberal Jesus with a dogmatic Christ-idea, Niebuhr observed, but this idea was every bit as subjective as the liberal Jesus. Two years later, while traveling in Germany, Niebuhr tried to debate a group of Barthians and gave up. "A positivism which stands above reason is not debatable so what's the use?" he wrote to John Bennett. "It is really hopeless to argue with Barthians." Barth and the Barthians renounced, while Niebuhr affirmed, the spiritual authority of reason and experience. They retreated to the Reformation way of revelation and faith alone, armed with a neo-Reformation doctrine of the Word of God, while Niebuhr believed that faith and salvation were intimately connected to current moral, social, and spiritual experience. Theologically, Niebuhr judged, Barthianism was a sophisticated form of otherworldliness; ethically it produced a Lutheran-like quietism; theologically and ethically it amounted to "sanctified futilitarianism." Niebuhr admired Barth's strident resistance to German Christianity after Hitler took power in 1933, but he never stopped thinking of Barthian theology as essentially a dogmatic retreat from the real world and the intellectual problems of modern Christian belief. Barthianism was an immunization strategy, but modern theology needed to face its critics, revise its beliefs, and defend its claims.[36]

In 1948 both theologians were overdue for a public airing of their differences. Barth understood that he and Niebuhr were far apart theologically, yet he expected Niebuhr to sympathize with his attack on the Council's moralistic reformism. He had not understood that, at bottom, Niebuhr was still a liberal advocate of social Christianity. Niebuhr still believed that the church was called to promote world order, freedom, and social justice. To him, "The Disorder of the World and God's Design" was exactly what the World Council needed to talk about.[37]

Niebuhr was appalled by Barth's refusal to engage secular criticism and ordinary political problems. He protested that Barth's otherworldly evangelicalism negated the church's capacity to defend its relevance and credibility. He added that it made Barth's ethical thought woefully deficient.

Barth's opposition to the Nazification of the German churches was admirable, Niebuhr acknowledged; it gave a "powerful witness to Christ." Barth was good at responding to a crisis. But his thundering, otherworldly approach to theology was not very good at discerning the moral meaning of Christianity in normal times. Niebuhr explained, "It can fight the devil if he shows both horns and both cloven feet. But it refuses to make discriminating judgments about good and evil if the devil shows only one horn or the half of a cloven foot." For Barth it was axiomatic that the church had no business fulfilling or accommodating the modern cultural enterprise. For Niebuhr it was axiomatic that "the Christian must explore every promise and every limit of the cultural enterprise."[38]

This debate had a cold war subtext. By 1948 Barth had made it clear that he did not endorse the West's cold war against communism in the name of Christianity.[39] Against Brunner, who contended that Christian churches were obliged in principle to oppose communist totalitarianism with the same fervor they aroused against Nazi totalitarianism, Barth insisted that the two cases were dissimilar from a Christian standpoint. The structural similarities between communist and fascist totalitarianism were not pertinent subjects of Christian ethics, he argued, for there was no such thing as a Christian political system. The church, when speaking as it should, did not endorse or condemn political systems as such. Since the church did not concern itself with ideologies, it was not to speak "on principle" about the legitimacy or illegitimacy of political systems. In Barth's view, the church had no business anathematizing the communist system as such because it had no business making "principled" judgments that identified Christ with or excluded Christ from any political ideology.[40]

Many critics, including Brunner, made the obvious objection that Barth had not talked that way in the 1930s; otherwise he would not have been kicked out of Nazi Germany. Brunner stressed that Barth condemned the Hitler regime in the name of Christ and called for its overthrow; Barth replied that he had not done so on the basis of a political principle. As much as he despised National Socialism, ideology was not the point. What made Nazism different was its power to overwhelm and corrupt Christian souls; it was an evil religion that subverted the soul of the German church. Niebuhr later claimed that Soviet communism, too, was an evil religion, but Barth denied that communism was religiously corrupting.[41] The German church nearly lost its soul to Nazism, but where was the spiritual threat that communism posed to North American or West European churches? In the countries where church leaders called for "Christian" crusades against communism, Barth asked, where was the spiritual threat to the church that the truth of an anticommunist crusade needed to extinguish? "Are they not already sure enough of the justice of their cause against Russia without this truth and our Christian support?" Barth left the implication hanging: because the U.S. had overwhelming economic and military power, the existence of a militantly "Christian anticommunism" in the U.S. was not a spiritually healthy phenomenon.[42]

Later he said it plainly, sometimes infuriating Christian anticommunists like Niebuhr and Brunner. In 1958 Barth declared, "I regard anticommunism as a matter of principle an evil even greater than communism itself."[43] The following year, after an East German pastor asked Barth if he should pray for the abolition of the communist government in East Germany, Barth cautioned the pastor to beware that such a prayer "might be awfully answered, so that some morning you would wake up among those 'Egyptian fleshpots,' as one obligated to the 'American way of life.'" He advised the pastor to pray for the East German government, not against it. From a Christian standpoint, Barth cautioned, the existence of a communist government in East Germany had to be regarded in some sense as the rod of divine punishment. Barth regarded communism as a dreadful but natural product of Western history. The Western nations were getting what they deserved for centuries of imperialism and war, and they had barely begun to pay the price.[44]

But that was never the heart of the matter for Barth. To him the crucial question was always: Who sits in the seat of judgment? The only judge to be taken seriously, he urged, was the gracious and merciful God who willed that all people—"Christians and the whole of mankind"—should be saved. Because God was above all things, God was certainly above the "legalistic totalitarianism" of communist governments. As a system of political rule, communism was limited precisely by its godlessness and inhumanity. Barth predicted that "one day its officeholders will halt at those limits, or else they will be destroyed." In either case, communism was not sustainable and not worth the spiritual price of committing the church to anticommunism. The church was not called to support or impose any political system: "She can only follow Jesus; that is, she cannot but keep her sights constantly fixed on the merciful God and on man who is to receive God's mercy and be set free."[45]

Niebuhr took Barth's "Egyptian fleshpot" crack about the American way of life as a sneering cheap shot. He took Barth's Christian neutralism as a provocation. He shot back that the East Germans were no more sinful than their West German kin. If the East Germans were suffering for their sins, why did West Germany have immunity? For the most part, Niebuhr allowed, Barth adhered to "the strategy of approximating divine impartiality." He recalled that during the Nazi period Barth dared to make "hazardous detailed judgments" regularly, but now only on rare occasions did Barth's "robust humanity" so betray him. Now Barth desperately aspired to be impartial, like God. "The price of this desperation is of course moral irrelevance," Niebuhr declared. Barth's pursuit of prophetic purity was necessarily a pursuit of moral irrelevance. Niebuhr did not grant, however, that Barth had actually attained impartiality in his moral judgments. He judged that Barth's writings were still loaded with "merely human political" sentiments, such as, most notably, his animus against the United States. He also believed that Barth overestimated his prophetic stature. These points built up to a vintage Niebuhr verdict: "Barth is a man of talent to the point of genius. But even a genius cannot escape the dilemma that the price of absolute purity is irrelevance and that the price of relevance is the possible betrayal of capricious human loves and hates even in the heart of a man of God."[46]

By then the differences between Niebuhr and Barth were much clearer. For much of Niebuhr's career he believed that England was the best country of all, but by the 1950s he inclined to the proud conclusion that his own country had become the model of the liberal democratic idea, its racial pathologies notwithstanding. In his later career he also judged that his attacks on liberalism were too sweeping and polemical. Liberal Christianity was a richer and more complex tradition than he had acknowledged, and his own thinking was obviously a type of liberal theology. He had spent most of his career fighting for a kind of liberalism that did not view the world entirely through its idealism. Unfortunately, in his zeal for polemical victories, he usually had not put it that way.[47]

In 1960 he put it ruefully: "When I find neo-orthodoxy turning into a sterile orthodoxy or a new Scholasticism, I find that I am a liberal at heart, and that many of my broadsides against liberalism were indiscriminate." He had never been theologically neo-orthodox, he explained; liberalism was his tradition, despite its faults. In politics and religion he believed in a chastened liberal empiricism: "On the whole I regret the polemical animus of my theological and political activities and am now inclined to become much more empirical, judging each situation and movement in terms of its actual fruits."[48] Elsewhere he explained that as a product of the social gospel he was predisposed to approach theology as a polemical enterprise, which he lived to regret: "There is no need for polemics today, and there was no need for them when I wrote. My polemics were of an impatient young man who had certain things to say and wanted to get them said clearly and forcefully."[49]

In his old age Niebuhr resisted sentimental entreaties from American acquaintances of Barth's to patch things up with Barth, but he reconsidered Barth's anti–anti-communism after America got stuck in Vietnam. In 1966 Niebuhr joined the antiwar opposition; the following year he wrote that America's illusion of omnipotence caused it to commit indefensible evils in the world. He told friends he felt ashamed of his beloved nation.[50] In that mood, in 1969 he returned to an old debate: "I must now ruefully change that decade-ago opinion of mine in regard to Barth's neutralism. While I do not share his sneer at the 'fleshpots of Germany and America,' I must admit that our wealth makes our religious anti-Communism particularly odious. Perhaps there is not so much to choose between Communist and anti-Communist fanaticism, particularly when the latter, combined with our wealth, has caused us to stumble into the most pointless, costly, and bloody war in our history."[51]

The critics who painted Niebuhr as an unremitting cold war ideologue, and the neoconservative Niebuhrians who did the same, would have done better to linger over that conclusion.

Chapter 3

The Niebuhrian Legacy

CHRISTIAN REALISM AS THEOLOGY, SOCIAL ETHICS,
AND PUBLIC INTELLECTUALISM

Reinhold Niebuhr is usually remembered as the last theologian and Protestant leader to make an important impact on American society and the church. This convention somehow forgets that Martin Luther King Jr. was a theologian and Protestant leader. Elizabeth Sifton, in her wonderfully vivid account of her father's career, registers another objection, that the usual rendering of Niebuhr's great influence is mostly fiction.

"I am regularly amazed when I read in this or that magazine that my father was a 'major leader' of postwar American Protestantism," Sifton remarks. Niebuhr spoke constantly in college chapels, but only a handful of churches invited him to preach in their pulpits. Although he dropped his socialism in the 1940s, it didn't matter: "Even twenty and thirty years later my father was still viewed in most churches as dangerously 'pink,' and their pastors didn't want to have anything to do with him." Most American Christians and clerical leaders ignored or shunned him: "They pussyfooted around feel-good mega-preachers like Norman Vincent Peale or Billy Graham—who like so many of their successors never risked their tremendous personal popularity by broaching a difficult spiritual subject, and rarely lifted a finger to help a social cause."[1]

Sifton recalls that Niebuhr wearied of the pious irrelevance and timidity of church people, which heightened his appreciation for the "atheists for Niebuhr." It was not merely that Niebuhr attracted admirers who ignored his theology; he came most fully alive in their company. In Sifton's words, Niebuhr's secular liberal friends in the Americans for Democratic Action

(ADA) were "a welcome relief from the sometimes inane, always piously cautious, and frequently self-congratulatory churchmen among whom he might otherwise have had to spend his time. Even at the seminary one had to guard against the constant threat of sanctimony, whereas the ADA people were exuberant, skeptical, and energetically committed, after all, to *democratic action*."[2]

Niebuhr's public influence, as Sifton rightly cautions, was quite small compared to that of Graham or Peale, and he generally took a dim view of liberal Protestant leaders. The very things that irritated him about them made them piously irrelevant in the public square. Niebuhr, by contrast, was never sanctimonious, which helped to make him unwelcome in church sanctuaries.[3]

But the most important parts of the Niebuhr myth are true. He was the greatest American theologian of the twentieth century. He made a tremendous impact on modern theology and ethics. He was the greatest American Christian public intellectual ever. And he made an important impact on American politics.

Had Niebuhr lacked the humility and intellectual flexibility to change his mind numerous times, he would not have become a towering figure. In his early career he implored his fellow German-Americans to support America's intervention in World War I. In the 1920s he became a leading advocate of pacifist social gospel liberalism. In the 1930s he dropped pacifism and blasted the New Deal as a militant Socialist. In the 1940s he dropped socialism and became a leader of the Democratic Party's "Vital Center" establishment. In the late 1940s and early 1950s he helped formulate and establish cold war ideology. In the late 1950s he protested that ideologues and militants had hijacked anticommunism. In the 1960s he turned against the Vietnam War and called for a policy of peaceful co-existence with the Soviet Union.

A few constants remained amid all the changes. Niebuhr took for granted the activist orientation of the social gospel, even as he criticized social gospel idealism. He was deeply political and never apologized for being so. He was a brilliant interpreter of human fallibility and ambiguity. And he was always determined to be realistic, even during his liberal pacifist phase. For Niebuhr, realism was fundamentally the recognition that good and evil are inextricably linked in human nature and society, and that politics is primarily about struggling for power.

Repeatedly he blasted his liberal Protestant tradition for being too moralistic and idealistic. Niebuhr's first attacks on liberal Protestantism called the church to throw off its moralism to join the class struggle against a dying capitalist order. Later he called the church to throw off its moralism to join the Allied military struggle against fascism. Later he called the church to throw off its moralism to support America's cold war against communism. Niebuhr's dialectical realism defined for much of his theological generation what the "realities" of politics and ethics were. He taught Christian ethicists to view the world as a theater of perpetual struggles for power among competing interests; realism sought to secure a balance of power among existing regimes and a stable correlation of forces.

In his prime he advised government officials, appeared on the cover of *Time* magazine, and dominated his field to the point where, as Alan Geyer observed, Niebuhr seemed "an omnipresent figure in theology and ethics." In his last years he lost his leadership role in Christian ethics on the ground that his realism was an American ideology serving the interests of American power. By the time Niebuhr died, liberation theologians James Cone and Gustavo Gutierrez had given notice that the reign of Christian realism was over in Christian ethics. From a liberationist standpoint, Niebuhrian realism was part of the problem because it viewed the world from the standpoint of white, male, middle-class, American political and economic interests. So-called Christian realism was functional to the prevailing system, just like the nationalistic secular realisms for which it provided ethical cover.[4]

But four decades after Niebuhr's death, debates over his method and position still preoccupy much of the field of Christian ethics, and Niebuhr's name has returned forcefully to public discussion, mostly because the Bush administration pitched realism aside after September 11, 2001. David Brooks, a *Weekly Standard* neocon with an editorial perch at the *New York Times*, invokes Niebuhr as his philosophical guide. So does Barack Obama, joining a vast array of liberal hawks, antiwar liberals, moderates, neoconservatives, and even old right conservatives. Niebuhr's many changes of position, his complexity and emphasis on ambiguity, and his pragmatism combined to earn him a varied legacy and to be claimed by contrasting political types.[5]

For Niebuhr personally, as for American theology as a whole, the turning point came in 1932 with the publication of *Moral Man and Immoral Society*. Niebuhr sharply contended that only individuals are capable of self-transcending moral decisions. Groups cannot organize for ethical ends. Politics is about struggling for power, always with some degree of violence, and defending gains toward justice, always with more violence.

Liberal appeals to rationality and goodwill in the political sphere, he assured, were stupid, and the love ethic of Jesus applied to the private sphere of the self, not the harsh business of managing the world.

Moral Man and Immoral Society evoked howls of outrage and shocked disbelief. Liberal Protestant leaders protested that Niebuhr ignored Jesus, he had no theology of the church or the kingdom, and he had no faith in the presence or regenerative power of God. Henry P. Van Dusen and Francis Miller could not find the gospel anywhere in the book. Norman Thomas, John Haynes Holmes, and the *Christian Century* magazine blasted Niebuhr's "defeatism." Charles Gilkey announced to his family that their dear friend Reinie had apparently lost his mind.[6]

In the face of this outcry, Helmut Richard Niebuhr saw an opportunity. Two years earlier he had begun teaching at Yale and started going by his "American" middle name. For many years Richard had competed with his brother, assisted him, argued with him, and looked up to him. Outside the public eye, the two regularly scrutinized each other's work; in public they debated only once, in 1932, in the *Christian Century* magazine, responding to the Japanese invasion of Manchuria. Richard spoke for non-intervention, invoking what he called "the grace of doing nothing." God had God's own plans for history, and Christians were not called to make history come out right. Reinhold replied that Christians are called to serve the cause of justice, and there is no grace in doing nothing. Richard replied that they had been having this argument for thirty years and it was pointless to say anything more; there would be no more public debates with his brother.[7]

But the following year he seized the opportunity to influence his brother. "I have no defense of idealism to offer," he told Reinhold. "I hate it with all my heart as an expression of our original sin." He found it commendable that Reinie had offended so many liberals, but Reinie was still one of them in his assumptions about human nature, religion, and activism. On the virtue of "moral man," for example, Richard asked him to consider brotherly love—for example, Richard's own. He took pride in Reinie's achievements, basked in his reflected glory, struggled to stand on his own feet, resented being compared to him, and felt jealous of him, all at the same time. If he could love his brother despite resenting him so much, it wasn't because any ideal or will to love prevailed over his selfishness or resentment. It was because something else that was not his will was at work long before he had a will or an ideal. Richard argued that human beings possess a moral gift of judging right and wrong, not a gift of goodness. All morally reflective people know they are bad. Therefore he rejected Reinhold's claim that individuals are morally superior to their groups. Individuals only appeared to have a higher capacity for moral self-giving because coercion works better in face-to-face relationships, and in the private realm it is easier to see that morality and enlightened self-interest go together.[8]

More important, Reinie was still a liberal in the way he thought about religion. For him, religion was a power for good or ill that he wanted to use for good. Richard admonished that true religion is directed toward God, not society: "I think that liberal religion is thoroughly bad. It is a first-aid to hypocrisy. It is the exaltation of goodwill, moral idealism . . . It is sentimental and romantic. Has it ever struck you that you read religion through the mystics and ascetics? You scarcely think of Paul, Augustine, Luther, Calvin. You're speaking of humanistic religion so far as I can see. You come close to breaking with it at times but you don't quite do it."

Luther and Calvin did not moralize Christianity or make it a vehicle for social activism, Richard urged. Reinhold's frenetic chasing after social causes was spiritually corrupting. Richard put it strongly: "I do think that an activism which stresses immediate results is the cancer of our modern life . . . We want to be saviors of civilization and simply bring down new destruction . . . You are about ready to break with that activism. I think I discern that."[9]

Richard Niebuhr was wrong about the last part. For Reinhold Niebuhr, the social gospel view of religion as energy for the social struggle was a core assumption. He would never say that social activism was the cancer of modern life. He took for granted that religion is a social construct; it is grounded in ethical and spiritual striving; it should be a power for social good; and it depends on human capacities for transcendence, good, and evil.

But Richard Niebuhr correctly perceived that his brother needed a theological basis. Reinhold had replaced the Reformationist language of grace alone, faith alone, and scripture alone with a pastiche of liberal theology and politics; then he turned to the left politically; then he turned against the idealistic parts of liberal theology. Richard protested that he wrote as though Paul and Calvin never existed. Reinhold took that objection to heart. His next book, *Reflections on the End of an Era*, was the most Marxist book he ever wrote, yet in its closing pages he reclaimed the language of divine providence and grace. Thereafter he drew more and more deeply on Augustine, Luther, and Calvin, remarking in 1939: "Even while imagining myself to be preaching the Gospel, I had really experimented with many modern alternatives to Christian faith, until one by one they proved unavailing."[10]

Niebuhr's mature theology was a profound refashioning of Reformation themes, though it had many shortcomings. Niebuhr took a pass on epistemology and hermeneutics. He had little to say about the trinity, Christology, the Holy Spirit, the Kingdom of God, and the church as the body of Christ. He described the incarnation and resurrection of Christ as "permanently valid" myths of Christianity without explaining what that meant. Are Christian symbols regulative principles in the Kantian sense? Do they have a more substantive reality? Niebuhr waved off such questions: "I cannot and do not claim to be a theologian . . . I have never been very competent in the nice points of pure theology; and I must confess that I have not been sufficiently interested heretofore to acquire the competence." His work reflected what he called "the strong pragmatic interest of American Christianity."[11]

On the other hand, Niebuhr went only so far in disclaiming the necessity of scholarly proficiency. His major work, *The Nature and Destiny of Man*, was based on a distinction between what he called the "classical" and "biblical" views of human nature and destiny. In his rendering, the classical view of Plato, Aristotle, and the Stoics held that human beings were unique within nature as spiritual beings gifted with self-reflective thought and reason. The biblical view was dialectical in conceiving the self as a created finite unity of body and spirit, a view that conflicted with idealist, rationalist, and romantic notions.

Niebuhr built his theology around this idea of the biblical view: God is beyond society and history, yet God is intimately related to the world. The human spirit finds a home and grasps its spiritual freedom in God's transcendence, yet the self also finds there the limit of its freedom, a judgment against it, and the divine mercy that makes judgment bearable. For Niebuhr, the heart of Christianity was the promise of salvation from humanity's enslaving egotism through divine grace, which was not a promise of deliverance or regeneration. The redemptive work of God's gift of grace was to enable egotists to surrender their prideful attempts to master their existence. Religiously, the cross was a symbol of God's judgment on human sin and God's loving forgiveness; ethically, it was the ultimate symbol of the importance and unattainability of the law of love.[12]

Niebuhr's creative profundity in expounding this perspective was more impressive than the scholarly foundation he built for it. Robert Calhoun was a legendary teacher at Yale and the most learned American historical theologian of his generation. Calhoun ripped apart the first volume of *The Nature and Destiny of Man*, blasting Niebuhr for distorting the past to dramatize his personal vision. In Niebuhr's telling, the prophets were always better than the Wisdom literature, Hebrew religion was better than Hellenism, Paul was better than the Synoptic Gospels, and the Reformation was better than the Renaissance. Calhoun replied: "He does not understand 'classical thought,' a chief villain throughout the book, and many of his references to it make painful reading." Niebuhr wrote shooting-gallery nonsense about classicism and the Renaissance; he oversimplified idealism and romanticism to refute them as well; he made a mess of Hellenistic Christianity; and he showed gross ignorance of philosophy and science. As a work of historical scholarship, Calhoun concluded, Niebuhr's magnum opus "cannot be taken seriously."[13]

This attack wounded Niebuhr deeply. Calhoun was a master of the data who never managed to write a major book. Niebuhr resented his superior attitude and his judgment that the valuable parts of Niebuhr's work were projections of his inner struggle. Yet on both points he surely realized that Calhoun was right. Niebuhr's penetrating descriptions of pride and will-to-power obviously drew on personal experience, and he lacked the temperament and training of a scholar. But Niebuhr did not reply, "Oh, well, I'm a public intellectual who can't be bothered with the scholarly finer points." *The Nature and Destiny of Man* was based on a two-semester course on Christian ethics that Niebuhr taught every year at Union. He cared deeply about getting the arguments right. Thus he replied to Calhoun and other critics by working harder on volume 2, toning down the shooting-gallery atmosphere, and enlisting his wife, Ursula, and Henry Sloane Coffin to restrain his polemics. Instead of blasting the Renaissance as in volume 1, he criticized Karl Barth and the Reformers for denigrating Renaissance humanism. In volume 2, Niebuhr began to clarify that he still belonged to the liberal tradition despite rejecting its idealism and rationalism.

Questioning the Nature of Man

The Nature and Destiny of Man brilliantly dissected the dilemmas of the isolated egocentric male. This creature was driven primarily by his struggle, conscious or not, with the sin of pride. In refusing to accept his dependence, he pretended to be adequate unto himself, and thus put himself in the place of God. He kept others at a distance, made himself the center of the universe, sought power over others, and usurped God's authority. For Niebuhr, as for Augustine and Calvin, hubris was the primary form of human sin, and salvation was deliverance from it. Christian salvation delivered isolated selves from their pride and self-absorption by defeating their self-will. In Niebuhr's words: "Christianity is a religion of revelation in which a holy and loving God is revealed to man as the source and end of all finite existence against whom the self-will of man is shattered and his pride abased."[14]

This understanding of the human situation and the Christian response to it was surely an insightful and illuminating description of something. But did it describe the universal human predicament, as Niebuhr claimed? How could it be said to account for people who were not self-centered and obsessed with power? The hallways of Union Theological Seminary were filled with women who put their husbands through seminary and sacrificed any hope of a career while taking care of their children. Were hubris and will-to-power their primary moral failings? Valerie Saiving, a doctoral student at Union in 1958, was the first to raise that question publicly. She observed that when Niebuhr described "man" as standing at the juncture of nature and spirit, he presumably had in mind all human beings, but in fact he generalized from his own experience and that of his colleagues. Men struggled with freedom, anxiety, and pride, but the women that Saiving and Niebuhr knew at Union were too close to nature to stand at the juncture of nature and spirit. Saiving observed that because pride and power were not really the issues for them, the remedy of self-sacrificial love was highly problematic.[15]

Union theologian Daniel Day Williams, upon reading her paper, told Saiving it had to be published; she later recalled that publishing it "never would have occurred to me, never." Two years later it was published in the *Journal of Religion* and then forgotten. Remembrance had to wait for the feminist movement and a popular anthology, *Womanspirit Rising*, edited by Carol Christ and Judith Plaskow, which republished Saiving's article and gave ballast to a powerful, rising tradition of feminist theology and criticism.[16]

Niebuhr died just as feminist theology arose. In his prime, during the decidedly pre-movement 1940s, he took a typically two-handed view of feminist ideology, claiming "balance." On the one hand, he argued, feminism was a liberating "new emergent in history" that corrected a universal wrong, for all societies of the past "unduly restricted" the right of women to "develop their capacities beyond the family function." On the other hand, patriarchy was organic and grounded in a deep moral wisdom, unlike the anti-organic rationalism and idealism of the modern age on which feminist ideology depended. Patriarchy understood that motherhood is a vocation grounded in nature, whereas fatherhood is merely an avocation. In its moral concern to protect the family's organic integrity, patriarchy "recognized the hazard to family life in the freedom of women."[17]

Niebuhr stressed that the meaning of justice in family life was elusive and paradoxical. In his telling, the problem was usually framed in public discussions by two extreme ideologies. Patriarchy was about organic repression, and modern idealism was about being liberated from nature. Both were seriously deficient, but the clash between them yielded an appropriate balance between women's rights and "natural obligations." Niebuhr believed, in 1944, that American society had fortunately achieved such a balance. The American bourgeoisie had shed "some of its appreciation of the organic integrity of the family," which was shortsighted and morally shallow, but also beneficial: "Had this error been prematurely suppressed, the new freedom of women would have been suppressed also." As always, the social good was to achieve "a proper balance between freedom and order," which usually occurred, in history's ironic way, by getting two mistaken ideas into a fight with each other.[18]

To Niebuhr, the paternally governed family was the bedrock of cultural order and the place where true human fulfillment was attainable. The private realm of home, family, and friends was the sphere in which moral values were generated and created, while the public realm was a zone of competition, power-lust, and comparative absence of values. It was not the business of the public sphere to nurture identity or instill values. Public business was about maintaining order and ensuring individual opportunity. To be sure, certain values were appropriate to the public sphere, but these were instrumental values serving society's quest for justice. The private realm was the sphere of true fulfillment; the public realm (overwhelmingly white and male) was the sphere for managing the outer world. This dualism, for better and worse, underwrote Niebuhr's realism whenever he construed the relation of Christianity to public business.

Defeating Fascism and Communism

He is best remembered for his attacks on liberal pacifism and idealism in the 1930s and his strong anticommunism in the 1950s. But memory is often fitted to our stereotypes, as in these cases. Contrary to the usual rendering, Niebuhr did not spend the 1930s urging the U.S. to arm for a battle against fascism. As late as March 1939 he was passionately opposed to preparing for war. In 1937 Niebuhr condemned Franklin Roosevelt's naval buildup as a "sinister" evil, declaring that it had to be "resisted at all costs." The next year he blasted Roosevelt's billion-dollar defense budget as "the worst piece of militarism in modern history," a stunning exaggeration considering what Hitler was up to. Right up to the Munich crisis, Niebuhr insisted that the best way to avoid war was not to prepare for one; collective security was the realistic alternative to war. He wanted the U.S. to enact neutrality legislation and voluntarily support League of Nations sanctions. That even Niebuhr stridently opposed Roosevelt's preparations for war is a measure of the revulsion for war that his generation felt after World War I. *Moral Man and Immoral Society* did not lead straight to the interventionism of 1940; Niebuhr had to struggle for eight years to get there. Then he had to fight to bring others along, and in doing so he became one of the giant figures of modern theology and a major public intellectual.[19]

Remarkably Niebuhr delivered his Gifford Lectures, *The Nature and Destiny of Man*, while Europeans prepared for war and Niebuhr faced up to the necessity of fighting fascism. On occasion the crisis of Western civilization poked through his Giffords, delivered in the spring and fall of 1939 at Edinburgh; otherwise he took the high road of doctrinal theology while pouring out magazine articles on Hitler and war. In both cases he warned that Europe lacked the moral and intellectual resources to resist modern cynicism, nihilism, militarism, and will-to-power. Modern alternatives to Christianity would never generate the realistic, reformist, spiritually powered defense of European civilization that was needed to save Europe from fascist barbarism.[20]

Niebuhr praised Roosevelt for grasping the terrible threat to democratic civilization posed by Hitler's militarism. In 1940, however, most Americans were determined to avoid another war, very much like their church leaders. Niebuhr blasted them furiously, charging that American churches had sunk to a new low of moral insensitivity and cowardice. The *Christian Century*, headed by Charles Clayton Morrison, was Niebuhr's main target. According to Morrison, Roosevelt was driving the U.S. straight to fascist rule and militarism. In May 1940 Morrison wanted the U.S. to convene a conference of neutral nations to formulate terms for an armistice. The following month he pleaded that it was too late for America to join the war. Hitler would either be stopped by the forces presently arrayed against him "or he will not be stopped." Niebuhr replied that Morrison's conference proposal was "fatuous" and his foreign policy "completely perverse and inept." The *Century*'s isolationism was a "shocking revelation of the disposition of Americans to close their eyes to the magnitude of the tragedy which has engulfed Europe."[21]

Morrison described himself as a pragmatic peacemaker, not an absolute pacifist; Niebuhr replied that if liberal Protestants could not summon the humanity and courage to defeat Hitler, they would never fight any evil aggressor. American liberal Christian pacifism was usually an "unholy compound of gospel perfectionism and bourgeois utopianism," he observed. Spurning sectarianism, it was "always fashioning political alternatives to the tragic business of resisting tyranny and establishing justice by coercion." But all the twisting and turning amounted to mere capitulation to tyranny, which was not very admirable. American Christianity needed to fight the fascist menace, Niebuhr implored, "lest we deliver the last ramparts of civilization into the hands of the new barbarians."[22]

In the name of gospel idealism, the *Christian Century* advocated connivance with tyranny and preached that slavery was better than war. "That any kind of peace is better than war," Niebuhr observed bitterly, was nearly a universal dogma of American Christianity. In this case, the terms of peace would require concessions to a tyrannical regime "which has destroyed freedom, is seeking to extinguish the Christian religion, debases its subjects to robots who have no opinion and judgment of their own, threatens the Jews of Europe with complete annihilation and all the nations of Europe with subordination under the imperial dominion of a 'master race.'" The appeasing moralism of America's liberal culture made the world safe for fascism: "It imagines that there is no conflict of interest which cannot be adjudicated. It does not understand what it means to meet a resolute foe who is intent upon either your annihilation or enslavement."[23]

Since the flagship magazine of American Protestantism was ethically bankrupt in the name of Christian ethics, American Protestantism needed a new magazine. *Christianity and Crisis* was Niebuhr's alternative. Launched in February 1941, it featured John Bennett, Sherwood Eddy, William Scarlett, Henry Sloane Coffin, William Adams Brown, John R. Mott, and Francis J. McConnell; above all, it was a vehicle for Niebuhr's politics. With its founding, Niebuhr sought to realign American liberal Protestantism. He already had one journal—*Radical Religion*, renamed *Christianity and Society* in 1940, published by the Fellowship of Socialist Christians—but it was too explicitly socialist to get much of an audience among pastors and church leaders. In 1941 Niebuhr got more political than ever, turning his attention to *Christianity and Crisis, The Nation,* and the newly formed Union for Democratic Action (UDA), a labor/socialist caucus of leftists disgusted by the Socialist Party's isolationism.

Niebuhr's seminary friends were only a piece of the progressive interventionist movement he envisioned; thus he built up *Christianity and Crisis* and the UDA at the same time. Theologians Henry Sloane Coffin and Henry Van Dusen were important to *Christianity and Crisis* and Niebuhr's vision of a realigned Protestantism, but they could never hang out with union leaders and Socialists. Under Niebuhr's leadership the UDA attracted union leaders Lewis Corey, Murray Gross, George Counts, A. Philip Randolph, and Franz Daniel. Niebuhr aspired to a national farmer-labor party; in the meantime he created a coalition of intellectuals, activists, and union officials that threw out the traditional socialist denigration of religion, excluded Communists from membership, and rallied Americans to fight fascism.

Niebuhr protested that bourgeois moralism was so pervasive in the U.S. that even Marxists were going soft. The American Left as a whole was nearly as cowardly and pacifistic as American Christianity. He warned that Hitler would not be deterred by the Atlantic Ocean: "If Hitler conquers Europe and penetrates into South America (which he may well do without much military effort) we would be forced to compete in the world with a slave economy, with an economy which would combine the efficiency of the modern machine with the low labor prices of slavery." Sometimes he doubted that Western democracy would survive anywhere: "The fact is that moralistic illusions of our liberal culture have been so great and its will-to-power has been so seriously enervated by a confused pacifism, in which Christian perfectionism and bourgeois love of ease have been curiously compounded, that our democratic world does not really deserve to survive."[24]

Shortly after Japan attacked Pearl Harbor and the U.S. entered World War II, Niebuhr switched gears. Very soon, he predicted, the same moralists that pleaded against going to war would be clothing America's war effort with insufferable visions of a transformed world order. He could hardly bear the idealistic calls to war that he knew were coming. Since Americans insisted on viewing themselves as righteous and benevolent, he complained, they had to moralize even their wars and imperial occupations.[25]

Repeatedly Niebuhr protested that Americans actually believed their country was the world's redeemer nation. Every president since Wilson felt obliged to pretend that America championed world democracy with no imperial designs or interests. Niebuhr replied in *The Irony of American History* (1952): "We cannot simply have our way, not even when we believe our way to have the 'happiness of mankind' as its promise." In *The Structure of Nations and Empires* (1959) he put it ruefully: "We are tempted to the fanatic dogma that our form of community is not only more valid than any other but that it is more feasible for all communities on all continents."[26]

To Niebuhr, a strong dose of realism about America's struggle for world power would have been redemptive. Realism without a moral dimension is corrupt, he argued, but any moral idealism not chastened by the world's evil is pathetic and dangerous. The cynically realistic "children of darkness" were wise in their recognition of self-interest and will-to-power, but evil to the extent that they recognized no transcendent moral law. The idealistic "children of light" were good by virtue of their obedience to moral law, but foolish in underestimating the pervasive and brutal power of collective egotism. In Niebuhr's reckoning the fascists and Soviet Communists were both children of darkness, with a significant difference. Fascists lacked an inspiring ideal that appealed to others; thus they could be smashed directly by armed force. But after World War II gave way to the cold war, Communists had the moral power of a utopian creed that appealed to deluded leftists and to millions in the Third World; thus they had to be fought differently.[27]

In essence, Niebuhr believed that communism was an evil religion. It was devoted to the establishment of a new universal order, not merely the supremacy of a race or nation. In 1954 he put it sharply: "We are embattled with a foe who embodies all the evils of a demonic religion. We will probably be at sword's point with this foe for generations to come."[28] Because the utopian element of communism made it more appealing and dangerous than fascism, Niebuhr reasoned, it had to be fought in the way that the Christian West should have fought militant Islam in the high Middle Ages. Crusading attempts to wipe out the enemy directly would not work; what was needed was a patient, forceful, selective policy of containment that put the Soviet state on the defensive. Like his friend George Kennan, Niebuhr believed that the Soviet Union would eventually self-destruct on its failures and internal contradictions. The chief purpose of cold war containment was to heighten the pressure on an unworkable Soviet system, although, unlike Kennan, Niebuhr judged that Soviet communism might survive for several generations. Kennan thought that successful containment might cause the Soviet Union to implode within fifteen years.[29]

These were the foreign policy keynotes of a "Vital Center" liberalism that claimed the mainstream of American politics in the late 1940s and 1950s. Niebuhr, Arthur Schlesinger Jr., John F. Kennedy, and Hubert Humphrey were its standard bearers. It combined a liberal internationalist commitment to the United Nations and international law with balance-of-power realism in diplomacy and an ideological abhorrence of communism. For the most part, Niebuhr's anticommunism was pragmatic and discriminating. In the late 1950s he protested that professional anti-Communists turned the cold war into an idolatrous and overly militarized religion, and he called for a policy of no-first-use of nuclear weapons. In the early 1960s, while accepting the Medal of Freedom from President Lyndon Johnson, Niebuhr lined up with other cold war liberals in support of America's war in Vietnam, warning that Southeast Asia would fall to the Communists if the U.S. gave up on South Vietnam. But the Niebuhr-quoting realists in the Kennedy and Johnson administrations created a disaster in Vietnam, and the Vital Center exploded, hurtling Niebuhrians to the right and left. To his sad surprise, Niebuhr tacked to the left, joining the antiwar movement. In 1966 he lamented that America had turned the Vietnamese civil war into an American imperial war. The following year he called for an American withdrawal from Vietnam and a public outcry "against these horrendous policies."[30]

The carnage and futility of the war sickened him. Niebuhr confessed, "For the first time I fear I am ashamed of our beloved nation." With Kennan, he disavowed "any simple containment of Communism," urging that the two superpowers had to work out a coexistence that lessened the threat of a nuclear war. In his last years Niebuhr worried that his country had become a reactionary world power through its arrogance of power.[31]

Thus did the cold war liberals back away from the ravages of anticommunist containment in Vietnam. A long succession of Kennedy and Johnson administration officials followed Niebuhr in repenting of imperial overstretch. The catastrophe in Vietnam fueled an explosion of new social movements challenging the legitimacy of America's dominant order. Two contrasting reactions to the exotic turbulence of the time had special pertinence for the fate of Niebuhrian theology: liberation theology and neoconservatism.

Liberationists charged that Niebuhrian realism was essentially an ideology of the dominant American order. Rubem Alves put it plainly, declaring that Niebuhr provided "ideological and theological justification" for American military and economic interests: "Realism has not yet recognized that it is an American ideology and yet [it] proceeds to pass universal judgment over the other 'regional' theologies." Cornel West put it strongly, describing Niebuhrian realism as a "form of Europeanist ideology that promoted and legitimated U.S. hegemony in the world." West explained that, for Niebuhr, Western Europe and the U.S. comprised a superior civilization, a prejudice that underwrote Niebuhr's support of U.S. domination of Latin America, European colonialism in Africa, and an Israeli state led by European Jews that oppressed the Palestinians. There were two streams of Niebuhrian realism, West observed. One sought to shore up a declining liberal Democratic Party establishment; West called them "desperate" defenders of a "discredited" perspective. The other group turned Niebuhr's Euro-American supremacism and cold war militarism into an ideology of American empire.[32]

The second stream was the neoconservative movement. Many of the original neoconservatives were longtime Old Left anti-Communists that hated the social movements of the 1960s.[33] Some were conservative-leaning religious thinkers close to Niebuhr's circle, such as Paul Ramsey and Ernest Lefever. Others turned to the political Right after dabbling in New Left radicalism; Michael Novak was a prominent example. In September 1972, one year after Niebuhr died, Novak wrote that it seemed like ten. Novak had worked recently for George McGovern's presidential campaign but revulsion was stirring within him. He hated feminism; it appalled him that white liberals deferred to Black Power; the antiwar movement had become unbearable; and McGovern's idealistic whining sent him over the edge. Novak didn't know where he was going politically, but he realized that he couldn't stand the new liberals, much less the radicals to whom they deferred. In his first phase of converting to what came to be called neoconservatism, Novak accused the Democratic Party of betraying real liberalism. McGovern symbolized this betrayal, just as Niebuhr symbolized what had been lost. More than ever, Novak argued, America needed Niebuhr's tough-minded, anticommunist, antimoralistic realism: "In many ways it is as if he had lived and worked in vain."[34]

At first the neocons proposed to restore the Democratic Party's aggressive anticommunist realism. That Niebuhr opposed the Vietnam War was sadly symptomatic. Ramsey lamented that the later Niebuhr signed petitions and editorials as if Reinhold Niebuhr had never existed. In 1966 Ramsey declared that because Niebuhr, John Bennett, and most Niebuhrians had turned against the war, it was time to say that Christian realism no longer existed. Its downfall had begun in the early 1960s, when the magazine *Christianity and Crisis* began to search for "a new liberal consensus."[35]

Novak expanded on that rendering of recent history. The real Niebuhr had torn apart America's idea of itself as a kind of church, "a movement of social goodness," Novak observed. But the Niebuhr of the 1960s was ill, and declining, and therefore unable to resist the tidal wave of another guilt-ridden, moralistic idealism. American liberalism desperately needed a renewal of the real thing that would repudiate the "unsupportable sense of guilt" over white racism and imperialism which defined the new progressives, the incredibly stupid slogan that "the personal is the political," and the popular conceit that liberals could make the world a better place through their idealism.[36]

On that basis the neocons claimed to be Niebuhrians. Niebuhr's closest ally and friend, John Bennett, begged to differ. In 1993, ten years before the neocons invaded Iraq, Bennett told me: "The only thing that Reinhold Niebuhr and the neoconservatives have in common is the word realism. The way they go on against feminism and environmentalism and gay rights—it's unbelievable. Their anti-feminism, especially, is horrible. This has nothing to do with Reinie or with how we understood Christian realism. I try not to take their meanness personally, but when they bring Reinie into it, that's more than I can take." Niebuhr would not have held out against feminism had he lived to see the emergence of a feminist theology movement, Bennett argued. All his life Niebuhr identified with the political Left, as did the Niebuhrians who shared his fundamental sympathies, such as Ronald Stone, Roger Shinn, Larry Rasmussen, Alan Geyer, Charles West, and Kermit Johnson. As for the neoconservative phenomenon, Bennett hoped it was over, having spent twenty-five years battling neocon Niebuhrians: "I think that neoconservatism is one of the worst movements in this country in my time. Those people are from my point of view wrong about everything."[37]

In later life Niebuhr regretted having spent so much of his career attacking liberalism. Repeatedly he stressed that he was a liberal in politics and theology. He took for granted that Christianity has a mission to build structures of social justice; that the wellspring of religion is humanity's unique capacity for good, transcendence, and evil; and that Christian scripture and teaching are pervaded by myth. Niebuhr criticized liberal theology for depending on philosophical idealism, but he relied on the idealistic concepts of self, consciousness, self-consciousness, self-transcendence, spirit, will, and personality. He rejected liberal rationalism, but he took for granted that reason and experience are the tests of religious truth. He had never been "neo-orthodox" in the Barthian sense of trumping reason and religious experience with a doctrine of scriptural authority, and he wished he had stressed his liberal underpinnings instead of giving comfort to religious and political conservatives.[38]

But the deeper problem of Niebuhrian realism lay elsewhere. The social gospelers tried to change society with moral appeals, but Niebuhr pleaded with them to stop, because politics is a struggle for power driven by interest and will-to-power. The social gospelers thought that a cooperative commonwealth was literally achievable; Niebuhr replied that the very idea of a just society had to be forsaken. These negations were costly for Christian ethics. The idea of a just society emerges from discussion and is always in process of revision. To let go of it is to undercut the struggle for attainable gains toward social justice, negating the elusive but formative vision of what is worth struggling for. Without a vision of a just society that transcends the prevailing order, ethics and politics remain captive to the dominant order, restricted to marginal reforms. The borders of possibility remain untested.

Moral Man and Immoral Society drew the lines that are still at issue. Niebuhr repudiated the liberal Protestant belief that the ethos of a moral community can be insinuated into the public realm. Politics was not about community or ethical aims, an assurance Niebuhr stuck to long after he stopped calling for socialist revolutions. Because the liberal Christian quest for a politics of community was an illusion, the only recourse for the church was to strengthen the capacity of the state to act as a secular moral guarantor.[39]

That was the welfare state version of Christian realism, which underwrote the merger of political liberalism and centralized state power. In the early twentieth century progressives like Henry Churchill King and Herbert Croly contended that American democracy would not survive if it did not make its peace with concentrated power. To defend democratic gains from concentrated economic power, the progressives called for a consolidation of countervailing political power. They supported centralized government, trade unions, and a nationalized politics. America would become more democratic only if it became more of a *nation* in its institutions and spirit. This strategy was consummated with the success of the New Deal, which effectively united liberalism and the national idea. The historic American democracy of small towns and civic republicanism gave way to the democracy of nationalized liberalism. In a society shaped increasingly by corporate economic power, the only effective progressive politics was that of the national republic.[40]

For the post-socialist Niebuhr these were basic political truisms. The progressives of Theodore Roosevelt's generation had fought for them, often with sentimental flourishes; the New Dealers put them in place, a bit haphazardly; the mid-century liberal realists defended them, emphasizing the need to consolidate state power for relatively good ends. To enlist the church in this enterprise, Niebuhr drove a wedge between the moral identity and social mission of the churches. The social mission was no longer the social gospel project of converting American society to the biblical vision of freedom, justice, community, and peace. Niebuhrian realism was about providing religious support for a secular liberal agenda serving the struggle for freedom and justice. Bennett observed that Niebuhr's central concern was always to influence the policy of the federal government on pressing issues. Because Niebuhr emphasized realistic limits and the clash of interests, Bennett noted, he had very little vision of a good society: "I think you get at Niebuhr negatively so much better than you do positively."[41]

Niebuhr's attentiveness to irony and paradox, his insistence on the inevitability of collective egotism, and his sensitivity to the complex ambiguities in all human choices made permanent contributions to Christian thought. His passion for justice roared through all his work through all his changes of position. He was better about racism than most theologians, writing nearly a dozen articles about racial injustice.[42]

But his dichotomizing between the moral identity and social mission of the church weakened the church's identity and social agency, helping to strip the public sphere of the language of moral value. The upshot was ironic, because no one struggled more brilliantly than Niebuhr to make Christianity relevant to modern society. Near the end of his life, Niebuhr warned Wolfhart Pannenberg and Richard John Neuhaus to steer clear of the kingdom of God. The social gospelers had proved that the kingdom idea was a loser, he urged. Any appeal to the biblical idea of the kingdom as an inbreaking spiritual and historical reality was bound to produce disasters. It made Rauschenbusch incorrigibly naïve about how to relate Christianity to politics. Niebuhr declared that were it up to him, he would tear the kingdom of God out of the Bible and Christian doctrine.[43]

That was an over-the-top expression of the problem of Niebuhr's realism. His theology had room for the sovereignty of a Creator God and the redeeming power of divine love mediated through the cross of Christ. But when Niebuhr invoked the authority of "reality" for Christian ethics, he did not mean the reality of God's presence in the Spirit of the resurrected Christ, nor was he prepared to cut against the grain of America's reality. Thus he never opposed a real American interest in the name of Christian ethics.

To a paternalistic Protestant culture that worried about its creeping softness and irrelevance, Niebuhr offered a powerful voice. Niebuhrian realism tried to save a place for the church in a secularizing society by accepting the liberal bourgeois dichotomy between a virtue-producing private realm and a hardball public realm. This strategy worked for a generation that still lived off the memory of a culturally enfranchised Protestantism.

But it had diminishing returns even in Niebuhr's lifetime. Mainline Protestantism never outgrew its ethnic families of origin, it failed even to replace itself demographically, and it gave up its hope of transforming the culture. No longer claiming a vision of its own in the public sphere, it was reduced to support work for anticommunism and other causes endorsed by the liberal establishment. This strategy sold short the social ethical vision of Christianity. It left progressive Christianity without enough to say or do in its own language, in its own way, and for its own reasons.

Niebuhr was always more complex and elusive than his positions, however, and so I end by accenting the positive on the very issue I have stressed critically, his signature dualism. For many years Niebuhr blasted everyone who tried to get a social ethic out of Jesus. Always he admonished that Jesus was no help with problems of proximate means and ends, necessary violence, and calculated consequences. But something nagged at him. Something was missing in his stark dichotomizing between love and justice. The later Niebuhr realized what it was: that the love ethic kept him and others in the struggle, whether or not they succeeded. *That* was its relevance.

Love was not merely the content of an impossible ethical ideal but the motive force of the struggle for justice. Love makes you care, makes you angry, throws you into the struggle, keeps you in it, and helps you face another day. In the 1930s Niebuhr equated justice with equality, or an equal balance of power. In his later thought he stressed that justice is a relational term; it depends on the motive force of love, and it cannot be defined abstractly. There are no definitive principles of justice, for all such instruments are too corrupt to be definitive. But Niebuhr judged that three regulative principles are useful: equality, freedom, and order. Social justice is an application of the law of love to the sociopolitical sphere, and love is the motivating energy of the struggle for justice. The meaning of justice cannot be taken directly from the principles. It is determined only in the interaction of love and situation, through the mediation of the principles of equality, freedom, and order.[44]

The upshot, this being Niebuhr, was of course paradoxical. Love is un-calculating concern for the dignity of persons; as such it asserts no inter-ests. But because love motivates concern for the dignity of persons, it also motivates a passion for justice overflowing with interests and requiring principles of justice. For decades many readers wondered how anyone as cynical and chastening as Niebuhr could be a prophetic social ethicist, or at least could be regarded as one. He seemed to revel in dispiriting proclamations. *An Interpretation of Christian Ethics* insisted that "the possibilities of evil grow with the possibilities of good." Any gain toward a good end simultaneously created new opportunities for evil. Every gain in equality, freedom, order, and democracy engendered new opportuni-ties for tyranny, squalor, and anarchy, giving rise to new kinds of unan-ticipated consequences and enabling greater numbers of people to do evil things.[45]

So how were people supposed to rally around that? Why would they even bother? Niebuhr skirted the question because it was never a serious one for him. He took for granted his own Christ-following passion for justice. Only in a few scattered references and interviews did he refer to the problem in a way that bordered on self-disclosure. For him the love ethic was always the point, the motive, and the end, even when it had no concrete social meaning. Christian ethics was about facing up to the ter-rible difficulty of being a disciple of Jesus and taking responsibility for society's problems at the same time. In his own way, sorting out the diffi-culty, Niebuhr was always rooted in, and sought to be faithful to, the love ethic to which the Word of the gospel called him.

Chapter 4

Ironic Complexity

REINHOLD NIEBUHR, BILLY GRAHAM, MODERNITY,
AND RACIAL JUSTICE

The image of Billy Graham that prevails in theology is the one Reinhold Niebuhr painted: a throwback to pietistic fundamentalism who over-simplified "every issue of life." In 1956, while Graham's fame soared to heights Niebuhr found incredible, not to mention embarrassing for American Christianity, Niebuhr panned that apparently there was still an ample market in American religion for simplistic preaching that reduced complex problems to pious slogans.[1]

Theologically, Niebuhr argued, Graham simply recycled the catch phrases of an outmoded Protestant individualism and literalism. His spectacular success at attracting an audience brought to mind the nearly forgotten reasons why liberal theology had been necessary. Niebuhr observed that liberalism was a needed improvement on the old evangelical religion, because it engaged modern criticism and had a sociological consciousness. Of course, the liberal social gospel was disastrously idealistic; Niebuhr had not spent twenty-five years attacking it for nothing.

But the masses had not flocked to Niebuhrian realism, and now the old pietistic literalism was packing football stadiums. Niebuhr commented ruefully: "Many of us, in our strictures against the Social Gospel, have forgotten the religious irrelevancies from which it saved us." Amazingly the old nonsense about hellfire, biblical inerrancy, and the Second Coming was back with a vengeance.[2]

Niebuhr was appalled that American Protestantism had come to this. As an apologist for Christianity to its cultured despisers, he was also embarrassed. Graham pronounced on theological and moral issues as though the past generation of theology did not exist. He simply ignored the tradition of social ethical analysis in which Niebuhr specialized, evoking Niebuhr's sarcastic response: "He thinks the problem of the atom bomb could be solved by converting the people to Christ." How could modern people take that seriously? For Graham, Niebuhr objected, every problem and story was a setup for an altar call; "come to Jesus" was the answer to everything.[3]

Niebuhr acknowledged that Graham had considerable virtues. He was obviously personable; by all evidence he was sincere in his faith and evangelistic calling; he mentioned social issues in his sermons; and he was not bad on the race issue. The latter point raised a possibility that maybe something good could be wrung from Graham's fame. Niebuhr remarked: "Though a Southerner, he has been rigorous on the race issue." Elsewhere he elaborated: "Though a Southerner, he is 'enlightened' on the race issue. He does not condone racial prejudice."[4]

In this context, "rigorous" meant that Graham personally opposed racial bigotry. Niebuhr observed that Graham did not preach against racism, and he treated the problem of racial justice with the same superficiality that he handled other complex theological and ethical issues. Graham did not tell his audiences that racial prejudice was incompatible with the gospel or an evil standing in need of repentance and redemption. He did not preach that white Americans needed to give "the Negro neighbor his full due as a man and brother." On racism, as on the atom bomb, Graham was oblivious to the "serious perplexities of guilt and responsibility, and of guilt associated with responsibility, which Christians must face."[5]

Niebuhr specialized in the serious perplexities, fashioning a modern neo-Reformationist realism drawing on Augustine, Luther, Calvin, Machiavelli, Hobbes, Marx, Weber, and William James. To Graham the devil was a literal agent of a literal hell; to Niebuhr these notions were symbols conveying true mythic import. Graham dichotomized between good and evil, while Niebuhr contended that evil was always constitutive in the good. To Niebuhr no human act, no matter how loving or seemingly innocent, was devoid of egotism. Purity of any kind was an illusion. Good and evil were always part of each other, not only as forces locked in dialectical tension but as interpenetrating realities. In the political sphere, Niebuhr taught, every gain toward a good end created new opportunities for evil. Democratic gains increased the possibilities for greater numbers of people to do evil things.

At the same time, Niebuhr roared for democracy and social justice reforms, because democracy was indispensable as a brake on human greed
and the will-to-power of elites, and justice was the ultimate end of Christian love in the social sphere. In Niebuhr's rendering, the love ethic of
Jesus was an impossible ideal. It was relevant as a reminder that an ideal
existed, even though sin made the ideal unattainable. The cross was the
ultimate symbol of this fundamental Christian truth. Religiously the cross
was the means by which God established God's mercy and judgment on
human sin; ethically it was the ultimate symbol of the importance and
unattainability of the law of love. God's redeeming love in the cross of
Christ reconciled human beings to their finitude, weakness, abasement,
and dependency.[6]

Niebuhr wanted Graham to draw from deeper wells of Christian orthodoxy than modern fundamentalism. Even if Graham had to have an
inerrant Bible, he could at least allow Augustine, Luther, Calvin, and
perhaps modern neo-orthodoxy to chasten his superficial revivalism and
perfectionism. How could Graham claim that the answer to every social
evil was to accept Jesus as your Savior? The South was rife with revivals,
which did not stop the slave masters from treating black Americans as
chattel. For Niebuhr it was galling to have fought against liberal perfectionism for decades, only to witness the resurrection of an older, backward, reactionary version.

Some of Niebuhr's friends counseled him to lighten up on Graham;
Union Seminary president Henry Pit Van Dusen was one of them. In June
1957 Graham conducted a crusade at Madison Square Garden in New
York, under the co-sponsorship of the New York City Protestant Council
of Churches. Van Dusen was a key supporter, writing in the *Christian
Century* that Graham offered "the pure milk of the Gospel in more readily
digestible form" than Niebuhr's dialectics. Most people needed the pure
milk before they could handle Niebuhr, Van Dusen observed; moreover,
many of Niebuhr's readers entered the orbit of theology and the church
through the evangelism of Billy Sunday, the Billy Graham of the previous generation. Van Dusen was one of them. Niebuhr summarized Van
Dusen's argument: "Billy will bring people into the Christian church, and
then the rest of us will have the opportunity to reveal all the duties and
possibilities that a Christian commitment implies."[7]

He didn't buy it. For Niebuhr it was obviously disastrous that millions
of people regarded Billy Graham as the exemplar of Christianity. Some-

thing terribly worrisome was happening in American Christianity if Graham was its leading voice.

Graham tried to meet with Niebuhr personally during the run-up to the New York crusade, but Niebuhr refused. Graham's friend George Champion, vice president of the Chase Manhattan Bank and chair of the Protestant Council of New York's evangelism department, made a power move, appealing to the chair of Union's board, also a leading banker, who assured that he would get Niebuhr to comply. Niebuhr still refused. He knew that Graham was good at defusing criticism with personal charm, and he took no interest in being charmed. When the crusade took place Niebuhr blasted it mercilessly, charging that Graham employed "all the high pressure techniques of modern salesmanship," selling Jesus in pretty much the same way that Madison Avenue sold soap and televisions. Watching the spectacle on television, Niebuhr was embarrassed for local pastors; in his telling they were reduced to carnival barkers to swell Graham's crowds. Van Dusen took a contrary view, loudly telling students and passersby in Union's lounge that Niebuhr's reaction was "pure hubris."[8]

Niebuhr saw four main problems with the ascension of Graham-style evangelicalism in American life. First, pietistic revivalism was not an improvement on the faith of the Reformation but a degeneration of it that led to sectarian enthusiasms, rank subjectivism, dumbed-down theologies, and a variety of perfectionisms. Niebuhr's favorite epithet was "stupid," followed closely by "naïve." He found a great deal of both in the pietistic strain of American Protestantism fueling the fundamentalist and holiness movements, the social gospel movement, and then a rebirth of evangelical revivalism.

Second, modern liberalism, though wrong about certain things, had been right to take the Enlightenment seriously. Christian theology had no credibility if it contradicted modern science or denied the legitim. cy of higher critical approaches to the Bible. To Niebuhr it was simply incredible that Graham, a college graduate living in the twentieth century, claimed to stand on the authority of an infallible, verbally inspired scripture. Fundamentalism and conservative evangelicalism ignored critical problems on every page of the Bible, exposing Christianity to ridicule.

Graham told his audiences that God did not inspire falsehoods. Thus there were no real contradictions in the Bible, only apparent ones, and every factual statement in the Bible was factually true. It was absurd to believe modern Bible scholars instead of God's Word.

Graham had flirted with that absurdity just before his famous 1949 revival in Los Angeles. In a story he retold for the rest of his life, he had read enough of Niebuhr and Karl Barth to doubt the evangelical orthodoxy of his youth: "The new meanings they put into some of the old theological terms confused me terribly. I never doubted the Gospel itself, or the deity of Christ on which it depended, but other major issues were called into question." If Niebuhr and Barth believed the Bible contained contradictions and factual errors, was he really so certain that the Bible was inerrant? If they believed an errant Bible could still be the Word of God, could he preach it that way?[9]

A close friend of Graham's, Chuck Templeton, had recently taken the latter path. For weeks Graham agonized over the trustworthiness of the Bible. It seemed to him that he had three options: preach an errant Bible, preach an inerrant Bible, or forsake preaching for dairy farming. A few weeks of inner struggle yielded one decision, that option one was not a real possibility for him. If he did not believe in the Bible's absolute trustworthiness, Graham resolved, he was still young enough—thirty—to take up dairy farming. He could not preach that the Bible was more or less the Word of God.

Graham's crisis of faith climaxed while he attended a conference at Forest Home, California, a retreat center east of Los Angeles. Taking an evening walk in the woods, he laid his Bible on a tree stump, tearfully confessed to God that the Bible was filled with problems he did not understand, and vowed in prayer to accept, by faith, the entire Bible as God's very Word. After that, in his telling, the matter was settled: "In my heart and mind, I knew a spiritual battle in my soul had been fought and won."[10]

Niebuhr thought he had witnessed the irrevocable downfall of fundamentalism in the 1920s. After Clarence Darrow humiliated William Jennings Bryan at the evolution trial in Dayton, Tennessee, it had seemed obvious that fundamentalist inerrancy doctrine and premillennial eschatology were on the downward path, to be claimed only by reactionary sects. Fundamentalists built a vast network of Bible institutes, radio programs, new denominations, and para-church ministries in the 1930s and 1940s, but all of it was off the map, and largely out of view, to Niebuhr and his colleagues. Nothing in the preaching or infrastructure of a defeated fundamentalism smacked of anything to be taken seriously.

Thus, for Niebuhr, Graham's stadium spectacles were hard to take, even if Graham and the new evangelicals avoided fractious debates over evolution.

Graham seemed to have come from nowhere, making a national sensation at the 1949 Los Angeles revival. He had caught the attention of newspaper tycoon William Randolph Hearst, who decided to make him famous, probably because of Graham's fervent anticommunism. Afterward Graham routinely drew enormous crowds, curried favor with presidents, dispensed political advice, and explained to millions the meaning of Christianity.

Niebuhr's annoyance and embarrassment showed through whenever he wrote about Graham. Always he conveyed snobbish disdain, even when enjoining Graham to preach against racism. Fundamentalist Protestantism, being Protestant, was right about some things, but fundamentalism should have passed away.

Though Niebuhr rejected liberal idealism and rationalism, he took for granted the liberal principle that truth questions cannot be settled by the word of an outside authority. In *An Interpretation of Christian Ethics* he declared that the old orthodoxies were no longer believable because they refused to acknowledge that Christian myths were myths. Instead of embarrassing Christianity by retaining "the dogmatisms of another day," conservatives needed to let the dogmas of verbal inspiration and infallibility, and the legalism of dogmatic morality, fall prey to "the beneficent dissolutions of the processes of nature and history."[11]

The third problem, closely related to the second, was that Graham-style evangelicalism was intolerant and theologically arrogant. It was one thing to say that the gospel is a source of grace and truth to all people, Niebuhr argued; it was something else to proclaim that one had to be a certain kind of Christian to avert eternal damnation in hell. Niebuhr pleaded for a Christianity with a more sensitive ethical spirit: "We must also have a decent modesty and humility about the righteousness of those whose common decencies contribute to our security, whether or not they have solved the ultimate mystery through faith or have made an ultimate commitment to Christ." The mystery of divine salvation transcended every theology, especially those that reduced God to provincial categories. Niebuhr allowed that Graham had more modesty than the average evangelist, but the practice of harping on "saved" versus "nonsaved" persons was morally repugnant, no matter how politely it was expressed. Niebuhr asked: What of the person who declined the altar call but outdid white

Christians in accepting racial equality? What sort of Christianity ignored or dismissed the moral difference? Instead of dwelling on the "unregenerate" status of unbelievers, American Christians needed to ask themselves whether they were good coworkers with the "decent secularists" in their midst.[12]

Niebuhr stressed the apologetic angle: "Whatever the church may do to spread the gospel, it must resist the temptation of simplifying it in either literalistic or individualistic terms, thus playing truant to positions hard-won in the course of Christian history." Graham had caught the public eye, but at serious cost to the moral and intellectual image of American Protestantism. Surging crowds of converts were not worth losing the integrity or soul of the church: "We cannot afford to retrogress in regard to the truth for the sake of a seeming advance."[13]

Niebuhr urged that it was still possible, in 1956, to combine the good parts of liberalism with the biblical message of redemption recovered by the Reformation. Unlike modern Pietism, the Reformers did not dwell on saved versus unsaved; they stressed that all people needed divine forgiveness equally. Neither did they give simplistic answers to complex problems. They recognized the limits of human knowledge and virtue, spurning easy answers and quack cures. They understood that "the ultimate dilemmas are universal" and the Word of Christ applied to all without exception. Claiming Luther and Calvin for his side, Niebuhr let Graham have the Awakening revivalists.[14]

But Graham did not burn for racial justice as the abolitionist revivalists did, which was the fourth problem (though Niebuhr did not mention the abolitionists). Graham's simplistic mentality was a stumbling block on other issues, Niebuhr judged, but the race issue was "fairly simple" on a moral level. It came down to the biblical principle that one cannot love God and hate one's brother. The moral root of the matter was as personal and individual as a typical Graham sermon. It should have suited revival preaching perfectly (as it did for abolitionists Charles Finney and Theodore Weld). So why did Graham's call to repentance not feature a condemnation of race prejudice?[15]

Niebuhr surmised that this question exposed a core weakness of conservative evangelicalism, which used a simplistic reading of select issues to pose a "crisis" that led to repentance and conversion. If Niebuhr had mentioned the abolitionists, he would have had to explain why their conversion preaching worked differently. As it was, he judged that contemporary evangelists went for obvious things that worked, like adultery and drunkenness. The most effective way to induce the crisis was to convict persons of sins that they and their peers regarded as sins. Race prejudice was a different kind of sin, Niebuhr reasoned, because its social basis was more important than its individual instantiation. Racism was embedded in the customs and social structures of communities. It was not a private sin committed one by one but something taught and approved by communities. Thus adultery worked better at evangelistic rallies than racial sinning, which induced no emotional crisis among its perpetrators.

Niebuhr had little hope for evangelicalism in this area, noting that the most violently racist sections of the U.S. had the most revivals. On the other hand, he saw something hopeful in Graham, who was well traveled and had a sense of justice. It was not impossible to imagine Graham taking up the cause of racial justice as an evangelistic priority. If he did so, he had a chance to become "a vital force in the nation's moral and spiritual life." Of course, Graham was already a vital force in American life; Niebuhr meant "a vital force for good."[16]

Unclaimed Ambiguity: Graham on Racial Justice

For the most part Graham went on to the career Niebuhr expected of him, lifting evangelicalism out of its sectarian ghetto, reducing social problems to matters of personal piety and morality, avoiding conservative debates over the extent of biblical inerrancy, and treading carefully on racial justice. Graham left it to his scholarly friends at Fuller Theological Seminary, Carl F. H. Henry and E. J. Carnell, to decide what inerrancy meant, staying above the fray of a draining, fractious, never-ending battle.

On the necessity of de-ghettoizing fundamentalism, his guide was Henry's *The Uneasy Conscience of Modern Fundamentalism*, which made the case for a new evangelicalism just before Fuller Seminary opened its doors in 1947. Henry depicted American fundamentalism as a sectarian retreat from the gospel mission to spread righteousness throughout the world. Fundamentalists hardly ever preached against "such social evils as aggressive warfare, racial hatred and intolerance, the liquor traffic, exploitation of labor or management, or the like," he observed. Ignoring centuries of Christian theology, biblical scholarship, and spiritual practice, they replaced the great hymns of the past with "a barn-dance variety of semi-religious choruses" and turned the world-changing gospel of Christ into "a world-resisting message" of apocalyptic deliverance.[17]

Henry called for a different kind of fundamentalism, one that reclaimed the social mission of the gospel and discarded shibboleths that "cut the nerve of world compassion." J. N. Darby-style apocalypticism, which ruled most of the fundamentalist movement, was a chief cause of the shibboleths. Darby's dispensational scheme turned the Bible into a strange guidebook of signs foretelling God's "rapture" of Christians out of the world and the inauguration of Christ's millennial kingdom on earth. Henry treaded lightly in this area, describing his position as "broadly pre-millennial," which placed him with the Puritans, not the sectarian dispensationalists. Moreover, he respected the sober a-millennialism of Reformed and Lutheran orthodoxy.[18]

Henry simply wanted fundamentalists to stop obsessing about signs of the end time. He proposed a truce between premillennialists and a-millennialists, allowing for a range of legitimate views on this issue, while ruling out the postmillennial fantasy of a Christianized world. The parties of orthodoxy needed to make room for one another on eschatology. They also needed to acknowledge that the postmillennial tradition was right about one thing: the church had a mission to transform society. That was a gospel theme, Henry urged, even though postmillennialists misconstrued it. The gospel was relevant to every world problem while the Lord tarried: "The main difference between the kingdom of God *now* and the kingdom of God *then* is that the future kingdom will center all of its activities in the redemptive King because all government and dominion will be subjected to Him. This difference overshadows the question, however important, whether the future kingdom involves an earthly reign or not."[19]

Graham drank more deeply than Henry from the dispensationalist well, avidly promoting Wilbur Smith's updated dispensational interpretations of biblical prophecy, which painted the threat of world communism in lurid colors. However, the fundamentalists who launched Fuller Theological Seminary and the "neo-evangelical" movement in the late 1940s—Henry, Smith, Carnell, Harold J. Ockenga, Harold Lindsell, and Everett F. Harrison—agreed with Henry not to fight over eschatology, at least not immediately. In its early years Fuller Seminary took a strict line on biblical inerrancy and basked in its association with the increasingly famous Graham. It also did very little to break the mold of fundamentalist conservatism in the political arena.

For years Henry was consumed with building up the seminary; afterward he steered the movement's flagship magazine, *Christianity Today*, which took conservative positions on social issues closely resembling Graham's. Henry was the movement's leading thinker, but to the general public Graham was the symbol of whatever difference there was between the old fundamentalism and the new evangelicalism.

As the public face of this transition, Graham had to figure out what it meant for evangelicalism to have a social mission, especially in dealing with America's original sin of racism. Here the ironies were thick. In writings and interviews scattered through his later life, Graham claimed to have supported the Civil Rights movement consistently. In reality, in the name of Christian morality and his imagined "voluntary integration," he blasted the movement's trouble-making demonstrations and condemned its advocacy of coerced integration.[20]

Though accused of simplemindedness, Graham's record in this area approached Niebuhrian levels of ironic complexity and strategic ambiguity. Keenly attuned to the white supremacist anxiety of his white conservative base, though of course he never called it that, Graham played a careful hand. He understood that his group had a very limited capacity to acknowledge wrongdoing against African Americans. On many occasions he showed that his own capacity was similarly limited. On the whole Graham played a role in the struggle for racial justice that redeemed some of Niebuhr's hope for him, even using arguments that sounded like Niebuhr. But they both fell short of giving racial justice the high priority it deserved, and Graham never accepted that the "race problem" was a white problem.

Niebuhr's appeal to Graham may have had some of the effect he sought. Years later Graham told his friend and biographer John Pollock: "I thought about it a great deal. He influenced me and I began to take a stronger stand." Graham may well have struggled internally with Niebuhr's critique and proposal, and he may have resolved to preach more directly about racism. But there was no point in his life at which he converted to a racial justice standpoint in his preaching or practices, and the only event that marked a clear change in his behavior was a Supreme Court decision. Recalling his upbringing in the rural South, Graham's autobiography disposed of a large topic in one sentence: "I had adopted the attitudes of that region without much reflection." Elsewhere he recalled: "If there were Negroes who chafed in their status as second-class citizens, I was not aware of them."[21]

Biographer Marshall Frady filled part of the gap, reporting Graham's boyhood use of racial epithets and his everyday support of Jim Crow. When Graham brushed near this subject he emphasized his boyhood respect for the black foreman on the Graham dairy farm, Reese Brown, and recalled that he never liked the white supremacist theme of his favorite books, the Tarzan stories of Edgar Rice Burroughs. At age sixteen Graham had a born-again experience at a segregated revival. Years later, as a professional evangelist, he often claimed that after his conversion he found American segregation incomprehensible, especially in the church. He could not treat blacks as inferior after he had come to Jesus. But that is not what happened. In 1960 Graham remembered his past more accurately: "Even after my conversion, I felt no guilt in thinking of my dark-skinned brothers in the usual patronizing and paternalistic way."[22]

Implicitly the latter remembrance undermined Graham's self-image as an agent of racial reconciliation and his vocational assurance that born-again conversion was the answer; thus he rarely verbalized it. But it fit Graham's personal trajectory, which included studying briefly at Bob Jones University, joining the staunchly segregationist Southern Baptist Convention, preaching at countless segregated Youth for Christ meetings, and, in the late 1940s, conducting numerous segregated crusades throughout the South. The first person to nudge Graham in the direction of supporting racial integration was Carl Henry, his classmate at Wheaton College in the early 1940s, but Graham said nothing about it while preaching constantly to segregated audiences in the later 1940s.

By 1949, when the Hearst papers made him a media star, Graham was a veteran evangelist with an ample record of ignoring racial injustice. He later explained that no one challenged segregation in the South before 1950, and he gave no thought to doing so. In the early 1950s, however, the media spotlight on Graham and the early rumblings of what became the Civil Rights movement raised the moral issue in his consciousness; Graham also wanted to reach black audiences. For two years he zigged and zagged on segregation, sometimes refusing to address segregated audiences, other times backsliding. In his memoir he retold a favorite story about tearing down the dividing ropes at a 1953 crusade in Chattanooga, Tennessee. He did not mention backsliding subsequently in Dallas, Texas, and Asheville, North Carolina. Michael Long aptly remarks that courageous anti-segregationist leaders were rare in the South, and Billy Graham, despite his progress on the race issue, "was not that rare."[23]

In 1954, twenty years after Graham's conversion, the Supreme Court settled the matter of segregation for him, in *Brown v. Board of Education*. Before the Supreme Court outlawed public school segregation, Graham assured his segregated audiences that the Bible had nothing to say about the issue. After the court ruled, Graham had the basis he needed to get on the right side of the Civil Rights movement. He spoke only to integrated audiences, reminded them that Jesus identified with the marginalized and segregated people of his time, and drew the connection to twentieth-century African Americans. Later he spoke against the stupidity of racist Christianity, admonishing white supremacists that Jesus was a Mediterranean Jew with a "swarthy" complexion. He also stressed that America's mistreatment of its black population handed Communists easy propaganda victories in their drive to conquer the world.[24]

By the 1960s Graham found it difficult to remember his early career correctly, sometimes claiming that only two or three of his crusades had been segregated. By the 1970s he had similar difficulties remembering his actual relation to the Civil Rights movement, which was equally ambiguous. Graham's version of his Civil Rights ministry featured an approving quote by Martin Luther King Jr. and a carefully vague self-placement between "extreme conservatives" and "extreme liberals." In his telling, King told him "early on" that he would best serve the cause of racial equality by preaching integrated crusades, not by joining King in the streets: "'You stay in the stadiums, Billy,' he said, 'because you will have far more impact on the white establishment there than you would if you marched in the streets. Besides that, you have a constituency that will listen to you, especially among white people, who may not listen so much to me. But if a leader gets too far in front of his people, they will lose sight of him and not follow him any longer.'" As Graham told it, he followed King's advice, which placed him "under fire from both sides" as extreme conservatives condemned his support of integration and "extreme liberals" found him too moralistic and solicitous of the establishment.[25]

That made Graham sound remarkably like King. At times he merited this self-description as the King-figure in the white evangelical community. Graham added a black evangelist, Howard Jones, to his team in 1957; he invited King to pray at the 1957 New York crusade, introducing King as the leader of "a great social revolution"; he conducted an integrated crusade in Birmingham, Alabama, a few months after the 1963 church bombing that killed four black girls; he served on a national citizens committee to help implement the Civil Rights Act of 1964; and in 1965 he made his strongest statement of support for King's nonviolent demonstrations, observing that they "brought about new, strong, tough laws that were needed many years ago."[26]

But King had ample reason to judge, as he did, that Graham was nowhere near the white evangelical leader that was needed. At the time that King made his "you stay in the stadiums" statement to Graham, at a planning meeting for the 1957 New York crusade, King dreamed of a Graham/King crusade that preached to integrated audiences in the North, proceeded to border states, and culminated in the Deep South. That dream foundered on Graham's anxieties about publicly cooperating with King and on his unwillingness to address the politics of racism. Graham never invited King to appear with him again, and within a year of the New York crusade, King had to plead with Graham to stop allowing segregationists on the platform of his Southern crusades.[27]

In public, and with King, Graham claimed to avoid politics, but he was a font of political advice to a succession of presidents. Unknown to King, Graham advised President Dwight Eisenhower in 1956 not to risk his reelection by appealing to Northern blacks, which would hurt him politically in the South. Besides watching out for Eisenhower's interests in the South, Graham repeatedly objected to Civil Rights campaigns there. King, realizing that he had very limited means of attacking a national and global problem, sought to dramatize the ravages of racism by conducting manageable campaigns in selected cities. Graham protested that this strategy stirred up racial animosity and scapegoated selected Southern communities. When King marched in Selma, Alabama, Graham decried singling out Selma; it was wrong to divert attention from a national problem by stigmatizing one particular community, he declared.[28]

These were exactly the high-minded arguments favored by moderate white ministers who opposed the marches and sit-ins of the Civil Rights movement while claiming to support its ultimate objective. King's "Letter from a Birmingham Jail" was a direct response to eight local ministers taking that line. On the one hand, Graham's team helped King orchestrate the timing and release of King's famous letter against going slow; on the other hand, temporizing ministers across the nation took comfort that Billy Graham was on their side. Graham legitimized the very reaction that King viewed as the greatest threat to the movement. Overall his record during the King years was only slightly more progressive than *Christianity Today*, which defended voluntary segregation, opposed coercive integration, and denounced the demonstrations and sit-ins of the Civil Rights movement.[29]

At times Graham not only legitimized clerical opposition but heightened its rhetorical ante. In 1958 he thundered in Charlotte, North Carolina, that Satan was the instigator of the current unrest over racial inequality: "We see the forces of evil stirring up racial tensions all over America . . . It seems as if the whole world is a pot and the devil has a big stick stirring everybody up. Why, he has even got the church stirred up."[30]

There were plenty of equally low points registering Graham's defensiveness as a white Southerner. He speculated that the Birmingham girls were killed by outside professionals to fan the flames of racial tension; he took offense at the Civil Rights movement's emphasis on white racism; most of his stories illustrating racial prejudice illustrated black racism; he warned repeatedly that "forced integration" would never work; right up to the Civil Rights Act of 1964 he protested that integrationists were pushing "too far too fast." Graham never quite explained how he could adamantly reject forced integration and yet claim to accept the *Brown* decision, which legalized and required forced integration. By the late 1960s, however, all was forgotten; in his later remembrances, Graham had supported King and the Civil Rights movement all along. Michael Long remarks: "No matter what he said in later years, Graham was no integrationist, at least in the sense that King and others in the civil rights movement were integrationists."[31]

The movement's short-term goal was government-enforced integration, but Graham supported only voluntary integration, which required nothing of whites and allowed them to feel righteous for whatever allowances they dispensed to blacks. Graham's sermons were long on the latter theme. In his telling, the moral revolution of the King years was mostly a white phenomenon. It was a story of whites letting go of customs that soiled their own virtue and of opening their institutions to blacks despite encountering so many ungrateful blacks. Graham might have struggled inwardly with the moral pitfall that frightened Niebuhr—that of proudly holding oneself above the prejudices of one's group—but there is little evidence of it. On the other hand, Niebuhr's anxiety about the latter species of moral pride inhibited him from following completely his own advice to Graham.

The Priority of Racial Justice

Niebuhr was better than most theologians about racism. He cared deeply about racial justice and wrote nearly a dozen articles about it, usually describing racism as a transcendently evil form of self-worship. But he never featured this subject in his major works or gave high priority to it in his activism. In his early career Niebuhr was devoted to pacifism and making a name for himself; in his middle career he burned for socialism and religious realism; in his later career he gave priority to antifascism, anticommunism, and Vital Center realism.

Niebuhr was sincere in challenging Graham to devote his crusades to racial equality; he was not just seeking another way to put down Graham. But the problem of liberal righteousness is a slippery, confounding one that has a way of turning on itself, as in Niebuhr's case. Uncharacteristically he failed to acknowledge the irony of his challenge to Graham. Niebuhr urged Graham to an extraordinarily difficult task, one entailing dangers and burdens from which Niebuhr was far removed. He had no contact with Graham's audiences, and by the 1950s he faced little prospect of confronting angry crowds of any kind. Yet even in Niebuhr's rarefied world of prestige lectureships and publishers, he did not take the risk that he asked of Graham, telling his group to interrogate its white supremacism.

Asking white liberals in the 1950s to interrogate their casual racism would not have gone well. It would have evoked, for Niebuhr, the kind of hostility that Graham confronted constantly, especially in the South, even as Graham tried not to offend the moral pride of his audience. Liberals took pride in having no racial biases; that was what made them liberals. For all his railing against liberal illusions, Niebuhr did not regard this as one of them. He took for granted that the problem was to eliminate racial bias, not to dismantle an entire national culture of white supremacism. He believed that liberals were closer than others to it and that America as a whole was moving, albeit belatedly, to the goal of a society without racial discrimination. On the way to that goal, he fretted more about the sin of liberal false righteousness than about liberals being too easy on themselves.

Niebuhr worried that when liberal white Christians apologized to blacks or Jews for the sins of white America, they won moral points for humility and contrition, but wrongly. Confessions of this sort were dictated by pride; thus they carried a whiff of hypocrisy. Instead of expressing a real confession, the penitent communicated his or her moral superiority. That scruple, plus the social punishments that would have fallen and his calculation of the practical politics, impeded Niebuhr from saying as much as he should have about white racism. More important, in the late 1950s this bundle of reservations prevented him from publicly supporting King on the crucial either/or of the moment.[32]

In 1957 King asked Niebuhr to support a petition asking President Eisenhower to enforce the *Brown* decision in the South. Niebuhr turned him down, explaining to Felix Frankfurter that he opposed anything smacking of Northern intervention. Pressuring the South would do "more harm than good," Niebuhr judged; plus, the moral problem of Northern presumption had to be taken seriously. Niebuhr informed Frankfurter that a group of Southern preachers was planning to urge Eisenhower to actively support the *Brown* decision. That was the way this difficult issue had to be dealt with, Niebuhr advised: "Anything from the North would seem like Yankee interference." Niebuhr cautioned liberal politicians and Civil Rights leaders to slow down and wait for "the slow erosion of racial prejudice" to do its work, an admonition that strengthened Democratic presidential candidate Adlai Stevenson's resolve to play down the integration issue. It also troubled Niebuhr that, in his experience, victims of racial discrimination rarely confessed their own shortcomings, though he allowed that this appearance could be a defensive reaction to the insincerity of white Americans' contrition for racism. Niebuhr's thought was a major influence on King, who grappled constantly with Niebuhr's dialectics. But Niebuhr did not catch up with King and a Civil Rights movement that forged ahead until the early 1960s.[33]

On the politics of Civil Rights, Niebuhr wanted change as soon as possible, but he was very cautious about what was possible, not unlike Graham. His understanding of America's racial pathology beyond the political level was also much closer to Graham's than his withering rebukes of Graham let on. Niebuhr argued that the problem of racial bigotry was ultimately a spiritual issue; thus it could not be cured by social engineering: "The mitigation of racial and cultural pride is finally a religious problem in the sense that each man, and each race and culture, must become religiously aware of the sin of self-worship, which is the final form of human evil and of which racial self-worship is the most vivid example." Racism was like every other form of evil in its egotistical presumption: "Religious humility, as well as rational enlightenment, must contribute to the elimination of this terrible evil of racial pride."[34]

In 1957, three years before Niebuhr retired from Union Seminary and shortly after he got heartburn from Graham's New York crusade, Niebuhr judged that his country was correcting its only serious social problem. The U.S. had solved the problems of liberty and equality "beyond the dreams of any European nation," he wrote. The New Deal was so successful that even Republicans accepted it. In domestic politics and society, there was only one major problem left to solve in American life: "We failed catastrophically only on one point—in our relation to the Negro race." Niebuhr believed, however, that even America's racial pathology was "on the way of being resolved." The Supreme Court finally recognized equality as a criterion of justice, and the *Brown* decision redeemed the promise of America for black Americans: "At last the seeming sentimentality of the preamble of our Declaration of Independence—the declaration that 'all men are created equal'—has assumed political reality and relevance."[35]

That even Reinhold Niebuhr could be naïve in celebrating America the good, even on the politics of the color line, is a measure of the bland optimism of the 1950s. When Niebuhr died in 1971 the Protestant mainline was still at the center of American culture, but there were signs of an impending downturn. The decades of annual membership losses had begun, and the college chapel circuit that made Niebuhr's fame possible no longer existed. He died barely in time not to witness the eclipse of his group by one he disdained, never imagining that the National Association of Evangelicals (NAE) would become a juggernaut. In Niebuhr's time the NAE was a decidedly marginal outfit; by 1980 it was a powerhouse that capitalized on Graham's fame and the success of *Christianity Today*.

The "Rightness" of Graham?

This chapter was originally composed for a book addressing the question of Graham's "rightness." Any such verdict must refer to different things. As the herald of a new evangelicalism he was phenomenally successful. As a temporizing advocate of racial integration he helped white evangelicals break free of segregation and, to some extent, white supremacism, although he felt compelled in later life to whitewash his record. It was not enough to say that his approach had worked; to feel good about it, Graham needed to revise what had happened, taking positions retroactively that he never quite managed when it mattered. As a theologian, however, he rested entirely on what had worked for him, which made his position intellectually impossible. Instead of struggling honestly with intellectual problems, Graham told the story of his 1949 walk in the woods. He preached and lived with winning conviction after vowing in faith to believe that the Bible contains no contradictions or factual errors. Believing in unbelievable things had worked for him; however, that strategy identified evangelicalism with fideistic escape.

The larger verdict rests on an outcome not yet known. From the beginning of the organized Christian Right in 1977, Graham has had an ambivalent relationship with it. Christian Right leaders are too nakedly partisan for him, and often too mean-spirited. He takes pride in the evangelical boon but steps back when evangelical leaders equate Christian faith with right-wing politics or make obnoxious pronouncements that embarrass him. Bailey Smith announced that God does not hear the prayers of Jews. Pat Robertson and Jerry Falwell opined that the fiendish attacks of September 11, 2001, were God's retribution for moral perfidy. Robertson added that God struck down Israeli president Ariel Sharon for giving back the Gaza Strip. Today Franklin Graham insists that Islamic terrorism is the essence of Islam, not a perversion of it.[36]

If evangelicalism of that sort prevails, it will be pointless to make a case for Billy Graham. But a great deal of American evangelicalism is temperamentally moderate, and there is such a thing as progressive evangelicalism. For the past thirty years *Sojourners* magazine has embraced progressive concerns and claimed its kinship with the antislavery, feminist, temperance, black church, and social gospel evangelicalisms of the nineteenth century. To the extent that progressives such as Jim Wallis, Tony Campolo, and Eugene Rivers have made inroads within evangelicalism, the reactionary spirit of evangelical fundamentalism has given way to the discourse of a generous orthodoxy, one that lives more peaceably and graciously within a religiously plural world. It speaks to the sensibility of young evangelicals who yearn for gospel-centered teaching that does not violate their own experience of living in a pluralistic, multicultural, postmodern society.

On these points contemporary evangelicals have reason to say, "It started with Billy Graham." Besides conducting racially integrated crusades, Graham broadened the ecumenical common ground within evangelicalism and sustained respectful relationships with Catholics, liberal Protestants, and Jews, which made him an object of loathing to fundamentalist leaders. He was a close friend of Rabbi Marc Tanenbaum, and in 1977 he won the American Jewish Committee's National Interreligious

Award for his efforts to strengthen mutual respect between evangelicals and Jews. In later life Graham surprised interviewers by calling himself a theological conservative and social liberal.[37]

But most of Graham's movement never shared much of his social conscience; his own was repeatedly compromised by his intimate access to power and lust for political influence; and today much of the evangelical movement is stridently dogmatic and mean-spirited. Graham's son Franklin preaches fundamentalist hellfire evangelism, disdaining ecumenical niceness: Jesus is the only way to salvation; every knee shall bow; most knees will bow in Hell, where it will be too late. The elder Graham preached the same theology but with better manners. That was the real difference between Graham-style evangelicalism and old-style fundamentalism: civility and the rejection of separatism, which led to the development of ecumenical and public skills. If Billy Graham is to be vindicated historically, evangelicalism must combine the liberationist spirit of its abolitionist past with Graham's ecumenical temperament.

Part II

Economic Democracy in Question

Chapter 5

Norman Thomas and the Dilemma
of American Socialism

Norman Thomas is usually remembered as an idealistic failure, an assessment he shared. He *was* idealistic, and he certainly failed to build a vital democratic socialist party in the United States. But "failure" is a harsh epitaph for a figure who fought valiantly for more good causes than any American of his time, and who sometimes pushed for winning causes, though never to his satisfaction.[1]

From the early 1920s to the late 1960s, Norman Thomas was America's foremost democratic socialist. From the beginning it was a dying cause; Thomas became a Socialist Party leader shortly after the party shattered over wartime politics and the opening round of America's faction fights over communism. For nearly fifty years he struggled to keep a tiny, quarrelsome, and defeated social democratic tradition alive in the United States while insisting, not always rightly, that his innumerable campaigns for social justice, civil liberties, and world peace did little good.

He was not a working-class militant like his socialist predecessor, Eugene Debs, or a Marxist of any kind, but a reformist who defended liberty above other values and championed social democracy on moral grounds. Thomas organized dozens of organizations and gave hundreds of speeches every year for more than forty years, including several thousand in the early 1930s across forty-four states. He fought in civil liberties cases throughout the nation, notably the Passaic textile strike of 1926, the anti-Klan campaign in Tampa in 1935, and the Hague machine in Jersey City in 1938. He was one of the first to campaign for Southern sharecroppers and helped organize the Southern Tenant Farmers' Union. At various times he was a leader or director of the Fellowship of Reconciliation, the American Civil Liberties Union, the League for Industrial Democracy, the Workers Defense League, the Post War World Council, the Socialist Party, and the Committee for a Sane Nuclear Policy. Six times he ran for the presidency on the Socialist ticket. When friends tried to console him that Franklin Roosevelt carried out much of the Socialist platform, Thomas invariably replied that he carried it out on a stretcher. That was his epitaph for American democratic socialism, which in his generation was called "Norman Thomas Socialism."

Norman Thomas Socialism was, in part, a product of the social gospel movement. Born in 1884 in Marion, Ohio, Thomas was the son and grandson of conservative Presbyterian ministers. After graduating from Princeton in 1905 he tested his religious vocation as a street minister on Manhattan's Lower East Side and later served as a pastor in a tenement district church bordering Hell's Kitchen. Enrolling at Union Theological Seminary, he studied Rauschenbusch avidly, learned the hermeneutical arguments that got him past a presbytery ordination hearing, and graduated in 1911. Though the New York presbytery voted overwhelmingly to ordain Thomas, his social gospel liberalism offended a conservative faction of the presbytery, causing his father to write that the sensational rumors of Thomas's heterodoxy were deeply painful to him. For Thomas, his father's old orthodoxy was a nonstarter; even liberal theology held little interest as theology. The point of being a Christian was to feed the hungry, shelter the homeless, comfort the afflicted, and build a just society. After his graduation from Union he received a pastoral call to a wealthy Fifth Avenue church, which he declined in favor of a poor, mixed-ethnic, Presbyterian parish in East Harlem. Thomas ministered there for seven years and became more radical, partly as a reaction against wealthy Presbyterian patrons who could not abide a pacifist and socialist pastor.

He came to pacifism by religion but later gave up on the church because of it. Thomas was fond of saying that Jesus was obviously a pacifist. In 1916 he joined the pacifist Fellowship of Reconciliation, which had been founded the previous year, and he soon became the organization's co-chair and founded its magazine, *World Tomorrow*. He campaigned ardently against conscription and preparedness for war, urging that the war was an imperial struggle to control markets in China, India, Africa, and the Middle East, and American progressives had to stand firmly against it. In January 1917, while conceding that war might be a tragic necessity in some circumstances, Thomas implored the New York presbytery to oppose America's looming intervention: "It is this which tempts me to despair for the future of the church. Even in war the church ought to stand for a form of society transcending nationalism and national boundaries." After the U.S. entered the war and many of Thomas's social gospel colleagues endorsed Wilson's slogans about putting an end to war and making the world safe for democracy, Thomas replied: "How can we accept Christ as Lord and Master and deny his spirit by sharing responsibility for the unutterable horrors of war? Shall we cast out Satan by Satan?" As for intervening for democracy: "Do you really think that our great papers like the *New York Times* which prate about war for democracy are fighting for democracy when they have devoted all their strength to oppose political and industrial democracy at home?"[2]

Alienated from the church, which joined a nationwide campaign to boost military recruitment, Thomas balked at making a home in the socialist movement. The Marxist rhetoric of the Socialist Party repelled him, and he feared that socialism might create new forms of government dictatorship. Thomas was allergic to authoritarianism of every kind, which ruled out most kinds of socialism. His commitment to civil liberties was even more uncompromising than his commitment to nonviolence. Moreover, international socialism had just failed stupendously in Europe, where solidarity lasted less than a day after war was declared. European Socialists gave barely a thought to working-class solidarity before reverting to slaughtering one another, making a mockery of the socialist claim to holding the solution to war.

But in the U.S. the Socialist Party of Eugene Debs and Morris Hillquit held fast to the socialist opposition to wars of empire, voting 140 to 36 in a national convention not to support Wilson's intervention. Hillquit declared that the wars of contending capitalists made no claim on American workers. Many American Socialists disagreed, resigning from the party, which lost its presidential candidate (Allan Benson) and all its native-born national leaders except Debs. Reeling from these resignations, Hillquit ran for mayor of New York in the hope of recruiting native-born supporters. He found his reward in Thomas, who supported Hillquit's campaign without joining the party. Thomas, having admired Hillquit from their work together in antiwar coalitions, gave a rousing speech for him at Madison Square Garden that drew the attention of the churchly patrons who kept his East Harlem ghetto parish afloat. In March 1918 Thomas learned that the patrons were pulling away from the congregation. To save the church he resigned his post; six months later he joined the Socialist Party, at the dawn of its self-destruction.[3]

Debs was imprisoned in Atlanta Penitentiary for speaking against the war. In 1920 the Socialists wore his federal prison number, 9653, as an electoral badge of honor, winning over nine hundred thousand votes in a symbolic antiwar campaign that confirmed Debs's status as the Grand Old Man of the Left. But the party that nominated him was rapidly disintegrating.

The Socialists were devastated by their party's stand against the war and then by a bitter faction fight over the Bolshevik Revolution. Their opposition to the war was fiercely denounced as anti-American; in the postwar hysteria of the Palmer raids, even militantly anticommunist Socialists were branded as subversives. It did not help that their antiwar stance attracted thousands of foreign-born Communists who walked out the following year, in 1919, after the Socialists refused to embrace Bolshevism. The party's right wing was militantly opposed to the new Russian government; Thomas identified with a centrist group that was both sympathetic and critical; and together they kept their distance from Bolshevism, which provoked a stormy factional schism. More than 30,000 members of the party's left wing walked out, forming the U.S. versions of the Communist and Communist Labor parties; John Reed and Jay Lovestone were among them. In 1918 the Socialist Party had 118,000 members; by 1923 it was down to 12,000.[4]

Thomas tried to look on the bright side of the second catastrophe, reasoning that by driving out the Communists the party had rid itself of pathological types who liked violence and intrigue, and dreamed of revolutionary glory. Leon Trotsky later sneered that the Thomas Socialists were a party of dentists, a reproach Thomas brushed off as the conceit of a manic totalitarian. Thomas became a party leader by exhorting beleaguered Socialists not to be cowed by conspiratorial types and not to regret having driven them away. He hated the revolutionary deviousness, violence, revenge fantasies, and doctrinal bickering of Trotskyists and Stalinists. Having joined the Socialist Party in the early days of the Red Scare, when most of the traffic was moving the other way, he offered a welcome voice of conviction and hope. Inwardly Thomas wavered on whether he had found a political home, but in public he urged that the future belonged to a democratic socialism that stuck to its core convictions about civil liberties, nonviolence, and economic democracy.

In 1922 he became co-director of the League for Industrial Democracy; two years later he ran for governor of New York as the Socialist candidate, though he and the party ignored their own campaign, concentrating on the newly founded Conference for Progressive Political Action (CPPA), a labor coalition advocating public control of natural resources and the railroads. The CPPA's model was the British Labour Party, but in 1925 it lost union support and fell apart. Thomas responded by saving his depleted party, undertaking exhausting speaking tours. He gave hundreds of speeches, ran for president in 1928, and for the next twenty-four years conducted presidential campaigns that were extensions of his personal campaign to eliminate exploitation and oppression.

Between 1931 and 1935 Thomas published six volumes of collected speeches. Often he implored that shrieking did little good and the Left shrieked too often. *America's Way Out: A Program for Democracy* (1931) made a case for nationalizing the big banks and major means of industrial production; *Human Exploitation in the United States* (1934) offered a massive account of the human ravages of the Depression; in a slightly lighter mood, *As I See It* (1932) counseled against making Marxism "a kind of slogan of salvation," attributing his party's image problem to that tendency: "I think that in some degree the comparative failure of the Socialist Party in America has been due to its iteration of dogmas in terms that were not self-explanatory and which antagonized farmers, intellectuals, and the majority of wage workers who would have been with us if they had understood."[5]

Thomas reported that although he admired the "crusaders for freedom and fellowship" who kept the social gospel alive, he no longer shared their faith: "Outstanding men in pew and pulpit are doing this very thing. That is good, but the promise of their power does not seem great. I doubt if they can win their own organizations. I have some hope of what the churches might do but very little for what they will do." He acknowledged that clergy were pouring into the antiwar movement, but Thomas had seen that another time, before America intervened in World War I. He expected the church to bless the next war "as it has blessed all wars." As for the "humanistic version of Protestant Christianity" that succeeded the social gospel, Thomas doubted it was "a valid development from Christianity," and he knew it was not very effective in the struggle for social justice. Fervent social gospel radicals like Rauschenbusch and Harry F. Ward were "definitely Christian," he judged, but many of their successors were religious humanists who did not really believe in God. Thomas was describing himself and some of his friends; thus he demitted from the ministry in 1931. Religion without a cosmic divine reality seemed pointless to him, and it lacked social power. If he no longer believed in God, it was pointless to make a home in the watered-down remains of liberal Christianity. Instead he cast his lot with mostly secular Democratic Socialists, though by doing so he made the Socialist Party accessible to radical social gospelers like Reinhold Niebuhr.[6]

Socialism was the last best hope of the world, "a society from which poverty and war are forever banished." That expression of faith retained the utopian aspect of socialism—Thomas urged that socialists must "hold up the vision of the classless society." But even at the depth of the Depression he admonished against radicalisms based on revenge, antidemocratic tactics, or popular explosions from below: "Wretched, half-starved children are not the builders of a beautiful cooperative commonwealth. Never was mere revolt, however justified, less likely to succeed in building the new order than today." Many leftists viewed the Depression as a political opportunity; Thomas replied that nothing good came from shredding bourgeois democracy. The Depression pushed Americans toward some kind of totalitarian salvation, he warned, and between the two competing options—communism and fascism—he had no doubt which one Americans would embrace. In the U.S. any political stampede was sure to rush to the right. From his speaking tours Thomas knew that much of his economically ravaged country was ripe for fascism, though he agreed with Huey Long that American fascism would have to be called something else. It galled him that with everything at stake in 1932, and demagogues like Long exploiting nativist prejudices, the Democratic Party was as mindlessly opportunistic as the radical leftists. Thomas complained that the Democrats lacked any ideas besides electoral posturing and catering to the business interests that financed campaigns. Their campaign slogan was "Hee, haw, we're coming back," which perfectly suited a party lacking vision, courage, principle, or, possibly, intelligence.[7]

"We drift, and we drift toward disaster," Thomas lamented. "There is a tragic amount of misery and great discontent in the United States but no proportionate amount of action, wise or otherwise." His presidential campaign of 1932 was reformist and far-reaching, advocating agricultural relief, unemployment insurance, public works projects, a pension system, slum clearance, a shortened work week, low-cost housing, a more progressive income tax, and the nationalization of basic industries. The victorious candidate in that election soon adopted all but the last of these proposals, but in 1932 Thomas considered Franklin Roosevelt little more than a wealthy opportunist and failed governor.[8]

The worst days of the Depression occurred between the November election and Roosevelt's inauguration in March. Thomas spoke to many gatherings of farmers that seethed on the edge of rioting, telling them that Roosevelt should nationalize the banks and issue a multibillion dollar bond for relief and public works. Upon assuming the presidency Roosevelt closed the banks; two weeks after his inauguration, he invited Thomas and Hillquit to the White House. The Socialists urged him to nationalize the banks and push for a $12 billion relief and public works bond issue. Roosevelt replied that nationalizing the banks was not in play; on the other hand, he impressed Thomas and Hillquit by taking their arguments seriously. A few months later, after Roosevelt had secured the Emergency Banking Act, the Federal Emergency Relief Act, the Agricultural Adjustment Act, the Tennessee Valley Authority (TVA) Act, and the National Industrial Recovery Act, Thomas observed with enthusiasm that the president's program resembled the Socialist platform, not the one on which he campaigned. Many observers made the same point, often bitterly; years later Herbert Hoover put it ruefully: "Students who wish to arrive at the subcurrents around Roosevelt would do well to examine the platform of the Socialist Party of 1932 and observe the uncanny fulfillment of its recommendations by Roosevelt's first administration." A stream of Socialists and progressives in Thomas's political orbit, recalculating the politics, suddenly became New Dealers. Paul Blanshard, formerly a socialist militant, joined the La Guardia administration in New York; socialist labor leaders David Dubinsky and Sidney Hillman became New Dealers as beneficiaries of the National Industrial Recovery Act. Exaggerating only slightly, Arthur M. Schlesinger Jr. later remarked that, by the end of 1933, "most of those who voted for Thomas were shouting for Roosevelt."[9]

If the New Deal delivered most of the platform that Socialists only talked about, why remain in the Socialist Party? Reinhold Niebuhr and the Marxist Left gave the "stretcher" answer: There was no third way after capitalism collapsed; sooner or later America would swerve to the fascist right or the socialist left; the New Deal was the apotheosis of opportunism. But even Niebuhr eventually decided that half a loaf was better than none and that staying in a New York socialist sect was impractical. Thomas, on the other hand, though never a militant, stuck with the stretcher answer. Roosevelt could have nationalized the banks without moving all the way to the socialist direction of credit toward production for use, Thomas stressed; a New Deal worthy of the name would have created nationalized institutions that produced for profit. Instead, Roosevelt closed the banks, patched up the system, "and gave it back to the bankers to see if they could ruin it again." The New Deal used public money and federal government power to shore up private enterprises for the sake of private profit. The nice name for that approach, Thomas observed, was state capitalism; more often it was called fascism. Roosevelt was not actually a fascist, Thomas acknowledged; America under Roosevelt was still a bastion of liberal democracy. Sometimes Thomas added that as long as Roosevelt was president the truly fascist strain in American society was thwarted. But Thomas was sufficiently impressed by the socialist either/or to believe that the New Deal was profoundly misguided. New Deal economics was a page from fascist ideology, and if history was moving toward either fascist barbarism or socialist democracy, the differences between socialism and New Deal liberalism were terribly important. There was no substitute for the socialist principle that public money should be spent directly on the public interest.[10]

Thomas contended that Democratic Socialists like himself also had a stronger conscience than liberals and conservatives about the "accustomed missionary work" of the U.S. American military in Latin America. Reviewing his country's long record of invading Latin America on behalf of bankers, oil speculators, and, ostensibly, civilization, Thomas called for a pledge to invade no more. He proposed to start by terminating the Platt Amendment, which caused "political misery" in Cuba, and by getting the Marines out of Haiti, "and in all Latin America cultivate in reality a Pan-Americanism which heretofore has been sentimental and occasional."[11]

In the early 1930s Thomas inveighed against union corruption and tolerating Communists in the unions, putting him in the crossfire of a raging battle on the Left. The Socialist Party's old guard, which was fiercely anticommunist, tended to ignore union racketeering while fighting to purge Communists from the unions. It took offense at Thomas's speeches against union corruption and bureaucratic tyranny. At the same time he insisted that because Communists were contemptuous of democracy and made a practice of sabotaging political coalitions, the democratic Left had no business cooperating with them. Thomas warned that American Communists sought a united front with the Socialist Party and broad American Left only because they were ordered by Moscow to do so as a means of destroying the Socialist Party. Since Communists and Socialists shared almost nothing, actual unity between them was impossible.[12]

But, above everything else, Thomas detested fascism, which conflicted with his opposition to a united front. It was terrible enough to witness the rise of fascist movements in Germany, Italy, and Japan; worse yet, a rising tide of racist violence and economic desperation in the United States made him fear for his country. His speaking tours hammered on the chilling parallels between fascist reactions abroad and at home. In the mid-1930s Thomas spoke in all but four states, giving him a keen sense of the country's mood. Faced with the growth of fascist sentiment in the U.S. and its alarming success in Germany, in 1934 he declared that allowing fascism to advance would be worse than linking arms with Communists. In an emergency situation, confronted with grave danger, America needed to form a united front with non-Stalinist Communists to defeat fascism: "I happen to belong to that group of Socialists, at present in a minority internationally, who believe that the urgency of the situation and the chances of success make it worthwhile to try boldly and carefully for a united front with Communists upon certain specific issues." Thomas did not blame the Socialist International and European social democratic parties for refusing to join forces with Communists. Since bad faith was a matter of policy for the Communists, it was impossible for democratic movements to actually join forces with them. But the supreme emergency of the moment necessitated a strictly limited coalition between American democrats and non-Stalinist Communists.[13]

That position set off a war in the American Socialist Party, eventually driving the old guard Socialists into Roosevelt's camp. The schism was triply ironic, because the old guard defected to someone who later formed an alliance with Joseph Stalin; Thomas had excluded Stalinists from the alliance in the first place; and three years later, in 1937, Thomas changed his mind about the desirability of linking arms with Communists even to fight fascism.

Until 1937, despite his conviction that Soviet communism was brutal and degrading, Thomas sustained a slight hope that it might liberalize. His trip to Russia in 1937 shredded what was left of that hope; Stalin's police state was even more tyrannical and murderous than Thomas had imagined. Former leftist Eugene Lyons published a searing indictment of the Soviet system, *Assignment in Utopia* (1937), which set off a bitter controversy on the Left. Thomas, upon returning to the U.S., told his audiences that the Soviet system was a left-wing form of fascism, just as

Lyons claimed. He was finished with mixing sympathy and criticism. In the distinctive tone of a disillusioned leftist, he began to say that the communist system was inherently evil. Two years before the Nazi-Soviet pact, Thomas declared that the increasing symmetry between the German and Soviet governments made a future alliance between them conceivable. The Moscow purge trials of the late 1930s sealed the point for him; Thomas urged that the trials displayed the brutality of communism itself, not merely Stalin's.[14]

Thus he stopped believing in the hope of a united front against fascism. The conspiratorial mendacity of American Communists had reached a new low in 1936, when, on orders from Trotsky, three hundred Trotskyists entered the Socialist Party to destroy it from within. Thomas originally supported the admission of the Trotskyists, but by August 1937, realizing they were subverting the party, he led a move to expel them. The excommunicated Trotskyists took one thousand members with them, including most of the youth section. For Thomas the experience was deeply humiliating; his failure as a party leader was undeniable. He resolved never to make a similar mistake. The Socialist Party was bound to be small with or without the hard Left, so it was better off without it. The party's biggest organizational problem was Roosevelt, not leftist factions. Thomas's 1936 campaign illustrated the problem. On the one hand, he showered praise on the TVA and the National Labor Relations Act; on the other, he implored Socialists and progressives not to sell out, stressing that Roosevelt did nothing for agricultural workers or racial justice. Thomas used his campaign to advocate for public banks, sharecroppers, tenant farmers, and the rights of African Americans.

But these issues attracted little attention in 1936, and Thomas was slow to admit that running against the president of the New Deal was bad politics for himself and his party. By 1936 the Socialist Party was a wreck; Thomas spent much of his campaign citing Roosevelt's accomplishments, and the following year his anticommunism was hardened by bitter experience. If not for the threat of war overshadowing everything else, Thomas might have faced political reality in the late 1930s, turning his party into a socialist caucus within the Democratic Party. But the threat of another world war kept him in a sect.

He had long since given up pacifism. Thomas conceded that his friend, Reinhold Niebuhr, was right about the necessity of using force to make and protect gains toward social justice. In 1937 Thomas supported the Eugene V. Debs Column, a group of antifascist volunteers who fought in the Spanish Civil War. Roosevelt dubbed the group "the Debutantes' Column"; Thomas, visiting battlefronts in May 1937, took it far more seriously. Though Thomas regretted that much of the Loyalist government was communist, he judged that Communists did not control it; in any case, fascism was the greater evil. Upon returning to the U.S. he urged Roosevelt to enforce the Neutrality Law against the Germans and Italians fighting an undeclared war against the legal Spanish government. World peace was at stake in Spain, Thomas warned. Franco had to be defeated; otherwise France would be bordered on three sides by fascists. Roosevelt listened intently, but laughed off Thomas's warning about a second world war and assured that few American arms were getting to Franco. Then he changed the subject to the Catholic vote in the United States. Thomas got the message; in this area, Roosevelt cared mainly about the implications for domestic politics. His respect for Roosevelt plummeted. For the rest of his life Thomas bitterly lamented that Roosevelt sold out the antifascist cause in Spain.[15]

Thus it was not as a pacifist that he campaigned against America's entry into World War II; on the other hand, Thomas was still passionately antiwar, which shaped his approach to international politics. By 1937 he believed that a war between the fascist and non-fascist nations of Europe was inevitable and imminent. After his unsuccessful meeting with Roosevelt he founded the Keep America Out of War Congress, warning that another European war was coming, it would be much like the last one, and America needed to stay out of it. Thomas and Niebuhr took essentially the same line, opposing Roosevelt's naval buildup, until the Munich Pact of September 30, 1938, when Niebuhr judged that League of Nations internationalism would never thwart Hitler. Thomas, like most Americans, welcomed the Munich Accords. It was grossly unfair for the British and French to hand the Sudetenland to Germany, he allowed; on the other hand, it was better to appease Hitler at Czechoslovakia's expense than to allow a war in which Czechoslovakia would be obliterated anyway.

But the Munich Pact merely whetted Hitler's appetite and fed his contempt for international law. Conceding the obvious, Thomas observed that the British and French appeasement of Hitler gave new prestige to his glorification of war and "put new minorities under his cruel and despotic power." Two huge moral decisions were at stake: fighting the Nazis and rescuing refugees. Thomas, paralyzed by his revulsion for war, got the first one wrong, as he subsequently admitted; Roosevelt was right to prepare for war. On the second issue, Thomas led a lonely crusade to rescue Jews and other minorities fleeing Europe, especially from the Sudetenland and Germany. He lectured constantly and testified to congressional committees about the moral necessity of saving threatened minorities and expanding immigration laws. He appealed directly to Roosevelt, who brushed him off again. In a few cases Thomas made a life-saving difference. Appealing to Assistant Secretary of State Adolf Berle Jr., Thomas saved former Communists Victor Serge, Marceau Pivert, and Julian Gorkin from execution by Stalin. But mostly he failed, for reasons that he loathed. The refugee cause had no visible constituency and was presumed to be generally unpopular; thus Roosevelt and most American politicians did nothing—at least that was Thomas's understanding of what happened, and it deepened his animosity for Roosevelt.

Meanwhile he was no match for Roosevelt in judging the moral necessity of fighting fascism. Thomas campaigned against American rearmament, conscription, aid, and intervention at every step of the road to war, even making alliances with right-wing isolationists. Viewing the next world war as an extension of the previous one, he warned that American liberties were more imperiled by intervening than by not going to war. When Hitler and Stalin signed a nonaggression pact in August 1939, much of the American Left was devastated; Communists resigned in droves and many Socialists withdrew from the antiwar movement. Thomas sympathized with the latter group, especially after Russia invaded Finland. Taking for granted that European Socialists would have to fight, Thomas did not press for an antiwar position on socialist grounds; politically he appealed to American isolationism, though he admitted to friends that he was conflicted about isolationism and isolationists. Emotionally Thomas was still a pacifist, describing war as "the monster I so utterly loathe." By the summer of 1940 he was not above arguing that it was too late to stop Hitler. By 1941 the Nazis had conquered Denmark, Norway, the Low Countries, and France, but Thomas railed against American professors who were "ready to fight for ideals, variously stated, to the last drop of blood of the last undergraduate." Fearing that American democracy was too fragile to withstand another major plunge into militarism, he warned that Roosevelt's military buildup paved the way to an American war machine state.[16]

Finally his worst fear came to pass. The day after Japan attacked Pearl Harbor, Thomas told his friend, Maynard Krueger, "I feel as if my world has pretty much come to an end, that what I have stood for has been defeated, and my own usefulness made small." He stewed for a day in despair, mulling his options, and then informed the party and the *New York Times* that he would support America's intervention, because an Axis victory would sink the world into an even deeper circle of hell. For weeks Thomas moaned about circles of hell, resisting patriotic gore; at the same time he redeemed a prewar promise. He had pledged that if the U.S. entered the war, he would do everything in his power to defeat his own prophecy that a militarized America would eviscerate liberal democracy. Thomas spent the war years giving highest priority to that cause.[17]

Antimilitarism and commitment to civil liberties were interrelated passions for Thomas; he never tired of warning that militarized states always targeted groups at home. After the U.S. entered World War II, Thomas lobbied the Selective Service for a wider definition of conscientious objection and, holding his nose, defended the rights of Communists and Fascists. In January 1942 he learned that "alien Japanese" had been forcibly removed from their jobs and homes in San Luis Obispo and Guadalupe, California. Thomas started with the American Civil Liberties Union, trying to leverage his authority as a founder and national board member, but the ACLU looked the other way. Next he appealed directly to Roosevelt, Attorney General Francis Biddle, and Assistant Secretary of War John McCloy, urging that it was plainly racist to persecute Japanese-Americans as a class. There was far more evidence of espionage among German-Americans and Italian-Americans, he noted; mercifully the government refrained from herding all German-Americans and Italian-Americans into concentration camps. Thomas told Roosevelt and McCloy, to no avail, that oppressing Japanese-Americans and other people of Japanese descent was immoral, illegal, totalitarian, and destructive, as well as certain to inflame Asians against the United States. Next he tried to arouse public opposition, imploring Americans that their country had stripped 116,000 Japanese descendents of their rights. Was that the kind of country they wanted to live in? One of Thomas's pamphlets on the plight of Japanese internees led to improvements in their condition, though Thomas and his group, the Post World War Council, failed to change the government's policy, which was upheld by the Supreme Court. At the same time he pressed Roosevelt to save European Jews, exhorting that the U.S. and England, by refusing to accept Jewish refugees, confirmed Hitler's conviction that no one cared about the Jews anyway.

These were lonely causes during the war. Thomas understood very well, from his speaking tours and hate mail, why Roosevelt had Japanese-

Americans in detention camps and refused to rescue the Jews. It was the same reason that he did not fight for the rights of American blacks or help the Spanish Loyalists. The politics were forbidding. Roosevelt saved his political capital for higher priorities and was careful not to race ahead of his political base. When the Allies firebombed German cities, erasing the distinction between combatants and civilians, Thomas protested again, warning that a fateful line had been crossed. On all these issues he sought allies wherever he could find them, but he found very few. Meanwhile he spoke against America's embrace of Stalin and constantly warned that the Soviet Union had a terrible plan for Europe.

Though Thomas anticipated much of the domestic and international fallout from the war, he was stunned by the American infatuation with Russia that arose after Hitler invaded Russia and the Soviets forged an alliance with the U.S. and Britain. Americans in both major parties suddenly developed tender feelings for Stalin and his nation. *Collier's* and *Life* magazines ran special issues that absurdly idealized Russian life, lauding supposed democratic trends in Soviet politics. Pundits, politicians, and captains of industry took to calling Stalin "Uncle Joe." Airline executive Eddie Rickenbacker returned from Russia praising the Soviet system's economic opportunities and lack of labor difficulties. The American Communist Party and its front organizations seized on Stalin's redemption, declaring themselves Roosevelt supporters and gaining thousands of new members. Demonstrating their loyalty to Roosevelt, they heckled Thomas and disrupted his speeches, charging that he hampered the war effort by criticizing America's concentration camps. For Thomas and the Norman Thomas Socialists, the "Uncle Joe" phenomenon was an unbearable absurdity; Stalin was the mass-murdering architect of a totalitarian perversion of socialism. They filled the Mecca Temple in New York to protest Stalin's execution of the Polish Jewish Socialists Viktor Alter and Henryk Ehrlich.[18]

In 1940 Soviet troops massacred fourteen thousand Polish prisoners of war in the Katyn Forest. The U.S. State Department and American media treated the story as Nazi propaganda, but Thomas urged Americans to take it seriously, warning that it was an augur of Stalin's designs for Europe. Repeatedly Thomas blasted Roosevelt's assurance that he knew how to handle Uncle Joe. Stalin was not a typical politician ready to cut a deal, Thomas protested, and Roosevelt was wrong to insist on an unconditional surrender by Germany, which played into Stalin's hands. Repeatedly Thomas warned that the Soviets were out to conquer Eastern Europe and that the U.S. was needlessly abandoning East Europeans to Soviet tyranny. He based his 1944 presidential campaign on that protest. Thomas wanted the Polish border of 1939 to be redrawn as part of a comprehensive settlement designed by an international federation. There was no reason to indulge Stalin's imperial ambitions, he argued. If Stalin were forced to settle for less, he would do so. He would not wage a bloodbath war with the U.S. and Britain to get Poland. The Western Allies could save the peoples of Eastern Europe from Soviet tyranny by standing up for them. But if Roosevelt did not stop Stalin from taking over Eastern Europe, "the President may be committing us and our sons after us not only to the prolongation of this war but to the certainty of the next."[19]

Of his six presidential campaigns, Thomas was proudest of this one, though he made his poorest electoral showing in it. For the rest of his life he smoldered at the way his arguments were brushed aside. The Katyn massacre, exactly as he claimed, was an augur of something terrible, as was the massacre on the banks of the Vistula, where the Soviet army waited while German troops exterminated the Warsaw insurgents. Yalta was the consequence, where the democracies sold out democracy and peace. Thomas wanted U.S. forces to meet the Russians as far to the east as possible. By the time Roosevelt, Churchill, and Stalin met at Yalta in the Crimea, however (February 4–11, 1945), the Soviets controlled Hungary, Romania, and Bulgaria, and Stalin rejected Churchill's demand for free elections in Poland. Formally the Yalta Accords committed the Allies to recognize freely elected governments in the liberated areas, but the Allies cut a secret deal dividing occupied Europe into spheres of influence reflecting the current military situation. Returning from Yalta in February 1945, Churchill strangely assured the House of Commons: "Marshal Stalin and the other Soviet leaders wish to live in honorable friendship and equality with the Western democracies. I feel also that their word is their bond. I know of no government which stands to its obligations, even in its own despite, more solidly than the Russian Soviet Government."[20]

For Thomas, that was an incredible betrayal. On the day after the Yalta agreements were announced he declared bitterly: "A war begun ostensibly to guarantee the integrity of Poland and entered presumably by the United States on the basis of the principles of the Atlantic Charter (which condemns 'territorial changes that do not accord with the freely expressed wishes of the peoples concerned') ends with Stalin in possession of the territory that he took forcibly from Poland in alliance with the Nazi aggressor and with a government in charge which is his creation." To Stalin,

Poland was merely a highway for invaders, and the call for elections in Poland by the West was a ruse to deny the Soviet Union a buffer state on its western border. For Thomas, Poland was the acid test of a decent peace. Five months later Churchill, Stalin, and President Harry Truman sealed the fate of Eastern Europe at the Potsdam Conference, though Churchill lost the British election halfway through the conference and was replaced by the new prime minister Clement Attlee. Thomas, though cheered by the election of a fellow Socialist in Britain, blasted the Labour Party's imperial policies in Burma, Malaya, and India. He urged the new American and British leaders not to sign the Potsdam Accords, which represented, in his equally unsparing view, "a triumph of vengeance and stupidity and in its inevitable application by the triumphant Kremlin turned eastern and central Europe over to the communists."[21]

Thomas believed that the rest of the war was concluded equally badly. He opposed Roosevelt's insistence on an unconditional Japanese surrender and Roosevelt's attempt at Yalta to draw the Soviets into the war against Japan. Both were terrible ideas for the same reason: the last thing the world needed was for the Soviet Empire to expand into Asia. When Truman became president in April 1945, Thomas urged him to reverse Roosevelt's policies on Eastern Europe, carpet-bombing, an unconditional Japanese surrender, and luring the Soviets into Asia. Japan was already prostrate; instead of inviting the Soviets into Asia, Thomas wanted Truman to negotiate a Japanese surrender.

Thomas and Truman subsequently developed a genuine respect for each other; Truman sought Thomas's advice on numerous issues, especially the cold war, and Thomas admired Truman's efforts to arrange a bilateral nuclear disarmament. But in 1945 Thomas was one of the few public figures to denounce Truman's atomic bombing of Hiroshima and Nagasaki. A decent society did not dispense with the prohibition against slaughtering civilians just because it had overriding military interests, Thomas protested. Japan was ready to negotiate a conditional surrender, and, even failing one, the U.S. could have dropped a demonstration bomb, and then dictated the terms of surrender. Instead the U.S. incinerated two crowded cities. Thomas was horrified. To him it was deeply shameful that the U.S. slaughtered one hundred thousand people without bothering to test the alternatives. Long before it became respectable to question Truman's decision to use the bomb, Thomas felt compelled to make his audiences consider the gratuitous horror of Hiroshima. For many years it was by far his most unpopular lecture topic.

Having protested the absurdity of "Uncle Joe" sentimentality, American pro-Sovietism, and the great betrayal at Yalta, Thomas might have seemed a perfect candidate for what became a significant social type: the cold war Socialist turned neoconservative. American neoconservatism first germinated within his circle of militantly anticommunist Socialists. But Thomas had warned all along that delusions about America's wartime Soviet ally could lead to a backlash and another avoidable war; thus he pleaded for a realistic view of Soviet Communism. When the pendulum swung back in 1946, he opposed that too. His speaking tours gave him a vivid and frightening sense of America's overreaction. At the end of 1945 Thomas lectured in California; in the spring of 1947 he spoke in many of the same places, and was appalled: "Then the tendency was too much complacency about Russia and too much appeasement. Now there is a high degree of rather hysterical anticommunism, which is being exploited by reactionaries."[22]

Thomas spent his remaining twenty-one years fighting both positions. In 1948 he ran for the presidency for the last time, directing most of his fire at the standard bearer of the fellow-traveling Left, former vice president Henry Wallace, whose Progressive Party was dominated by Communists. Thomas's contempt for Wallace was long-standing. In the 1930s, when Wallace was Secretary of Agriculture and Thomas helped the Southern sharecroppers organize a union, he tried to persuade Wallace to take an interest in America's most exploited workers; Wallace refused to meet with him. Later Thomas was disgusted by Wallace's alliances with Communists and his ludicrous description of Stalinist communism as "directed democracy." In the 1948 campaign Thomas repeatedly challenged Wallace to a debate, calling him an "apologist for the slave state of Russia, and preacher of peace by appeasement." He ridiculed Wallace's faith that peace could be achieved "by submission to the mightiest tyranny which has ever appeared on this earth." Communism was not a militant version of liberal democracy or progressivism, Thomas implored; it stood for the annihilation of liberal decency. For Thomas the Wallace candidacy was repugnant because it threatened to ruin the very idea of a progressive, third-party Left in American politics. He attacked it accordingly, while Wallace refused to debate him. Though Thomas won only ninety-five thousand votes, he got wider press coverage than usual, and was often lauded as the voice of America's conscience.[23]

After the war he tried to write a major work summarizing the case for a progressive, anticommunist, generally antimilitaristic, democratic socialism. Thomas started to write *A Socialist's Faith* in 1945, but he stopped two years later after his wife Violet's death left him too depressed to complete it. By 1948, when he returned to the manuscript, he had to make extensive revisions. The political context had so changed that he had to rewrite almost the entire book. His first draft stressed the threat of communist totalitarianism, but by 1948 that was unnecessary. His first draft, like his 1948 campaign, blasted parlor-pink anti–anti-communism, but Thomas realized that a major work should be aimed at the long term, taking a higher road. The Wallace-types were not worth more than a few sentences. *A Socialist's Faith*, finally published in 1951, ruefully observed: "The change in the American attitude is so extreme that it is hard for me to remember how coldly my warnings about the essential nature of communism inside and out of the Soviet Union were received in the years 1944–46."[24]

Thomas pressed hard for a progressive anticommunism. "The evidence of the essential evil of communism is strong," he contended; on the other hand, the Western democracies handed cheap propaganda victories to the Soviet Union every time they bullied weaker nations or embraced Third World dictators. Communism was growing in the Third World because Britain and the U.S. appeased Stalin from Casablanca to Potsdam *and* because communism shrewdly exploited the hopes of downtrodden populations: "Despite its own worse crimes—which are still widely disbelieved—it has the towering advantage of being in a position to say to millions of resentful colonials and to the disinherited masses generally: 'Our enemies are your enemies. Let us make common cause!'" To fight communist expansion, the democracies needed the "propaganda of the truth" about communist salvation, Thomas urged; even more, they needed to change the bitter truth about their own racism and imperialism. To him, democratic socialism remained the only comprehensive strategy of achieving and pulling together freedom, equality, community, racial justice, and a decent world order.[25]

"For myself, socialism has always seemed primarily a doctrine and movement consciously concerned with the common good," he wrote. In the economic sphere Thomas advocated a commanding heights strategy in which public corporations controlled essential industries, consumer cooperatives controlled most retail outlets, and nonessential industries remained under private control. During the Depression his list of essential industries needing to be socialized was naturally longer than afterward, but critics such as Bernard Johnpoll and Dwight Steward exaggerated the difference, claiming that Thomas abandoned socialism after the war.[26]

In 1934 Thomas advocated the immediate socialization of all banks, railroads, coal mines, and power and oil companies, as well as all other monopolized or semi-monopolized firms such as the dairy trust.[27] By 1940 he favored consumer cooperatives over public corporations but treated this issue as a matter of emphasis and contextual judgment. Thomas believed, in any case, that all natural monopolies should be socialized as public corporations and all other essential industries should be socialized in some form.[28]

That remained his position for the rest of his life. In *A Socialist's Faith* (1951) and *Socialism Re-examined* (1963) Thomas advocated the socialization of natural resources, the system of money, banking, and credit, and the monopolies. Private firms should be allowed to profit from the mineral wealth they discover or extract, he judged, but not to own what they did not make. Mineral wealth should be public property and available to everyone. Similarly, it was outrageous for citizens of an advanced democracy to pay interest to banks "for no other service than what ought to be the social function of the creation of money in the form of credit." One of the state's essential functions is to create money parallel to the creation of goods on noninflationary terms, he reasoned. Socialized credit is a fundamental necessity that promotes investment for the public good. Moreover, socializing natural monopolies such as water and electrical power systems and the steel, coal, and oil industries was a basic matter of serving the common good by privileging the principle of production for use. Thomas gave little attention to how democratic control of the economy should be organized. He thought that workers should be represented directly on company boards, not through unions, and that public representatives should be selected by consumer associations and government appointments, but his arguments in this area were never more than suggestions. He understood, as he wrote in *Socialism Re-examined*, that "socialism needs new answers," but social theory was not his calling, and he died before economic democracy theorists opted for public bank models of market socialism.[29]

Thomas supported America's military intervention in Korea on anticommunist containment grounds and as a show of support for the United Nations. In Korea, he believed, the U.S. had an important chance to teach Stalin that containment was real and that further Soviet aggression would be resisted.[30] Thomas brooked no revisionism on who started the cold war. Stalin conquered Eastern Europe, launched the Berlin blockade, refused to cooperate with the Marshall Plan, and rejected American proposals for nuclear disarmament. If another world war was to be averted, Thomas urged, American leaders had to meet the challenge of resisting further aggressions of the type that launched the cold war. A just peace required a realistic understanding of Soviet goals and a will to prevent their realization.[31]

Like Niebuhr and George Kennan, however, Thomas judged that anticommunist containment doctrine acquired an overly militarized and ideologized meaning in the 1950s, especially in the nuclear field. Despite his friendship with Secretary of State John Foster Dulles, he condemned Dulles's doctrine of nuclear brinkmanship, urging that America needed to work at preventing war, not dancing on the edge of a nuclear abyss. The new generation of nuclear realists such as Herman Kahn, Henry Kissinger, and William F. Buckley Jr. appalled him; Thomas debated all of them, criticizing their complacency about the apocalyptic destructiveness of nuclear weapons. He also disliked that his country routinely applied anticommunist containment to the Third World, propping up fascistic regimes, though his reaction to the CIA-sponsored coup in Guatemala in 1954 was surprisingly mild. Thomas thought the State Department did it to prevent a communist beachhead. His idea of anticommunism pressed for multilateral disarmament, multilateral disengagement, and a strengthened United Nations.[32]

In 1957 Thomas cofounded the Committee for a Sane Nuclear Policy, which he expected to become another tiny peace group. Instead it mushroomed into a major national organization that attracted communist infiltrators. Formally Sane barred communist members, but when Thomas realized that the organization had been infiltrated he demanded that the Communists be removed. Senate investigators eventually subpoenaed thirty-seven members of the New York City chapter. At Thomas's insistence, Sane's national board did not defend the ousted members, which infuriated much of the Left, including the *Nation* magazine. Thomas replied that it was difficult enough to sustain a national antiwar organization without having to cope with the sabotage tactics of inside totalitarians.

He was much less circumspect, however, about the opposite threat. By 1961 it was widely rumored that for many years the CIA had secretly funded the Socialist International and the Congress for Cultural Freedom. Thomas, active in both organizations, asked CIA director John McCone about the rumors, but he failed to pursue the matter after McCone refused to comment on it. In 1967 the web of secrecy on CIA subsidies came unraveled, revealing that the CIA had funded a Socialist International agency that Thomas chaired—the Institute for International Labor Research—through the J. M. Kaplan fund. On occasion Thomas had asked Kaplan about the CIA rumors, always believing Kaplan's denials. When the truth came out, Thomas was deeply embarrassed. He apologized for his gullibility but defended the institute's work and record, noting that the previous year the institute attacked the Johnson administration's 1965 invasion of the Dominican Republic: "The CIA didn't get much for that money."[33]

By then he was deeply involved in another antiwar movement. In 1964 Thomas told friends that he supported Johnson for president but not his war in Vietnam, because Vietnam was "the kind of war in which an American plane can stray over a line and destroy a Cambodian village. It is a war which cannot be won." The following January he joined the public antiwar movement, hoping to stop Johnson from escalating America's involvement in Vietnam. Thomas spoke across the country, still roaring in a booming voice at two hundred words per minute, at the age of eighty-one, warning that Vietnam was a civil war of the unwinnable guerrilla variety. Johnson's massive escalation of the war repulsed him. Vice President Hubert Humphrey, an old friend, proved equally disappointing; Thomas said of him: "He could contradict himself and then deny doing it." Thomas wrote a blistering letter to Johnson, asking if he did not see how the slaughter of innocents damaged America's reputation in the world.

He had similar feelings about the violence and lewdness of much of the antiwar movement. In 1967 Thomas exhorted the New Politics Convention to turn away from the destructive vulgarity of "Burn, Baby, Burn!" in favor of a fraternal spirit and a constructive program. Afterward he told friends that his feelings about "big chunks" of the Left had hit an all-time low. He recoiled at the ugly treatment of soldiers and police officers that prevailed at "peace" demonstrations. Speaking to the National Students' Association, Thomas declared that the freedom to dissent was a precious right, enjoyed only by a minority of the world's students, and carried special moral responsibilities: "I don't like the sight of young people burning the flag of my country, the country that I love. If they want an appropriate symbol they should be washing the flag, not burning it."[34]

He died the following year, eight months after the assassination of Martin Luther King Jr., whom he admired and whose religious faith he envied. Long after he demitted from the ministry, Thomas admitted that he never ceased to be "obsessed" with religion. Often he asked his many friends who were clerics or theologians if they still "really believed." It amazed him when they said yes, but usually they did not identify "really believing" with supernatural orthodoxy, as Thomas did.[35]

He offered a rare public word about that impression in 1932, after demitting from the ministry, in the form of a tribute to his grandfathers and father. Of his paternal grandfather Thomas wrote: "As we sat quietly around him, with his large-type Bible in his lap—one of his few concessions to advancing age—dimly at least we understood from him the sources of a light which gave meaning, yes, and glory, to the humdrum task, and all the vicissitudes of the year, a light which bathed, in beauty greater than the sun's, the fields, the shining river, the wooded hills, the cottage and the cherished garden in which this Preacher of the Word lived out his days." None of his "fathers" would have comprehended nor found comfort in the sophisticated concepts of modern theologians, Thomas observed: "Their God was a Father . . . who gave man dominion over the world which He had made and in that world occasionally had walked and talked with men." He never shook the feeling that that was real Christianity.[36]

Thus he counted himself among the unbelievers, even though he had a religious worldview. In 1955 Thomas wrote a head-clearing essay on the subject for his own edification, not for publication. He observed that his perspective was surely as Christian as Paul Tillich's; what puzzled him was that Tillich was accepted as a Christian theologian.[37] Elsewhere he wrote: "There is undoubtedly a Power, not ourselves, behind the universe whom or which we may call God." In a letter to his 1948 running mate, Tucker Smith, Thomas explained: "I cannot become sophisticated enough philosophically to be satisfied with a purely philosophic concept of God." Thomas accepted Tillich's argument that all theological language is symbolic, but he yearned for the anthropomorphic deity of his father who was, as Tillich noted, less than Being itself because "he" was one object among others. Having thought himself into a concept of God that he found emotionally unsatisfying and supposedly too rationalistic to be Christian, Thomas left the church and offered his bemused respect to friends who stayed in it.[38]

For him, Marxist intellectualism held even less meaning than theology; thus, for many Americans of his generation, Thomas was the one who made it possible to be a Socialist. Liberating socialism from its Marxist straightjacket, he conceived it as a compelling doctrine and movement of the common good. Thomas lived to see much of his program become part of American life, including old-age insurance, civil rights, public housing, a national health plan, union organizing and collective bargaining rights, control of stock market specialization, and much more, though he found it incredible that his country lacked national health insurance. Above all he held high the vision of a better world that was always within reach—a cooperative commonwealth, defended on moral and practical grounds, that appealed to common experience and the common good.

This vision was old-fashioned, moralistic in the social gospel sense, idealistic, and not so wild a dream. Thomas was right about the limitations of the New Deal. Roosevelt never really believed in demand-side economics; he practiced just enough of it to keep capitalism alive in the mid-1930s; and the Depression was still on when World War II, not the New Deal, solved the employment problem. But Thomas repeatedly failed to grasp that his often correct opinions about matters political failed to register the politics. Setting himself against the New Deal was the showcase example. The New Deal mobilized a mass movement of the working class that sparked a nationwide political realignment. When the Socialist Party opposed this movement and called for a different one in the name of the same working class, it condemned itself to political exile and futility. Arthur Schlesinger put it well: "He raised his voice courageously and insistently on questions of civil liberties and civil rights. His essential contribution, indeed, was to keep moral issues alive at a moment when the central emphasis was on meeting economic emergencies. At his best, Thomas gave moving expression to an ethical urgency badly needed in politics, to a sense of the relation between means and ends and of the inestimable value of the human being." But on economic matters Thomas blundered into the either/or camp, claiming that capitalism could not be reformed, when obviously the New Deal was doing exactly that.[39]

Thomas came late to the realization that the American democratic Left advances only during periods of liberal resurgence, and only then if it does not cut itself off from liberalism. In 1951 he founded an educational society within the party that he called the Union of Democratic Socialists; Thomas hoped that this revamped Fabian model would eventually replace the party. But the institute expired after only three years and Thomas stuck with the party, despite the fact that its failure, as he told friends, was a source of constant pain for him. In the early 1960s, when Michael Harrington began to argue that Socialists should work as an educational caucus within the Democratic Party, Thomas found himself in reluctant agreement.

He made numerous mistakes and met nearly constant failure, often struggling alone. But he fought for nearly every good cause of his time. Social critic Murray Kempton, in his memoir *Part of Our Time*, aptly remarked on Thomas's significance for his generation: "The old libertarian dream of spending one's life in lonely combat against every form of enslavement, to the extent that it was not a Communist confusion, appeared to us to have no vessel but Norman Thomas." Literary critic and Socialist Irving Howe put it more personally: "Even after he died Thomas remained, so to say, in my head, setting a standard of right action, pointing to the elusive path where the 'ethic of ultimate ends' and the 'ethic of responsibility' join. When I did something unworthy in politics, it was to his memory I had to answer; when I acquitted myself well, it was his approval I would most have wanted." That was a high standard.[40]

Chapter 6

Michael Harrington and the "Left Wing of the Possible"

Nearly a hundred times per year for more than thirty years Michael Harrington heard himself introduced before he launched into an earnest, learned, humorous, sometimes scintillating speech on some aspect of his democratic socialist politics. Gifted with charm and a quick wit, he was adept at handling hecklers; the low point of these events, from his perspective, usually came during the introduction. Nearly always he was described as "the author of *The Other America*, the book that sparked the War on Poverty," while his other books got short shrift. Harrington cringed, hating to correct a welcoming host, but these introductions were hard to bear. Sometimes he reintroduced himself. "I've written quite a few books since *The Other America*, some of which might interest you," he would say. His major works were very important to him, and *The Other America* was not one of them. He could see his epitaph in the making: "Wrote *The Other America*, downhill after that."

That, indeed, is how Harrington is usually remembered. He generally gets a page or two in books on the Johnson administration and a brief mention in books on the Civil Rights movement, but since American socialism gets few books of any kind, the rest of his work is downgraded or forgotten. Even Maurice Isserman's otherwise splendid biography of Harrington, *The Other American*, says almost nothing about the aspect of his career that mattered most to him.[1]

Had Michael Harrington been born anywhere in Western Europe, he would have become a major social democratic party leader. Having been raised, instead, in Missouri, and then transplanted to New York, he could have become America's leading liberal political intellectual, but he was committed to building a serious social democratic tradition in his country. Thus he settled for being America's leading Socialist, which, as William F. Buckley Jr. once teased him from a podium, was something like being the tallest building in Kansas.

Edward Michael Harrington was born in St. Louis in 1928 to a securely middle-class family that was Irish Catholic on both sides. His father, Edward Harrington, was a mild-mannered patent lawyer whom Harrington described, in his writings and public interviews, as a gentle soul. His mother, Catherine Harrington, was a domineering personality whom Harrington described, with more reserve, as a "public-spirited" volunteer in Catholic and civic organizations. In private Harrington explained that his mother was a militant Catholic whose dogmatism and forcefulness gave him much to overcome, though even to friends he refrained from commenting on the irony of being an only child in a conservative Catholic household. Edward Harrington Sr. taught his son by word and example to do what Catherine wanted. After Harrington achieved fame for *The Other America*, Catherine recalled to an interviewer that when Michael was seven years old, "We were both reading in bed. He was reading Dickens and he turned to me and said, 'My, this author expresses himself well.'" That was a true picture, even if Catherine Harrington improved the quote.[2]

Michael Harrington was educated by the Jesuits at St. Louis University High School, where he was called Ned, and by the Jesuits at Holy Cross College, where friends called him Ed. At both places he was very young, having started high school at the age of twelve. Harrington later recalled that he grew up "in a pleasant Irish Catholic ghetto, which made the death of God particularly poignant for me." He also acknowledged that his training in Thomist scholasticism probably had something to do with his later attraction to Marxist scholasticism.[3]

After graduating from Holy Cross at the age of nineteen, near the top of his class, he took a few years to find himself. To please his parents Harrington spent a year at Yale Law School, which bored him, and a year studying English at the University of Chicago, which he liked but not enough to hang on for a doctorate. He later claimed that he converted from Taft republicanism to socialism near the end of his law schooling and that his "Damascus Road" conversion to social activism occurred during a summer job in St. Louis, where he worked for the public school system's

Pupil Welfare Department. Standing in a decayed building that reeked of garbage, broken toilets, and overcrowded habitation, he recalled: "Suddenly the abstract and statistical and aesthetic outrages I had reacted to at Yale and Chicago became real and personal and insistent. A few hours later, riding the Grand Avenue streetcar, I realized that somehow I must spend my life trying to obliterate that kind of house and to work with the people who lived there." Perhaps it did happen that way, since Harrington featured this story in both of his autobiographies. But Isserman could not find a Yale classmate who remembered him as a Socialist, and Harrington worked for the Pupil Welfare Department for a total of three days.[4]

He started to become Michael Harrington on his next stop, Greenwich Village, where he aspired to become a socialist poet. Moving to New York in 1951, Harrington made his way to Dorothy Day's Catholic Worker House of Hospitality, in the Bowery, where he promptly took over the *Catholic Worker* newspaper and became a favorite of the founder. Though Harrington spent little time actually ministering to the poor— the newspaper proved more interesting—he repeated the *Worker's* standard answer to inquirers: he was there to become a saint. For nearly two years he tried to adopt Day's anarcho-pacifist politics and her devotion to Catholic orthodoxy, while spending his evenings at the White Horse Tavern, which was locally famous for the poets and writers who drank there—Dylan Thomas, Delmore Schwartz, Norman Mailer, William Styron, and Dan Wakefield. Young Democratic Party operative Daniel Patrick Moynihan was another regular; for ten years Harrington was a fixture at the White Horse. He fancied himself a poet and Bohemian, smoked and drank every night, held court on politics and literature, took home many women, and dropped Day's anarchism, pacifism, and religion, in that order. Under the influence of a young operative in the Young People's Socialist League, Bogdan Denitch, Harrington joined the socialist "movement," as the YPSL cadre called its grouplet. Trading one unworldly sect for another, Harrington told himself that instead of merely ministering to human misery, he was working to abolish the system that produced it.

For twenty years he thrived in that world, outgrowing the youth section to become the eloquent golden boy of a quarrelsome, factional, New York socialist environment, in Harrington's case as a Shachtmanite. Max Shachtman was a charismatic autodidact, party hack, and orator who left his mark on a peculiar mixture of radicals and conservatives. He began his political pilgrimage as a Communist and ended it as a father figure to the generation of right-wing Socialists and neoconservatives who won high positions in the Reagan administration. In the 1920s he was a Soviet-style Communist; in 1929, as a close associate of Leon Trotsky, he co-founded American Trotskyism; in 1940 he founded the post-Trotskyist Independent Socialist League, which espoused what Shachtman called "Third Camp" revolutionary socialism; in the 1950s his theory of "democratic Marxism" provided the ideological scaffolding for democratic Socialists who considered themselves too "hard" to be Norman Thomas Socialists; in the 1960s he moved to the right, joined the Socialist Party, and cozied up to the leadership of the AFL-CIO; subsequently he was revered by neoconservatives as a champion of militantly anticommunist trade unionism.

Harrington got his political education in the 1950s phase of the Shachtmanite school, which debated abstruse points of Marxist doctrine in sessions often lasting through the night. There were always rallies and "actions" to attend, but mostly Shachtmanite socialism was about getting the arguments right. Harrington's comrades were all Marxologists; he later described them as "determined, but unhysterical anticommunists engaged in seemingly Talmudic exegeses of the holy writ according to Karl Marx." From Shachtman he inherited his signature theories of democratic Marxism and bureaucratic collectivism, as well as his socialist outrage at the communist perversion of socialism. Harrington recalled that when Shachtman gave one of his three-hour speeches on the evils of communism, reeling off the names of socialist leaders murdered by Stalin, "it was like hearing the roll call of revolutionary martyrs who were bone of our bone, flesh of our flesh." This schooling in the intensely anticommunist faction of the Old Left shaped Harrington's early concept of the socialist project and, in the early 1960s, undercut his relationships with youthful leaders of the New Left.[5]

In 1960 the non-youthful Socialists of the League for Industrial Democracy (a socialist youth-outreach vehicle with ties to the Shachtmanites and the Socialist Party) tried to regenerate their youth division by funding a new student organization later named Students for a Democratic Society (SDS). Harrington had spent the past two years lecturing at colleges and universities across the country, helping to build YPSL into a national organization boasting one thousand members and a YPSL coalition project, the Student Peace Union, into a ten-thousand-member organization. He was the obvious choice to be the Old Left's bridge to the student generation. In early 1962 Harrington glowed when student movement leader Tom Hayden declared that his generation trusted only three people older than thirty: Norman Thomas, leftist sociologist C. Wright Mills, and Harrington. Hayden's fledgling protest organization, SDS, had a few hundred members at the time; Harrington set out to educate them about leftist politics and building a serious student-based left-wing movement.

But to Hayden, Al Haber, Richard Flacks, and other SDS leaders, YPSL was not a model of anything to emulate; meanwhile, Harrington could not resist lecturing them about things they did not understand owing to their deficient backgrounds in leftist politics. YPSL specialized in factional disputes over fine points of ideological purity. Marxology prevailed, in the form of mimeographed, single-spaced position statements by rival caucuses. All of that repelled the SDS leaders. To them it was obvious that the American Left needed a different kind of student movement, one that dropped the Old Left's esoteric debates about Marxism and socialism, its obsessive hatred of communism, and its nostalgic alliances with trade unions and Democratic Party liberalism.

In 1962 fifty-nine SDS delegates met at the United Automobile Workers camp in Port Huron, Michigan, to draft a soon-famous manifesto, the Port Huron Statement, where they clashed with Harrington and YPSL leaders Richard Roman, Rochelle Horowitz, and Tom Kahn. The SDS leaders wanted to break free from anticommunism and the Democratic Party establishment; Harrington railed against them on both points. To him, making socialism American was paramount. Democratic socialism would never get anywhere in the U.S., nor should it, if it was not militantly anticommunist and friendly to liberal Democrats and unionists. To the SDS leaders, Harrington seemed obsessed with battles from another time and place. Making socialism American was not their cause; they took a low view of socialism and a lower one of America. To them, anticommunist was simply the excuse that liberals and reactionaries used to justify America's wars and its expanding military empire. Harrington later recalled, "My notion of a progressive, Leftist anti-Communist made as much existential sense to them as a purple cow." Since liberals were part of the problem, the SDS took little interest in working with them: "They were in favor of political realignment, but dismissed the liberals who were essential to it."[6]

Briefly, at Harrington's urging, the League for Industrial Democracy cut off funding for the SDS, an episode that grew with retelling in New Left lore. Harrington had been the youngest member of his high school class, his college class, his drinking gangs, and his socialist sects. Now he confronted younger student leaders who spurned his counsel, and he took it badly, damaging his reputation among young radicals just as they began to build a new Left worth naming. That he was right on the two main issues didn't help: the student radicals needed to recognize that communism was oppressive, murderous, and squalid, and that denigrating liberals was not the way to build a healthy progressive movement. But Harrington unnecessarily alienated the SDS leaders by talking down to them. He was too defensive about YPSL to acknowledge its repellent features, and the SDS leaders turned out to be perceptive about the upshot of his anticommunism. The Port Huron Statement acknowledged that Soviet communism was ugly and oppressive; it also blasted the reigning cold war militarism that turned the entire planet into an anticommunist battlefield. After Vietnam became the issue, Harrington took the wrong side nearly to the end of the 1960s, exactly as SDS expected.

Contrary to most accounts of this subject, however, Harrington never lost his access to most New Left leaders. He worked hard at rebuilding damaged relationships, and by the late 1960s he was well practiced at apologizing for his rift with the SDS, an apology he repeated on the lecture trail for the rest of his life. He regretted having botched his chance to influence the student movement. For the most part, he also resisted the "I told you so" mode after SDS degenerated into Maoist vanguardism and hooliganism. Self-righteousness was not Harrington's style, and he grew better at confessing that his group missed its opportunity to bond with and restrain the New Left. More important, by the early 1970s he sorely regretted that it took him so long to oppose the Vietnam War. Harrington did not speak at an antiwar rally until October 1969, and he did not call for the U.S. to withdraw from Vietnam until January 1970.

Despite these regrets and mistakes, he connected with a large swath of the sixties generation as "the man who discovered poverty." *The Other America* gave Harrington an identity to a mass audience that knew nothing about Max Shachtman or even the Port Huron Statement. To a smaller number he also became the symbol of a humane, democratic socialist politics, even as many leftists gagged on his anticommunism.

The Other America had inauspicious beginnings. As a professional activist, Harrington was adept at writing and speaking on topics he knew little about. In 1959 he knew a lot about communism, literary criticism, and civil liberties, his staple topics for *Commonweal* and *Dissent* magazines. About poverty he knew very little, aside from his brief experience at the *Catholic Worker* and occasional glimpses of urban poverty on his speaking tours. Liberal journals rarely mentioned poverty in the 1950s. To the extent that poverty still existed, liberals took it to be a marginal hangover, lacking any importance as a political issue. In 1959 most liberals believed that the basic structural problems of how government and business should work together had been solved. Economic growth would mop up residual "pockets of poverty" left over from the Depression. John Kenneth's Galbraith's *The Affluent Society* and Arthur Schlesinger Jr.'s *The Vital Center* were the Bibles of the new prosperity-liberalism. Though Galbraith later pleaded for a different reading of his celebrated book, it had perfect pitch for the Vital Center's blend of optimism and complacency.[7]

The Affluent Society brought out a few nay-sayers. Economist Leon Keyserling suggested that establishment liberalism might be too complacent by half. In 1958, noting that more than a quarter of American families reported annual incomes below $4,000, Keyserling suggested there was a stronger case to be made for a new New Deal–style employment policy than Galbraith and Schlesinger let on. A few months later Senator Paul Douglas of Illinois, in a speech published by the *New Leader*, called for a more aggressive government response to America's lingering poverty problem. *Commentary* editor Anatole Shub, sensing a hot topic, asked Harrington to write an article on poverty as a social and political issue.

Harrington was always a quick study. Using statistics from the Federal Reserve Board and the U.S. Commerce Department, he argued that America had fifty million poor people. To explain how the affluent society of 1959 could still have that much poverty, he appropriated anthropologist Oscar Lewis's "culture of poverty" thesis: The problem was not mere unemployment and underemployment; rather, America's poor constituted "a separate culture, another nation, with its own way of life." This notion had a leftist spin in Lewis's and Harrington's usage, though in later years Harrington had to dissociate it from neoconservative usage, which employed the "culture of poverty" as a club to attack antipoverty programs. In a second article in 1960, on urban slums, he decried America's housing policy as cheap and lacking in compassion.[8]

Even Harrington did not regard poverty as a top priority issue, however. As an activist he gave first place to the Civil Rights movement and second place to building a socialist movement; poverty was a secondary matter. By 1960 there were two full-fledged Civil Rights movements, which worked together but operated differently. The northern movement was centered in New York, rooted in long-standing organizations, and professional in its structure and style. It handled fund-raising and publicity for the movement as a whole, emphasized coalition building with sympathetic groups, and organized large national events such as the March on Washington. Harrington was a stalwart of this group of leaders and organizers, which included black socialists A. Philip Randolph, Bayard Rustin, and James Farmer. The southern movement grew out of the Montgomery Bus Boycott of 1955 and the student sit-ins of spring 1960. It was younger, less professional in style, structure, and ideology, and more radical tactically. Harrington shared the qualms of northern Civil Rights leaders about the expressive, theatrical style of the southern movement, but he also appreciated its advantages. Northern Civil Rights leaders were sometimes constrained by their institutions and professionalism, and they had to cope with the decline of an existing student movement. In the South the movement was new and comparatively uninhibited, if ideologically undeveloped. As Harrington put it, "They came fresh to their rebellion." He treasured his friendships with Rustin and Martin Luther King Jr., often remarking that he knew from his first meeting with King in 1960 that King was a Democratic Socialist in all but name.[9]

Years later King enjoyed teasing Harrington about having discovered poverty. In the early 1960s, however, Civil Rights and socialism were consuming for Harrington, and he had no intention of turning his articles on poverty into a book, even after Edward R. Murrow's documentary, "Harvest of Shame," drew attention to the plight of migrant farm laborers. Harrington brushed off requests from publishers to write *The Other America*, until Macmillan offered a $500 advance, an enormous sum to a movement activist always pinched for bus fare. For it he wrote the book that changed his life.

The Other America explained that the land of the poor was invisible to middle-class Americans because it existed mostly in rural isolation and crowded urban slums. This America, its invisibility notwithstanding, numbered fifty million fellow citizens who belonged to a different society than the middle-class culture of affluence. It was also the product of social neglect: "Until these facts shame us, until they stir us to action, the other America will continue to exist, a monstrous example of needless suffering in the most advanced society in the world."[10]

Dwight Macdonald praised the book for forty pages in the *New Yorker*, setting off a flood of media attention and speaking requests for Harrington. The book became required reading for social scientists, government officials, student activists, and intellectuals. Economic adviser Walter Heller gave a copy to President Kennedy, who may have read it before ordering a federal war on poverty three days before his death.

Shortly afterward Lyndon Johnson declared war on poverty, telling Heller that abolishing poverty was his kind of program. To head the new Office of Economic Opportunity Johnson appointed Peace Corps director Sargent Shriver, who then appointed Harrington to the program's organizing group. Shriver briefed Harrington on the agency's mandate and budget, prompting Harrington to object that America would not abolish poverty by spending merely "nickels and dimes." Shriver archly replied, "Oh really, Mr. Harrington. I don't know about you, but this is the first time I've spent a billion dollars." That exchange, a staple of Harrington's subsequent lecture touring, explained for him why the U.S. lost its war on poverty. Government spending increased significantly between 1965 and 1968, he allowed, but that was to pay for the war in Vietnam and increases in Social Security and Medicare. The war on poverty got less than 1 percent of the federal budget.[11]

Harrington wore his fame uneasily. He could have used it as a ticket to individual stardom as a liberal—*The Other America* never mentioned socialism—but instead he promoted democratic socialism and tried to build new social democratic organizations. He could have written trade market best-sellers to boost his name and income—publishers pleaded for a sequel to *The Other America*—but he persisted in writing scholarly books on socialism and the crises of late capitalism. He was a sensational speaker—expressive, flowing, affable, gifted at humorous asides, always making three well-outlined points—and he enjoyed his lecture touring. Yet in March 1965, while striding to a podium in San Diego, he nearly collapsed from the first blast of a nervous breakdown, which, he later described, felt like a combination of vertigo and a heart attack.

At first he blamed his overcrowded lecture calendar and the stresses of the Civil Rights campaign; Harrington joined King a few days later in Montgomery, Alabama, for the last day of the march from Selma. Later that spring he realized that he was not merely suffering from stress but was violently depressed from repressed conflicts, for which he undertook four years of psychoanalytic treatment. As far as he could tell, parental influences aside, the culprit was his unexpected fame. It was absurd, to Harrington, that he became a minor celebrity by writing about poor people. He pretended that nothing had changed; he was still a servant of social justice causes, not a star who floated above them. But denial merely intensified the war within. For many years, long after he crawled out of denial, every time Harrington walked to a podium he felt a flash of anxiety about another meltdown. He felt guilty about the money he earned from his lectures and books, was embarrassed by the star treatment he received, and in 1979 disconcerted many of his comrades by spending the money on a move to suburban Larchmont in Westchester County, for the sake of his wife and children, all the while lamenting that they suffered from his long lecture-touring absences.

When the activist organizations that Harrington subsequently founded garnered media attention, the spotlight nearly always fell on Harrington, for which he routinely apologized to the group. For much of his media coverage and many other observers, it was strange that Harrington wasted his time building up socialist organizations; obviously he could have risen higher without them. But Harrington never considered his organizational work optional; it was central to his identity as a socialist activist and intellectual. To him, the key decision of his life had to do with opting for the right kind of anticommunism.

In the late 1960s Harrington agonized over Vietnam. His Shachtmanite comrades were mostly pro-war, but Harrington sympathized with Norman Thomas and other critics. He wanted to oppose the war, but was held back by the Old Left's embattled anticommunism and disgusted by the New Left's tendency to romanticize the Vietnamese revolution. He warned that the forced collectivization of North Vietnam offered a nasty preview of what a communist victory would look like in South Vietnam. Those who waved Vietcong flags had to ignore a great deal of North Vietnamese history: "They ignored, for instance, the fact that Ho Chi Minh had by his own admission carried out a bloody collectivization in the North over the dead bodies of some tens of thousands of 'his' peasants." Later he noted that those who disrupted peace rallies by waving Vietcong flags never tried out the same theatrics on less tolerant groups like the American Legion.[12]

In 1969 Harrington belatedly joined the antiwar movement, which set off an explosion in the Socialist Party. To many Old Left Socialists and unionists, Harrington's conversion on Vietnam was a betrayal. Shachtman argued that the war should be judged on a political basis, not a moral one. What mattered was the political outcome—a communist victory. Harrington replied that America's intervention legitimized communism as a political force, effectively recruiting Vietnamese peasants to its ranks. It was too late to prevent the Vietnamese revolution from being overtaken by Stalinists as a response to popular resentment of French colonialism, the corruption of Vietnamese governments, and American imperialism, all of which the Communists successfully exploited. American intervention gave propaganda victories to Communists and secured their credibility as proponents of national liberation. Moreover, Harrington did not share the Shachtmanites' denigration of the moral issue or their revulsion for the American antiwar movement as a whole. He loathed the movement's pro-communist and vulgar anti-American sideshows but judged that its mainstream had an ethical anti-imperialist basis.[13]

These disagreements played out in two successive conventions of the Socialist Party. At the 1972 convention Harrington listened incredulously as longtime friends declared their hope that Richard Nixon would smash George McGovern in the presidential election. For Harrington, that marked the sorry end of the party of Eugene Debs and Norman Thomas. Leading a dissident faction out of the party, in 1973 he formed a new organization, the Democratic Socialist Organizing Committee (DSOC). Harrington was finished with the right-leaning Shachtmanites but not the dream of building a vital democratic socialist movement.

To him and his friends at *Dissent* magazine, the phenomenon of Socialists for Nixon deserved a name. Harrington reached for the term "neoconservative," a disputed label that stuck to Sidney Hook, Emanuel Muravchik, Arnold Beichman, Arch Puddington, John Roche, Bayard Rustin, Harry Overstreet, Carl Gershman, Rochelle Horowitz, Tom Kahn, Penn Kemble, Joshua Muravchik, and, later, a sizable group of others including Irving Kristol, Midge Decter, Jeane Kirkpatrick, Michael Novak, Norman Podhoretz, Paul Wolfowitz, Richard Perle, and George Weigel. The neoconservatives derided the sixties generation of progressives as a "New Class" of self-seeking bureaucrats and opportunists. Harrington saw the same group as the hope of a new "conscience constituency" in American politics. He sought to bring together the McGovern wing of the Democratic Party, the social movements left over from the sixties, the progressive unions, and the progressive wing of the Socialist Party, urging that it was not too late to make socialism American.

Harrington's new group was more progressive and good-spirited than the one he left behind, but much less successful politically. Its early leaders included sociologist Bogdan Denitch, literary critic Irving Howe, school administrator Deborah Meier, union chief William Winpisinger, feminist icon Gloria Steinem, and Congressman Ron Dellums. DSOC worked primarily as a socialist caucus in the liberal wings of the trade union movement and the Democratic Party. It enjoyed strong support from the Machinists, Communications Workers, and American Federation of State, County and Municipal Employees, and in the mid- and late

1970s it made impressive inroads in the Democratic Party, especially at the national party's mid-term conventions. A further step toward healing and moving beyond the generational Old Left–New Left split occurred in 1982, when DSOC merged with a predominantly New Left organization, the New American Movement, to form Democratic Socialists of America. This merger brought feminist writer Barbara Ehrenreich, labor historian Stanley Aronowitz, and Black Studies scholar Manning Marable into the new organization and reversed the long-standing American socialist tradition of splintering into ever smaller sects. Until his death in 1989, Harrington chaired or co-chaired DSA, a "multi-tendency" group with as many greens and more feminists than the holdover reds from which it had come.

From the beginning the band of battle-scarred progressive Socialists that followed Harrington out of the Socialist Party strove to create a socialist organization that spurned ideological fanaticism, cold war militarism, and male domination. From the mid-1970s on, DSOC mostly attracted members who knew and cared very little about the sectarian Old Left. Their frame of political reference had begun too recently to have a stake in the history of the Shachtmanites. They joined DSOC, or later DSA, because they heard Harrington give an inspiring speech at their university. On occasion Harrington would make a scholastic point as an aside ("Here's a note for the Marxologists among you") but generally he was careful to keep his sectarian socialist past in the past. Some of his books rehashed Marxist debates at length, but not his campus lectures. He knew there was little in the Old Left to commend to young activists, and he learned the hard way that they were not interested anyway.

The eleven books Harrington wrote after *The Other America* were terribly important to him, especially *Socialism* (1972), *The Twilight of Capitalism* (1976), *Decade of Decision* (1980), *The Next Left* (1986), and *Socialism: Past and Future* (1989). Most are forgotten now, and Isserman barely mentions them, settling for a footnote that refers the reader to one of my early books and a monograph by Robert Gorman. This bifurcation of Harrington's life and thought underwrites the usual dismissal of Harrington's socialism, even if Isserman intended otherwise. Sociologist Alan Wolfe typifies the usual dismissal, declaring that Harrington's books after *The Other America* were failures "because Harrington was too busy fighting forgotten battles to concentrate on the writing of them." Harrington kept plugging for democratic socialism long after he should have gotten his clock fixed.[14]

To some degree Wolfe is certainly right; whether he is wholly right depends on one's politics. Among the "forgotten battles" that Harrington might better have let go was his persistent defense of Karl Marx, to which he devoted his two major mid-career works, *Socialism* and *The Twilight of Capitalism*. In essence, Harrington argued that Marx was a Democratic Socialist very much like Harrington. Old fixations were hard to break; Harrington had to have Marx on his side, even if that blocked the view of Harrington's thoroughly democratic and freedom-supporting socialism. Harrington claimed that the real Marx was a "foe of every dogma, champion of human freedom and democratic socialism." Marx wrote some things that gave a very different impression, Harrington allowed, but the bad parts of Marx were temporary lapses, and Frederick Engels compounded the problem with his unfortunate invention, dialectical materialism.[15]

In Harrington's rendering, the *Communist Manifesto* featured a "schizophrenic" exaggeration of capitalist achievements and communist promise. Its opening line, that the "specter of communism" haunted Europe, was absurd, since Europe in 1848 was at war over bourgeois freedoms, not communism. Marx and Engels knew they were blowing smoke, Harrington argued. In section 2 they announced the funeral of the bourgeoisie, but in the final section they advocated an alliance with it. Marx furiously denounced the bourgeoisie while trying to bring it to power. Harrington explained the contradiction by granting Marx a weakness for dramatic motivational language. Marx's specter and funeral language was obviously premature; thus he advocated tactical alliances with Chartists in England, agrarian reformers in the United States, petty-bourgeois radicals in France, and the bourgeoisie itself in Germany.[16]

But what kinds of alliances did he want? Near the end of the manifesto Marx contended that the bourgeoisie was fundamentally hostile to proletarian interests and in Germany the bourgeois revolution would be the "immediate prelude" to a proletarian revolution. That sounded like Leninism: an immediate transition from a bourgeois to a communist revolution, skipping an intervening period of bourgeois government. Was Leninism Marxist? Harrington urged that instead of taking Marx's "immediate prelude" statement literally, it was better to understand Marx by what he did in 1848, advocating long-term alliances with bourgeois democrats. But that was not much of a difference, because only a few months later, still in 1848, Marx urged workers to form secret armed organizations that prepared for immediate class war. And in 1850 he urged workers to set up revolutionary proletarian regimes alongside the victorious bourgeois governments, for "from the very first moment of the victory, the workers must distrust not only the defeated reactionary party, but its former comrades as well, and fight that party which will try to exploit the common victory on its own."[17]

Harrington used a stage theory to dispose of these counterfactuals, explaining that the bad Marx prevailed between 1849 and 1850. For two years Marx was an ultra-leftist who envisioned the proletarian revolution as a popular explosion or insurrection from below. But even during Marx's bad phase, Harrington argued, he was a Jacobin democrat, never a Leninist. Marx advocated independent revolutionary regimes to stoke popular explosions, not vanguard dictatorships that deceitfully manipulated the proletariat or that conspired coups. Admittedly, on several occasions during this phase, Marx used the fateful phrase, "dictatorship of the proletariat." In April 1850 he and Engels signed the declaration of the World Society of Revolutionary Communists, which announced: "The aim of the association is the overthrow of all privileged classes, their subjugation by the dictatorship of the proletariat which will maintain the revolution in permanence until communism, the last organizational form of the human family, will be constructed."[18]

Harrington dealt with the latter problem by invoking the early Sidney Hook's explanation that Marx had a peculiar understanding of dictatorship. For Marx, Hook explained in 1933, "dictatorship" referred to the class basis of pre-communist societies, not revolutionary repression. Every state was a dictatorship, including the bourgeois democracies, because the purpose of the state was to uphold the economic and political power of the ruling class. Marx believed that the state was necessary only in class societies, to uphold and defend class privileges. Once the proletarian revolution overthrew capitalism and smashed the capitalist state, the state would not be necessary; thus a communist state was a contradiction in terms. Even revolutionary states were dictatorships in this sense. Marx described the Paris Commune as a dictatorship because its property forms organized a proletarian type of class rule; it favored the working class over the bourgeoisie. Establishing revolutionary governments was never really the point for him, Harrington argued, following Hook; neither was repressing civil liberties. For Marx the point was for a revolutionary majority to overthrow capitalism and set up a government favoring its own interests. Then the revolution would abolish the state, too.[19]

That was a plausible exegesis, but it did not exactly advance Harrington's purpose of making Marxism attractive to Americans. In the Marxist sense, Harrington argued, a dictatorship brought about the fulfillment of democracy. Just as the triumph of the bourgeois revolutions brought about gains in civil liberty, the proletarian revolution brought about the fulfillment of economic freedom. Marx's example was the Paris Commune, a failed insurrection of city workers. Though a fiasco, Marx defended it forcefully. In the Paris Commune all official jobs at all levels were paid the same wages as workers received, and all administrative, judicial, and educational officers were elected and recallable by universal suffrage. To Marx that was a model of proletarian dictatorship as democracy; Harrington contended that Marx advocated dictatorship only in this sense, as the fulfillment of democracy.

But Marx's faith in the withering away of the state under communism was utopian and stupendously destructive; he was never a good democrat in terms of practicing humane democratic values; and at times he resorted to violent tactics and vicious rhetoric that flunked minimal tests of democratic principle. He flirted with the vanguard conspiracy theories of Louis Auguste Blanqui, called for massive insurrections from below, advocated secret societies, and repeatedly skewered opponents, factional rivals, and hapless followers with violent invective, calling them "toads," "vermin," "emigrant scum," and the like. His violent exhortations to take up revolutionary violence are hard to construe as democratic, especially since the proletarian movement was pitifully small and disorganized in the late 1840s. Moreover, Marx continued to call for the dictatorship of the proletariat well after passing through his ultra-Left phase. In 1852 he told Joseph Weydemeyer that his central discovery was the structural development of the class struggle, which "necessarily leads to the dictatorship of the proletariat," and that "this dictatorship itself only constitutes the transition to the abolition of all classes and to a classless society." That formulation combined the three planks of what came to be called "vulgar Marxism": determinism, the dictatorship of the proletariat, and utopianism.[20]

When Harrington was not writing about Marx, he was a staunch opponent of revolutionary utopianism. Repeatedly he repudiated the utopian impulse as incipiently totalitarian. Yet he passed over the rather large problem of utopianism in Marx's thought with a quick assurance and dismissal. In *The German Ideology* Marx fantasized that under communism, because general production would be regulated by society, it would be possible for a worker "to do one thing today and another tomorrow, to hunt in the morning, fish in the afternoon, rear cattle in the evening, criticize after dinner, just as I have a mind, without ever becoming hunter, fisherman, cowherd, or critic." Marx dropped the lyricism in his later career but not his faith in the classless and stateless utopia. His anarcho-syndicalist idea of communism was pure utopianism and his last word on the subject. He had no theory of the revolutionary state beyond the promise of withering away. Marx put it plainly in his 1874 review of Bakunin's *Statism and Anarchy*: "When class rule has disappeared, there will no longer be any state in the present political sense of the word." Communism meant self-government for all; when the revolution brought about collective property and the abolition of classes, "the so-called will of the people disappears in order to make way for the real will of the co-operative."[21]

Marx actually believed that a proletarian revolution would abolish class domination and therefore the need for a political state. This was hardly a minor aspect of his thought, but Harrington brushed it aside as a negligible slip-up. In the twentieth century, he assured, "Marxism must be more chastened, but not less militant." Similarly Harrington claimed that Marx was not an economic determinist, except on occasions when he was "unjust to his ideas." Marx's preface to the *Critique of Political Economy* (1859) was a notable example: "The mode of production determines the social, political, and spiritual life processes in general." That was clear enough, but Marx amplified: "It is not the consciousness of men that determines their existence but, on the contrary, their social existence determines their consciousness." All intellectual, political, and religious phenomena were superstructural rationalizations of economic interests. In Harrington's view this formulation fell under the rule, "Even Homer nods." The real Marx was not the economic determinist of the preface, but the anti-mechanistic Hegelian of the *Grundrisse* who taught that the economic, political, and cultural dimensions of society interact and mutually determine one another.[22]

Harrington was surely right that Marx, a thinker of enormous power, was more sophisticated than vulgar Marxism and that the preface to the *Critique of Political Economy* oversimplified his argument by trying to summarize it concisely. But here the rule of watching what Marx actually did is instructive. Marx published the preface, stood by it, repeated it in other contexts, and republished it; meanwhile he did not publish the

Grundrisse. Had he shared Harrington's concern to absolve Marxism of economic determinism, he would not have disseminated and recycled his formulation about it so determinedly, which supported his concept of class. Harrington did not believe that the mode of production determined the organization of slave and feudal societies, but Marx did believe it. For him, a class was defined precisely by its function in the mode of production; thus, as he declared in the *Communist Manifesto*, "the history of all hitherto existing society is the history of class struggles."[23]

In Harrington's telling, Marx was a sophisticated social scientist who tolerated Engels's vulgar Marxism out of loyalty to him and because Engels accepted the disagreeable task of defending Marx/Engels from their critics, especially German Socialist rival Karl Eugen Dühring. Engels promoted a crude base-superstructure theory that popularized Marxism, with unfortunate results. But Harrington wrongly played down Marx's role in developing the Marxist tradition. Besides being a sophisticated social scientist, Marx was a revolutionist who read and approved the entire manuscript of Engels's *Anti-Dühring* and even wrote one of its chapters. Marx did not achieve a reputation for economic determinism only because he tolerated Engels's defense of him. He wrote and promoted the works that shaped the Marxist tradition on this issue. Harrington was certainly right that Marx's totalitarian "followers" distorted and abused his thought. To Marx, communist transformations were possible only in industrialized societies that had gone through capitalist accumulation; moreover, it was a terrible irony of history that "Marxism" came to be associated with repugnant forms of state collectivism. But Marx's utopianism, determinism, rhetorical violence, and advocacy of secret societies and vanguard strategies all had something to do with that outcome.

Harrington's sensibility and vision were vastly better than Marx's. Sadly he burned too much time and effort trying to convince readers that Marx shared his politics. He made better use of the theory of bureaucratic collectivism, which he always attributed to Shachtman. The idea of bureaucratic collectivism originated as an attempt to explain what went wrong in the Soviet Union. As early as the mid-1920s Marxists and anarchists— some of them in Stalin's concentration camps—began to refer to the Soviet system as a state capitalist regime run by a "New Class" of professional bureaucrats. Christian Rakovsky, drawing on the pre-Bolshevik anarchism of Michael Bakunin, Peter Kropotkin, and Waclaw Machajski, described the Soviet leadership as a New Class of dictators whose rule was based on a new type of private property: collectivist state power. In the 1930s the theory of the New Class was refashioned by American Trotskyists James Burnham, Joseph Carter, and Max Shachtman, and Italian Trotskyist fellow-traveler Bruno Rizzi, all in opposition to Leon Trotsky.[24]

Trotsky contended that the Soviet regime—a degenerated workers' state under Stalin—would either move forward to socialism or backward to capitalism. At the founding congress of the Socialist Workers Party in 1937, however, Burnham and Carter challenged this premise, arguing that the Soviet regime was taking on a viable structure of its own. It was not a bourgeois state degenerating into outright capitalism or a workers' state moving forward to socialism but something else, a bureaucratic deformation of a workers' state. In the factional Trotskyist debates of the later 1930s, Burnham and Shachtman argued that the traditional definition of a class did not cover the new form of social organization invented in the Soviet Union. Shachtman put it bluntly: "What we have called the consummated usurpation of power by the Stalinist bureaucracy was, in reality, nothing but the self-realization of the bureaucracy as a class and its seizure of state power from the proletariat, the establishment of its own state power and its own rule." Before the Bolshevik Revolution, Trotsky warned that merely socializing poverty in a backward nation would never create a workers' state; to succeed, the Bolshevik Revolution would have to depend on the aid of the international proletariat. But the Bolsheviks were left on their own, Shachtman explained, and the workers' state *was* overthrown, though not by a bourgeois restoration. The Soviet regime amounted to a new kind of counterrevolutionary class: "The old crap was revived in a new, unprecedented, hitherto unknown form, the rule of a new bureaucratic class."[25]

When the state takes over the means of production, the question changes to, "Who owns the state?" That question eventually drove Shachtman, after a prolonged bout with quasi-Trotskyism, to a form of democratic state socialism. The only true workers' state had to be democratically owned and controlled by workers, he argued. Soviet communism had no place in the history of socialism, because democracy was the essence of socialism. Just as the defining feature of capitalism was private ownership and the defining feature of communism was totalitarian ownership, the defining feature of socialism was democratic ownership and control. Having co-founded American Trotskyism in 1929, Shachtman was compelled by the first glimmerings of this conclusion to start over, forming a new Workers Party in 1940 (originality in nomenclature was little known in these circles), which later morphed into the Independent Socialist League (where he became Harrington's mentor), which he later led into the Socialist Party, where he became a right-wing Socialist and guru to the original neoconservatives.[26]

Harrington's major works featured the idea of bureaucratic collectivism as a critique of late capitalism. For him the serious question was not whether economic planning would take place in the future, but the form in which it would take place. Corporate capitalism was increasingly a top-down form of bureaucratic collectivism, Harrington argued, in which huge oligopolies administered prices, controlled the politics of investment, bought off the political system, and defined cultural tastes and values while obtaining protection and support from the state. It shook down the state for subsidies and favors, and was happy to socialize its losses with government bailouts, but it preached private enterprise and the right to free capital flows when its profits were questioned. Most important, capitalism granted control over investment, credit, and social planning to unelected elites holding quite particular interests in the increase of their own wealth and power. It was fine to bail out too-big-to-fail capitalist enterprises with public money, as long as the public interest got no stake in the companies.[27]

For Harrington, democratic socialism was essentially a vision of an alternative future in which an inevitably collectivized society was effectively democratized. It had almost nothing to do with economic nationalization and everything to do with economic democracy. The mission of democratic socialism was to democratize the collectivist logic of modernity. In 1986 he put it bluntly: "The issue of the twenty-first century and of the late twentieth century is, can that collective tendency be made democratic and responsible? Can it be made compatible with freedom?" He believed that freedom would survive the ascendance of globalized markets and corporations only if it took the form of decentralized economic democracy. Harrington opposed economic nationalization on both philosophical and programmatic grounds. Unlike state socialism, corporate capitalism, and other forms of authoritarian collectivism, Harrington-style economic democracy promoted decentralized worker and community ownership and regionally based economic planning. In the 1970s and 1980s his vision became greener and more insistent on human-scale community forms of socialization, ratcheting down the economism of his Old Left past. On the lecture trail he was fond of admonishing old leftists that "any idiot can nationalize a bank," which became his judgment on France's bank nationalizations of the 1980s. That, to some comrades and critics, smacked of selling out socialism; Harrington replied: "To think that 'socialization' is a panacea is to ignore the socialist history of the twentieth century, including the experience of France under Mitterand. I am for worker- and community-controlled ownership and for an immediate and practical program for full employment which approximates as much of that ideal as possible. No more. No less."[28]

For Harrington, the purpose of democratic socialism was to empower ordinary people and thus preserve and extend democratic freedom. He pointed to public bank models, such as the Meidner Plan for Economic Democracy in Sweden, and other experiments in worker and social ownership as examples of the decentralized democratic socialism of the future. Democratic empowerment was the prize, which an increasingly global, predatory capitalism devoured: "I would argue that the bureaucratizers, the collectivizers, the anti-freedom tendencies of modern society are the corporate capitalist tendencies of late capitalism, and that the alternative of freedom is represented by the democratic socialist movement for which I speak."[29]

Harrington took very seriously the necessity of believing in ordinary people and his own moral obligation to inspire hope. Often he told campus audiences: "If you consider your country capable of democratic socialism, you must do two things. First you must deeply love and trust your country. You must sense the dignity and humanity of the people who survive and grow within your country despite the injustices of its system. And second, you must recognize that the social vision to which you are committing yourself will never be fulfilled in your lifetime." That was a far cry from the party of Debs and Thomas, which promised "socialism in our time" even when it knew better. After the lecture was over and Heineken time had commenced at a local hotel bar, Harrington could be bleak about where history was going. He hated the kind of leftism that paraded self-righteous superiority and tagged every opponent as a "fascist," but in private he would allow that the emerging system of global corporate giants wedded to pliant governments was "a kind of fascism."

His final book, *Socialism: Past and Future*, expounded his "visionary gradualist" strategy, which conceived democratic socialism as a stubborn, persistently reformist pressure for further gains toward democratic self-determination: "I insist that the political, social, and economic development of modern society points socialism toward an ethical, multiclass, and decentralized conception of its goal based on the democratization of the workplace and the creation of new forms of community, both within and throughout the world. That vision has a remarkable continuity with the basic republican values that derive from both the French and the American revolutions." Harrington understood very well how far that was from Marx, though he insisted that the core of his vision was still Marxist. In his closing paragraph he declared that if the socialist movement could learn from the failures of its past about how to create the future, "then there is hope for freedom, solidarity, and justice. And perhaps there will be a visionary gradualism equal to the challenge of the 'slow apocalypse' in which we live."[30]

In my introduction to this book I noted that religion gnawed at Harrington. As a reasonably good Marxist, Harrington believed that religion was passing into oblivion, but he also worried that the passing of legitimizing religious authority left Western societies without a moral basis to inspire virtue or define common values. He proposed that the job of providing a legitimizing, integrating principle of Western culture should be taken up by democratic socialism. Specifically, in *The Politics at God's Funeral* he called for a new "united front" of religious and secular Socialists to redeem the values of religious socialism and fill the void left by terminal Western religions. The new socialist united front would recover the values of progressive Judaism and Christianity, he wrote, "but not in religious form." It would require religious activists to subordinate their religious concerns to the needs of the movement in order to promote the values it held in common with other Socialists. Harrington believed that progressive religious values would survive without religion and he assumed that religion was dying anyway. Socialism was a vehicle to keep progressive religious values alive.[31]

"But Mike," I would say, "what if religion isn't dying after all? What if the survival of religion is far more certain than that of socialism? And what if the movement that you want needs living, vital religious currents to sustain itself?" Mike didn't like these questions, so he usually changed the subject or shifted to scholastic points about philosophers and theologians. But he was an example of the possibility that he hoped for. Though not a religious believer, Harrington *was* religiously musical, and deeply influenced by Christian ethical teaching. He welcomed and respected religious comrades, and his organizations had quite a few of them, most notably Cornel West, Rosemary Radford Ruether, and Michael Eric Dyson.

Harrington had a tendency to substitute belief in Marx for his loss of religious belief, but the list of Marxist notions that he disbelieved grew longer with age. He could hear the ghost of Marx ridiculing his "visionary gradualist" politics as a revival of the utopian socialism Marx ridiculed in the 1840s. But the failures of twentieth-century "socialisms" bearing Marx's name undercut the force of this criticism. Socialism was no longer innocent and could not afford to ignore Marx's mistakes. Marx mistook the rise of capitalism for its decline and mistakenly assumed that the middle-classes in industrialized societies would become proletarianized. Worse yet, his revolutionary utopianism made it possible for generations of totalitarian thugs to call themselves Marxists. Harrington said all of this plainly in his last years, without disavowing his conviction that democratic Marxism was the last best hope of humankind.

He died of cancer in 1989, carrying on until the end with a full calendar of lectures, organizing, and writing. Irving Howe later remarked that Harrington's gentleness seemed almost a flaw. There was not a trace of meanness in him; he lacked the hardness of the typical political leader and was thus extremely reluctant ever to criticize a comrade. Near the end of his life, after one of my books strongly criticized some of Harrington's arguments, I waited anxiously for his reaction. "So you think I don't know how to read Marx, do you?" he teased. "Well, you're in good company." He relinquished the hope of ever straightening out people like me. But what delighted him in his last years, he said, was that he finally belonged to a leftist organization in which people could criticize one another without generating destructive intrigues, factional schisms, and personal attacks.

That was, in large part, his personal achievement. It is not only the Left that is poorer today for having no one like him. American politics as a whole is poorer. Bill Clinton's presidency suffered from lacking a strong progressive flank in his party compelling him to do something about inequality, energy, and health care. Lacking any ballast on the left, Clinton's triangulating politics predictably tilted away from core progressive concerns. Whatever illusions Harrington may have indulged on other subjects, he would have understood very keenly that Clinton needed a strong left flank, and that Barack Obama needs one now.

Chapter 7

Christian Socialism as Tradition and Problem

For more than a century, Christian theologians have dreamed of a transformed economic order based on democratic empowerment and the common good. A century ago the social gospel movement reverberated with calls for economic democracy. In the 1930s, after global capitalism crashed spectacularly, theologians stressed the necessity of finding an alternative to capitalist boom and bust. In the 1970s the rise of liberation theology resurrected the dream of a transformed economic order.

But the dream failed, and today capitalism prevails in more global and predatory forms than ever. Today the idea of a fundamental alternative seems quaint at best, even though global capitalism has crashed again. The idea of a systemic alternative has lost its coherence in a world of mega-byte monies zipping across the planet at the speed of light, delinked from real production. There is no major structural movement to replace the predatory impulses of capitalism. There is only the necessity of creating one, recognized by thousands of disparate organizations and communities. For the very problems that gave rise to socialist movements still exist, still matter, and exist among new problems threatening the very survival of the planet.

Almost every important theological movement of the past century called for a different future, especially liberal theology, the social gospel, Barthian neo-orthodoxy, modern Catholic social thought, Christian realism, ecumenical social ethics, liberation theology, progressive evangelicalism, and radical orthodoxy. The social gospel expounded a vision of decentralized economic democracy or, sometimes, democratic socialism. The Barthian movement was explicitly socialist, though it usually tried to keep theology and politics in different compartments. The papal encyclical *Rerum novarum* (1891) introduced the idea of a "solidarist" third way between capitalism and socialism in Catholic social teaching, which was expounded explicitly in *Quadragesimo anno* (1941). For decades the ecumenical movement kept alive the social gospel hope of a social democratic transformation of capitalism, until liberation theology helped to push the World Council of Churches further to the left in political economy. Liberation theology advocated a revolutionary Marxist or, sometimes, democratic socialist vision of liberation from structures of oppression and dependency. Repeatedly twentieth-century theologians and social ethicists dreamed of an economy based on human need and the common good.

In every case the social mission of Christianity had something to do with replacing capitalist selfishness and inequality with something better. Virtually all the progressive-era social gospelers spoke an optimistic language of progress and social evolution, even if they were radical Socialists, which they couched in third-way terms that kept their politics from sounding scary. Reform-oriented progressives like Washington Gladden, Francis G. Peabody, Shailer Mathews, and Catholic ethicist John A. Ryan favored a third way between capitalism and socialism, advocating cooperatives and guilds, while radicals like Walter Rauschenbusch and Harry F. Ward struggled to make Christian socialism not seem dangerous.[1]

In 1908 the newly founded Federal Council of Churches, comprising approximately thirty-one Protestant and Eastern Orthodox denominations, issued the Social Creed of the Churches. A few denominations had partial or associate memberships; thus the member number was variously reckoned between twenty-nine and thirty-three denominations. Since the churches did not agree on doctrine, American Christianity had many denominations. But the social gospel leaders of the ecumenical movement urged that all Christians should be able to band together to do something about social justice. The Social Creed had fourteen points: it stood up for "equal rights and complete justice" for all human beings; the abolition of child labor; a "living wage as a minimum in every industry"; social security; an equitable distribution of income and wealth; the abatement of poverty; and eight other planks focused mostly on economic justice.[2]

The Great Depression yielded a sterner kind of Christian radicalism that spurned third ways, speaking a binary language of revolution versus barbarism. There was no third way between state socialism and reaction;

for Reinhold Niebuhr and his followers, economic democracy was serious only if it stood for a revolutionary state control of the economy. In the name of realism and relevance, the Niebuhrians of the 1930s and other radical Socialists propounded a host of bad ideas, rejecting markets and production for profit, claiming that state planners could replicate the pricing decisions of markets, and equating socialization with nationalization.

On these issues Rauschenbusch ended up looking better than the radicals that panned him for being too idealistic. He contended that democratic worker control was the heart of the matter and that markets cannot be abolished in a free society. He had a strong concept of personal and collective evil coupled with an overcoming message of social salvation. On the other hand, even Rauschenbusch recycled the totalizing rhetoric of state socialism, embraced the Marxist theory of surplus value, claimed that prices under socialism would be based entirely on services rendered, and trusted too much in the overcoming tide of social idealism.[3]

To the major theologians of the progressive era and the Great Depression generation, the capitalist devotion to individual self-interest was plainly hostile to Christian teaching. Some who were far from being Marxists were unsparing about the predatory immorality of capitalism. Christian Socialists usually acknowledged, like Marx, that capitalism marked a great leap forward, and that capitalist accumulation and industrialization were necessary preconditions of a desirable social order. To Barthian theologian Emil Brunner, however, capitalism was not a prelude to anything except moral and social catastrophe. In *The Divine Imperative* he pronounced that capitalism "is that system in which all that we can see to be the meaning of the economic order from the point of view of faith is being denied: in which, therefore, it is made almost impossible for the individual to realize, in any way through his economic activity, the service of God and his neighbor. This system is contrary to the spirit of service; it is debased and irresponsible; indeed we may go further and say it is irresponsibility developed into a system."[4]

Anglican bishop William Temple pressed similar feelings about capitalism into a theory of guild socialism. In 1941, shortly before he was named Archbishop of Canterbury, Temple called for an excess-profits tax to create worker and community-controlled enterprises. The following year his book *Christianity and the Social Order* enlisted natural law against the spirit and logic of capitalism. Production naturally exists for consumption, Temple argued, but capitalism reversed the natural order of things by making consumption depend on production, while production depended on finance. Temple's alternative put a higher value on fellowship than profits, calling for withering capital investment, mutual export trade, economic democracy, a socialized monetary system, and the social use of land. He observed: "It is important to remember that the class-war was not first proclaimed as a crusade by Marx and Engels; it was first announced as a fact by Adam Smith. Nothing can securely end it except the acquisition by Labour of a share in the control of industry. Capital gets its dividends; Labour gets its wages; there is no reason why Capital should also get control and Labour have no share in it."[5]

One of the ironies of modern theology is that the American social gospelers of the 1930s and 1940s are nearly always treated as naïve idealists, because many of them were pacifists, whereas Niebuhr is treated as the hero of the story. Yet Niebuhr was wrong about the New Deal and the social gospel progressives were right. The social gospelers supported the Emergency Banking Act of 1933, which allowed the new Reconstruction Finance Corporation to buy bank equity. Over the next year the RFC bought more than $1 billion of bank stock, about one-third of the capital invested in U.S. banks. Speaking through the Federal Council of Churches, the social gospel progressives called for "subordination of speculation and the profit motive to the creative and cooperative spirit" and for "social planning and control of the credit and monetary systems for the common good." They supported mortgage restructuring, social security, public works employment, and selective nationalization, while Niebuhr replied that these were mere Band-Aids to make middle-class moralists feel better and the New Deal was a form of quackery.[6]

The social gospelers told a story about the necessity of gradually democratizing society; Niebuhr told a more dramatic story, that history would either move forward to socialism or backward to barbarism. Radical socialism, communism, and fascism were supposedly more realistic than the tame progressivism of the social democratic, social gospel, and New Deal movements. But the radical alternatives crashed and burned, and afterward Niebuhr retreated to welfare state reformism and the liberal democratic mainstream.

With notable exceptions such as Walter Muelder and Martin Luther King Jr., ecumenical social ethics trimmed its sails in the 1950s, taking a similar tack as Niebuhr. But in the 1960s and 1970s socialist idealism made a comeback in social ethics and theology through the rise of German political theology, Third World liberation theology, black theology, and feminism. German theologian Jürgen Moltmann described democratic socialism as the historical form that Christian hope had to take, "given the present poverty of capitalism and its democracies as well as socialism and its dictatorial governments." Peruvian liberationist Gustavo Gutierrez proclaimed that Christian theology needed to speak "of social revolution, not reform; of liberation, not development; of socialism, not modernization of the prevailing system."[7] Argentine liberationist José Míguez Bonino declared that the struggle for socialist transformation "concretely defines my Christian obedience in the world."[8]

African American social critic Cornel West positioned himself to the left of democratic socialism, embracing the neo-Marxist councilism of Rosa Luxemburg and Karl Korsch, while feminist theologian Rosemary Radford Ruether advocated "a democratic socialist society that dismantles sexist and class hierarchies, that restores ownership and management of work to the base communities of workers themselves, who then create networks of economic and political relationships."[9]

Visions of this sort were commonplace in the theologies of the 1970s and 1980s. Many theologians explicitly advocated democratic socialism, notably Harvey Cox, Gregory Baum, Leonardo Boff, Robert McAfee Brown, Beverly W. Harrison, Kenneth Leech, Johannes Metz, Arthur McGovern, Delores Williams, Ronald Preston, Dorothee Soelle, Franklin Gamwell, Phillip Wogaman, Gibson Winter, Daniel Maguire, and Joe Holland.[10] Others propounded a similar vision while avoiding the language of socialism, notably Letty Russell, Larry Rasmussen, M. Douglass Meeks, Douglas Sturm, Preston Williams, Harlan Beckley, Alan Geyer, and Warren Copeland.[11]

Most of these thinkers made it clear that good socialism had little or nothing to do with communism. American social gospeler Harry Ward and English Anglican cleric Hewlett Johnson were cautionary figures in this area, having ruined their reputations by fixating on the star of Soviet communism. At its best, Christian socialism also held out against state socialist ideology. For decades the central policy proposal of most Western socialist parties was centralized government ownership of the major means of industrial production. "Socialism" meant top-down government planning, economic nationalization, and what the British Fabians called the rationalization of society—that every act of collectivization furthered the socialist cause of rationalized economic planning.

The best versions of Christian socialism replied that exalting state power was not the answer. The Anglican socialism of Temple, Charles Raven, R. H. Tawney, and Charles Gore was rooted in the pre-Marxist Anglican cooperativism of F. D. Maurice, Charles Kingsley, and John Ludlow, just as the American decentralized socialism of W. D. P. Bliss, Justin Wroe Nixon, and Walter Muelder was rooted in the economic democracy of the social gospel. Paul Tillich, more indebted to Marxist theory than most English and American Christian Socialists, shared the Christian socialist aversion to state collectivism. Tillich warned against the "bureaucratization of the economy," took for granted the necessity of market discipline, and contended that only the market knew how to get prices right.[12]

The debate that advocates of decentralized economic democracy always wanted was the one between themselves and state Socialists; communism was a perversion of anything deserving to be called socialism. But after the Soviet Union imploded, decentralized Socialists did not get the debate they wanted. The differences between the various democratic socialisms seemed irrelevant in a world seized by the manic logic of capitalism. Economic globalization pushed aside socialist concerns about equality and humane community. Nations crawling out from decades of communist rule in the former Soviet bloc did not aspire to democratic versions of anything smacking of socialism, which raised the question as to whether anything was left of Christian socialism. How much of the vision of a democratized social order could be saved or reconstructed in a political culture in which "socialism" mostly conjured up repulsive images of state authoritarianism? How was it possible to reclaim the social Christian vision of democratized economic power at a time when corporate capitalism was turning the planet into a single economic market?

For some Christian ethicists, the dream of economic democracy was exhausted and refuted. Lutheran neoconservative Robert Benne contended that the time had come for Christian ethicists to break from their democratic socialist heritage: "I believe that Christian ethicists should rather turn their attention to the possibilities for justice within liberal capitalism."[13] Neoliberal realists Max Stackhouse and Dennis McCann urged that the death of communism bore unavoidable implications for Christian social ethics. Stackhouse and McCann observed that "the Protestant Social Gospel, early Christian realism, much neo-orthodoxy, many forms of Catholic modernism, the modern ecumenical drive for racial and social inclusiveness, and contemporary liberation theories all held that democracy, human rights and socialism were the marks of the coming kingdom." But modern theology and social ethics were wrong about socialism: "The future will not bring what contemporary theology said it would and should." According to Stackhouse and McCann, the verdict of history had come down not only against the communist mistake but against even the forms of democratic socialism that militantly opposed communism. Socialism was dead, which marked the end of liberal Christianity's attempt to give it a human face.[14]

For neoconservatives and some Niebuhrian realists the project that remains for Christian social ethics is to apply the chastening lessons of Niebuhrian realism to the economic order. Neoconservative social critic Michael Novak disavows the social Christian project of breaking down existing concentrations of economic power. Noting that Niebuhr failed to press his political realism into a critique of social democratic economics, Novak says that neoconservatives like himself complete this essential Niebuhrian task by repudiating the progressive Christian tradition of economic democracy: "Niebuhr did not give much attention to economic issues. Precisely in Niebuhr's neglect, I found my own vocation. Surely, I thought, the next generation of Niebuhrians ought to push some of Niebuhr's deeper insights into the one major area he neglected."[15]

Novak's assumption of this neglected task drew him deeply into the political Right, where, in the 1980s, he became a Reagan supporter and a chief mythologist of American capitalism. To apply Niebuhr's realism to the economic realm is to relinquish the progressive Christian dream of democratizing economic power, Novak argued. Neoconservatives contend that the values and legitimizing principles of democracy are pertinent only to the political sphere. To face up to modernity is to exclude democratic tests of legitimacy, equality, and accountability from the economic realm. Realism emphasizes wealth creation and allows the market to take care of distribution. It opposes government regulation of the financial sector and assures that wealth creation at the top will eventually trickle down to middle-class and working-class communities. It accepts and celebrates the triumph of corporate capitalism. Faced with the dissolution of the only serious alternative to capitalism, modern Christians must face up to modernity in the economic realm.[16]

Problems with Christian Socialism

A significant stream of religious thinkers has taken that option, supporting the upsurge of global, capitalist ideology. This ideological upsurge is grounded in dominant real-world social and economic forces, which cannot be seriously challenged by merely recycling leftist slogans of the past.

Unfortunately a great deal of progressive theology settled for slogans, featuring a dreamy utopian air that vaguely defined its subject and only rarely addressed the political and economic problems associated with economic strategies favoring equality and environmentalism. Liberation theology was a conspicuous example. Repeatedly liberationists advocated socialism without clarifying what the term meant to them, leaving the impression that liberation theology was compatible with any kind of socialism.

Gustavo Gutierrez, for example, declared that the political goal of liberation theology must be to create a society "in which private ownership of the means of production is eliminated." Contending that a just society could be created "only by installing a political power at the service of the great popular majorities," he never moved beyond bare assertions about "eliminating the private appropriation of wealth" to describe the kind of political economy that liberation theology sought to create. Though Gutierrez was quite precise in describing ideologies and social systems he opposed, he resorted to slogans in describing his alternative.[17]

Like most liberationists he failed to discuss the relationship between democracy and socialism, or to explain how the mistakes of communist or other revolutionary movements could be avoided, or to distinguish between different types of socialism, or to address the problems of creating socialist economies in pre-industrialized societies. Like Marx, his writings on political economy were consumed with his critique of capitalism. The parallel should be instructive, for it was precisely Marx's vagueness and utopianism about the revolutionary alternative that allowed generations of totalitarian thugs to call themselves Marxists. A great deal of liberation theology has failed to make the most elementary point against socialisms of the latter sort—that democracy is an indispensable brake on utopianism and left-authoritarianism.

But the problem of Christian socialism is deeper than that of demonstrating its commitment to democracy and human rights. Tens of millions have died in prison camps, killing fields, and torture chambers in the name of building "socialism," smearing the word with repugnant associations. "Socialism" is no longer even remotely the name of an innocent ideal. In much of the world, it is synonymous with totalitarian brutality, terror, bureaucratic stagnation, economic backwardness, and moral squalor. In its democratic forms, socialism has strained national economies with bloated welfare systems. Where social democratic parties have attained power they have created the world's most humane and efficient systems of health coverage, education, and social insurance, but always by expanding centralized government bureaucracies. Wherever it has sought power, democratic socialism has lost the radical communitarian spirit that fueled the Christian socialist, syndicalist, and even social democratic movements of the early twentieth century. Under these historical circumstances it is crucially important, but far from enough, for the successors of Walter Rauschenbusch and Martin Luther King Jr. to explain that their socialism is democratic and devoted to human rights.

This dilemma was anticipated by Temple in the 1930s and early 1940s. Temple generally avoided the language of socialism, even as he produced some of the most creative Christian socialist thinking of the twentieth century. He worried that "socialism" was already indelibly associated with left-authoritarian politics. Communism was a factor in that judgment; so was the centralizing tendency of democratic socialism. Temple opposed state socialism while appreciating that, for most people, socialism meant economic nationalization. Thus he eschewed the language of socialism in making his case for decentralized economic democracy. As he explained in *Christianity and the Social Order*, he hoped that all Christians would accept his arguments for economic democracy. However, he realized that few Christians outside the trade unions and the political Left embraced socialism.

Temple was not interested in bolstering a suspect ideology with the prestige of Christian faith. Most important to him was to elucidate what it meant for Christians of his generation and social context to follow the way of Christ. He appropriated guild socialist ideas in discerning and practicing the prophetic meaning of Christianity, but he never reduced the social ethical meaning of the gospel to his politics nor turned Christianity into an endorsement of socialism. For him, socialist ideology was a barrier to the modern Christian project of democratizing social and economic power. Temple promoted economic democracy as a Christian ethical project while eschewing the progressive Christian tendency to sanctify socialist ideology.[18]

The difference is crucial. Progressive Christianity has to stand for social justice, but the ideology of socialism is dubious and unitary. It smacks of "one size fits all" dogmatism even when modified by democracy, cultural difference, and pluralism. Too much of the liberationist tradition and other radical theologies have done what Temple feared, undercutting the moral influence of progressive Christianity by clinging to socialist ideology. Progressive Christianity today needs to be more pluralistic, contextual, and pragmatic than that, standing for radical democracy and decentralized economic democracy in ways that suit particular social and cultural contexts.

The social vision of economic democracy cannot be imposed or transplanted. It can only take shape over the course of decades, as hard-won social gains and the cultivation of cooperative habits and knowledge build the groundwork for a better society. Such a project does not call for large-scale investments in any particular economic model; it does not rest upon illusions about human nature; nor does it envision or require a transformed humanity. Reinhold Niebuhr's epigrammatic justification of democracy suffices for economic democracy: The human capacity for justice makes democracy possible, but the human inclination to injustice makes democracy necessary.

Niebuhr did not deny that the human capacity for fairness is often moved by genuine feelings of compassion and solidarity, but to him it was obvious that all such feelings are mixed in human nature with more selfish motives. The critical point was that democracy is necessary precisely because virtually everyone is selfish. Because human beings are so easily corrupted by the attainment of power, democracy is necessary as a restraint on greed and the human proclivity to dominate others.[19]

By the time he elaborated this argument, in *The Children of Light and the Children of Darkness* (1944), Niebuhr was no longer inclined to press it as a case for economic democracy. Having belatedly given up Marxism, Niebuhr gave up on Christian socialism a few years later. In the early 1940s, when he tentatively held out for a socialism stripped of its Marxist illusions, he did not explore the possibilities of a politics that democratized and decentralized economic power. For Niebuhr there were only three serious possibilities—free market capitalism, socialism, and New Deal capitalism—and socialism meant economic nationalization and state-planned production for use. He supported the Delta Farm Cooperative movement, but there were never enough experiments of this kind for him to take them seriously as prototypes of an alternative politics. Realism compared liberal capitalism with existing historical alternatives, not with a fantasized economic democracy.

This conclusion remains a serious possibility for Christian ethics. Whether it is the only possibility depends largely on the viability of decentralized, social market alternatives that Niebuhr did not seriously consider. To persist in struggling for the democratization of social and economic power is to hold out for a battered, marginalized, increasingly countercultural vision of the common good that is deeply rooted in the history of American progressivism and progressive Christianity, and which has chapters yet to be written.

Chapter 8

Breaking the Oligarchy

GLOBALIZATION, TURBO-CAPITALISM,
ECONOMIC CRASH, ECONOMIC DEMOCRACY

What would a just society look like? What kind of country should the U.S. want to be? For more than two centuries U.S. American politics has featured two fundamentally different answers to these questions. The first is the vision of a society that provides unrestricted liberty to acquire wealth. The second is the vision of a realized democracy in which democratic rights over society's major institutions are established. In the first vision, the right to property is lifted above the right to self-government, and the just society minimizes the equalizing role of government. In the second view, the right to self-government is considered superior to the right to property, and the just society places democratic checks on social, political, and economic power.[1]

Both of these visions are ideal types, deeply rooted in U.S. American history, reflecting inherent tensions between classic liberalism and democracy. Both have limited and conditioned each other in the U.S. American experience. But, in every generation, one gains predominance over the other, shaping the terms of political possibility. Today, confronted with a colossal economic crash of global proportions, there is an opening for a democratic surge, one that puts into play new possibilities for social justice and the resurrection of economic democracy.

To the founders that wrote the U.S. Constitution, "liberal" was a good word, referring to the liberties of white male property owners, whereas "democracy" was a scare-word, referring to the vengeance and stupidity of the mob. From the beginning, democratic movements countered that liberty must be fused with democracy. The building blocks of American liberal democracy emerged from the early struggles between the parties of liberty and democracy: an open society, checks and balances, enumerated powers, consent of the governed, due process, the republican safeguards of *Federalist* Number Ten, separation of church and state, and disagreements over who deserved to be enfranchised, whether liberty could tolerate much democracy, and whether the American idea included republican democracy or a strong federal state.[2]

In the nineteenth century the Jeffersonian/Jacksonian party of democracy prevailed about republican democracy; the Federalist/Whig party of the state prevailed regarding a federal state; both parties compounded the U.S.'s original sins against Native Americans and African Americans; the Republican Party emerged to challenge chattel slavery; and the progressive movement embraced the idea of a centralized government. The latter development turned the party of democracy into the party of the state, changing the meaning of "liberal" in American politics. Before the progressive era the Federalist/Whig/Republican tradition stood for the consolidation of the national union, while Jacksonian and populist democrats stood for decentralized power, small-town values, and farming interests. The progressive movement changed this picture by democratizing liberal ideology; progressives converted to national governance, laying the groundwork for the New Deal, while Republicans became the party of antigovernment individualism and big business. The party of democracy, despite its racist and sexist history, made gains for social justice by demanding that society recognize the rights and humanity of groups lacking privileged status. The logic of democracy put the question to privileged groups: Why should only you have access to education, property, wealth, health care, and other social goods?

Every presidential election of the past century has replayed some version of this debate, but from 1980 to 2008 the individualistic-capitalist vision prevailed in American politics, rendering even the idea of a common good as something un-American. A politically skilled Democrat, Bill Clinton, won two terms in the 1990s, yet found it impossible to fix Social Security, stem accelerating inequality, make a breakthrough on energy and green technology, or attain universal health coverage. Clinton might have had enough political capital to fix Social Security, but he spent it on other things. He chose fiscal conservatism and financial deregulation over social investment and curbing Wall Street, which exacerbated inequality. Instead of enacting a major gas tax that reduced pollution, gas-guzzling cars, driving, and dependence on foreign oil, he had to fight for a measly 4.3-cent increase in the federal tax per gallon, which left the U.S. federal levy on gasoline twenty times less than the standard rate in Europe. Instead of universalizing Medicare, a health plan worth fighting for, he proposed a bureaucratic mess that left the insurance companies in charge, a political disaster that killed the issue for more than a decade.

To his credit, Clinton put the U.S.'s fiscal house in order, ringing up budget surpluses of $70 billion in 1998, $124 billion in 1999, and $237 billion in 2000, which whittled the national debt to $5.7 trillion. According to the Congressional Budget Office, had the U.S. stuck with Clinton's fiscal policy, the cumulative budget surplus would have reached $5.6 trillion by 2011. But all that was quickly squandered by George W. Bush's tax cuts for the rich and ramped-up military expenditures. On Bush's watch the bill for total new debt and new accrued obligations soared to $10.35 trillion and the national debt climbed to $11.3 trillion, not counting the $5.4 trillion of debt inherited from the federal takeovers of Fannie Mae and Freddie Mac after the U.S. housing market crashed. When crashing and bailing commenced in September 2008, Federal Reserve chair Ben Bernanke told members of Congress that the U.S. financial system was "perilously close to collapse." An era of U.S. American politics should have ended with that announcement, and perhaps it did; Barack Obama's presidency, even more than his election, is the best test of whether we have entered a new era. But America's economic oligarchy, which is thoroughly enmeshed in the government, is determined to carry on without changing, and Obama has no intention of challenging it.[3]

The first wave of what is now called economic "globalization" began in the 1870s and faltered in the 1930s. The second wave began in the late 1970s and faltered in 2008. Karl Marx and Frederick Engels, foreseeing the first wave in *The Communist Manifesto*, famously predicted: "All that is solid melts into air." Suddenly that has an existential ring. But Marx's point cut deeper than the threat of vaporized pensions and jobs, namely, that global capitalism commodifies everything it touches, including labor and nature, putting everything up for sale. Nothing is exempt from the pressure of competition. Social contracts and places of rest have vanished under threats of obsolescence and ruin, while the global market exploits resources, displaces communities, and sets off wealth explosions in wild cycles of boom and bust. Political journalist Thomas Friedman, a celebrant of the second wave, calls it "turbo-capitalism." Economic globalization— the integration of national economies into the global economy through trade, direct foreign investment, short-term capital flows, and flows of labor and technology—has "flattened" the world, Friedman says.[4]

In Friedman's telling, global capitalism reduces national politics to minor tweaks. There is no third way in political economy anymore; there isn't even a second way. Any nation that wants a growing economy has to wear a one-size-fits-all "golden straightjacket" that unleashes the private sector, keeps inflation low, minimizes government bureaucracy, sustains a balanced budget, eliminates tariffs on imported goods and restrictions on foreign investment, abolishes quotas and domestic monopolies, privatizes state-owned industries and utilities, deregulates capital markets, and allows direct foreign ownership and investment. Once a nation takes this path, Friedman says, "its political choices get reduced to Pepsi or Coke—to slight nuances of taste, slight nuances of policy, slight alterations in design to account for local traditions, some loosening here or there, but never any major deviation from the core golden rules." Friedman wants the U.S. to spend more on green technology and science education, but he advises liberals to give up on nostalgic dreams of social justice and equality. Right up to the crash of 2008, he marveled at the wealth-breeding ingenuity of what he called "the electronic herd."[5]

Social critic Mickey Kaus, a longtime advocate of a similar prescription, distinguished himself in a crowded field by pitching his argument specifically to liberals. For twenty years Kaus has contended that global capitalism sharply reduces the scope of national politics and that no amount of government engineering will arrest the accelerating inequality trend or the "Hollywood Effect" of lavishing absurd rewards on celebrities and corporate executives. Capitalism is a culture, he stresses, not merely an economic system. Before capitalism went global, it was possible to keep top performers from earning the full measure of their economic value. Unions restrained wage disparities, and cultural values of loyalty and trust restrained the predatory impulses of the market. But these restraints have been routed. Turbo-capitalism feeds on inequality and obliterates cultural values and communities that get in the way. It shatters the cultural taboos that once restrained corporate headhunting and firm switching, even in the communitarian cultures of East Asia. Nothing that ruthless and technocratic is going to be tamed by government reforms.[6]

Kaus acknowledges that America's accelerating inequality has created serious social problems. Liberals usually respond by trying to raise the minimum wage and make the tax system more progressive, he observes, but these strategies do not change the predatory race to the bottom. In a world market, good wages no longer exist for unskilled work and the disparity between skilled and unskilled income is increasing. Low-skilled manufacturing jobs paying middle-class wages are disappearing in the United States, because corporations can make more money in the cheaper labor markets of Mexico and East Asia. As routine production jobs move overseas, unskilled American workers are reduced to competing with one another for minimum wage jobs in the service sector, exacerbating inequality. On the other hand, globalization is a bonanza for plugged-in "symbolic analysts," Robert Reich's term for the global economy's winners.[7]

Kaus contends that American progressives need to give up their attachment to progressive taxes and wealth redistribution, for economic justice is no longer possible even in theory. No conceivable amount of government engineering will change, soften, or re-channel the fallout from the global economy's race to low tax and cheap labor havens. What government can and must do, instead, is attend to the social effects of economic globalization by circumscribing the sphere in which money matters. America needs a new equality, which Kaus calls "civic liberalism."

R. H. Tawney, the great British economic historian and Fabian socialist, is ostensibly Kaus's inspiration on civic liberalism. Tawney argued that the problem with inequality is not so much that some people earn more money than others but that some people are excluded from the heritage of civilization. This is the crucial issue for American democracy, Kaus argues. Liberalism should strive for social equality, not economic equality. The purpose of liberal politics should be "to prevent the income inequality inevitably generated by capitalism from translating into invidious social distinctions." A civic liberal politics would strengthen and expand civil society, creating more opportunities for people of different classes and races to share common space, institutions, and concerns. It would counter the privatizing dynamic of commercial society and limit the social importance of money by making investments in programs that promote social equality. Toward this end Kaus supports national health insurance and compulsory national service, as well as investments in community day care, infrastructure maintenance, low-cost housing, parks, and other community enterprises. He also endorses public choice in education. An American liberalism that pursued this agenda would begin to repair and reintegrate a badly fragmented society, he urges. America is unavoidably unequal but not unavoidably mean: "We can't stop the basic tides of our economy. But we can build dikes." A smarter liberalism would stop chasing the social democratic illusion of economic justice. It would put money in its place and save the more precious form of equality that is be-ing lost.[8]

This is a strong argument for a neoliberal politics of community. Many Democratic and even Republican campaigns have taken a page from Kaus's playbook since the 1990s, translating neoliberal and communi-tarian ideas into a viable political program. With some justification he views the affirmative side of his argument as an application of American political theorist Michael Walzer's "spheres of justice" approach to poli-tics and Tawney's civic liberalism. Walzer's theory of "complex equality" defines justice as the elimination of domination, not the elimination of differences in wealth, capital, education, ethnicity, or other social goods, and Kaus's plea for a stronger public sphere of community life is an echo of the Fabian "social wage." For Tawney and other British Socialists, a good society made public provisions that recognized the equal dignity and rights of all citizens. In a good society, persons were entitled to certain basic social goods as citizens, not as consumers. These entitlements in-cluded health care, education, and child care, which could be provided only if citizens accepted their corresponding obligations to society. Social equality was even more important to a healthy democracy than economic equality, Tawney urged, for the flourishing of human fellowship was the highest social good.[9]

But Kaus's dismissal of "money liberalism" does not fit Walzer, a Social Democrat for whom the purpose of a just politics is to ensure that no social good serves as a means of domination. And Kaus's denigration of economic equality is inimical to Tawney's strong egalitarianism. Tawney advocated democratic socialism as a bulwark against the two essential fea-tures of capitalism: privilege and tyranny. Privilege is a function of inter-related social and economic power, he argued. Typically it is a by-product of wealth converting to social power, whereas tyranny is a function of the distribution of power. Tawney viewed equality as an antidote to privilege, but, against tyranny, he argued for the democratization of power. Demo-cratic socialism democratized economic and social power and thus made it possible for human fellowship to flourish.

In a just society, Tawney argued, people respect one another for what they are, not for what they own. A just society abolishes the reverence for wealth that capitalism feeds upon by abolishing the very existence of an upper class. That was too socialistic for England, turning the political sphere into a church of heroic moral demands. Yet Tawney's ethical radi-calism, despite overreaching politically, rested on a truism, that economic inequality and social inequality are deeply interrelated. The social wage is a democratic antidote to privilege, but social equality is impossible amid gross disparities in economic power. American society today exemplifies the truism in its lift-the-drawbridge municipal arrangements, beggar-thy-neighbor tax policies, and white flight from racially integrated schools and neighborhoods. In a radically unequal society, the rich are able to buy their way out of dealing with others while middle-class people feel pressured to insulate themselves from poor and working-class neighbors.[10]

Kaus asks: "Once we've failed to draw a line between equality and inequality, between 1 to 1 and 2 to 1, what's the basis for so self-confidently taking a stand at 8 to 1 or even 1,000 to 1?" But no particular ratio is the point. What matters is that U.S. American society is racing to 1,000 to 1 and making a mockery of American democracy. Today the wealthiest 1 percent of American households has an average level of wealth two hundred times greater than the median U.S. household, a rise of 50 percent since the 1970s. Democracy cannot flourish or endure in a society with a large underclass living in poverty, acute disparities of income, and an extreme concentration of wealth at the top.[11]

In Kaus's reading, every possible strategy to arrest the inequality trend is doomed to failure. Progressive income taxes will not do the job, training programs will never turn most Americans into symbolic analysts, American unions are weak and defensive, and protectionism is self-destructive. Flexible production strategies create collaborative and participatory enterprises in some fields but only for innovative workers with the requisite skills, creativity, and computer smarts. No solution is strong enough to turn the tide in favor of social justice, and some solutions make the problem worse.

Kaus and Friedman have plenty of company in either cheering for neoliberal globalization or assuring that nothing can be done about it. Many celebrants of globalization and neoliberal theory repeat the assurances of Kaus and Friedman that globalization shrinks our politics; at least, they did for twenty years. *The Economist*, the *Wall Street Journal*, and Columbia University economist Jagdish Bhagwati are especially active in this field, aggressively defending neoliberal policies. Like Kaus and Friedman, they exaggerate the futility of political attempts to channel economic forces. Often they ignore that unionism and government intervention have globalizing capacities, too. Routinely neoliberals take a "don't worry about it" attitude toward huge unbalances racked up between economies relying on debt-financed consumption and those promoting over-saving

and production-oriented exports. For twenty years they were far too cred-
ulous about the self-correcting capacities of the market, which supposedly
made it unnecessary to regulate banks and investment firms. Above all,
they wrongly supposed that America's ever widening chasm between productivity and wages could be bridged with more and more borrowing.

Contrary to Friedman, the U.S. did not ensure its prosperity by don-
ning the golden straightjacket and relinquishing its manufacturing base.
From the late 1940s to 1975, productivity and wages soared together
in the United States, creating a middle-class society. But wages flattened from 1975 on while productivity kept soaring. The rich got fantastically richer in the 1980s and 1990s while everyone else fell behind,
taking on debt to keep from drowning. During that period nearly every
manufacturing-oriented society outperformed the U.S. in income growth
and did so with more equitable distributions of income. Then the global
integration of two radically different models of growth—debt-financed
consumption and production-oriented export and saving—created a
wildly unstable world economy featuring asset bubbles and huge trade
imbalances. In the U.S. credit card debt increased sevenfold (adjusted for
inflation) from 1975 to 2008, and outstanding household debt exploded
from 47 percent of the GDP in 1975 to 100 percent in 2005.[12]

Manufacturing is concrete and rooted in communities, whereas the
non-manufacturing "new economy" depends on skill premiums, opposes
unionization, and is vulnerable to outsourcing, all of which exacerbate
inequality. The U.S. cannot write off manufacturing and wage equity
without shredding its social and economic fabric, exactly the path it took
in the "prosperity" of the market religion era. Most world trade is still
in goods, especially manufacturing goods. The massive trade deficits of
George W. Bush's presidency were fueled by policies, some preceding his
administration, which favored the financial industry and real estate over
manufacturing.

First the U.S. hollowed out its industrial base that paid decent wages,
providing incentives to firms that made things to make them elsewhere.
Then it rang up enormous trade deficits that left the U.S. dependent on
China to finance its debt. In 2006 the U.S. amassed record trade deficits with China ($239 billion), Japan ($170 billion), Germany ($146 bil-
lion), Saudi Arabia ($96 billion), and others adding up to $857 billion.
Then the nations that built up the deficits came with sovereign wealth
funds to buy up U.S. companies and factories. In 2007 foreign investors
spent $414 billion buying up U.S. American enterprises, a 90 percent in-

crease from 2006 and more than double the average for the previous decade. Then the entire economy cratered after the debt resort reached its outer limit in the U.S. housing market, the mortgage bubble burst, and world credit markets froze. Huge financial firms perished or were bailed out; stocks worldwide lost 42 percent of their value in 2008, erasing more than $29 trillion; in the U.S. the Dow Jones industrial average fell 33.8 percent and the broader Standard & Poor's index fell 38.5 percent, the worst stock losses since 1931.[13]

Contrary to Friedman and other celebrants of the global market, governments were far from passé in this area before the global economy crashed; after the crash governments stepped up dramatically, spending trillions of dollars to save capitalism from itself. Germany put up more than $700 billion and Britain spent one-fifth of its national GDP to save its banking systems. By March 2009 the governments of Europe, North America, and the leading Asian capitalist powers had spent or guaranteed over $11 trillion to prevent global economic suffocation. All of this was impossible to foresee or imagine in Friedman's picture of an electronic herd of global investors zipping capital around the world with no regard for governments or nations, taking orders from no one, guided only by economic attractions he likened to laws of nature.

Friedman-style boosterism for neoliberal globalization overlooked that governments played huge roles in setting up this system, defending and perpetuating it, deciding whether to regulate it, and dealing with its implications for equality, trade agreements, human rights and the rights of workers, immigration, and the environment. Neoliberal boosterism overlooked that economic oligarchies in emerging and advanced economies entrenched themselves in national governments, rigging the game whenever possible. It played down the roles of the International Monetary Fund (IMF) and World Bank in enforcing the golden straightjacket. It overlooked that lacking strong institutions and policies regulating capital flows, turbo-capitalism everywhere is vulnerable to the kind of meltdown that occurred in East Asia in 1997.

East Asia's capitalist dynamos achieved model records on the very things stressed by the IMF: budget surpluses, strong investment and growth rates, low inflation, and low trade deficits. Taiwan, South Korea, Singapore, and Hong Kong racked up phenomenally high rates of productive investment, while Malaysia and Thailand sought to catch up by following the IMF's prescription of keeping governments out of the financial restructuring business. All of that did not stop these nations and others from crashing to negative growth rates as a run on short-term capital set off a panic that fed on itself. It didn't help that the IMF doled out bad fiscal advice and pushed for unsustainably fast capital market liberalization. The East Asian economic take-off was fueled by free-trade policies managed by state-dominated economies that selected and nurtured key industries. Economic oligarchies enriched themselves by taking advantage of their connections to governments. But the oligarchies overreached in good times and the lack of monitoring and regulatory mechanisms allowed the entire "miracle" to collapse in a few months.[14]

All of that was a prelude to the crash of 2008. From the perspective of Economics 101 every bubble mania is basically alike, but from the beginning this one has been harder to swallow, because it started with people who were just trying to buy a house of their own; who usually had no concept of predatory lending; and who had no say in the securitization boondoggle that spliced up various components of risk to trade them separately. It seemed a blessing to get a low-rate mortgage. It was a mystery how the banks did it, but this was their business; you trusted that they knew what they were doing. Your bank resold the mortgage to an aggregator who bunched it up with thousands of other subprime mortgages, chopped the package into pieces, and sold them as corporate bonds to parties looking for extra yield. Your mortgage payments paid for the interest on the bonds.

For twenty years securitizations and derivatives were great at concocting extra yield and allowing the banks to hide their debt. Broadly speaking, a derivative is any contract that derives its value from another underlying asset, such as buying home insurance. More narrowly and pertinently, it is an instrument that allows investors to speculate on the future price of something without having to buy it. Modern derivatives were developed to allow investors to hedge their risks in financial markets—essentially to buy insurance against market movements. In each case they quickly became major investment options in their own right, allowing executives to claim "earnings" for contracts in which money exchanged hands only at a designated, sometimes far-off future date.

Option trading—paying for the right to exercise an option in the event prices move in a set direction—soared in the 1970s, aided by the growth of computers, which helped to gauge the volatility of assets. The more prices move, the more buyers exercise their options. Currency swaps, and then interest-rate swaps, emerged in the 1980s. Currency swaps exchange bonds issued in one currency for another currency, enabling both parties to seek lower interest rates; interest rate swaps pair variable rate borrowers with borrowers on a fixed rate, as both parties try to manage their risk exposure.

From there it was a short step to the credit-default swaps pioneered in the late 1990s, in which parties bet on, or insured against, defaults. Credit-default swaps are private contracts in a completely unregulated market that allow investors to bet on whether a borrower will default. In theory they are a form of insurance, because sellers guarantee to pay investors if their investments go bad. In reality, the credit default mania of the 2000s was pure gambling exempted from standard insurance reserve requirements and state gaming laws. Credit default sellers are not required to set aside reserves to pay for claims, and in 2000 the Commodity Futures Modernization Act exempted credit default swaps (CDSs) from state gaming laws and other forms of regulation.

For ten years credit default swaps were fantastically lucrative. In 1998 the total value of credit-default contracts was $144 billion; by 2008 it was $62 trillion, and at the very heart of the financial crash. The derivatives market as a whole was equally spectacular and concentrated. In 2003 seven banks owned 96 percent of the derivatives in the banking system, which had a total value of $56 trillion; by 2008 the market was estimated to be $520 trillion. Alan Greenspan, Federal Reserve chair from 1987 to 2006, was a major proponent of derivatives, contending that the big banks and financial firms, being highly leveraged, needed a market vehicle to transfer their risks. An ardent libertarian, Greenspan worried when he took the Federal Reserve post that he would clash with Fed professionals who believed in regulation. To his delight he found that the Federal Reserve governors shared his strong opposition to most forms of regulation, and he took pride that the derivatives market exploded on his watch.[15]

But these instruments offered dangerous incentives for false accounting and made it extremely difficult to ascertain a firm's true exposure. By design, they generated huge amounts of leverage in which investors controlled assets far exceeding the original investment. The financial products unit of American International Group (AIG), a corporation of U.S.-based insurance companies, virtually bankrupted the conglomerate by trafficking in derivatives tied to subprime mortgages. In the aftermath of the September 2008 meltdown AIG consumed four government bailouts totaling $175 billion and doled out $165 million of bonus payments without finding a bottom to its sinkhole of toxic debt exceeding $1 trillion.

Derivatives created dangerous incentives for false accounting and made it extremely difficult to ascertain a firm's true exposure. They generated huge amounts of leverage by design and were developed with virtually no consideration of the broad financial consequences. Securitization, contrary to what it sounds like, practically ensured unaccountability by creating new types of information asymmetries. Mortgage bundlers knew more than the buyers about what was in the bundles, but nobody knew very much, which left nobody responsible for what happened to them. Essentially securitization allowed banks to set up off-balance-sheet vehicles to hide their debt. If financial institutions could parcel out their risk, supposedly there was nothing to worry about, since housing values always went up.

The big investment banks had complex mathematical models for measuring risk, which provided a false assurance of safety, and still do despite the meltdown. The leading model, VaR (Value at Risk), was developed at JPMorgan in the early 1990s. It uses statistical ideas and probability theories to quantify portfolio risks as a single number. Traders prize its unique ability to picture short-term trends by measuring normal probabilities. The big firms measure VaR every day. But VaR, for all its mathematical complexity, is only as good as the information fed into it, which has a very limited scope. The benchmarks for VaR modeling are usually a few days or weeks; even the "historical" variations of standard VaR measure risks only for a year or two.

If, before 2008, your historical benchmark was what happened in almost any two-year period from 1990 to 2007, your research was reassuring. It showed that housing values always went up and unprecedented levels of debt could be sustained. Greenspan later lamented to Congress that if the risk models had been fitted to normal historical periods, Wall Street might have known better than to keep piling on debt. With "shocked disbelief" he observed that apparently the big banks could not be trusted to protect shareholder equity, a discovery that contradicted his "fundamental worldview." Greenlight Capital founder David Einhorn and best-selling author and options trader Nassim Nicholas Taleb take dimmer views of risk modeling. Einhorn compares risk models to air bags that work except in the event of a car accident, creating a false sense of security. Taleb contends that VaR is an outright "fraud," as it cannot detect unexpected calamities; the greatest risks are the "black swans" that cannot be seen or measured.[16]

In any case, greed and historical amnesia prevailed. Banks got leveraged up to 50-to-1 (Bear Stearns's ratio at the end) and kept piling on debt, stoking the mania for extra yield. In some cases subprime mortgage bonds were actually created to allow investors, using credit-default swaps, to bet against them. There was so much money to be made that firms could not bear to leave it aside for competitors to grab. The mania for extra yield fed on itself, blowing away business ethics and common sense.

For nine years Harry Markopolos, an investment officer with Rampart Investment Management in Boston, warned the Securities and Exchange Commission that Bernard Madoff's $50 billion investment empire had to be fraudulent because his constant high profits were impossible. But the SEC did no better with Madoff's outright Ponzi operation than it managed with Wall Street's high-yielding securitization trading. One pyramid-style breeder of paper gains and bonuses looked too much like another.[17]

So many plugged-in bankers, investors, brokers, and traders rode this financial lunacy for all it was worth, caught in the terribly real pressure of the market to produce constant short-term gains. Speculators gamed the system, and regulators looked the other way. Mortgage brokers, bond bundlers, rating agencies, and corporate executives made fortunes selling bad mortgages, packaging them into securities, handing out inflated bond ratings, and putting the bonds on balance sheets. At every link in the chain, every time a loan was sold, packaged, securitized, or resold, transaction fees were charged and somebody's "wealth" increased. Bonuses were paid for short-term paper gains on money held up for as long as ten years. The chief rating agencies, Moody's and Standard & Poor's, instead of exposing financial risk, handed out Triple-A ratings that stoked the lunacy, being paid by the very issuers of the bonds they rated.

Warnings of a day of reckoning were not lacking. Chris Dialynas, a managing director at the investment firm Pimco, warned in October 2002 that credit default markets were especially vulnerable to insider-trading abuses, bankers could not be trusted to safeguard their clients' interests, and mere self-policing without regulation would not work. Pimco founder and bond investment star Bill Gross cautioned that derivatives multiplied leverage like the Andromeda strain: "When interest rates go up, the Petri dish turns from a benign experiment in financial engineering to a destructive virus because the cost of that leverage ultimately reduces the price of assets." Prominent left-liberal political journalist William Greider warned repeatedly that America's financial system was imperiled by its dependence on fallible computer models and its extreme oscillations between excess and panic. India's Reserve Bank governor Y. V. Reddy, a sharp critic of derivatives and securitizations, limited these instruments for years before banning them outright. Indian bankers howled against Reddy right up to September 2008, when all was forgiven; Reddy saved India from being swept into the worst of the derivatives catastrophe.[18]

Investment guru Warren Buffett was another critic of the derivatives revolution. In 2002 Buffett warned that derivatives were time bombs that threatened to blow up Wall Street and the economy. His investment group, Berkshire Hathaway, pulled out of most derivatives markets, explaining that derivatives pushed companies into a "spiral that can lead to a corporate meltdown." Buffett stressed that the value of a derivative contract usually depended on the creditworthiness of its counter-party and that earnings on derivatives were "often wildly overstated." Since inaccurate estimates could take many years to expose, executives made off with huge bonuses and options for phony earnings. The problem wasn't just greed or false optimism, he noted; the deeper problem was that derivatives were opaque, risky, and loaded with destructive incentives. There was no real market, and money did not change hands immediately; thus executives substituted mark-to-model accounting schemes for standard mark-to-market accounting to determine the value of their assets. Buffett cautioned that mark-to-model accounting virtually invited "fanciful assumptions." In the worst cases it was better called "market-to-myth." He warned: "The derivatives genie is now well out of the bottle, and these instruments will almost certainly multiply in variety and number until some event makes their toxicity clear. Central banks and governments have so far found no effective way to control, or even monitor, the risks posed by these contracts. In my view, derivatives are financial weapons of mass destruction, carrying dangers that, while now latent, are potentially lethal."[19]

When the housing bubble burst in August 2007, Wall Street gasped but kept piling on debt. The following spring Bear Stearns went down, stunningly, but it was still plausible to many that Buffett had exaggerated about destruction and lethality. In September the crashing and bailing commenced; even Berkshire Hathaway was burned, losing 36 percent of its share value in two months, as Buffett turned out to be deeper into derivatives than advertised. U.S. Treasury Secretary Henry Paulson engineered an emergency $700 billion cash-for-trash bailout called the Troubled Assets Relief Program (TARP), which was supposed to buy toxic assets at market prices. But the stock market continued to fall, market prices for bad debt were frighteningly low, credit remained nearly frozen, and Europe got caught in the meltdown, with the rest of the world in its wake. Numerous European officials, appalled that Paulson allowed Lehman Brothers to go down, declared they would not let a similar crash occur in their country. British Prime Minister Gordon Brown half-socialized Britain's banking sector, declaring that he opposed mere giveaways to the parties that created the mess, though he was a major facilitator of deregulation and derivatives trading as Chancellor of the Exchequer in Tony Blair's Labour government from 1997 to 2007. Other European nations followed suit; Paulson suddenly agreed, sort of, changing his strategy, and on October 13, 2008, the Bush administration invested $250 billion in senior preferred bank stock in Wells Fargo ($25 billion), JPMorgan Chase ($25 billion), Citigroup ($25 billion), Bank of America ($15 billion), Goldman Sachs ($10 billion), Morgan Stanley ($10 billion), Bank of New York ($3 billion), and State Street ($2 billion). Two weeks later twenty-one additional banks received taxpayer infusions, notably Sun Trust and Capital One (each for $3.5 billion); the following week there were twenty-three more.[20]

Paulson reasoned that the banks would start lending again if he gave them money. But this approach did not satisfy either part of Brown's objection. Paulson's arrangement *was* a mere giveaway, overpaying for preferred stock with no control rights, and it went to the very people that created the crisis. Also, it did not work. Had Paulson given the banks tangible common equity instead of preferred stock (which is essentially a loan) and told them to invest it in the real economy or write off their toxic debt, they would have had to do so. As it was, they didn't know what their assets were worth, so they sat on the taxpayers' money, not being required to do anything else with it, and subsequently went back to gambling on derivatives, which is more lucrative than lending. Citigroup, within weeks of receiving its first $25 billion gift from taxpayers, got another $20 billion of TARP money in late November and a whopping $306 billion guarantee (2 percent of America's GDP), all with no public stake, no management changes, and no annoying demands to do anything for the public with the public's money. Treasury and Fed officials managed not to take an equity stake in Citigroup by structuring the deal like an insurance program, which concealed the amount of risk that taxpayers took on. Bank of America got a similar deal just before the Obama administration took office, receiving a fresh $20 billion capital injection and a guarantee of up to $118 billion in losses on toxic assets.[21]

Smaller banks socked away their TARP money, too, or used it to repay short-term loans from the Federal Reserve. Some of them used taxpayer money to buy rival banks. Wells Fargo acquired massive exposure to California mortgage failures by taking over Wachovia, and JPMorgan Chase took on similar liabilities by taking over Bear Stearns and Washington Mutual. The Federal Reserve Bank of New York, chaired by Timothy Geithner, paid AIG's partners one hundred cents on the dollar to terminate their contracts with the insurance conglomerate, apparently on the premise that well-connected financial giants were exempt from the haircuts that auto companies and their unionized employees had to take after Geithner succeeded Paulson as Treasury Secretary. In the last eighteen months of the Bush administration $13 trillion in net worth evaporated from the U.S. economy and the government pledged $9 trillion in loans, investments, and guarantees to fill the chasm. When Obama took office, half the $700 billion TARP money had been spent, spread among 257 financial institutions in forty-two states, and only a trickle of it was getting invested in a disintegrating economy.[22]

The Obama administration inherited a global deflationary spiral ravaging nearly every nation connected to the global economy, although the powerhouses in the emerging market group—China, India, Brazil, and Argentina—fared better than others. Deflation, once started, has a terrible tendency to feed on itself. Income falls in a recession, which makes debt harder to bear, which discourages investment, which further depresses the economy, which leads to more deflation. In 2008 twenty-five failed banks in the U.S. were deemed small enough to fail; by October 2009, one hundred and three banks had joined them. These are modest figures compared to the thousands of bank failures of the 1930s, and most of the too-big-to-fail banks bailed out by Bush and Obama should be able to repay U.S. taxpayers eventually, as the nineteen largest banks have assets totaling $8 trillion in mostly performing loans. But the current crisis is more dangerous than the Depression in one respect. This time it is the very pillars of America's financial system—the giant banks and mortgage companies—that collapsed and screamed for rescue. Some will never repay taxpayers. Citigroup and AIG are good candidates for that group, as are the mortgage giants Fannie Mae and Freddie Mac. AIG's derivatives unit was a huge casino selling phantom insurance with hardly any backing, for which taxpayers are left having to cover over $1 trillion of debt. Fannie Mae and Freddie Mac, with combined assets of $5.4 trillion—all in mortgages—will cost taxpayers more than $400 billion over the next ten years. These firms, for years to come, will borrow government money merely to pay dividends owed to the government on money borrowed previously.[23]

The U.S. financial regulatory system has to be reorganized, new regulatory regimes for individual dealers of derivatives and for the marketplaces where derivatives are traded must be created, and the global economy needs a new system of rules. But the big banks and other Wall Street powers are dead against even mild reforms, let alone radical changes in the way they operate. They are returning headlong into the very practices that caused the crash, lobbying shamelessly against all serious proposals to regulate derivative dealing. Instead of requiring the Commodities Futures Trading Commission and the Securities and Exchange Commission to regulate derivatives, as the Obama administration mildly proposes, the big banks are insisting that oversight of the dealers must be left to the same banking regulators that did nothing to prevent the derivatives explosion. The banks are more interested in gambling for high returns with their taxpayer bailouts than in making boring low-return investments in the real economy, which has fueled the Wall Street surge of 2009 at the same time that unemployment topped 10 percent nationally. They are against forcing over-the-counter derivatives to be traded on open exchanges, or centrally cleared, or subjected to the margin requirements that cleaned up the corporate bond market at the end of the 1990s. And they want nothing to do with an updated version of Bretton Woods.

Regulatory authority in the U.S. is divided among federal and state governments, the Security and Exchange Commission, the comptroller of the currency, and the Federal Reserve. The global economy is even more fragmented and dysfunctional, having lacked a system of road rules since the early 1970s. After World War II the Bretton Woods Agreement established a system of fixed exchange rates that limited capital flows from one country to another. In 1971, however, Richard Nixon, struggling with a large trade deficit and a costly war in Vietnam, suspended the dollar's convertibility into gold, which ended the Bretton Woods system. Now currencies could float. Capital flows rushed across national borders, the world changed, and the financial futures business was created, centered at the newly founded Chicago Mercantile Exchange. Currency trading led straight to the electronic herd's world of zippy derivatives trading, far eclipsing the commodities market.

The sheer ungovernability of free-flowing global capitalism seemed like heaven to the electronic herd. Today the ravages of that illusion are crushing poor nations and driving millions from richer nations into homelessness. The most vulnerable nations of the global South, which once managed to feed themselves before their economies became totally dependent on the world market price for two or three commodities, have been hit hardest by the crash. They need substantial debt forgiveness to be able to breath again; at the same time, huge trade imbalances between major powers have to be reduced to restore some measure of functional equilibrium.

The U.S. has a savings rate of almost zero and a skyrocketing national debt equal to the size of its entire economy, plus recent annual trade deficits exceeding $200 billion with China, while China has a savings rate of nearly 50 percent, a consumption rate of only 35 percent, and a beggar-thy-neighbor policy of subsidizing exports, racking up huge trade surpluses with its regional neighbors. To attain something resembling a functional global trading system, both sides of this picture have to change. The U.S. has to relearn how to save, live within its means, and get along without cheap money and easy credit. China has to ease up on the very strategy of cheap money and exports that lifted it to superpower status over the past fifteen years; otherwise the existence of an open global trading system is imperiled.

Every major and middle-sized trading power in the world, except one, allows its currency to float against other currencies, permitting the relative value of its currency to fluctuate depending on market forces. Tactical exceptions and adjustments are commonplace, as when a government limits capital flows to head off a currency run or limits capital inflows caused by excessive speculation. But as a rule, active trading nations keep the value of their currency in line with economic fundamentals.

China is playing a different game, a dangerous one. China keeps its currency, the renminbi, artificially low, mostly by buying hundreds of billions of dollars annually in the currency markets; in 2009 China added $300 billion to its dollar-denominated reserve assets of $2 trillion. This strategy keeps China's currency undervalued by twenty to thirty percent, fueling its constant export growth, which is great for Chinese exporters and terrible for weaker trading powers and everyone else trying to crawl out from a depressed world economy. In this situation, it should not have to fall to progressives alone to demand a new system of global economic rules, though they have this issue pretty much to themselves thus far. Progressives have a distinct role to play in demanding a twenty-first century

version of Bretton Woods that upholds principles
rights, systemic functionality, fiscal responsibility,
protection.

The TARP program probably saved the financia
pletely collapsing in the last months of 2008, but it
flawed, and the banks had serious reasons for sitti
funds, since they did not want to go broke again. W   .....α ͻ presidency began, the banks held at least $2 trillion of toxic debt. The bank-
ing system was paralyzed because the big private equity funds and hedge
funds refused to pay more than thirty cents on the dollar for the mortgage
bundles and the banks were afraid to book such huge losses on their holdings. A year later, as this book goes to press, the banks are still holding
out for sixty cents and the problem of the toxic debt is not resolved.

One option is Henry Paulson's original plan, which Princeton economist Paul Krugman dubbed "cash for trash," this time with more accountability. Another is to ramp up the insurance approach, "ring-fencing" bad
assets by providing federal guarantees against losses. But these are more-
of-the-same options that coddle the banks and do not solve the valuation
problem, that nobody trusts anyone else's balance sheet. A third option,
the "bad bank" model, creates transitional banks that soak up bad debt.
Here the risk of getting prices wrong is daunting, assuming that assets
are valued immediately. If the government overpays for toxic securities,
taxpayers are cheated; if it does not overpay and the banks take mark-to-
market prices, many are sure to fail. In theory, a bad bank could stall on
the price issue, waiting until values rise, but Treasury Secretary Timothy
Geithner and Federal Deposit Insurance Corporation (FDIC) chair Sheila
Bair judged that that smacked too much of alchemy, floating assets into
ether.

Geithner and Bair settled on an "Aggregator Bank" that blends the
original Paulson plan with some elements of the bad bank topped off with
an auction scheme to find private buyers for the toxic debt. The FDIC
created a pilot program featuring cheap financing for investors to buy up
bad assets, which it canceled in June 2009 after the banks proved unwilling to book losses on their holdings. The centerpiece of the Geithner plan
is a $1 trillion public-private investment fund to be run by the FDIC and
Treasury Department. The government will team up with hedge funds
and private equity firms, subsidizing up to 95 percent of deals partnered
with them, to buy up bad loans and toxic securities. The FDIC will hold

...s and do most of the partnering work, and Treasury will hire four ...ive investment management firms.[24]

Since this is what we are doing, I certainly hope it works. But the Geithner plan is obsequious to Wall Street. It coddles the banks and showers shareholders with taxpayer-funded gifts exceeding a trillion dollars. It is based on the dubious hope of finding enough private buyers for rotten goods. And it is the most cumbersome and nontransparent of the main options. Essentially this is a scheme to pay huge bribes to private investors to buy the bad loans and toxic securities for more than they are worth. The big banks are balking anyway, because they don't want to be hamstrung by the government as they resume the very practices that caused the crash.

Two years from now, speculative corporate debt in the U.S. is going to explode as the reckoning for high risk loans, bonds, and leveraged buyouts transacted five to seven years ago arrives. In the bond business this is called a maturity wall. This year $21 billion is coming due for junk bonds that were sold before the credit crisis hit in 2007. In 2012 that number will soar to $155 billion; the following year it will exceed $212 billion; and the year after that it will be over $340 billion. This coming avalanche of over $700 billion of speculative debt was created, just like the mortgage crisis, with collateralized debt obligations (CDOs) that sliced and diced corporate loans, and it will come due at a time when the U.S. government needs to borrow almost $2 trillion to bridge its budget deficit and refinance its existing debt. Another credit crunch is coming, and we still haven't solved the bank problem that the Obama administration inherited.[25]

We ought to be talking about abolishing derivatives, but that would require fighting with the big banks that want to sell them and financial players that want to use them to hedge their risks, something not in Obama's game plan. CDOs are not investments; they are like side bets at a casino, pure gambling on whether somebody's bonds will succeed. The fallback reform is to put derivative trading on an open exchange, where it will be subject to margin requirements that show customers what they are buying. As this book goes to press, Democrats in Congress are pushing a reform bill to put most derivative trading on an open market. This bill, if it passes, will be a major achievement for the Obama administration and U.S. American democracy. The joint lobbying powerhouse for the nine biggest banks, the CDS Dealers Consortium, has lobbied furiously to thwart regulations on derivatives. Seven of these banks control 65 percent of the U.S. gross domestic product. It is no easy thing to defeat them on something they want badly. On the other hand, the reform bill is loaded with carve-outs for select corporate users of derivatives, exemptions for foreign exchange swaps, and restricted scrutiny of corporate pension funds. It does not abolish gambling with CDOs, nor does it address the biggest problem of all: that the big banks are too big to fail, and thus too big.

I am for biting the bullet. It is obscene to reward the very people who created this disaster. At some point moral fairness and accountability have to enter this picture. When a too-big-to-fail bank goes bankrupt, the government's appropriate response is to take it over, transfer the bad assets to a reincarnation of the 1980s Resolution Trust Corporation, and sell off the sellable parts to new owners. Nationalization is cleaner and more transparent than the alternatives. It takes hold of the valuation problem by finding the bottom. It cuts off the gusher of taxpayer gifts to shareholders and failed bankers. It puts an end to mergers between zombie banks, which create more zombie banks that are too big to fail. And it breaks the grip of the economic oligarchy that made fortunes on the way to causing disaster.

There are significant differences between the South Korean and Indonesian crashes of 1997, the Malaysian crash of 1998, Japan's lost decade, the recurrent crashes in Russia and Argentina, and our current meltdown. But they hold in common the crucial thing: a financial oligarchy that rigged the game in its favor, built an empire on debt, overreached in good times, and brought the house down on everybody. When the house collapses, elites do what they always do: they take care of their own. To get a different result, a nation has to take control of the problem and break the grip of the oligarchy. Otherwise you muddle along in a lost decade of your own, further entrenching the oligarchy.

MIT economist Simon Johnson served in 2007–2008 as chief economist of the IMF. He was skeptical about the power of economic elites in Western democracies, until he went to the IMF and got a close look at the symbiotic relationships between economic elites and their governments. In the U.S. it goes far beyond mere access or even collusion, he observes. Here the two career tracks of government and high finance are thoroughly melded together, which is problematic when the oligarchy screws up and the economy implodes.[26]

Johnson stresses that when the IMF enters the scene of a crash, the economic part is usually straightforward: nations in crisis are told to live within their means by increasing exports, cutting imports, and breaking up bankrupt enterprises and banks. Every endangered country that is not the U.S. would get this prescription. But the U.S. controls the IMF, it has a very powerful and well-connected oligarchy, and it pays its foreign debts in its own currency. So the U.S. recovery, even under a liberal Democratic administration, begins with paying off Wall Street.

Johnson's analysis is compelling on the latter point. But his prescription is straight out of the IMF playbook: find a bottom, clear out the clutter, get the fiscal and monetary houses in order, and shake up crony capitalism. There is always going to be an economic oligarchy, he says, so the best we can do is to shake it up from time to time. To this end he recommends new antitrust laws, though he cannot say what they would look like, and he notes that we will probably try to cap executive compensation, though he says that won't work. Meanwhile the U.S. is not facing up to the crisis of capitalism, because our oligarchy has immense political and economic power, our economy is based on ever expanding consumption, and if we opt for muddling through, the Federal Reserve can just print more money.[27]

If we take the existing system for granted, Johnson's prescription is about the best we can do. But this crisis will be wasted if we do not push for structural changes that expand the cooperative sector and democratize the process of investment. An aggressively democratic strategy puts into play something more creative and constructive than merely taking bankrupt firms into temporary receivership: Establishing publicly funded venture capital banks. If we can spend trillions of taxpayer dollars creating bad banks or aggregator banks we ought to be able to talk about creating publicly owned good banks to do good things. Public banks could finance start-ups in green technology that are currently languishing and provide financing for cooperatives that traditional banks spurn. They could be financed by an economic stimulus package approved by Congress or by claiming the good assets of banks seized by the government, or both.

Obama must be pushed for anything like that, as he is surrounded by centrist establishment types eager to placate Wall Street and averse to wiping out shareholders. His chief economic advisor, Lawrence Summers, was a major player in tearing down the wall between commercial and investment banking during the Clinton administration and prides himself on being adored by Wall Street. Obama will have to be pushed, as well, to stick to a social investment strategy throughout his presidency, instead of backing off from it as Franklin Roosevelt did.

When Roosevelt took office in March 1933, banks were closed in thirty-eight states, withdrawals were limited in the other ten, unemployment was officially 25 percent but in reality was higher, manufacturing output was down 35 percent from 1929, farm foreclosures were averaging twenty thousand per month, and currency values were dramatically deflated. In three months Roosevelt signed fourteen major acts of legislation, including an Emergency Banking Relief Act which Congress passed without reading. The New Deal stopped the bleeding, whittling unemployment to 14 percent by 1937.

But Roosevelt never really believed in social investment. He fretted about budget deficits, refused to nationalize failing banks or create public banks, and low-balled his spending programs. Then he reduced unemployment spending in 1937, which helped send unemployment soaring to 19 percent the following year. By 1940, after seven years of New Deal economics, unemployment stood at 14.5 percent and the New Deal was not a candidate for iconic status. It became a great success only by gearing up for World War II.[28]

Now we are in a 1930s-like political moment, and we must not hope for the perverse "deliverance" of a World War III. The U.S. needs to fill a $2 trillion hole in the economy that is sucking ordinary wage-earners into unemployed despair even as Wall Street regains its swagger. We need huge investments in green technology, infrastructure rebuilding, high-speed trains, education, and health care to meet our human and environmental needs and to revive the economy's productive capacity. Deficit spending, in the long run, is inflationary, which is why we must not let up on progressive causes that restore fiscal sanity even in a moment when job creation is the highest priority. We need to scale back the U.S. global military empire, break our addiction to oil, get control of health care costs, and fight for a tax system that restores and extends the principle of progressive taxation. We need to break the grip of America's economic oligarchy and build a movement for economic democracy. And we need a national discussion about the kind of country the U.S. might prefer to be.

In the 1980s Sweden and Japan had national discussions about the tolerable limits of inequality. Swedish conservatives and progressives debated whether the wage differential between corporate executives and laborers permitted by the nation's solidarity wage policy should be increased to eight to one or maintained at four to one. In Japan, where worker share-holder plans were commonplace, a similar debate occurred over the tolerability of allowing more than the existing ratio of sixteen to one. In the United States the ratio climbed to 145 to 1 and there was no debate. The right to attain wealth was exalted over other values. The Reagan administration cut the marginal tax rate for individuals from 70 percent to 28 percent and cut the top rate on capital gains from 49 percent to 20 percent. These measures had very large effects on the kind of society the U.S. became, fueling a huge surge for inequality. By the end of the decade, the top fifth of the population earned more than half the nation's income and held more than three-quarters of its wealth while the bottom fifth received barely 4 percent of its income.[29]

Today these numbers look rather moderate, because we have just had twenty years of unleashed greed in the financial sector and eight years of tax policy redistribution for the rich. First the derivatives market was allowed to soar and multiply. Then the Clinton administration tore down the regulatory walls between commercial banking and investment firms and exempted credit default swaps from regulation. Then the Bush administration refused to enforce protections within the law, pushed for more deregulation, cut the capital gains rate to 15 percent, and gave enormous tax windfalls to the top 5 percent of earners. Nearly all of America's economic growth under Bush went to the top 5 percent, while the middle and working classes kept borrowing to stay afloat. Then the debt resort reached its outer limit and drowning commenced.[30]

An entire generation of economists, trained to spurn the New Deal and Keynesian theory, has to retool its worldview to help rebuild the economy by investing in human needs and green technology. Having ignored public spending in their research, mainstream economists are short on the requisite expertise. Berkeley economist Alan Auerbach remarks, "We have spent so many years thinking that discretionary fiscal policy was a bad idea that we have not figured out the right things to do to cure a recession that is scaring all of us." Dealing with that challenge throws us way beyond Pepsi-or-Coke options, as even Thomas Friedman acknowledges. On the day of Obama's inauguration, Friedman urged Obama to be a radical—spurning cautious choices and putting everything on the table.[31]

In the 1990s Kaus ruled out almost every strategy for economic justice in a globalized world, with one caveat. He allowed that a serious case could be made for one strategy: a strong progressive income tax combined with a serious push for worker ownership and shareholding.

Kaus doubted that this would work, either, and a subsequent decade of manic capitalism in the financial sector did nothing to change his mind. Economic democracy had two major problems in addition to its obvious political problems in the American context, he observed. Worker/owners tend to be biased toward capital intensive investments, and they spurn efficiency decisions (like moving to Mexico) that ruthless corporations would take.

But the latter problem is one of the virtues of social ownership; the former problem can be dealt with by instituting tax incentives that promote full employment; in many cases worker ownership is a community's only chance of combating runaway plants and deindustrialization; and Kaus overlooked that worker ownership is not the only form of economic democracy. Economic democracy, to be sure, is a wilder dream today than it was a century ago. Any proposal to expand the cooperative and social market sectors must address the problems of worker, community, and public bank ownership. For worker and social ownership strategies to succeed, they have to build upon the advantage that, as Kaus conceded, workers are typically "more creative, energetic, and responsible when they have a stake in their employer's success."[32]

Decentralized economic democracy cannot abolish the predatory logic of "creative destruction" that economist Joseph Schumpeter vividly described in the 1940s and which second-wave globalization dramatically unleashed. But for those who refuse to accept the givens and outcomes of the race to the bottom, it is still the best bet for getting something better.[33]

Chapter 9

Rethinking and Renewing Economic Democracy

Economic democracy, in my conception, is not a nicer-sounding stand-in for state socialism, though the phrase was sometimes used as such by twentieth-century Socialists. Neither is it compatible with blueprint dogmatism, though some theorists of economic democracy are devoted to their blueprints. In my conception it is communitarian, radically democratic, pluralistic, environmentalist, as decentralized as possible, and a compound of realism and idealism. The roots of economic democracy theory go back to the cooperative and guild socialist movements of the nineteenth and early twentieth centuries, notably the French section of the First Socialist International, which stressed cooperative networks of production and consumption, and the guild socialist section of the British Labour Party, which advocated a decentralized third way between syndicalism and state socialism. But contemporary theorists usually start with Oscar Lange.

A Polish economist and diplomat who taught at the University of Chicago in the late 1930s, Lange served as the Polish delegate to the United Nations Security Council in the mid-1940s and published his major work, *On the Economic Theory of Socialism*, in 1936. He rejected the Marxian labor theory of value, contending that Socialists needed to accommodate neoclassical price theory. Essentially he showed that market mechanisms and incentives could be integrated into socialist theory.

In Lange's proposal, a large state sector coexisted with, and benefited from, the pricing and market discipline of a private sector of small enterprises. State planners simulated and were instructed by the private sector's pricing system, and central planning boards set prices by adjusting to shortages and surpluses. When shortages occurred, prices would be raised to encourage businesses to increase production; when surpluses occurred, prices would be lowered to encourage businesses to prevent losses by curtailing production.[1]

But that was still a form of state socialism. Lange showed, more rigorously than previous theorists had, that market mechanisms and social ownership were compatible, and he granted a larger role for the market than state socialists. But he had centralized planners trying to replicate the innumerable and enormously complex pricing decisions of markets—a task exceeding the competence, time constraints, and knowledge of any conceivable planning board. Lange-style blueprints for "market socialism" invariably founder on this problem and the authoritarian politics that inevitably go with it.

Economic democracy has to break from the unitary logic of state socialism, featuring mixed forms of worker, community, and mutual fund or public bank enterprises. It is about democratizing economic power and creating environmentally sustainable economies. I do not believe that factors of production trump everything else. Any serious attempt to democratize power has to take "living place" issues such as housing, health care, and the environment as seriously as it takes the democratization of the investment process. It requires a feminist, interracial, multicultural, ecological, and anti-imperial consciousness that privileges liberationist and environmental issues.

In the 1990s economics fell into disfavor among progressives because it seemed too depressing to deal with. Capitalism was more aggressive and triumphant than ever, trade unionism was devastated, and liberals fought rearguard battles over social programs. But economic justice is fundamental to every form of social justice, and no serious challenge to existing relations of power can ignore the factors of production. Those who control the terms, amounts, and direction of credit have a huge say in determining the kind of society that everyone else lives in. Thus the question of who controls the process of investment is enormously significant. Gains toward social and economic democracy are needed today for the same reason that political democracy is necessary, to restrain the abuse of unequal power.

Economic democracy, like political democracy, is messy and time-consuming. Democratically controlled capital is less mobile than corporate capital, and the return to democratically controlled capital tends to be lower than in corporations, because worker-controlled enterprises are more committed to keeping low-return firms in operation. Producer cooperatives are often too slow, small, and humane to compete with corporations, and they require cooperative habits and values that cut against the grain of American individualism. In the U.S., any strategy to break down concentrated economic power by expanding the cooperative sector confronts difficult economic trade-offs, political opposition, and cultural barriers.

But economic democracy also has pragmatic considerations in its favor. Economic losses caused by worker participation can be offset by gains in productivity made possible by it. People often work harder and more efficiently when they have a stake in the company. Worker ownership is a key option for communities threatened by runaway plants and deindustrialization. Experiments with various kinds of worker ownership increased dramatically in the late 1980s and early 1990s, aided by a growing network of policy experts, and some unions began to bargain for worker ownership, worker control over pension funds, and worker management rights. These developments are not yet, but have the potential to become, the building blocks of a serious movement for economic democracy.

The showcase example of cooperative management is the Mondragon network in the Basque region of Spain. In the 1950s a Catholic priest, Fr. Jose Maria Arizmendi, inspired twenty-five students to launch a cooperative stove factory (Ulgor) that grew into a network of worker-owned, democratically managed foundries incorporated as agricultural cooperatives. Between 1966 and 1975 sales rose from $47 million to $336 million; in the 1980s Mondragon became Spain's largest exporter of durable goods; by 1997 it had total sales of $5 billion, held $7.5 billion of assets, and had experienced only two closings. Today Mondragon firms export half their industrial sales and are Spain's leading producer of domestic appliances and machine tools.[2]

Mondragon employs more than one hundred thousand workers in an integrated network of more than 125 financial, industrial, and service companies in virtually every economic sector, including robots and mass transit. It contains over 75 industrial firms, an agricultural cooperative, five schools, a technical college, and a central bank—the Caja Laboral Popular—that is half-owned by its own employees and half-owned by other cooperatives. The bank, founded in a church basement in 1958, specializes in loans to cooperative firms and industry-specific consulting assistance. Each Mondragon worker/owner holds one share of voting stock, and profits are distributed in the form of additions to a capital account on which 6 percent interest is paid annually. Seventy percent of annual profits are distributed to worker/owners on the basis of salary scale and seniority, 10 percent are donated to charity, and the remaining 20 percent are reinvested. Because members cannot withdraw money from their capital accounts until they retire, Mondragon is able to make long-term investments in expansion, diversification, research and development, and reinvestment from its accumulated capital stock.

The Mondragon network consistently outperforms comparable European capitalist enterprises, demonstrating that worker empowerment and cooperation can be turned into economic advantages. Beginning as an attempt to apply Fr. Arizmendi's Catholic personalism to a local community, its early success was aided by the community's common ethnic and Catholic heritage. Researchers have repeatedly judged, however, that neither culture nor ideology is crucial to Mondragon's continued success. George Benello remarks, "The secret of Mondragon is not ideological, but organizational: it is 'how to' knowledge that makes it work." Mondragon succeeds because it trades on the advantages of worker empowerment and cooperation.[3]

Any experiment in economic democracy, to be successful, has to acquire distinct skills, habits, and technical knowledge. Some U.S. American unions and worker associations began to acquire it out of necessity after capitalism went global. In 1980 there were fewer than two hundred worker-owned enterprises in the U.S. The manager-owned United Parcel Service was one of the few large ones, in addition to a few networks of producer cooperatives such as the sixteen-firm plywood mills of the Pacific Northwest. Most cooperatives and worker/community-owned firms were small, isolated, and restricted to a handful of economic sectors. The cultural and political factors were forbidding. Worker and community ownership, like universal health care, seemed out of reach for American individualism and capitalism.

Globalization drove many communities and a few unions to give economic democracy a second look, trading wage restraint for worker ownership or, more ambitiously, worker control over investment and enterprise management. In the 1990s thousands of firms converted to worker ownership, bringing the total number to approximately twelve thousand by the end of the decade, where it has stayed. In addition to small producer cooperatives, this group included large enterprises such as Republic

Engineered Steels, America West Airlines, Publix Supermarkets, Chicago Northwestern Railroad, and Northwestern Steel and Wire.

For decades United Parcel Service was the crown jewel of the worker-owned list, renowned for its size, efficiency, and high employee morale. Founded in 1907 by James Casey, who established a system of manager ownership, by the 1990s UPS was owned by fifteen thousand of its managers and supervisors, and was the dominant player in its market. For ninety years it avoided strikes, but its first one in 1997 helped pave the way to going public two years later; UPS was no longer a company that prized equality and cooperation. Today it is a powerhouse in the global delivery business, a pioneer of "insourcing" synchronization that services supply chains globally, and a symbol of the difficulty of sustaining a cooperative ethos in an aggressively capitalist environment; in 2006 the company's net income was over $4 billion.[4]

Worker ownership and the movement for it are both more modest affairs usually. Most employee ownership plans offer shares without voting rights; most assure that employees will be kept in a minority ownership position; few provide educational opportunities to help worker/owners develop management skills; and virtually none offers programs to build solidarity or help worker/owners forge links with other cooperative enterprises or raise awareness of economic democracy issues. Most worker ownership schemes in the U.S. offer stock ownership to workers while excluding them from obtaining managerial control or economic coordination. Worker ownership without democratic control is a nominal version of economic democracy, thwarting the real thing. American unions have a generally dismal record in this area, reinforcing the shortcomings; for the most part unions have not pressed for workplace democracy or new forms of democratic capital formation.

With all its limitations, however, worker ownership in the U.S. is a growing idea. Several thousand firms have converted to employee ownership, hundreds of others have been launched with worker-ownership plans, and approximately one thousand companies in the U.S. are worker-controlled. Employee stock ownership plans cover more than 10 percent of the U.S. workforce, and numerous firms have adopted labor-management cooperation schemes. In addition, industry-wide unions such as the United Steel Workers and the Amalgamated Clothing and Textile Workers promote worker ownership through the AFL-CIO Employee Partnership Fund, which provides capital for union-led conversions to worker ownership. The Midwest Center for Labor Research, Ohio Employee Ownership

Center, National Cooperative Business Association, Employee Share Ownership Plan Association, U.S. Federation of Worker Cooperatives and Democratic Workplaces, and Industrial Cooperative Association facilitate worker buyouts and develop sector-specific expertise that was unavailable to earlier generations of American cooperatives.[5]

A movement for full-orbed economic democracy that dramatically expands the cooperative sector and substantially democratizes the process of investment is obviously far off. On the way to it, economic democracy is about building up institutions that do not belong wholly to the capitalist market or the state. It begins by expanding the traditional cooperative and social market sectors. Producer cooperatives take labor out of the market by removing corporate shares from the stock market and maintaining local worker ownership. Community land trusts take land out of the market and place it under local democratic controls to serve the social needs of communities. Community finance corporations take democratic control over capital to finance cooperative firms, make investments in areas of social need, and fight the redlining policies of conventional banks. These strategies widen the base of social and economic power by expanding the cooperative and social market sectors, mixing together cooperative banks, employee stock ownership plans, producer cooperatives, community land trusts, and planning agencies that guide investments into locally defined areas of need such as housing, soft-energy hardware, infrastructure maintenance, and mass transit.[6]

But merely expanding the cooperative and social market sectors is not enough. Cooperatives prohibit nonworking shareholders, so they usually attract less outside financing than capitalist firms. They are committed to keeping low-return firms in operation, so they tend to stay in business even when they cannot afford to pay competitive wages. They are committed to particular communities, so cooperative capital and labor are less mobile than corporate capital and labor. They smack of anti-capitalist bias, so they have trouble getting financing and advice from capitalist banks. They tend to maximize net income per worker rather than profits, so they tend to favor capital-intensive investments over job creation. Cooperative worker/owners often have their savings invested in a single enterprise, so they tend to avoid risky innovations.

These problems can be mitigated with tax incentives and regulations promoting job expansion, reinvestment, innovation, and bank lending to cooperatives. Internal capital accounts, such as Mondragon's retirement accounts, facilitate reinvestment of savings and enable worker/owners to plan for the long term. Tax incentives promoting expansion and innovation counteract the cooperative tendency to fixate on share income per worker. Moreover, the commitment of cooperatives to particular contexts and communities is one of their best assets, and the lack of an expansionary dynamic should be counted mostly on the plus side as well.

Traditional capitalist firms have structural incentives to grow under conditions of constant returns to scale. When costs-per-item are constant, capitalist firms are predisposed to grow to increase profits. Doubling the size of a capitalist firm doubles its profits. But democratic firms do not expand production automatically when demand increases, because they maximize share income per worker, not total profits. Unless sizable economies of scale are involved, individual worker/owners in a cooperative have little to gain by doubling the size of their firm. A cooperative hardware store run by thirty people will have the same per-worker share income as one run by sixty people. Thus democratic firms are structurally suited to counteract the manic capitalist logic of bigger is better. Cooperative economics and ecological sustainability are naturally linked by the necessity of creating structural alternatives to the capitalist fantasy of unlimited growth. The kind of economic development that favors the needs of poor and disenfranchised communities and does not harm the earth's environment will require a dramatically expanded cooperative sector consisting of worker-owned firms rooted in communities, committed to sustainability, and prepared to accept comparatively lower returns.[7]

But even a cooperative sector aided by better financing and entrepreneurial incentives will carry special risks for workers and a bias toward capital-intensive investments. Cooperatives are a big piece of the answer to environmental destruction and predatory boom-and-bust economics, but they don't do enough for job creation or equality.

Most cooperatives require members to sell out to the company rather than allow members to sell out to the highest bidder and take their capital gains, and most cooperatives operate on the traditional principle that those who own a company's capital have the right to control the company. The former policy guards against reverting to traditional investor ownership, and the latter policy sustains the traditional assumption that property rights determine the right of effective control; workers must be the primary investors in a firm to control it. But the most successful cooperatives succeed by imposing high borrowing fees on new members, which excludes workers lacking the entrepreneurial nerve or resources to buy in. For cooperatives featuring share prices ranging up to $100,000, only the determined and prosperous need apply. Moreover, absolutizing property rights measures human value in terms of exchange value, leaving out people who are unable to earn wages.

One might address the equality problem by universalizing cooperation, but that would ruin a mostly good thing. If everyone had to belong to a cooperative, the entry fees would be waved and many enterprises would fail, forcing the state to socialize the economy's losses. Economic democracy has a place for Mondragon-style cooperatives, but it cannot succeed by requiring workers to join them. And it must have greater ambitions for social justice and the common good than merely enabling hard-charging types to buy into attractive cooperatives. Full-orbed economic democracy treats all citizens as stakeholders in the economic system, placing a social mortgage on property. It makes democratic institutions major players in the investment process, creating structures of public investment and control that break the dominance of the investor class.[8]

Economic Democracy as Throwback Socialism

Unfortunately there are more theorists of a full-orbed approach to economic democracy than concrete examples of it. The theorists include Peter Abell, Joanne Barkan, Frank Cunningham, Robert Dahl, Saul Estrin, Julian Le Grand, David Miller, Alec Nove, John Roemer, Frank Roosevelt, David Schweickart, Radoslav Selucky, Thomas Weisskopf, David Winter, and Rick Wolff. Some are keepers of the socialist dream of a fundamentally different economic system, fashioning blueprints of a world relieved of corporate capitalists and private financial markets. Most are more realistic, taking for granted that private financial markets are inevitable in a free society and that economic democracy must be pragmatic and pluralistic. Estrin, an economist at the London School of Economics and specialist on comparative economic systems, and Nove, an emeritus economics professor at the University of Glasgow, have made notable contributions to the economics of market socialism. Miller, an Oxford social and political theorist, and Dahl, an eminent political philosopher retired from Yale, have made notable contributions to economic democracy as a political philosophy. Schweickart, a Loyola University philosopher, is a leading advocate of economic democracy as old-time socialism.[9]

Rightly Schweickart stresses that the current economic meltdown is a crisis of overproduction tellingly like the one Marx predicted. From

1956 to 1972 the Dow Jones average doubled (from 500 to 1,000) as did wages. Then the Dow soared by fourteenfold, reaching 14,000 in 2007, despite thirty years of flat wages. Working and middle-class people fell increasingly further behind for three decades, but they felt richer, holding ever rising assets against which they borrowed deeply to keep spending and borrowing. "But what can't go on, doesn't," Schweickart observes. Credit lines finally maxed out and major pillars of the American financial system crashed overnight.[10]

Schweickart aptly contends that Keynesian pump-priming is a coping strategy, at best, that fizzled in the 1970s. The Kennedy, Johnson, and Nixon administrations used Keynesian stimulus schemes to tamp down unemployment but government spending, combined with union-negotiated wage increases and slow growth, led to the stagflation of the 1970s, which set the stage for Federal Reserve chair Paul Volcker's war against inflation in the 1980s. Unemployment reached 10 percent and corporations went on the offensive against trade unions, relocating to the non-union Sunbelt. Later, after globalization took hold, corporations moved anywhere they could find cheap labor and minimal taxes. Keynesian pump-priming is not much of a solution to the problem of low wages in a global economy, Schweickart cautions, because it does not stop firms from racing to the bottom. Any plan that increases taxes or wages is sure to set off another surge of runaway plants.

In Schweickart's analysis, the environmental crisis compounds the necessity of creating an economy not based on ever increasing consumption. We cannot solve the terrible problems of global warming, ozone depletion, acid rain, deforestation, and pollution by focusing on consumption, he argues. The real culprit is the mode of production. Human beings are not naturally voracious; otherwise Americans would not have to be subjected annually to $300 billion worth of advertising designed to make us consume far more than we need. The economy that we have is based upon constant "propagandizing on behalf of consumption," he remarks. The economy that we need would feature workplace democracy, social control of investment, full employment, capitalism within socialism, socialist protectionism, and economic stability and sustainability.[11]

Schweickart's version of workplace democracy is in the mainstream of economic democracy theory; something like it is a nearly universal feature of economic democracy. Essentially it is the organization of democratic governance, one of the two main structural differences between economic democracy and traditional capitalism. In workplace democracy, enterprises are democratic communities, not properties to be bought, moved to cheap labor havens, or sold. Workers elect representatives to a workers council that performs the usual functions of a shareholder-serving board of directors in corporations: appointing managers, establishing terms of employment, and approving major business decisions. Workers receive a variously designated share of the company's profit, not a fixed salary, as income, and companies compete for business in a free market. Since wages are not a cost of production in democratic enterprises, workers receive all the productivity gains of their labor.

The second key structural feature of economic democracy concerns the control of investment. Here Schweickart's socialist utopianism takes over. Real economic democracy completely severs the connection between saving and investment, he argues. Instead of relying on the hunches, desires, interests, and private savings of a capitalist class to decide how much societal investment is needed and where it should be invested, economic democracy socializes the entire business of business loans. All funds for business investment should be raised from taxes, and all private financial markets should be abolished. Individuals would be allowed to save money in savings and loan banks paying modest interest on deposits, he allows, but all funds for business investment should be raised publicly, relying on a flat-rate tax on the value of a firm's tangible property. Revenue from the property tax would be kept separate from general tax revenues and allocated to networks of regional and local banks on a regional per capita basis. Regions would not compete for capital, which eliminates the business-attracting race to the bottom between regions, though enterprises within regions would compete with one another for capital. Each region of the nation would get its fair share of the national investment fund annually; investment plans devised by local, regional, and national investment boards would be approved or revised by appropriate legislatures; and profitability would be a major criterion of success in judging the performances of public loan officers.[12]

If we took economic democracy this far, Schweickart urges, there would be no more economic crashes, because full-blown economic democracy has no stock markets, bond markets, hedge funds, private investment banks, or private financial markets of any kind. There would still be markets for goods and services, but mortgages would stay with their banks of origin and speculative financial gambling would be abolished. In his foundational work, *Capitalism or Worker Control?*, Schweickart argues that private property itself should be abolished, since owning property is socially regressive and not economically productive.[13]

But if one is going to go that far, one might as well come out for world pacifism and the abolition of selfishness. Schweickart fails to absorb that private financial markets and private property cannot be abolished in a free society. Utopian fantasies about abolishing capitalism have a poor track record, to put it mildly, though some of Schweickart's policies brush closer to the real world of actual possibilities. He argues that government should be the employer of last resort, since no market economy can guarantee full employment. He allows that anyone should be permitted to start a business and run it as she desires, but if the business exceeds a certain size, it has to be sold to the state after the entrepreneur is finished with it so that it can be converted to a cooperative. He advocates socialist protectionism: charging a tariff on goods imported from poor nations to eliminate the difference and advantage of cheaper labor costs in the exporting nations, then rebating the tariff to the government, unions, or NGOs of the exporting nation. Above all, Schweickart rightly stresses that capitalism is beset with the classic collective-action problem of individual rationality leading to collective irrationality. Because wages are a cost of production in traditional investor-owned firms, capitalist economies are vulnerable to the problem of insufficient effective demand. Every capitalist owner has a vested, rational interest in holding down the wages of her own workers. At the same time the wages of working- and middle-class earners are the major source of the economy's consumer demand. Ideally every capitalist owner would prefer to have customers with high wages who stoke sufficient demand. But the same owners have control only over their own workers, whose wages they hold down as much as possible.[14]

Economic democracy is a more stable and sustainable option. Democratic firms are committed to their own communities. The face-to-face democracy of worker-owned firms nurtures solidarity and social trust, causing them to resist reducing their ranks in economic downturns. And wages are not a cost of production in democratic firms, because worker-controlled firms are geared to maximize net income per worker, which constitute shares of the firm's profit, not wages. In democratic firms, all productivity gains go to the worker/owners that produce them. Building on these advantages would create a healthier and more humane economy, as Schweickart contends. But the way to actually build it is step-by-step, pragmatic, and contextual. It begins with expanding the cooperative sector, adds public bank models to the mix, and rejects utopian fantasies and blueprints of a new world order requiring coercion over holdouts and departures from political reality.

Economic Democracy, Democratic Realism, and Public Bank Theory

There is such a thing as a full-orbed economic democracy that works from the bottom up and does not make heroic demands on the political system or sinful human beings. It is undeniably visionary, challenging the borders of possibility and imagining new forms of social and economic organization. But it is fundamentally about creating concrete and viable new democratic choices, not imposing anybody's blueprint of a perfect system.

We need forms of social ownership that facilitate democratic capital formation and are more entrepreneurial. Specifically we need forms of economic democracy featuring public banks and mutual funded holding companies. This approach can take a variety of forms, but the essential idea is to establish competing banks or holding companies in which ownership of productive capital is vested. The companies lend capital to enterprises at market rates of interest and otherwise control the process of investment, including decision-making power to initiate new cooperatives and shut down unprofitable enterprises. Equity shareholders, the state, and/or other cooperatives own the holding companies or public banks.

The central bank at Mondragon, the Caja Laboral Populaire, a cooperative half-owned by other Mondragon cooperatives, is a prototype of this idea. It lends financial capital, monitors the performances of Mondragon's vast network of cooperatives, and finds outlets for their funds. The most ambitious experiment of this kind, thus far, was the Meidner Plan in Sweden, named after German economist Rudolf Meidner, which was enacted in 1982 by the Social Democratic government.

The Meidner Plan called for an annual 20 percent tax on major company profits to be paid in the form of stock to eight regional mutual funds. Worker, consumer, and government representatives controlled the funds, and as their proportion of stock ownership grew, these groups were collectively entitled to representation on company boards. Locals and branch funds jointly held voting rights of the employee shares. In the compromised form of the plan that was enacted by the Swedish government, a 40 percent ceiling was placed on the amount of stock that the eight funds in total could own of any single firm, and the funds were managed conventionally. True believers considered these compromises a defeat, but even with a 40 percent ceiling the Meidner Plan, if carried out, would have rendered effective control over profitable firms in Sweden to the worker and public organizations.[15]

Since the funds represented part of workers' compensation, the plan contained a built-in system of wage restraints and facilitated a new form of capital formation. It required no program of nationalization, and investors still sought the highest rate of return. Like most mutual fund or public bank models, the Meidner Plan separated risk in production from entrepreneurial risk, assigning production risks to worker-managed enterprises and entrepreneurial risks to the holding companies. Most important, it offered a way beyond the welfare state, by expanding the base of economic power, while saving the social and political gains of social democratic liberalism.

The fate of the Meidner Plan is a symbol of our time. Its original backer in Sweden was the Confederation of Swedish Trade Unions (*Landsorganisationen i Sverige*, or LO), which stressed in the mid-1970s that benefits from the capital fund should accrue to all wage earners and that the plan traded wage restraint for greater control over investment capital. Business groups howled against it, using the issue to help defeat the Social Democrats in the 1976 election, even though the Social Democrats had not yet embraced it. In 1982, when the Social Democrats regained power, they enacted a version of the Meidner Plan but made little effort to educate the public about it or to win popular support for it.

For eight years Sweden's corporate elites railed against the worker funds constantly, inveighing against their loss of control over finance. Stock markets are the home turf of financiers, a privilege that Sweden's capitalist class was not shy in defending. Managers of the worker funds, trying to legitimize themselves to the financial class, managed like ordinary fund managers, but that made the whole enterprise abstract to the general population. Princeton economist Jonas Pontusson observed that it was hard to generate popular enthusiasm "when collective shareholding funds are reduced to deciding whether to buy shares in Volvo or Saab." To stir popular support, the Social Democrats needed to back up the Meidner Plan with industrial policies targeting specific needs—things that ordinary people could see at work in their communities during the very period that Sweden's shipbuilding industry collapsed, the steel industry specialized, wood pulp was integrated into modernized paper production, and other pillars of the manufacturing base were restructured. Instead, the charter for the Meidner Plan expired in 1990 and the Social Democrats lost the 1991 election. Sweden had a frightening banking crisis in 1992, which it resolved by nationalizing the banks, and in 1994 the Social Democrats regained power as the party best suited to manage the turbulence of economic globalization and nationalized banks. They stabilized the currency, got the government's fiscal house in order, dropped the Meidner Plan, and scaled back their historic achievement, the Swedish welfare state.[16]

That option made political sense in Sweden at the outset of second-wave globalization. It may prove to be the death knell for national-scale experiments in full-orbed economic democracy. But less ambitious forms of economic democracy have succeeded in many places, and the scale question rests more on politics and culture than economic viability. Economic democracy theorists such as Raymond Plant, Alec Nove, Saul Estrin, David Miller, Joanne Barkan, Robert Dahl, and David Winter take seriously the failures of state socialism, the limitations of worker ownership, and the necessity of building up highly capitalized forms of economic democracy. The distinct advantage of the mutual fund approach is that it diversifies forms of risk sharing and promotes greater efficiency by forcing firms to be financially accountable to a broad range of investors. Essentially it is a solution to the entrepreneurial deficiencies of worker-owned firms, addressing conflicts of interest between cooperative owners and profitability that often cause cooperatives to miss market signals.

This approach does not rest on idealistic notions about human nature and should not be the next progressive blueprint. Economic democracy is a brake on human greed and domination; the whole point of it is to fight the universal propensity of dominant groups to hoard social goods and abuse disenfranchised people. Neither should progressives absolutize any particular model of economic democracy, for the blueprint mentality is inherently problematic. Socialists were wrong to equate socialization with nationalization. They were wrong to reject production for profit. They were wrong to think that state planners could replicate the complex pricing decisions of markets. They were wrong in believing that worker-owned cooperatives could organize an economy not linked by markets. Not all socialist traditions made these mistakes, but the blueprint mentality was deeply ingrained in virtually all of them.

From a democratic perspective, the key problem with the mutual fund model is that it weakens workers' power at the firm level and increases the power of the agents that invest collectively owned social capital. To the extent that the holding companies are granted supervisory control over their client enterprises, worker control is diminished. To the extent that the holding companies are kept in a weak position, the advantages of the mutual fund model are traded off as the client enterprises essentially become cooperatives. The radical democratic and communitarian impulses of economic democracy theory tend to cause its theorists to place as much control as possible in human-scale organizations in which the distance between management and workers is minimized. However, this egalitarian, community-oriented preference can be a sizable disadvantage in competing with huge, aggressive, integrated corporations that focus ruthlessly on the bottom line. Any experiment in full-orbed economic democracy has to grapple with difficult trade-offs between the responsibilities of the holding companies or public banks and the rights of worker-managed enterprises. And some economic sectors, especially those with large financing requirements, are very difficult for democratic firms of any kind.[17]

There is no unitary answer to these problems; there is only the variable and challenging work of making gains toward democratizing the factors of investment and production in particular contexts. On the control problem, I favor a circular model that is biased toward upholding the authority of the public banks or holding companies. To minimize trade-offs between democratic control and efficiency, cooperative firms become shareholders in the holding companies or public banks. At Mondragon the authority and efficiency of the Caja Laboral Populaire is indispensable. Mondragon's "second degree" cooperatives, in which cooperatives hold shares in other cooperatives, offer a useful model of circular ownership and control, one that diversifies risk and builds up new sources of investment capital.

But more important than any model or theory is the willingness to expand the social market in different ways and find out which models work best in particular circumstances. Washington Gladden believed that profit-sharing industrial partnerships would put an end to the class struggle, until he lived long enough to see otherwise. Many social gospelers shared Francis G. Peabody's conviction that cooperatives were obviously the progressive Christian solution. Walter Rauschenbusch believed that a combination of state and cooperative ownership would create a good society. William Temple developed a type of guild socialism that featured a Meidner-like plan for creating worker-controlled collective capital funds. Reinhold Niebuhr stood for radical state socialism before opting for the welfare state. Many liberationists and social ethicists have promoted "socialism" without describing what it is.

Most of this tradition wrongly operated with unitary ideas of capitalism and socialism, as though each were only one thing, culminating in the liberationist tendency to condemn "capitalism" categorically while employing "socialism" as a magic wand. The latter approach is too vague, monolithic, and evasive, but neither should social justice movements embrace any particular model or mixture of models as the next sign of the divine commonwealth. Just as it would be disastrously misguided to claim that all capitalist firms should be turned into cooperative or mutual fund enterprises, it would be equally wrong to claim that new enterprises must follow a Mondragon or Meidner model.

Decentralized, economic democracy must be a project built from the ground up, piece by piece, opening new choices, creating more democracy, building an economic order that does not rest on selfishness, consumerism, and the prerogatives of shareholders. It allows for social contracts, common goods, and ecological flourishing. It nurtures and sustains social trust, the form of social capital that no healthy society can do without. It is a project that breaks from the universalizing logic of state socialism, taking seriously that there are different kinds of capitalism. Social theorist Roberto Mangabeira Unger aptly calls for "alternative pluralisms," step-by-step constructions of alternative political and economic institutions. Abstract concepts of a monolithic "capitalism" or "market" obscure the variety of possibilities within really existing capitalism and markets, Unger stresses; "capitalism" has no necessary content but is always the product of particular historical configurations, contingencies, and struggles.[18]

The tests of any experiment in economic democracy are pragmatic. To impose something like a universal Mondragon on a capitalist society would require coercion over workers who do not want to belong to cooperatives. Today in the U.S. Pacific Northwest, some plywood workers choose employment in conventional firms over membership in the plywood cooperatives. No political economy worth building would force them into a different choice.

The issue of choice, however, is the key to the better alternative. A politics that expanded the cooperative and mutual fund sectors would give workers important new choices. The central conceit of neoclassical economics could be turned into a reality if meaningful choices were created. The neoclassical conceit is that capitalism doesn't exploit anyone, because labor employs capital as much as capital employs labor. But in the real world the owners of capital nearly always organize the factors of production. To expand the cooperative, mutual fund and other social market sectors would give choices to workers that neoclassical theory promises but does not deliver. It would begin to create a culture that is more democratic, egalitarian, cooperative, and ecologically conscious than the one we have now.[19]

The earth's ecosystem cannot sustain a U.S. American-level lifestyle for more than one-sixth of the world's population. The economy is physical. There are limits to economic growth. Global warming is melting the Arctic ice cap at a shocking pace, as well as large areas of permafrost in Alaska, Canada, and Siberia, and destroying wetlands and forests around the world. The manic logic of corporate capitalism pays little heed to communities and the environment, and none to equality, reenacting the tragedy of the commons. Corporate giants like ExxonMobil succeed as businesses and investments while treating the destructive aspects of their behavior as someone else's problem.

Better government and the struggles of a profusion of social movements are indispensable to solving these problems. So is creating a more just and ecologically sustainable economy. For thirty years one had to be a stubborn type to sail against the religion of the market. Now one only needs to be awake. If the stubborn types can seize this terrible moment as an opportunity to build a better social order, we may actually do it.

Part III

Neoconservatism and American Empire

Chapter 10

The Neoconservative Phenomenon

AMERICAN POWER AND THE WAR OF IDEOLOGY

In the early 1970s American socialist Michael Harrington and his friends at *Dissent* magazine hung the label "neoconservative" on an assortment of former liberals and leftists that had recently moved to the political right. Many of these new conservatives were bitterly attacking longtime friends who remained in the Left. Former freedom riders were condemning affirmative action and Black Power for "destroying" the Civil Rights movement. Former Socialists and Liberals were denouncing Lyndon Johnson's War on Poverty program for creating a "New Class" of parasitic bureaucrats and social workers. *Commentary* magazine was running furious assaults on antiwar, feminist, and environmental causes it previously supported. The phenomenon seemed worth naming, especially as an act of dissociation.

Many of the neoconservatives had, until recently, been Harrington's comrades in the Socialist Party; some called themselves Socialists for Nixon. Others were old liberals (some of them former Socialists) who hated what liberalism had become since the mid-1960s. The socialist group included veteran old leftists Arnold Beichman, Sidney Hook, Emanuel Muravchik, Arch Puddington, John Roche, and Max Shachtman, plus younger activists Tom Kahn, Rochelle Horowitz, and Joshua Muravchik. The liberal group included political figures and intellectuals Daniel Bell, Nathan Glazer, Henry Jackson, Max Kampelman, Jeane Kirkpatrick, Irving Kristol, Daniel Patrick Moynihan, and Ben Wattenberg. A few refugees from the New Left, notably Richard John Neuhaus, Michael Novak, and Norman Podhoretz, also migrated to the neoconservative camp, as did politically homeless conservatives Peter Berger and James Q. Wilson.

Most of the neoconservatives supported America's war in Vietnam, but, more important, all were repulsed by America's antiwar movement. To them it was appalling that the party of Harry Truman and John Kennedy nominated George McGovern for president in 1972. The neoconservatives had long battled the pinkish-liberal, anti–anticommunist wing of the Democratic Party; now they protested that something even worse had overtaken the party, which they called "McGovernism." McGovernism stood for appeasement and the politics of liberal guilt, whereas good liberalism stood for an aggressive, patriotic Americanism that fought communism wherever it spread.

The neoconservatives were deeply alienated from what they called the "liberal intelligentsia" and the "fashionable liberal elite." To them, the only American liberalism deserving of the name was nationalistic and fiercely anticommunist. It prized patriotic values sneered at by the liberal elite. Often the neoconservatives protested that they had not changed; they were not the ones that needed to be renamed. It was liberalism that had changed, having been perverted by the social movements of the sixties. Harrington and the *Dissent* Socialists had changed, too, selling out the cause of socialist anticommunism. Worse yet, Harrington's group had done it to win over the New Left children of the sixties, who had reduced liberalism to guilt-breeding, antiwar, anti-American idealism.[1]

Harrington and his friends sought to make clear that a parting of ways had occurred. They were no longer associated with the neoconservatives. In the wake of McGovern's crushing electoral defeat the Socialist Party had imploded, the Old Left launched a new organization called Social Democrats USA, Harrington formed a new organization called the Democratic Socialist Organizing Committee, and the cold war liberals founded the Coalition for a Democratic Majority to take back the Democratic Party from McGovernism. Harrington wanted to convert the McGovern liberals to democratic socialism. Ten years earlier his emotional and ideological ties to Old Left anticommunism had alienated the youthful leaders of the New Left; now he envisioned a party-realigning coalition of baby boom liberals and progressive Social Democrats.[2]

But first he had to excommunicate his rightward-moving former comrades from the Left, partly to establish his separation from them. By calling them "neoconservatives," he implied that the old Social Democrats were not the right wing of the Left, but the left wing of the Right. The difference was crucial, as the labeled party keenly understood. At first the neoconservatives objected that they had nothing in common with American conservatives. Many of them didn't know any conservatives personally. To them conservatives were country clubbers, reactionaries, racists, and Republicans, nothing like cold war Democrats or tough Social Democrats.

In addition to being militantly anticommunist, nationalistic, repulsed by the new social movements, and rooted personally in the American Left, the neoconservatives supported democratic rule by elites and, unlike most conservatives, lacked conservative nostalgia. They did not yearn for medieval Christendom, Tory England, the Old South, or Gilded Age capitalism. The neoconservatives were modernists, longtime supporters of the Civil Rights movement, comfortable with a minimal welfare state, and schooled in the social sciences. Many were New York Jews who shuddered at the anti-Semitism and xenophobia of the Old Right. They may have voted for Richard Nixon but only because the Democratic Party had lost its bearings and the Socialists had stopped running presidential candidates. Calling them conservatives of any kind was insulting.

But the name stuck because they were changing more than they acknowledged. Despite lacking conservative friends, the neoconservatives went on to align themselves with the political Right and make it more like themselves. Having begun as a reaction against the antiwar and social movements of the 1960s, neoconservatism gradually shifted to the right on economics, too. Two journals stood at the center of the neocon reaction: *The Public Interest*, founded by coeditors Irving Kristol and Daniel Bell in 1965, which debunked liberal dreams of a big-government Great Society, and *Commentary*, the flagship of the American Jewish Committee edited by Norman Podhoretz, which Podhoretz turned sharply to the right in 1970.

Kristol regarded himself as a "neoliberal" like Reinhold Niebuhr and literary critic Lionel Trilling, not a conservative. In the 1950s he blasted squishy liberals for abetting the communist conspiracy, notoriously suggesting that Joseph McCarthy was more loyal to America than most liberals. By the mid-1960s he believed that liberals were equally naïve about eradicating poverty. He and Bell, judging that government policymakers were operating with a shortage of hard information, founded *The Public Interest* as an antidote to idealistic social engineering.[3]

Harrington's celebrated *The Other America* was Example A of what they were against. Relying on personal anecdotes and a strong moral argument in a field lacking hard information, Harrington called for massive government efforts to eliminate poverty. *The Public Interest* was decidedly more cautious, quantitative, and skeptical. Bell's recent work with the Commission for the Study of Automation had convinced him that the social policy field was producing "a lot of sloppy thinking." Kristol reasoned that the best research was not getting filtered to government policymakers; Bell stressed that the academy needed to produce better research; together they stood against a rising tide of social idealism, declaring that *The Public Interest* was willing to appear "a middle-aged magazine for middle-aged readers." At the beginning, however, they had no concept of launching a new kind of conservatism; years later Kristol recalled: "Conservatism in the United States at that time was represented by the Goldwater campaign against the New Deal, with which none of us had any sympathy, and by *National Review*, which we regarded as too right-wing. We considered ourselves to be realistic meliorists, skeptical of government programs that ignored history and experience in favor of then-fashionable ideas spawned by the academy."[4]

The wet-blanket empiricist phase of the neoconservative reaction was a brief affair, however, for neoconservatism was rooted in a long tradition of ideological combat, and it became politically powerful as a new species of hard-line Republican ideology. The roots of neoconservatism went back to the American Left's fractious debates over Stalinism in the 1930s, where Big Thinking polemics about where history was going prevailed. America's first anticommunist intellectual movement was fashioned by New York Socialists later fabled as the "New York intellectuals." *Partisan Review*, a communist journal, became home base for the New York intellectuals after William Phillips and Philip Rahv, in 1937, turned it into an independent Marxist forum. The new *Partisan Review* blended anti-Stalinist politics and modernist aestheticism, featuring Rahv, Sidney Hook, James Burnham, Lionel Trilling, Diana Trilling, and Lionel Abel. A second group of New York intellectuals was younger by ten to fifteen years; it included William Barrett, Irving Howe, Irving Kristol, Alfred Kazin, and Delmore Schwartz. A third generation subsequently included Hilton Kramer, Steven Marcus, and Norman Podhoretz. The New York intellectuals were deeply politicized thinkers who believed in the social and political power of ideas. Though some were trained in the social sciences, they did not allow deterministic social scientific analyses to quell their belief that powerful ideas could change the world—a faith that later gave them considerable advantages over liberal academics in the political realm. Adept at launching magazines, especially when their politics changed, they scattered across the map politically but always with a style that reflected their background in the Old Left.[5]

The Public Interest was the first venue of the neoconservative reaction. It warned that social engineering often had predictable bad consequences and worse unanticipated ones. Nathan Glazer, Edward C. Banfield, Roger Starr, and Aaron Wildavsky sharply criticized Great Society housing and welfare policies; James Q. Wilson censured liberal strategies to overcome racism; in 1967 Daniel Patrick Moynihan judged that the war on poverty was faring as badly as America's war in Vietnam. The following year John H. Bunzel inveighed against black studies. In the name of promoting equal opportunity—a liberal ideal—*The Public Interest* warned that a bad mutation of liberalism was breeding dependency in the welfare class, legitimizing reverse racism through affirmative action, impeding America's economic growth, and creating a vast "New Class" of parasitic public-sector functionaries.[6]

At first the neoconservatives made a point of distinguishing their critiques from standard fare on the right, contending that they were social scientists, not ideologues. They opposed social engineering only if the evidence weighed against it, not because they opposed government programs on principle. But by 1970 the difference was already blurred. *The Public Interest* increasingly took on a movement character, blasting social justice as a goal of government policy. Kristol later recalled that the rise of the antiwar counterculture drove his group to draw lines and make unexpected alliances: "Suddenly we discovered that we had been cultural conservatives all along. Now, we had to decide what we were for, and why. Cool criticism of the prevailing liberal-left orthodoxy was not enough at a time when liberalism itself was crumbling before the resurgent Left."[7]

Many others joined the neoconservative reaction. In the early 1960s Podhoretz featured New Left writers in *Commentary* magazine, but he had second thoughts after American youths chanted slogans against their country. His generation of Jewish New Yorkers had struggled to assimilate to American society and to be accepted as "Americans" not requiring a hyphen. It galled him when a slightly younger generation denounced America in the streets. By 1970 Podhoretz was embarrassed to have encouraged the antiwar movement and counterculture.[8] In his telling, he tried to return to the liberal anticommunist establishment of the 1950s, only to find that it no longer existed. The old "Vital Center" liberals had lost their will and coherence. Arthur Schlesinger Jr. and John Kenneth Galbraith accommodated feminism, Black Power, and other radicalisms, while the fiasco in

Vietnam and a burgeoning antiwar movement sapped the will of liberals to fight communism anywhere. Podhoretz lurched to the right in reaction, setting *Commentary* against the progeny of the New Left.[9]

He drew an ideological line on issues that the magazine had previously debated freely. The new *Commentary* was defiant, aggressive, and often harsh, specializing in personal attacks on former friends. Samuel McCracken blasted the new academic leftism, Dorothy Rabinowitz took aim at activist professors and clergy, Midge Decter and Arlene Croce contended that feminism was destructive to American families and society, and Kristol skewered the liberal "religion of democracy." A bit later Jeane Kirkpatrick denounced the politics of "McGovernism," and Michael Novak condemned the moralistic hypocrisy of the New Class. Podhoretz later explained that his writers enjoyed a crucial advantage over *National Review* conservatives in their polemics against the Left: "We knew what they really thought and felt, which did not always coincide with what they considered it expedient to say in public; and we knew how to penetrate their self-protective rhetoric." The new conservatives stressed that all the new social movements had an anti-American core.[10]

It helped that many neoconservatives were veterans of the struggle in the 1930s to drive Communists out of the unions, which was fought with guns and clubs. The neocons brought a highly developed sense of politics as polemical tournament to the fight against a rising counterculture progressivism. Kristol put it vividly:

> The neoconservatives are the political intellectuals, and that's what the Trotskyists were. The Trotskyist movement produced political intellectuals, which is why so many went into sociology and achieved distinction. It was much more rigorous intellectual training than you could get in college. If someone came up with some matter on which you were not well read, my God, you were humiliated. It was Jesuitical. The Republican Party, meanwhile, produced antipolitical intellectuals. Those people are not in my tradition.[11]

Reviving standard tropes of the Old Left, neoconservatives railed against the "New Class" of government functionaries, contended that ideology trumped everything else in the struggle against communism, and insisted that communist ideology had huge advantages over liberal democracy. In the early 1970s they urged that it was not too late for the Democratic Party to regain its self-respect and anticommunist militancy;

otherwise the U.S. would lose the struggle for the world. In their telling, the Soviet Union was preparing to fight and win a nuclear war against a cowardly America that feared the Soviet Union too much to resist it. Neocons opposed the Strategic Arms Limitation Treaty because they opposed détente; arms control agreements and Henry Kissinger-style diplomacy merely helped the Soviet Union stabilize its empire. To revive the fervently anticommunist wing of the Democratic Party, most neocons supported Henry Jackson in the 1976 presidential primaries, and in March 1976 they founded the Committee on the Present Danger (CPD) to warn that Kissingerian coexistence had dangerously weakened the United States.[12]

The Committee on the Present Danger, which included Republican hard-liners Richard Allen and William Casey in addition to Democratic neocons Norman Podhoretz, Richard Perle, and Max Kampelman, became the vehicle of the neocons' entry into the Republican Right. It blasted President Gerald Ford, a pure conservative, for kowtowing to Kissinger and weakening American power. Ford, desperate to appease his far-right critics and facing a primary challenge from Ronald Reagan for the Republican nomination, responded by appointing three groups of hard-liners to evaluate the CIA's recent National Intelligence Estimates.

One group analyzed Soviet low-altitude air defense capabilities; another studied the accuracy of Soviet intercontinental ballistic missiles (ICBMs); a third group focused on Soviet strategic objectives. All three groups were collectively named "Team B," but group 3 alone stirred a huge controversy, thus earning the name exclusively. Chaired by Harvard historian Richard Pipes, the group included political scientist William R. Van Cleave, retired army lieutenant general Daniel O. Graham (a former head of the Defense Intelligence Agency), retired air force general John Vogt, Air Force Major General Jasper Welch, Ambassador Foy Kohler, Ambassador Seymour Weiss, Rand analyst Thomas Wolfe, neocon heavyweight Paul Nitze, and neocon upcomer Paul Wolfowitz. It met during September and October 1976, issued its report in December after Jimmy Carter had been elected president, and warned that American intelligence analysts failed to grasp that the Soviets sought to fight and win a nuclear war, not to deter one.[13]

According to Team B, Soviet leaders did not distinguish between war and peace, confrontation and détente, offense and defense, strategic and peripheral, or nuclear and conventional war. Since the Soviets did not regard nuclear war as an unthinkable evil, they were not deterred by a so-called balance of terror. The CIA routinely overemphasized hard data about Soviet capabilities and ignored the Soviet objective of conquering the world. This was a terrible mistake, and a lazy one, Team B warned. The American intelligence community, taking for granted that Russians and Americans shared the same fear of nuclear war, specialized in perfectly wrong examples of "mirror-imaging." In Team B's view, Soviet and American leaders differed radically. American society was commercial, democratic, and insular. It assumed that peace and profit seeking were normal, war was an aberration, human nature was the same everywhere in the world, social equality was natural, the military was a marginal factor in politics, and using weapons of mass destruction was "something entirely outside the norms of policy." But in fact, the hard-liners asserted, this outlook was sui generis. No nation in the world shared the American worldview, yet American intelligence analysts projected their beliefs onto the Soviets. The real Soviet enemy was a giant conglomerate that fused its military, political, and economic institutions into a single arsenal of power, "all administered by the same body of men and all usable for purposes of persuasion and coercion."[14]

By this reading, CIA officials consistently missed the point, underestimating the ideological component of Soviet policy and the monolithic nature of the Soviet system. They assumed that Soviet nuclear strategy was defensive because they could not imagine assuming anything else. To American leaders, the Strategic Arms Limitation Treaty (SALT) of 1972 (which froze nuclear arsenals at current levels) was a big deal, but to Soviet leaders it was "a minor sideshow" that had little effect on their drive for world dominion. Team B warned that when Soviet leaders looked at American society, they liked their odds of success: "A population addicted to the pursuit of consumer goods rapidly loses its sense of patriotism, sinking into a mood of self-indulgence that makes it extremely poor material for national mobilization."[15]

Team B persistently described the worst possible case as the reality. It projected that by 1984 the Soviets would have 500 Backfire bombers; in fact, the Soviets built 235. It predicted that by 1985 the Soviets would have replaced 90 percent of their long-range bombers and missiles; in fact, they replaced less than 60 percent of their long-range force. It warned that a test site for nuclear-powered rocket engines was developing nuclear-powered beam weapons; in fact, this claim wildly overestimated Soviet capabilities. It charged that the CIA ignored "an intense military buildup in nuclear as well as conventional forces of all sorts, not moderated either by the West's self-imposed restraints or by SALT"; in fact, the rate of growth in Soviet military spending slowed in the mid-1970s and was flat for the next decade. Some parts of the report, especially Wolfowitz's section on mobile missiles, were not so alarmist, but even Wolfowitz warned that the CIA was too sanguine about the Soviet SS-20 force, overlooking that it might be upgraded to intercontinental capability and that SS-X-16s could be concealed and launched from mobile launchers. Wolfowitz cautioned that the latter fact posed "a serious potential threat" that the CIA had barely begun to address.[16]

According to Team B, Americans used force only reluctantly as an occasionally necessary departure from normal life, but Soviet leaders embraced and admired force: "The Soviet Union, to an extent inconceivable to the average Westerner, relies on force as a standard instrument of policy. . . . Militarism is deeply ingrained in the Soviet system and plays a central role in the mentality of its elite." Admittedly, during the Khrushchev years, Soviet leaders may have flirted with "Western concepts of deterrence," but that was only because the U.S. had strategic superiority at the time. By 1976 the Soviets no longer doubted their capacity to achieve clear superiority. They placed a high priority "on the attainment of a superiority that would deny the U.S. effective retaliatory options against a nuclear attack." Team B did not spell out what the latter statement meant; it lacked a consensus on what strategic superiority was actually good for. Some neocons worried that Pipes communicated a stronger hatred of Russia than of communism. But with commanding self-assurance, Pipes and his colleagues pictured the Soviet enemy as a towering dynamo that not unreasonably believed it would conquer the world.[17]

Team B and the CIA were both wildly wrong about the crumbling Soviet economy. The burden of superpower-level military spending on the Soviet Union was much greater than was recognized by the CIA or its hard-line critics, and eventually it destroyed the Soviet system. In December 1976 the Team B report was both dead on arrival and the basis of a powerful political reaction. Confined to classified secrecy, it had no public life and was rejected by the incoming president Jimmy Carter. A month before his inauguration, Carter indicated that he might replace George H. W. Bush as CIA director; Bush responded by leaking the existence of the Team B report to the *New York Times* and discussing it on *Meet the Press*. That gave the neocons the public exposure and uproar they wanted, lighting the fuse of a controversy that simmered throughout Carter's presidency.[18]

To the neocons, the chief arguments of Team B (which remained classified until 1992) were factual imperatives. They lobbied hard for positions in Carter's administration, presenting Carter with a list of sixty names headed by Jeane Kirkpatrick, Max Kampelman, and Richard Perle. Carter gave them one position, special negotiator for Micronesia. The neocons turned on him furiously, using the Team B report as a political weapon. *Commentary* led the charge for an aggressive foreign policy. Richard Pipes, Edward Luttwak and Walter Laqueur warned that Soviet military strength was superior to America's and that Soviet communism was winning the struggle for the world. New *Commentary* writers Robert Jastrow, Patrick Glynn, and Angelo Codevilla made the case for a massive nuclear rearmament leading to strategic superiority.[19]

The key figure was Pipes, who began to write for *Commentary* during Carter's first year in office. For fifteen years Pipes pleaded for the declassification of the Team B report; in the meantime he reprised its themes and spelled out its vision of a Soviet nuclear victory. Pipes insisted that because the Soviets did not believe in nuclear deterrence, Americans were foolish to believe in it. Unlike the United States, which relied on countervalue deterrence (targeting Soviet cities), the Soviets built land-based counterforce missiles to launch a first strike on America's counterforce arsenal. Americans thought that threatening to incinerate tens of millions of people constituted an ample deterrent, Pipes observed, but Soviet leaders did not think that way. They did not share the "middle-class, commercial, essentially Protestant" notion that nuclear weapons were primarily useful for their deterrent value. America's Protestantized governing elites assumed that resorting to force was a sign of weakness or failure, but Soviet leaders were Russians who admired force and domination. To a Russian, Pipes explained, failing to use force revealed a fatal inner weakness.[20]

American and Soviet nuclear doctrines differed accordingly. Soviet rulers did not place nuclear weapons in a separate category or assume that the main reason to possess them was to prevent nuclear war. They sought to build a superior counterforce arsenal because they believed that a surprise counterforce attack would lead to a successful nuclear war. The Soviets sought "not deterrence but victory, not sufficiency in weapons but superiority, not retaliation but offensive action." American defense strategists were reluctant to adopt the Soviet view, or even to accept that the Soviets subscribed to it, because it was alien "to their experience and view of human nature." For Pipes, the chief threat to American security lay in this reluctance.[21]

He did not deny that even a fantastically successful Soviet attack would leave part of America's counterforce arsenal intact, as well as thousands of submarine-based countervalue missiles. To obliterate every city in the Soviet Union, the United States would need fewer than three hundred of its ten thousand countervalue missiles. Assuming even the most horribly imaginable attack, the United States would retain enough nuclear overkill capacity to incinerate the Soviet population more than thirty times over.

But that wasn't enough to deter Russian Communists. Because the United States overemphasized the retaliatory capacity of its countervalue arsenal, it tempted the Soviets to launch a surprise attack. They were seriously tempted, Pipes claimed, because they were fully prepared to accept tens of millions of casualties to win a nuclear war. Having lost tens of millions in World War II, the loss of forty million more in World War III was a tolerable prospect. The American squeamishness about committing nuclear genocide was precisely what made a Soviet nuclear attack conceivable. American officials would have approximately thirty minutes to retaliate with their own counterforce missiles. The Soviets had to assume that millions of citizens living near the silos along the trans-Siberian railway would be killed.

Their next assumption was the crucial one. Soviet leaders counted on America's unwillingness to take the next step, initiating countervalue warfare. Though the Soviets were prepared to sustain massive losses, they knew that an all-out countervalue war would incinerate both countries. Their wager, Pipes contended, was that nuclear war would not go that far. A successful Soviet attack would leave America with the choice of launching its countervalue missiles or submitting to a Soviet dictat.[22]

This was the ultimate Present Danger, which rested on highly dubious claims about the feasibility of a successful first strike—an attack covering thousands of miles in the teeth of winds, rough weather, and gravitational fields. *Commentary* and the Committee on the Present Danger argued for the MX missile and, later, the Strategic Defense Initiative on the basis of this supposed danger. Pipes was right in believing that the most important issue was personal, but he avoided the most important part of it. In his portrait, Soviet leaders were so depraved that the deaths of tens of millions of Soviet citizens meant nothing to them and fighting an all-out counterforce war was a serious temptation. Neoconservatives failed to explain why Soviet leaders would not become more likely to start a nuclear war if they saw the U.S. building toward strategic superiority.[23]

The insecurity of Soviet leaders would have presumably heightened at the spectacle of an American government that did not believe in deterrence. Neoconservatives also failed to explain why a Soviet counter-force strike would leave the United States and its allies with only two (suicidal) options. Even with forty million dead and the loss of most of its counterforce arsenal, the U.S. would have retained thousands of countervalue missiles, its military forces, its superior industrial capacity, its remaining counterforce arsenal, and its network of highly armed and technologically advanced allies. A Soviet attack would have provoked the combined force of this economically and technologically superior alliance in a protracted conventional war, backed by the threat of countervalue nuclear strikes. Neoconservatives insisted that Soviet leaders regarded this as a tempting prospect. A "window of vulnerability" invited Soviet leaders to launch a suicidal attack. What neoconservatives ultimately failed to explain was how *any* defense strategy would have worked if Soviet leaders were so thoroughly depraved.

The Team B episode vividly displayed the political power of alarmism. It paved the way for neoconservatives to join the Reagan Right and gave them a Scripture-like basis for attacking Carter's foreign policy, making "Carterism" an epithet. In a speech at Notre Dame, Carter announced that Americans were overcoming their "inordinate fear of communism." Podhoretz replied that Carter epitomized the stupidity and corrupted spirit of America's "culture of appeasement." Using virtually the same words that *National Review* pundit James Burnham, a former Trotskyist, had employed since the late 1940s to shame American politicians, Podhoretz charged that American leaders surrendered to Soviet power because they secretly feared it, cowering before a superior Soviet enemy.[24]

This reading of America's situation and its stigmatizing rhetoric of "appeasement" and "Finlandization" had little place in the Democratic Party, but it perfectly suited Ronald Reagan, who stocked his foreign policy team with neoconservatives. In 1979, after the Soviet Union invaded Afghanistan, Carter dramatically increased U.S. military spending, but by then most neocons had given up on the Democrats. Carter authorized a 5 percent increase in military spending for 1981, and Congress authorized an additional 4 percent increase; neocons replied that enhanced firepower would be wasted if Carter were reelected. They had found a presidential candidate who understood that America was losing the cold war. Attracted by Reagan's candidacy and the hope that he would "take the fight to the Soviets," neocons streamed into the Republican Party for the 1980 election. By then they had embraced Harrington's name for them, which legitimized their Republican standing.

The neoconservatives had come to the Right by conversion, not in-heritance. With the passion of converts they urged Reagan to heap new spending increases on top of Carter's escalated military budget, thus cre-ating what Reagan's Office of Management and Budget director David Stockman later called "the giant fiscal syllogism" that doubled American military spending in five years. Neocons assured Reagan that Republican conservatives weren't much better than Democrats at fighting commu-nism, because standard-issue Republican conservatives lacked the requi-site smarts and aggressiveness for the job. To take the fight to the Soviets and clean up American culture, Reagan needed to load his administration with neoconservatives.[25]

The neocons were stunningly successful in this venture, which infu-riated many old-style conservatives that were pushed aside. Thirty-two members of the Committee on the Present Danger were appointed to high-ranking foreign policy positions, including neocon stalwarts Max Kampelman, Jeane Kirkpatrick, Elliott Abrams, Richard Perle, Eugene Rostow, Kenneth Adelman, Frank Gaffney, and Richard Pipes. William Bennett, Chester Finn, William Kristol, Linda Chavez and other neocons were appointed to domestic policy offices. *The New Republic* warned half-seriously that "Trotsky's orphans" had taken over the government. Neoconservatives provided the intellectual ballast for Reagan's military build-up and his anticommunist foreign policy, especially his maneuvers in Central America.[26]

They were the last true believers in Communism. In the mid-1980s neo-conservatives brushed aside any suggestion that the Soviet economy was disintegrating, that dissident movements in the Soviet bloc revealed cracks in the Soviet empire, or that Mikhail Gorbachev's reforms should be taken seriously. For them, the absolute domestic power of the Communist party and the communist duty to create a communist world order precluded the possibility of actual change anywhere in the Soviet bloc. Neocons insisted that Communist totalitarianism gave the Soviets immense advantages in struggling for global hegemony and that the Soviets were winning the cold war in every way that mattered. They wanted Reagan to push back aggressively; instead he disappointed them.

Despite his militant speeches, skyrocketing military expenditures, and neocon appointments, Reagan governed as though he didn't really believe the U.S. was losing the cold war. His invasions were tiny and inconsequen-tial, and he relied on surrogates to fight communism in Central America. Neocons complained that instead of pushing back, Reagan seemed to take seriously the realist portrayal of the Soviet Union as a competing super-power wracked by internal problems. Though he opposed all previous arms control agreements, Reagan waxed with alarming enthusiasm about the hope of eliminating entire classes of nuclear weapons.[27]

To the neocons, the U.S. was in grave danger. Against conservative re-alists, they insisted that conventional foreign policy factors were trivial compared to the cold war struggle for the world. To conceive the Soviet Union as a competing superpower was to undermine America's will and capacity to *fight* communism. The Nixon, Ford, and Carter administra-tions had disastrously undermined America's life or death mission. The U.S. needed a courageously ideological leader who recognized the impla-cable hostility of the Soviet state and faced up to the necessity of making life intolerable for it. Reagan officials Adelman, Perle, Gaffney, Pipes and Rostow pushed hard on this theme, while Perle and Defense Secretary Casper Weinberger coped with Reagan's disarmament-utopian streak by fashioning a "zero-option" policy that Perle considered bizarre. Mean-while *Commentary* and other neocon journals railed that the struggle for the world was being lost.[28]

Neocons invoked the doctrine of totalitarianism as an article of faith. It taught that the Soviet system had immense competitive advan-tages over democracies by virtue of not being a democracy and that Soviet power was invulnerable to internal challenges. The Soviet state was a fearsome monolith that surpassed the United States in military power and global ambition. Repeatedly *Commentary* blasted the cul-ture of appeasement that called for a nuclear freeze and refused to fight communism in Central America. Podhoretz heaped scorn on antiwar church leaders, gay and lesbian pacifists, and liberal politicians; he also attacked big business appeasers who wanted to do business with the So-viets, complaining that Reagan was too solicitous of the capitalist class to fight the Soviet Union. In his rendering, liberal church leaders and politicians were cowardly moralists and fools, homosexuals opposed war out of their lust for "helpless, good-looking boys," and the capitalist class perversely sold Soviet leaders the rope that would be used to hang America.[29]

Podhoretz charged that the new peace activists were motivated by fear, which made them more loathsome than the fellow traveling dupes of an earlier generation who actually liked the Soviet Union, or at least their fantasy of it. The new pacifists felt no attraction to the Soviet Union, he explained; they were simply terrified of it and lacked the courage to resist it. The new movements for nuclear arms control and disarmament were fueled by the cowardly fear that the evils of war outweighed the worth of any objective for which a war might be fought. But sadly, even Reagan had no stomach for actually fighting communism; thus, everywhere he was losing the cold war.

Podhoretz's disappointment in Reagan turned to outright contempt during Reagan's second term. In 1985 he complained that Reagan was repeating the worst mistakes of his predecessors. Reagan's emerging arms control agreement was a throwback to the Basic Principles of Detente of 1972; his approach to Central America resembled the ill-fated resolution of the 1962 Cuban missile crisis; his approach to Nicaragua, in particular, recycled the disastrous 1962 Declaration on the Neutrality of Laos, which called for the withdrawal of all foreign troops from the area. A truly anticommunist president would have crushed the Nicaraguan Sandinistas and Salvadoran guerrillas, Podhoretz admonished, but Reagan played political games with them. Podhoretz warned that if Reagan continued down this road in his second term, he would cruelly disappoint those who had believed in his commitment to fight communism.[30]

In Reagan's second term, the titles of Podhoretz's articles told the story of his bitter disappointment: "Reagan: A Case of Mistaken Identity," "How Reagan Succeeds as a Carter Clone," and most plaintively, "What If Reagan Were President?" When Gorbachev surprisingly accepted the zero option proposal and Reagan agreed to take yes for an answer, Podhoretz thundered that Reagan betrayed the cause of anticommunism. He was incredulous that Reagan bought the "single greatest lie of our time," that arms control served the ends of peace and security. In 1986 Reagan traded a Soviet spy for the release of an American journalist; Podhoretz protested that Reagan "shamed himself and the country" because of his "craven eagerness" for an arms agreement with Gorbachev. The culture of appeasement was winning. By playing on the fear of war, Podhoretz claimed, the culture of appeasement turned even Ronald Reagan into a servant of the Big Lie.[31]

Some neocons resisted this verdict, gamely relieving Reagan of responsibility for the foreign policies of his administration. Under the slogan, "let Reagan be Reagan," they blamed a series of Reagan officials—Alexander Haig, James Baker, Michael Deaver, and finally George Schultz—for pushing Reagan toward a policy of "Finlandizing" appeasement. Some of them also blamed Nancy Reagan. But Podhoretz spurned these pious evasions. The Reagan administration was craven and foolish because that was Reagan's character, he charged. The real Reagan was not the courageous anticommunist of Reagan speeches, but a vain politician whose greed for popularity drove him into the arms of the Soviets. Reaching for the ultimate insult, in 1986 Podhoretz desperately announced that Reagan had become a Carter clone. But while poor Carter never got away with being Carter, he complained, it seemed that Reagan would get away with it. The only hope for his administration was for Reaganites to stop ganging up on scapegoats like Shultz and vent their rage at Reagan himself: "Maybe if they did, the President would think twice before betraying them and his own ideas again."[32]

To Podhoretz, Gaffney, Michael Ledeen, and other hard-line neocons, America stood in greater danger than ever before, because it faced a Soviet leader who had figured out how to strengthen the Soviet empire and disarm the West. Gorbachev was a cunning Leninist who seduced America into lowering its guard. He softened up Western opinion by making the world less afraid of the Soviet Union. Neocons relied on the doctrine of totalitarianism to explain what was happening. The twin pillars of communism were the absolute domestic power of the Communist Party and the duty to create a communist international order. It was absurd to believe that any Soviet leader would try to democratize the Soviet system or curb its drive for world domination. Just as Lenin loosened economic restraints during the 1920s to impede an economic collapse, Gorbachev opened the Soviet system just enough to entice Western aid and save his totalitarian structure.[33]

The neocons debated whether Gorbachev had found a cunning way to disarm America. Near the end of Reagan's first term the zero-option, a Machiavellian stratagem that synthesized Reagan's peculiar combination of beliefs, became the centerpiece of the debate. In his entire career Reagan had never supported an arms control agreement. He opposed the Limited Test Ban Treaty of 1963, the Non-Proliferation Treaty of 1968, the SALT I agreement and ABM Treaty of 1972, the Peaceful Nuclear Explosions Treaty of 1976, and the SALT II agreement of 1979. But he insisted to Perle and Weinberger that he believed in arms control agreements that abolished entire classes or deployments of nuclear weapons; thus they devised the zero option.

Perle assumed that the Soviets would never remove actual missiles in return for a promise not to install weapons that were still in production. Though Perle was widely believed to oppose arms control in principle, he denied it when pressed on the question. He told aides that because arms negotiations lulled Americans into complacency, they were harmful to American interests; the only merit of arms control was its propaganda value. At the same time he was the chief arms control policymaker for a president who claimed to support real disarmament. In public, at least, Perle professed to agree with the president. The trick was to indulge Reagan's utopian side and get the propaganda value of pursuing arms control while pursuing military superiority. The zero option set the model for Reagan's novel blend of hard-line militarism and utopian disarmament, which bewildered conservatives, liberals, American allies, and American critics alike.[34]

The sheer strangeness of Perle's situation attracted ample notice during Reagan's first term. Shortly after he joined the administration Perle told an interviewer, "It's not in our interests to sign agreements that do not entail a significant improvement in the strategic balance." Since Perle did not expect the Soviets to sign agreements that damaged their strategic position, the implication was that no agreement was conceivable. Critics protested that Perle's "significant improvement" principle guaranteed that the arms race would continue. In 1983 Perle observed to a special panel of the House Armed Services Committee that "it has become commonplace for the Administration's critics to accuse it of a lack of seriousness about arms control." He complained that according to the conventional wisdom, the "good guys" who supported arms control were blocked by "bad guys" led by himself "who are secretly opposed to arms control and block it at every turn but go through the motions in a false show of seriousness." By various turns Perle reinforced and denounced this image of him while waiting for a stable Soviet leadership with which he might at least make a show of pursuing arms control.[35]

The Reagan administration had begun just as the Soviet economy and the Brezhnev generation of Soviet leaders began to expire. Leonid Brezhnev died in November 1982; his successor Yuri Andropov died in February 1984; his successor Konstantin Chernenko died in March 1985. Later in 1985, while Reagan prepared to meet Mikhail Gorbachev, he quipped that he had always been willing to negotiate with Soviet leaders but they "kept dying on me." Reagan's eagerness to negotiate with Gorbachev surprised many Americans and horrified his right flank, which smelled a Soviet ruse to disarm the U.S. After Gorbachev took office, Perle had to take an unlikely "yes" for an answer on the zero option, though Gorbachev bargained for concessions on the strategic defense initiative, Soviet SS-20s in Asia, counting British and French nuclear weapons, and on-site verification. Gorbachev feared the deployment of American Pershing II missiles in Europe, which could hit Soviet targets very quickly, and Soviet leaders were frightened that the U.S. might be capable of building an effective missile defense system. But after two years of stalling Gorbachev relinquished all the Soviet Union's "non-negotiable" positions, accepting Perle's zero option of 1981. In 1987 Perle resigned from the government; later that year the Intermediate Nuclear Forces Treaty was signed; and on January 20, 1989, the day that Reagan left the White House, he declared to the great discomfort of cold war hard-liners and the incoming Bush administration: "The Cold War is over."[36]

Neoconservative and conservative hard-liners were glad to see him leave. During Reagan's last years in office, while Podhoretz accused him of betraying anticommunism, conservative columnist William Safire acidly remarked that Reagan "professed to see in Mr. Gorbachev's eyes an end to the Soviet goal of world dominance." Conservative columnist George Will was harsher: "How wildly wrong he is about what is happening in Moscow . . . Reagan has accelerated the moral disarmament of the West—actual disarmament will follow—by elevating wishful thinking to the status of political philosophy." Reagan's successor, George H. W. Bush, did not like the neocons; he especially hated their leaking against Reagan's policies and ideological bullying. Thus he gave them only a handful of positions. But Bush also tried to live down Reagan's parting declaration, spending the first year of his administration denying that the cold war was over. After things turned out differently than everyone expected, Perle commented on the ironic legacy of his career, explaining that Reagan's policy was concocted by taking the worst parts of contradictory options and fusing them "into a single, incoherent proposal." Since Perle was usually credited with inventing the zero option, he could afford to be jocular about it. Weinberger wanted history to be remembered differently: "My memory is that Richard was able to conceal quite well any enthusiasm he may have felt for my idea. Later, however, he supported it loyally and effectively."[37]

The early Bush Administration, dominated by conservative realists, was a chilly workplace for its handful of neocons and hard-line conservatives. Defense Secretary Dick Cheney, an old-style conservative, and his policy chief Paul Wolfowitz lost argument after argument within the administration, contending for cold war militancy. Neocon columnist Charles Krauthammer, while doubting that Gorbachev had suckered the West, pined for

American leaders who matched Gorbachev's commanding skills. Podhoretz and Gaffney implored that America was losing the cold war because Gorbachev seduced Reagan and Bush to stop fighting it. The doctrine of totalitarianism taught that Soviet leaders were not free to assess the national interest. Thus it was inconceivable that Gorbachev would undermine the basis of his rule by actually opening the Soviet system or dismantling the Soviet empire. Podhoretz inveighed against the Arias Peace Plan for Central America on the same grounds, arguing that it was "naive to the point of dementia" to believe that the Nicaraguan Sandinistas would ever permit a legitimate election.[38]

Why was the West falling for Gorbachev's peace offensive? Podhoretz darkly suggested that the answer lay in the warning he had issued ten years earlier. Unless America committed itself to attaining strategic superiority, he had warned, the West would become Finlandized in the name of peace. An unspoken fear of Soviet power would lead the West to sign trade agreements with the Soviets involving the transfer of technology, grain, "and anything else the Soviets might want or need . . . negotiated on terms amounting to the payment of tribute." Reagan's military build-up was too small and had come too late. Thus he crawled to Moscow "with bags of tributary gold." Having lost the Cold War, the West frantically negotiated the terms of its Finlandization. It was a species of surrender.[39]

In the fall of 1989 the "totalitarian" regimes of Eastern Europe collapsed overnight, most of them without violence, and the theory of totalitarianism perished with them. To the neocons the experience was exhilarating, confounding and deflating all at once. In June 1990 I asked Podhoretz why he had stopped writing; he replied that he no longer knew what to think. He still did not believe the cold war was over, but he didn't know how to argue that it wasn't. He had lost his compass. The moment for politics had passed; he found himself losing interest in it. He laughed that Irving Kristol moved to Washington just before the spirit blew out of the Beltway.[40]

For a moment there was such a thing as a somewhat chastened neoconservatism; at least, a few neocons said so. Irving Kristol and Jeane Kirkpatrick argued that the downfall of Communism permitted the U.S. to return to foreign policy realism. America did not need a world crusade that transcended the U.S.'s economic and security interests. The U.S. was not some kind of church that had to have a moral or creedal mission. Sustaining American dominance was one thing—all neocons were for that—but missionary enterprises to democratize the world and remake it in America's image were no longer necessary. Kirkpatrick spoke wistfully of becoming a normal nation.[41]

But for most neoconservatives that prescription was too small and provincial. They urged that the U.S. needed a new ideological creed and cause, one that exported capitalist democracy throughout the world and sustained America's global dominance. Podhoretz told me that younger neocons like Wolfowitz and Krauthammer would have to lead the battle for American global dominion. The crusade of the founding generation was over, and the founders were getting old. Yet the greatest challenge lay ahead. Podhoretz called it "keeping America Number One." Krauthammer called it "unipolarism."[42]

The neocons regretted that the unipolar moment arrived on the watch of a Republican president who did not like them. The 41st president (hereafter, Bush 41, to be distinguished from Bush 43) was a bitter disappointment, though he appointed Wolfowitz, Constance Horner, Bernard Aronson and William Kristol to high-ranking positions. Having little use for quarrelsome intellectuals of any kind, Bush took no interest in the grand designs of neoconservatives. He gave them a burst of hope at the outset of the Gulf War by referring fleetingly to a "New World Order," but quickly reverted to realist power-balancing. By 1992 a few neoconservatives were so disgusted with Bush that they supported Bill Clinton's presidential candidacy, hoping that he would pursue what he called an aggressive foreign policy "infused with democratic spirit." But Clinton appointed no neocons to major offices, he quickly put aside his campaign rhetoric about exporting democracy, and for most neocons, returning to the Democratic Party was unthinkable anyway. The Republican Party was their political home, for better or worse.[43]

From the beginning they had been controversial in their Republican home; later they became more so. Old Right conservatives complained bitterly that neocons beat them out for positions, raided the right-wing foundation money, and were not good conservatives. They told stories of losing foundation money after the neocons smeared them as reactionaries, old fogies, and bigots. By the mid-1980s *National Review* regularly featured Old Right complaints about neocons, as did George Panichas's *Modern Age*, a highbrow journal of conservative elitism, and Thomas Fleming's *Chronicles*, a populist journal of the Old Right. Russell Kirk, the dean of American intellectual conservatism, rebuked neoconservatives for their "ideological infatuations" ("the neoconservatives are often clever, but seldom wise") and commented wryly on their industry: "How earnestly they founded magazine upon magazine! How skillfully they insinuated themselves into the councils of the Nixon and Reagan Administrations!"[44]

Many traditional conservatives embraced the term "paleoconservative" to mark themselves off from the neocons. In their telling, neocons were opportunistic, devious, power-hungry, ideological, and not very religious. Kirk observed that neoconservatives behaved like the cadre of a political machine, "eager for place and preferment and power, skillful at intrigue, ready to exclude from office any persons who might not be counted upon as faithful to the Neoconservative ideology." They were "clever creatures, glib, committed to an ideology, and devious at attaining their objects," which included global imperialism. Having started as Marxists, they were now reverse-Marxists who acted as though they invented conservatism. Stephen Tonsor declared that neocons had no business leading any part of the conservative movement: "It is splendid when the town whore gets religion and joins the church. Now and then she makes a good choir director, but when she begins to tell the minister what he ought to say in his Sunday sermons, matters have been carried too far."[45]

To many old conservatives the hardest part to swallow was the neocon march on the Old Right institutions, especially the American Enterprise Institute, Hoover Institution, Heritage Foundation, Scaife Foundation, Bradley Foundation, Smith Richardson Foundation, and John M. Olin Foundation. "We have simply been crowded out by overwhelming numbers," Clyde Wilson protested. "The offensives of radicalism have driven vast herds of liberals across the border into our territories. These refugees now speak in our name, but the language they speak is the same one they always spoke . . . Our estate has been taken over by an imposter, just as we were about to inherit."[46] Pat Buchanan protested that neocon staffers steered "thirty million dollars a year to front groups, magazines, scholars and policy institutions who toe their party line." Paul Fleming complained that neocons were gaining "a lock on all money and the institutions created by the Right." Paul Gottfried put it harshly: "The neoconservatives created an enemy on the right by vilification and exclusion. The enemy lives increasingly for revenge and is trying to subvert the neoconservative empire. Few old rightists believe the foundations now run by neoconservatives will become theirs as soon as their enemies fall. Far more likely such resources will go to opera houses and other civic charities than to supporting old right scholars. It is burning hate, not uncomplicated greed, that fuels the old right war against the neoconservatives."[47]

In the early going, neocons mostly kept their heads down and muttered off the record about the burdens of working with bigots and reactionaries. This was a fight they could not win, at least in public, during the Reagan administration. Later they drew lines and slugged it out in public, after Old Right conservatives charged that neocons were not to be trusted in foreign policy. Kirk speculated that neocon imperialism was a function of neocon utilitarianism. Unlike genuine conservatives, he explained, neoconservatives had little sense of the mundane order as a realm subordinate to the transcendent order: "They are focused on the struggle for power, and are using power for their mundane purposes." In Kirk's telling, genuine conservatism found its home in history, theology and humane letters, but neoconservatives were social scientists and ideologues, which caused them to be every bit as self-promoting and power-oriented as the New Class liberals they denounced.[48]

To the neocons, this sort of criticism and the barely veiled anti-Semitism of some conservative writers, especially Joseph Sobran, displayed why a *new* conservatism had been needed in the first place. Podhoretz, Midge Decter, and Richard John Neuhaus charged that the traditional Right was still rife with racism, anti-Semitism and xenophobia. Neuhaus, having worked closely with paleoconservatives, reported knowingly that many were comfortable only with governments led by white males of tested genetic stock. Like Henry Adams, the Old Right conservatives feared that America's experiment in republicanism would not survive its vulgar economic system and the unrefined immigrants it attracted. This was an old story on the Right, Neuhaus allowed. The new wrinkle was that paleoconservatives used the neocon ideology of democratic globalism as a foil for their own reinstatement of repressed bigotries into America's public discourse: "The list includes nativism, racism, anti-Semitism, xenophobia, a penchant for authoritarian politics, and related diseases of the *ressentiment* that flourishes on the marginalia of American life." Neuhaus brushed off conservative complaints that neocons were cultural imperialists and militarists. American conservatives did not have delicate sensibilities on these matters, he noted; they simply clung to a small and mean image of what America should be. Old Right intellectuals still distrusted democracy, they wanted to restrict immigration to northern Europeans, and they couldn't bring themselves to work with Jews and other "ethnic" conservatives. They apparently needed to be reminded that the evils of racism and anti-Semitism were not "merely figments of the fevered liberal imagination."[49]

To paleoconservatives, being lectured about prejudice was as hard to take as losing the foundation money. Fleming replied that neoconservatives specialized in "the last resort of the calumniator: 'code words' and 'insensitivity.'" These were leftist sins, he implied. It was the Left that judged and excluded people on the basis of a sensitivity code, demonizing opponents with charges of racism, anti-Semitism, and misogyny. Real conservatives did not appeal to political correctness. Neoconservatives savaged the code of political correctness when they attacked liberals, but were quick to invoke it against conservatives. Podhoretz, blasting the "nativist bigotry" and "other abominations" of *Chronicles*, angrily declared: "I know an enemy when I see one, and *Chronicles* has become just that so far as I personally am concerned." To Fleming, that pronouncement proved that neocons did not belong in the conservative movement. They were more like conspiracy theorists, in his view: "If they know where a man stands on nuclear energy, the Trilateral Commission, the Palestinians, or the gold standard, they can locate him precisely on the grid of their paranoia."[50]

Neoconservatives thus entered the 1990s as a splintering faction of a disintegrating intellectual Right. On the level of mass politics, "conservatism" remained a potent electoral force. Among its intellectual elites, where the movement's ideological contradictions were less tolerated, American conservatism was a shambles. The unifying force of the Soviet threat was gone, which magnified the cracks in the Reagan/Bush coalition. Old Right isolationist nationalism made a comeback, as represented by Buchanan's presidential campaigns, while neoconservatives crusaded for a "unipolar" foreign policy that claimed American dominion over the entire globe. Conservatives wanted to relinquish the empire and expand it; they wanted to make America the universal nation and severely restrict immigration; they identified America's interests with Israel's and resurrected the dual loyalty smears of the 1940s; they celebrated the triumph of corporate capitalism and condemned the commercial culture it created; they celebrated the universality of American democracy and repudiated the imperialism of democratic globalist ideology.

At the height of the faction fight between neocons and paleoconservatives, Stephen Tonsor remarked, "It has always struck me as odd, even perverse, that former Marxists have been permitted, yes invited, to play such a leading role in the Conservative movement of the twentieth century." He mused that if Stalin had spared Trotsky's life, Trotsky would be holed up at the Hoover Institution writing neoconservative tracts for *Commentary*. Neoconservatism was culturally unthinkable apart from the history of New York Jewish leftism, he contended, which was the root of the problem. Trotsky's orphans had never made good allies and they never would. They belonged too much to the modern world to make good conservatives.[51]

This verdict was exaggerated and ungenerous, but it reverberated in the rage that neocons evoked on the right, which erupted again after George W. Bush invaded Iraq. Neoconservatives made sizable contributions to the American Right that only they could have made. Despite the frequent suggestion that "neoconservatism" was really a euphemism for "Jewish conservatism," many neocons were not Jewish; William Bennett, Peter Berger, Francis Fukuyama, Zalmay Khalilzad, Jeane Kirkpatrick, Paul Ramsey, Ernest Lefever, James Nuechterlein, Michael Novak, Richard John Neuhaus, George Weigel, and James Q. Wilson were prominent examples. More importantly, neoconservatives helped to create a new American right that played down its segregationist and anti-Semitic past. In the 1990s many youthful interns at neocon institutions described themselves simply as conservatives. They were products of the neoconservative reaction, but had little acquaintance with the experiences that created neoconservatism. They described Kristol and Novak as "the grandpas," but did not share the grandpas' need to distinguish their conservatism from bad-smelling older versions. Neoconservatives succeeded politically by making the Republican Right more like themselves. They attacked affirmative action in the name of individual rights and blasted multiculturalism without the baggage of a nativist past, helping the American right defend its claim of not being racist.

To neocons the language of democracy and rights was second nature. The Old Right had been wrong to oppose the civil rights movement, but the new liberalism disastrously legalized reverse discrimination through affirmative action. According to neocons, affirmative action helped only those that did not deserve their attainments and stigmatized those that deserved them. To many white Americans who resented affirmative action but were anxious to avoid seeming racist, the neoconservative approach was exactly right. Defending the American establishment that actually existed, neocons blasted liberals constantly for promoting anti-American ideas and refusing to stand up for America. In their telling, American liberals coddled the criminal class (which was disproportionately black) and welfare class (also disproportionately black) and betrayed American sovereignty (by indulging foreign nations and the United Nations). Liberals discriminated against white Americans through affirmative action and created public sector jobs for themselves. And they kept America weak against a superior Soviet enemy.

The first generation of neocons turned to the Right at the same time and for the same reasons that millions of white ethnics and middle-class taxpayers began to vote Republican. This was the historical moment when working- and middle-class Americans could no longer expect to live better than their parents. In the 1970s Americans increasingly thought of themselves as beleaguered taxpayers, not beneficiaries of government programs. America's decline as a world economic power cost Jimmy Carter his second presidential term and propelled most neoconservatives to adopt Reaganomics. To explain to Americans why their country was in economic decline, neocons joined Reagan in blaming "labor elites" that strangled American productivity, a New Class of public sector functionaries that benefited from expanded government, and a welfare class addicted to government largesse. The image of a burgeoning welfare class that physically and economically threatened other Americans lurked behind neoconservative and Old Right rhetoric about the culture of poverty.[52]

In its first generation neoconservatism was primarily a politics of militant anti-communism and only secondarily a politics of economic conservatism, the rule of traditional elites, and a return to conservative values. In its post-Cold War phase it was fundamentally a vision of global American empire and only secondarily an economic and social ideology. Yet its secondary work was indispensable to its political success. Kristol explained that neocons became influential by defending an American economic and social establishment that did a poor job of defending itself: "We had to tell businessmen that they needed us. Business understands the need for intellectuals much more than trade unionists understand it, but not enough. Basically, it wants intellectuals to go out and justify profits and explain to people why corporations make a lot of money. That's their main interest. It is very hard for business to understand how to think politically."[53]

It was the neoconservatives who taught the Right's wealthy benefactors and corporate class how to think politically. The neocons transformed the role of think tanks and policy journals in American politics, showing the potential of intellectual activism. They took over sleepy conservative institutions and built a vast array of new ones, creating the Right's mighty Wurlitzer of institutes, magazines, media outlets, foundations, and lobbying agencies.

In both of its historic phases neoconservatism was distinguished by the passion and scale of its global ambitions. American military spending doubled between 1980 and 1985 on the basis of neocon claims that Soviet totalitarianism had immense competitive advantages, Soviet military strength and strategic geopolitical power surpassed America's, and Soviet leaders were preparing to fight and win a nuclear war. Neoconservatives subsequently claimed that the collapse of the Soviet Union owed much to Reagan's military build-up, which purportedly convinced Soviet leaders that they could not afford to perpetuate the arms race.[54]

The pace of Soviet disintegration was, indeed, accelerated by the pressure of heightened American military spending in the 1980s, with which the Soviets could not compete. But the costs of America's global military empire were staggering and unnecessary. Neoconservatives grossly overestimated the Soviet government, economy, and military. They demanded enormous military increases to outstrip a fantasized opponent. When Reagan's military build-up began, the United States was the world's leading creditor nation, providing the largest source of capital for national economies across the globe. By the end of Reagan's presidency, the United States was the world's largest debtor nation, dependent on other nations to finance its debt.

The military expansion of the 1980s crowded out vital national investments in infrastructure, education, housing, health care, and energy. Federal aid to education was slashed by a third while workforce training and retraining were gutted. The U.S. spent more than $2 trillion on the military without raising the money to pay for it, leaving debts that devoured nearly half of every subsequent tax dollar. The Reagan military budgets sent a fantastically expensive message to a Soviet leadership that could not ignore its disintegrating economic base no matter who was president. As early as 1983, Soviet General Staff chief Marshal Nikolai Ogarkov told former American officials that the cold war was over because Russia was too backward economically and technologically to compete. Many Soviet officials recognized that their system was too rigid to compete with societies that put computers in the hands of every student. In an increasingly global economy, the inferiority of the Soviet economic and educational systems was too obvious even for Soviet leaders to ignore. A more realistic assessment of the Soviet threat would have allowed the United States to husband its resources. Neoconservative polemics against "appeasement" made such an assessment politically impossible in the 1980s.[55]

Neoconservatism marked the last stage of the Old Left, being the last movement in American politics to define itself principally by its opposition to Communism. But generational experience cannot be replicated. The second generation of neocons was less insistent on the "neo" than the first; in 1989 the Cold War ended; and the movement's third generation had little sense of joining a distinctive movement. Neoconservatism was identified with bygone debates, and in 1992 it fell out of power. It seemed to be fading indistinguishably into the Republican Right. It was still adept at culture war, but neocons were nowhere near as effective as the Christian Right in that area. Neocons were good at defending capitalism, but that was not their strong suit, and they had plenty of company in it. Irving Kristol and Norman Podhoretz reasoned that their movement had faded by succeeding. The neocons had joined and changed American conservatism, making it possible for their children to call themselves, simply, conservatives.[56]

But that was not quite right. Even though the neocons merged into the mainstream American Republican right, the term persisted. It referred to something that was still too important not to be named. The neocons had a more dramatic idea of politics than other kinds of conservatives, one that featured a radical, expansive faith in American power. Even the realist-leaning neocons had messianic ambitions for the United States, and most neocons were idealists. Their blend of ideology, idealism, and an increasingly frank neo-imperialism offered a coherent view of what the United States should do with its unrivaled economic and military power. Dwelling on crisis, and also thriving on it, they had a ready-made worldview when the second President Bush unexpectedly found need of one on September 11, 2001.

Chapter 11

Imperial Designs

NEOCONSERVATISM AND THE IRAQ WAR

In the waning months of the cold war, shortly before an expiring Soviet Union finally dissolved, a group of American neoconservatives urged that the time had come to create an American-dominated world order. Some of them called it the "unipolarist imperative." Instead of reducing military spending, they contended, the United States needed to expand its military reach to every region of the world, using its tremendous military and economic power to consolidate America's global supremacy. At the very moment that neoconservatism was widely claimed to be finished in American politics, a sizable group of neocons devised a new rationale for their movement, one that propelled them a decade later to political power, and wreaked colossal harm.

Charles Krauthammer, in a seminal article of 1989, "Universal Dominion: Toward a Unipolar World," took an early pass at spelling out the unipolar idea. At first it was a vision of the U.S. as the leader of a "super-sovereign confederated West," not a unipolar hegemon by itself. In the mid-1980s Krauthammer had been a leading advocate of democratic globalism, which he likened to something he called the "Reagan Doctrine." Ronald Reagan never proclaimed a doctrine bearing his name, but Krauthammer attributed one to him that welded together the containment and rollback approaches to anticommunism. The Reagan Doctrine settled for containment in Europe, where a threat of world war existed, and supported anticommunist rebellions in the Third World, where there was no threat of world war. To Krauthammer, democratic globalism was merely the positive side of the Reagan Doctrine, helping cold war proxies like Angola and El Salvador fight off communism by becoming democracies. Unlike many neoconservatives, he did not play up the idealistic side of democratic globalist theory. Since democratic globalism was primarily a way to fight communism, he dropped it after the cold war ended, reasoning that the U.S. no longer had a vital stake in exporting democracy. The structure of America's obligations had changed. Instead of focusing on the periphery, the unipolar strategy focused on the center, unifying and strengthening the democratic West. Krauthammer urged: "America's purpose should be to steer the world away from its coming multipolar future toward a qualitatively new outcome—a unipolar world whose center is a confederated West."[1]

The following year, enthralled by the U.S. mobilization to expel Iraq from Kuwait, Krauthammer refined the unipolar idea, judging that "confederated West" was an evasive euphemism for the real thing. There was no such thing as collective security, he contended; the United Nations would not have driven Iraq out of Kuwait. What was real was American power and resolve; America's so-called multilateral coalition against Iraq was mere political cover for reality. Krauthammer had nothing against cover, but he warned Americans not to dispense with real power by making a fetish of multilateralism. Americans were overdue to relinquish their innocent denial that they had an empire. They needed to accept and appreciate that the unipolar moment had arrived. A single pole of world power, the United States, now dominated the world, which was a very good thing. The business of a serious American foreign policy was to sustain that dominance. Krauthammer allowed that building democracy and keeping the peace in Third World nations was a worthy occupation for third-rate democratic powers like Canada and Sweden. A unipolar superpower, however, to maintain self-respect, did not do windows. The next mission of the United States was to create a world order shaped by American power.[2]

To most neoconservatives Krauthammer's prescription was exactly right, an inspiring vision, and too cynical by half. They embraced the idea of unipolar dominance while usually qualifying or rejecting Krauthammer's haughty disregard for missionary enterprises. Sustaining American dominance and planting more democracies went together, they contended. Norman Podhoretz told me that he had been a unipolarist for more than twenty years, though he recognized that politically it represented a new movement within neoconservatism that would have to be led and defended by younger neocons like Krauthammer and Paul Wolfowitz. Michael Novak stressed that unipolarism was the positive side of anticommunism and that the vision of pro-American global democracy was an indispensable feature of it. Ben Wattenberg urged nervous politicians not to be shy about asserting American superiority: "We are the first universal nation. 'First' as in the first one, 'first' as in 'number one.' And 'universal' within our borders and globally." Because the U.S. was uniquely universal, Wattenberg claimed, it had a unique right to impose its will on other nations on behalf of a democratic world order.[3]

Wattenberg was unabashedly buoyant and sloganeering on the theme that America needed to do something grand, interventionist, and American with its victory in the cold war. There had to be a bigger payoff from defeating communism than merely watching the Soviet Union dissolve. After all, "American taxpayers didn't put up trillions of dollars in the Cold War to create a few more Swedens." In Wattenberg's telling, America was the only mythic nation, and its primary myth was Manifest Destiny: "Only Americans have the sense of mission—and gall—to engage in benign, but energetic, global cultural advocacy. We are the most potent cultural imperialists in history, although generally constructive and non-coercive." As a description and objective, he believed, "unipolarism" was exactly right: "A unipolar world is a good thing, if America is the uni." But Wattenberg preferred "neo-manifest destinarian" for its historical resonance and emotive coloring. America's struggle for the world was a crusade to fulfill the manifest destiny of America itself, making the world more like the United States while remaining subordinate to it.[4]

Joshua Muravchik, the movement's most scholarly advocate of democratic globalism and unipolar supremacy, put it plaintively in his 1991 book, *Exporting Democracy: Fulfilling America's Destiny*: "For our nation, this is the opportunity of a lifetime. Our failure to exert every possible effort to secure [a new world order] would be unforgivable. If we succeed, we will have forged a Pax Americana unlike any previous peace, one of harmony, not of conquest. Then the twenty-first century will be the American century by virtue of the triumph of the humane idea born in the American experiment." Like Krauthammer and Wattenberg, Muravchik sought to create a new ideological grammar for neoconservatism, stressing that ideological wars began with new creeds. The cold war rhetoric of totalitarianism, Finlandization, Present Danger, fifth columnist, infiltration, and choke point went down the Orwellian memory hole; only "appeasement" survived the death of communism. The new neoconservatism spoke of neo-universalism, neo-manifest destiny, benevolent global hegemony, waging democracy, democratic idealism, liberal imperialism, declinism, and unipolarism. Wattenberg explained that new ideological wars required new bumper stickers: "An American foreign policy, to be successful, must quicken the public pulse. Americans have a missionary streak, and democracy is our mission."[5]

Not all the neoconservatives went along with this transition. A few defected from the neoconservative movement, notably military strategist Edward Luttwak and political writer Michael Lind. Neoconservative sociologist Peter Berger shook his head at the imperial chauvinism of his friends. Some neocons distinguished between defending American superiority and assuming the burdens of a global Pax Americana. From the beginning there were key differences between the movement's nationalistic realists (such as Krauthammer, Jeane Kirkpatrick and Irving Kristol) and its democratic globalists (the vast majority of neocons). For a while Kirkpatrick and Kristol claimed to be holdouts from neocon overexpansiveness, urging neocons to settle for great power realism. Kirkpatrick counseled in 1990 that it should be enough for the U.S. to be more like a normal nation, as long as it was the greatest of nations; Kristol puckishly opined in defense of George H. W. Bush, who declined to invade Iraq, "No civilized person in his right mind wants to govern Iraq." But for most neoconservatives, normal great power realism was not nearly enough, and even Kirkpatrick and Kristol eventually signed on for global empire militarism, though not for missionary movements to export democracy.[6]

By the early 1990s, when I wrote the first of my books on neoconservatism, neocons were debating whether to give highest priority to global dominion or culture war; their embrace of unipolarism was already a settled matter for most of them. In addition to Krauthammer, Wattenberg, and Muravchik, the leading neocon unipolarists were Kenneth Adelman, Elliot Abrams, John R. Bolton, Stephen Cambone, Angelo Codevilla, Eliot Cohen, Devon Cross, Eric Edelman, Douglas Feith, Frank Gaffney, Donald Kagan, Robert Kagan, Lawrence F. Kaplan, Robert Kaplan, William Kristol, Michael Ledeen, I. Lewis Libby, Michael Novak, Richard Perle, Daniel Pipes, Norman Podhoretz, George Weigel, and James Woolsey. Unipolarism was not an exclusively neoconservative enterprise. Old-style conservative hawks such as Donald Rumsfeld, William F. Buckley Jr., and Dick Cheney were unipolarists but not products of the neoconservative movement. The same was true of conservative realists Colin Powell, Dick Armitage, Condoleezza Rice, and Henry Kissinger. The Democratic Party eventually sprouted its own versions of unipolarism, notably in the writings of Zbigniew Brzezinski, Peter Beinart, and Michael Ignatieff (some of whom had second thoughts after America invaded Iraq). But the ideology of American unipolarism was largely a neoconservative phenomenon, which caused Cheney to strengthen his alliances with neoconservatives.

In a turbulent, surprising, and confusing historical moment, the neocons had a vision. Ironically the Republican Party's first debates over unipolarism occurred in the administration of George W. Bush's father. Dick Cheney, serving as defense secretary under George H. W. Bush, was forced to cut back on the military after the Soviet Union imploded, which he did very grudgingly. Cheney was the only hard-line conservative at the top level of the Bush 41 administration. To him the neoconservatives were the only group with a serious view of American power. In 1990, facing demands for a sharp decrease in U.S. military spending, Cheney commissioned his policy chief, Paul Wolfowitz, to devise a new strategic plan for the United States, which became the Defense Policy Guidance of 1992. Wolfowitz, working principally with his protégés Zalmay Khalilzad and I. Lewis Libby, outlined a global empire strategy that rationalized unilateral interventions, preemptive strikes, and new military bases. Eschewing bureaucratic vagueness, it asserted that America's central objective was to prevent any nation from becoming a serious rival. The point was not merely to suppress any unfriendly regime; it was to assure that no nation became a superpower and thereby diminished America's global supremacy. Neither was it a question of maintaining military supremacy only; the plan was equally committed to sustaining America's political and economic supremacy. The U.S. had to thwart even the desire of other nations for great-power status: "We must maintain the mechanism for deterring potential competitors from even aspiring to a larger regional or global role."[7]

Unfortunately for Wolfowitz the plan was leaked to the *New York Times*, sparking an unwelcome uproar for the Bush administration, which had a low threshold of tolerance for its neocon faction in the Defense Department. President Bush disavowed the plan, and Wolfowitz feared that his government career was over. But two senior officials defended the plan: Colin Powell, who endorsed it publicly, and Dick Cheney, who tinkered with it until the end of the Bush 41 administration. In the wilderness years of the 1990s after Republicans lost the White House to Bill Clinton, Wolfowitz became a hero to a neoconservative movement plotting its return to power.[8]

The neocons and their hard-line conservative allies were frustrated by the first Bush administration, and in 1992 they fell out of power. They seemed to be fading. Their political obituary was published many times. Always it said that neoconservatism was nothing without a Soviet enemy, which no longer existed. The neocons would have to blend into the Republican mainstream, where they were small-to-middling players in the fights over economic and social issues. But the neocons kept their name and standing in the Republican Party by contending for unipolar Americanism. For many of them, this faith was their operative religion. Many neocons were not religiously observant; many were not Jewish, contrary to the stereotype; and their ideology was not a cover for hard-line Zionism, though nearly all of them were supporters of the Netanyahu wing of the Likud party. The hallmark of neoconservatism was its radical faith that the maximal use of American power is good for America and the world.

The neocons despised Clinton for wasting America's hegemonic power. Clinton was solicitous of world opinion; he intervened in nations that didn't matter, like Somalia and Haiti; and he indulged Iraq, Iran, North Korea, China, and the Palestinians. Fueled by their intense dislike of Clinton and the opportunity to overtake the Republican Party's realist establishment, the neocons refined their strategic vision and regrouped organizationally. They tightened their hold over conservative think tanks and magazines, cultivated alliances with Cheney and Rumsfeld, founded the *Weekly Standard* magazine with Rupert Murdoch money, and got a huge boost from the rise of the Fox network, also a Murdoch production. They were deeply involved in the culture wars of the 1990s, which enhanced their standing in the Republican Party.

In 1996 Clinton beat the Republicans again, this time by co-opting most of their winning issues, and the neocons declared that establishment Republican realism was bankrupt. The following year Bill Kristol founded the Project for the New American Century (PNAC), which called for a foreign policy of global dominion, and the next year the PNAC issued a public letter to Clinton calling for the overthrow of the Baathist regime in Iraq. In the 2000 Republican presidential primaries, most neocons supported Senator John McCain, a unipolarist who shared their core conviction that militarism was integral to the greatness of the nation.

But Wolfowitz and Richard Perle judged that George W. Bush looked more electable and teachable. Joining his team, they urged other neocons to take Bush seriously, and Wolfowitz became one of Bush's two chief foreign policy advisers, along with Condoleezza Rice. The neocons rallied to Bush after he won the nomination. Two months before the election of 2000, the PNAC issued a position paper spelling out the particulars of a global empire strategy: repudiate the ABM treaty, build a global missile defense system, develop a strategic dominance of space, increase defense spending by $20 billion per year, establish permanent new forces in Southern Europe, Southeast Asia, and the Middle East, and reinvent the U.S. military to "fight and decisively win multiple, simultaneous major theater wars." They also remarked that it might take "a new Pearl Harbor" for Americans to realize the necessity of dramatically expanding America's military force and strategy.[9]

When Bush won the presidency, the unipolarists came with him. Of the eighteen figures that signed the PNAC's 1998 letter to Clinton calling for regime change in Iraq, eleven took high-ranking positions in the Bush administration, including Wolfowitz, Rumsfeld, Elliott Abrams, Dick Armitage, John Bolton, Paula Dobriansky, Zalmay Khalilzad, Richard Perle, Peter W. Rodman, William Schneider Jr., and Robert B. Zoellick. Other PNAC associates and prominent unipolarists who landed high-ranking positions included Stephen Cambone, Devon Gaffney Cross, Douglas Feith, John Hannah, Robert Joseph, Scooter Libby, William Luti, Abram Shulsky, and David Wurmser.

Cheney was the key to this incredible windfall of appointments. During the campaign Bush zigged and zagged between realist and unipolarist positions, but Cheney was determined to exclude the *realpolitikers* who had frustrated him in the first Bush administration. Colin Powell was too prominent not to be named Secretary of State, and he believed in the ideology of global preeminence, but Cheney and the neocons rightly viewed him as a reluctant warrior and foreign policy realist. Thus Cheney limited Powell's influence by tabbing Rumsfeld for the Pentagon, which became a neoconservative stronghold led by Wolfowitz and Feith, and Cheney loaded his office with neocons.

For seven months the neocons found the Bush administration very frustrating despite their prominence in it. Bush rejected neocon demands for a big increase in the Pentagon budget. He talked about invading Iraq but spent his political capital on a tax cut for the rich. He quashed the ABM Treaty and American support of the Kyoto Protocol and the International Criminal Court, but these were second-rate issues. He took little interest in scattered terrorist groups like al Qaeda, as former National Security Council counterterrorism coordinator Richard Clarke later recounted bitterly, though the neocons shared that predisposition. They wanted Bush to overthrow Iraq, Iran, and Syria. By July the *Weekly Standard* magazine was so frustrated that it called upon Rumsfeld and Wolfowitz to resign in protest.[10]

All of that was quickly forgotten after the United States was attacked on September 11, 2001. Suddenly Bush needed a worldview; he was surrounded by people who had one; and they were obsessed with invading Iraq. In a real sense Bush joined his own administration. I do not mean that he became a puppet of Cheney or the neocons. His administration was very short on sustained policy discussion of any kind, and Bush prided himself on being "the decider." He apparently made up his own mind to scuttle the doctrine of deterrence, pursue antiterrorism as a world war, propound a radical doctrine of preventive war, and invade Iraq. But these were long-standing neocon fantasies that became American policies at the urging of Cheney, Rumsfeld, and the neocons. In the days immediately following September 11, Wolfowitz and Rumsfeld urged Bush to respond to al Qaeda's fiendish attacks by invading Iraq. That Iraq had nothing to do with 9/11 was inconsequential; what mattered was getting rid of Saddam Hussein and imposing a pro-American regime in the Middle East. Bush pressured Richard Clarke to find a link between Saddam and 9/11, and on ten separate occasions Rumsfeld pleaded with the CIA to find one.[11]

The Bush administration had a sloppy list of reasons to invade Iraq, which it never bothered to subject to serious internal criticism. To question any of them was to betray one's lack of right-thinking pro-Americanism. In public the administration stressed that the war was about Saddam Hussein's supposed weapons of mass destruction and links to al Qaeda. On occasion Bush officials also invoked the benefits of creative destruction in the Middle East, consolidating American power there to secure the oil supply, and changing the political culture of the region. But the latter reasons were hard to talk about in a democratic republic known for its innocent self-image, and the reasons that got a stampede going were based on conjectures.

Bush officials realized that Saudi Arabia did not provide a secure basis for American influence in the region or ensure a stable oil supply for the West. Fifteen of the September 11 hijackers were Saudis; the Saudi people despised the ruling regime of their country; and they resented the presence of American troops there. The war was a species of social engineering. Bush wanted to change the Middle East, creating a pro-American Iraq that gave the U.S. a direct power base, ensured the oil supply, set off a chain reaction of regime changes, gave relief to Israel, and got rid of a thuggish enemy. At Bush's first National Security Council meeting, on the eleventh day of his administration, he put Iraq at the top of his foreign policy agenda, urging that it was the key to reshaping the entire Middle East. Two days later Donald Rumsfeld put it this way at a National Security Council meeting: "Imagine what the region would look like without Saddam and with a regime that's aligned with U.S. interests. It would change everything in the region and beyond it. It would demonstrate what U.S. policy is all about."[12]

The visions of a new pro-American government in the Middle East and the political/cultural transformation of the region were tightly intertwined. Bush wanted Arab leaders to get the picture. During the war in Afghanistan they kept their heads down; afterward they carried on as though the world had not changed. Bush wanted to smash into their terrorist-breeding world at its center. Iraq was the best candidate, because Iraq had a vast oil supply, it was a warm-water port with seventy-two airfields in the middle of the Middle East, it was under UN sanctions, its tyrannical leader had tried to assassinate Bush's father, and Bush's key advisers had been long determined to overthrow the Baath party. They convinced Bush that Iraq would break without much of a fight and a pro-American government would be readily imposed.

But Bush officials were not free to say "what U.S. policy is all about." The war could not be sold by calling for a new American power base and the transformation of the Middle East, and it would not have been credible to suddenly claim a humanitarian ground. The transformationist argument smacked of naked imperialism and grandiose fantasy, and the world had known for fifteen years that Saddam held the country together by sheer thuggery. That hadn't stopped the U.S. from arming him, or later from inciting the Shiites and Kurds to rebel against him. Thus the U.S. was deeply implicated in both of Saddam's mass-killing rampages, and both were long past when the second Bush administration claimed it was an urgent necessity to invade Iraq. Upon setting out to do so, the Pentagon neocons ignored State Department warnings about the perils of invading and occupying the Arab world's Yugoslavia. Rumsfeld, Wolfowitz, and Feith had a privileged vision of how things would go, which they did not allow to be challenged. Their arrogance in stampeding to war would be hard to exaggerate. It included not bothering with normal intelligence roundtable debates and telling the first American overseer in

Iraq, Lt. General Jay Garner, not to bother reading the State Department's study of what might go wrong.

To secure public support, the Bush administration told Americans that Saddam Hussein threatened their safety. It claimed to know that Saddam possessed huge stockpiles of chemical and biological weapons, a nuclear weapons program, and links to al Qaeda, and that all of this posed an immediate threat that could be removed only by a full-scale war of aggression. Though Bush officials undoubtedly believed these claims, they knew the evidence for them was very weak. Intelligence analysts protested that reports were distorted by Bush officials, who cherry-picked the intelligence and pressured the CIA to deliver politically correct estimates. The Pentagon had to create its own intelligence unit and rely on stories from exiles just to claim that it had some new evidence.

In his 2003 State of the Union Address President Bush recycled a howler about uranium yellowcake from Niger that had already been discredited. Rumsfeld announced that he had "bulletproof" evidence of Saddam's collusion with al Qaeda. Cheney assured there was "no doubt" that Saddam had amassed weapons of mass destruction to use against Americans. Cheney claimed to know that Saddam had an advanced nuclear program. Condoleezza Rice claimed that the only possible use of Saddam's aluminum tubes was to enrich uranium.[13]

Colin Powell, realizing that his colleagues were selling the war with bad information, tried to make a more credible case in his dramatic presentation to the U.N. Security Council in February 2003. He spurned several pages of the draft that Cheney's staff wrote for him, angrily declaring that he wasn't going to read that "bullshit." But his galvanizing performance recycled weak and disputed evidence, and injected still more. Powell charged that Iraq tried to buy magnets for centrifuge enrichment, but the International Atomic Energy Agency showed that the magnets would have been for telephones and short-range missiles. He claimed that "classified documents" discovered at the home of a Baghdad nuclear scientist offered "dramatic confirmation" of administration claims about concealment, but U.N. nuclear inspectors later judged that the documents were old and worthless. Powell presented satellite photos of industrial buildings, bunkers, and trucks that he described as chemical and biological weapons facilities and decontamination vehicles, but these very sites and others had been inspected nearly four hundred times by Hans Blix and his U.N. inspections team. On February 4, 2003, two days before Powell testified at the U.N., Blix told the U.N. that his team found no sign of contraband. Powell claimed that the Tariq State Establishment in Fallujah was a chemical weapons facility, but this facility, inspected six times between December 2002 and January 2003, was a chlorine plant. Powell warned that Iraq produced four tons of the nerve agent VX but most of it was destroyed under U.N. supervision in the 1990s.[14]

Citing testimonies by defectors, Powell charged that Iraq had mobile biological weapons factories. After the invasion the U.S. found two trailers that the CIA judged to be part of a bioweapons production line, but the CIA's report was rushed and politicized, no trace of biological agents was found, and the DIA, the Institute for Science and International Security, and the intelligence bureau of the State Department all judged that the trailers were used to inflate weather balloons for Iraqi artillery. Powell claimed that Iraq had a stockpile of up to five hundred tons of chemical weapons agent and that "key portions" of Iraq's chemical weapons infrastructure were embedded in its civilian industries, but no such agents and no chemical weapons infrastructure were found. Powell warned that chemical warheads found by U.N. inspectors in January might be the "tip of an iceberg," but the warheads were empty, and on June 16 Blix reported that the stray rocket warheads were uncrated debris from the 1980s. Powell alleged that Iraqi field commanders had been recently authorized to use chemical weapons, but seven months later the CIA's Iraq Survey Group, co-chaired by David Kay, acknowledged that there was no evidence to support this assertion.[15]

Most of the problem was that Powell relied on the same bad information from the intelligence agencies as the rest of the administration. Part of the problem was that he relied on some raw data that had not been analyzed. He was forced to build his own case because he knew better than to rely on the hyped intelligence that the White House and Pentagon were demanding from the CIA. The politicization of intelligence began at the outset of the war on terrorism, after the CIA failed to deliver the kind of intelligence that Bush officials demanded. Richard Perle declared that the CIA's analysis wasn't worth the paper it was written on. Cheney and his aides intimidated analysts at the CIA, DIA, and National Security Agency. Rumsfeld and Wolfowitz, needing better evidence for the administration's public claims, created their own intelligence unit, the Policy Counterterrorism Evaluation Group, which consisted largely of Perle and Wolfowitz protégés.[16]

Launched in October 2001 as a small operation in Feith's office, the Policy Counterterrorism Evaluation Group was originally headed by Perle disciple David Wurmser, who called himself one of Perle's "fiercely loyal group of followers." In 1999 Wurmser had written a book advocating the overthrow of Iraq. The doctrinal differences between Middle Eastern terrorist groups were increasingly irrelevant, Wurmser argued, and Iraq was the best place to fight terrorism. In 2002, under new leadership (Perle protégé Abram Shulsky and Feith's deputy for Near East and South Asia William Luti), the group grew into an eighteen-member nerve center at the Pentagon called the Office of Special Plans. Formally focused on relationships between terrorist organizations and state sponsors, this office politicized the transmission of intelligence and stood as a bureaucratic rebuke to the intelligence agencies. It was a throwback to the Team B episode of 1976 and Rumsfeld's 1998 committee on missile defense, both of which Wolfowitz worked on. Just as Team B argued that the CIA was overly concerned with facts, and thus overlooked the evil character of the Soviet regime, the Office of Special Plans argued that the CIA overlooked intentions and anecdotal evidence. Relying on anecdotes and assurances from Ahmed Chalabi's Iraqi National Congress (INC), the Pentagon group fed politically useful intelligence to Pentagon officials and Cheney, the group's key administrative supporter. In 2002 Cheney intervened in a feud between the State Department and Pentagon over funding increases for the INC, contending that it provided "unique intelligence" on the Iraq situation.[17]

The Special Plans unit was skilled at bureaucratic warfare. Jocularly calling itself "the Cabal," it portrayed itself as a tougher outfit than the fuddy-duddies at the CIA and DIA. At the same time it specialized in softer material than the traditional agencies. CIA analysts groused to reporters that Wolfowitz's group was arrogant, relentless, and not to be trusted, but CIA chief George Tenet, desperate not to be left behind by the winning team, accommodated the Pentagon and Vice President's office, which required selling out his analysts. Many analysts did not keep their frustration and humiliation to themselves. One reported: "As an employee of the Defense Intelligence Agency, I know how this administration has lied to the public to get support for its attack on Iraq." Another remarked of Rumsfeld: "He's an ideologist. He doesn't start with facts, even though he's quite brainy. He has a bottom line, and then he gathers facts to support the bottom line." An army intelligence officer told *Time* magazine more bluntly: "Rumsfeld was deeply, almost pathologically, distorting the intelligence."[18]

The Office of Special Plans contributed mightily to the Bush administration's grossly unwarranted claims about Iraq's weapons of mass destruction, partly by relying on the Iraqi National Congress. It also had a hand in the administration's disastrous lack of planning for the post-invasion occupation and insurgency, partly by relying on the Iraqi National Congress. In addition to assuring that Saddam still possessed a nuclear program and large quantities of chemical and biological weapons, the exiles claimed that Saddam was involved in the September 11 attacks and that they would be happy to run the Iraqi government after the U.S. overthrew Saddam.

Former U.N. weapons inspector Scott Ritter gave a different picture of the weapons issue, contending that 90 to 95 percent of Iraq's weapons of mass destruction were destroyed in the 1990s. "We had an incineration plant operating full-time for years, burning tons of the stuff every day," he recalled. Even if Iraq managed to hide some of its Sarin or Tabun, the shelf life of these nerve agents was only five years, the shelf life of anthrax was three years, and Iraq lacked the complex aerosol dispensing systems to deliver biological toxins such as anthrax beyond artillery range. Against an onslaught of misinformation about the status of Iraq's nuclear weapons program, Ritter insisted that Iraq could not have reconstituted its nuclear program without setting off detectable heat and gamma radiation. The U.N.'s exacting inspections made nuclear progress doubly impossible. But Ritter destroyed his credibility with the Pentagon after he joined the antiwar opposition. Wolfowitz dismissed his arguments as "simply amazing," Ritter was vilified as a traitor, and Blix was similarly condemned for stating that Bush's claims about weapons of mass destruction were exaggerated.[19]

Why didn't Saddam show that he had no weapons of mass destruction? He apparently held the disastrously mistaken idea that keeping the world guessing about whether he had them would be a deterrent against being invaded. He couldn't stand not being feared in the Middle East and the Pentagon; he especially wanted Iranian leaders to fear him; and he miscalculated the deterrent effect of possessing dangerous weapons. U.N. inspectors had reasons to believe that he retained some. In 1995 they found ballistic missile gyroscopes at the bottom of the Tigris River, and three years later they discovered an Iraqi document indicating that Iraq may have dropped six thousand fewer chemical bombs during the Iran-Iraq War than it claimed. But chemical and nuclear weapons cannot be produced without large-scale facilities, and Saddam's capacity to produce or even hide mass destruction weapons was destroyed by the combined effects of the Gulf War, nine years of U.N. inspections, thirteen years of U.N. sanctions, and the 1998 Desert Fox air strikes.

Meanwhile the very monster that the Bush team conjured to scare Americans into supporting an offensive war came into being as a result of the war. Iraq was not a haven for terrorists before the U.S. invaded and occupied the country, but it quickly became one afterward. The war created a perfect breeding ground for insurgents and a magnet for foreign terrorists by creating a broken state unable to control its borders or meet the essential needs of its people. And it offered 140,000 American troops as targets.

For years neoconservatives had dreamed of overthrowing half a dozen Middle Eastern governments; after 9/11 they demanded it. Krauthammer's target list of Afghanistan, Syria, Iran, and Iraq served as a template for the early discussion. During the buildup to the war, Angelo Codevilla argued that the second phase of the war on terrorism had to include the overthrow of Iraq, Syria, and the Palestinian Authority. Frank Gaffney believed that Iraq, Iran, and the Palestinian Authority headed the list. Laurent Murawiec told the Defense Policy Board that Iraq was the "tactical pivot" of America's war in the Middle East, Saudi Arabia was the "strategic pivot," and Egypt was the "prize." Michael Ledeen wanted America to overthrow Iran first, then Iraq, then Syria, then Saudi Arabia.[20]

Norman Podhoretz argued that the U.S. had to begin by killing the regimes in Iraq, Iran, and North Korea; that Syria, Lebanon, Libya, and the Palestinian Authority had to be overthrown as soon as possible; and that Egypt and Saudi Arabia belonged on the list of enemy regimes. Podhoretz allowed that disastrous victories were possible in each case. "There is no denying that the alternative to these regimes could easily turn out to be worse, even (or especially) if it comes to power through democratic elections," he wrote. For that reason, the United States had to find "the stomach to *impose* a new political culture on the defeated parties." America had to find the will and means to remake its defeated enemies from top to bottom as pro-American social, cultural, and political entities.[21]

Neocons in the Pentagon and vice president's office envisioned creative destruction on a similar scale before getting stuck in Iraq. Nine days after the 9/11 attacks, former NATO Supreme Commander Wesley Clark was told by a three-star general who had previously served under him that Bush officials were determined to invade Iraq even if Saddam had nothing to do with the attacks. Two months later Clark returned to the

Pentagon, where he was told that the administration had a five-year plan to overthrow the governments of Iraq, Syria, Lebanon, Libya, Iran, Somalia, and Sudan. The general explained, "We're not that good at fighting terrorists, so we're going after states." Tellingly, the worst state harborers of terrorists—Egypt, Pakistan, and Saudi Arabia—were not on the Pentagon's hit list, because they were allies. That briefing inadvertently launched Clark's 2004 presidential candidacy.[22]

The neoconservatives were relentless in pressing this extraordinary agenda. They stressed the logic of perpetual war implicit in Bush's declaration of global war, especially the "double or nothing" logic of having smashed into the Middle East. Syria allowed anti-American fighters to pass into Iraq, and Shiite leaders in Iraq were tied by faith and recent history to Iran. Syria possessed chemical weapons and supported Hezbollah, and Iran had ballistic missiles superior to Syria's, strong connections to Hezbollah, and an abandoned nuclear program. By the logic of perpetual war, Syria and especially Iran were therefore linked to Iraq as a double or nothing problem. Shortly after the U.S. marched into Baghdad the *Weekly Standard* put it plainly, that Iran was next: "We are already in a death struggle with Iran over the future of Iraq . . . Iran is the tipping point in the war on proliferation, the war on terror, and the effort to reshape the Middle East."[23]

History Applied: Conservative Nationalists, Liberal Hawks, and the Road to Empire

Meanwhile a sizable chunk of the American intellectual Right begged off from invading more nations and reshaping the entire Middle East. The Bush administration blasted into Iraq as though the history of previous imperial ventures there did not apply to the United States. But history was quickly applied. The U.S. marched straight into the mess left by previous empires, and for very similar reasons.

From the beginning the paleoconservative and realist sectors of the American Right were wary of the historical parallels. Pat Buchanan launched *American Conservative* magazine in the summer of 2002 to draw attention to them, warning that Islamic peoples excelled at expelling imperial powers through terrorism and guerrilla war: "They drove the Brits out of Palestine and Aden, the French out of Algeria, the Russians out of Afghanistan, the Americans out of Somalia and Beirut, the Israelis out of Lebanon . . . We have started up the road to empire and over the next hill we shall meet those who went before. The only lesson we learn from history is that we do not learn from history."[24]

During the invasion, the *National Review* tried to expel Buchanan and other critics from the respectable right. Buchanan found that ridiculous, replying that neoconservative imperialism was the opposite of good conservatism. Conservatism was prudent, wise, and historically grounded, he contended. It was tough but not rash or arrogant. Neoconservatism, however, was all about intervening rashly and arrogantly: "The neoconservatives are marinated in conceit, and their hubris may yet prove their undoing . . . What neoconservatives are about is the antithesis of strategy. They do not want to narrow America's list of enemies to those who attack us. They want to broaden the theater of war and multiply our enemies." Buchanan urged that because it was terribly important to defeat al Qaeda and protect America's interests in the Middle East, Americans needed to prevent the war on terror from being "conflated and morphed into the neoconservatives' war for empire. If we do, we will lose our war, isolate America, and bankrupt our republic."[25]

Buchanan's magazine gathered Old Right and realist conservatives around this reading of the situation, including Andrew Bacevich, Doug Bandow, Samuel Francis, Paul Gottfried, Owen Harries, Peter Hitchens, James Kurth, Christopher Layne, Scott McConnell, Eric Margolis, James P. Pinkerton, Justin Raimondo, and Taki Theodoracopulos. Harries, revisiting Krauthammer's thesis that the U.S. took a "holiday from history" in the 1990s, begged to differ. Nine military interventions in one decade did not strike him as much of a vacation. Harries also judged that the Iraq War was more important than the fate of Iraq, because it tested the Bush Doctrine of preemptive, unilateral, liberal imperialism, which Harries considered an unfortunate departure from "the best way to play a hegemonic role." Kurth argued that America's ambitious attempt to transform Iraq into a democracy was likely to fail because Iraqis lacked the cultural values, social conditions, and historical experience to construct one; or because Iraqis associated democracy with American occupation and humiliation; or because there was no Iraqi people, "only three peoples who will use democracy to break away from each other"; or because the combined effect of all these factors was too much to overcome.[26]

Repeatedly the *American Conservative* conservatives echoed Buchanan's admonition that wars are the death of republics and empires. The twentieth century alone was a graveyard of empires that died at war. World War I finished off the Austro-Hungarian, German, Russian, and

Ottoman empires; World War II ended the Nazi and Japanese empires; the two world wars together exhausted the British Empire; and the Soviet Empire cracked apart in Afghanistan. As a presidential candidate in 2000, Buchanan warned that the U.S. could not meddle constantly in other nations without sparking "some horrible retribution." Two years later his magazine belabored this theme in a dramatically new context. The anti-imperial conservatives warned that America could not intervene repeatedly without becoming a target of blowback terrorism, the weapon of the weak. But the neoconservative Bush Doctrine of sustaining hegemony and waging preventive wars was a prescription for permanent war.[27]

Other conservatives offered milder reproaches after it became clear that America's venture in Iraq was not going well. In May 2004 George Will declared that Bush needed to reclaim the genuinely conservative dedication to things as they were, not as they should be: "Traditional conservatism. Nothing 'neo' about it. This administration needs a dose of conservatism without the prefix." Robert F. Ellsworth and Dimitri K. Simes faulted the U.S. for dismantling the Baath party government and Iraqi army before having anything to replace them. In their view, Bush also needed to drop his universal democracy rhetoric, which trumpeted democracy "as an imperial command" and paraded the "demonstrably false pretense" that all cultures had the same values. Even sadder was Fouad Ajami's lament that the first twelve months of America's occupation killed the dream of a democratic showcase in Iraq: "A year or so ago, it was our war, and we claimed it proudly." Now he was embarrassed when Bush mouthed the slogans about why America invaded, because in truth, "we are strangers in Iraq, and we didn't know the place."[28]

The leading liberal hawks who supported the war—John Kerry, Joe Biden, Richard Gephardt, Joseph Lieberman, and Hillary Clinton among the politicians; Thomas Friedman, Peter Beinart, Paul Berman, Kenneth Pollack, Leon Wieseltier, Michael Ignatieff, and Jonathan Chait among the pundits—offered similar renderings of how the Bush team botched a necessary enterprise (though Wieseltier declared that he would not have supported the war had he known the truth about Iraq's nonexistent weapons). The politicians, all of them presidential aspirants, held fast to the implications of their belief that an antiwar Democrat could not be elected to the presidency. Kerry undoubtedly voted for the war because he was planning to run for president. By the time that Kerry won the nomination in 2004, the situation in Iraq was so awful that he may have doubted the certainties of his poll-driven advisers. Kerry tried to turn Iraq to his advantage, but his tortured explanations of his record lessened the damage of the issue to Bush's campaign. In the end Kerry was reduced to claiming that he would have run a better occupation because America's allies didn't hate him.[29]

Jonathan Chait, two years removed from his strident pro-war editorials in the *New Republic*, conceded the obvious—that the war was going very badly—but insisted that the liberal hawks' "prescription" had been right. Social realities were often governed by "tipping points," he argued, not proportional returns. If Rumsfeld had sent enough troops to secure and rebuild Iraq, fewer Iraqi males would have joined the resistance, which would have led to greater political stability. Had Bush occupied Iraq in the way that the liberal hawks called for, with plenty of troops and international support, the Iraq occupation might have resembled those of East Timor, Germany, and Japan. Instead the country quickly descended into a vicious cycle of chaos, insecurity, stagnation, and resentment.

Chait allowed that the Bush team never feigned any interest in doing it right. Bush, Cheney, Rumsfeld, and Wolfowitz had assured that Iraq would be transformed quickly and cheaply. Chait figured that was stampede boilerplate. In other words, "I simply thought they were lying." The Bush team routinely lied about the costs of its tax cuts and other initiatives, so how were liberal hawks to know that this time "the Bushies actually believed their own propaganda?" It made no sense that Bush would allow Iraq to descend into chaos, but that was what happened. Moreover, unlike many liberal hawks, Chait never believed in the democratization argument anyway. Iraq was not a good candidate for democracy, and he had figured that the Bush administration would settle for a stable illiberal regime in Baghdad.[30]

With each year of Bush's second term, the ranks of defiant liberal hawks diminished; John Edwards and Hillary Clinton recanted in 2007 in time to run for the 2008 Democratic presidential nomination as critics of the war. The neocons, meanwhile, though shaken by the savage violence of Iraq's insurgent and sectarian wars, did not go in for doleful second thoughts.

The Neoconservative Moment: Podhoretz, Muravchik, Krauthammer, and Fukuyama

Norman Podhoretz kept refashioning the same essay, lionizing the Bush Doctrine, blasting its "anti-American" critics, mythologizing the war on radical Islamism as World War IV, and updating his list of governments that had to be smashed. If the U.S. could transform Nazi Germany and imperial Japan into capitalist democracies, there was no reason why it could not do the same to the entire Islamic world. Conservative realists replied that things were different there; Podhoretz countered that "things were different everywhere, and a thousand reasons to expect the failure of any enterprise could always be conjured up to discourage making an ambitious effort."[31]

In September 2004 he compared the upcoming presidential election to that of 1948. The issues in 1948 were the necessity of World War III and the right way to fight it, Podhoretz explained. World War III had begun in 1947. Truman's narrow victory the following year established that the U.S. would not shrink from fighting communism; eventually the Republican Party and the liberal wing of the Democratic Party joined the cold war consensus. Podhoretz urged that the 2004 election was equally significant. John Kerry was not committed to fighting World War IV; if elected he would return to antiterrorism as law enforcement. Podhoretz urged that, fortunately, America already had a president who understood the reality and necessity of World War IV. Bush had recently bestowed on Podhoretz the Presidential Medal of Freedom, the nation's highest civilian honor. Podhoretz pleaded that America needed Bush to remain president. Like Reagan, there were times when Bush failed to act in full accordance with his convictions, but Podhoretz vowed not to repeat the mistake he had made with Reagan. Having condemned Reagan's opportunism and mistakes during his presidency, only to realize afterward that Reagan got the big things right, Podhoretz judged that Bush was like Reagan; in 2005 he described Bush as "the amazing leader this President has amazingly turned out to be." Bush made historic changes in America's approach to the world; he gave hope to reformers in the Middle East, just as Reagan inspired dissidents behind the Iron Curtain; and he reduced the number of rogue governments. For years Podhoretz had ranked Afghanistan, Iraq, and Libya among the governments that had to be overthrown as soon as possible. Now all three were off the list because Bush smashed Afghanistan and Iraq, while Libya's Qaddafi, not wishing to be next, gave up his nuclear program. To Podhoretz that left Iran, Syria, the Palestinian Authority, and North Korea at the top of the list; Lebanon came off after Syria withdrew from it; Egypt and Saudi Arabia still had to go but were not as urgent.[32]

Joshua Muravchik adopted Podhoretz's trope that the war on Islamic terrorism was actually World War IV. Like Podhoretz, he stressed that radical Muslims had been waging this war for decades with little response from Americans: "The jihadists have murdered our diplomatic personnel in numerous countries, hijacked our airliners and cruise ships, blown our civilian aircraft out of the sky, killed our Marines in their barracks, soldiers in their beds, sailors in their berths. They have kidnapped, tortured, and murdered us by the ones, the tens, and the hundreds." In 2001 they finally killed enough Americans to get America's attention; thus World War IV began on September 11, 2001. Muravchik cautioned that radical Islamists already held more support among the world's billion-plus Muslims than Americans found it "diplomatic" to acknowledge. If the radicals defeated the U.S. in Iraq, their prestige would skyrocket throughout the Muslim world, forcing moderates to cater to them.[33]

Faced with a world-historical crisis in Iraq, the neocons seemed to become more alike, adopting the same jargon and tone. They blasted their critics and did not labor their philosophical differences with one another. The exception to the rule—a speech by Charles Krauthammer on February 10, 2004—sparked a rare controversy among neoconservatives. The occasion was the annual board dinner of the *National Interest*, a gathering of prominent neocons and conservatives; the site was the epicenter of neoconservatism, the American Enterprise Institute; the forum was the Irving Kristol Lecture. Reprising his "holiday from history" thesis, Krauthammer asserted that Americans were rudely awakened from their vacation slumbers on 9/11, after which they had to think seriously about how the U.S. should relate to the world.

In his rendering there were four major schools of thought. Isolationists wanted to pull back to Fortress America; liberal internationalists believed in multilateral webs of treaties and international cooperation; realists stressed the primacy of power in a Hobbesian world of nation states; democratic globalists believed in the moral and geopolitical power of exporting democracy. For neoconservatives the serious options were realism and democratic globalism, but Krauthammer cautioned that pure realism lacked any vision besides power, while democratic globalism was too ambitious and idealistic. Because it stressed the universal right to freedom, democratic globalism tended to erase the crucial, chastening, prudential calculation of national interest and limits. It was too open-ended in its idealism not to plant the flag of democracy everywhere. Krauthammer warned that the high-flying rhetoric of Bush and British Prime Minister Tony Blair exemplified this danger. Because many neocons were democratic globalists, neoconservatism was usually identified with it, and Bush was often called a neocon for having embraced it. But Krauthammer urged that good neoconservatism was something else, a fifth approach he called "democratic realism."[34]

Democratic realism applied the brakes of national interest and limits to the religion of democracy. It spent blood and treasure to create democracies only in places where the American hegemon faced an "existential" challenge to its unipolar status or its very existence. The object of an empire's foreign policy is to maintain its dominance, Krauthammer admonished; thus the U.S. had to defend its unipolar dominion wherever it was challenged. However, America needed to fight for democracy only in places where it confronted challenges to its existence and identity. Currently the existential enemy of the United States was radical Islamism. America had no business exporting democracy to non-Islamic nations, but it had a compelling reason to create democracies in the Islamic crescent stretching from North Africa to Afghanistan. Krauthammer stressed that radical Islamism presented the same challenge to America's existence and identity that Soviet communism posed during the cold war. For that reason it had to be fought in the same way that America fought communism. During the cold war the crucial test of any foreign-policy decision was whether it helped America defeat communism. Fighting for democracy was sometimes a means to the anticommunist end; often it was not. The same test of democratic realism applied to the new struggle for the world.

This prescription refashioned Krauthammer's familiar themes from the 1980s and 1990s in a new context. In the 1980s he conceived democratic globalism as a means to fight communism; in the 1990s he urged that the lowly mop work of exporting democracy was not a proper task for a self-respecting unrivaled superpower; after America invaded Iraq he conceded that democracy building was back on the agenda because the threat from radical Muslims had risen to a world-historical level. America had to use democracy as a weapon against radical Islamism in much the same way that it used democracy during the cold war.

Most of Krauthammer's audience was well versed in the twists and turns of his foreign policy thinking, and his latest turn was not surprising. But the immediate context triggered a surprising reaction from one of his listeners, Francis Fukuyama. A Wolfowitz protégé and professor of international political economy at Johns Hopkins, Fukuyama's heralded 1989 article on the "end of history" had provided the point of departure for Krauthammer's first version of unipolarity. If history was ending, Krauthammer reasoned, there was no longer any reason to focus on the periphery. The death of communism changed America's structure of obligations. Instead of converting Third World nations to democracy, the focus of American foreign policy should be to strengthen and unify "a super-sovereign West." Later he judged that, in fact, the super-sovereign center of things was the United States.[35]

Fukuyama and Krauthammer shared the same network of neoconservative journals and institutions, but by 2004 Fukuyama was distressed at the influence of Krauthammer-style unipolarism. Often it was simply identified with neoconservatism; more important, as Fukuyama observed, it had "strong influence inside the Bush Administration foreign policy team and beyond." Krauthammer received invitations to the White House, where he was taken very seriously. Listening to him lecture, Fukuyama was struck by Krauthammer's seemingly arrogant disregard of the turmoil in Iraq. The invasion of Iraq was "the archetypal application of American unipolarity," Fukuyama observed, yet Krauthammer felt no obligation even to mention its challenge to his thesis:

> There is not the slightest nod towards the new empirical facts that have emerged in the last year or so: the failure to find weapons of mass destruction in Iraq, the virulent and steadily mounting anti-Americanism throughout the Middle East, the growing insurgency in Iraq, the fact that no strong democratic leadership had emerged there, the enormous financial and growing human cost of the war, the failure to leverage the war to make progress on the Israeli-Palestinian front, and the fact that America's fellow democratic allies had by and large failed to fall in line and legitimate American actions *ex post*.[36]

Fukuyama worried that most observers equated neoconservatism with Krauthammer's imperious attitude about such things. If those holding to a different idea of neoconservatism did not step forward, the neocons were sure to be replaced by old-style realists like Brent Scowcroft, Old Right nationalists like Pat Buchanan, or liberal internationalists like John Kerry. Neoconservatism was on fire in Iraq, and neocons were foolish to ignore it. Thanks especially to Krauthammer, Fukuyama observed, neoconservatism was known for spurning diplomacy, advocating outright imperialism, and claiming that Arabs respected power above all; he recalled hearing Krauthammer say that to win the hearts and minds of Arab leaders, the U.S. had to grab a lower part of their anatomy and squeeze hard. To Fukuyama, Krauthammer's realism and idealism were both strangely exaggerated, as were his views of the radical Islamic threat and the capacity of American power to control world events.

Under the category of exaggerated realism, Fukuyama doubted that radical Islam posed an existential threat to Americans. Thus he was skeptical of Krauthammer's claim that destroying it was America's highest-priority strategic necessity. The Soviet Union certainly had been such a threat; it could have annihilated America physically or perhaps subverted American democracy. Fukuyama observed that radical jihadists had no such power over American civilization. Under the category of exaggerated democratic idealism, it astonished him that Krauthammer recycled grandiose neocon assurances about the power of American democracy to transform Arab societies. How had this faith emerged from the very movement that spent decades condemning the social engineering schemes of Great Society liberals? If the U.S. could not eliminate poverty in Baltimore, how was it supposed to create liberal democracy in Iraq? Krauthammer accused skeptics of believing that Arabs were not capable of democracy; Fukuyama replied that no one said that. His own writings were rather strong on the theme that history moved toward liberal democracy. But democracy had strong cultural prerequisites, he remarked, "something that is usually taken to be a conservative insight." Democracies were not created through sheer political willpower. In its history since conquering the Philippines in 1899 the U.S. engaged in approximately eighteen nation-building projects. Only three were definitely successful—Germany, Japan, and South Korea—all of which required very long military engagements; moreover, Germany and Japan were highly developed states before the American democratizing began. In all other cases, Fukuyama cautioned, U.S. power established no self-sustaining institutions, and sometimes it made matters considerably worse.[37]

As for Krauthammer's constant boasting about the enormity and disparity of American power, Fukuyama appealed for a bit more modesty. America had vast military and cultural power, but Americans generally lacked Krauthammer's imperial ambitions and self-image. Since Krauthammer acknowledged the latter point, why was he so eager for Americans to assume "this unbelievably ambitious effort to politically transform one of the world's most troubled and hostile regions?" If Americans really wanted their country to be a commercial republic, not an empire, why should neoconservatives insist on expanding America's domain? Fukuyama cautioned that the destructive chaos of Iraq showed what was likely to happen when a nation of reluctant imperialists played at empire: "We have been our usual inept and disorganized selves in planning for and carrying out the reconstruction, something that was predictable in advance and should not have surprised anyone familiar with American history."[38]

It troubled Fukuyama that, thanks to Krauthammer, Podhoretz, both Kristols, the Bush administration, and a host of others, neoconservatism was known for snubbing its nose at world opinion. Krauthammer was good at blasting the wooly-minded types that made the United Nations an object of faith, but he was not very good at listening to what many European critics of the Iraq war actually said. Often they stressed prudential concerns, Fukuyama noted. Europeans questioned the wisdom of invading the Muslim world; they doubted that Iraq was as dangerous as the Bush administration claimed; they argued that al Qaeda had no operative connection to Saddam's regime; they worried that invading Iraq would detract from the struggle against terrorism; they did not trust that the U.S. would be a good occupying power in Iraq; they were incredulous that the U.S. proposed to democratize the entire Middle East; and they preferred to see the U.S. concentrate on solving the Israeli-Palestinian problem, which was a worse source of conflict than Iraq. Fukuyama conceded that these positions were debatable. But by the summer of 2004, there was little room for doubt that the European critics were closer to the truth than was the Bush administration.[39]

Neoconservatism abounded in strident depictions of a world war between good and evil. Krauthammer portrayed the radical Islamic threat to the United States as immense, bitter, pervasive, remorseless, immediate, implacable, and potentially catastrophic; Fukuyama replied that that described Israel's situation, not America's. Israel was locked in a remorseless struggle with most of the Arab and Muslim world, its very existence was threatened, and it seemed to have few options besides an iron fist. The American situation was very different, for the U.S. was incredibly powerful, not surrounded by enemies, and not hated by most of the Muslim world. The radical jihadists hated America, but they were a small fraction of the world's 1.2 billion Muslims. Fukuyama wanted neoconservatives to pay more attention to the feelings of ordinary Muslims, because "Krauthammerian unipolarity has increased hatred for the United States in the broader fight for hearts and minds." It was not a good thing for

America to adopt Israel's aggressive, pre-emptive approach to the Middle East, for Israel's strategy did not scale well.[40]

Fukuyama wanted neoconservatism to be known for practicing vigorous diplomacy and building new institutions. On the national level he wanted the U.S. government to create a permanent office devoted to nation building. On the global level he wanted the U.S. to get behind the Community of Democracies founded during the Clinton administration. On the regional international level he wanted the U.S. to create overlapping multilateral organizations such as the six-power configuration that the Bush administration stumbled into in dealing with North Korea. China and Japan were especially eager to create new regional multilateral organizations, he observed. It was wrong for the U.S. to ignore or oppose opportunities for new free-trade networks, information sharing, and security pacts, especially in East Asia. As a neoconservative, Fukuyama assured that he held no brief for the United Nations and did not believe in multilateralism for its own sake. He told the *New York Times* that he retained his neoconservative belief in the "universal aspiration for democracy and the use of American power to spread democracy in the world." But he wanted the neoconservative movement that he had long supported to become known for its constructive impulses.[41]

This broadside was curiously confused on key points. Fukuyama failed to distinguish between the democratic globalist and democratic realist wings of neoconservatism; he wrongly described Krauthammer as a democratic globalist, criticizing him on this basis; yet in his closing paragraph Fukuyama identified himself with democratic globalism. Based on Fukuyama's description one would not have known that, nor been able to explain why, Krauthammer opposed Clinton's interventions in Bosnia and Kosovo. Neither would one have realized that Krauthammer's enthusiasm for democratizing the Middle East was a recent development. Had he explained Krauthammer's thinking more precisely, Fukuyama's critique of his selective realism and democratizing turn would have been more effective. Skilled at debate, Krauthammer replied that it was "odd in the extreme" to be criticized for taking a position he had criticized for nearly fifteen years, especially since Fukuyama apparently aspired to that view.[42]

Despite getting some of the positioning wrong, however, Fukuyama made telling points on matters of greater importance, and from a unique standpoint. It was a novel development for a self-identified neoconservative to judge that America had overreached in Iraq. Having sparked a firestorm of blowback resistance and terrorism in Iraq, the neocons concentrated reluctantly on rearguard battles but did not back down from "double or nothing" claims about the bigger picture.

Richard Perle and David Frum wanted a comprehensive air and naval blockade of North Korea and a buildup of ground forces on the Korean peninsula to force a North Korean capitulation, compel a Chinese intervention, or start a shooting war. They wanted to overthrow the Iranian, Syrian, and Libyan governments, explaining that Iran and Syria colluded with terrorists on their own soil and Libya had "an implacably hostile regime" that would never change without being overthrown (the following year Libya did so). They wanted similarly aggressive policies toward Lebanon, the Palestinian Authority, Somalia, Sierra Leone, Yemen, Venezuela, and Paraguay, explaining that Lebanon was a vassal of Syria; the Palestinian Authority existed to collude with terrorists; Yemen, Somalia, and Sierra Leone were failed states; and Venezuela and Paraguay had gotten into the terrorist collusion business. They bitterly rejected the State Department's distinction between al Qaeda's terrorism against America and that of Hamas and Hezbollah against Israel, contending that Hamas and Hezbollah deserved the same treatment as al Qaeda. And they wanted Bush to enroll Saudi Arabia in the axis of evil.[43]

Like most neocons Perle and Frum treated the problem of anti-imperial blowback as a test of American seriousness. Reuel Marc Gerecht, a former Middle East specialist for the CIA, took it slightly more seriously. Gerecht urged that bombing Iran was the "only option that passes the pinch test" and that the U.S. also needed to attack Syria. Like many neocons he believed that Syria would be easy and Iran much less so. Gerecht acknowledged that there was one serious reason not to attack Iran—the Iraq-scale potential for terrorist blowback that existed in Iran. However, that argument "takes us back to the pre-9/11 world, where we preempted ourselves because of our fear of our enemies' potential nastiness." The neocons enthused that with George W. Bush in the White House, America no longer backed away from creative destruction and its side effects.[44]

Later they plugged hard for John McCain on the same grounds.

Chapter 12

Militaristic Illusions

THE IRAQ DEBACLE AND THE CRISIS OF AMERICAN EMPIRE

Our subject is the crisis of American empire, especially in Iraq. One of the central problems of U.S. foreign policy today is to modulate the natural tendency of an unrivaled power to regard the entire world as its geopolitical neighborhood. This would have been a defining challenge for the Bush administration even if terrorists had not struck the U.S. on September 11, 2001. The U.S. at the turn of the twenty-first century was overdue for a moral and political reckoning with the compulsive expansionism of unrivaled power. But the problem of world empire increased by several orders of magnitude with the election of George W. Bush, his selection of a neoconservative foreign policy team, their urging after the fiendish attacks of 9/11 to conceive the struggle against terrorism as a world war, and his decision to do so. Thus our country finds itself struggling to extricate itself from an imperial debacle in Iraq.

Five years of war have ripped apart Iraqi society, Prime Minister Nouri al-Maliki's government barely exists in most of the country, and the U.S. has no exit plan, all of which leave Iraq with only a distant hope of real sovereignty. On the other hand, mercifully, the violence in Iraq has declined dramatically in recent months, and last August the Maliki government began to press the U.S. for an exit agreement. As bad as things look today in Iraq, for three years it was dreadfully worse. Though the media and even the peace movement have stopped talking about Iraq, this is the moment to make a real breakthrough for peace and anti-imperialism.

From March 2005 to April 2007 the eruption of a civil war in the midst of a ferocious insurgent war produced huge numbers of weekly attacks and killings in Iraq, averaging two thousand attacks per month. In the past seven months violence has declined because the recent "surge" of U.S. forces restricted the flow of explosives into Baghdad, ethnic cleansing was completed in many areas, the Mahdi Army suspended its attacks, and the U.S. co-opted Sunni insurgents. However, the surge was temporary, ethnic cleansing is unfinished in many areas, the Mahdi Army may be biding its time, and it's a perilous business to pay people to stop shooting at you, especially when it involves meddling in tribal conflicts and favoring some tribes over others. More importantly, the fundamental problems that fueled the insurgency and civil war still exist in Iraq, while the U.S.'s total-expenses price tag is approaching $2 trillion.

President Bush's surge strategy was controversial when he announced it last year, because it smacked of desperation and quagmire after four years of failed military strategies. But cutting off the supply lines into Baghdad was an achievable objective with enough forces; General David Petraeus used the surge's five extra combat brigades to build a military ring around Baghdad. At the same time Bush officials called the escalation a "surge" because it had to be temporary; the U.S. lacks the forces to sustain it. Moreover, the high death tolls of 2006 and early 2007 reflected vicious campaigns of ethnic cleansing that are now completed in key areas. We may be witnessing a mere lull of ethnic cleansing before it resumes elsewhere, just as the cease-fire by Moktada al-Sadr's Mahdi Army, the main anti-American Shiite militia group, may not be permanent. Last August the Mahdi Army had a dangerous clash with the Badr Organization, the Shiite militia group that dominates the Iraqi Army and police force, which raised the specter of a civil war between Shiites.

All of this will take decades to play out, well beyond the blink of an American news cycle. Iraq is broken into rival groups of warlords, sectarian militias, local gangs, foreign terrorists, political and ethnic factions, a struggling government, and a deeply corrupted and sectarian police force. In Bosnia it was possible to settle a civil war by turning the country into a loose confederation, because at least Bosnia had leaders of coherent political factions that cut deals and delivered their factions. Iraq is broken worse than that.

The Sunnis are enraged at being invaded, having their homes destroyed, losing their privileged status, and being subjected to a foreign power. As the nation's traditional elite they assume their right to govern. Many of them believe that only Sunnis are true Muslims. They are appalled that the Western invader has paved the way to a Shiite government allied with Iran. They regard the Shiites as collaborators with the invader. They are deeply opposed to the new constitution. They want a strong central government that distributes oil revenue from Baghdad, and they are incredulous that the U.S. has enabled Iran to become the dominant force in the Middle East. The Shiites are embittered by decades of Sunni tyranny in Iraq and centuries of Sunni dominance in the Middle East. Arab Shiites have not tasted power for centuries, and Iraqi Shiites are determined to redeem their ostensible right to rule Iraq that was denied them in 1920.

Both sides and the Kurds have militia groups that are the real powers in Iraq. Two million Iraqis have fled the country, in a nation of twenty-seven million; another two million have fled their homes within the country. The Kurds want their own country, and in the meantime they have enacted their own oil law, cut a deal with the Hunt Oil Company of Dallas, and are demanding 17 percent of the national income.

The Bush administration put forth a grab bag of rationales for invading Iraq and a series of strategies for converting it into a unitary democracy. All of them failed, so the administration fell back on the slogan that when the Iraqi Army stands up, the American Army will stand down. Today Iraq has over fifty battle-tested battalions, and its army and police force are approaching a combined force of four hundred thousand.

But after five years Iraq still has few battalions that can fight and hold without American support, and to the extent that a military force is being built up, it's a Shiite army. The Sunnis will not stand for that. For two years, the creation of a national Shiite army was the number one factor fueling the civil war in Iraq; it drove the middle section of the country to a barbaric state beyond politics where all that mattered was fear and revenge. This fear of a Shiite army and police force, and the Shiite determination to retain both, remain central facts of life in Iraq.

As recently as February 2005 the war against the Sunni insurgency was consuming for the U.S. and the problem of foreign terrorism was growing but small. Then the civil war erupted in mid-February, creating a new worst problem, and the problem of foreign terrorism got worse, because the Sunni tribes gave refuge to foreign fighters. The foreign terrorists thrived on the chaotic aftermath of the war, the lack of a stable government and police force, and the intense Sunni desire for revenge. They swam in a sea of disorder and alienated hostility that the American occupation constantly refueled. Today some terrorist groups in Iraq are on the run, because their Sunni tribal sponsors have belatedly turned against them, but others are still swimming, especially those connected to Shiite Iran.

Last summer the Bush administration and Army made a stunning policy change by arming Sunni insurgents. Al Qaeda in Mesopotamia, a homegrown Sunni Arab insurgent group led by foreign terrorists, alienated Sunni tribal sheiks by bombing marketplaces, killing Iraqis indiscriminately. General Petraeus capitalized on the alienation by giving weapons to tribal police forces and other militia groups in Anbar Province that promised to use them against foreign terrorists. Attacks on American troops went down after the policy was instituted, so Petraeus rolled the dice in the entire Sunni triangle, despite the opposition of the Maliki government. Sunni tribal sheiks call this co-optation program the "Awakening Movement." The very groups the U.S. fought for four years are now getting U.S. weapons if they promise to use them against foreign terrorists.

This measure has bought significant relief for U.S. troops, but the strategy of arming the Sunni insurgency is loaded with perils and tricky long-term consequences. Trying to co-opt insurgent groups is not new in counterinsurgency warfare. The French, British, and U.S. tried it, respectively, in Algeria, Malaya, and Vietnam. In every case the weapons given to insurgent groups ended up being used against the forces providing them. Major General Rick Lynch, commander of the Third Infantry Division, explains the mentality of the Sunni militants he is trying to co-opt: "They say to us, 'We hate you because you are occupiers, but we hate Al Qaeda worse, and we hate the Persians even more.'" In this lexicon, Iraqi Shiites are Persians, like the Iranians.[1]

So the U.S. is arming Sunni fighters in the hope that they will spend most of their time killing people in the middle group, even as they profess to hating the Shiites most of all. The Shiite-dominated government, naturally, pleaded against this scheme. Last July, during a video conference, Maliki implored Bush to terminate the policy and fire Petraeus. He also threatened to arm Shiite militias with government funds in response; Bush told Maliki to calm down and get with the American program. In public Maliki's top political adviser, Sadiq Rikabi, is more plaintive. There are too many militias already, he says: "Why are we creating new ones?"[2]

The answer is that nothing else worked, so the Bush administration put one hundred thousand "Awakening Leaders" on the weekly payroll. It's not clear how they will be removed from the dole, and Shiite leaders are not sympathetic to the U.S.'s predicament. The co-optation strategy has deeply enmeshed the U.S. in Iraqi tribal politics, lifting up (and corrupting) certain tribes, such as the newly powerful Abu Risha tribe in Ramadi, which is fueling tribal resentments throughout the Sunni triangle region. Tribes are forming their own militias, undermining the Iraqi Islamic Party (the main Sunni political party) and creating new leaders adept at cutting deals and getting access to money that was supposed to pay for reconstruction projects. Very little reconstruction that actually helps Iraq has occurred. It's very hard to find evidence of the $150 billion of aid the U.S. has poured into Iraq, aside from a handful of gold-plated projects that American contractors were eager to build, and the predatory corruption of government officials and well-connected tribal leaders in Iraq is pervasive, direct, and unrelenting.

American military commanders warn that Iraq could explode again at any time, because Sunni leaders are demanding real power, the Shiite parties are determined not to yield it, and intra-sectarian resentments are boiling. For two years Shiite leaders sat back, bided their time, gave lip service to a unity government, thwarted any real attempt at one, and trusted the Americans to kill off their Sunni enemies. But the Americans failed, and civil war erupted. Today the Shiites and Kurds see total victory within their grasp. They are stonewalling against integrating Sunnis into the army, and they are gathering the fingerprints, retinal scans, and home addresses of every Awakening fighter. They are convinced that another year or two of lip service to a unity government will pave the way to a Shiite-dominated government and a U.S. withdrawal from Iraq. Maliki observes: "There are two mentalities in this region: conspiracy and mistrust."[3]

He would know. The key to Maliki is that he survived twenty-four years of brutally difficult exile in Iran and Syria as a functionary in a tiny, persecuted, ferociously anti-American, Islamist party, the Dawa Party. He developed close ties with Iran and Hezbollah but learned to trust only tiny cells of Dawa exiles. Maliki owes his political prominence in Iraq to his alliance, only recently severed, with Moktada al-Sadr and the Mahdi Army, the very force he is now trying to put down to prove his mettle as a unifying nationalist leader.

Last year his government set up a constitutional review committee. The group was given four months to recommend changes to the constitution, which is so flawed that it doesn't give the government the right to collect taxes. The group met for seven months, wrangled over taxes, revenue distribution, Kirkuk, whether Iraq is an Arab country, and the scope of the presidency, and gave up; it no longer meets. Last spring the Reconciliation and Accountability Law was supposed to allow former Baathists to collect government pensions and open hundreds of government jobs to Sunnis. But the plan was quashed in the Iraqi Parliament after Ahmad Chalabi, Ayatollah Sistani, and other Shiite leaders rallied against it. To many Shiite leaders, Paul Bremer's purge of thirty thousand Baathists and his disbanding of the Iraqi Army were not disastrous miscalculations that fueled the insurgent war; they were merely a good start toward a Shiite victory that must not be squandered.

On many days the Iraqi Parliament cannot manage a quorum, and nearly all of Maliki's proposals are bogged down in parliamentary committees. His government could fold on any given day, because it lacks a majority in the National Assembly. All it would take is a no-confidence motion in the parliament. Last summer, the Accordance Front (a Sunni alliance) and Iraqiya (a secular alliance) resigned from the government, both protesting the government's alliance with Iran, which left it even more so.

The Maliki government is a shrinking coalition of pro-Iranian Shiite parties and militias, and the militia groups are the basis of political power and loyalty in Iraq. Formally Maliki's cabinet has thirty-six ministers, but he can rely on only three or four, and his cabinet vacancies have oscillated between fifteen and twenty over the past year. His power rests on the Bush administration and the Supreme Islamic Iraqi Council, formerly known as the Supreme Council for the Islamic Revolution, led by Abdul Aziz al-Hakim, which controls the Badr Organization that dominates the Iraqi police and army.

Thus far the parliament has accomplished precious little, and its legitimacy is disputed even when it passes something. Most Sunnis boycotted the 2005 election, as did Moktada al-Sadr's followers, leaving much of the country unrepresented in parliament. Understandably in a nation with a smashed state, a shredded civil society, and no democratic tradition, there is little acceptance that obeying the rules is more important than winning. Last month Speaker Mashhadani, the Sunni leader of Iraq's parliament, threatened to disband the legislature, protesting that sectarian gridlock prevailed. The government still had no budget for 2008, he observed, it could not agree on a date for provincial elections, and the Baathist reconciliation bill passed in January was already being subverted. Mashhadani declared that Iraq's parliament was too dysfunctional to do anything except reinforce sectarian agendas.

This is a grim picture, which won't improve as long as Iraqi Sunnis and Shiites don't find a way to cooperate politically. But there are some recent signs of political progress. The parliament is grappling seriously with the Baathist reconciliation process, an extremely difficult problem that requires tough political bargaining. An election law is in the works, and Mashhadani's dramatic threat to disband the parliament broke a logjam on the budget issue, freeing up millions of dollars for reconstruction projects. To make further political progress that makes a real difference in the country, Iraq needs an oil deal, a new constitution, a resolution over Kirkuk, and an election that brings more Sunnis into the government and more secular-leaning Shiites that resist depending on Iran. Most difficult of all, it needs to integrate large numbers of Sunni forces into the army and police force. Above all, it needs to pull off a deal with the United States to get American troops out of Iraq.

We are approaching a turning point on the last issue. For Iraq, the question is whether Iraqi leaders will restrain their sectarian factionalism enough to stand up for their own sovereignty. For the U.S., the question is whether it will commit to a definite departure date from Iraq. Once a nation takes the path of empire, there are always reasons why it thinks it cannot leave a place it has invaded. The Bush administration is loudly admonishing on this subject because pressure is mounting to make a different choice. The U.N. authorization for the U.S.'s presence in Iraq will run out in December, and Maliki is under pressure from Shiite and Sunni factions to get American troops out of the country. But his army is weak, like his government, and Iraq may well explode in a civil war when the U.S. leaves. So Maliki is having trouble settling on a position. His administration is wavering back and forth over how much longer it wants the U.S. military to stay in Iraq, while the Bush administration adamantly opposes any commitment to an exit date and it has no intention of relinquishing most or all of the fourteen military bases we've built there.

That's where the peace movement comes in. This is not a moment to downplay the Iraq issue or to lose interest in it. We must demand that the U.S. start planning its exit from Iraq with a definite ending date. As long as the U.S. Army is the ultimate power in Iraq, Iraq will have no sovereignty; Shiites will be viewed in the Sunni provinces as collaborators with the invader; Sunnis will view the Iraqi Army as a creation of the invaders that puts their enemies in charge; and Sunni leaders must fear that any cooperation they extend to the occupier will brand them as traitors. When the occupier pulls back, the toxic politics of collaboration and betrayal

will be lessened. The civil strife in Iraq is going to play itself out no matter what the U.S. does. But the U.S. set it off; we are refueling it every day
that we are there; and sooner or later even a stubborn, clueless invader
has to leave, to let conquered peoples breathe on their own.

Admiral Michael G. Mullen, chair of the Joint Chiefs of Staff, told
Congress last July that if Iraq does not soon achieve a breakthrough that
unifies the country politically, "no amount of troops in no amount of time
will make much of a difference."[4] There is no military solution to the
debacle of Iraq, and all the options are bad. The best thing we can do is
find our way out so that Iraq can regain its dignity as a sovereign country. President Bush warns that if we commit to an exit strategy in Iraq,
Iranian-backed radicalism will gain the upper hand there and all will be
lost: "For all those who ask whether the fight is worth it, imagine an Iraq
where militia groups backed by Iran control large parts of the country."
But that is exactly what is happening now. Iranian agents are everywhere
in Iraq, buying off politicians and military leaders, and financing para-
military groups. The American military is not the long-term or even the
present-day solution to that problem, as we have failed to contain it even
with 165,000 troops there. If Iraq is to stand up for its own sovereignty
against Iran, it will have to do so on the basis of Iraqi nationalism and
culture.[5]

We got into this situation because the Bush administration invaded Iraq
with no regard whatsoever for the cultural and historical variables. The
Pentagon, vice president, and president had a privileged vision of what
was going to happen and did not allow it to be challenged. With an arrogance that would be hard to exaggerate, they dismissed warnings from
the State Department and others about the perils of occupying the Arab
world's Yugoslavia.

They didn't want to know that the process of modernization and urbanization was only an inch deep in Iraqi society. They had no idea that
tribal values, born of surviving a harsh environment for centuries, held
sway for so many Iraqis. They didn't even know the names of the tribes.
Donald Rumsfeld, Dick Cheney, Paul Wolfowitz, and Douglas Feith
looked at their exile informants, especially Ahmad Chalabi, and blithely
assumed that democratizing Iraq would be easy. They actually believed
they could create an instant pro-American democracy by destroying the
Iraqi state and paving the way to a government led by Chalabi. Instead,
lacking inside contacts and familiarity with the cultural signals, they blundered into an inferno of insurgent and sectarian violence. The U.S. could

not get Iraqi Sunnis to spy upon or kill fellow Sunnis, and Iraqi Shiite informers were not effective in Sunni provinces. In a nation of Assyrians, Chaldeans, Kurds, Sunnis, Shi'a, Turkmen, Yazidis, and a mixture of foreigners, American soldiers were unable to identify the provenance of those whom they guarded and fought.

Today many Americans want to believe the U.S. can have its way wherever it uses enough force. So we are told that if only Rumsfeld had occupied Iraq with twice as many troops, everything would be fine in Iraq; John McCain says it every day on the campaign trail. But even a competent occupier would not have prevented the insurgency or the sectarian violence in Iraq. Invading Iraq was not a good idea that the Pentagon mismanaged. It was an atrocious idea dreamed up by people who did not want to know that the American invader would be radioactive there.

Rumsfeld came to symbolize the contradictions in this picture. For years his neoconservative friends made lists of the half-dozen governments they wanted to overthrow. But Rumsfeld tried to show that the U.S. could overthrow governments at minimal cost, without a Colin Powell–sized fuss. Even the U.S. didn't have a large enough military to combine the Powell Doctrine of overwhelming force with neocon ambitions for several wars.

Today the Bush administration is caught in the aftermath of this contradiction. The U.S. is spending hundreds of billions anyway, but with little to show for it. We are warned that all of it will be wasted if the U.S. does not pour massive new resources into Iraq *and* overthrow Iran and Syria. Hard-liners want a cold war–sized army, a sustained surge in Iraq, military strikes against Iran and Syria, and the next generation of high-tech weapons. The war plan for Iran was finished three years ago, and in April 2006 *New Yorker* political journalist Seymour Hersh reported that Bush and Cheney fought with the Joint Chiefs over the necessity of bombing Natanz with a tactical nuclear weapon; Bush and Cheney were dead serious about doing it.[6]

Meanwhile the U.S. is officially spending $11 billion per month in Iraq, nearly all of it from emergency spending bills, and the total bill for five years of Iraq (counting long-term costs) is expected to run at least $2 trillion, all of it added to the federal debt. That comes out to $18,000 per household. Columbia University economist Joseph Stiglitz and Harvard University public finance specialist Linda Bilmes have been tracking the total costs since the U.S. invaded Iraq; their new book is titled *The Three Trillion Dollar War*. The U.S. could have fixed Social Security or provided health insurance for all uninsured Americans for the next half-century with the amount it is spending in Iraq.[7]

An Exception to History?

"We come to your cities and lands not as conquerors or enemies, but as liberators." These eerily familiar words were spoken by General F. S. Maude, as the British Army invaded Baghdad in March 1917. Then, as now, the assurance was a half-truth. The British, having secured a League of Nations mandate, could say they were freeing the people of Mesopotamia from Turkish oppression, but the whole world knew they did it for the sake of their empire, to secure British control over the Persian Gulf and its oil. Their occupation led to a rather unhappy experiment with what we, today, call Iraqification. The British occupied Iraq with a force of 120,000 troops, but that didn't stop Sunni and Shiite nationalists from revolting in 1920. The occupiers responded by inventing Iraq as a quasi-independent entity. They rigged a plebiscite and phony parliament, installed a Hashemite puppet regime that the Shiites and Kurds never accepted, and paved the way to Sunni tyranny.

Today, having ignored all the relevant history, the U.S. is pouring staggering sums into Iraq while denying that we invaded for oil, influence, or geopolitical advantage. President Bush says the U.S. is fighting a global war to eliminate terrorism, but Iraq was not a haven for terrorists before the U.S. invaded, and terrorism is primarily a tactic of the desperate to repel foreign intruders.

The ancient Britons used terrorism against the Romans. For 900 years the Irish used it against the British. The Chechens began using it against their Russian occupiers in 1731 and are still at it. The Algerians used it against the French for 130 years; the Zionists used it against the British; and the Basques are still trying to terrorize Spain into giving up.

Robert Pape's book, *Dying to Win*, contains a database of all suicide terrorist campaigns from 1980 to 2004. He found that every campaign had the strategic objective of expelling a democratic foreign power (France, the U.S., India, Israel, Russia, Sri Lanka, Turkey, and England). In only a tiny fraction of cases were Islamic terrorists motivated primarily by their adherence to Islamic fundamentalist ideology. Obviously radical Islamic ideology is a large factor in this picture, but it matters that it is not the primary strategic objective or motivation. Almost every suicide attack, and *every* campaign, sought to compel foreign nations to withdraw their military forces. When U.S. troops occupied the Arabian Peninsula from 1990 to 2001, the statistical likelihood of attacks against Americans increased ten to twenty times. The terrorists come from places in which campaigns of resistance to foreign intervention have been organized by large militant organizations.[8]

If we wish to reduce terrorism, the first thing we might do is reduce the imprint of the invader that sets off the terrorist reaction. But our leaders don't think that way, any more than they consider the analogies to imperial Rome or England. They believe the U.S. needs to have a military presence everywhere and that history does not apply to the United States. The U.S. is superior in goodness and power; therefore the experiences of other nations are not relevant. Neoconservative writings are emphatic on this theme, but the idea is woven deeply into the American consciousness. Every time the U.S. invades a sovereign nation, American presidents announce that the American democracy invades only to liberate, never to conquer. Invading for oil or geopolitical advantage is what grubby empires of the past have done, never the benevolent American Republic. The U.S. has overthrown fourteen governments since the 1890s and played a subsidiary role in overthrowing numerous others. Yet until very recently, most Americans truly believed that their armed forces should be welcomed whenever they invade another country.

Today Americans are absorbing contrary evidence and turning against the war in Iraq. How serious is that shift? My neoconservative friends are convinced it won't survive another patriotic call to war. They want a sustained escalation in Iraq, a straightforward overthrow of the Syrian government, a bombing campaign against Iran, military campaigns against North Korea and Hezbollah, the next generation of high-tech weapons, and a huge expansion of the military to conduct all this smashing and killing, preferably without a draft. Fifteen years ago, neoconservatism was said to be finished in American politics because it was too stuck in a cold war mentality to have a role in a post–cold war world. Today the neocons are said to be finished again, because they ruined Bush's presidency.

But the neoconservatives are still the strongest foreign policy faction in the Republican Party. They hold the advantage of being clear and unabashedly nationalistic, which covers a multitude of shortcomings in American politics. They have a strange yet effective alliance with the Christian Right, which lacks a foreign policy brain trust of its own. The neocons have the best network of think tanks, journals, and media connections in

Washington and New York. They are firmly ensconced in the Pentagon and defense industry. They have a presidential candidate, John McCain, whose top foreign policy adviser, Randy Scheunemann, is a card-carrying neocon, and a McCain administration would be loaded with neocons like Daniel McKivergan, Marshall Wittmann, and Michael Rubin.

Above all, neoconservatism is based on powerful tides of opinion about the U.S.'s special character and supremacy. It trades on the historic American myths of exceptionalism and manifest destiny, offering a vision of what the U.S. should do with its unrivaled power. Fundamentally it is the belief that the maximal use of American power is good for America and the world. In its most rhetorically seductive versions, this vision conflates the expansion of American power with the dream of global democracy, as in President Bush's second inaugural address. In other words, neoconservatism is merely an explicit, think-tank version of American supremacism, one that defends the U.S.'s routine practices of empire while upping the ante on what is routine.

Today the Republican Party's realist flank, which still thinks of itself as the establishment, is vying for a larger place at the table, and realists in the Democratic Party are making a similar push. Five years ago, when I wrote *Imperial Designs*, I had a section on the explicitly anti-imperial conservative realists, people like Chalmers Johnson, James Kurth, and Andrew Bacevich. Today that group is flourishing. The Republican realists who ran the first Bush administration are resurfacing, notably Brent Scowcroft, James Baker, Lawrence Eagleburger, and Robert Gates. Hardcore, hawkish, nationalistic realism is also ascending on the right, as represented by Dov Zakheim, Daniel Pipes, and Robert Kaplan. Democrats like Peter Beinart and Jonathan Chait who pushed hard for invading Iraq are rediscovering the chastening aspects of realism, sometimes with appeals to Reinhold Niebuhr. All are trying to cope with the debacle of Iraq while disclaiming any responsibility for it.

Realism is not my tradition—I belong to the explicitly anti-imperialist wing of the liberal internationalist school—but I recognize there is such a thing as progressive realism, and I believe that any viable approach to foreign policy must absorb the realist emphasis on personal and collective evil, the will-to-power of nation-states, and the limits of politics. I believe that we need to get out of Iraq, create an international peacekeeping force there, and relinquish U.S. control of the military bases. We need a peace movement that is pledged to cooperation, multilateralism, human rights, and creating structures that transcend nationalism. We need a foreign policy that holds out for a two-state solution in Israel/Palestine with borders approximately along the Green Line. And we need to support and strengthen the United Nations, doubling the Security Council and getting rid of the veto power on the Security Council.

I have trouble accepting Fareed Zakaria as a guru of realistic wisdom, which is how *Newsweek* treats him. It's hard for me to forget that Zakaria defended the war for three years, he was a major cheerleader during the invasion, and before that he was a member of the Bletchley II group organized by Wolfowitz that mapped out the global war on terror. But in the past year Zakaria, like Thomas Friedman, has begun to deal with the reality of what we've done in Iraq, and last summer he put it quite well: "Having spooked ourselves into believing that we have no option but to act fast, alone, and pre-emptively, we have managed in six years to destroy decades of international good will, alienate allies, embolden enemies and yet solve few of the major international problems we face."[9]

On September 11, 2001, and for weeks following, the U.S. had a precious opportunity, a moment with new possibilities. Not since the end of World War II had there been such a moment when a huge step forward was possible toward a community of nations. If the U.S. had responded to 9/11 by sending NATO forces and Army Rangers after Al Qaeda, rebuilding Afghanistan, and building new networks of collective security against terrorism, it would have gained the world's gratitude. Instead it took a course of action that caused an explosion of anti-American hostility throughout the world, a torrent of bitter feeling that has not abated.

Having made a terrible mistake by invading Iraq and destroying the Iraqi state, the U.S. is now faced with bad choices. But the hope of finding the best one, which gets the U.S. out of Iraq, is getting stronger as Americans turn against the war.

The Baker-Hamilton Commission called for a strategy of pulling back to air, ground, and naval deployments in Kuwait, Bahrain, and other bases in the Middle East, while maintaining some residual U.S. forces in Iraq to fight terrorism and stabilize the Kurdish region. That is the main alternative at play in Washington. The Republican presidential field stood by the president's policy of holding out for "victory" in Iraq and refusing to broker an exit plan, and the apparent nominee, John McCain, outflanks everyone to the right on this issue. Bush has to worry about providing political cover for Republicans running this November, and he has a legacy to think about. Thus even he has begun to talk about winding down in

Iraq, which leaves McCain hanging out by himself as a "victory or bust" true believer.

The Democratic field offered variations on the Baker-Hamilton strategy. Of the two remaining Democratic contenders, Barack Obama, having opposed the war from the beginning, supported the Baker-Hamilton approach before it had a name, and Hillary Clinton changed her position last spring in favor of it. There are five main issues to deal with: the insurgency and civil war, which are tied together; terrorism, the prospect of a humanitarian crisis, and the U.S.'s military presence in the Middle East.

The insurgency has made its point: the U.S. is an occupying force that cannot win the hearts and minds of the occupied. The Sunni opposition is too small to win the insurgent war but too large, well armed, and fiercely determined to be defeated. The same thing is true of Sunni prospects in the battle with Iraqi Shiites, which is still causing, despite being in a low-burn mode, approximately two hundred deaths per month. Last summer five U.S. sergeants and one army specialist serving in Iraq offered a grim description of sectarian warfare from what soldiers call "the battle space." Any claim that Iraqi Army commanders are reliable partners is simply "misleading rhetoric," they warned: "The truth is that battalion commanders, even if well-meaning, have little to no influence over the thousands of obstinate men under them, in an incoherent chain of command, who are really loyal only to their militias."[10]

The original Sunni militias fought the U.S. occupiers and Shiite beneficiaries; the Shiites overmatched them with deadly militias of their own and took up the anti-American cause; in the past year the U.S. helped the Sunnis achieve balancing leverage. In effect, the U.S. has created a Sunni Army. The fate of this entity trumps a long list of daunting variables in Iraq. The Shiites have decades of grievances fueling their resistance to sharing power with the Sunnis, but the Sunnis have reason to protest, as they constantly do, that the nation's interests against Iran are not being defended.

If the Sunnis and Kurds can be integrated into what is euphemistically called the Iraq Army, Iraq has a chance of holding together as a semi-federalized state. There is no other option that averts another upsurge of death and destruction. Advocates of breaking Iraq into three countries, such as Senator Joe Biden, stress that parts of the country are already partitioned, all three of the major groups have their own military, and the Kurds have their own government and oil deal, too. But the majority of

Iraqi cities and provinces still have Sunni and Shiite communities living side by side. Iraq cannot break apart without igniting a very ugly civil war, one that Iran, Syria, Turkey, and Saudi Arabia would not sit out. The best hope is that Iraq will decide for integration and sovereignty, enabling it to tell the U.S. to leave Iraq, and that the U.S. will elect a president and Congress this fall that is committed to getting out by a definite date. I hope very much that the next president will be Barack Obama. But it is up to Iraqis to decide whether they want a unitary state, a decentralized federation, three countries, or something else. I don't want President Bush or President Obama to decide whether Iraq should press hard for full integration or allow a modus vivendi among the three armies that determines which groups will control which areas. It cannot be the business of the U.S. to manage the outcome of Iraq's civil strife, even if that conflict leads to a civil war that the U.S. set in motion.

On terrorism, the U.S. needs to return to a police model that practices counterterrorism through the force of law and international cooperation. Neoconservatives mapped out the Bush Doctrine in the 1990s, long before Bush thought about such things, and in his early months as president, Bush was onboard for neocon unipolarism, spurning the world court, and military full-spectrum dominance. He also flirted with a neocon line on the Middle East, especially Iraq, but angered his neocon supporters by temporizing on the big things. After 9/11 he adopted the rest of the neocon playbook, except for China policy: unilateral regime change, preemptive war, ramp up the military, denigrate the police model, rally the nation to a perpetual war on terror. On the weekend after 9/11 Bush told Richard Perle at Camp David that first the U.S. would hit Afghanistan, then Iraq.

For months afterward neocons were frantic that Colin Powell was not onboard. Powell talked about coordinating international police action against Al Qaeda and working through the United Nations. Neocons attacked him ferociously, charging that Powell was stuck in the outmoded counterterrorism of the past. Repeatedly they demanded that Powell had to accept the president's policy of unilateral war or get out of the administration. In January 2003 Bush gave Powell the same choice, telling him to put on his war uniform. Today Powell probably wishes that he made a different choice. Invading Iraq was a supercharger for terrorism, inflaming an endless supply of suicide bombers. Today we, as a nation, need to return to Bush's original mistake of elevating antiterrorism to the level of global war. The police approach views terrorists as criminals, refusing them the status of combatants. It hunts down terrorists and prosecutes them as criminals in concert with law enforcement agencies throughout the world, using the tools of detection and prevention in concert with governments.

On the prospect of a humanitarian crisis, President Bush warns of chaos if we leave Iraq. Indeed, if we simply leave, there will be chaos. Leaving chaos behind is what happens when imperial powers refuse to take responsibility for planning a decent exit after they are finished with a country. In the 1940s the British refused to accept, until the very end in 1947, that their imperial rule in India was over. When they finally emerged from denial they cleared out in seven weeks, the country was partitioned between Muslims and Hindus, twelve million people were displaced, and half a million were killed. In Algeria the French hung on until 1962, then departed rapidly; refugees poured into France, while many of the one hundred thousand Arabs who had worked for the colonial government met a savage end.

The U.S. withdrawal from Vietnam was a more prolonged affair than these precedents, but it was equally flawed. The U.S. sent Americans to die for years after Americans stopped believing in the war, it spurned international peacekeeping, it destabilized the Cambodian government, and it betrayed its Vietnamese collaborators upon clearing out.

A few years later the Soviet Union apparently learned nothing from the U.S. experience. Soviet leaders invaded Afghanistan in 1979, got stuck in a quagmire of their own, and staggered on for eight years. They tried a new constitution, a new leader, and a new policy of national reconciliation. Finally they found something that did work—getting a better Soviet leader, Mikhail Gorbachev, who faced up to reality and got out. If the Soviets had departed in the early 1980s, Afghanistan might not have descended into civil war. By 1987 a civil war was inevitable, one that gave birth to Al Qaeda.

This lesson of history is so obvious and yet so hard for great powers to accept: if you stagger along as an occupying power, all you do is delay the inevitable, run up the casualties on both sides, empower your enemies, and disgrace yourself in world opinion. Today the U.S. government should be planning how to get out of Iraq and make the best of a bad situation instead of babbling nonsense about "winning" there. We should make it clear that we are leaving; that the U.S. understands its responsibility for setting off the violence in Iraq; that the U.S. will offer asylum to Iraqis endangered by their cooperation with U.S. forces; and that the U.S. will provide massive economic assistance for all humanitarian work undertaken by the United Nations, NATO, other governments, and international agencies. We should hammer out a departure agreement with the Iraqi government that relinquishes U.S. military bases by a certain time; that requires the application of human rights standards to Iraqi detainees; and that contains protections against sectarian policing and prison procedures.

Politically speaking, we are at least ten months and one election away from doing that. When we finally get to that point, I would favor getting the U.S. military footprint down to a minimum in the entire Middle East. To put it negatively, I believe that installing thousands of U.S. troops anywhere in the Middle East is a recipe for disaster. The U.S. has two strategic objectives in the Persian Gulf: to protect its allies and secure its oil interests. It can do both these things without stationing troops on the ground.

Obviously the U.S. needs to break its addiction to Persian Gulf oil, but that is not happening. And the U.S. has to rethink what it is doing in Afghanistan, where it has suffered from the draining debacle in Iraq; I have a cautionary word to say about that. But concerning the two strategic objectives, both are best secured by maintaining a strong naval presence in the Indian Ocean and some naval forces in the international waters of the Persian Gulf. The main thing is to make sure that ships get through the Straight of Hormuz. That can be done by stationing forces in the Indian Ocean and at bases outside the Middle East. In other words, the U.S. could go back to the policy it had in the 1980s after it lost Iran.

In the 1980s the U.S. was locked in a cold war with the Soviet Union and faced adversaries in the Middle East that were armed militarily by the Soviets. And yet, despite these threats, American leaders were sufficiently chastened to avoid inflaming anti-American feeling in the Middle East. We need to recover that sensibility and improve upon it.

My word about Afghanistan is wary and somewhat contrarian. Obama proposes to add thousands of U.S. troops there, perhaps nearly doubling the current force total of thirty-two thousand. I appreciate that it plays well for him politically to say the U.S. needs to escalate its military effort. But after nearly seven years of war, Afghanistan has "quagmire" written all over it. The government is corrupt from top to bottom. It barely exists outside Kabul except as an instrument of shakedowns and graft, beginning with the family of President Hamid Karzai. The Afghan army is no exception to the corruption plague; civilian fatality rates from the war have doubled in the past year; and the acreage of the nation's farmland devoted to opium production is expanding dramatically. More than two-thirds of the economy is centered on opium traffic. The United States has a vital interest in preventing Al Qaeda and other terrorist groups from securing a safe haven in Afghanistan. But we don't need fifty thousand troops in the country for that. If the U.S. is going to pour more troops into a country featuring a chronically dysfunctional government, treacherous terrain, and a soaring narcotics trade, it needs to spell out what, exactly, this escalation is supposed to accomplish and how the U.S. will know it has succeeded enough to get out or even scale down. So far the advocates of escalation, including the presidential candidate I support, haven't come through.

In 2002 the Democrats that wanted to run for president thought they couldn't do so if they opposed the war in Iraq. Two years later they still thought so. Today John Kerry and John Edwards wish they had stood for something better. So does Hillary Clinton. We need a peace movement that will help wobbly politicians find their nerve.

Since this is a secular gathering I have kept my deepest wellspring of motivation and perspective out of this speech. It's very difficult even to mention that I have a religious wellspring without setting off mistaken impressions, so let me begin by saying: I don't believe that one has to be a Christian to accept or care about anything that I've said tonight. Most of my friends are secular, which may go without saying, as I am an academic. But I do not believe that people like me are obliged to keep their religious feelings out of view on occasions like this one. When I was a college student in the early 1970s, it occurred to me that the people I admired most had a religious center or taproot: Martin Luther King Jr., Mohandas Gandhi, Jane Addams. I always had the mystical germ, but no expectation of a ministerial or theological career. What launched me on the path I have taken was the recognition that the people who inspired me had a spiritual impulse that was deeper than their politics.

The response of any Christian or other religious tradition to world politics must feature a strong presumption against war and a predisposition to view the world from the perspectives of the poor, the excluded, and the vulnerable. In biblical teaching, the test of ethical action is how it affects the struggles of oppressed and excluded people. Christianity must be a movement that shows the peaceable and justice-making way of Christ and that asks at all times, "How does this policy affect oppressed or vulnerable people?"

For me the normative gospel ethic of peacemaking, loving one's enemies, and what Jesus called the "weightier matters of the law"—justice and mercy—is integrative and contextual. I take questions about war and foreign policy one at a time, and I reserve a place for humanitarian intervention. At the same time the presumption against war must be very strong for an ethic to be Christian, and it must see the face of Christ in the faces of the world's disinherited. The way of Christ has been conflated with empire and militarism many times in church history but never without betraying Christ.

We need new forms of community that arise out of but transcend religious affiliation, culture, and nation. All our traditions have propensities for dogmatism and prejudice that must be uprooted. If we fail to interrogate the violence that is in our religious traditions, religion will remain part of the problem. If those of us who are Caucasian fail to interrogate white supremacism and its privileges, we will resist any recognition of our own racism. If those of us who are male fail to interrogate our complicity in sexism, we will perpetuate it. If those of us who are Christian fail to repudiate anti-Semitism and Christian supercessionism, we will perpetuate the evils that come with them. If those of us who are heterosexual fail to stand up for the rights of gays, lesbians, bisexuals, and transsexuals, we will have an oppressive church and society. If we swear our highest loyalty to our nation, we will perpetuate American imperialism.

Today we need a peace movement that says, "I don't want my country, the country that I love, fighting wars of aggression. I don't want my country to spurn the hard work of collective security. I don't want my country to be dragged into wars that don't come remotely close to being a last resort, inflaming resentments that will last for centuries. I don't want my country to plant permanent military bases for itself anywhere in the Middle East. Not in my name do you invade any more Muslim nations in the name of making America safe."

Ruether had just cause to ask for a more accurate remembering, though she failed to grasp that her feminist critics *did* make an advance by interrogating whiteness, repudiating the essentialism of (white) "sisterhood" rhetoric, and bringing feminism into conversation with deconstructionist theory. Some of them told stories of being gruffly treated by her on their way up. But they also told stories of her modeling feminist scholar-activism, bustling to conferences and speaking engagements, holding advising meetings in the car on her way to the airport, building up liberationist movements. "Everything is related" is a maxim of every feminist generation; Ruether epitomized it.

Chapter 13

Empire in Denial

AMERICAN EXCEPTIONALISM AND
THE COMMUNITY OF NATIONS

Belatedly, confronted with an imperial debacle in Iraq and an expensive global military, Americans have begun to debate whether their country is some kind of empire, an idea foreign to the nation's historic idea of itself as a benevolent republic. Most of the world has no doubt that the U.S. is an empire, but today it holds plenty of uncertainty and concern about the kind of empire the U.S. wants to be. For U.S. Americans, emerging from denial that we are an empire is a crucial first step toward becoming something better.

Setting aside its Native American reservations, the United States is not an empire in the classic sense of the term. It does not exercise direct dominion over conquered peoples. It does not formally rule an extensive group of countries under a single sovereign authority. Official U.S. colonies have been few and scattered, most U.S. occupations have been brief, the largest of the U.S.'s fourteen dependent entities is Puerto Rico, and its domination of Latin America has been mostly indirect. Most U.S. Americans have little imperial consciousness, and they are not militaristic in the sense of glorying in their wars or military might.

Yet the United States has been on a neo-imperial trajectory since its founding. It conquered nearly an entire continent and waged genocidal violence against Native Americans, colonizing the surviving tribes in reservations. For nearly a century, when the U.S. was a slave state, many of its leaders wanted to create a Western empire based on the extension of slavery throughout the Caribbean. From the Monroe Doctrine to the

Bush Doctrine, presidents have made doctrinal pronouncements about their putative right to dominate or invade sovereign nations. Theodore Roosevelt, who viewed his imperial ambition as a natural outgrowth of the U.S. American story, was fond of saying that his country's entire national history was one of expansion. His corollary to the Monroe Doctrine, announced in 1906, declared that the U.S. was entitled to invade any Latin American nation that engaged in "flagrant wrongdoing." Latin Americans took that to mean any action that conflicted with U.S. interests, which helped explain how the U.S., between 1906 and 1945, found it necessary to invade Colombia, Panama, Honduras, the Dominican Republic, Cuba, Nicaragua, Haiti, Mexico, and Guatemala.

Americans have long imagined that their country is an exception to history. American history is replete with self-images of superiority and divine favor—God's New Israel, the Redeemer Nation, the City on a Hill, the New Order of the Ages, Manifest Destiny, the Pax Americana, the Arsenal of Democracy, the Leader of the Free World. But for more than a century Americans regarded their country's exceptionalism as something to be protected by avoiding foreign entanglements. The American Revolution was an anti-imperial rebellion; George Washington famously cautioned against foreign wars and alliances; James Monroe, in an 1823 address to Congress authored by John Quincy Adams, warned the European powers to keep their colonizing hands off Latin America; in the same spirit, Adams proclaimed in his July 4 oration of 1821 that the American democracy "does not go abroad in search of monsters to destroy." Like many Americans, Adams saw no contradiction between proclaiming the Monroe Doctrine and claiming the mantle of anti-imperialism.[1]

After 1898 the United States could no longer say it was the occupier of none, but it claimed insistently that it never acted out of imperial self-interest. Upon winning the Spanish-American War, the United States became, in its self-image, the world power that occupied only for the sake of freedom. President William McKinley annexed and occupied Cuba, Puerto Rico, Guam, and the Philippines; in the excitement of imperial expansion he also annexed the Hawaiian islands, thus requiring a real navy; in 1899 he partitioned the Samoan Islands; in 1900 he helped suppress the Boxer Rebellion in China; in 1902 Theodore Roosevelt inserted the Platt Amendment into the Cuban Constitution, rendering Cuba a U.S. colony in all but name.

This sudden imperial maneuvering and Roosevelt's colorful statements about it forced Americans to relinquish a bit of their innocent self-image.

Some contended that there was such a thing as good imperialism; others insisted that it wasn't really imperialism if the occupying power had good intentions. Indiana Republican Senator Albert J. Beveridge admonished that God spent a thousand years preparing the English-speaking and Teutonic people to redeem the world; thus it would be sinful for Americans to luxuriate in domestic contentment instead of following "the Star of Empire." Every great nation became a colonizer of inferior peoples, Beveridge instructed, great nations became greater by colonizing widely, and they declined when they abandoned "the policy of possession and administration." The United States was called by God to be history's greatest empire: "We cannot retreat from any soil where Providence has unfurled our banner; it is ours to save that soil for liberty and civilization."[2]

Social gospel leader Lyman Abbott concurred that it was "the function of the Anglo-Saxon race" to confer the civilizing gifts of law, commerce, and education "on the uncivilized people of the world." Against William James, social gospeler Graham Taylor, and other anti-imperialists, Abbott proclaimed:

It is said that we have no right to go to a land occupied by a barbaric people and interfere with their life. It is said that if they prefer barbarism they have a right to remain barbarians. I deny the right of a barbaric people to retain possession of any quarter of the globe . . . Barbarism has no rights which civilization is bound to respect. Barbarians have rights which civilized people are bound to respect, but they have no right to their barbarism.[3]

Other liberals said the same thing more nicely. Washington Gladden admonished imperialists and anti-imperialists alike for wrongly assuming that self-interest was the basis of U.S. foreign policy. In 1898 Gladden held out for the primacy of good intentions: "We are not going to be dragged into any war for purposes of conquest—neither for the acquisition of territory nor for the extension of trade. And those who are preaching this jingoism to-day should be warned that the Nation has a conscience that can speak and make itself heard, and that will paralyze its arm whenever it is lifted to do injustice to any weaker people."[4] To Gladden it was "morally unthinkable" that the U.S. might set free the Philippines, Puerto Rico, and Guam after these colonial possessions were relinquished by Spain. "Degraded races" never worked their way up to freedom, he explained; they had to be lifted up to civilized standards of behavior by stronger races. Gladden rejoiced that his country had linked arms with imperial England in this redemptive mission. The American democracy sought no empire, and to the extent that it acquired one, it did so only to promote the freedom and self-determination of weaker nations.[5]

America's most exuberantly imperial presidents of the twentieth century, Theodore Roosevelt and Woodrow Wilson, exulted in their nation's redemptive expansionism. At the turn of the century they spoke of Christianizing the world and fulfilling the global destiny of the Anglo-Saxon race. For TR and Wilson, expansion was about civilization, democratization, and liberation, not merely territorial advance and acquisition. Both wanted to save the world in approximately the same way that the U.S. transformed its continental frontier. TR bristled with imperial spirit, expanded the Monroe Doctrine, called for a U.S. canal across Central America, and vowed to "civilize" the Filipinos. He played down that all this expanding and civilizing had anything to do with economic gain, though he zealously guarded the sea lanes that led to America's new naval bases in the Pacific. Wilson told audiences that the entire Eastern world was destined to be "opened and transformed" by the West and that "the standards of the West are to be imposed upon it; nations and peoples which have stood still the centuries through are to be quickened, and made part of the universal world of commerce and of ideas which has so steadily been a-making by the advance of European power from age to age."[6]

When Wilson took the U.S. into World War I, he had to have idealistic reasons for doing so, as did his country; the war was a crusade for democracy and liberal internationalism. American presidents subsequently rationalized their occupations of Nicaragua and Haiti with similar assurances. Shortly after the United States entered World War II, Reinhold Niebuhr lamented that the same American moralists who had resisted going to war could now be counted upon to clothe America's war effort with insufferable visions of a transformed world order. To Niebuhr it was a source of continual regret that Americans had to turn even their wars and imperial occupations into moral causes. The benevolent American republic could not be an empire; thus Americans refused to acknowledge that they had built one by serving their self-interests.[7]

In 1945 the U.S. began to amass a global military empire, beginning with its new military bases in Western Germany, Japan, Korea, and the Eastern Mediterranean. Afterward American leaders contended that Soviet communism was evil because it was ideologically driven to rule the world. Trying to dominate the world was a bad thing, they assured; the

U.S. played this game only to prevent the Soviet Union from succeeding at it. The world had nothing to fear from the expansion of American power and everything to fear from Soviet totalitarianism. Along the way the U.S. created a new kind of empire that vastly outstripped its Soviet rival.

This novel empire, which dwarfs all colonizing types of the past, is not based on the conquest of territory. The United States is the most awesome world power that the world has ever seen. It floods the world with its culture and technology. Its economy out-produces the next eleven nations combined, accounting for 32 percent of the world's output, which put off for twenty years the day of reckoning for being the world's greatest creditor nation. The Pentagon alone spends more on defense than the next 25 nations combined, and when total military spending is taken into account, the U.S. outspends the rest of the world combined. It employs 5 global military commands to police the world; it has 750 military bases in 130 countries, covering two-thirds of the world; it has formal military base rights in 40 countries; each branch of the armed services has its own air force; the U.S. Air Force operates on 6 continents; the U.S. deploys carrier battleships in every ocean; and the U.S. Special Forces conducts thousands of operations per year in approximately 170 nations.

Just before the U.S. invaded Iraq in March 2003 the *New Republic* marveled: "There is no more significant fact about the present-day international order, no more sensational fact about it, than the prominence of the United States. We are staggeringly huge. The century that just passed was not the American century. This is the American century, and everybody knows it, and everybody loves it or hates it." At the time the mostly Democratic *New Republic* was fervently for the war, blasting fellow liberals who lacked the patriotism and common sense to support it. A few weeks later the magazine's editors had second thoughts about the war, publishing some of the earliest exposés of how the Bush administration manufactured phony intelligence. But the editors betrayed no conflicted feelings about what they called "the liberal power." They wanted Americans to love the dream of a world remade in America's image. They enthused that the best American century was still to come.[8]

That American century was very brief, as the U.S. got stuck in Iraq, inflamed anti-American feeling throughout the world, disgraced itself in New Orleans, and leveraged and gambled its way to an economic crash. Yet the U.S. remains not only a predominant power but an imperial one that assumes global responsibilities and reaps the benefits that derive from them. The U.S. is imperial in the sense of enforcing its idea of world order in the U.S. interest, presuming the right to lay down the rules of trade, commerce, security, and political legitimacy. It rewards or punishes nations on the basis of their willingness to create open markets, support U.S. military policies, and establish pro-U.S. governments.

After the U.S. invaded Iraq it radically redesigned that nation's economy, ignoring long-standing Iraqi laws curtailing foreign ownership and principles of international law limiting the powers of occupiers. In May 2003 Paul Bremer banned thirty thousand former Baath Party leaders from employment in Iraq's public sector and disbanded the Iraqi Army, decisions that became controversial for disastrously fueling the Sunni insurgency against the U.S. But in the same month Bremer took other drastic measures that were rarely noted. He abolished nearly all of Iraq's laws, issuing a hundred binding decrees that sold off state enterprises, suspended tariffs on imports and exports, allowed for 100 percent foreign ownership of Iraqi businesses, reduced corporate taxes to 15 percent, and permitted businesses to repatriate 100 percent of their profits. Somehow all this went down with hardly any protest or even commentary in the U.S. If we were going to invade and occupy Iraq, radically redesigning its economy was taken for granted as a spoil of empire, even as the U.S. denied being one.

Today the U.S. is spending $2 billion per week in Iraq, nearly all of it from emergency spending bills, which exceeded $800 billion by November 2009. These figures do not include disability and health payments for returning troops, inducements for soldiers to serve additional deployments, extra pay for reservists and National Guard members, and additional foreign aid to supportive nations. When all that is factored in, along with the Pentagon's unprecedented dependence on expensive private contractors, one gets a figure exceeding $2 trillion, as explained by Joseph E. Stiglitz and Linda Bilmes in their book, *The Three Trillion Dollar War*.[9]

Meanwhile the defense budget for 2009, which covers normal personnel, procurement, and operational expenses, is up to $513 billion. In addition to not including the costs of the wars in Iraq and Afghanistan, this figure does not include nuclear weapons, which are assigned to the Energy Department, or the defense expenditures of the National Defense Stockpile, Selective Service, FBI, and Coast Guard, or the State Department's security programs, or Homeland Security programs not in the Pentagon budget, or the Department of Veterans Affairs, or interest payments on the national debt related to defense spending. When these items are counted, military spending for 2009 comes to approximately $1 trillion. President Obama's official defense budget for 2010 is $664 billion, bringing the real number to well over $1 trillion. That exceeds what the rest of the world combined spends on defense—a stupendous disparity incomparable to any historical parallel.[10]

Despite these immense outlays, budget analysts warn of a coming financial train wreck, because the appropriations in virtually every category fall short of the true costs of America's military posture. The U.S. is caught in the classic imperial dilemma of spending fantastic sums on the military yet lacking enough military to cover its foreign policy. In November 2006 Army Chief of Staff General Peter Schoomaker withheld his required 2008 budget plan as a protest against what his staff called a "disastrous" and "unsustainable" situation in the army. The army's regular budget in 2007 was $99 billion, but Schoomaker demanded a 41 percent increase, eventually settling for 19 percent that included a 55 percent increase in procurement. A senior army official observed, "Yes, it's incredibly huge. These are just incredible numbers." Having been limited by law to 482,400 troops in the 1990s, the army added 30,000 troops on a temporary basis in 2004, which became permanent. Today an army expansion of 65,000 troops is making its way through Congress, fueled politically by the army's struggle to sustain rotations in Iraq and its institution of what amounted to a back-door draft by relying on the National Guard and extending many tours of duty. At present over half the army's forty-three combat brigades are deployed overseas, and President Obama is committed to expanding the army.[11]

Donald Rumsfeld bitterly disappointed his neoconservative comrades by occupying Iraq with a light force and refusing to push for a larger expansion of the army. But in both cases he sought to increase America's military power. He left behind a restructured military that reflects his vision of how to sustain the U.S.'s global military dominance without instituting a draft. For six years Rumsfeld pursued a plan called "military transformation" that significantly globalized America's military reach. Robert Kaplan, in his book *Imperial Grunts*, celebrates this plan, according to which the heart and soul of the new American military is its expeditionary force, especially its Marine Corps commando component, the Special Operations Command (SOCOM).[12]

Rumsfeld was infatuated with the vision of a global military empire combining high technology with adaptable, rapid force projection. He seeded the military with officials who shared this vision. Dividing the globe among regional combatant commanders, he gave new responsibilities and financing to specialized commands, shifted regional war-fighting plans away from cold war bases in Europe, and obtained easier access to the Middle East and Central Asia. More provocative and costly, he launched a high-tech program called Future Combat Systems, an integrated structure of manned and unmanned air and ground vehicles that communicates with each other and other units through a global military network.[13]

The Future Combat Systems program includes unattended ground sensors and munitions, unmanned aerial and ground vehicles, robotic vehicles, a mounted combat system, and ten other systems acting as a unified combat force on a 16-to-1 ratio: 16 high-tech units per soldier. The army describes it as the "core" of its mission to be able to strike any region of the world quickly and powerfully. GlobalSecurity.org describes it as a revolutionary "leap ahead" system and the "centerpiece" of the next army: "lightweight, overwhelmingly lethal, strategically deployable, and self-sustaining." The cost is expensive even by defense industry standards. The first phase of the program, covering one-third of the U.S. Army's present force, will cost $160 billion; $4 billion for it was allocated in 2007; the whole thing will add over $500 billion to military expenses.[14]

Along the same line, Pentagon budgets have gotten "blacker" in recent years, to use the defense and intelligence jargon. Over 20 percent of the Pentagon's current acquisition budget is devoted to secret, classified programs, a return to the cold war–level of classified spending. Kaplan explains the necessity of doing so, contending that the U.S. must bring back the pre-Vietnam rules of engagement using twenty-first century technology. Impending technologies such as warhead-like bullets and neurobiological signature-tracking satellites will make it easier to carry out assassinations; more important, covert war evades most of the politics of intervention and imperialism. To the extent that the U.S. is able to handle its global management problems with Special Forces and the CIA's military wing, it circumvents having to deal with domestic politics and the U.N. Security Council. Thus the CIA is getting "greener" (increasing its uniformed military wing) and the Special Forces are getting "blacker" (emphasizing super-clandestine operations).[15]

A further variation on this trend is the U.S. investment in programs that could lead to the development of dual-use space weapons. In 2008 the Pentagon spent $1 billion on space weapons. Until recently the U.S. had no formal policy on new military missions in outer space; now it has a stunningly imperial one. On October 13, 2006, President Bush signed a National Space Policy ruling out any future arms control agreements that might limit U.S. operations in space. The new policy, which was vetted quietly in Congress, asserted that the U.S. has a right to deny access to space to any nation that the U.S. government deems to be "hostile to U.S. interests."[16]

That is the Monroe Doctrine applied to outer space. There are no codes of conduct about how military missions in outer space would be conducted, nor any rules about how space weapons would be operated. The Bush administration's position was that since there is no space arms race, there is no need of an arms control agreement in this area. Congress has never voted on, nor even debated, whether it wants to invest in space weapons. But the Bush administration quietly funded programs that created "facts in orbit"—the development, testing, and deployment of space weapon technologies.[17]

The most explicitly militaristic faction of the American political establishment, the neoconservative wing of the Republican Party, has been defined since the cold war by its doctrine of "full spectrum dominance." Neoconservatives could not be more explicit in espousing the vision of American global domination. Yet the idea of "full spectrum dominance" is not unique to neoconservatives. It was a staple of defense industry and Pentagon literature in the 1990s. The Joint Chiefs of Staff, in their *Joint Vision* statements of 1996 and 2000, declared that the U.S. is committed to sustaining full spectrum dominance on a global scale as a primary military policy. *Joint Vision 2020*, issued on May 30, 2000, put it this way:

> The overall goal of the transformation described in this document is the creation of a force that is dominant across the full spectrum of military operations—persuasive in peace, decisive in war, preeminent in any form of conflict . . . Full spectrum dominance [is] the ability of U.S. forces, operating unilaterally or in combination with multinational and interagency partners, to defeat any adversary and control any situation across the full range of military options.[18]

That put it as plainly as possible, and that was under the Clinton administration. For eight years neoconservatives railed against President Clinton for wasting America's dominance. They wanted a huge military expansion and what they called "creative destruction" in the Middle East. Upon gaining power they were relentless in pressing their extraordinary agenda of global warfare. But all this was simply a more explicit and aggressive version of America's normal practices of empire.

The neocons are often dismissed as ideologues and overreachers, but they have a record of pushing American policy in their direction. They overreached on Iraq for years before getting their way. They are entrenched in the Pentagon and defense industry; they are the strongest foreign policy faction in the Republican Party; and they have an extensive infrastructure of think tanks and media outlets. They specialize in calls to toughness, lists of things that America will not tolerate, and appeals to American greatness.

But just below the surface of the claim to toughness lurks a persistent anxiety. This anxiety is inherent in the problem of empire and, in the case of the neocons, is heightened by ideological ardor. Normal countries worry about their own neighborhoods, but a global hegemon is not a normal country. For the empire, every conflict is a local concern that threatens its control. However secure it may be, it never feels secure enough. Every threat feeds a constant howling of alarm.

For many Americans the alarm obliterates any capacity for merely coping with a foreign policy threat. They believe in abolishing problems, not coping with them. It is never enough to piece out a difficult problem and contain it. The howling of alarm and the smashing impulse go together. If America has overwhelming power at its disposal, how can it not use that power to wipe out regimes that want to hurt the United States? If the smashing approach requires top-to-bottom assaults on foreign civilizations, so be it. And if America lacks the military means to fight two or three wars at once, it must acquire the means.

Neoconservatives stoke the fear and smashing impulses assiduously, taking no pause between crusades. The anxiety is unquenchable. Bill Kristol's magazine, *The Weekly Standard*, piles one crisis upon another. In Bush's first term Kristol demanded wars against Afghanistan, Iran, Iraq, Syria, and North Korea simultaneously, plus a cold war with China. Was he serious? How could an overstretched American military fight so many wars? Kristol always replied that he was dead serious and the problem of the overstretched military was terribly real; that was why neocons implored for years that America needed a massive military upgrade. Under Clinton the U.S. wasted eight years, coasting foolishly on its preeminence, taking a vacation from history. In the name of sustaining America's dominance, neocons vowed to wage a great deal of creative destruction when they gained power.

But this preoccupation with sustaining America's dominance and waging creative destruction is self-defeating. It undermines the structure of international trust that allowed the U.S. to flourish in the first place. The United States got to be an unrivaled power largely by escaping the downward drag of rival power blocs. Throughout the twentieth century the United States was the strongest power in the world, and it stirred its share of resentments by supporting dictatorships, exploiting its economic leverage, and bragging about its greatness. Yet the U.S. was remarkably free of rivals. It was not afflicted with great power antagonists in the manner of imperial England, France, Germany, or Japan, and it had to be dragged into both world wars. After World War II the United States finally acquired a great power rival, the Soviet Union, but it never faced a united challenge from a rival coalition, even in the Soviet bloc countries. Despite its support of dictatorships and neocolonial exploitation, and despite "ugly Americanism," many interventions, military bases around the globe, the Vietnam War, and a hard-to-take rhetoric of superiority and patriotic self-righteousness, the United States was not challenged by rival powers, mainly because it was not viewed as an external threat. America's reputation for not being a threatening, colonizing, aggressive power was its most precious attribute. But that was shredded by eight years of Bush 43.

Liberal Internationalism and the Logic of War

Two months before the United States invaded Iraq, Pope John Paul II declared that the future of humanity depended in large measure on the courage of the earth's peoples and their leaders to reject "the logic of war." The pontiff asked: "And what are we to say of the threat of a war which could strike the people of Iraq, the land of the prophets, a people already sorely tried by more than 12 years of embargo? War is never just another means that one can choose to employ for settling differences between nations." Appealing to just war theory, international law, and the U.N. charter, he admonished that "war cannot be decided upon, even when it is a matter of ensuring the common good, except as the last option and in accordance with very strict conditions." During the military buildup he implored diplomats to stop the war, urging that resorting to military force must be "the very last option."[19]

Two weeks after the U.S. toppled Baghdad the Italian Jesuit journal *Civilta Cattolica*, a mouthpiece of the Vatican, declared that the war was "a wound and a humiliation for the entire Islamic world that, sooner or later, could be revenged through terrorist acts." Invading Iraq ripped apart any hope of a decent world order, the Jesuit editors lamented. Iraq posed no real danger to the U.S. and its allies, and invading deprived the United Nations of its rightful function. It was also incredibly "wounding" and "humiliating" to Muslims. How did Western leaders manage to believe they could invade a Muslim country without causing a great convulsion in the Muslim world? To the Jesuit editors, the war was obviously a catastrophe: "The Iraqi conflict did not end with the Anglo-American military but likely will continue to nourish, especially among Islamic fundamentalists, hatred against the West and proposals of revenge and vendetta that may be translated into acts of terrorism."[20]

Other church leaders and institutions condemned the war on similar grounds. The Central Committee of the World Council of Churches deplored the invasion and occupation as a violation of international law and the U.N. Charter, condemned the Bush Doctrine's policy of preemptive war for the same reasons, and opposed the occupying powers "taking advantage of their military force to establish military bases in Iraq for their own use, and from benefiting from rebuilding Iraq or from sale of its resources." The (U.S.) Global Ministries office of the World Council of Churches, representing nine denominations and three Catholic religious orders, emphasized that the war was illegal under international law and that it jeopardized the struggle against terrorism. The Collegium of Officers of the United Church of Christ (USA) declared that attacking Iraq "will not serve to prevent terrorism or defend our nation's interests. We fear that war would only provoke greater regional instability and lead to the mass destruction it is intended to prevent." U.S. Episcopal Church presiding bishop Frank Griswold declared that the war was nothing like a last resort and that it "could profoundly destabilize the Middle East and set in motion a situation disastrous for all of us."[21]

Pope John Paul's opposition to war, like that of other church leaders, was rooted in the gospel ethic of sacrificial love and the scriptural command not to kill. For the Pope and many Christian leaders, the tests of just war were to be stringently applied, containing as they did the gospel presumption against war. Others opposed the war on pacifist or realist lesser-evil grounds, but church leaders shared an emphasis on international law and real-world consequences, not utopian ideals. They did not sentimentalize morality, minimize the evil of Saddam Hussein's regime, or picture the United Nations as the bearer of the world's hope. The statements of ecumenical bodies took seriously the pervasive reality of evil in individuals and society and the realist maxim that all nations are self-interested and power-seeking.

The case for liberal internationalist collective security has a realistic basis, that the benefits of multilateral cooperation outweigh the costs and risks of not working together. A superpower that insists on absolute security for itself makes all other nations insecure. All parties are better off when the most powerful nations agree not to do everything that is in their power and nations work together to create new forms of collective protection. In an increasingly interdependent world, single nation-states have to cooperate with one another to address security issues that exist primarily in the interstices between states. Political philosopher Benjamin Barber observes that terrorism is a feature of an interdependent world; it cannot be smashed on the model of nineteenth-century warfare between states, because it has no address or nationality. The U.S. destroyed the Taliban, but al Qaeda moved on; the U.S. destroyed the Baathist regime in Iraq, and drew terrorists to Iraq. To fight terrorism, nations must create new forms of collective security that reflect the interdependence of the real world.[22]

To be sure, nations do not subordinate their national interests to the common good of an abstract international community. When north European governments make decisions about war and trade policy they calculate their own interests, just like governments that make less of a show of multilateralism. In the buildup to the Iraq War, France and Germany sought to balance American power, while Spain and Italy viewed the United States as a check on the regional ambitions of France and Germany. For much of Europe, the key calculation was what it would cost to oppose the United States. Western nations make similar calculations when they impose import fees on agricultural goods that condemn African farmers to misery. International community of the ideal type is impossible precisely for the reasons that Reinhold Niebuhr stressed. But Niebuhr's defense of democracy applies to multilateralism. Collective security is valuable not so much as an ideal to be realized but as a brake on human greed and will-to-power.

What passes for democracy in the twenty-first century is usually very thin, and so is the international system. But it is better to have thin democracy and collective security than none at all, and it is not unrealistic to imagine a more effective United Nations. The UN could be significantly strengthened by reforming structures that have gone unchanged since 1945. The Security Council could abolish the veto power for permanent members and make its decisions by a two-thirds majority vote, preventing a single member from paralyzing the UN in a crisis. The Security Council could increase the number of rotating seats and double its permanent membership to include Germany, India, Brazil, Japan, and South Africa. In the 1990s the U.S. supported permanent membership status for Germany and Japan and sought to expand the council to twenty-one members, but assorted rivalries got in the way of making the Security Council reflect today's world. Pakistan and Italy refused to be left out if India and Germany got in.

Besides the structural reforms on Security Council membership and veto power that the United Nations would do well to make, the UN must reconsider the priority of human rights relative to national sovereignty. The UN Charter identifies threshold exceptions to the sovereignty of nations, but the UN is better at preventing wars between states than at rescuing people trapped in bad states. The International Commission on Intervention and State Sovereignty holds that intervention is justified against nation-states that perpetrate or allow occurring or imminent large-scale loss of life or ethnic cleansing. Political philosopher Michael Ignatieff goes much further, contending that regime-changing intervention is justified when it (1) stops mass killing and ethnic cleansing, (2) or restores an overthrown democracy, (3) or overthrows a state that violates nonproliferation protocols regarding chemical, biological, and nuclear weapons, (4) or stops terrorist attacks, (5) or expels invaders.[23]

Ignatieff goes too far, and even modest attempts to expand emergency thresholds are fraught with peril. If the United States intervened every time that a nation violated the massacre/ethnic cleansing standard, the U.S. would currently occupy or recently have occupied Abkhazia, Afghanistan, Angola, Bosnia, Burundi, China, Colombia, Congo, East Timor, El Salvador, Guatemala, Haiti, India, Indonesia, Iraq, Israel/Palestine, Kosovo, Lebanon, Liberia, Nagorno-Karabakh, Nigeria, Pakistan, Peru, Russia, Rwanda, Sierra Leone, Somalia, Sri Lanka, and Zimbabwe. The candidates for invasion would double or triple if Ignatieff's aggressive vision of humanitarian interventionism were adopted. To wage war as an instrument of policy rather than as a last resort in a supreme emergency is to make a mockery of the last-resort criterion. The murderous violence of war is a greater evil than failing at democracy or seeking the same murderous weapons that every nation on the Security Council possesses in large supply. Ignatieff's proposal is unwittingly a prescription for perpetual war, this time waged by a U.S.-led United Nations; tellingly, he supported America's invasion of Iraq.

Ignatieff admits to liberal imperialism, though as a political liberal, not a neocon. A Canadian believer in U.S. exceptionalism, he wants the U.S. to accept its global hegemonic burden, which "is more than being the most powerful nation in the world or just the most hated one. It means enforcing such order as there is in the world and doing so in the American interest. It means laying down the rules America wants (on everything from markets to weapons of mass destruction) while exempting itself from other rules (the Kyoto Protocol on climate change and the International Criminal Court) that go against its interest." Ignatieff does not blush at the arrogance of arrogating American interests above global environmental problems or the enforcement of human rights, but, unlike the neocons, he realizes the U.S. will lose its soul if it does all this smashing and laying down unilaterally. The new Pax Americana has to be multilateral or it will fail: "Without clear principles for intervention, without friends, without dreams to serve, the soldiers sweating in their body armor in Iraq are defending nothing more than power."[24]

Democratic policymakers Madeleine Albright and Richard Holbrooke advance milder versions of this argument, contending that a strengthened United Nations would strengthen the Pax Americana; Ignatieff says it plainly to provoke fellow liberals. In his rendering, it is a good thing that America is so powerful, but power does not endure if it lacks legitimacy and support. Ignatieff wants the U.S. to imagine the possibility of sustaining global preeminence *while* cooperating with others and *through* doing so. The alternative to building a new international community, he cautions, is the imperialism of the unilateralists, "a muddled, lurching America policing an ever more resistant world alone, with former allies sabotaging it at every turn."[25]

That is essentially the foreign policy approach that Americans voted to take in electing Barack Obama, though he would never put it so bluntly. Obama stands for stabilizing American empire and making it more palatable to the rest of the world, not scaling it back. He wants a more constructive relationship with the United Nations without having to offend Americans who are hostile to it.

Meanwhile, the U.N. keeps alive the principle of collective security and brings humanitarian relief to millions. With all its failures and defects, the United Nations is the world's leading humanitarian organization and its most important source of international legitimacy. It feeds more than seventy million people each year through the World Food Programme, leads the fight against AIDS through the Joint U.N. Programme on HIV/AIDS, coordinates the global response to SARS through the World Health Organization, and rescues the international homeless through the U.N. High Commissioner for Refugees. It leads the world's resistance to nuclear proliferation through the International Atomic Energy Agency and has led successful peacekeeping operations in Cambodia, Cyprus, East Timor, Haiti, Mozambique, Sierra Leone, and eastern Slavonia. It is the world's most important source of international legitimacy. And it does all this on an annual budget of $2.5 billion. The Pentagon spends that much every day.[26]

The liberal internationalist commitments to democracy, cooperative problem solving, and universalistic human rights are indispensable to a constructive foreign policy, as is the liberal internationalist commitment to create structures that transcend nationalism and provide collective security. These commitments are compatible with a realist perspective on the will-to-power of political entities. Though some states are more evil than others, all are self-interested and power-seeking.

Today the foreign policy journals are awash with debates about the kind of realism we need, because the disasters of the Bush 43 administration have awakened a yearning for it. In my view this is an ambiguous enterprise, because foreign policy realism is inherently nationalistic and it usually excludes ethical factors, including human rights.

For Hobbes, Machiavelli, and other founders of the realist tradition, the whole point of realism was to divorce politics from ethical factors. In the past half-century realism has justified U.S. support for apartheid in South Africa and alliances with dictators in Indonesia, the Philippines, Chile, Argentina, and a long list of others, always in the name of strategic interests.

Foreign policy realism is too nationalistic and ethically thin to be something with which anti-imperial progressives like me can identify, but we need to find as much common ground as we can with realists and also recognize that there is such a thing as progressive realism. That common ground includes a deep skepticism about the moral and ideological claims of empires and the selfish interests of all states. It distinguishes between international police action and preventive wars against nations. It rejects the fantasy of beneficial transformations flowing from wars of aggression and comprehends that terrorism can only be minimized, not eliminated.

In November 2008 Americans voted for a return to a foreign policy based on realistic diplomacy and cooperation. Obama combines Niebuhr's cold-eyed emphasis on the limits of politics and the clash of interests with a liberal internationalist emphasis on collective action. In Iraq he is slowly withdrawing U.S. military forces, building up the Iraqi army, and trying to help Iraq create a unified state. In Afghanistan he has nearly tripled U.S. forces in the name of building up a real army and a functional government, all within eighteen months, so the U.S. can withdraw. That will not happen. It will take years to create a viable Afghan army, and the goal of creating a functional Afghan government is so far out of reach that Obama has to deny being committed to it, even as he escalates America's commitment to killing and dying for the discredited Karzai government. Obama has taken the path of Lyndon Johnson and Mikhail Gorbachev, doubling down on a mess he inherited, just as Johnson and Gorbachev escalated in Vietnam and Afghanistan, respectively, upon taking office. In both of the latter cases everything got worse, though at least Gorbachev recognized it and reversed course.

Afghanistan is a minefield of bad choices. We are smashing the third poorest country in the world, where the Bush administration complained eight years ago that there were no hard targets to destroy, only shacks and tents. Instead of sending fifty thousand additional troops to Afghanistan, I would prefer to build fifty thousand schools there, where the cost of building twenty schools is equal to deploying one soldier per year. Instead of propping up a corrupt nongovernment in Afghanistan and treating the Taliban as a mortal threat to the U.S., I would rather see the U.S. and its allies campaign for hearts and minds, buy off the approachable segments of the Taliban, test whether the Taliban and Al Qaeda can be separated, and go after Al Qaeda where it actually exists, in Pakistan. Obama has taken the option that has "sinkhole" written all over it, notwithstanding his promise to escalate only to enable withdrawing.

But no matter what Obama does in Afghanistan, the work is going to be grinding, perilous, and ambiguous. There are no good choices there and no major diplomatic breakthroughs coming. In Afghanistan, as in Iraq, the fix is in and there is only the arduous work of achieving a decently tolerable outcome.

The situation in Iran, where the Bush legacy is disastrous, is equally perilous. Yet there is a real chance of a breakthrough with Iran. In 2001 Iran had a few dozen centrifuges and the government of President Mohammad Khatami helped the U.S. overthrow the Taliban regime in Afghanistan. Khatami negotiated with the U.S. in the wake of 9/11, closed Iran's border with Afghanistan, deported hundreds of Qaeda and Taliban operatives who had sought sanctuary in Iran, and helped establish the new Afghan government. The Bush administration could have spent the succeeding years further negotiating with Iran, limiting Iran's nuclear program, allowing it to buy a nuclear power reactor from France, and restraining it from flooding Iraq with foreign agents. Instead, Bush arbitrarily ended talks with Iran and consigned it to the axis of evil. Iran responded by electing an eccentric extremist, Mahmoud Ahmadinejad, to the presidency, developing more than five thousand centrifuges, and threatening Israel. We barely averted a catastrophe in 2006, when Bush and Cheney wanted to bomb Natanz with a nuclear weapon and the Joint Chiefs rebelled against Bush and Cheney.

Today there is a serious possibility that the Netanyahu government in Israel will carry out the bombing option. If it does, the entire region could explode into a ball of fire. That's the apocalyptic scenario. The hopeful one is a game-changer based on two or three years of sustained diplomacy. The U.S. could declare that it recognizes the legitimacy of the Islamic Republic of Iran. It could acknowledge Iran's right to security within its present borders and its right to be a geo-political player in the region. It could accept Iran's right to operate a limited enrichment facility with a few hundred centrifuges for peaceful purposes. It could agree to the French nuclear power reactor and support Iran's entry into the World Trade Organization. And it could return seized Iranian assets. In return Iran could be required to cut off its assistance to Hezbollah and Hamas, help stabilize Iraq and Afghanistan, maintain a limited nuclear program for peaceful ends verified by the International Atomic Energy Agency, adopt a non-recognition and non-interference approach to Israel, improve its human rights record, and stop its campaign of persecution and culture war against the political opposition it defrauded in the election of 2009.

Any deal of this sort would be a dramatic breakthrough in the Middle East. It would have a positive impact on nearly every major point of conflict in the region. It would be the opposite of the Bush-neocon approach, which demonized Iran and plotted attacks on it. It would demonstrate that the United States understands that it cannot advance the cause of peace in the Middle East by isolating Iran. The election of 2009 embarrassed the clerical, political, and Revolutionary Guard reactionaries that rule Iran, leaving them in a weakened position politically, to which they responded by mounting a futile campaign of cultural warfare against a majority of Iranians. To the extent that these weakened rulers make concessions to the U.S. and the United Nations, the game will change. If they defy genuine diplomatic initiatives then that will strengthen the youthful majority opposition that wants Iran to have constructive relations with the rest of the world. Obama may be the ideal president to pull off a game-changing deal with Iran or to at least ratchet up the pressure on Iran's rulers to make gains for peace in the Middle East. If he tries, he will have to stand up to a firestorm of opposition in the U.S. and overrule his key officials in this area, Hillary Clinton and Dennis Ross. And he will have to risk offending most of Israel's political establishment, to get something that is actually better for Israel.

Regardless of what Obama does or does not do, we need a defiantly anti-imperial peace movement that seeks to scale back the military empire, rejects the American obsession with supremacy and dominance, and insists that planting thousands of U.S. troops anywhere on Middle Eastern soil is not the answer to our security problems.

Liberal Internationalism and the Wilsonian Tightrope

Toward that end it is worth remembering that Theodore Roosevelt and Woodrow Wilson, besides bequeathing a toxic strain of imperial supremacism to the U.S., were burned by anti-imperial rebellions that somewhat chastened them as presidents. More important, the idea of collective security, which belongs to history with Wilson's name affixed, is an anti-imperial notion at its best and indispensable to anti-imperialist movements.

Roosevelt, while serving as Assistant Secretary of the Navy in 1898, two months before the Spanish-American War, sent Commodore George Dewey to Hong Kong to attack the Spanish fleet in the Philippines. Dewey made quick work of the Spanish occupiers, TR became famous as a hard-charging colonel in Cuba, and the "splendid little war" delivered the Philippines to the United States. President McKinley promised to train the Filipinos in the discipline of self-government and to make Christians of them, never mind that they were Catholic; in the succeeding four years, America's pacification of the Philippines required 126,000 American troops.

The Filipino rebellion against the American occupiers killed 4,234 Americans, approximately 16,000 insurgents, and 200,000 civilians. Near the end of it, President Roosevelt fretted over atrocity stories. General Nelson A. Miles, a political rival and former Indian fighter, pressed the atrocity issue; TR rebuked him, recalling that Miles and his soldiers at Wounded Knee "killed squaws and children as well as unarmed Indians." Characteristically Roosevelt folded both episodes into a progress narrative. In his telling, the U.S. gained the Philippines "at a time so opportune that it may without irreverence be called providential." America had to show that it was strong and peaceful, and the surest way of doing so was "to show that we are not afraid of war."[27]

But TR's zest for expansion faded in his second term. He wearied of colonial maintenance in the Philippines, the American empire contracted on his watch, and in 1914 he urged Wilson to end America's colonial experiment in the Philippines.

Wilson's encounter with nationalist rage occurred in Mexico, which teetered on the edge of civil war at the time he became president in 1913. In 1911 revolutionary leader Francisco Madero, a liberal Constitutionalist, overthrew the dictatorship of Porfirio Diaz, under whose regime U.S. and British companies controlled Mexico's railroads and 90 percent of its oil industry. Madero was opposed by the army, the landed aristocracy, reactionary business interests, and the Catholic Church, as well as by U.S. Ambassador Henry Lane Wilson. In February 1913 he was murdered and replaced by General Victoriano Huerta. The new American president, an author of several books on constitutional government, was appalled. Ambassador Wilson contended that only a dictator like Huerta could hold Mexico together and could protect American investments; President Wilson fired the ambassador, imposed an arms embargo on Mexico, and sought to mediate between the Huerta regime and the revolutionary Constitutionalists.

Wilson shocked prominent Democrats and Republicans by taking the side of Constitutionalist leader Venustiano Carranza and his radical lieutenant, Francisco "Pancho" Villa. In April 1914 he dispatched the Marines to Mexico to overthrow Huerta, vowing that he would teach Mexico to elect good leaders. The Marines, seeking to prevent the delivery of weapons from an approaching German steamer, occupied the coastal city of Veracruz and were attacked. Nineteen Marines and 126 Mexicans were killed in the battle, and Mexicans exploded in outrage. Wilson's show of democratic idealism united Mexico's warring factions against the United States. Carranza, desperate not to be identified with the Yankee invaders, rebuffed Wilson, who responded by withdrawing the Marines.

Wilson was stunned and embarrassed, plus galled that he gave Roosevelt an easy shot at him. He and Roosevelt despised each other. Roosevelt blasted him for disgracing the U.S. Wilson, reeling from criticism, lamented to his secretary of war that he walked into a revolutionary cauldron as hot as the French Revolution. But Wilson's moralism, where it existed, ran deep in him. It was not merely a self-righteous impulse. His presidency was atrocious on racial justice because he was very short on moral feelings for African Americans. In other areas, where his moral feelings ran strong, he had trouble recognizing that the morally right action was not always politically right. In a July 4 oration Wilson defended his Mexican fiasco by comparing it to his (ostensible) opposition to economic imperialism. When American companies exploited "the mass of the people" in a foreign country, he claimed, especially a country that was "not strong enough to resist us," he believed that the American government needed to intervene on behalf of the weaker parties. Just as he believed in capitalism, but not its right to suppress the rights of vulnerable people, he regretted the violence of his Mexican adventure, but "back of it all is the struggle of a people to come into its own."[28]

This moral impulse, though ridiculed in 1913, was an asset for Wilson four years later when he took his country to war. Elected to the presidency at the height of the social gospel movement, he accepted the challenge of Protestant leaders to champion the movement's progressive idealism. As late as January 1917 Wilson personally assured progressive internationalists that he was determined to obtain conditions for peace negotiations and keep America out of World War I. On January 22, 1917, he gave a dramatic address to the U.S. Senate, calling for a "peace without victory" and the creation of a "League of Peace." The war needed to be resolved in a way that did not produce bitter losers, he urged, and the new federation of nations would keep the peace: "The equality of nations upon which peace must be founded if it is to last must be an equality of rights. Only a peace between equals can last."[29]

Instead, the warring parties on both sides were determined to prevail. Germany sunk the American *Housatonic* and schemed for Mexico to enter the war, Britain used the Zimmerman Telegram to pull America into the war, and five U.S. ships were sunk without warning. On April 2 Wilson told a joint session of Congress that America had to join the war to make the world safe for democracy. His call to war was a disaster for American progressivism that shredded radical movements and sparked an explosion of jingoistic intolerance calling itself "One Hundred Percent Americanism." Radical critic Randolph Bourne hauntingly asked his progressive friends who supported the war, "If the war is too strong for you to prevent, how is it going to be weak enough for you to control and mould to your liberal purposes?" But most progressive internationalists accepted Wilson's famous assurance of January 8, 1918—the Fourteen Points Address—that the war would be molded to good purposes.[30]

Speaking to a joint session of Congress, Wilson offered proposals on border and sovereignty issues, implored the Allies to eschew "jealousy of German greatness," and called for freedom of the seas, elimination of trade barriers, equality of trade conditions, adjustment of colonial claims, and the establishment of a community of nations to provide collective security for "great and small states alike." The League of Nations came last because Wilson considered it his most important point. The key to the Fourteen Points, as in the "Peace without Victory" speech, was Wilson's anti-imperial principle of collective security and justice. He described it as "the principle of justice to all peoples and nationalities and the right to live on equal terms of liberty and safety with one another, whether they be strong or weak."[31]

Wilson had claimed upon entering the war that German aggression was the sole cause of the war, but he knew better. The problem was imperialism and imperial rivalry, not merely Germany's form of it. The great powers claimed that imperial expansion aided world peace by eliminating unstable regimes. Wilson recognized that that stood the truth on its head. Imperial rivalry was the main cause of modern wars; the Great War was merely the worst example. It was caused chiefly by clashes between the great powers for imperial control over Africa and Asia. Wilson wanted to prevent future wars and end the current one by creating an international federation of nations, "the very principle of which is equality and a common participation in a common benefit." A worthy peace would make Germany an equal player and partner among the world's civilized nations, not humiliate Germany or impair its claim to greatness.[32]

America's European allies took no interest in being equals with Germany. French Prime Minister Clemenceau sniffed that even God had only ten points. At Versailles the victors shredded Wilson's ideals in a vengeful display of Old World politics, blaming Germany entirely for the war, punishing it with $15 billion of reparations, and rejecting Wilson's pleas for free trade and an end to colonialism. Wilson fared just as poorly at home, botching the politics with a Republican Congress that wanted nothing to do with collective security and ruining his health in a failed effort to link his nation to the League of Nations. Wilsonian collective security had to wait for the failure of a weakened League of Nations and the horrible destruction of another world war.

The victors of World War II, especially Franklin Roosevelt, recognized that Wilson was right about the causal link between imperial rivalry and world war. Imperialism itself was the primary cause of war. As long as there were imperial powers that dreamed of conquering Africa, Asia, and Europe, world wars would continue. The victors established the United Nations; the British, Dutch, French, Germans, and Italians gave up their empires; the European Union was formed; and a host of international economic and security institutions were founded.

The liberal internationalist idea of collective security to which Wilson gave historic expression has more than a century of advocacy behind it and more than six decades of institutional practice. Always it has battled a potent combination of prejudice and anxious fear of the loss of national control. Loathing of the United Nations runs deep and wide in American society. Madeleine Albright, speaking from her experience as an ambassador to the UN, observes that most complaints about the United Nations' usurpation of American sovereignty come from "people aggrieved to find the United Nations so full of foreigners." Her appropriately tart reply: "That, I am constrained to say, simply cannot be helped."[33]

Collective security is essential to liberal internationalism; it is the anti-imperial heart of a cooperative and diplomatic approach to the clash of nations. Neoconservatism is often described as Wilsonian because its democratic globalist wing features a militaristic retrieval of Wilson's vision of world democracy, but neocon militarism is nationalistic and imperialist. It dismisses collective security as a dispensable offshoot of believing in the possibility of world democracy. Wilson had a better idea, building cooperative institutions, on which depended the hope of world democracy and abolishing war. International institutions were and are the fallible, indispensable means by which democratic principles advance in world politics.

Democracy has to do with the character of relationships that are constructed on the principles of freedom and equality. Robust democracies are pluralistic, egalitarian, peaceable, and cooperative; they seek to maximize freedom and equality for all people and to build effective structures of collective security. They develop from within. Neoconservatives lay claim to the language of democracy but spurn its essential values of equality, cooperation, and diversity. They ignore the contradiction between advocating American unipolar dominance and upholding the United States as the model for other nations. President Bush's National Security Strategy of 2002 declared in its opening sentence that there exists "a single sustainable model for national success." Leaving aside that actually there is no single model of national success, the president and his supporters ignored that the U.S. cannot be a unipolar hegemon and a model for other nations at the same time. The American colossus, if devoted to maintaining its dominant position in the global capitalist system, cannot be the exemplar of a way that encourages or yields to imitators.[34]

The presumption that America invades and fights only to liberate, never to conquer, is deeply woven into the American consciousness. It was a staple of July 4 orations long before Woodrow Wilson, and it is a large part of Wilson's national legacy. American presidents trade on this partly true, partly ridiculous national self-image whenever they take their country to war. The United States was founded on a genocidal conquest, but, unlike most countries, the United States itself has never been occupied, which is a clue to America's counterfactual insistence on its innocence. For decades Americans felt safe from the problems and dangers of other nations without noticing the resentments and harms that their country piled up within them. On September 11, 2001, Americans lost the former illusion, but their political leaders in both parties invoked that experience to reinforce American hubris and obliviousness, a cunningly stoked reaction that led straight to the flag-waving invasion of Iraq.

Forty years ago Senator William Fulbright warned that the U.S. was well on its way to becoming an empire that exercised power for its own sake, projected to the limit of its capacity and beyond, filling every vacuum and extending American force to the farthest reaches of the earth. As the power grows, he warned, it becomes an end in itself, separated from its initial motives (all the while denying it), governed by its own mystique, projecting power merely because we have it. That's where we are today, still overdue, even with a better president, to arrest the compulsive expansion of American power.

Postscript: Empire and Globalization Theory

At academic venues I am asked occasionally whether my focus on scaling back the U.S. military empire does not cut against the recent trend in postmodern social theory to discount nationalism and the nation-state in a globalized world. Michael Hardt and Antonio Negri, in their respective works *Empire* and *Empire and Multitude,* contend that such concerns are outdated in an age when globalization itself is the ruling empire. They argue that globalization has rendered old forms of imperialism obsolete as it creates a new type of global sovereignty based on the network power of transnational corporations, a global financial class, nation-states, and other powers.[35]

I agree with Hardt and Negri that globalization is changing empire itself into something more fluid, intertwined, and trans-governmental than the older state-centered imperialisms. The new imperialism of neoliberal globalization is, as they claim, like the classic one in prizing a universal order that accepts no boundaries or limits; yet, on the other hand, it is a new phenomenon by virtue of its capacity to transform sovereignty into a sprawling, global system of diffuse national and supranational institutions.

But Hardt and Negri, in the manner of academic fashions, press this compelling description of something terribly real into an exaggerated thesis. Like Thomas Friedman, only with contrasting politics, they describe a triumphant global capitalism that is essentially immune from ordinary politics. Contrary to Hardt, Negri, and Friedman, nationalism and nation-states remain powerful forces in the world, a point dramatized by the trillions of dollars that governments marshaled to save capitalism from itself in 2008. Moreover, there is no structural substitute for democratizing economic power, which means that there is no substitute for the old-fashioned socialist concerns with democratic politics, breaking up economic oligarchies, and democratizing the process of investment.

Hardt and Negri contend that globalization-as-empire has brought progressive democratic theory to grief by undermining the capacity of states to channel economic forces and create structures of social justice. Today, in their telling, two progressive theoretical orientations and two conservative ones dominate the field: social democracy, liberal cosmopolitanism, Old Right conservatism, and neoconservatism. Social democracy is a weak throwback to the age of nation-based class conflict; liberal cosmopolitanism is sophisticated and relevant but lacks transformative power; Old Right conservatism gets certain things right in a bad way; and neoconservatism is repugnant all the way down.

Social Democrats such as Paul Hirst and Grahame Thompson view democracy as being eviscerated or threatened by globalization. To strengthen democracy, they support policies that refortify the sovereignty of nation-states, taking greater political control of the economy at national and supranational levels. Liberal cosmopolitans like David Held and Mary Kaldor view globalization as a generally good thing that, with a bit of liberal management, fosters democracy. In their view globalization can be a powerful force for progressive change because it enhances economic growth, encourages nations to get along with one another, and liberates individuals and groups from the rule of nation-states. In foreign policy, liberal cosmopolitans support using and strengthening multilateral institutions.[36]

On the right, similar attitudes toward globalization provide ballast for very different political agendas. Old Right conservatives like Patrick Buchanan and Samuel Huntington take a negative view of globalization, mainly because it undermines traditional values and national sovereignty. Globalization exports the worst parts of American culture, they argue; it fosters a radical expansion of U.S. hegemony at the expense of traditional American values and the best meaning of American exceptionalism; and it engenders imperial war, which is the graveyard of republics and empires. On the other side of contemporary conservatism, neoconservatives Bill Kristol and Michael Novak acknowledge that globalization tends to export the worst of American culture, but they stress its capacity to boost America's unipolar dominance. For neocons, to be pro-American is precisely to prize America's global economic and military dominance.[37]

Hardt and Negri emphasize that the high tide of globalization in the late 1990s and early 2000s shredded the hopes of Social Democrats, which set off a stampede toward the liberal cosmopolitan view. If the tides of globalization are too powerful to be restrained or channeled, they argue, and if war has become a perpetual fact of life no longer confined to interstate conflicts, the best hope for progressives may be a cosmopolitan liberalism that builds on the best aspects of globalization and strives for a democratic world government, or at least a strengthened United Nations.

Rightly Hardt and Negri want us to dream more ambitiously than that. What is needed, and happening, they argue, is a movement for radical, bottom-up, participatory democracy on a world scale. They call it "the possibility of a unified global people." Inspired by the protest movements against the IMF and World Bank, Hardt and Negri envision a global multitude of postmodernized hybrid identities creating a new world society through its various engagements with and struggles against empire. The aim and hope of the world is a global democracy created by a unified global people.[38]

This is a utopian vision, which evokes dispositional arguments about the value of utopian projects. From a Christian perspective a dose of utopianism is always in order, exactly along the line that Hardt and Negri take in describing the multitude. We are capable of imagining the multitude as a long-term political project only because it is already latent in our social existence, they say. We can only hope to realize it "because it already exists as a real potential." The multitude has "a strange, double temporality: always-already and not-yet." That is an echo of the biblical kingdom of God, which the social gospel and liberation theology translated as the eschatological commonwealth of freedom. Hardt and Negri aptly describe and support the "motley crew" politics of some of today's best anti-poverty and anti-globalization movements, which prize unruly protest and disrupting normal flows in public space.[39] But motley crew leftism is notoriously fragmented, lacking social justice organizations and strategies that scale up. Hardt and Negri, besides exaggerating the demise of national governments under globalization and over-relying on protest politics, ignore democratic socialism. When they discuss social democracy, they hold in view the European social democratic parties that integrated themselves into the capitalist system and abandoned even the pretense of advocating for the working class. When they discuss socialism, they emphasize the radical socialist and communist traditions that took a vanguardist approach to practical politics, conceived the revolutionary party as the representative of those lacking representation, and wanted the state to be abolished. Democratic socialism gets barely a sentence in this account of the relevant options. Walter Rauschenbusch, Eugene Debs, Michael Harrington, and Martin Luther King Jr. apparently wasted their time advocating it.

But the democratic socialist vision of economic democracy, by whatever name, is not as wild a dream as the one conjured by Hardt and Negri of a global democracy forged by a unified global people. It is always about giving substance to the principle of self-determination for all people. It extends this principle across all sectors of social existence, including racial and sexual justice, and refuses wars of empire and aggression, forging a common ground for social justice movements. Before taking a leap into a vision of postmodernized multitudes discovering and producing their oneness on the way to global democracy, we should account for what economic democracy gets right and wrong.

Part IV

Social Ethics and the Politics of Difference

Chapter 14

The Feminist Difference

ROSEMARY R. RUETHER AND ECO-SOCIALIST CHRISTIANITY

My first encounter with Rosemary Radford Ruether occurred in 1974, during my first semester of divinity school, when she spoke at Boston College. To me she was already a theological star: prolific, brilliant, radical yet perfectly sane, obviously the best of the feminist theologians. Her books had exciting titles that exuded revolutionary anticipation— *The Radical Kingdom, Liberation Theology, Religion and Sexism*—and at Boston College she polled the audience on provocative titles for her next collection, which became *New Woman, New Earth*. Feminist theology, Ruether declared, was the "next great revolution" in theology and religion; I remember thinking that "next" seemed surprisingly modest, since the revolution was well under way.

Fifteen months later she was the featured speaker at a University Christian Movement conference that I organized in Cambridge. The church hall was packed with students from local congregations and divinity schools, Ruether expounded on women as "the first and final proletariat," and she admonished a dissenter that "God created a world, not a church." None of my professors at Harvard would have drawn such a large or politically active crowd. She seemed supremely confident in herself and her message, exhorting women not to settle for whining; feminism was a revolution, not a pity-party. Ruether roared against sexism, racism, militarism, and other oppressive isms, sometimes breaking a heavy feeling in the air with a caustic expletive. For many of us it was thrilling just to be in the same room with her.

She teased me about studying at a school that had no feminist theologians, and I agreed that Harvard's lack of one was incredible. How could it be that Harvard Divinity School had no place for feminist criticism? How could it be, after feminism had blasted male-stream theology so convincingly for excluding and demeaning half the human race, that Harvard did not teach feminist theology or scholarship? Several years passed before it occurred to me that Ruether could not have been as confident as she seemed. For feminist theology barely existed anywhere in the mid-1970s, and even Ruether, for all her books and speaking engagements, had almost no experience teaching it.

She was born to a cultured, humanistic, Catholic mother and an Anglican, Republican, Virginia gentleman father who died when she was twelve. After an early childhood in Georgetown, Ruether spent her adolescent years in California, where her primary role models were women. She later credited her mother Rebecca Cresap Ord Radford, her mother's friends, and Scripps College as the formative influences on her development. From her mother she inherited a "sense of secure self-confidence" in her abilities and opportunities, as well as a Catholic background that, as Ruether later stressed, was more cosmopolitan than the "ghettoized" type in which radical feminist Mary Daly grew up. At Scripps College—a Claremont, California, women's institution featuring a humanities core curriculum—she majored in classics, which set her on the path to religious studies.[1]

Ruether's college professors taught her to understand Christianity as an alien development within the ancient Mediterranean world that ultimately became the preserver of its legacy. Her favorite teacher, classicist Robert Palmer, regarded Christianity as a poor replacement for the humanism, balance, and splendor of classical culture. Others denigrated Catholicism as inferior to classical culture and Protestantism. In four years of college Ruether rarely peered beyond the fifth century. She absorbed the outlook of her teachers but also reacted against them, discovering an unexpected loyalty to her mother's church. Near the end of her doctoral studies at Claremont Graduate School it also dawned on her that her admired undergraduate professors had not taken her seriously. Scripps professors took for granted that they taught future wives and society matrons, not scholars. That realization filled Ruether with a "profound sense of betrayal," pushing her toward feminism.[2]

Well into her college career she was clueless about politics. In 1956, while her college friends supported Adlai Stevenson for president, Ruether didn't know if she was a Democrat or Republican. Two years later she married Herman Ruether, a political scientist whose liberal politics rubbed off on her, and her increasing participation in campus ministry activities drew her into racial justice and antiwar causes. "Once exposed to these issues, I seemed instinctively to gravitate to the Left," she later recalled. Intrigued by the prophetic stream of biblical proclamation, Ruether studied Hebrew prophecy in the context of Mediterranean religious development, forming three conclusions: the only scholarship worth reading on this subject was liberal Protestant; she preferred the ethical religion of biblical monotheism over pagan theophanies of the gods; and Protestant scholarship was too much like the Bible in denigrating pagan religions. Ruether warmed to the prophetic witness of the Bible but not its polemic against Ba'alism; the genius of Catholicism, she judged, was that it synthesized the entire complex of religious heritages of the ancient world. It also helped that Vatican II took place during her doctoral studies at Claremont Graduate School; Ruether later reflected that she probably would not have remained in the Catholic Church had the council not occurred. In graduate school she deepened her identification with Catholic political activism, while writing a dissertation on Gregory of Naziansus, the Cappadocian monk, and Bishop of Constantinople who defended the Nicene faith at the Council of Constantinople in 381. Ruether argued that Christian monasticism made a mistake by defining itself as a spiritual elite of celibates with lifelong vows and vocations rather than a stage of life (as in Asian monasticism) or a source of periodic renewal.[3]

Her involvements in movement politics shaped her entire theological career. In 1965 Ruether joined the Civil Rights movement as a Delta Ministries summer worker in Beulah, Mississippi; the following year she began her teaching career at Howard University, where she taught from 1966 to 1976; in the later 1960s and early 1970s she was deeply involved in Washington, D.C.'s church-based antiwar movement, getting arrested at numerous pray-ins and sing-ins: "One lived in a constant atmosphere of political awareness that made any other part of the country appear asleep."[4]

By 1968 she was already a prolific essayist, though her early work contained little hint of a feminist perspective. Ruether's first post-dissertation book, a collection of essays on ecclesiology titled *The Church Against Itself* (1967), contended, in the "secular city" spirit of the time, that the church as triumphant colossus and sacramental fortress was disintegrating; to make its way in the new world the church had to learn to live with "radical cultural insecurity." Her first glimmer of feminist consciousness was a critique of the Catholic prohibition of artificial contraception. In 1964 Ruether noted that as a graduate student and mother of three children she experienced the church's command as a psychological impossibility. In effect, the church told her to abandon her academic dreams in order to have an unlimited number of children. That amounted to "a demand that I scuttle my interests, my training, and in the last analysis, my soul." The hardness of Catholic teaching in this area was not a virtue, Ruether admonished; she respected moral rigor when it served worthy moral values, but the church's position yielded merely "weariness and disgust."[5]

On the shifting politics of race she wrote about the generational feud between integrationist liberals and liberationist radicals, but treaded lightly in faculty meetings and class. Her status at Howard was tenuous simply by virtue of being a white female professor and lacking female students. It grew more complex and tense as she identified with the feminist uprising of the late 1960s. Along with Letty Russell (Yale Divinity School) and Beverly Harrison (Union Theological Seminary), Ruether was one of the first to develop a feminist theological critique of the Civil Rights movement, the New Left, and everyday sexism. More than any feminist besides Mary Daly, she inspired a feminist movement in theology through her writings and speaking engagements. But all of Ruether's feminist scholarship and movement building was on her own time, for at Howard she had no opportunity to teach feminism or even talk about it: "Every time I raised the issue, I was accused of being racist." At Howard University the issue of sexism had to be raised by African Americans; meanwhile "it was clear my feminist work needed to happen somewhere else." That verdict caused Ruether to move to Garrett Evangelical Theological Seminary in 1976, where she could teach what she was known for.[6]

In her early years at Howard she labored over a massive manuscript on the roots of Jewish messianism in Near Eastern kingship and New Year rituals. Ruether's publisher rejected it, partly because her account of the Canaanite origins of messianic ideas offended a peer reviewer, and she never published it. Yet her research for the book proved to be a wellspring for many years, fueling her writings on Christology, anti-Semitism, goddess religion, and political theology. Ruether made her early renown as a critic of Western dualism. By 1970 she had a signature lecture on this theme that inspired and framed much of the feminist theology movement. Judith Plaskow and Carol P. Christ, who heard it as graduate students at Yale, later remembered the lecture as "almost miraculous." Ruether's definitive version of it, published in 1972, described sexism as a by-product of the breakdown of tribal culture.[7]

For the first two millennia of recorded history, she recounted, religious culture reflected the holistic worldview and primitive democracy of the neolithic village. The earth goddess and sky god played complementary roles, as did females and males. The salvation of the individual was not divorced from that of the community or the renewal of the earth. New Year's festivals celebrated the annual death and resurrection of the cosmos; the king (personifying the community) played the role of the dying and rising god; his female counterpart (a virgin and mother, and wife and sister) rescued the dying god from the netherworld. At the end of the celebration the two united to form the divine child of the new year's life. However, the communal neolithic worldview of a sacred cosmos began to break down in the first millennium BCE, partly as a consequence of imperial invasions that swept the peoples of the Mediterranean into alien civilizations. To the extent that the old religions of the earth survived, they became private cults for individuals, "no longer anticipating the renewal of the earth and society but rather expecting an otherworldly salvation of the individual soul after death." Nature became an alien reality; individuals imagined that their bodies were foreign to their true selves; the idea of a heavenly escape to a true home displaced the idea that the earth is humanity's home.[8]

In Ruether's rendering, early Christianity synthesized the Hebrew and classical myths of redemption. The Hebrews clung tenaciously to their tribal identity in resistance to a succession of imperial powers, claiming the land as a divine legacy, reinterpreting the earth festivals as historical events in their communal journey, and looking forward to a renewal of earth and society in a messianic age. But they also repressed the feminine imagery of the old religions (aside from symbolizing Israel as the bride of Yahweh), divorced the cycle of death and resurrection from the sacred cosmos, and refigured death and resurrection as historical wrath and redemption. Classical philosophy further alienated the individual from the world, viewing the body as an obstacle to clear knowledge, moral integrity, and spiritual refinement. Platonism was a myth of liberation to a "changeless, infinite world beyond," which Christianity absorbed. In Christianity the old myths of the new year and the virgin-mother goddess, the historical consciousness of Israel, and the anti-feminine spirituality of late antiquity were refashioned, synthesizing the best and worst of late classical civilization. Accenting the down side, Ruether remarked: "What we see in this development is a one-sided expression of the ego claiming its transcendental autonomy by negating the finite matrix of existence."[9]

In language that had not quite caught up to her vision of feminist transformation, she exhorted that "women must be the spokesmen for a new humanity arising out of the reconciliation of spirit and body." The crucial challenge and "secret power of the women's revolution" was to liberate women from patriarchal oppression without buying into the "masculine ethic of competitiveness." Unlike men, Ruether explained, women typically cultivated an ethic of "communal personhood" that allowed them to participate in the successes of others instead of viewing others as threats to their own success. The revolution that was needed, and occurring, achieved women's liberation without losing women's superior capacity for community.[10]

By 1971 feminist theology was hot enough that Harvard Divinity School wanted to teach it, if only on an occasional basis. Ruether, having never taught it herself, welcomed the opportunity to do so as a one-year visiting professor. Later she put it more caustically, recalling that Harvard was willing to patronize feminist liberationists as visiting lecturers but "never to embrace" them as members of its club. Ruether's first experience of teaching feminist theology was rather bruising. She shook her head at the faculty: "These scholars had kept their eyes determinedly averted from the collapse of the society around them, never allowing it to impinge upon or question their segregated mental world." At the same time she had troubling encounters with radical feminist students. "As a feminist theologian I was regarded as the 'coming thing,' riding the new wave of critical thought," she recalled. But Harvard's student body had a contingent of radical feminists for whom Mary Daly represented the real thing.[11]

Daly raged against universal patriarchy, described feminism as the ultimate revolution, and was well on her way toward repudiating Christianity. Ruether later recalled of her encounter with Daly-feminism: "To be concerned about class and race was seen as distracting from 'pure' feminism. The influence of Mary Daly was evident here." Radical feminists responded to Ruether's politicized feminism "in a slightly pitying manner, as though I was 'still back in the sixties.'" Her research on patristic anti-Semitism was even more incomprehensible: "Anti-Semitism was not even a fad become passé for them. It simply did not make any sense at all." Judaism held no interest except as the grandfather of "patriarchal misogyny." For Ruether the experience was chastening: "I came to realize how faddish 'social' theologies are apt to be." It was also clarifying about the kind of feminist that she wanted to be—one that stressed the interrelationships between feminism and other justice causes.[12]

In her early years at Garrett the lack of a systematic text in feminist theology troubled Ruether, forcing her to devise makeshift course packs. In the meantime she labored on the first feminist systematic theology, *Sexism and God-Talk*, which was published in 1983. Twenty-five years later it was still the only work of its kind. Ruether described her critical principle as "the promotion of the full humanity of women" and identified five sources of feminist theology: (1) the Bible, especially its prophetic-liberating stream; (2) marginalized Christian traditions such as Gnosticism and Quakerism; (3) primary themes of classical Christianity; (4) non-Christian "Near Eastern" and Greco-Roman religion and philosophy; and (5) critical post-Christian perspectives such as liberalism, romanticism, and Marxism. Since all these traditions were sexist, she cautioned, all had to be judged by the feminist critical principle. Feminist theology was a type of liberation theology in which women were included in the prophetic norm: "Feminism sees what male prophetic thought generally has not seen: that once the prophetic norm is asserted to be central to Biblical faith, then patriarchy can no longer be maintained as authoritative."[13]

Feminist theology, like liberation theology as a whole, appealed to the prophetic-liberating stream of biblical religion, in her rendering. It had four defining themes: proclaiming God's favor for the oppressed, criticizing the dominant systems and holders of power, proclaiming the vision of a coming new age of peace and justice, and criticizing ideologies that sanctified an unjust social order. In political terms it contained intimations of a social order founded on the principles of freedom, equality, cooperation, and sustainable development. Ruether stressed that feminist theology was not based on "unprecedented ideas." It renewed and deepened the ethical conscience of biblical religion by applying the prophetic-liberating principle to women: "Feminist theology makes explicit what was overlooked in male advocacy of the poor and oppressed: namely, *women* of the oppressed. This means that the critique of hierarchy must become explicitly a critique of patriarchy. All the liberating prophetic visions must be deepened and transformed to include what was not included: women." Just as Paul grasped the necessity of erasing the barriers between Jews and Greeks, feminist theology took up his unfinished vision of equality between females and males.[14]

Ruether's development of these themes virtually defined the mainstream of feminist liberation theology in its first generation. For those who embraced radical feminist criticism but stopped short of opting for spiritual utopianism, the prominence of Daly-type feminism made it necessary to explain why radical feminists went too far. Ruether contended that radical feminism was attractive in many respects but wrong in its separatism and Gnostic tendencies. Her brand of feminist theology affirmed the radical emphasis on transformations of consciousness but also affirmed aspects of liberal politics and theology.[15]

In Daly's type of feminism, Ruether observed, "the history of women becomes a trail of crucifixions, with males as the evil archons of an anticosmos where women are entrapped." Seeking an alternative world "within their inner selves," radical feminists engendered a new language of inner transformation that broke apart the dominant language of patriarchy: "They escape together through the holes rent in the fabric of patriarchal ideology into a separate and higher realm of female interiority." Ruether noted that Daly's radical feminism replicated the spiritual dualism of ancient Gnosticism, except that, in her version, feminism was built "on the dualism of a transcendent spirit world of femaleness over against the deceitful anticosmos of masculinity."[16]

To Ruether it was one thing, and absolutely needed, to condemn the ravages of male domination; it was something else to dehumanize all males. Separatism reversed the logic of misogynistic patriarchy, treating women as normative humanity and males as defective humans. This strategy was no more liberating or life-affirming than its enemy, since it projected moral responsibility for all the world's evils onto an alien group: "Such enemy-making of men would ultimately subvert the whole dream of a women's culture based on mutuality and altruism. The very process of projecting the negative part of their own psychic potential onto males, and failing to own these themselves, would tend to make such women's groups fanatical caricatures of that which they hate." Ruether cautioned that to dehumanize the other is to dehumanize oneself, since "one duplicates evil-making in the very effort to escape from it once and for all, by projecting it on the 'alien' group."[17]

Her alternative blended elements of liberal, socialist, and radical feminism, prophetic Christianity, and ecological holism. In some contexts Ruether distinguished between liberal feminism (which stressed that women and men share the same essential humanity), romantic feminism (which valorized distinctive feminine qualities), and the third way that was needed, which neither ghettoized women's concerns (as in romanticism) nor kept racial and class hierarchies intact (as in liberalism). Elsewhere she sought a dialectical synthesis of liberal, socialist, and radical feminisms. Ruether upheld the liberal feminist doctrine of a common human nature and its derivative principle of equal rights for all people, but she criticized liberal feminism for its reformist politics and its preoccupation with equal opportunity gains for middle-class and professional women. Liberal feminism impeded the struggle for equality whenever it overlooked the structural impediments to equality for working-class, minority, and poor women, she argued. Like liberal politics generally, liberal feminism was not enough, yet the liberal doctrine of equal rights was the foundation of any progressive feminism. Building on Zillah Eisenstein's thesis in *The Radical Future of Liberal Feminism*, Ruether contended that the liberal feminist pursuit of social equality was unattainable on liberal terms. Liberal demands for federally funded child care, parental leave, flextime, work sharing, and comparable worth were not viable without structural socioeconomic changes in the direction of democratic socialism. The liberal demand for equality held redistributive implications that outstripped liberal politics.[18]

Since liberal feminism lacked the class perspective of socialism, it typically became a vehicle for the interests of middle- and upper-class women. Ruether stressed that it benefited privileged women who, wanting the same social goods as men of their class, hired domestic workers to do their "women's work" for them: "This is then touted as the fulfillment of the promise of liberal feminism, although actually the economic position of the white upper middle class is being reinforced against women and men of lower classes and races. The glitter of feminist 'equality,' as displayed in *Cosmopolitan* and *Ms.*, both eludes and insults the majority of women who recognize that its 'promise' is not for them."[19]

Her idea of a good feminist politics was democratic socialist, communitarian, and participatory. It decentralized ownership and authority while creating a society that valued cooperation, community, and the common good over material success or power. Ruether urged: "Feminism needs to ask whether, instead of making the male sphere the human norm and attempting to assimilate women into it, it is not necessary to move in the opposite direction. Should we not take the creation and sustaining of human life as the center and reintegrate alienated maleness into it?" Instead of reinscribing the androcentric myth of the workplace as society's locus of meaning and importance, feminism needed to work on getting males more involved in their families.[20]

The middle piece of Ruether's triad of liberal, socialist, and radical feminisms was the controlling one, holding together a fusion of perspectives, but she stressed that the liberal and radical contributions were indispensable. Liberalism was a bulwark for individual rights, while radical feminism rightly insisted that the feminist revolution was about something deeper than equal opportunity or distributive justice. Radical feminists contended that gender oppression was the fundamental historical form of enslavement and that liberation from it required a new spirituality, not merely a new politics. Just as patriarchy subordinated women's bodies, sexuality, and reproduction to male ownership and control, radical feminism liberated women from patriarchal laws and social roles. Just as patriarchy made women emotionally dependent upon controlling males, radical feminism liberated women from maleness itself. For radical feminists, feminism was revolutionary, not merely radical; it was a revolution of consciousness.

Ruether agreed that feminism did not reduce to politics. She did not agree that gender oppression was more fundamental or important than other forms of oppression. She agreed that gender had to be regarded as a fundamental organizing variable in social structure, culture, and personal life. Any feminism that failed to attack patriarchy as a social system would also fail to liberate women from the shackles of male domination, she contended. Her ideal was to integrate the liberal concern with equal rights, the democratic socialist commitment to distributive justice, and the radical emphasis on gender feminism. Though each of these perspectives was deficient by itself, she argued, each was necessary and generative to the extent that it remained open to the liberating capacities of other perspectives.[21]

Ruether stressed that feminist theology rested on the central tradition of the scriptural witness, the one by which biblical faith "constantly criticizes and renews itself and its own vision." By claiming the Bible's prophetic-liberating stream as a norm for criticizing Christianity and patriarchy, feminist theology operated in the same fashion as other liberationisms, stripping away layers of ideology and misunderstanding that concealed Christianity's emancipatory content. In the typical fashion of liberation theologies that refashioned liberal christology, Ruether conceived Christ as the symbol of regenerated humanity. Jesus is not necessarily male, she taught, for as the symbol of a new humanity and representative of God's Word, Jesus manifests the self-emptying of God, the "kenosis of patriarchy." The dynamic relationship between redeemer and redeemed is intrinsic to Christianity, for Christ's identity continues as the symbol of liberated humanity. Christic personhood continues in the struggles of faithful people: "Redemptive humanity goes ahead of us, calling us to yet incompleted dimensions of human liberation."[22]

Sexism and God-Talk was vague and evasive about its ultimate referent, but when Ruether finally developed her operative idea of divine reality, in *Gaia & God: An Ecofeminist Theology of Earth Healing* (1992), she turned out to be a process theologian. Explaining the Whiteheadian distinction between primordial and consequent divinity, she observed that for each actual entity the most life-enhancing choice is always made possible by its participation in God's primordial nature. Because each entity has its own subjectivity, however, it possesses the power to actualize or negate the life-enhancing aim of God's primordial nature. The gift of divine freedom makes it possible for subjective selves to choose evil. Ruether liked Alfred North Whitehead's idea of a divine matrix that lures its subjects to make choices creating new life-giving possibilities: "The reality of God is thus shaped through interrelation with self-actualizing entities. God not only lures and offers new life, but also suffers, experiencing the pain of destructive choices as well as the pleasure of good choices."[23]

Her appropriation of process theology gave her a basis for navigating between different kinds of ecofeminism. Ruether identified with ecofeminist critiques of classical theism but rejected ecofeminist theologies that replaced a monotheistic, transcendent, male-identified religion with a multicentered, immanent, female-identified one. Feminist theology needed a "more imaginative" alternative to androcentric monotheism than simply its reversal, "something more like Nicholas of Cusa's paradoxical 'coincidence of opposites,' in which the 'absolute maximum' and the 'absolute minimum' are the same." In physics, Ruether observed, the distinction between matter and energy no longer holds at the subatomic level; matter is conceived as energy moving in defined patterns of relationality:

At the level of the "absolute minimum," the appearance of physical "stuff" disappears into a voidlike web of relationships, relationships in which the whole universe is finally interconnected and in which the observer also stands as part of the process. As we move below the "absolute minimum" of the tiniest particles into the dancing void of energy patterns that build up the "appearance" of solid objects on the macroscopic level, we also recognize that this is also the "absolute maximum," the matrix of all interconnections of the whole universe. This matrix of dancing energy operates with a "rationality," predictable patterns that result in a fixed number of possibilities. Thus what we have called "God," the "mind," or rational pattern holding all things together, and what we have called "matter," the "ground" of physical objects, come together. The disintegration of the many into infinitely small "bits," and the One, or unifying whole that connects all things together, coincide.[24]

For Ruether, the task of an ecologically conscious feminism was to connect the meaning of human living to these absolutely minimal and maximal worlds, "standing between the dancing void of energy" that underlies the atomic structure of all entities in the universe. To seek religious meaning in a possibly meaningless world is to commune with the universe as heart to heart, or between I and Thou, she argued. Human beings are connected to all living creatures past, present, and future through matter and consciousness; thus all creatures are linked to Gaia, the living and sacred earth/organism. To bear compassion for all living things is to break down the illusion of otherness with the power of spirit: "Surely, if we are kin to all things and offspring of the universe, then what has flowered in us as consciousness must also be reflected in that universe as well, in the ongoing creative Matrix of the whole."[25]

Ruether called for new hymns and liturgies to awaken in human hearts an awareness of the deep kinship between humanity and the natural world. The imperative of finding new ways of organizing the world was intrinsically connected to that of perceiving God and the world in new ways. "God is not a 'being' removed from creation, ruling it from outside in the manner of a patriarchal ruler," she wrote. "God is the source of being that underlies creation and grounds its nature and future potential for continual transformative renewal in biophilic mutuality." In her later career she traveled widely in support of ecofeminist and justice causes, writing extensively on the plight of Palestinians and helping women's groups in a variety of contexts to "legitimize their questions," as she put it.[26]

Routinely Ruether was lauded as the most influential and accomplished feminist theologian of her generation. Letty Russell called her longtime friend "a very wise woman" and partner in "the work against racism and in subversion of church hierarchy." Theologian Susan A. Ross remarked that Ruether's books endured as landmarks in the field because they stressed the interrelatedness of oppressions, criticized the Christian tendency to "totalize and dualize," repudiated the "insidious misogyny" of Christianity, and featured strong historical research. Jewish liberationist Marc H. Ellis commended her opposition to Christian anti-Semitism and Jewish oppression of the Palestinians. Brazilian ecofeminist Ivone Gebara called her an "intellectual for our contemporary time committed to justice with love." Religious historian Rosalind Hinton, Ruether's former student, noted that Ruether's writings were always timely and relevant because they were rooted in her global activism. Every Ruether book had a community behind it, because she forged friendships with activists in various fields and wrote books out of her activist commitments.[27]

Ruether was the epitome of a scholar-activist, advocating the contextualization of feminism in global communities. However, to many feminist colleagues, her perspective smacked too much of liberal theology, especially her rendering of Christianity's usable past. Among feminists schooled in poststructuralist criticism, the problem was repeatedly described as Ruether's "essentialist" theological method, "reformist" theological agenda, and "essentialist" feminism. Feminists of her generation sometimes blasted her assurance that feminist theology simply adopts and extends the method of liberation theology; feminists of the next generation often added that Ruether operated with old-fashioned categories of experience and binary sexuality. On occasion she was also criticized for overpoliticizing theology or showing little sign of spiritual feeling or religious belief or both.

Mary McClintock Fulkerson judged that Ruether's version of gender criticism was "a kind of 'me, too' theory" that reproduced the heterosexual binary of liberal essentialism and that her rendering of experience wrongly implicated women's experience "in a realm prior to language." Ellen T. Armour judged that Ruether's writings were structured "by an assumed feminine identity" to which distinctions of race and class were mere additions. By casting patriarchy as the father of oppression, Armour contended, Ruether added to the oppression experienced by women of color and poor women, conceiving race and class as further means of subjecting and dividing the objects of the father's attention, women. Delores Williams charged that Ruether was a primary culprit of the white feminist universalization of white women's experience, which obscured the racism and privileges of white feminists. In Williams's view, virtually everything that Ruether said about feminism privileged the beliefs of white feminists, including her claim that "encountering the divine as goddess" was a point of unity for feminists of various races and nationalities; Williams countered: "This is exactly the problem. The 'divine as goddess' is a concern emphasized in *white* feminist theology." Daphne Hampson described Ruether as a classic "golden thread" essentialist who privileged her version of a "sacred history" of liberating praxis; moreover, "one is hard pressed to see how hers is a theology, as opposed to simply a political agenda for the liberation of people." Sheila Greeve Davaney described Ruether as a guardian of the liberal experientialist school that "enhanced the credence of its norms by providing them with an ontological or divine foundation." Kwok Pui-lan judged that Ruether's essentially "reformist" approach to theology gave "too much power to the theological categories established by the patriarchal tradition."[28]

Elisabeth Schüssler Fiorenza offered an especially influential variation on these themes, charging that Ruether presented an idealized picture of prophetic Christianity that overlooked its oppressive elements. Ruether, rather than subject prophetic religion to historical and ideological criticism, simply appealed to it as an interpretive pattern abstracted from biblical history, playing down the patriarchal character of biblical prophecy and its repression of Goddess religion. Schüssler Fiorenza admonished that it was not enough to assert that biblical prophecy "can be used in the interest of feminism." Neither was it enough to say, nor even true, that feminist theology "can transform this social-critical androcentric tradition into a feminist liberating tradition and use it to its own ends." To her, "its own ends" trumped any religious apologetic or warrant. Just because the Bible promotes "freedom" and "social justice" does not mean that scripture implicitly supports feminism. Biblical patriarchy had a social conscience but not one that supported feminism.[29]

Schüssler Fiorenza concluded that Ruether's approach was not even liberal. It was essentially a neo-orthodox attempt to rescue biblical religion from its feminist critics. But what feminist theology needed was a radical feminist hermeneutic that incorporated "Wicca's feminist spiritual quest for women's power."[30]

Ruether gave short shrift to critics of her religious temperament. She had no interest in calibrating her spiritual tone to that preferred by unsympathetic critics, and she preferred to have a major biblical tradition on her side than to spurn any such connection to the biblical witness or other forms of liberation theology. But she took sharp exception to the charge of essentialism. It galled her to be lumped repeatedly with Daly as an essentialist who excluded the claims of race and class. "There is a group of scholars that is very competitive within the academy and are making their careers by critiquing all that came before them as essentialist without making any distinctions between scholars' work," Ruether protested. "Some have not even read much of my work. They don't have an understanding of how we got started. Race and class were central to what we were doing and then we added a gender critique."[31]

She stressed that the founding Christian feminists began in the Civil Rights movement and the New Left. "We did not start with a univocal 'woman' and then seek to add race and class difference." From the beginning Christian feminists viewed race, class, and gender as interconnected variables that created multiple differences. For the most part, the first generation's feminism was not a Daly-type essentialism or even a liberal version of one: "Mary Daly wasn't even around. She was in Europe studying Catholic theology and Thomism and trying to become a Catholic theologian." Ruether protested that her legacy was "distorted by these claims of essentialism." Perhaps the generation of feminists behind hers, which was trained in the academy, universalized its own experience, "but that is what we were fighting against. Men were universalizing their experience and white people were universalizing their experience. We were not going to do it too. That is what we were critiquing."[32]

Admittedly early feminist theology was white, but that was because there were no women of color in the field. When African American women began to enter the field in the early 1980s, Ruether observed, the discourse changed. Having come to the academy from outward-reaching activist movements, she and her Christian feminist colleagues deserved better than to be remembered wrongly, especially by a generation that belonged to the academy and spoke the language of French deconstruction: "It's telling that so many people thought they had to trash me in order to have something to say. If they were really making an advance, why was it necessary to distort what I said?"[33]

Ruether had just cause to ask for a more accurate remembering, though she failed to grasp that her feminist critics make an advance by interrogating whiteness, repudiating the essentialism of (white) "sisterhood" rhetoric, and bringing feminism into conversation with deconstructionist theory. Some of them told stories of being gruffly treated by her on their way up. But they also told stories of her modeling feminist scholar-activism, bustling to conferences and speaking engagements, holding advising meetings in the car on her way to the airport, building up liberationist movements. "Everything is related" is a maxim of every feminist generation; Ruether epitomized it.

Chapter 15

Pragmatic Postmodern Prophecy

CORNEL WEST AS SOCIAL CRITIC AND PUBLIC INTELLECTUAL

Cornel West, our greatest religious public intellectual since Reinhold Niebuhr, is difficult to categorize, partly because so many categories apply to him. He is a philosopher but does not write for or in the manner of the philosophical guild. He is not a theologian, yet liberation theology is at the heart of his work and vision. He is a pragmatist, a Socialist, a postmodern historicist, and a black Christian liberationist, but he is all of these things in his own inimitable way. His favorite self-description, aptly, is "Jesus-centered intellectual bluesman." West has become America's greatest religious public intellectual by practicing liberation theology as a form of philosophical and social criticism.

He came to Christian social criticism through his upbringing in an African American Christian family and church and his exposure to the Civil Rights and Black Panther movements. West's grandfather, C. L. West, was a Baptist minister in Tulsa, Oklahoma, where West was born in 1953. Both of his parents were raised in Louisiana; his father was a civilian air force administrator, which necessitated moving frequently when West was young; eventually the family settled in a segregated section of Sacramento, California. West later recalled that he was a beneficiary of California's version of Jim Crow, because he did not have to deal with white people or struggle for a place in the world: "Whiteness was really not a point of reference for me because the world was all black . . . That was a very positive thing, because it gave me a chance to really revel in black humanity." Because he grew up relatively free of direct experiences with whites, he reflected, he was able in later life to perceive whites as human beings without being affected by negative experiences or preconceptions: "I didn't have to either deify them or demonize them . . . I could just view them as human beings, and I think that was quite a contribution of my own context."[1]

As a youth he reveled in the preaching of Shiloh Baptist Church pastor Willie P. Cooke, admired Martin Luther King Jr., was hooked by Søren Kierkegaard's struggle with melancholia and mortality, and came to political consciousness by listening to Black Panther meetings. From Kierkegaard he took the lifelong conviction that philosophy should be about the human experiences of living, suffering, and finding hope. From the Panthers he took the lifelong conviction that politics should combine the best available theory with concrete strategies: "They taught me the importance of political philosophy *and* strategy."[2]

At the age of seventeen he graduated from John F. Kennedy High School in Sacramento and enrolled at Harvard. Aside from Kierkegaard, West's knowledge of philosophy rested on Will Durant's *Story of Philosophy* and other popular histories; philosopher Robert Nozick assured him that Harvard would expose him to more "high-powered" fare, especially in the analytic tradition. In more important ways, however, West already knew who he was and what he aimed to do: "Owing to my family, church, and the black social movements of the 1960s, I arrived at Harvard unashamed of my African, Christian, and militant decolonized outlooks." He was determined to shape his own image, not have it shaped for him by Harvard University: "I've always wanted to be myself, and, of course, that is a perennial process." At Harvard he studied philosophy under Nozick, John Rawls, Hilary Putnam, and Stanley Cavell; history under Samuel Beer, H. Stuart Hughes, and Martin Kilson; and social thought under Talcott Parsons, Terry Irwin, and Preston Williams—all in addition to his major, Near Eastern languages and literature, which he undertook so he could read ancient religious texts in their original languages and also graduate in three years.[3]

That made him twenty years old when he began his doctoral program in philosophy at Princeton University. West worried that Princeton philosophers would undermine his Christian faith, disabuse him of his attraction to Wittgenstein, and look down on his equally strong attraction to Frankfurt School neo-Marxism. Instead, his teachers took no interest in religion, which allowed him to keep Kierkegaard and African American mystic Howard Thurman close to his heart. West's teachers at Princeton included Richard Rorty, David Lewis, Thomas Scanlon, Raymond Geuss, and Sheldon Wolin. Rorty's pragmatic historicist turn reinforced West's commitment to Wittgensteinian anti-foundationalism, while Wolin, his thesis adviser, encouraged him to plunge deeper into the Hegelian Marxist tradition. West started with a dissertation on English idealist T. H. Green's neo-Hegelianism, switched to one on Aristotelian aspects of Marxist thought, and settled on one exploring Marx's ethical commitments that he finished eight years after reaching the dissertation stage. He argued that Marx's appropriation of historical consciousness and critique of capitalism were informed by ethical values of individuality and democracy, notwithstanding his attacks on moral reason. By the mid-1970s West was already acquiring a reputation as an intellectual spellbinder. The first time I saw him, in 1975, he had attracted a sidewalk crowd of a dozen people at Harvard Divinity School and was expounding exuberantly on the varieties of black nationalism. The crowd expanded as passersby judged, as I had, "That must be Cornel West." Two years later he began his teaching career at Union Theological Seminary, which seemed to him the perfect home for his broad intellectual and activist interests.[4]

"You know, my aim was always to teach at Union Seminary," he later recalled. "Union Seminary, for me, was the real institutional site that brought together all of my interests. It was a Christian seminary, it was deeply shaped by progressive politics, Marxism, feminism, antihomophobic thought and black liberation theology." Elsewhere he put it more precisely:

> I decided to teach at Union Seminary for three reasons: It was (and still is) the center of liberation theology in the country; it was one of the best places for black theological education in the country; and it allowed me to teach and read widely in philosophy, social theory, history, literary criticism and cultural thought. Union was the perfect place to become a broadly engaged cultural critic with a strong grounding in the history of philosophy and criticism.

At Union he formed friendships with colleagues James Cone, James Forbes, Beverly Harrison, Tom Driver, Dorothee Sölle, and especially James Washington. Equally significant for West's intellectual trajectory were his friendships with Socialists Stanley Aronowitz and Michael Harrington, his involvement with Aronowitz's journal *Social Text*, which related leftist thought to the cultural politics of difference, and his collaboration with cultural theorists associated with the editorial collective *Boundary 2: An International Journal of Literature and Culture*, especially Paul Bové, William Spanos, Michael Hayes, Donald Pease, and Nancy Fraser.[5]

For West it was crucial to get his bearings about the kind of Socialist he was, the kind he was not, and the kinds with which he could work collaboratively. Michael Harrington's Democratic Socialist Organizing Committee, formed in 1973 after the breakup of the Socialist Party, smacked too much of its anticommunist, social democratic background to be something that West could join. In 1982, however, Harrington's organization merged with the New American Movement (NAM) to form Democratic Socialists of America (DSA). NAM, a socialist offshoot of the New Left, emphasized cultural politics, anti-anticommunism, and radical democracy. Most of its leaders were veterans of the 1960s social movements, including Aronowitz and social critic Barbara Ehrenreich. Black studies scholar Manning Marable joined DSA, as did West, though both of them battled for years with DSA's social democratic mainstream, especially its right flank of Old Left anti-Communists. Challenging DSA to fulfill its claim to be a "multi-tendency" organization, West propounded a Gramscian, black liberationist socialism as an alternative to social democratic gradualism. For seven years he served on DSA's political committee; afterwards, following Harrington's death in 1989, West served as DSA's honorary co-chair.[6]

In his telling, democratic socialism was like liberal theology, a valuable project that had outlived its usefulness. Though West always cautioned that he was not a theologian, he described Marxism in theological terms and clearly favored liberation theology. Democratic socialism was too compromised by its historic identification with middle-class electoral reformism to provide the emancipatory vision that was needed, he argued. Like liberal theology, democratic socialism was a creative project of the past that represented, at best, a "crucial stepping-stone" to something better: a Marxist, feminist, Garveyist, ecological, and antimilitarist revolutionary vision.[7]

West delineated six types of Marxism—Stalinism, Leninism, Trotskyism, Gramscianism, social democracy, and revolutionary councilism—and assigned a theological analogue to each. Stalinism, a total perversion of its founding symbols, was the Ku Klux Klan of Marxism. The Leninist and Trotskyist traditions were fundamentalist, marshaling proof-texts for truncated versions of Marxist norms. West admired the left-romanticist tradition of Italian theorist Antonio Gramsci, especially his emphasis on cultural forms of hegemony, but he acknowledged that Gramsci was only slightly democratic. Gramsci defended freedom on strategic grounds, not principle; thus his version of socialism was still essentially Leninist. To West, that made Gramscian Marxism analogous to theological neo-orthodoxy, "an innovative revision of dogmas for dogmatic purposes." As for European social democracy, it was too much like the social gospel. One could get an impressive critique of capitalism from it but not a revolutionary praxis. Though social democracy retained the Marxist concepts of the class struggle and the dialectic of history, it sold out revolutionary consciousness, concentrating on electoral reformism and anticommunism. Like the social gospel, it accommodated bourgeois modernity too deeply not to be compromised by it.[8]

For West, the real thing was the councilist Marxism of Rosa Luxemburg, Anton Pannekoek, and Karl Korsch, which he viewed as analogous to liberation theology. Against the class collaborationism of social democracy and its anticommunist animus, the councilist tradition was revolutionary and pre-figural. Instead of viewing workers as wage earners, voters, and consumers, it viewed workers as collective self-determining producers that prefigured the coming socialist order. Councilist Marxism was about workers seizing power through revolutionary organizations that already prefigured a socialist society. Because the councilist tradition was anti-collaborationist and internally democratic, West prized it as the authentic expression of revolutionary Marxism: "Councilism is to Marxism what liberation theology is to Christianity: a promotion and practice of the moral core of the perspective against overwhelming odds for success."[9]

Since the point was to actually change society, however, not merely to adopt a position, the overwhelming odds were a serious problem. As theory, revolutionary councilism was an important tradition of socialist thought. As anything else, it barely existed. The social democratic tradition that West dismissed at least had actual parties and worked in solidarity with existing trade unions; Councilism, on the other hand, represented solidarity with an imaginary movement. In two books I argued for an updated guild socialist idea of economic democracy, contending that if democratic socialism was too defeated to be worth considering, that did not speak well for the utility of revolutionary councilism, which existed only as the fantasy of Left intellectuals.[10]

West spent his early years in DSA debating variations of that argument. On short-term practical grounds, he allowed, Democratic Socialists had a strong case; on the other hand, since that option would never build real socialism, it was a loser. Democratic socialism stood for the betrayal of revolutionary consciousness and the very idea of radical democracy. Instead of building a true alternative to capitalism it settled for electoral reformism, extending the welfare state, and denouncing communism. I replied that West's radical democratic vision was unattainable on councilist terms, he was wrong to identify liberation theology with a single form of Marxism, and democratic socialism was not identical with welfare state social democracy. Democratic socialism also included a guild socialist stream that was closely related, structurally and historically, to the councilist tradition. Councilism needed democratic socialism in the same way that liberation theology needed to be informed and limited by earlier forms of Christian socialism, especially those in the guild socialist tradition.[11]

To a considerable degree West moved in that direction without giving up his preferences for the councilist revolutionaries of an earlier generation. He drew increasingly on current theories of "market socialism," especially by Branko Horvat, Wlodzimierz Brus, and Alec Nove, which acknowledged the necessity of market mechanisms and establishing mixed forms of ownership. Any feasible model of socialism had to get prices right, just as it had to abolish racial, sexual, and economic hierarchies, he argued. In the name of "wholesome Christian rejection of such hierarchies," he advocated a mixed-model democratic socialism featuring "a socio-economic arrangement with markets, price mechanisms, and induced (not directed) labor force, a free press, formal political rights, and a constitutionally based legal order with special protections of the marginalized." In structural terms that entailed an economy with five major sections: (1) state-owned industries of basic producer goods (electricity networks, oil and petrochemical companies, financial institutions); (2) independent, self-managed, socialized public enterprises; (3) cooperative enterprises controlling their own property; (4) small private businesses; and (5) self-employed individuals.[12]

Harrington argued that the future, inevitably, would be collective; the question was whether the collectivism of the future would be democratic or authoritarian. West, joining Harrington in lecture tours for DSA, found himself adopting Harrington's signature theme. Centralization was as inescapable in modern society as the market, he argued; the struggle was to democratize collective structures. In 1986 West put it programmatically: "The crucial question is how are various forms of centralization, hierarchy, and markets regulated—that is, to what extent can democratic mechanisms yield public accountability of limited centralization, meritorious hierarchy, and a mixture of planned, socialized, and private enterprises in the market along with indispensable democratic political institutions."[13]

Elsewhere he put it more plainly, noting that for Harrington the choice was not between the bureaucratic collectivism of command economies and the "free enterprise" competition of capitalism: "Rather, the basic choice in the future will be between a democratic, or 'bottom-up' socialization, and corporate, or 'top-down,' socialization." The point for Harrington, and eventually for West, was to broaden the participation of citizens in the economic, political, and cultural dimensions of the social order "and thus control the conditions of their existence." By the end of the 1980s West believed that Harrington's focus on democratizing the process of investment was exactly right and even that his democratic socialism was inspiring, "indeed visionary." On the other hand, West still preferred revolutionary Councilism and he found Harrington ironically lacking at the cultural level. Harrington, having attained fame by describing American poverty in *The Other America*, subsequently concentrated on structural economic analysis, social theory, and political strategy. He lived too far above the everyday, grasping, vacuous, nihilistic, television-watching, sometimes violent culture of ordinary consumers to write about it. Harrington was eloquent about the structural injustices of capitalism, but he passed over its equally devastating operations on the cultural level.[14]

That was never true of West, who emphasized cultural criticism, writing about popular music, television, sexuality, identity politics, black culture, white supremacism, the culture of nihilism, and the cultural limitations of progressive organizations dominated by whites. West's pamphlet for DSA, "Toward a Socialist Theory of Racism," was a signature statement for him and the organization. Stressing the Marxist bias of most American socialist theorizing about racism, West delineated four main types. The first viewed racism as an epiphenomenon of the class struggle, subsuming racial injustice under the general rubric of working-class exploitation. Eugene Debs, an icon of this approach, had a simple answer to the question of what socialism offered blacks: "Nothing, except socialism." Debs took for granted that racism was a divide-and-conquer ruse of the ruling class. To him, a socialist revolution was the only solution to racial injustice and all other social evils; any solution outside the labor framework was racism in reverse. West acknowledged that Debs, having fought racism bravely, was an honorable example of the color-blind strategy; nonetheless, socialist reductionism was not the answer, since it ignored the complexity of the problem.[15]

The second approach, usually taken by the socialist wing of the union movement, stuck to the class exploitation thesis while acknowledging that blacks were subjected to a second dose of exploitation through workplace discrimination and exclusion. This acknowledgment of racism as "super-exploitation" marked an improvement on Debs-style color-blindness, West allowed, but it still limited the struggle against racial injustice to the workplace.

The third approach was the "Black Nation" thesis of the Garveyite movement, the American Communist Party, various Leninist organizations, and a variety of black nationalist organizations and individuals including James Forman. Contending that blacks constituted an oppressed nation within the United States, proponents usually cited Joseph Stalin's definition of a nation in *Marxism and the National Question* (1913): "A historically constituted, stable community of people formed on the basis of a common language, territory, economic life and psychological make-up manifested in a common culture." In the case of Marcus Garvey, the Black Nation thesis fueled a powerful "back to Africa" movement in the 1920s. West commended the Garveyite and communist traditions for taking the cultural dimension of the freedom struggle more seriously than other socialist approaches; in this respect, most black nationalists were "proto-Gramscians." But as theory it was shot through with ahistorical special pleading, and as practice it was backward looking, if not reactionary.[16]

The fourth socialist approach, identified chiefly with W. E. B. Du Bois and neo-Marxist Oliver Cox, arose as an alternative to the Black Nation thesis. It argued that racism was a product of class exploitation and of xenophobic attitudes not reducible to class exploitation. For Du Bois and Cox, West explained, racism had a life of its own, depending on psychological factors and cultural practices that were not necessarily or directly caused by structural economic injustices. Du Bois and Cox had the right project, West argued; they pointed to the capitalist role in modern racism while stressing psychological and cultural aspects of the problem. The contemporary struggle against racism needed to move further in that direction, stressing that the roots of racism lay in conflicts between the civilizations of Europe, Africa, Asia and Latin America before modern capitalism arose, while retaining the Marxist emphasis on class exploitation. Moreover, all four of the dominant Marxist approaches operated largely or exclusively on the macrostructural level, concentrating on the dynamics of racism within and between social institutions. But a full-orbed theory of racism also had to deal with the genealogy of racism, the ideological dimensions of racism, and micro-institutional factors.[17]

In other words, the best socialist theory of racism would be Gramscian, stressing culture and ideology, while extending beyond Gramsci's particular formulations. It would assume that cultural practices of racism had a reality of their own that did not reduce to class exploitation; that cultural practices were the medium through which selves were produced; and that cultural practices were shaped and bounded by civilizations, including the modes of production of civilizations. It would offer a genealogical account of the ideology of racism, examining the modes of European domination of non-European peoples. It would analyze the micro-institutional mechanisms that sustained white supremacism, highlighting the various forms of Euro-centric dominance. And it would provide a macrostructural analysis of the exploitation and oppression of non-European peoples, tracking the variety of and relationships between the various types of oppression.

That was a project for theorists of a scholarly bent, a title West declined. He was an intellectual freedom fighter, not a scholar, theologian, or professional philosopher, he explained. For twenty years he averaged more than 150 lectures per year, speaking to academic and nonacademic audiences on his broad range of topics. To social activists he often waxed on the cultural limitations of progressive organizations dominated by whites. DSA was, for him, a primary case in point. Since African Americans and other people of color usually perceived progressive white organizations as racially and culturally alien, West observed, they did not join them, which ensnared these organizations in a vicious circle. Even when white progressives made serious attempts to diversify, they failed because of their geographical and cultural remoteness from the everyday lives of people unlike themselves. This failure desensitized white organizations to the necessity of struggling against white supremacism, further widening the cultural gap between people of color and white activists.

West urged that the only way to break this vicious circle was for progressive organizations to privilege the issues of people of color, taking the liberationist option of siding with the excluded and oppressed. Strategies based on white guilt were paralyzing, both psychologically and politically, while strategies based on making white organizations more attractive to racial minorities had little effectiveness. The answer was for activist organizations and progressive religious communities to make a commitment of will to the specific struggles of people of color. It was pointless for progressive organizations to pursue diversity campaigns if they did not make the struggle against white supremacism their highest priority, he argued. There had to be a transformation of consciousness, one that was practical, convinced of the priority of racial justice, and not overburdened with useless guilt: "What is needed is more widespread participation by predominantly white democratic socialist organizations in antiracist struggles—whether those struggles be for the political, economic, and cultural empowerment of Latinos, blacks, Asians, and North Americans or anti-imperialist struggles against U.S. support for oppressive regimes in South Africa, Chile, the Philippines, and the occupied West Bank."[18]

In liberation theology, West explained, this transformation of consciousness was called "conscientization." It occurred only through an act of commitment that brought about a new awareness of marginalization, exclusion, or oppression from the perspective of those victimized by it. Only by taking the liberationist option would white activists comprehend or sustain their awareness of the crucial importance of struggling against racism in all its forms. Bonds of trust across racial lines would be forged only within contexts of struggle in which white activists privileged the concerns of people of color. West cautioned:

This interracial interaction guarantees neither love nor friendship. Yet it can yield more understanding and the realization of two overlapping goals—democratic socialism and antiracism. While engaging in antiracist struggles, democratic socialists can also enter into a dialogue on the power relationships and misconceptions that often emerge in multiracial movements for social justice in a racist society. Honest and trusting coalition work can help socialists unlearn Eurocentrism in a self-critical manner and can also demystify the motivations of white progressives in the movement for social justice.[19]

West's involvement with DSA evoked a range of reactions that he encountered weekly on the lecture trail. White liberals blanched that he limited his effectiveness by identifying so explicitly with a socialist organization; conservatives Red-baited him for it; black nationalists heaped scorn on him for it; and radicals of various kinds chided him for hanging out with Social Democrats. West replied: "I've got to be organized with some group." Socialism alone would never eradicate racism, and antiracist struggle was fundamental to any progressive politics worth pursuing:

"Yet a democratic socialist society is the best hope for alleviating and minimizing racism, particularly institutional forms of racism." He chose DSA because it was multiracial, multi-tendency, and comprehensive, standing for racial justice, economic democracy, feminism, environmentalism, and anti-imperialism: "We need the groups highlighting connection and linkage in a time of balkanization and polarization and fragmentation. There's got to be some group that does this."[20]

In his early career West shared the black radical and conventional leftist assumption that Martin Luther King Jr. was, at best, "a grand example of integrity and sacrifice," and not much more. Malcolm X was the more inspiring figure: "Malcolm X's voice was as fresh as ever. We were all convinced that Malcolm X would hold *our* position and have *our* politics if he were alive." In the 1970s King was not someone to be claimed for the road ahead, West recalled: "King was for us the Great Man who died for us—but not yet the voice we had to listen to, question, learn from and build on."[21]

That began to change in the 1980s as West, Cone, David Garrow, and others played up King's socialism and anti-imperialism. West rediscovered in King an exemplar of most of the things he cared about:

King's thought remains a challenge to us principally in that he accented the anticolonial, anti-imperialist, and antiracist consequences of taking seriously the American ideals of democracy, freedom, and equality. He never forgot that America was born out of revolutionary revolt and subversive rebellion against British colonialism and imperialism and that while much of white America viewed the country as the promised land, black slaves saw it as Egypt; that just as Europe's poor huddled masses were attracted to America, the largest black mass movement (led by Marcus Garvey) was set on leaving America! Through his prophetic Christian lens, King saw just how far America had swerved away from its own revolutionary past.[22]

In 1986, speaking at a King symposium at the U.S. Capital, West disavowed the conventional underestimation of King, observing that he embodied "the best of American Christianity." King was an exemplary organic intellectual, nonviolent resister, prophet, and egalitarian internationalist, West declared: "As an organic intellectual, he exemplifies the best of the life of the mind involved in public affairs; as a proponent of nonviolent resistance he holds out the only slim hope for social sanity in a violence-ridden world; as an American prophet he commands the

respect even of those who opposed him; and as an egalitarian internationalist he inspires all oppressed peoples around the world who struggle for
democracy, freedom, and equality."[23]

In 1984 West moved to Yale Divinity School, where he won a joint appointment in American Studies, took part in campus protests for a clerical
union and divestment from apartheid in South Africa, and was arrested
and jailed. As punishment for his jailing the university canceled his leave
for spring 1987, which forced him to spend the semester commuting between Yale and the University of Paris. The following year he returned to
Union Seminary, but in 1988 he moved to Princeton University as Professor of Religion and Director of Afro-American Studies. Princeton asked
what it would take to get him; West replied that it would take a serious
commitment to build a premier black studies program. He gave six years
to building one centered on novelist Toni Morrison, then moved to Harvard in 1994 to join its black studies program, with a joint appointment
at the Divinity School; literary theorist Henry Louis Gates Jr., the architect of Harvard's program, famously called it the "Dream Team" of black
studies.

Each of these moves escalated West's renown in the academy. Fundamentally he was a liberationist critic, but to the extent that he hung
his reputation on familiar academic categories he did so as a religious/
philosophical proponent of "prophetic pragmatism." His chief academic
work, The American Evasion of Philosophy (1989), argued that the task
of a revolutionary intellectual was to develop a counternarrative to the
hegemonic texts and narrative of the prevailing order. In the U.S. American context, he contended, the best resources for this project were the
pragmatist, Marxist, and Christian intellectual traditions. West prized
pragmatism as the distinctive American contribution to Western philosophy; more important, it underwrote historicist social criticism pressing
toward social transformation.

In West's rendering of the American pragmatic tradition, Charles S.
Peirce was the founder and methodologist, concerned chiefly with the
pragmatic rendering of clear and distinct ideas; William James was an
Emersonian moralist preoccupied with the powers and anxieties of individuals; and John Dewey was the theorist of pragmatic historical consciousness and creative democracy. Following Rorty, West embraced a historicist neo-pragmatism that rejected all reductionist claims to objective
knowledge. Unlike Rorty, however, West was religious, and unlike Gramsci, who took religion seriously only for political reasons, West's political

reasons were trumped by existential concerns. He explained that the central narratives of the Bible and the insights of Christian thought into "the crises and traumas of life" were indispensable for his sanity. Christian narrative and insight held at bay, for him, "the sheer absurdity so evident in life, without erasing or eliding the tragedy of life." As a pragmatist, he focused on transient and provisional matters, not believing in extrahistorical justifications or in defending faith with rational arguments. Yet, as a Christian pragmatist, his hope transcended the transient matters. Logical consistency mattered, West allowed; however, in the realm of faith, the ultimate issue was life or death, not the risk of logical inconsistency.[24]

At the level of practical politics, where solidarity with the oppressed was at issue, it also helped to be religious. West allowed that one did not have to be religious to appreciate how oppressed people coped with their situation, "but if one is religious, one has wider access into their life-worlds." Similarly he was a pragmatist without claiming that one had to be one to be effective. Some of his favorite thinkers were pragmatists, especially Du Bois, Gramsci, Dewey, James, Reinhold Niebuhr, sociologist C. Wright Mills, literary critic Lionel Trilling, and political philosopher Roberto M. Unger. But some of the greatest modern prophets had no truck with pragmatism: King, Rauschenbusch, Sojourner Truth, Elizabeth Cady Stanton, and Dorothy Day. That didn't matter, West assured; what mattered was to struggle against oppression everywhere: "Prophetic pragmatism worships at no ideological altars. It condemns oppression anywhere and everywhere, be it the brutal butchery of third-world dictators, the regimentation and repression of peoples in the Soviet Union and Soviet-bloc countries, or the racism, patriarchy, homophobia, and economic injustice in the first-world capitalist nations."[25]

For all his success, and to some degree because of it, despair was a real option for West. He wrote constantly about "keeping faith" and "sustaining hope," partly as an admonition to himself. In 1993, the year before he moved to Harvard, he published two books that differently registered his deepening gloom about U.S. American culture and democracy, the condition of black America, and his deepening unease about both. One of these books, *Keeping Faith: Philosophy and Race in America*, collected his recent articles on pragmatism, Marxism, racial justice, and progressive politics. The other book, *Race Matters*, launched him into the realm of American public celebrity just as he began to talk about taking leave of the U.S.A.

Keeping Faith disclosed that West felt increasingly exiled from the black community and in despair about American society. To be a black American intellectual was to be caught "between an insolent American society and an insouciant black community," he lamented. White America as a whole was unwilling to learn much of anything from people of color, while black America took little interest in the life of the mind. Thus "the African American who takes seriously the life of the mind inhabits an isolated and insulated world." West cautioned that the problem was objective, not something that anyone could avoid with sufficient sincerity or skill. Because America was racist, and because there was no African American intellectual tradition to support black intellectuals, the ones that came along were condemned to "dangling status." Black America had only two organic intellectual traditions, he explained: musical performance and black church preaching. Both were oral, improvisational, histrionic, and rooted in black life. Both traditions contained canons for assessing performance and models of past achievement. In the intellectual field, there was nothing to compare. West allowed that black America managed to produce a few remarkable intellectuals—W. E. B. Du Bois, James Baldwin, Zora Neale Hurston, E. Franklin Frazier, and Ralph Ellison—but they were exceptions and did not compare to the best black preachers and musicians. The only great black American intellectual thus far was novelist Toni Morrison. Aside from the handful of exceptions, black American intellectuals either capitulated to the white academy or catered to the "cathartic provincialism" of a black community that had no use for real intellectuals.[26]

This dreary picture was getting worse, West warned: "As we approach the last few years of this century, black literate intellectual activity has declined in both quantity and quality." Integration merely integrated black youths into decaying public high schools, bureaucratized universities, and "dull middlebrow colleges" that cared nothing about developing black intellectuals. More broadly, West found it "depressing and debilitating" to realize that race still mattered tremendously in virtually every sphere of U.S. American life. The "decline and decay in American life" seemed irreversible to him, making him grateful for his refuge in Addis Ababa, Ethiopia, the homeland of his wife, Elleni Gebre Amlak. West reported that he was strongly tempted to make Ethiopia his home, not merely a refuge: "Not since the 1920s have so many black folk been disappointed and disillusioned with America. I partake of this black zeitgeist; I share these sentiments. Yet I try to muster all that is within me, including my rich African and American traditions, to keep faith in the struggle for human dignity and existential democracy."[27]

With the same mixture of gloom and willful hope, he wrote a cry from the heart for the trade market, *Race Matters*, which made him famous far beyond the academy. Many of West's new readers must have expected a sermon on the evils of white racism; instead he barely mentioned it, spending much of the book showing how the "decline and decay in American life" applied to black America. West took a hard-line on what he called "nihilism in black America" and the shortcomings of contemporary black leaders. America as a whole shared the problem of nihilism, he assured, but it applied with a special vengeance to black America. Two sentences in the book's introduction prepared readers for the jeremiad that followed: "We have created rootless, dangling people with little link to the supportive networks—family, friends, school—that sustain some sense of purpose in life . . . Post-modern culture is more and more a market culture dominated by gangster mentalities and self-destructive wantonness."[28]

Capitalist culture bombarded its youthful consumers with titillating images designed to stimulate self-preoccupation, materialism, and antisocial attitudes, West contended; moreover, most American children lacked adequate parental guidance: "Most of our children—neglected by overburdened parents and bombarded by the market values of profit-hungry corporations—are ill-equipped to live lives of spiritual and cultural quality." In a word, postmodern capitalist culture was deeply nihilistic. Philosophically, nihilism was the doctrine that there are no credible grounds for truth statements or standards; at the street level, it was the experience of "horrifying meaninglessness, hopelessness, and (most important) lovelessness." In West's telling, the culture of nihilism was especially toxic in poor black urban neighborhoods. It was the "major enemy of black survival in America," more destructive than oppression or exploitation. The black American struggle against nihilistic despair was hardly new, he acknowledged. It was as old as the slave ships and auction blocks that ripped apart black families and condemned blacks to chattel servitude. Yet, as recently as the early 1970s, black Americans had the lowest suicide rate in the U.S. A generation later, young black Americans had the highest rate. What had changed? What accounted for "this shattering of black civil society"?[29]

West was not sure how much to blame the bitter ironies of racial integration or the collapse of black optimism after the King years had passed.

He was more certain about two factors: "I believe that two significant reasons why the threat is more powerful now than ever before are the saturation of market forces and market moralities in black life and the present crisis in black leadership." The flood of violence and sexual titillation that poured through the culture industries of television, radio, video, and music was disastrous for black America, he argued. All Americans were influenced and degraded by the decadence of the media, which bombarded them constantly with images of depravity. The black underclass, however, facing special threats to its survival in the first place, was especially vulnerable to being damaged by it: "The predominance of this way of life among those living in poverty-ridden conditions, with a limited capacity to ward off self-contempt and self-hatred, results in the possible triumph of the nihilistic threat in black America."[30]

More than ever, West argued, black America needed compelling black leaders; unfortunately contemporary black leaders were grasping and morally unimpressive: "The present-day black middle class is not simply different than its predecessors—it is more deficient and, to put it strongly, more decadent. For the most part, the dominant outlooks and life-styles of today's black middle class discourage the development of high quality political and intellectual leaders." In fact, the worst aspects of America's general cultural decadence were "accentuated among black middle-class Americans."[31]

The great black leaders of the past carried themselves with moral dignity, West explained. They wore suits and white shirts, conveyed a serious moral purpose, treated ordinary blacks with humble respect, and projected a bold, gut-level anger at the condition of black America. "In stark contrast, most present-day black political leaders appear too hungry for status to be angry, too eager for acceptance to be bold, too self-invested in advancement to be defiant." On occasion they took a stab at prophetic speech, but that was "more performance than personal, more play-acting than heartfelt." Like other new entrants to the middle-class culture of consumption, they were obsessed with status and addicted to self-gratification. Instead of raging against "the gross deterioration of personal, familial, and communal relations among African-Americans," they looked away from it, knowing they were poorly suited to condemn it.[32]

Contemporary black political leaders sorted into three types, West argued: race-effacing managers, race-identifying protest leaders, and race-transcending prophets. The first type, epitomized by Los Angeles mayor Thomas Bradley, relied on political savvy and personal diplomacy to claim a place at the establishment table. Those of the second type confined their attention to "black turf" and assiduously protected their hold over it. West cited Nation of Islam leader Louis Farrakhan as an extreme example, but also assigned to the second category black nationalists and most leaders of the Civil Rights organizations. The third type was the ideal, which stood boldly for racial justice while transcending race as a category of personal identity and collective loyalty. Harlem civil rights leader Adam Clayton Powell Jr. was one example; more recently Harold Washington, Chicago's mayor in the mid-1980s, was another; Jesse Jackson tried to be one in his 1988 presidential race but never quite overcame his opportunist past; West judged that his own generation had yet to produce one.

Black intellectuals sorted into similar types, by his account: race-distancing elitists, race-embracing rebels, and race-transcending prophets. The first type, impressed by their own cultivation and accomplishments, held themselves above other blacks; West cited the "mean-spirited" cultural critic Adolph Reed Jr. as an example. The second type rebelled against the snobbish insularity of the white academy by creating a black-space version of it which they themselves headed; West put most Afrocentrists in this category. The ideal, the race-transcending prophets, courageously fused the life of the mind with the struggle for justice without paying heed to social standing, career advancement, or intellectual fashions. West's exemplar was James Baldwin; Oliver Cox also qualified; on the contemporary scene, only Toni Morrison deserved to be called a race-transcending prophetic intellectual. West stressed the negative: "This vacuum continues to aggravate the crisis of black leadership—and the plight of the wretched of the earth deteriorates."[33]

Anticipating the charge that he was too harsh, ungenerous, or opportunistically playing to a white audience, West admonished: "The crisis in black leadership can be remedied only if we candidly confront its existence." He was not calling for a Messiah figure to replace Malcolm or King, because that was not the point, and there were always problems with messiah figures anyway. Malcolm said nothing about "the vicious role of priestly versions of Islam in the modern world," and King was sexist and homophobic. West did not even believe that the answer was to build an organization dedicated to race-transcending prophetic politics, although he still hoped to see one emerge. What really mattered was to develop "new models of leadership and forge the kind of persons to actualize these models." Black America needed race-transcending prophets that raged for racial justice and social justice for all: "To be a serious black leader is to be a race-transcending prophet who critiques the powers that be (including the black component of the Establishment) and who puts forward a vision of fundamental social change for all who suffer from socially induced misery."[34]

Race Matters brought West such a crush of national and international publicity that he moaned to friends about the ravages of overexposure. The book's 1994 paperback edition was adorned with gushing reviews from major media outlets. *Newsday* called it "exciting," "illuminating," and filled with "profound and unsettling thoughts." The *New York Times* applauded its "ferocious moral vision and astute intellect." *Newsweek*, describing West as "an eloquent prophet with attitude," enthused that his book was "devoted to kicking butt and naming names." In a single sentence that placed West in the highest company imaginable, the *Washington Post Book World* declared that his book was as moving as any of King's sermons, as profound as Du Bois's *The Souls of Black Folk*, and as exhilarating as Baldwin's early work. *Time*, in a quotable estimate that somehow did not make the book's cover, declared: "Cornel West is one complex dude: brilliant scholar, political activist, committed Christian and soul brother down to the bone. At 40 he has become one of the most insightful and passionate analysts of America's racial dilemma to emerge in recent years, the architect of a post–civil rights philosophy of black liberation that is beginning to be heard across the country."[35]

From there West climbed to higher levels of public renown, attaining fixture status in the mass media through countless profiles, interviews, and guest appearances while confining his writing, for nearly a decade, to co-authored books on topical themes. He seemed to be too busy to write them on his own. A book that he co-authored with liberal rabbi Michael Lerner, *Jews & Blacks: Let the Healing Begin* (1995), which called for a new alliance between progressive Jews and blacks, got a whopping $100,000 advance. A book that he co-authored with Harvard economist Sylvia Ann Hewlett, *The War Against Parents: What We Can Do for America's Beleaguered Moms and Dads* (1998), made a trade-market pitch for liberal economic and social policies while urging parents to strengthen their marital commitments. Meanwhile West appeared regularly on C-SPAN and other television networks, commented weekly on Tavis Smiley's National Public Radio program, served as a senior adviser to presidential candidate Bill Bradley in the 2000 Democratic primaries, campaigned for Ralph Nader in the 2000 presidential election, supported

Al Sharpton's brief presidential bid in 2004, cut two rap CD's, *Sketches of My Culture* (2001, Artemis) and *Street Knowledge* (2004, Roc Diamond), and played the role of Councilor West, a member of the Council of Zion, in two of the *Matrix* movies, *The Matrix Reloaded* and *The Matrix Revolutions*. [36]

He obviously enjoyed being famous, yet West was mindful of its perils. He was wary of being corrupted by adulation and enrichment. He winced at the obvious conflict between social justice militancy and celebrity success. And he understood that the more famous he became, the more *he* became the subject instead of anything that he said. Often he became an object of jealousy or resentment. Having stressed the shortcomings of others on his way up, West got a stream of tart responses. Sometimes it happened during the introduction of the speaker, after he had put himself out to speak at somebody's conference or group; often it happened in the discussion period after a lecture. Black nationalists and black radicals charged that he sold out his race; in 1993 the African United Front tagged West as an "Uncle Tom," claimed that he was "far more favorable to Jews than to Blacks," and protested that he never presented "the Black side" of the conflict between American blacks and Jews. On the right, where West's blistering critiques of white supremacism were noticed, he was often accused of epitomizing the radicalization and corruption of the academy. Meanwhile the hazards of his fame were noted by figures closer to him. One of his friends told *Time* magazine that part of West really wanted to be "the next H.N.I.C. [Head Negro in Charge, a satiric acronym with a long history]. It's not just white folks holding him up." James Cone told the same reporter that his friend's celebrity was spiritually perilous: "One of the best ways to destroy someone is to expose and promote him. It's very hard to be critical of a system that makes a hero out of you."[37]

Friendly reviewers more or less in West's intellectual orbit mixed critical jabs with the compliments. African American studies scholar Randal Jelks, in the *Christian Century*, considered *Race Matters* an effective "popularization of West's thought," but protested that West was too gloomy, showed no sense of humor, and put a misleading title on the book; *Race Matters*, the title, smacked of racial essentialism. Womanist theologian Delores Williams, in *Theology Today*, lauded West's "brilliant analysis" before criticizing his claim to speak the truth to power with love. It was one thing for King to talk about loving white people into repentance, Williams admonished, but King had millions of supporters to back up his challenge to white supremacy. Who was West anyway, and what did he have compared to that? And if West really cared about ordinary people, why were his writings loaded with Latin terms and academic jargon?[38]

Friends and foes alike questioned the quality of West's scholarship. Stanley Aronowitz, one of his closest friends and collaborators, was fond of saying in the 1990s that West's scholarship had not started yet. *Time* magazine echoed a common complaint that his writings were vague and utopian. In 1995 *New Republic* literary editor Leon Wieseltier put it much worse, declaring that West's work was "noisy, tedious, slippery . . . sectarian, humorless, pedantic and self endeared." In Wieseltier's telling, West did not make arguments, he merely declaimed. He was not a philosopher but merely cobbled together snatches of philosophies. West's eccentricity was surpassed only by his vanity, which was enormous, Wieseltier opined. His books were monuments "to the devastation of a mind by the squalls of theory." In sum, in a quote immortalized by repeated citation: "They are almost completely worthless."[39]

The latter attack was delivered by a prominent neoliberal in the flagship journal of neoliberal politics. Its parade of mean-spirited exaggerations made West more vulnerable to attacks not deriving from the political Right, usually without citation. It also inspired and fueled ferocious ridicule from the Right, where Wieseltier was nearly always cited gleefully. Conservative activist David Horowitz offered a typical rendering. In 1999, reviewing the *Cornel West Reader*, Horowitz invoked Wieseltier's charges, added a few of his own about West's "intellectual superficiality" and "blasts of hot air," and condemned West's friendships with Sharpton and Louis Farrakhan. In the 1990s West cultivated friendships with Farrakhan and other black nationalist leaders in an attempt to build bridges between them and other groups. He especially tried to mediate the hostility between black nationalists and Jews. To Horowitz, that was the key to West's eminent stature: his oxymoronic capacity to pose simultaneously as a racial healer and a "bedfellow of racial extremists." West got away with it, Horowitz contended, only because no one took him seriously: "He is the quintessential non-threatening radical, an African American who can wave the bloody shirt to orchestrate the heartstrings of white guilt, while coming to dinner at the Harvard faculty club and acting as a gentleman host."[40]

Horowitz's right-wing activism was beyond the pale for anyone in West's intellectual orbit. However, many of West's usual allies concurred that he took his mission of racial reconciliation a step too far in courting influence with Farrakhan. In his early writings West condemned Farrakhan's characterization of Judaism as a "gutter religion" as "despicable." Later he spoke more guardedly about the "underdog resentment and envy" that fueled black anti-Semitism, and in 1995 he supported Farrakhan's Million Man March. Trading on his public prominence, West told black national-ists that overcoming white supremacism was something they could not do by themselves. He urged Farrakhan to repudiate anti-Semitism and acknowledge the equal humanity of all persons. Michael Lerner, discuss-ing with West the possibilities of reconciliation between blacks and Jews, drew the line at Farrakhan, calling him a "racist dog." West replied char-acteristically, "I wouldn't call the brother a racist dog but a xenophobic spokesperson when it comes to dealing with Jewish humanity."[41]

If racial healing was to extend beyond the ranks of liberals, the human-ity of persons on all sides of the conflict had to be acknowledged as a first principle. Stepping straight into the crossfire between black nationalists and Jews, West urged friends on both sides to stop the vicious cycle of vituperation, realizing that he risked his reputation and his efficacy as a racial healer by doing so. Ironically he took his greatest risk during the same period in which he received a barrage of criticism for selling out.

Conservative magazines regularly complained that only conservatives and a smattering of (usually Jewish) neoliberals like Wieseltier had the nerve to criticize Cornel West. That was a plausible impression if one relied on television and conservative magazines for information. In the academy and political left, however, criticizing West was a favorite pas-time. Many scholars blasted him for blaming the victim in his critique of black nihilism. Cultural critic Nick De Genova protested that West sounded "like the classic example of a colonized elite, trapped in an ex-istential condition of self-hatred and shame because he has come to view his own people as undignified, indecent, backward, and uncouth." Social critic Eric Lott similarly ripped West for coming perilously close to deny-ing the humanity of poor blacks; Lott contended that West's entire "lexi-con of urban savagery" was disastrously wrongheaded, frightening, and reactionary, as well as unsupported by evidence.[42]

Political scientist Floyd W. Hayes III, black studies scholars Lewis Gordon and Peniel E. Joseph, and philosophers Charles Mills and Clevis Headley concurred that West's critique of Afro-nihilism was hard to dis-tinguish from blame-the-victim conservatism. Hayes protested that instead of stressing the ravages of white supremacism and capitalist exploitation, West recycled the old "culture of poverty" elitism that blamed "impoverished Black Folk for their own predicament and for being unable to rid themselves of it." Gordon added that West underestimated Du Bois and denigrated the black Marxist tradition, especially C. L. R. James and Walter Rodney. Joseph put it more hotly, blasting West for his "victim-blaming and excoriation of contemporary Black leadership." West's account of black intellectualism rested on a method of "demonization and invocation," Joseph argued. He lifted Toni Morrison above all others by invocation, with no argument, put down everyone else, and did not bother even to mention the radical black humanist tradition of Angela Davis, Huey Newton, Fred Hampton, and Vicki Garvin.[43]

Headley admonished that West's evasion of philosophy was literal and not something to be proud of. West never developed a serious argument, Headley contended; he merely patched together "various rhetorics of liberation for the purpose of building progressive coalitions." In Headley's judgment, West's writings amounted, at best, to "an impressive collage of political slogans" that infused pragmatism with his magnetic personality: "He substitutes intellectual seduction in place of rational persuasion." Adding to the objections of Hayes, Gordon, Joseph, Mills, and Headley that West spent much of his breakthrough book blaming blacks for their nihilism, feminist theorist Iris M. Young protested that West and Hewlett stooped to a similar antifeminism in their critique of American family life. It was offensive enough when conservatives made alarmist statements about the downfall of marriage, Young contended, "but coming from supposed progressives, they are frightening! Privileging marriage and genetic ties of parenting in this way is heterosexist and insulting to adoptive parents, and wrongfully supports continued stigmatization of single mothers."[44]

Philosopher John Pittman chided West for conjuring a pragmatic ethical Karl Marx remarkably like Cornel West. Philosopher George Yancy worried that West relied too heavily on religion, which in his case rested on a thin crypto-fideism. Since West's claims for religion were merely pragmatic and historicist, how could much of a religion come from that? Comparative literature scholar Nada Elia advised West to stop complaining about feeling exiled. For one thing, he exaggerated his suffering; for another, to the extent that he was truly marginalized, he was free to do the work of criticism that radical intellectuals were supposed to do. Political philosopher Lucius Turner Outlaw Jr. suggested, disapprovingly, that West criticized Du Bois for failing to deal with major European thinkers because West wanted to lift himself above Du Bois.[45]

West endured the attacks from the right with as little replying as possible. There was little to be gained by defending himself from ridicule or by debating people with whom he shared nothing. He engaged his other critics wholeheartedly, without noting the irony of the personal offense that his writings of the early nineties caused. No one was more generous with praise or charitable affection than West. He poured himself out for a constant stream of colleagues and students seeking his help, opened doors for them professionally, remembered personal things about them, and routinely greeted them as treasured sisters and brothers. Often he explained that public intellectualism and original scholarship were different things. Contrary to Aronowitz's implication, West had no plans for a scholarly phase. The Gramscian task of engaging the dominant culture from a left-intellectual standpoint and the personal relationships he cultivated on the lecture trail were vocation enough for him.

On most points of criticism he was a model of respectful engagement, though West made an exception for the charge that he blamed the victim in *Race Matters*. To him, this charge was a "bizarre," "sophomoric," and "leftist knee-jerk" myth that somehow survived his many writings on white racism, a response that ignored the point of his critics that *Race Matters* vastly outsold his other writings. As for the black intellectual tradition, he respected it greatly, but not to the point of indulging Gordon's filiopiety. Du Bois produced outstanding work in historical sociology, West acknowledged; on the other hand, Du Bois was a Victorian elitist and Enlightenment rationalist who did not compare intellectually to the great musical geniuses of black America. Moreover, most of the black Marxists extolled by Gordon were Leninists. As for Joseph's charge that West dismissed black nationalism, West replied, "ludicrous." *Prophesy Deliverance!* lauded the black nationalist tradition, and West's comradely friendships with black nationalist leader Maulana Karenga, Afrocentric theorist Molefi Asante, and "the beloved Minister Louis Farrakhan" were matters of public record. He added that his $10,000 contribution to the Black Radical Congress surely said something about his respect for black nationalism; to Joseph he appealed, "please do more homework."[46]

To academic critics of his improvisational style, he gave short shrift. West told Headley that obviously he did not share Headley's devotion to philosophical professionalism, cognitive models, formal analysis, and the positivist distinction between reason and emotion. Thus it was not surprising that Headley and others like him did not comprehend West's intellectual style, though West wished they would recognize its legitimacy. To

Young he replied that it should be possible to defend the progressive possibilities of heterosexual marriage from a feminist and egalitarian standpoint without being accused of bigotry against gays, lesbians, and single parents. Repeating a central argument of his book on the family, West contended that children did best when raised by two biological parents that were married to each other. The empirical evidence on this point was terribly clear and important, he urged. To set progressivism against it was disastrous for progressivism and for children: "We make it clear that this does not stigmatize single mothers and fathers, disqualify loving gay or lesbian parents, or preclude successful adoption of children." He took no interest in bolstering discrimination against gay or lesbian parents. Progressivism had to be against that, just as it had to "put a premium on the well-being of children."[47]

To Pittman he replied that every insightful interpretation of Marx had background premises. Georg Lukacs described a neo-Hegelian Marx, Alexandre Kojeve described a Heideggerian Marx, and Louis Althusser described a structuralist Marx. It would have been odd if ethical pragmatist West had not played up the ethical aspects of Marx's thought. To Yancy he acknowledged that he tended to be silent about the philosophic and religious "more" beyond utility and politics. To pursue the more was to lapse into metaphysics or onto-theology, which he eschewed. That did not make him a pragmatic reductionist, West cautioned. He treasured the irreducible mystery of being and emphasized the tragicomic "funk" of living, suffering, struggling, and dying. West prized Anton Chekhov above all thinkers, often calling himself a "Chekhovian Christian." To him, Chekhov was the greatest literary artist of the modern age because he was "the pre-eminent poet of the funk of life, its tragicomic darkness, mystery, and incongruity, with a blues conclusion: keep lovin' and fightin' for justice anyway, i.e., regardless of the situation." Chekhov inveighed against evil while spurning the aid of religion; as a Chekhovian Christian, West held to a "blues-ridden gospel" of resistance to evil that trusted in the possibility of divine goodness: "Ours is in the trying—the rest is not our business."[48]

To Elia he replied that he reveled in his marginality from the black community and American culture while feeling estranged from neither. To Outlaw he denied that he was driven by his considerable "notoriety" or even his ambivalence about it to place himself above Du Bois. West criticized Du Bois only because Du Bois deserved it, not to make himself number one: "My Chekhovian Christian voice simply cuts deeper and thereby is more truthful than Du Bois's Goethean Enlightenment view that under-girded his marvelous scholarship."[49]

Repeatedly, realizing that being exalted made him a target, West ad-monished friendly critics not to judge him by an inflated standard of ex-pectation. In particular he asked them not to imagine that he aimed "to save American civilization or achieve greatness owing to white recogni-tion." He did not expect to be remembered as a historic figure, and he doubted there was a "Westian" ideology or position. Intellectually he was someone who looked at the world through various lenses, not a grand theorist. He was keenly aware that his prominence had much to do with having come along at the right moment: "My sheer level of privilege and scope of exposure is unprecedented."[50]

West's immense goodwill and generous spirit helped him get on with academics who thought they were more deserving of fame. By 1999, when he annotated and published *The Cornel West Reader*, he was long practiced at explaining that he rejected the narrowly academic view of academic work. He believed that the academy needed to address audi-ences and topics outside the academy, a view that he featured prominently in the reader. In 2001, however, he acquired a president at Harvard who had a narrow idea of what a Harvard professor should be and an amaz-ingly obtuse understanding of West's value to the university.

West had never met Harvard's new president, economist Lawrence Summers, before being summoned to a fateful meeting with him in Oc-tober 2001. Though Summers had not read West's books, he had strong opinions about them that closely resembled the Wieseltier genre of ridi-cule. He blasted West for producing a rap CD that embarrassed Harvard, reproached him for missing classes to campaign for Bradley, opined that "no one in his right mind" supported Sharpton, admonished him to write a major scholarly work that established him as a real academic, chas-tised him for giving too many A's to students, and exhorted West to start writing the kind of books that academic journals would review. In other words, West needed to legitimize his appointment as a distinguished Uni-versity Professor. Summers proposed to have regular meetings with West to monitor his progress. In reality, West had not missed any classes while campaigning for Bradley or anyone else, one of his courses had an enroll-ment of 700 students, and he had already written a scholarly tome, *The American Evasion of Philosophy*, and published a collection of academic essays, *Keeping Faith*.[51]

Feeling attacked and insulted, West decided to resign quietly from Harvard and return to Princeton. It seemed pointless to fight with Summers, nor did he relish the prospect of a media spectacle. For two months he refused to speak to reporters about the rumored episode, but the story exploded into a page-one spectacle anyway. As West later recalled, the dominant story line was of a principled president "upholding standards and refusing to give in to an undeserving and greedy professor." Though many Harvard students defended West, a student newspaper, *The Harvard Crimson*, fed the press frenzy by recycling Wieseltier's polemic and mocking West's purported vanity and hypocrisy. Recalling his attack on the hedonism of the black middle class, the paper found a contradiction "between West's prophetic contempt for material gain and his exquisitely tailored suits, comfortably tenured lifestyle, lucrative speaking gigs and fancy cars." Fareed Zakaria piled on in *Newsweek*, recycling Wieseltier's litany yet again; *Newsweek* readers were assured that "noisy, self-endeared, completely worthless" and all the rest were exactly right. The *New Republic* added that West epitomized the contemporary mutation of the public intellectual: a celebrity master of public relations. Brilliantly packaging himself as a brand, the magazine explained, West kept himself in the news and choreographed his controversy with Harvard. Instead of producing serious scholarship, he offered "tossed-off books, rap CDs, and shallow public disputes over the respect due to him."[52]

The Summers episode set up West for a media bashing far beyond his total past experience, a point West made vividly in his second meeting with Summers. By then Summers realized that the media controversy was bad for Harvard and his presidency; he thanked West for not playing the race card. West replied that in the U.S. "the whole deck was full of race cards," but there were additional issues at stake. He would have welcomed a serious exchange about academic freedom and the public responsibilities of the academy. As it was, he found himself pilloried in the media, because Summers "had authorized every xenophobic and conservative or neoliberal newspaper writer in the country to unleash pent-up hostility toward me." In West's telling, Summers apologized to him for setting off a damaging "misunderstanding," then told a reporter he had not apologized, then told West the reporter misquoted him. West, after learning otherwise from the reporter, blasted Summers on the Tavis Smiley Show as "the Ariel Sharon of American higher education," an arrogant bully unsuited for his position. That set off another media explosion, this time featuring the charge that West had to be anti-Semitic for linking Harvard's first Jewish president with Sharon. West later recalled ruefully that most of his Harvard colleagues sat back and said nothing while he was roasted in the media, which showed the typical "spinelessness in the academy." Undergoing surgery for cancer, he waited for the controversy to burn itself out and returned to Princeton.[53]

To West the entire episode was pathetic and damaging. He later reflected that it should have been possible for him to disagree with Summers "without being subjected to slightly veiled threats and overt disrespect." Harvard was supposed to stand for academic freedom. Having sought to facilitate greater mutual respect between American blacks and Jews, West regretted the symbolism of having clashed with Summers. Above all, he regretted that for all his fame as a public intellectual, the controversy offered a chastening warning to others who shared his belief in the necessity of academic engagement with popular culture. In a sequel to *Race Matters*, titled *Democracy Matters* (2004), he put it with a slightly defiant edge: "As one who is deeply committed to the deep democratic tradition in America and to engaging youth culture, I have no intention of cutting back on my academic and outreach activities, because the effort to shatter the sleepwalking of youths who are shut out of the intellectual excitement and opportunity of the academy is such a vital one for our democracy."[54]

Race Matters was about the social ravages of white supremacy; *Democracy Matters* was about the degradation of American democracy in the age of American empire. Writing against the background of the Bush administration's imperial disaster in Iraq, but also implicitly reflecting his vigorous opposition to Al Gore in the 2000 presidential election, West declared: "The rise of an ugly imperialism has been aided by an unholy alliance of the plutocratic elites and the Christian Right, and also by a massive disaffection of so many voters who see too little difference between two corrupted parties, with blacks being taken for granted by the Democrats, and with the deep disaffection of youth." Since the Republican and Democratic parties were both owned by corporate money and interests, choosing between them was like choosing between "the left-wing and right-wing versions of the Dred Scott decision."[55]

Three dogmas of modern American life played the leading roles in degrading American democracy, he contended. Capitalist fundamentalism (the glorification of unfettered markets and market rationality) cast aside the public good while delivering the world to the corporations. Aggressive militarism (the pursuit of global military empire) imposed the will of American elites on other nations. Escalating authoritarianism (the diminishment of individual rights) betrayed hard-won liberties in the name of national security. Taken together, West argued, "we are experiencing the sad American imperial devouring of American democracy," which amounted to "an unprecedented gangsterization of America."[56]

In West's view, the Republican Party was myopically mendacious in promoting capitalist fundamentalism, aggressive militarism, and authoritarianism, while the Democratic Party was pathetically spineless in promoting weaker versions of the same thing. "The saturation of market forces in American life generates a market morality that undermines a sense of meaning and larger purpose," he wrote. Capitalist fundamentalism reduced all values to market value, pitting government institutions against each other in a race to the bottom that shredded social safety nets and corrupted societies "all the way up." Worst of all, fifteen years after the end of the cold war, America was more deeply and pervasively militaristic than ever.[57]

Nihilism in America was a two-sided coin, West observed. On one side it was the despair of worthlessness and believing in nothing that afflicted Americans of all races and classes, which was especially devastating in poor communities. On the other side it was the ruthless abuse of power that nihilistic elites waged daily, which also fell heaviest on America's most vulnerable communities: "Political nihilism now sets the tone for public discourse, and market moralities now dictate the landscape of a stifled American democracy." For West the administration of George W. Bush was the showcase example, serving up fear and greed, tax cuts for the rich, and imperialism: "A political nihilist is one who is not simply intoxicated with the exercise of power but also obsessed with stifling any criticism of that exercise of power. He will use clever arguments to rationalize his will to power and deploy skillful strategies, denying the pain and suffering he may cause, in order to shape the world and control history in light of the pursuit of power."[58]

In theory, the Democratic Party existed to "fight the plutocracy," exacting concessions from the corporate class that benefited the majority. In fact, West lamented, contemporary Democratic leaders fell woefully short of Franklin Roosevelt and even Lyndon Johnson. At least Johnson recognized and cared that poor whites and most blacks had the same fundamental interests. By contrast, current Democrats like John Kerry and Hillary Clinton were "paternalistic nihilists," slick professionals who spoke blandly for democracy with no heart-felt rage at the injustices of the system.[59]

West had a version of American exceptionalism that contrasted with America's self-congratulatory versions. The American democratic experiment was unique only in the sense that most Americans refused to acknowledge "the deeply racist and imperial roots of our democratic project," he argued: "No other democratic nation revels so blatantly in such self-deceptive innocence, such self-paralyzing reluctance to confront the nightmare of its own history." Despite having grown huge and powerful, American civilization refused to grow up. It was stuck in an adolescent refusal to face painful truths about itself, which made America unable to negotiate tempting options that were bad for America itself and others. West put it bluntly: "Race has always been the crucial litmus test for such maturity in America. To acknowledge the deeply racist and imperial roots of our democratic project is anti-American only if one holds to a childish belief that America is pure and pristine, or if one opts for self-destructive nihilistic rationalizations."[60]

Though he was often accused of selling out racial justice to further his own celebrity, or of imagining that he was the only "race-transcending prophet" of his time, West was emphatic that ignoring or minimizing the matter of race would not make anything better. There were many issues to address in struggling for social justice, he urged, but race was nearly always intertwined with them: "Niggerization in America has always been the test case for examining the nihilistic threats to America. For so long niggerization has been viewed as marginal and optimism central to America. But in our time, when we push race to the margins we imperil all of us, not just peoples of color."[61]

Democracy Matters got the usual mix of praise and brickbats. The *Village Voice* lauded West as "a thinker of dazzling erudition, whose critiques are inevitably balanced by an infectious optimism and magnanimity of spirit." The *Seattle Times* called him "a compelling and sought-after deep thinker in a nation weaned on five-second sound bites." Womanist ethicist Cheryl Sanders enthused in the *Christian Century* that the book was an inspiration and blessing to her: "What I love about his new book, *Democracy Matters*, is how deeply motivated and illuminated I felt when thinking through his formulation of democratic solutions to the problem of American imperialism." *Daily Princetonian* arts writer Hamid Khanbhai lauded West as "a polemicist with all the pizzazz of a passionate gospel preacher," though he worried about West's eagerness to implant democracy in the Middle East. Historian Daniel Levine, writing in *America*, commended West's politics, but criticized his "platitudinous" style, "outright banality," and "sloppy thinking." *New Criterion* reviewer Mark Bauerlein, upholding a conservative tradition, recycled Wieseltier yet again before assuring that West's latest book was no better. West never reasoned his way to conclusions or even appealed to empirical evidence, Bauerlein complained; he simply made charges and declared things with overheated language. In Bauerlein's judgment, *Democracy Matters* showed what happened when an intellectual was hailed by the mass media, "courted by rival universities, and invited, interviewed, and idolized without end. The process is fatal to the scholarly intelligence."[62]

As a writer West sometimes did not get through; the torrential riffs that made him a sensational speaker often did not sing as well on the page. Many of his reviewers would have done better, however, had they acknowledged that they did not know what to make of someone who glided effortlessly from Matthew Arnold to C. L. R. James to Socrates to John Coltrane to Kierkegaard to Michel Foucault to Toni Morrison to Dostoyevsky to Alain Badiou to Jay-Z and Outkast, finding juxtapositions that only he would have perceived. There was simply no one to compare to West, until his protégé Michael Eric Dyson made a similar splash. West enthralled lecture audiences like no other intellectual of his time, taught in prisons, wrote about hip-hop, and recorded CD's that sought to convey the greatness of the black tradition to youths who would not have touched his books. Most reviewers that chastised him lacked even a fraction of his intellectual range. Somehow reviewers who knew nothing of postcolonial theory knew that his use of it had to be worthless.

On the right, the need to disparage West was an ideological necessity; for many others, the jealousy factor played a role; in addition, his dramatic expansiveness made him easy to caricature. He persistently overdressed in informal contexts while criticizing other black intellectuals for wearing "shabby" clothes. Sometimes a serious point got lost in his maze of allusions. *In These Times* writer Salim Muwakkil noted that there was "something excessive about him," a point that West confirmed in his memoir, *Brother West*, by disclosing that he had never spent a weekend at his home in Princeton, never used a computer, and never been satisfied in his romantic relationships with anything less than "full-blast mutual intensity, fully-fledged mutual acceptance, full-blown mutual flourishing, and fully felt peace and joy with each other." This rather high standard was hard on his three marriages, he acknowledged, as it required "a level of physical attraction, personal adoration, and moral admiration that is hard to find." But West's proclivity to excess also worked for him, driving him to unsurpassed achievements cutting across multiple fields and publics. In a generation that produced excessive wailing about the decline of public intellectualism, the lack of engagement between the academy and public, and the loss of a progressive Christian voice in the public square, he was the towering exception. West made himself a target for criticism by achieving what others claimed was no longer possible.[63]

He never really changed, notwithstanding the Left critics who liked his early writings and claimed that he sold out later. From the beginning West was committed to a Christian liberationist vision of social justice and reconciliation, though some readers wrongly took his early writings to be Marxism dressed up as Christian thought. West was not "really" a Marxist who used Christianity; it was more the other way around. He began as a liberationist social critic committed to building progressive multiracial coalitions, and he remained one. He moved easily among groups that had little in common with one another and that sometimes could not abide one another: *Monthly Review* Marxists, postmodern deconstructionists, black nationalists, Civil Rights leaders, anti-imperialist activists, conservative and liberal academics, DSA Social Democrats, black church pastors and congregants, churchgoing white Protestants and Catholics.

But West was not satisfied with bringing together likeminded progressives from different backgrounds. He worked at the boundaries of his wide-ranging social existence, struggling above all to bring black nationalists and black radicals into dialogue and solidarity work with white progressives. West realized that he jeopardized his favored standing with white progressives and some black civil rights leaders by cultivating bonds of trust with Farrakhan and the Nation of Islam. That he took the risk was typical of him. "The tensions between blacks and Jews are so volatile and our national discourse regarding difficult issues is so stunted that thoughtful dialogue is nearly impossible," he lamented. By playing close to the edge of the field, he jeopardized his capacity to be a racial healer. For West, however, the spiritual principle at issue trumped the questionable politics of the situation. The love ethic of Christianity compelled him to appeal to the humanity of anti-Semitic black nationalists just as it compelled him to look for it in the racist beneficiaries of white supremacism.[64]

In the spring of 2009 I co-taught a course and public forum with Serene Jones and Cornel at Union Theological Seminary titled "Christianity and the U.S. Crisis." Each week one of us was supposed to give the featured lecture with the other two responding, but the responses often turned into full-length lectures of their own. Cornel was always on—dazzling a huge crowd with improvised riffs on theory and practice, marshaling his boundary-less arsenal of information, blasting America's refusal to deal with its white supremacism, and waxing with sermonic poetry on suffering and hope. Often after a sermonic riff, trying to decompress, he would turn introspective or self-explanatory, emoting "I love this seminary" or "I'm a blest Negro tonight" or, more than once, "You see, I'm just a bluesman who loves Jesus." His generosity and loving spirit overflowed. Each class lasted two and a half hours; there was always a post-class gathering of responders with whom he conversed; then he gave three hours to whatever group of Union guests or doctoral students that Serene and I put together. Every week he was the last one still animated, wise-cracking, and exuberant after six hours of holding forth; sometimes he continued with passersby on the sidewalk after the evening had ended. Every week he told our guests and students it was a great blessing for him to meet them. And every week he meant it.

Chapter 16

As Purple to Lavender

KATIE CANNON AND WOMANIST ETHICS

The necessity of a black feminist Christian social ethic was obvious long before anyone knew what it would be like. When I was a seminarian in the mid- and late 1970s all the black theologians we studied were male and all the female theologians were white. This anomaly did not go unnoticed; many times, when my classes discussed black and feminist theology, the point was made that one group would be in a position to meld these perspectives together, if only there were any black women in the field to do so.

At the time there were a few black women in the classrooms. Sometimes they raised the issue; more often, uncomfortably, they had to deal with others raising it in their presence; too often they were pressed to declare which perspective took priority for them. The discursive tradition they created, womanism, was distinguished by its determined refusal to make an either/or answer. In social ethics the pioneer was Katie Geneva Cannon, who studied under Beverly Harrison and Cornel West at Union Theological Seminary, and who spent much of her graduate school career pondering what a black feminist ethic would be. The key to her answer appeared in 1983, when Alice Walker published *In Search of Our Mothers' Gardens: Womanist Prose*.[1]

Katie Cannon was the first African American woman to earn a doctorate at Union Seminary and the first African American woman to be ordained in the United Presbyterian Church, U.S.A. In her early career she taught at Episcopal Divinity School in Cambridge, Massachusetts; later she taught at Temple University in Philadelphia; later, moving closer to home, she taught at Union Theological Seminary and Presbyterian School of Christian Education in Richmond, Virginia. Born and raised in Kannapolis, North Carolina, she came to Presbyterianism by family heritage, came to her "firsts" through an urgent desire to grow beyond her roots, and came to her later spiritual perspective by reclaiming her Southern, poor, extended family heritage.

In Kannapolis, a segregated rural town near Charlotte where the Ku Klux Klan was an oppressive force, Cannon began at an early age to plot her escape. Her mother, Corine Lytle Cannon, worked as a domestic; her father, Esau Cannon, was a truck driver; in addition to their seven children, the Cannons lived among large groups of relatives. Corine Cannon was the nineteenth of twenty children, each of whom had at least seven children, and her husband's family was almost as large. The slave tradition dichotomy between house servants and field hands was a palpable reality to them. The Lytle family was churchly, literate, and inclined to look down on the field laboring, hard partying, less religious types from which Esau Cannon came. The Lytles lamented that Corine married beneath her status, and the Cannons regretted that Corine was dark-skinned. Cannon later recalled that she knew little of her father, however, because her mother claimed him exclusively: "That was her man. 'He's mine, get your own man,' she'd say. We were appendages to their marriage; we could never come between them."[2]

Elsewhere she recalled, with slight exaggeration, "We all live there . . . We dominate the place . . . There are thousands of us." Cannon coped with the sprawling chaos of her family situation, which included many alcoholic relatives, by embracing the rules of school and church, finding comfort in institutional structures. "I liked the rules," she remarked of her early attraction to school, which extended to church: "I was overendowed with Christianity. This was linked with education." In her world, black women worked as domestics or teachers; later they were also allowed to work in the mills. Cannon aspired to be a teacher, but she also fantasized about saving blacks from self-destructive behavior. For most of her youth she judged that blacks were poor and backward because they were promiscuous: "I figured this whole thing out—the curse of blackness had to do with SEX . . . We drink, we party, we dance, we have children out of wedlock—all of this animalistic behavior—no wonder we are enslaved."[3]

If that was the problem, salvation was deliverance from licentiousness. Cannon resolved to be a missionary, perhaps a nun: "The energy needed to be controlled . . . I'd go to Africa . . . I'd save us!" In high school, however, she discovered to her astonishment that white youths got drunk and formicated just like her black classmates: "That is when I became a militant." If whites behaved the same way with no apparent social consequences, there had to be another reason why blacks suffered "so brutally." Cannon's remembrance of November 22, 1963, was, for her, a telling marker of the difference. On the day that President John Kennedy was assassinated, Cannon was a ninth grader at George Washington Carver High School. "It was a *comical* day at Carver," she recalled. Her civics class, watching the television coverage of Kennedy being whisked to a Dallas hospital emergency room, laughed at the attempts of "these white people to . . . do this resurrection thing on Kennedy." Cannon and her classmates were not candidates for the great national grieving over Kennedy: "Our lives were worth nothing to these white people. In ninth grade, we were already working on organically critiquing society. We knew the country was evil and violent. None of us really mourned Kennedy's death." Social criticism had begun to trump moralistic reproach.[4]

Five years later she was a freshman at Barber-Scotia College (a liberal arts college seven miles from her home) when Martin Luther King Jr. was assassinated. Infuriated at the government, Cannon and her classmates took for granted that King was killed by a conspiracy, not a lone assassin: "Naivete has never been our privilege." Swiftly she converted to Black Power radicalism: "I had on my dashiki. I had my Black Power fist dangling from my neck . . . It was like a transfusion of blackness. I was high on it. I *loved* it." She consumed Black Power literature, but fell into depression and had a second transforming experience as a college intern at Ghost Ranch in Santa Fe, New Mexico, a Presbyterian retreat. Luxuriating in the beauty of the ranch's twenty-three thousand acres, Cannon became physically active for the first time in her life, met friendly white people for the first time, and realized that getting out of Kannapolis was a genuine possibility for her: "The ranch is what gave me hope . . . It opened up the horizon and pushed it toward the sun."[5]

During her college years Cannon was recruited by James Costen, a Presbyterian minister and president of Johnson C. Smith Seminary in Atlanta, to study for the ministry. Cannon had never known a female pastor; Costen helped her imagine herself as one. Enrolling at Interdenominational Theological Center (ITC) in Atlanta, she discovered a ministerial vocation, majored in Old Testament, and undertook an archaeological dig in Israel, which bruised her enthusiasm for the land of the Bible. The Israelis she met were virulently racist, hurling epithets at her that she had never heard directly in the U.S. Stunned at the bigotry she encountered, Cannon felt intensely lonely, driven to the wilderness: "You know, you give up your slave experience and depend upon God." She returned to seminary still wanting to study Hebrew scripture, though with conflicted feelings.[6]

Her next academic stop was the doctoral program at Union Theological Seminary in New York, where Cannon eventually, and painfully, relinquished her ambition to be a biblical scholar. Her searing experience in Israel had been hurtful and alienating but not too humiliating to overcome. Her first encounter with the white academy was thoroughly humiliating. Enrolling at Union in 1974, Cannon felt completely out of place. To her, Union was impossibly arid, erudite, white, and elitist. Even the black students seemed unreal to her. At Interdenominational Theological Center the free-wheeling, high-spirited unpretentiousness of black culture had prevailed; at Union Cannon's awkward attempts to deflate scholarly decorum elicited eye-rolling embarrassment and disapproval: "All I was trying to do was cut through the bullshit. I'd come from all-black schools, and whenever anybody was talking this highfalutin kind of stuff, people would say, 'Come on, let's be real. Be real!'" Union Seminary did not confirm her sense of what was real, nor indulge her aversion to abstract theory; it only made her feel loud and frivolous. At ITC she had been the gatekeeper of student study groups, deciding who got in: "I had *controlled* them. I dominated." At Union students shunned her, excluding her from study groups. Moreover, the Hebrew Bible division at Union was noted for its air of academic seriousness. "It's only by grace that I didn't crack," Cannon later recalled. "I mean, suddenly the ground was opening up and I was falling down into the descent into Hell."[7]

It didn't help that she felt guilty about being there, supported by scholarships that exceeded the combined incomes of her parents. Cannon anguished over the contradictions between her privileges and the hard-pressed lives of her parents and relatives. Often her mother told her that if she really hated Union so much, she could return to Kannapolis and work in the mill. Otherwise, Corine Cannon exhorted, "You must do it for all of us!" Failing to win a mentor in Hebrew Bible, Cannon switched reluctantly to social ethics, where she found mentors in Roger Shinn and Beverly Harrison.[8]

An East Side therapist helped Cannon realize that she was too traumatized by white people to see any differences between them: "I would say, 'All white people,' and she would say, 'Well, wait a minute, Katie.

Not *all* white people.' Our work together helped me start to make sense out of this big ball of whiteness that was scaring the hell out of me." White society was a menacing world to her; Union's culture of academic whiteness seemed doubly menacing. Cannon had to learn "to make the white world more livable." The white feminism of her therapist helped Cannon make the transition. To Cannon's surprise, the feminist rhetoric of individual freedom and equal rights for women struck chords of recognition. Warming up to feminism, she loosened her exclusive identity with blackness. Cannon's black male classmates, by disliking her dramatic persona and challenging her right to ordination, caused further loosening. She responded by joining the seminary's Women's Caucus, becoming, in her telling, "an honorary white person." On the one hand, it troubled and perplexed her to find her primary community of support among white women; on the other hand, at least they respected her right to be at Union: "I had been trained all my life to deal with race and white supremacy . . . but nobody had conscientized me in terms of what it meant to be born a female, a black female."[9]

The writings of Zora Neale Hurston and Alice Walker helped Cannon get her social ethical bearings on what it meant to be a black female. In 1983 Walker provided the concept of "womanism," which Cannon called "the new gatekeeper in my land of counterpain." Meanwhile Cannon's doctoral dissertation featured Hurston's life and work. The dissertation came first, in 1983, but its book version had a Walkeresque title, *Black Womanist Ethics* (1988).[10]

Walker offered a four-part definition of a womanist. First, she was a serious, morally responsible adult, as in the black folk expression of mothers to female children, "You acting womanish." A womanist was a black feminist or feminist of color; the term was also interchangeable with the folk expression, "You trying to be grown." Second, a womanist loved other women, "sexually and/or unsexually," preferred women's culture and the personal qualities of women, and sometimes loved individual men. She was committed to survival and the wholeness of people, and was not a separatist, "except periodically, for health." Third, a womanist loved music, dancing, the moon, the Spirit, love, food, roundness, struggle, and herself. Lastly, Walker wrote, "Womanist is to feminist as purple to lavender."[11]

Walker's previous writings, especially *The Color Purple*, were already important to Cannon and other black women who had recently entered the theological field. Then Walker offered "womanism," which for Cannon was "philosophically medicinal." It named the elements and contours of her black, female, Southern, spiritual, overcoming sensibility, expressing her preference for the company and folkways of black women. For many black women who entered the American Academy of Religion and the Society of Biblical Literature in the 1980s and 1990s, the idea of womanism was personally and collectively definitive. Cannon was the first to explain it as a type of theological ethics.[12]

African American women needed and possessed distinctive virtues, she argued. White Americans prized self-reliance, frugality, and industry, and white ethicists provided philosophical and religious reasons for doing so, because these virtues worked for whites, facilitating their success. But they did not work for black Americans, Cannon argued. To subscribe to white values was to legitimate the power that whites held over blacks, thereby worsening black humiliation. In racist America, the game was rigged against blacks that tried to acquire finance capital or climb a career ladder. Even when blacks adopted white individualism and frugality, they were put down anyway, which was humiliating, adding to the "evidence" of their supposed inferiority. Cannon remarked: "Racism does not allow Black women and Black men to labor habitually in beneficial work with the hope of saving expenses by avoiding waste so that they can develop a standard of living that is congruent with the American ideal."[13]

Cannon stressed that black women worked for lower wages than men and white women, doing jobs that others refused to do. For them, to embrace work as a prime value was to risk their emotional and physical health. Moreover, the range of their moral agency was severely limited by racism and poverty. White theologians described a self with a wide capacity for moral agency, taking for granted that each person is free and self-determining. The assumption that each person holds self-determining power underwrote the white Christian idea of Christian virtue, which prized the choice of bearing one's cross. White Christian ethics treated voluntary suffering as a moral norm. The virtuous Christian chose to follow Jesus to the cross, making personal sacrifices as a voluntary commitment. The Christian followed Christ by choosing to suffer for the sake of others.

Cannon replied that for blacks, however, suffering was not a choice or a desirable moral norm. It was a repugnant everyday reality to overcome: "The vast majority of Blacks suffer every conceivable form of denigration. Their lives are named, defined and circumscribed by whites." Since black Americans lacked the moral agency and freedom of whites, it was wrong to apply the ethic of voluntary suffering to them. Moreover, it was also obscene, because blacks owed their lack of moral agency and freedom to the oppression they suffered at the hands of whites. For Cannon, black faith and liberation ethics were responses to these conditions, helping blacks "purge themselves of self-hate" and throw off the judgment of an ethic that did not rightly apply to them: "The ethical values that the Black community has construed for itself are not identical with the body of obligations and duties that Anglo-Protestant American society requires of its members. Nor can the ethical assumptions be the same, as long as powerful whites who control the wealth, the systems and the institutions in this society continue to perpetuate brutality and criminality against Blacks."[14]

Repudiating the myth of black inferiority and the application of white ethical standards to black people, Cannon argued that black folk culture, as described by Walker and Hurston, possessed a distinct ethical character. Womanist ethics began with the experiences of black female survivors, deriving its moral norms from the study of black female culture and experience. *Black Womanist Ethics* did not get to the business of ethical construction, pointing merely to how it might be done. "For too long the Black community's theological and ethical understandings have been written from a decidedly male bias," Cannon declared. Womanist thought was a type of black liberationism, but one that privileged the distinctive experiences and moral agency of black women.[15]

Cannon walked a fine line between stressing the objective ravages of racism and denying that black women were emotionally stunted by it. To a degree she lauded Hurston on the latter theme, though Cannon would never say, as Hurston insisted of herself, that she lacked any interest in "the race problem." Hurston famously wrote in 1928: "I am not tragically colored. There is no great sorrow damned up in my soul, nor lurking behind my eyes. I do not mind at all. I do not belong to the sobbing school of negrohood who hold that nature somehow has given them a lowdown dirty deal and whose feelings are hurt about it." Cannon had a different voice, but she loved Hurston's saucy flair and her portraits of complex, psychologically integral black women.[16]

Hurston's characters labored long hours, held families together, danced and partied, had affairs, protected vulnerable black males, and loved and raged at them, all with little sense of being defeated or victimized. Since Hurston did not experience black people or herself as humiliated or degraded, she did not portray blacks in that way. Subtly refuting the white supremacist slander of black inferiority, she portrayed emotionally healthy characters that did not think of themselves as a "problem" and gave almost no thought or time to white people. Adopting critic Mary Burgher's description of black female novelists as a whole, Cannon praised Hurston for showing that black women turned their lost innocence into "invisible dignity," sustained a "quiet grace" despite being refused the possibility of feminine delicacy, and converted their unchosen responsibilities into "unshouted courage."[17]

For Hurston, as for black women generally, Cannon argued, suffering was an everyday reality, not something to be prized as a moral value. Virtue was not about experiencing suffering, or even enduring it. To be virtuous was to sustain a robust, self-respecting, feisty affirmation of one's life and life itself. Borrowing a term favored by Walker, Cannon noted that Hurston was long on "unctuousness," the virtue of taking the good and bad together in stride; Hurston called it "soaking up urine and perfume with the same indifference."[18]

The invisible dignity of black women enabled them to maintain self-respect despite being treated as the "mules of the world." Their quiet grace enabled them to persist against forces that denied their humanity. Their unshouted courage enabled them to calibrate the effects of human wills besides their own and to accept accountability for occurrences beyond their control. In all this persisting and resisting, Cannon stressed, black women acquired a wily sense of the relativity of truth, using whatever means they found to hold off the threat of violence and death: "For Black people the moral element of courage is annexed with the will to live and the dread of greater perpetrations of evil acts against them."[19]

Cannon allowed that Hurston ended badly, lapsing into reactionary politics and isolation in her last years. But her best work offered the best depiction of the folk wisdom of black women: "Across the boundaries of her own experience, Hurston wrote about the oppressive and unbearable, about those things that rub Black women raw. Her richness and chaos, her merits and faults witnessed to an ethic that can be lived out only in community."[20]

Cannon was fond of Hurston's self-description: that she tried "to hit a straight lick with a crooked stick." Cannon wrote womanist ethics in the same manner. On the one hand, as a Christian social ethicist she spoke to and about "the universality of the human condition," transcending her blackness and femaleness. On the other hand, as a womanist liberation ethicist, her blackness and femaleness were very much in play; woman-ist liberation was determinately situated, deconstructive, and perspectival: "In other words, my role is to speak as 'one of the canonical boys' and as 'the noncanonical other' at one and the same time." Canonical notions about ethical scholarship had "nothing to do with the realities of Black women," she judged. To qualify for membership in the scholarly guild of Christian ethicists, one had to demonstrate proficiency in abstract theory, philosophy, and the classical canon of ethical texts and problems. Can-non put it ruefully: "To prove that she is sufficiently intelligent, the Black woman as Christian ethicist must discount the particularities of her lived experiences and instead focus on the validity of generalizable external an-alytical data."[21]

The dilemma was obvious and perplexing. If she spoke the canonical language of abstraction and Euro-American concerns, she risked betray-ing black women. But if she spoke as a pure liberationist, she risked being devalued by the guild as "a second-class scholar specializing in Jim Crow subject matter." It was one thing to include black women in the field, Cannon observed; it was something further to recognize black women's moral reasoning as an important aspect of the field. Both ideas were new, but the field resisted the second more than the first. The experience of black women was routinely ignored, even in black theology. On the rare occasions when black women were mentioned, their moral agency was hardly ever respected or accurately described.[22]

Cannon conceived womanist ethics as a corrective enterprise that worked within and outside the guild, interpreting traditional paradigms from the perspectives of the black, female noncanonical other. As a criti-cal enterprise, womanist ethics pointed to the silencing and denigration of black women, including the sexist content of black male preaching; as a constructive enterprise, it described the genius of black women in cre-atively shaping their destinies. "The womanist scholar stresses the role of emotional, intuitive knowledge in the collective life of the people," study-ing the consciousness of black women as reflected in their literature and institutions.[23]

The womanist alternative for which Cannon called in the 1980s was al-ready a blooming garden by the end of the decade. When Cannon started seminary in the early 1970s, just one African American woman was en-rolled in a seminary doctoral program. By 1990 womanist theology and ethics was a rising movement led by Cannon, M. Shawn Copeland, Jac-quelyn Grant, Cheryl A. Kirk-Duggan, Cheryl Townsend Gilkes, Clarice

Martin, Marcia Riggs, Cheryl Sanders, Emilie Townes, and Delores S. Williams. Cannon remarked of their road to academic recognition:

> Even with the requisite credentials for matriculation in hand, we were constantly barraged with arrogance and insults, suspicion and insensitivity, backhand compliments and tongue-in-cheek naivete. The worlds of divinity school, denominational headquarters, regional adjudicatory offices, and local parishes, between which we negotiated, demanded different and often wrenching allegiances. But we continued to study, struggling for our rightful places in the church and in the academy.[24]

As the womanist community grew in size and productivity, Cannon defended her inside-outside concept of womanist method from criticism. Cheryl Sanders, in 1989, enthused that womanist scholars relied on their own experience and sources. Womanist scholarship focused commendably on black women and womanist scholars, Sanders observed; in fact, nearly all the footnotes in womanist scholarship cited the writings of black women. To Sanders, that showed that most womanists were free of self-hatred, needing no approval from outside authority figures: "To see black women embracing and engaging our material is a celebration in itself."[25]

Cannon took that as a direct challenge. Unlike many womanists, she observed, her writings often cited white scholars, especially Harrison and Elisabeth Schüssler Fiorenza. Did that make her a self-hater? Worse yet, "Did it make me a fraud?" Cannon exhorted womanists to avert the path of exclusion and insularity. If womanism was to remain a liberationist discourse that supported the emancipation of "a whole people," it could not cut itself off from white feminist thought. The same was true of its relation to black theology, though Cannon mentioned only feminism: "As one of the senior womanist ethicists, I am issuing advance warning to new womanist scholars, both actual and potential, that Sanders's devaluation of credibility consequent on such a conservative framework of Black-sources-only encourages guesswork, blank spots, and time-consuming busy work, the reinvention of the proverbial wheel over and over again." Womanism would not flourish as an intellectual or spiritual departure if it imposed purity tests on the sources that womanists could cite. Cannon urged womanists to take the long view, and an open one: "Staying open-minded as heterogeneous theoreticians may prove to be the most difficult ethical challenge in securing and extending the legacy of our intellectual life."[26]

In her early career she wearied of being told to choose between blackness and womanhood; later she tried not to be defensive when a postmodernized generation resisted her essentialism; in both cases she protested against being marginalized in the academy. Being black was no more and no less important to her than being female, Cannon asserted. Womanism was the refusal to make this false choice. Womanist ethics refused to surrender to either/or dichotomies that spurned the necessary, difficult, messy work of appropriation and reciprocity. Attending always to the interrelationships of race, gender, and class, it drew on the "rugged endurance of Black folks in America" to fulfill new possibilities of human flourishing. Cannon protested that after twenty years of womanism, the academy was as rife as ever with "androcentric, heteropatriarchal, malestream, white supremacist culture. From 1983 until now, storms of opposition, bigotry and suspicion mount." The mere legitimacy of the womanist enterprise had to be defended daily from academics that "experience our very presence as colleagues as a cruel joke." Thus the existence of the womanist tradition was not something to be taken for granted, she cautioned.[27]

Critiques of Cannon's essentialism and confessional approach by younger womanists and black feminists belonged to a different category. Cannon's former doctoral advisee Stacey Floyd-Thomas, describing herself as a second-generation womanist, urged womanists to move beyond the confessional mode of discourse pioneered by Cannon, Jacquelyn Grant, Emilie Townes, Delores Williams, and Marcia Riggs in favor of a distinct ethical method that non-womanists could use. Her proposal reformulated Walker's four tenets of womanism as radical subjectivity, traditional communalism, redemptive self-love, and critical engagement. It employed the methods of literary analysis, sociological analysis, and historiography, plus practical engagement strategies for each method, to construe the meanings of the three virtues described by Cannon and to overcome racial, economic, and gender-based oppression. Womanist ethics, Floyd-Thomas argued, though rooted in black liberation theology and feminist theology, needed to be an essential discourse about "what it means to be in right-relationship," not an oppositional discourse: "I am convinced of the need to avoid the field being marginalized as viable for exploration only by black women. In light of the groundbreaking work done by first-generation womanists, it is now important to unearth these epistemological treasures so that students and scholars of all backgrounds can *do* womanism even if they cannot *be* womanists."[28]

Some womanists argued that if Floyd-Thomas stood for the second wave, there was already a more culturally diverse group that should be called the third wave. Melanie Harris, noting that nearly all the first- and second-wave womanists were Christians, stressed that the founder of womanism—Walker—was not. Womanist scholarship needed to be "more self-critical of its appropriation of Christian categories," Harris argued; for example, her own commitment to humanism deserved to be viewed as an equally valid option for womanists. Monica Coleman agreed that there had to be a third wave; otherwise she could not be a womanist: "When I read Walker's definition, I feel at home, but the trajectory of womanist religious scholarship has left me in a house without enough furniture."[29]

Walker privileged love between women, Coleman observed, but the church-based womanist movement privileged hetero-normativity and tended to settle for being quietly friendly to gays and lesbians. Moreover, womanism was overwhelmingly Christian, typically assuming "that black women's religious experiences are Christian," and it rarely took strong positions on political issues, settling for self-referential descriptions that curtailed the movement's public relevance. In Coleman's telling, the first and second waves had a very limited range of concerns, having little or nothing to say about "bisexuality, colorism and standards of beauty, eating disorders and obesity, class realities (after all, if we're writing books, we can't be too far down on the class scale), mental health, progressive Christianity, paganism, indigenous spirituality, and participation in other world religions—like Baha'i and Buddhism. These are the issues I want to read about."[30]

Social ethicist Traci C. West and social critic bell hooks took a further step, declining to call themselves womanists of any kind, contending that "black feminist" was a more open-ended and liberating category. West appreciated the womanist movement, having studied under Delores Williams at Union Theological Seminary and begun her academic career as womanism developed into an important perspective. She treasured its achievement of a vital space in the academy that privileged black female subjectivity. But the problem of parochialism was obvious in womanist writing, she judged. It began with the womanist notion that accountability was "exclusively tied to one's own racial/ethnic group" and included the assumption that black women like herself were not supposed to call themselves feminists. West replied: "If there is such a consensus being promoted by womanists, how can they avoid the contradiction of circumscribing conformity and policing black womanhood while claiming to free it from the bondage of too few acceptable forms?" Remarking on the "narrowing" tendency of womanist thought, West pointed to its repeated conflation of feminism with whiteness, which had the unfortunate effect of "erasing the contributions of a generation of black feminist foremothers." Much as she admired the womanist movement, West refrained from identifying with "this exclusively black community-based tradition of intellectual work."[31]

Cannon acknowledged that her generation of womanists was not very diverse religiously and it had a quite limited range of concerns. She respected that young black feminist scholars often found womanism to be too essentialist in its stress on "blackness" and too identified with southern folk wisdom to speak for them. If black women who came of age in the 1990s favored hip-hop, an iconographic aesthetic, and hybrid identities, Cannon would not tell them they had a moral obligation to be womanists. Womanism was a "self-naming sensibility," not something handed down by coercion, she assured. It needed to be more diverse and politically relevant, as the third wavers contended; it also needed the kind of methodological development that Floyd-Thomas advanced. On the other hand, Cannon cringed at the term "post-womanist," asking young scholars not to spurn twenty years of labor: "Those of us who have been busy doing womanist work from the moment that we enrolled in seminary believe we have built a solid womanist foundation. We officially began constructing this womanist house of wisdom in 1985, and as intellectual laborers we continue to work day in and day out so that our scholarly infrastructure is built on solid rock instead of shifting sand."[32]

Erasing the liberationist work of previous generations was a serious matter, she cautioned. If womanism seemed too stodgy and smacked too much of 1970s polemics, that could be fixed; it did not have to be stuck in the 1970s or 1980s. The womanist house of wisdom was an ongoing project: "The real challenge before us is not to become 'post-womanist' but to investigate feasible ways to actualize the definition of *womanism*." The idea of building on the wisdom of ordinary black women could not be wrong and was not outdated, she believed. It was the ultimate example of taking liberation theology seriously in a North American context.[33]

Chapter 17

Religious Pluralism as a Justice Issue

CATHOLICISM, PROTESTANTISM, JUDAISM, AND ECUMENISM

My assignment is to talk about the problems of religious pluralism, prosyletism, and ecumenism from a liberal Protestant perspective, which I am happy to do, notwithstanding that this convention is filled with people who know more about Jewish-Christian dialogue than I do. When I think about the matrix of issues addressed by this convention I think about Gregory Baum, Charles Clayton Morrison, John Courtney Murray, and a long line of liberal theologians beginning with Friedrich Schleiermacher.

"Proselytism" is an alien concept to me and to most liberal theologians. For me, the idea of a gospel imperative to proselytize Jews, Muslims, and other non-Christians belongs to a category-heap of rejected notions from the past that includes biblical inerrancy, substitutionary atonement, and Christian supersessionism. But liberalism developed differently in the Protestant and Catholic traditions; a great deal of contemporary Christianity vehemently insists on the necessity of aggressive proselytism, not to mention inerrancy, satisfaction theory, and supersessionism; there are negative factors to negotiate no matter where you come from or end up; and some of the key ones are illuminated by the thinkers just named.

Gregory Baum is a renowned Catholic theologian and social ethicist who made his early mark as a liberal-leaning interpreter of Vatican II. In his early career he sought to make the Catholic Church more modern and inclusive without deconstructing Christian doctrine in the manner of liberal Protestantism. A Canadian, and for many years an Augustinian priest, his personal journey to a North American context was dramatic and unusual, but his subsequent theological pilgrimage was representative for many of his generation.

Baum was born in Berlin, Germany, in 1923 to a secular Jewish family. His parents were thoroughly assimilated in the manner of the German bourgeoisie, believing in the cultural ideals of urbanity and refinement, admiring Goethe above all others, and taking no interest in religion. To the extent that they thought about such things, they considered themselves nominal Protestants. As an adolescent Baum witnessed the destruction of their world in Nazi Germany. He later recalled: "I felt that my world had gone under. The people I knew, my family and friends, had become mute. They had nothing to say. None of the inherited values shed light on the new situation. Life had lost all meaning." With the help of a British refugee organization he fled to England in 1939, just before World War II, leaving his family behind.[1]

He found work on a farm in England, but was arrested in 1940 as a German citizen and sent to Canada along with other civilian internees. For two years Baum was held in an internment camp, where he completed the requirements for a junior matriculation program sponsored by McGill University. His score on the final exam stunned him. In Germany he had been a mediocre student; at the camp he placed third. Baum told the person reading the names that there had to be a mistake; later he struggled to absorb that he had excelled. In a chaotic world, he felt rescued.[2]

Identifying himself as a nominal Protestant, he won a scholarship to McMaster University, majored in mathematics and physics, and studied Augustine. In 1946 he became a Canadian citizen and joined the Catholic Church. Baum was deeply impressed by Augustine's description of the good as a miracle that transcends an ocean of refuse. That was his experience, that the good is the surprising and gratuitous sign of God's gracious presence. Intellectually and emotionally he grappled with being gifted in a senseless world. Joining the Augustinian order, which sent him to Fribourg for doctoral studies, Baum took for granted that Jesus is the only way to salvation and that there is no salvation outside the Catholic Church.

His graduate studies sowed a few doubts, but Baum's faith was challenged more deeply by a stint as a parish priest in Switzerland. If the point of being Catholic was to share the "higher life" of holiness that came with belonging to the church, how was he to make sense of the lack of difference between Catholics and non-Catholics? To Baum's surprise it didn't seem to matter whether people received the sacraments or not; in either case they had the same deficiencies, anxieties, and virtues. Holiness was apparently no less universal than sin. It occurred to Baum that believing in the superiority of one's group could be spiritually damaging: "The pretense to have access to a higher life not available elsewhere tended to make Catholics blind to the holiness present in others and, with more damaging effects, insensitive to their own failings and vices. It was difficult for Catholics to learn from others and come to self-knowledge."[3]

At the time, not coincidentally, Baum was studying the history of Christian anti-Semitism. It disturbed him that Catholic scholars took little interest in the subject; for Baum the issue was personal. Some of his relatives and family friends had perished in the Holocaust, and by the laws of Nuremberg he was Jewish. That hadn't stopped him from preaching that God chose the Gentiles over the Jews. With little self-consciousness and no hesitation, Baum repeated stock clichés about God's preference for the younger Abel, Isaac, Jacob, and Gentiles over the older Cain, Esau, Ishmael, and Jews. His background as a designated "other" made him sensitive to the treatment of others, but only slightly; the church's supersessionism was his own. For him the Christian mistreatment of Jews was a personal issue; on the other hand, he didn't think about it very much. Later he explained: "Though I come from a Jewish family, I had never reflected on this topic. I have no childhood memory of Jewish religion . . . To be Jewish had only a secular meaning to me."[4]

His second conversion was prompted by an invitation to lecture on the relationship between the Catholic Church and the Jewish people. Baum did a bit of reading, recycled his usual clichés, and came across Jules Isaac's eloquent critique of Christian anti-Semitism, *Jésus et Israel*. Years later he recalled: "The book shattered me." Isaac attributed the church's anti-Semitism to a constitutively Christian prejudice. Baum, repelled at discovering the anti-Jewish bigotry of numerous church fathers, questioned whether Isaac was right to accuse the New Testament of anti-Semitism. Although he lacked the training for biblical scholarship, could find no biblical scholars who addressed the question, and needed to finish his dissertation on Catholic ecumenism, Baum couldn't wait to find the answer. He spent the last two years of his doctoral program pursuing it. Later he acknowledged that if his answer had been yes, he could not have remained a Christian.[5]

His book, *The Jews and the Gospel* (1961), gave a negative answer; in a subsequent edition, Baum titled the book *Is the New Testament Anti-Semitic?* (1965). He argued, in both editions, that anti-Jewish prejudice was deep, prevalent, and early in Christianity but was not rooted in the New Testament or apostolic tradition. Baum explained that the New Testament contained three types of problem passages: admonitions to the Jews of Jesus' time who rejected Jesus; exhortatory and polemical utterances by Jewish-Christian writers to their fellow Jews; and denunciations of the scribes and Pharisees. The New Testament never condemned Jews or Jewish religion as a whole, he contended. All negative passages were particular in reference and purpose; passages of the second type acquired their anti-Semitic connotations only after gentile Christians recycled them as repudiations of Jewish religion; and condemnations of the third type applied to all forms of bad religion, not merely Jewish legalism.[6]

Baum allowed that the final redaction of the gospels showed signs of a struggle between the synagogue and apostolic church, but he insisted that "no degradation of the Jewish people, no unjust accusation, no malevolent prophecy is ever suggested or implied." Matthew and John, being Jewish Christians, did not denigrate Jews as "a castaway people to be despised," a notion existing only in the heads of later readers. The early church was too Jewish and its scripture too inspired by the Holy Spirit to have been anti-Jewish. By contrast, St. John Chrysostom and St. Ambrose were violently anti-Jewish. They cursed Jews as a class and Jewish religion as a whole, called Jews the enemies of Christ, and read their own prejudices into the New Testament. Baum admonished that Christian anti-Judaism was a terrible thing; besides its oppressive impact on Jews, it prevented Christians from comprehending their own scripture and faith: "We have been unjust to the Jews in our thought. We have removed the Jews from the origins of Christianity; they have become for us its opponents. Jesus is no longer a Jew; he is simply man, universal, belonging to no people . . . In our imagination Judas is more Jewish than Mary, Caiphas more Jewish than Peter, the spiteful crowd more Jewish than the daughters of Jerusalem weeping for Christ."[7]

Baum defended the gospel against the charge of anti-Jewish bias, the Jewish people from centuries of Christian denigration, and the Catholic doctrine of the church. In his telling, the Catholic Church was the true home of Israel. The church could not be anti-Jewish were it true to itself, he argued. Moreover, Jews did not forsake their Jewish vocation when they became members of the church, and they did not deserve to be treated as deserters. Baum urged that Catholicism was "built upon the Israel of the spirit," the Jews that accepted Jesus. A faithful Jew could not be a stranger in the church after joining it; that was a spiritual impossibility. Baum wasn't sure what defined a Jew, since Jews were not a race, belonged to many nations, lacked a common language or culture, and were not bound by religion. He knew only that Christianity was inherently Jewish, Jews could be Christians without ceasing to be Jews, and Jews were bound together by a common memory and destiny.[8]

To Baum, the ecumenical movement was the key to a better religious future, especially Catholic-Protestant and Christian-Jewish dialogue. Though he was still a religious exclusivist, and also because of it, he committed himself to overcoming exclusivism. As a youth, and at McMaster, most of his friends had been Protestants. Baum never shared his Catholic friends' feeling that Protestantism was alien. He hated that Catholics and Protestants routinely insulted each other, and he lamented that his church lagged far behind Protestantism in accepting modern science and culture. To him it was obvious that the Catholic Church had much to learn from Protestant thought, a conviction that set him on a modernizing path.[9]

It gnawed at Baum that liberalism, not the church, led the way in condemning anti-Semitism; meanwhile the church condemned liberalism, abetted anti-Semitism, and proclaimed its own righteousness. By the late 1950s Baum seriously doubted that he could remain a Catholic. How could he take the anti-modernist oath after he learned from modern liberalism to value intellectual freedom and the critical spirit? In that mood, he read Karl Rahner, whose theology kept him in the Catholic Church. For Baum, the crucial thing was Rahner's double affirmation of the church's unique spiritual authority and the mystery of divine grace in every human being. Baum rejected liberal theology, because it negated the unique authority of the church; his ideal was to be like Rahner—orthodox and radical at the same time.[10]

His first book was his doctoral thesis, "That They May Be One," which he published in 1958. Baum argued that the Catholic Church is the earthly body and one true church of Jesus Christ, and there is such a thing as separated membership. Many Eastern Orthodox and Protestant Christians were separated in good faith from the true church, he judged. Pius X and Pius XII described them as "separated brethren"; Baum stressed that separated brethren could not be Christian sisters and brothers and at the same time be heretics. If they were Christian sisters and brothers, their faith was saving. The true church included dissident Christians who did not count themselves as belonging to it. Baum wanted the Catholic Church to say it explicitly, not merely imply it.[11]

The book version of Baum's dissertation was fortunately timed, making him a player in ecumenical circles and winning a papal appointment to the Secretariat for Promoting Christian Unity, a new Vatican office that played a key role at Vatican II. In 1959 he began his teaching career at St. Michael's College, University of Toronto; three years later, shortly before Vatican II, Baum wrestled with the question whether ecumenism and proselytism were compatible. There was only one legitimate starting point for a Catholic on this question, he asserted. If the Catholic Church was the only true church and way to salvation, the apostolate of conversion was not negotiable. It was axiomatic that Protestants and other non-Catholics had to be targeted for conversion.[12]

Baum admonished that this was where liberal Protestantism had lost its mind. At the time his knowledge base in this area was rather thin, but he didn't need to be an expert on Protestant theology to know how the story turned out. Liberal Protestantism had liberalized to the point of relinquishing any faith that anybody really needed. It was merely a religious option for people who liked its kind of cafeteria religion. Though on most points Baum felt closer to liberal Protestants than to fundamentalist or conservative evangelical Protestants, on the most important point there was no comparison. At least conservative Protestants respected their faith enough to convert others to it. Baum shook his head at the idea of a "liberal theology." How could you have a Christian theology with no external authority and no missionary impulse?

That was, and is, a serious question, though the liberal backstory was more important than Baum thought at the time. The idea of a liberal approach to Christianity is, at root, a simple one and, I believe, a necessary one. In essence it is the idea of a theology based on reason and experience, not external authority, which offers a third way between orthodox authority religion and secular disbelief. There are many varieties of liberal theology, but these two factors define the category: the authority principle and the principle of integrative mediation. Liberal theology conceives the meaning of religious faith in the light of modern knowledge and ethical values. It is reformist in spirit and substance; it is deeply shaped by modern science, humanism, and historical criticism; and in its Christian expression it is committed to making Christianity credible and socially relevant. In liberal theology the Bible remains an authority for faith, but its authority operates within Christian experience, not as an outside force that establishes or compels belief.

There were five dominant schools of liberal theology in its formative century, all pioneered by Germans. Immanuel Kant located religious truth in the moral claims of practical reason. G. W. F. Hegel formulated a dialectical system of metaphysical idealism inspired by the doctrines of the Incarnation, Trinity, and Holy Spirit. Friedrich Schleiermacher located the essence of religion in spiritual "feeling" or intuition. Albrecht Ritschl interpreted Christianity as a socio-historical movement with a distinct ethical-religious character. Ernst Troeltsch launched a de-Christianized form of Ritschlian historicism that became the history-of-religions school.

All these approaches inspired early forms of inter-religious dialogue or comparative theology, but none of them got far on that project, as the strength of each approach was geared to something else. Kantian theologies defended religion as the ground of moral truth. Hegelian theologies treated Christianity as a wellspring of images requiring metaphysical reinterpretation. Schleiermacherian experientialism had the richest legacy but was limited by its subjectivism and a-historicism. Ritschlian historicism swept the field in the late nineteenth and early twentieth centuries, but it was too specifically Christian to look beyond Christianity. The history-of-religions school flourished as a method but gradually gave up its claim to a theological perspective.

Most of these theologies shared the Enlightenment prejudice against the ostensible narrowness and provincialism of Jewish faith. Ritschl was an exception, but most of the leading Ritschlians were not. A few liberals, usually combining Schleiermacher with some kind of historicism, made creative contributions to a theology of inter-religious dialogue; Rudolf Otto and Wilhelm Bousset were the major pioneers.[13]

But liberal theology as a whole, especially in the United States, did not give high priority to engaging other religions. The American tradition of modern liberal theology is nearly as old as the German one, and in the nineteenth century it featured some distinguished thinkers: William Ellery Channing, Theodore Parker, Horace Bushnell, Washington Gladden, Theodore Munger, Charles Briggs, and Borden Parker Bowne. Of this group, only Parker imagined a theology of world religions, and his was merely another name for his radical Unitarianism, which he called "Absolute Religion." Nineteenth-century liberals rejected the doctrines of double predestination, substitutionary atonement, and biblical inerrancy. They accepted biblical criticism, Darwinian evolution, and an idea of God as the personal and eternal Spirit of love. Some were believers in universal salvation, and others said they wanted to believe it but weren't sure. Above all, liberal theologians denied that religious arguments should be settled by appeals to an infallible text or ecclesial authority.[14]

In the early twentieth century a few American liberals tried to conduct inter-religious theology in something like Rudolf Otto's spirit. James Pratt was an early proponent; Bernard Meland was a later one. But most American liberals were too fixated on their own world to look far beyond it. Their anxieties, cultural privileges, and custodial duties were absorbing. Though they spoke a self-confident language of optimism and cultural progress, most liberals were terribly anxious about the fate of religion in a secularizing world. They believed that most religions had no future, because modernity obliterated religion wherever it spread. The only kind of religion that had any chance of surviving the onslaught of Enlightenment rationalism, historical criticism, scientific empiricism, capitalism, and modern technology was one that made its peace with modernity. To the liberal Protestants, only liberal Protestantism had a good chance of accomplishing that. Liberal forms of Jewish and Catholic theology were at least conceivable, but not likely to succeed, and no other religion had any chance. Borden Parker Bowne, writing in 1896, put it plainly, assuring that non-Christian religions had no future worth discussing: "As soon as they come into contact with our Western thought, science, and individualism, it becomes apparent that their day is done." Inter-religious dialogue was a waste of time if modernity was obliterating religion; the real challenge was to make Christianity modern and thus avert the fate of other religions.[15]

Logically and historically, liberal theology was a fusion of Protestant evangelicalism and Enlightenment rationalism and humanism. From its Enlightenment heritage, liberal theology emphasized the authority of modern knowledge, affirmed the continuity between reason and revelation, championed the values of humanistic individualism and democracy, and was usually too Kantian or empiricist to make metaphysical claims. From its evangelical heritage, it affirmed a personal transcendent God, the authority of Christian experience, the divinity of Christ, the need of personal redemption, and the importance of Christian missions.

The figures that made liberal Christianity compelling to millions were evangelical liberals who held together both heritages. In the nineteenth century the towering example was Henry Ward Beecher; in the twentieth century it was Harry Emerson Fosdick. To the evangelical liberals, there was no reason to choose between being modern and gospel-centered, for the whole idea of liberal theology was to hold these things together.[16]

American liberal theology had schools of thought just like its German counterpart, but nearly all American liberals contended that spirit or personality holds primacy over the things of sense.[17] Fosdick, for example, preached every week at Riverside Church that Christianity is fundamentally about the care and flourishing of personality. He was not a religious philosopher; Fosdick could not have taught a seminar on metaphysical idealism, but his sermons conveyed a popular version of it to millions. He taught that Christianity is the best major religion in the world and that Buddhism is the worst, because good religion is about the flourishing of personality. The divine is present wherever goodness, beauty, truth, and love exist. Human beings are divine to the extent that they embody and mobilize these qualities. Jesus was uniquely divine because he embodied these qualities fully. To Fosdick, divinity was the perfection of immanent love that every person is capable of mobilizing. Sin was the victory of bad social influences and bodily impulses over the instincts of a higher self. Good religion brought people to an awareness of their better nature and mobilized their capacity to live out of it.[18]

Almost every liberal theologian of the nineteenth and early twentieth centuries expounded a version of this Victorian gospel about the triumph of spirit over nature as mediated by the example of Jesus. Liberals were evangelical in spreading this gospel, but they assured that you could get it to some degree in every religion.

I am eager to get to pluralism, but first I need to say something about what happened to liberal theology in the 1930s and 1940s. In Europe, World War I obliterated the moral idealism and cultural optimism that fueled liberal theology. The United States, however, experienced World War I very differently, and thus the war did not destroy liberal idealism there. It took the Great Depression to do that. By 1932 a new generation of American theologians began to say that liberal Christianity was not a good idea.

Reinhold Niebuhr was the leading debunker. Repeatedly he bewailed that his group equated Christian faith with utter nonsense about believing in progress and ideals. Liberal Christians actually believed that the world could be saved by reason and goodwill, Niebuhr stressed. To him that was pathetic. To make any sense in the 1930s, American Protestantism had to move sharply to the left politically—he was a radical Marxist at the time—and considerably to the right theologically, though he was vague about what that meant.[19]

Niebuhr was not really anti-liberal, even as he scorned liberal idealism and rationalism. But he blasted liberal theologians, who struggled to keep their tradition alive. They were a stubborn bunch—Fosdick, Brightman, Benjamin Mays, Georgia Harkness, James Luther Adams, George Buttrick, Norman Pittenger, Bernard Meland, Nels Ferre. They identified with Fosdick's self-description; for them it was either liberal religion or no religion at all. Whatever its problems, they believed in the liberal faith of reasonableness, openness, modernity, and the social gospel.

The old liberals understood that their language of progress and idealism seemed like sentimental mush in the Depression era of collapsing economies and political turmoil. But the "mystery X" dialecticism of Karl Barth and neo-orthodoxy was not an option for them. Liberal theology, whatever its problems, was still the only option that held together reason and faith. It had the right project, even if it did not have all the answers. If liberalism was too deferential to modern culture, it had to be more critical. If the social gospel was too idealistic and sentimental, maybe it needed a dose of realism. If liberal theology read too much of its middle-class moralism into the gospel, that could be fixed. The mid-century liberals were willing to make adjustments of that kind, but they would not disown liberalism because, to them, there was no better place to go.

Most of them never bought the apocalyptic Jesus of German scholarship, although for decades they were ridiculed for holding out. Many of them proudly asserted that liberal Protestantism was the best religion in the world, but all of them assured that you didn't have to be one to be loved and accepted by God. Most important to the liberals was to be able to follow Jesus and worship God as the divine Spirit of love without having to believe any particular thing on the basis of authority. Some alternative to orthodox over-belief and secular unbelief was still needed, even if liberalism required better answers.

That was the attitude of the *Christian Century* magazine in the mid-twentieth century, when Martin Marty joined the magazine as an editor. Liberal Protestantism was bruised by criticism but zealous in guarding its role as the custodian of America's spiritual culture. For decades liberal Protestants had sought to "Christianize" American society by projecting their social and religious ideals onto all Americans without apology. In 1908 Charles Clayton Morrison founded the *Christian Century* magazine, giving it a name that reflected the ambitions of the social gospel. Nearly half a century later, when Marty joined the magazine, its editors were beginning to accept that religious diversity was inevitable in the United States. But they made no pretense of believing that cultural pluralism was a good thing.

The term "pluralism" had very little currency in American English before the mid-twentieth century. It played a small role in philosophical debates about monism and the plurality of worlds, as in William James's book *A Pluralistic Universe*. In the 1920s Jewish philosopher Horace Kallen pioneered the modern use of the word by speaking of "cultural pluralism." In his usage it referred to the preservation of multiple cultural heritages within a single republic featuring civil interactions between groups. By the early 1950s the *Christian Century* was one of the first journals to use the word "pluralism" in this sense, which it stridently opposed. Pluralism was a "national menace," the magazine contended. If the American experiment had been a culturally pluralistic enterprise, it would have failed disastrously. America was able to build a modern, liberal democratic republic featuring religious freedom because it was founded and built by Northern European Protestants. Culturally speaking, America worked only as a Protestant project informed by Enlightenment ideals, to which immigrant newcomers were welcome to assimilate.[20]

If you talk to Martin Marty about this today, he will caution that his bosses were not bigots and they saw no contradiction between their liberalism and their cultural/religious chauvinism. They played a leading role in urging white Protestants to support racial integration and the Civil Rights movement. They were advocates of Jewish-Christian dialogue, but they were very clear about wanting blacks and Jews to assimilate to white Protestant America. They assumed that the only kind of pluralism worth having assimilated outsiders into white liberal Protestant ways. The *Christian Century* belabored this theme in the 1950s, stressing the negative: in the name of protecting the rights of various minorities, American lawmakers were infringing on the right of a Protestant majority to maintain a common American faith.[21]

Here the contrast between Morrison and the American Jesuit theologian John Courtney Murray is illuminating. Morrison was a quintessential social gospel progressive. He believed in social and economic democracy; he was passionately antiwar; he was a fervent ecumenist; and he was theologically liberal. Yet, for all that, he was a Protestant chauvinist bordering on bigotry, while Murray, who was very conservative on almost everything, was a rebel on one hugely important thing, which he got right—that religious pluralism is a justice issue, and an enormously significant one.[22]

In 1948 Morrison wrote a manifesto titled *Can Protestantism Win America?* In his usage, "Protestantism" meant liberal ecumenical Protestantism. Fundamentalism was too backward and reactionary to be worth more than a quick dismissal; Billy Graham was not yet famous. Morrison never imagined that conservative evangelicalism would become powerful. However, he was very worried that secularism and Catholicism were getting stronger. Atheists and Catholics had every right to vie for cultural influence, he allowed. What galled him was that liberal Protestants refused to fight or even recognize that they were in a fight for America's soul. The *Christian Century* was losing the argument, even within its own audience of liberal Protestant ministers.[23]

Morrison admonished that winning converts was the mark of any serious faith: "The missionary spirit is of its essence." But liberal Protestantism no longer had a missionary spirit or even tried to win converts. It stopped trying after the social gospel petered out. Morrison stressed that most liberal Protestants had no missionary vigor; they shunned words like "proselytism" like the plague; they liked to pretend they were not in competition with Catholicism; and they took pride in being secular, which was a self-liquidating attitude. Liberal Protestantism was too secular, ecumenical, and soaked in relativism to proselytize the masses. Within Protestantism, Morrison argued, ecumenism was a good thing; in fact, it was desperately necessary. But liberal Protestants were making ecumenism look ridiculous by asking Catholics to join it. Protestantism was about freedom and democracy, whereas Catholicism was about dogmatism and authoritarianism: "Protestantism cannot cooperate ecclesiastically with a dictatorship. It must make a clear-cut decision to accept its task of winning America to Christ without any illusion that it has a collaborator in Roman Catholicism."[24]

Morrison urged liberal Protestant leaders to stop minimizing their core beliefs in the hope of gaining ecumenical relationships with Catholics. That was a losing strategy. It would not modernize Catholicism, and it would never win America. Moreover, the greatest threat to America's soul was its ascending secularism. Protestantism was not losing members to the Catholic Church, but it was losing multitudes to the culture of disbelief. There was a bitter irony here, which Morrison stressed. The Protestant mainline had tried valiantly to accommodate modern culture, only to be snubbed by it. He declared: "The assumption that modern culture has been moving toward a Christian goal has been the undoing of Protestantism. It has weakened its will and confused its faith. Too long has Protestantism stood in awe of modern culture. Its sense of mission has been obfuscated by the messianic pretensions of science, by the prestige of public education, and by the benefits which technology and an ever enlarging state paternalism were conferring upon the people."[25]

That was in 1948, when mainline Protestants were building churches across the landscape and setting attendance records that would climb for another decade. By most appearances Protestantism was doing very well, but Morrison was not impressed. He was an old social gospeler who remembered what it felt like to dream of a good society, a Christian America, a cooperative commonwealth. Postwar America, oozing superficial religiosity, didn't come close. It had no spiritual depth and no passion for social justice. Moreover, the Protestant churches were disadvantaged from lacking a competitive history. They had never had to "win" America, since they assumed that America was culturally Protestant.

Now the Protestant churches were paying the price for their privileges and secularism. Morrison urged that they had to give up their inherited ease and their liberal qualms about converting people; otherwise they would sink into irrelevance. To join the struggle for America's soul, modern Protestantism had to renounce its denial that it competed to win anything. It had to become reacquainted with the language of evangelism, conversion, and victory. In Morrison's vision, the resurgent Protestantism that was needed would be militant, united, and theologically purified. It would get rid of all the mainline denominations, form an ecumenical superchurch, and confess only that Christ is Lord. The sovereign authority of Christ was the only principle that could unify ecumenical Christianity. Everything else was divisive and sectarian, and had to go.[26]

Can Protestantism Win America? was an echo from a lost world, written during Morrison's last year at the *Christian Century*. A few years later the term "WASP" gained currency in American society, as did the term "mainline Protestantism." Both were markers of a changing cultural consciousness. The first term reflected the startling, unsettling idea that white Anglo-Saxon Protestants constituted one American ethnic group among others. The second term registered that there were other kinds of Protestantism worth mentioning. With this shift in consciousness, Morrison's dream of a victorious "Protestantism" became an object of ridicule. The bland unconsciousness of hegemonic white Protestant Americanism was no longer possible.

John Courtney Murray was a keen observer of this development. A member of the New York Province of the Society of Jesus, Murray taught at Woodstock College in Maryland from 1937 until his death in 1967. In his early career he believed that the chasm between Protestantism and Catholicism was so deep and wide that dialogue between them was pointless. Protestantism had lost or rejected so much of classical Christianity that there was no basis even for analogical discussion. At the time Murray had similar feelings about the Anglo-American tradition as a whole and the fate of Catholicism within it.

But, to his surprise, Murray found himself drawn to the problem of religious freedom, which led him to an unexpected standpoint and career. Instead of writing technical theology, he wrote increasingly about religious freedom, venturing into a field he called "religion and society." It helped at first that the Jesuits assigned him to run two journals, *America* and *Theological Studies*, though Murray eventually begged out of *America*. Pursuing a career he had not expected, he became the first major American Catholic theologian by rethinking the Catholic theory of religious freedom, which led him to think creatively about religious pluralism, which led him to a deeper appreciation of the Anglo-American tradition and a new model of public theology.

Murray is like Niebuhr, an enormously complex subject unto himself. I've wrestled elsewhere with the complexities; here I aim straight for the payoff. For ten years Morrison's book stuck in Murray's craw, stoking a belief that Murray was trying to give up, that the differences between Catholicism and Protestantism were incommensurable. Repeatedly Murray struggled with the deep disagreements between American Protestants, Catholics, Jews, and secularists that seemed, to him, to obviate meaningful discussions between them. Yet Murray burned at Morrison's prejudiced way of putting it; he countered that no group should have dominant cultural privileges; and he insisted that pluralism was a justice issue.[27]

Murray was sensitive to the irony of Morrison's argument that Protestantism wrongly accommodated secular culture and thus lost its spiritual and public power. Like Morrison, Murray believed that American Christianity was in a life-or-death struggle with secular disbelief. Like Morrison, Murray believed that nearly everything precious in the American experiment was at stake in the secularization of American culture.

But Murray had a contrasting strategy for holding off the tide of secular destruction. It was to make a creative response to religious pluralism. He argued that whenever Americans spoke their historic language of unalienable rights, constitutionalism, and limited government, "the Catholic joins the conversation with complete ease. It is his language. The ideas expressed are native to his own universe of discourse." The strongest hope of a new consensus was for more Catholics to join the conversation. Murray stressed that the Catholic Church spoke the universal language of moral rights and responsibilities long before the U.S. existed, and it would go on speaking it even if non-Catholic Americans settled for the thin soup of positivism, majoritarianism, and disbelief. In that case, "it would be for others, not Catholics, to ask themselves whether they still shared the consensus which first fashioned the American people into a body politic and determined the structure of its fundamental law."[28]

That sounded like special pleading to many American non-Catholics who demanded to know whether Catholics really believed in the First Amendment. Murray replied that this question seemed relevant only because misunderstanding abounded on this subject. The American Constitution was not an object of faith. It prescribed law, not dogma, containing articles of civil peace that Americans were required to observe, not articles of faith that they were required to believe.

Three groups dominated the discussion on this topic, he judged, all of which vested the Constitution with authority that compelled belief. The first group interpreted the Constitution as prescribing distinctly Protestant religious or cultural beliefs rooted in free-church Puritanism. For them the First Amendment contained articles of faith with a definite religious content. The second group, descendants of American deism and rationalism, interpreted the Constitution in terms of Enlightenment secular liberalism. For them the articles were vested only with the rationality that attached to law, not any religious meaning, and rationality was the highest value of law. The third group, the "secularizing Protestants," melded its religious faith with American secular culture, trying to bridge the differences between the Puritan and rationalist traditions. For them religion was true and relevant to the extent that it embraced the norms of modern secular culture, including its concept of freedom.[29]

Murray took no interest in adjudicating the relative historical merits of these traditions. What mattered was that all three were deeply rooted in American history, all of them viewed the Constitution as expressing a worldview or ideology, each of them contradicted the other two, and all were wrong in assuming that the Constitution called for some kind of assent. The U.S. was not some kind of church, and Americans did not have to believe in the First Amendment, Murray contended. Otherwise the Constitution became a religious test, and the republic was a fellowship of believers in free-church Protestantism or naturalistic humanism. Instead, the United States was "simply a civil community, whose unity is purely political."[30]

The U.S. was a pluralistic republic that had no business insinuating religious teaching of any kind into its law; at the same time, American democracy needed very much to take its religious pluralism more seriously. If the First Amendment was a religious test, thirty-five million American Catholics were officially dissenters. If the First Amendment meant what the secularists said, Catholics were officially denigrated. It was not enough to have a pluralistic political philosophy, Murray urged. America was overdue to make good on the acceptance of diversity implied in the Declaration of Independence. Most critical was to respect the diversity of religions. To move in that direction was to reject the usual options of watering down Protestantism, stripping religion from the public square, treating democracy as a substitute for religion, or reducing religion to values. Murray got many things wrong, in my view, and some of his claims are still up for grabs, but the crucial thing about respecting religious diversity, he got brilliantly right.

I am near the end of my time, but I cannot leave Gregory Baum where we left him. In his later career Gregory became a major liberal theologian; his fundamental theme was the gracious presence of God in all human life; and to me he is a model ecumenical theologian. When we took leave of him, in the early 1960s, Baum was still a Catholic triumphalist, which he softened by saying that Catholics, as the stronger party, needed to make a unilateral show of goodwill to advance the ecumenical movement. Greater charity from the true church would bring out a like reaction from Protestants. He liked the World Council of Churches' distinction between good-spirited "witness" to the faith and bad-spirited "proselytism." Evangelism is inherently Christian, he argued, but not the use of pressure tactics, manipulation, intimidation, or demeaning characterization. Fifty years later that remains a useful distinction. I take for granted the categorical difference between exuberantly witnessing to one's faith and forcing it on others.[31]

But Baum went on to expound the fundamental theme that he took from Karl Rahner and Maurice Blondel, that the divine mystery of redemption is operative everywhere in human life. Under Rahner's influence, Vatican II spoke of the possible salvific status of non-Christian religions, reasoning that if divine grace is prevenient everywhere, God must be active in other religions and movements. Baum heralded this statement for many years, but gradually he also relativized his Catholic identity. The gospel is not an extrinsic piece of knowledge, something added to human life from without, he stressed. Rather, the gospel makes explicit the divine self-communication that is offered universally. Christian faith is a new consciousness, the specification of the gracious and saving divine mystery that takes place everywhere at all times.[32]

The free choices of a self are co-constitutive of the self's being. By making choices, one co-determines the person that one becomes. Each person needs others to become oneself; every person comes to be through dialogue and communion with others; God is revealed in the interpersonal process of self-creation.

Baum's thinking and career went through three stages. Though he remained deeply involved in ecumenical affairs, serving for decades as editor of *The Ecumenist*, by the late 1960s he began to weary of committee ecumenism. He had little patience for give and take on small points of doctrine, and he disliked the self-perpetuating professionalism of the dialogue enterprise. His second stage was a therapeutic turn, which lasted only a few years, but through which he became more attentive to the psychodynamics of social interaction. Then he took a social-ethical turn in the 1970s, writing his many books on social theory, liberation theology, and politics.[33]

The later Baum moved to the left theologically and politically, nowhere more significantly than in his rethinking about Judaism and Christianity. Baum credited Vatican II for recognizing that Jews continue to be God's chosen people. But the council did not repudiate supersessionism nor acknowledge the anti-Jewish aspects of New Testament Christianity. By 1974, influenced by Rosemary Ruether's critique of Christian anti-Semitism, Baum no longer believed that anti-Judaism was late and peripheral in Christianity. Anti-Jewish trends were "woven into the core" of the Christian message, he judged. Paul and the gospel writers did not recognize Jewish religion as a way of grace, and, until Vatican II, neither did the Catholic Church: "What Paul and the entire Christian tradition taught is unmistakably negative: the religion of Israel is now superseded, the Torah abrogated, the promises fulfilled in the Christian Church, the Jews struck with blindness, and whatever remains of the election to Israel rests as a burden upon them in the present age."[34]

It was nice that Vatican II ended the church's litany of insults against Judaism, but the problem of Christian anti-Judaism was deeper than bad

manners. Baum urged that the problem was the supersessionist exclusivism of Christian theology. Christianity was long overdue to repudiate its
conceit that the Christian covenant with God supersedes the Jewish covenant: "As long as the Christian church regards itself as the successor of
Israel, as the new people of God substituted in the place of the old, and
as long as the Church proclaims Jesus as the one mediator without whom
there is no salvation, no theological space is left for other religions, and,
in particular, no theological validity is left for Jewish religion."[35]

Ruether described the early church's repudiation of the synagogal interpretation of scripture as the "left hand of Christology." To first-century
Jews, the messianic promises remained to be fulfilled. To the early Christians, the promises were fulfilled in the kingdom inaugurated by Jesus.
Christology was born in the church's insistence that only it, not the synagogue, rightly interpreted the Jewish scriptures. Following Ruether, Baum
traced the origin of Christian anti-Semitism to this claim that the synagogue turned away from its own scripture.[36]

Christianity has had more than its share of destructive dualisms, but the
one between the believing Church and the blind Synagogue has yielded a
distinctly destructive legacy. The later Baum must have winced at seeing it
in his own well-meaning early writings on the Israel of the spirit and the
Israel of the flesh. To take seriously the ethical and spiritual imperative
of undoing this legacy is to take on the very agenda of the centers represented here today: learning from Jewish commentary and scriptural interpretation, correcting the New Testament's stereotypes of the Pharisees
and Torah, perceiving the rabbinic aspects and contexts of the teaching
of Jesus and Paul, teaching the history of Christian persecution of Jews,
conducting inter-religious dialogues among all faiths, supporting the widest possible ecumenism, and disavowing supersessionist theology without
denying the claim of the gospel to religious truth.

My colleague at Union Seminary, Mary Boys, is an important contribu-
tor to this work; I am merely an observer. I am indebted to, and deeply
grateful for, the many centers represented here today for carrying on this
indispensable work, and I am equally grateful to have shared your company today.

Chapter 18

The Obama Phenomenon and Presidency

"Hope or Hype?"

The Obama phenomenon is hurtling past the best analogies that we have for it. Three years ago Obama shot into the national political scene with a sensational speech at the Democratic Party Convention. Two years ago he joined the U.S. Senate as its only African American member. A year ago he was still admonishing admirers to give him time to accomplish something before talking up an Obama presidency. Today he is running for president because he has generated too much excitement to wait for another political season.

In some respects, the echoes of Robert Kennedy in 1968 are strong. No candidate has stirred such an intense reaction on the campaign trail since Kennedy, who might have won the White House had he not been assassinated. Like Obama, Kennedy ran against a controversial war and tapped the repressed hope and idealism of millions in a presidential campaign that he had not expected to wage. But Bobby Kennedy was already a totem of national memory and feeling when he ran for president. Most Americans remembered him as a former U.S. attorney general, many regarded him as the successor to the tragically interrupted Kennedy presidency, some hoped that he stood for something even better, and every American knew him as the brother of a martyred president.

In other respects, the Obama phenomenon is an echo of the political boon for Colin Powell that peaked in 1995. Powell might well have won the presidency had his wife Alma not declared that he would have to campaign as a divorcé; Alma Powell feared the part of white America that would not stand for a black president. Colin Powell's memoir, *My American Journey*, sold nearly three million copies while he contemplated a run for the presidency; today Obama is a beneficiary of the fact that many Americans got used to imagining a black president more than a decade ago.[1]

But Powell, like Kennedy, had an ample public grooming before he seemed presidential. Americans did not need to read his memoir to learn that he had been President Reagan's National Security Advisor and served as chair of the Joint Chiefs of Staff during George H. W. Bush's presidency. By the end of the Bush 41 administration Powell was the most admired figure in the nation, a stature that has become hard to remember after his fateful role in the Bush 43 administration.

Barack Obama is acutely aware that he rocketed into national politics with a swiftness and apparent ease that outstrips even these analogies. His book, *The Audacity of Hope*, is charmingly candid on the matter of swiftness and only slightly defensive on the matter of ease. He points out, echoing the protests of his 2004 campaign staff, that he wasn't just lucky; he worked hard to get elected and had an appealing message. On the other hand, he acknowledges, it would be pointless to deny "my almost spooky good fortune."[2]

Instead of getting hammered with negative ads like other candidates, Obama found himself in a seven-way Democratic primary campaign that produced not a single negative ad. In the final weeks of the primary campaign his opponent flamed out in a divorce scandal. A few weeks later the same thing happened to his Republican opponent. Then John Kerry handed him a convention keynote slot. Then the Illinois Republicans inexplicably selected Alan Keyes, an eccentric ideologue, to run against him. By the time that Obama took office the following January he had to deal with hyperbolic media coverage treating him as the savior of politics while insiders treated him, in his telling, as "an outlier, a freak . . . I felt like the rookie who shows up after the game, his uniform spotless, eager to play, even as his mud-splattered teammates tend to their wounds."[3]

On the day that he moved into his Senate office a reporter asked him to assess his place in history; Obama noted that he had yet to cast a vote. For months afterward he played the story for laughs in his speeches, and does so again in *The Audacity of Hope*. The book stakes out a pragmatic middle ground between edgy, risky, or exaggerated positions that he does not hold, and it deflates the impression that he has no flaws. Poking gentle fun at himself repeatedly, Obama admits to political "restlessness," enjoying private jets, preferring Dijon mustard, being grumpy in the morning, and fretting that he might have had chicken crumbs on his face when he met Laura Bush. He confesses that for years he overtaxed the patience and support of his wife Michelle in pursuit of political success. He admits that in the summer of 2003 he doubted whether he had been right to oppose the invasion of Iraq. He acknowledges that his speaking style "can be rambling, hesitant, and overly verbose." But Obama's endearing lightheartedness about himself is, of course, another virtue, and as he continues to draw enormous crowds, the media hyperbole about him begins to seem not so exaggerated.[4]

The Audacity of Hope was written before he knew it would be a presidential campaign book, which may account for its chief defect as one. Because Obama shot into political prominence so quickly, and because his background is more complicated and exotic than that of most U.S. politicians, his campaign book needed to lay out the gist of his life story in an early chapter. That doesn't happen. If you don't know the story from his previous book, *Dreams from My Father* (1995), or from an article like this one, you will have a difficult time piecing it together from asides scattered throughout the new book.

So for those who don't know the story: Barack Hussein Obama was born in Honolulu, Hawaii, in 1961 to a Kansas-born mother, Ann Dunham, and a Kenyan-born father, Barack Hussein Obama, both of whom were students at the East-West Center at the University of Hawaii. When Obama was two years old his parents separated and later divorced. His father completed a doctorate in economics at Harvard and returned to Kenya; his mother married an Indonesian foreign student and moved to Jakarta, Indonesia, in 1967; years later she earned a doctorate in anthropology; in 1982 his father died in a car accident. For five years, Obama lived with his mother and stepfather in Jakarta, where he attended Catholic and Muslim schools. In 1972 he returned to Hawaii to live with his maternal grandparents, where he graduated from high school in 1979.[5]

In *Dreams from My Father* he recounted that in early life he barely noticed that his mother and maternal grandparents were white, his absent father in the photographs was black, he was biracial, and his extended family was multiracial. As a teenager he found all of it perplexing and unsettling, especially his uncertain identity. Obama struggled to define his racial and cultural selfhood, or at least determine the significance of doing so; sometimes he used alcohol and drugs to help him not think about it.

For two years he studied at Occidental College; in 1981 he transferred to Columbia University, where he earned a degree in political science, specializing in international relations; for three years after college he worked as a community organizer in Chicago, helping churches organize job training programs in poor neighborhoods. The latter experience was formative for him, giving rise to his sustained interest in urban policy, early childhood education, and urban cultural initiatives. It was also formative because he decided that he didn't want to live without faith and a spiritual community.

Obama's father was an atheist from a Muslim background. His maternal grandparents dropped evangelical Protestantism for skeptical unbelief, just as they subsequently dropped Kansas for Hawaii. His mother mixed personal secularism with an anthropologist's interest in comparative religion as a cultural phenomenon. With typical grace Obama expresses tender respect for his parents and grandparents while noting gratefully that he took a different path. He wanted to be a Christian before he became convinced that doing so with integrity would be possible for him. Obama questioned whether joining a church would require him to suspend his critical reason or temper his passion for social justice. Worshipping at Trinity United Church of Christ, he listened to Jeremiah Wright Jr.'s sermons and became friends with Wright, finding assurance on both questions. Describing his baptism, he writes: "It came about as a choice and not an epiphany; the questions I had did not magically disappear. But kneeling beneath that cross on the South Side of Chicago, I felt God's spirit beckoning me. I submitted myself to His will, and dedicated myself to discovering His truth."[6]

In 1988 he enrolled at Harvard Law School, where he flourished. Both of Obama's memoirs barely mention his law school experience, yet it was there that he acquired his radiant self-confidence and diplomatic skills. At the time, the law school's student body was sharply divided along ideological lines. Bitter fights over affirmative action, diversity, critical race theory, liberalism, feminism, and getting published in the *Harvard Law Review* were commonplace. Law School professor Derrick Bell resigned dramatically from the faculty as a protest against the school's lack of faculty diversity.

In this environment, Obama became the first African American in the 104-year history of the *Harvard Law Review* to be elected to its presidency. Then as now, he showed a gift for expressing a basically liberal perspective in a sunny, respectful, thoughtful, congenial manner that won the trust and respect of others from a variety of perspectives. Avoiding extreme positions and, as much as possible, volatile subjects, he stressed the non-political necessity of the virtues and was known for his seemingly tireless capacity to search for common ground. At the same time, when the issue of faculty diversity roiled the law school, Obama sided clearly with diversity advocates, lauding Bell as a latter-day Rosa Parks.

After graduating from Harvard in 1991 he returned to Chicago, directed a voter registration drive, practiced civil rights law, served in the Illinois state senate, and for eleven years taught at the University of Chicago Law School, where he excelled at classroom performance and case analysis.

The Audacity of Hope has many words in favor of audacity and transformation, though its policy sections are very cautious. The only risky position in Obama's portfolio is his opposition to the Iraq War, which was risky indeed when he committed himself to it in October 2002. Speaking to a crowd at Chicago's Federal Plaza, he declared that he could not support "a dumb war, a rash war, a war based not on reason but on passion; not on principle but on politics." However, Obama was far from a national figure at the time, and he admits that he had doubts afterward about stepping out so far. When challenged for evidence that he can take a sizable political risk, he points to his opposition to the war.[7]

Otherwise he holds carefully to liberal-leaning middle ground. The presidents that he admires most are Franklin Roosevelt and John Kennedy, he says, because they represented "transformative politics." By that standard, Obama needs to decide what he is for that compares to the New Deal or even the Peace Corps. He will not lead the fight for single payer health coverage or scaling back the U.S. military empire; at the moment he is deciding whether he can afford even to advocate a gas tax. Obama thinks that a health care solution must be voluntary and that military spending must be increased, notwithstanding that, as he notes, the U.S. is currently spending more on defense than the next thirty nations combined.

He understands that his appeal is mostly personal. Though Obama is a liberal Democrat, he says that too many liberal Democrats are stuck in "the old-time religion, defending every New Deal and Great Society program from Republican encroachment, achieving ratings of 100 percent from the liberal interest groups." Though he is a lawyer, he says there are too many of them in Congress. Most people in Washington are either law-yers or political operatives, he observes—professions focused on winning, not solving problems. America needs politicians of goodwill who are de-voted to solving the problems of Americans as a whole. And although he knows that some white Americans still harbor hostility toward blacks, "I don't want to confer on such bigotry a power it no longer possesses."[8]

The latter refusal is a key to the surging crowds that greet him wherever he speaks. Thus far, Obama has generated intense excitement among vast crowds of white listeners and a decidedly more reserved, though support-ive, response from African Americans. *Time* magazine writer Joe Klein asked him about his unusual appeal to college-educated white voters. Were white Americans desperate for validation from prominent blacks like Oprah Winfrey, Tiger Woods, and him? Did his success show the im-portance of not stoking the racial guilt of whites? Before Klein could get the words out, Obama answered: "There's a core decency to the American people that doesn't get enough attention. Figures like Oprah, Tiger, and Michael Jordan give people a shortcut to express their better instincts. You can be cynical about this. You can say, 'It's easy to love Oprah. It's harder to embrace the idea of putting more resources for young black men—some of whom aren't so lovable.' But I don't feel that way. I think it's healthy, a good instinct. I just don't want it to stop with Oprah. I'd rather say, 'If you feel good about me, there's a whole lot of young men out there who could be me if given the chance.'"[9]

In *The Audacity of Hope* he puts it more politically, recalling a former Illinois state senate colleague who was prone to charge racism when peo-ple voted the wrong way. A white liberal colleague remarked to Obama: "You know what the problem is with John? Whenever I hear him, he makes me feel more white." Obama, characteristically, starts with a one-handed defense of his former black colleague, noting the difficulty of finding the exact tone that is angry enough but not too angry. Then he switches to the other hand: "Still, my white colleague's comment was in-structive. Rightly or wrongly, white guilt has largely exhausted itself in America; even the most fair-minded of whites, those who would genu-inely like to see racial inequality ended and poverty relieved, tend to push back against suggestions of racial victimization—or race-specific claims based on the history of race discrimination in this country."[10]

"Rightly or wrongly" is a telling caveat. Obama was a civil rights lawyer who specialized in civil rights law as a law professor. He under-stands very well that racial prejudice and white supremacism are deeply entrenched in our society; otherwise we would not need civil rights law-yers to fight discrimination cases against corporations, trade unions, and the government. The problem is not merely racial bias but a structure of power based on privilege that prizes white people and their culture above people of color.

Obama would never say that in public. However, in his own way he makes the point that the problem is entrenched in white attitudes and social structures. The political Right has caused some of the "push back" against racial justice, he observes. More importantly, the cause is losing for a larger reason, the "simple self-interest" of most white Americans, who, he writes, "figure that they haven't engaged in discrimination them-selves and have plenty of their own problems to worry about."[11]

That makes it imperative for those who care about racial justice to talk about the common good, not about racial "us" and "them," he argues. No measure aimed at helping racial minorities will get more than short-term support from whites, and no measure bearing high costs for whites will be supported for any period of time. Although Obama supports affirmative action, he prefers to talk about universal programs that "disproportion-ately help minorities," such as creating better schools, jobs that pay, and access to health care. He assures that he understands the fears of the civil rights establishment. According to the "old" thinking, he observes, racial discrimination has to stay on the front burner; otherwise, "white America will be let off the hook and hard-fought gains may be reversed."[12]

Obama replies that in the past generation the black middle class has grown fourfold and the black poverty rate has been cut in half. Latinos have made comparable gains. Most blacks and Latinos, he argues, have already climbed into the middle class or are on their way, despite the bar-riers thrown in their way. A good politics will help others get there. It will stress work and opportunity, not racism. As a state senator during the Clinton administration Obama was a Clinton liberal, not the kind that lived, as he puts it, by "old habits." He supported welfare reform, fought for day care provisions, and advocated work requirements for welfare recipients.

On the campaign trail people often recite to Obama, gratefully, his line at the 2004 Democratic Convention: "There is not a black America and white America and Latino America and Asian America—there's the United States of America." That struck a chord for many who show up at his rallies. He ended that address with an eloquent, slightly cheeky, and utterly characteristic peroration on national unity: "The pundits like to slice-and-dice our country into Red States and Blue States; Red States for Republicans, Blue States for Democrats. But I've got news for them too. We worship an awesome God in the Blue States, and we don't like federal agents poking around in our libraries in the Red States. We coach Little League in the Blue States and, yes, we got some gay friends in the Red States. There are patriots who opposed the war in Iraq and patriots who supported the war in Iraq. We are one people, all of us pledging allegiance to the stars and stripes, all of us defending the United States of America."[13]

Only someone who had sung "Awesome God" more than a few times at religious gatherings would have understood the resonance of claiming that phrase for the blue states. That sentence alone launched a wave of editorial comment on the possibility of Democrats speaking the language of faith. Obama is fond of saying, "There are a whole lot of religious people in America, including the majority of Democrats." To scrub public language of all religious content, he cautions, is to forfeit the imagery through which most Americans conceive social justice and their personal morality. And when progressives shy away from using religious language in the public square, they allow "insular views of faith" to dominate it.[14]

Obama is reflective and reasonably clear about the difference between being religiously faithful in an open-ended way and claiming religious certainty in a publicly problematic way. He is "anchored" in his faith, he explains, but not rigid or dogmatic about it. He disposes of two difficult subjects—abortion and gay marriage—by using them as illustrations of his point about religion. Obama believes that abortion should be legal and gay marriage should not be legal. However, he accepts some restrictions on late-term abortion, supports civil unions for gays and lesbians, and does not claim absolute certainty for the positions that he takes on either subject. As an elected official in a pluralistic society and as a Christian, he acknowledges, he might be wrong about abortion and gay marriage. Perhaps he will learn that he has internalized society's prejudices on one, the other, or both: "I don't believe such doubts make me a bad Christian. I believe they make me human, limited in my understandings of God's purpose and therefore prone to sin." To him the Bible is a living Word that opens to new revelations, "whether they come from a lesbian friend or a doctor opposed to abortion."[15]

Today the U.S. is a profoundly more diverse and multicultural society than the one that produced forty-two white Protestant presidents and one Catholic one. For a growing, diverse American constituency, Obama is a symbol of the multicultural, multiracial, cosmopolitan America of the future that already exists.

By the time that he finished writing *The Audacity of Hope* last year, he might have realized that he could not resist running for the presidency already; the buzz was too strong to put off. Three months ago he announced his candidacy and steeled himself for the first real pummeling of his political career, having no idea what form the attacks would take.

The early returns on that pummeling have been meager. To take them in reverse order: in March the *Chicago Tribune* questioned Obama's purchase of stock in two companies whose investors included donors to his 2004 Senate campaign (he denies having known that his broker bought the stocks, which were held in a quasi-blind trust). On the day that Obama announced his candidacy for president he put some campaign distance between himself and Wright, who is prone to jeremiads, but they remain friends and allies. And last fall it was reported that he purchased land on Chicago's South Side in June 2005 from subsequently indicted political fund-raiser Tony Rezko (he had purchased the land from the owner of the lot next door to his own to enhance the aesthetic balance of his own home and property; later he apologized for this "boneheaded" mistake, donated the amount of the seller's campaign contribution to charity, and vowed to pay closer attention to appearances in the future).

For three years political pundits and comedians have complained that Obama is an untouchable icon better named "Obambi." Today the complaining is mounting again because Obama has withstood the first barrage of national campaign scrutiny and he is setting attendance records on the campaign trail. When Illinois Republicans drafted Alan Keyes for their Senate race, one of them told Obama that they figured the voluble, volatile Keyes would be able to knock the halo off his head.

Obama has no halo, but if media vetting and opposition research don't come up with something considerably worse than they have thus far, it will seem to his opponents that he is indeed graced with one.

"Yes We Can . . . Change the Subject?"

Barack Obama cannot help that the election campaign until now has been mostly about him—his background, his personality, his race, his politics, his oratory, his church, his newness, his inexperience, his family, his primary victories, his victory over Hillary and Bill Clinton, his rock star tour of Europe. His star power and unprecedented attainment of the Democratic nomination have made him, inevitably, the chief subject of the campaign thus far, with or without Republican attack ads.

But the Democrats have two chief tasks at their convention this week. One is to shift the focus to the Republican record of the past eight years and the unacceptable prospect of a third Bush-like term. The other is to make a favorable impression on the tens of millions of Americans that haven't paid enough attention thus far to make a decision about Barack Obama. The fact that these goals are contradictory does not lessen the urgent necessity of either one.

This is a blowout election year for the Democrats. Seventy percent of Americans say the incumbent Republican administration has done a bad job. Approximately the same percentage say the same thing about the administration's handling of the economy and the war in Iraq, two things that go together, given the staggering costs of the war.

In a normal election year, any one of these three issues would be enough to dispatch the incumbent party, and the watershed elections of the past seventy-five years have been two-for-three affairs: 1932 was a referendum on a disastrous economy and a failed presidency, but no war; 1968 was about a disastrous war and a failed presidency, but the economy grew anyway; 1980 put Jimmy Carter's presidency and economic performance on trial, but it was mere piling-on to claim that Carter botched the cold war and embarrassed the U.S. in Iran. This year marks the first legitimate three-for-three election of modern times, and Democrats are going to clean up, except, perhaps, at the top of the ticket.

The possibility that Democrats will lose the presidential race despite their enormous advantages is scaring many of them. I hear it all the time on the lecture trail. "Do you really think Obama can win?" anxious liberals ask me, especially academics. The question is not, "Will he win?" but, "Do you really think it's even possible?" Some are convinced that the polling data are meaningless because the Bradley Effect is worth up to fifteen points. Many are already bracing themselves against disappointment, muttering quietly, "You know he's going to lose, don't you?"

No, I believe he can win. I believe he will win. I think he is the most compelling candidate and human being to be nominated by either party in my lifetime. But I understand the anxious foreboding of many Democrats, because I have a good deal of it. The Republican field, the weakest in memory, had only one candidate, John McCain, who had any chance of winning the presidency this year, but the Republicans lucked into nominating him. If the Democrats had nominated one of their usual bland, white male, career politicians—think John Kerry, Al Gore in 2000, or Walter Mondale, or, this year, Joe Biden or Chris Dodd—they would be leading in the polls handily. Hillary Clinton probably would be leading by a smaller but still sizable margin at this stage, too. Obama, the candidate I have supported since the day he entered the race, has a much steeper mountain to climb, even among Democrats. If polling is to be believed, approximately 27 percent of Hillary Clinton's supporters say that they are not willing to switch to Obama. That is the third most pressing problem that Democrats have to deal with this week.

Michelle Obama's luminous, beautiful address at the convention went as far as one speech could to deal with the personal side of the electoral equation. Her buoyant expression of her faith and hope had perfect pitch for the occasion and its urgent necessity of reaching across a disturbing popular divide in the American electorate. According to a mid-July New York Times/CBS News Poll, 30 percent of white Americans hold a favorable view of Barack Obama and 24 percent view Michelle Obama favorably. These pitiful numbers are the yield, thus far, for the Obamas among white Americans after two years of overwhelmingly favorable news coverage, countless magazine cover stories, and dozens of primary and caucus campaigns that ended with a soaring victory speech.

Michelle Obama obviously understands that she and her husband must reach the reachable in a personal way before they change the subject to the Bush debacle and John McCain's guardianship of it. To the extent that one speech can do that, it was done on Monday night. Now we will see how many Americans are actually reachable, and if the Democrats are able to highlight Obama and change the subject at the same time.

"Visible Man Rising"

By the time that The Speech of August 28, 2008, ended with an artful allusion to the March on Washington of August 28, 1963, the Democratic Convention had belatedly made a case for ending the rule of the Republicans. By then Barack Obama also knew that he had won his medium-sized convention gamble. The only thing that didn't go right was losing the day-after media attention to John McCain's stunningly desperate gamble.

It didn't rain in Denver, and after an outpouring of predictions that Obama would look physically diminished at Invesco Field, or look egotistically inflated at his Greek temple, or prove unable to hold the attention of a stadium audience, he gave a sensational speech watched by forty million viewers that looked as impressive as it sounded. Obama worked a typical Obama theme, this time calling it "the American Promise" of opportunity and responsibility for all, but he was tougher and more specific than much of his campaign rhetoric. Stressing the struggles of working people, he called for tax cuts for the non-rich and higher taxes on corporations that ship jobs overseas. He made a strong case for strengthening the middle class, investing in renewable energy, universalizing health coverage, and repairing America's international image. He amplified Bill Clinton's skillful summary of the current miserable economic situation and John Kerry's forceful summary of John McCain's retreat to Republican establishment orthodoxy. He stressed his differences with McCain and gave a clear picture of what an Obama presidency would be about.

Except that an Obama presidency would also represent something magnificent that his campaign, and now his convention, have assiduously played down. Obama has run a decidedly post-racial campaign. He talks about racial justice as little as possible, and he requires his workers not to discuss publicly the racial antagonism they have encountered while campaigning for him. Yet on the rare occasions that he speaks about post-racial politics, he denies that the moment for it has arrived or even that he is a symbol of it. His favorite image of how we should think about racial justice is a split screen that holds in view the just, multi-racial society that must be created and the reality of an America that is not a just society. On the second screen, race remains a major marker of inequality and social privilege. As long as the two screens are so glaringly different, you cannot have a genuinely post-racial politics.

Obama's very argument for not rubbing the noses of white Americans in the history and reality of white racism is that the problem is too entrenched in white attitudes and social structures to be remedied by race-specific policies.[16]

Since even the most fair-minded whites have a low threshold for anything smacking of black grievance, better not go there in a political campaign. Better not evoke the Civil Rights movement in prime time at the convention. And better not let on that you understand the racial subtext of the accusation that you are a proud type with overweening self-regard, which calls up centuries of needing to put down the "uppity" blacks that dared to defend themselves and their families.

Shelby Steele's bestselling new book, *A Bound Man*, was written just before the primary and caucus voting began. Steele said that Obama cannot win because he is caught in the historic double bind between African American bargainers and challengers. Bargainers bargain for acceptance in white America by not presuming that white Americans are racist, while challengers challenge white Americans to prove themselves innocent of racism. Bill Cosby, Colin Powell, and Oprah Winfrey are bargainers, in this telling, while Al Sharpton and Jesse Jackson are challengers. Had Steele written his book a few months later, undoubtedly Jeremiah Wright would have played a larger role; here he gets less than a page without being named.[17]

The bargainer/challenger debate takes place between and within the races, setting guilt-as-impotence against innocence-as-power, Steele argues. America needs to be delivered from this sorry either/or, which is why Obama has generated so much excitement. However, Steele says that Obama is too hopelessly bound by the social forces behind these categories to find a voice of his own. Obama is a racial cipher, not an actualized individual. He has a talent for inauthenticity that makes him good at fashioning a racial persona, which is not the same thing as achieving selfhood. According to Steele, Obama constantly negotiates the either/or in a vain attempt to grant racial innocence to white Americans at the same time that he withholds it from them. Thus, like the fictional Tod Clifton in Ralph Ellison's *Invisible Man*, Obama has not achieved visibility as an individual. Since he lacks a real self, it is not clear that he has any real beliefs. This is why Obama cannot win, Steele wrote so recently. If he bargains zealously, he cannot win black majorities; if he opts for challenge, making himself "black enough," he cannot win a majority of any other group. Steele advised Obama to give up what he was doing in favor of finding out who he was.

One might have thought that Obama's remarkable blend of discipline, equanimity, and charisma stood in his favor. *A Bound Man*, however, is a Swift-boat operation, spinning strength into weakness, unwittingly raising the question: How ridiculous can you get? The reflective, searching, complex, and sometimes painfully honest author of *Dreams from My Father* has no sense of self? His unprecedented march to the nomination was conducted by a cipher projecting the illusion of personhood? His very success at transcending the morality play of challengers versus bargainers proves that he must be a fraud?

Steele is insightful in describing parts of his subject. He notes that challengers are granted distinct roles on special occasions to arbitrate who is racist and what racism looks like, and he rightly stresses that bargainers often have to hide their anger at whites for fear of wrecking the bargain. But his attack on Obama's personal character is absurd, and his political forecast is spectacularly not turning out.

We await polling data on how the Democratic Convention played in Ohio, Michigan, Pennsylvania, and other election-in-their-hands states. But John McCain may have anticipated that it is going to play too well. For on the day after the convention, McCain undermined his chief argument against Obama—lack of relevant experience—by choosing the most inexperienced running mate ever selected by either party. McCain's desperation should be a sign to nervous liberals of how very winnable is this campaign to elect Barack Obama as the forty-fourth president of the United States.

"Impulsive Distractions"

By the end of the Democratic Convention, John McCain knew that his campaign was in deep trouble. Hillary and Bill Clinton had rallied her followers to get behind Barack Obama; Obama closed the convention with a spectacular speech in a stadium spectacle; all of McCain's vice-presidential contenders were either boring or unacceptable to the evangelical Right or both; the Republican right-wing base was sour and depressed; and the Republican Convention was scheduled to begin with George W. Bush and Dick Cheney night.

McCain realized where all of that was leading, and it galled him that so many Democratic speakers dismissed his claim to maverick status as laughable. John Kerry chided that his friend McCain, before trying to debate Obama, needed to have one with himself. Others suggested that McCain abandoned his independence so long ago that he represented a third Bush term in all but name; supporting Bush 90 percent of the time was not quite the mark of a maverick.

That must have hit close to home, since McCain prizes his (outdated) reputation for independence. He wants to be recognized as a clean-government reformer almost as much as he wants to be president; plus, the two things go together in this year's electoral aftermath of the Bush debacle. So at the last moment McCain made the most important decision of his campaign by opting for an unknown running mate whom he had met a single time.

Sarah Palin's vetting was apparently a one-day affair, occurring the day before McCain offered her the nomination. The process was too rushed to have covered much of anything. Did McCain realize how little Palin knows about the world? Did he know that she had never traveled abroad until 2007? Did he even know that she assiduously promoted the "bridge to nowhere" before she became the clean-government governor that turned against it?

Too much of the early media scrutiny along this line has fixated on a family issue that should be out of bounds in a political campaign; no candidate deserves to have her or his children roasted in the media. And McCain may well have stumbled into lifting up the next star of the Republican Party. Palin has already electrified the party's base and provided a godsend-distraction from eight years of job losses, disappearing health coverage, massive budget and trade deficits, a two-and-a-half-trillion-dollar mortgage meltdown, a two-trillion-dollar disaster in Iraq, and a damaged American image in the world.

But whatever Palin's strengths or weaknesses as a political performer may turn out to be, McCain's turn to her confirms the most unsettling thing about him, his impulsive temperament. I opposed Howard Dean's candidacy for the presidency in 2004, despite sharing his opposition to the war in Iraq, because he struck me from the beginning as lacking the requisite self-discipline and emotional maturity for the job. McCain has similar problems on a larger scale. He has an amply founded reputation for shooting first and thinking later; even his friends describe him as volatile and quarrelsome. Though considerate to staff underlings, McCain's hair-trigger rages against colleagues are legendary in the Senate. These tendencies correlate with his militaristic mind-set and his distinctly self-righteous view of himself as a crusader for the public interest surrounded by corruptible types.

On the first night of the convention, Hurricane Gustav rescued the Republican Party from an entire night of George Bush and Dick Cheney. On the second night the party featured its patriotic militarism as a party-unifying theme and told the story of McCain's war heroism. That is not much of a platform for a presidential campaign, but the party has the immense distraction of Palin's novelty on its side, which will at least allow the McCain campaign to survive its own convention.

"Back to the Subject"

When the Democratic Convention started, Barack Obama's main challenge was to change the focus of the election from himself to a miserably failing economy, including its energy-and-environment dimension. By the time that the Republican Convention started, Obama had the same problem with the Sarah Palin phenomenon. The McCain campaign would love to have an election that revolves around Obama and Palin. More than ever, Obama needs to turn the election into a referendum on larger matters.

John McCain had no chance of uniting the Republican Convention by himself, let alone of energizing and elating the party's right-wing base. He was the first Republican since 1948 to win the nomination without the support of the party base, and he knew that flag-waving militarism would take him only so far at the convention and in the election campaign. He struck a political gusher by turning to Palin, which electrified the party base and improved McCain's chances with evangelicals, Reagan Democrats, Westerners, hunters, non-feminist women, and perhaps suburban independents.

Palin does not help McCain in his weakest area, his bankruptcy on economy/energy/ecology. Her knowledge base about the world beyond Alaska is worrisome. And it is very much in question whether McCain's Janus-faced convention strategy will play for two months of everyday campaigning. The Republican Convention featured three nights of right-wing bombast for the base, all approved by the candidate, followed by the candidate's assurance that he floats above partisanship and attack politics. That dubious combination smacks of the Fox Network's claim to be "fair and balanced," which no one takes seriously. McCain needs to be careful not to flunk the laugh test.

For the Republican base, Palin's nomination is a realized fantasy and a delicious play to Hillary Clinton's supporters. For the Obama campaign, it is a distraction from what the election needs to be about. For Democrats, the economy is the key to winning the election. For Republicans, the key is to drive up voter unease with Obama.

On the edge of the worst financial crisis since the Great Depression, the Republicans had astonishingly little to say about skyrocketing mortgage foreclosures and job losses. The exception was former presidential contestant Fred Thompson, who ridiculed Democrats (with an echo of whiner-hating Phil Gramm) for complaining about economic stress. Former presidential contestant Rudy Guliani, warming up the crowd, tossed out red meat. Former presidential contestant Mitt Romney won the prize for red meat, declaring that even the Roberts Supreme Court is liberal, like the rest of "liberal Washington."

But Romney had his eye on 2012, not this November. Still envisioning himself as the favorite of the party's culture-warring base, he had in mind Goldwater in 1960 and Reagan in 1976, passionate cries from the far right that paid dividends four years later. Somehow Romney has not absorbed that the evangelical Right will never rally behind a Mormon, especially him. In the meantime Palin sailed past Romney, Mike Huckabee, and all other claimants to the favor of the religious Right, shoring up a presidential nominee who was never in the running for it.

The case for throwing out the ruling party is awfully strong; thus the Republicans rarely mentioned George W. Bush or even used the word "Republican." The U.S. economy needs to create at least 100,000 jobs per month to keep up with a growing population. This year the economy has lost jobs in every month, totaling 605,000 lost jobs in 2008 thus far. McCain, mindful of his friend Gramm's eruption against whiners, aptly remarked that the Bush administration seems not to care about the human suffering behind these figures. But McCain has no plan that differs from that of Bush or Gramm.

The mortgage meltdown is colossal, totaling two-and-a-half trillion dollars of lost value thus far. One of its major causes was the Bush administration's ideologically driven refusal to sensibly regulate the mortgage industry, but McCain has the same ideology. The Bush budget deficits are similarly enormous and self-inflicted, fueled chiefly by Bush's tax cuts for the rich and five years of consequences for invading Iraq. But McCain would make the deficits worse by cutting corporate taxes, eliminating the alternative minimum income tax, ramping up military spending, and making permanent Bush's tax cuts for the upper class.

Keeping Bush's tax cuts would cost the federal treasury $1 trillion over four years. McCain's only idea for cutting the budget deficit is to cut earmarks. If he somehow managed to cut all of them, the savings would total only $19 billion per year, and now he has a running mate who specializes in them. As mayor of tiny Wasilla, Palin lobbied for earmarks totaling $27 million, and in less than two years of governing Alaska she sought nearly $750 million of special federal funding, by far the largest per-capita request by any U.S. governor. Her gas pipeline for Alaska would be a monument to her skill at the earmark game.

McCain once had a sensible position on the Bush tax cuts, which he dropped to make himself competitive in Republican presidential prima-ries. He once aspired to be known as a green conservative, but on his way to the nomination he deliberately avoided voting on all eight attempts to pass a bill that would expand America's wind and solar industries. He once opposed offshore drilling on the ground that the environment mat-ters, but he dropped environmentalism on the way to the nomination. He still opposes drilling in the Arctic National Wildlife Refuge, savoring his last dissent from Bush-style oil politics, but now he has a running mate who advocates drilling in ANWR [Arctic National Wildlife Refuge].

McCain's alliance with a drill-everywhere enthusiast is apparently a case of one thing leading to another, not a coincidence. One of Palin's chief boosters for the vice-presidential nod was neoconservative pundit and *Weekly Standard* editor Bill Kristol, who touted her brassy toughness and urged McCain operatives not to rule her out. In mid-August, *Weekly Standard* writer Stephen Hayes urged McCain to meet with Palin to hear her case for drilling in ANWR. McCain indicated that he was willing to do so. The *Weekly Standard*, not content to wait for an actual meeting, announced McCain's promise in a splashy article by Hayes featuring a picture of Palin. Now lightning has struck for Palin.

That gives the Obama campaign two enormous distractions to overcome—the endless fascination of Obama and the explosion of fas-cination with Palin. This week, while Palin studies up on the world, the election is mostly about her. A certain amount of time has to be spent highlighting her howlers and extremism. For example, in her convention speech Palin claimed that Obama has never authored a single major law or reform, "not even in the state senate." Either she did not know the truth or did not feel constrained by it. Obama pushed through two major bills in Illinois dealing with racial profiling by police and the recording of interrogations in potential death penalty cases, and in the Senate he has been a leader on ethics reform legislation and intercepting illegal ship-ments of weapons of mass destruction.

But dwelling on Palin, her worldview, and all that she does not know is not what the Democrats need to be about. They need to summon the discipline and moxie to swing the discussion back to jobs, homes, credit, energy, the environment, and the world.

Democrats should not assume that an electoral windfall awaits Palin's debate with Joe Biden. Palin is sharper than George W. Bush in give-and-take exchanges, and the mention of Bush calls up painful memories. In 2000 Al Gore wiped the floor with Bush in the first debate, but the media fixated on Gore's grunts and sighs. In the second debate Bush relied on slogans to cover his ignorance of foreign policy, but it didn't matter; Gore shut down and the story was still about his strangeness. By then Gore's lead was gone and the election was a toss-up. The debates will be equally important this year, and Biden will need to prove that he is capable of disciplining his tendency to bluster and bloviate.

"Taking Social Investment Seriously"

From 1980 to 2008 only stubborn types held out for economic justice and regulating the financial sector. The market always knew best, trickle-down economics prevailed, and social justice was off the table politically. Adam Smith's invisible hand was said to dispense general well-being, never mind that his conclusions depended on sound information, which was impossible to attain after Wall Street fell in love with derivatives and securitizations. For nearly thirty years the religion of the market ruled U.S. American politics and looked past the embarrassments of Enron and WorldCom, where the heedless pursuit of self-interest led to something quite contrary to societal well-being.

No more. In September 2008 the self-inflicted meltdown of U.S. American and European banks and investment firms ended the era of market fundamentalism. In October 2008 a Republican government took up bailing like it was 1933. In November 2008 the election of Barack Obama and a strong Democratic majority in the Congress raised the possibility of a real change in U.S. American politics. Most of Obama's presidency will necessarily consist of cleaning up a financial mess and coping with a bad recession. But beyond the necessities of cleaning up and coping, the U.S. is overdue for a renewal of common good politics, this time with a global perspective, and a fundamental discussion about the kind of country it wants to be.

On November 5 I felt that I woke up in a better country. To me, Barack Obama's election is the most beautiful and historically important event of my lifetime, rivaled only by the March on Washington of August 1963. Many of us would prefer to linger in the glow of that event and feeling, but Obama has inherited the worst economic crisis since Franklin Roosevelt in 1933 and a worse set of foreign policy challenges than anything Americans knew about in 1933.

The economic crisis is systemic; we are caught in a global deflationary spiral that won't be reversed by a policy. The banks have faked themselves out from knowing what their assets are worth, credit lines are frozen, unemployment is soaring, the real economy of production is suffering structural damage, and the wreckage in foreign policy is similarly vast. Dealing with all of this, plus coping with racial attacks veiled as something else, will require the most competent and creative administration in memory, supported by supporters with backbone.

I do not doubt that Obama will lead this country with intelligence, dignity, discipline, integrity, and eloquence. I do worry that he will be too cautious. His cabinet and advisers are mostly center-right retreads from the Clinton administration who are comfortable with the system and their places in it. He has no prominent consumer advocate among his economic advisers. He has no figure in his cabinet that spoke out strongly against the deregulatory mania of the past decade. His choice for Treasury secretary, New York Federal Reserve Bank president Timothy Geithner, was the regulator closest to Wall Street over the past five years, when Wall Street's gambling binge wrecked the economy.

Being cautious and temperate is a good thing. Obama's calm reasonableness inspired confidence before Wall Street collapsed in mid-September, and afterward it was the main difference-maker in the election. John McCain was stuck with an anti-regulation record and an ideological kinship with a failed administration; then he doubled his trouble by appearing emotionally unstable in responding to the financial crisis. Obama's steady, disciplined temperament was and is enormously important.

But cautiousness will not rise to the challenge or opportunity of this moment. This disaster was thirty years in the making. Government was denigrated and private wealth was prized over the public good. Wall Street invented increasingly fanciful and opaque derivatives schemes, speculators gamed the system, and regulators took a light pass at regulating. People made fortunes at every link of Ponzi-like schemes that ensured unaccountability. Greed and irrational exuberance abounded. Credit default swaps, invented barely a dozen years ago, skyrocketed to a $62 trillion completely unregulated market.

Now the global system is caught in a deflationary spiral producing portfolio contractions of 30 to 40 percent. Obama will have to stoke the economy with a trillion dollars of stimulus just to keep it alive. One hopes that he will do it in a way that prizes accountability and inspires investor confidence. Opaqueness and unaccountability were intrinsic to the mortgage meltdown, plus a decided obsequiousness to the big banks, and in the last weeks of the Bush administration we are getting bailouts that are equally opaque and short on accountability.

The Treasury and Federal Reserve are managing the TARP [Troubled Asset Relief Program] process in secret, and as far as anyone can tell, obsequiousness continues. Banks are getting tax exemptions for mergers; banks taking taxpayer money are still paying generous dividends; and banks large and small are sitting on their TARP money, not being required to do anything with it. Public money is bailing out corporations lacking public voting rights or even voice on corporate boards. When the Bush administration injected capital into nine of the biggest banks in October, it bought preferred stock at above-market prices with no control rights and no stipulations about doing anything for the public with the public's money. As the Bush years run out, the national debt has tripled in eight years from $4 trillion to $12 trillion; it will get worse if Fannie Mae and Freddy Mac turn out to be as toxically ill as they appear; and the total bill for Bush's recent loans, investments, guarantees, and other forms of bailing is up to $8 trillion—a figure half the size of the nation's entire economy.

The echoes of the Great Depression and the New Deal are awfully strong. We must hope that Obama will stop the bleeding in something like the way that Roosevelt did, but with stronger conviction and consistency. Roosevelt was skittish about social investment and he refused to nationalize the banks or create public banks. In 1937 he disastrously reduced employment spending, which unraveled the employment gains of the New Deal. It took World War II to solve the Great Depression's scourge of unemployment.

We do not know if Obama really believes in social and environmental investment, or only half-believes like Roosevelt. He will surely go further than Roosevelt or George W. Bush in ensuring that taxpayer bailouts benefit the taxpayers, but we don't know by how much. If taxpayers are going to bail out Citigroup and Bank of America, or eat their toxic debt through publicly owned "bad banks," the public good should factor into how these companies operate. Obama may have to nationalize the biggest too-dumb-to-fail banks just to establish a bottom in a free-falling economy. The same thing is true of too-big-to-fail companies that make things.

Instead of pouring tens of billions more into dysfunctional companies like Chrysler, in some cases we're overdue for tough love: nationalize them, fire the managers, wipe out the shareholders, break up the enterprises, and sell off the parts worth buying and saving. That would put an end to lemon socialism, the kind the corporate class has long preferred.

"Health-care Fix: The Role of a Public Option"

Health care reform, a cause left for dead in 1993, is suddenly hurtling down the political track with breathtaking speed. Both branches of Congress may have a bill by August, and a reconciliation bill is on schedule for September.

Longtime advocates of single-payer insurance like me are thrilled, anxious, and deflated simultaneously. The debate that we wanted has finally come, and it is coming with a legislative rush, but the plan that we wanted is being excluded from consideration. Should we hold out for the real thing, or get behind the best politically possible thing?

I am for doing both: standing up for single payer without holding out for it exclusively; supporting a public option without denying its limitations; and hoping that a *good* public plan will lead eventually to real national health insurance.

Single payer basically means Medicare for everyone, without the co-pays and deductibles of the current Medicare system. It is not socialized medicine, as in England or Spain, where doctors and hospitals work for the government. It does not violate the Takings Clause of the Fifth Amendment, which bars the government from taking private property for public use without appropriate compensation, since it does not nationalize any private firms. The single-payer plan is a system of socialized health insurance similar to that of Canada, Australia, and most European nations. Essentially it is an extension and improvement of the Medicare system in which government pays for care that is managed and delivered in the private sector.

We don't need private health insurance companies. We certainly don't need a system that wastes $450 billion per year in redundant administrative costs and leaves 45 million Americans without health coverage. We could do without a system that excludes people with preexisting medical conditions and limited economic resources. We don't need a system that cherry picks profitable clients and dumps the unprofitably ill in HMOs featuring lousy care and little choice. Businesses and other employers would do much better not having to provide health coverage for their employees, who often end up under-insured. We could do better than a system that ties people fearfully to jobs they want to leave but can't afford to lose because they might lose their health coverage.

Health care is a fundamental human right that should be available to all people regardless of their economic resources. A society that takes seriously this elementary principle of social justice does not relegate the poor and underemployed to second-class care or status. The only Western democratic society that doesn't even try to live up to this principle is the United States. When wealthy and middle-class people have to rely on the same health system as the poor, as they do throughout Europe, they use their political power to make sure it's a decent system.

But single-payer deliverance is not on the agenda for President Obama and this Congress. The insurance companies are too powerful and politically aggressive to be retired in one legislative stroke. The House bill for a system that replaces for-profit insurance companies, H.R. 676, has seventy-nine co-sponsors, and the Senate bill, S. 703, has only Bernie Sanders. Obama, who deserves immense credit for pushing this issue forward, rightly urges that significant health care reform has to happen this year if it is to happen on his watch. In May he told a town hall meeting in Rio Rancho, New Mexico, that if one were starting from scratch, a single-payer system might be the best option. However, he observed, "The only problem is that we're not starting from scratch." The system that we have comprises 14 percent of the nation's gross domestic product. Reinventing something that big and politically connected has no chance of happening this year.

The best we can hope for this year is a public Medicare-like option that competes with private plans. This reform would save only 15 percent of the $350 billion insurance overhead costs that converting to single payer would achieve. Most versions currently being touted would not get everyone covered, though Obama suggested recently that he might be open to changing his position on requiring all Americans to have health coverage. In any case, even the better proposals along this line, like the one that Senator Ted Kennedy has championed for years, would not get us close to equality in health care. But a strong reform bill would offer an important alternative to private health insurance that might pave the way to real national health insurance.

The insurance companies are gearing up to prevent a public plan because they don't want to compete with one. The American Medical Association doesn't want one either, which preserves its bad-smelling record in this area. The AMA was against Medicare, it has opposed every previous proposal for universal coverage, and today it is against providing a public option even for people lacking the economic means or opportunity to buy health insurance.

Princeton economist and *New York Times* columnist Paul Krugman is almost right in contending that the crucial either/or of the battle over health care is whether reform delivers a public option. But Krugman's point needs to be put more precisely. The acid test is not whether reform delivers a public plan but whether it delivers a good one. A good public plan would be open to all individuals and employers that want to join. It would allow members to choose their own doctors. It would eliminate high deductibles. It would allow members to negotiate reimbursement rates and drug prices. The government would run it. And it would be backed up by tough cost controls and a requirement that all Americans have health coverage.

A bad public plan, however, is not worth supporting. A plan that isn't open to everyone or that prevents choice or negotiation would be a plan designed to fail. It would take the pressure off private companies to do something about the uninsured and under-insured without solving the problem. It would be like Medicaid—poorly funded and managed because its beneficiaries lack political power. The failure of a designed-for-failure plan would kill the cause of real national health insurance for another sixteen years. Some insurance industry leaders, having figured this out, are ready to indulge a bad plan. The political task for health care reformers is to create and push through a public plan worth having.

We are still in the phase of the debate where the political and industry opposition to health care reform is mostly warning that a public option means "socialized medicine" that won't work. A fair amount of time has to be spent repeating over and over that single payer is not socialized medicine, and a public option among private competitors is even farther from it. But we are approaching a tipping point where opponents of health care reform will stress the opposite. The problem is not that a government program won't work. The real problem, for all who want to keep the present system, is that a government program will work too well.

Overwhelming majorities in blue and red states alike would love to dump their policies containing high deductibles and health exclusions. A public plan could be a magnet for health care workers that got into this business to serve human needs, not to be cogs in a profit machine. If that happens, opponents will have been right about one big thing. Mere reform could lead to the real thing, a single-payer system where real savings and equality are achievable. Medicare's average overhead cost is 3 percent, and provincial single-payer plans in Canada average 1 percent. HMOs range between 15 and 25 percent. If we create a public plan that people want to join, we may well go the rest of the way, toward savings and equality, too.

Chapter 19

Social Ethics in the Making

HISTORY, METHOD, AND WHITE SUPREMACISM

An inaugural celebration, I am told, is supposed to highlight something about the speaker. But I couldn't think of anything about myself that I wanted to feature, except that I love Union Theological Seminary and am amazed to have been called to it. So this lecture will be almost as Union-centric as the rest of the service.

I have a lot of friends here and if I start naming them I'll have to go row by row. So I will limit myself to four friends from my Kalamazoo years. Dr. Romeo E. Phillips and Dr. James F. Jones Jr. are my cherished friends and former colleagues at Kalamazoo College. Romeo Phillips is an emeritus professor of education and music, served on the Portage City Council, and is a legend in Southwest Michigan. Jimmy Jones was formerly president of Kalamazoo College and is currently president of Trinity College in Hartford, Connecticut. An equally treasured friend, the Reverend Chuck Kutz-Marks, now of Austin, Texas, is here. Chuck is a Disciples of Christ pastor, formerly of Kalamazoo, and he is sitting next to the Reverend Becca Kutz-Marks, a force of nature whose ordination is in the United Church of Christ. Becca is the dearest friend I have ever had. We came together through our daughters; for years Becca, Chuck, Brenda and I were two pairs of couples, all four of us ministers, God help our kids. Then came the years of grieving and grace, when Becca looked out for me. I am ineffably grateful to these dear friends, and so many others, for being here tonight.

This day holds a many-layered amazement for me. I grew up in a semi-rural area of mid-Michigan called Bay County, a mish-mash of lower-class and working-class families, where my parents eked out a spare living. They had come from poor families in the Upper Peninsula of Michigan, where my father endured years of abuse for his Native American bloodline, and where, he claims, his family was slightly better off than my mother's, though this remains a matter of dispute. My family was nominally Catholic, but I had a mystical streak, and from an early age I was drawn to the icons in our church and family Bible.

From an early age I had a strong feeling that my brothers and I had won the birth lottery. We had cousins and neighbors that didn't make it past junior high school, and nobody that we knew talked about going to college, but my parents said that school was important and we should aim for college. When the local school system went down to half-days, my parents moved three miles in the other direction, so their kids would go to decent schools. I would love to say that I seized this opportunity, but, in fact, the idea of *studying* never occurred to me before my senior year. Though I was an avid reader, the idea of reading schoolbooks was unthinkable. I paid just enough attention to pass the courses, because you had to pass to be eligible for varsity sports. For me, athletics was as necessary as breathing. And so, because my parents cared, and because I played sports year-round, I squeaked into college.

My unlikely interest in things intellectual sprouted near the end of my senior high school football season. It dawned on me that I would not be able to play varsity sports forever; school might be less tiresome if I took an interest; and preparing for college academics, not merely college sports, was probably advisable. These insights led to an unsuspected attraction to ideas, which set me on a path my relatives and friends found impossible to fathom. They still do, and to this day I assure them I'm still a jock, masquerading as an intellectual.

Partly because of this background, I am mindful every day of what an immense privilege it is to be a professor. It astonishes me that I have the privilege to teach and write for a living, much less to occupy the Reinhold Niebuhr chair.

This lecture is titled "Social Ethics in the Making," and so is the book I am currently writing. This was not my plan. I had meant to write a meaning-of-it-all book titled *The Spirit of Liberal Theology* after I finished my trilogy on the history of American theological liberalism, but then my daughter Sara started college, Joe Hough called, I moved to Union, and my students promptly asked me what, exactly, *is* social ethics. Unfortunately there is no book that describes the history of the field and its methods. There is a book titled *Soul in Society* that is often *used* as a history of the field, but that is embarrassing to me, because I was not trying to cover the field when I wrote it. That book starts a generation too late to be a history of the field, it deals with only three social ethical traditions, and the history part is a setup for my theory of economic democracy. So we need a book that interprets the history of social ethics, or at least, I need one to do my job.

Social ethics was invented in the early 1880s, right along with the social gospel, sociology, modern socialism, Social Darwinism, the term "social justice," the social gospel idea of social salvation, and the trade unions. The founders of social ethics were founders of the social gospel but not the ones that history remembered. The famous social gospelers were bracing personalities who operated primarily in the public square—Washington Gladden, Richard Ely, Josiah Strong, George Herron, Jane Addams, and Walter Rauschenbusch. They got to be renowned by preaching the social gospel as a form of public homiletics.

The founders of social ethics also spoke to the general public, but they were absorbed by a cause that belonged to the academy: making a home for Christian ethics as a self-standing discipline of ethically grounded social science. They urged that society is a whole that includes an ethical dimension; thus there needed to be something like social ethics. This discipline would be a central feature of liberal arts and seminary education. It would succeed the old moral philosophy, replacing an outmoded commonsense realism with a socially oriented idealism.

Intellectually the founders of social ethics belonged to the U.S. American generation that reconciled Christianity to Darwinism, accepted the historical critical approach to the Bible, and discovered the power of social ideas. They believed that modern scholarship had rediscovered the social meaning of Christianity in the kingdom-centered religion of Jesus. As early advocates of sociology, they also believed in the disciplinary unity of social science and its ethical character.

The founders of social ethics were Francis Greenwood Peabody, a Harvard professor and Unitarian theologian; William Jewett Tucker, an Andover Seminary professor who later achieved distinction as president of Dartmouth College; J. H. W. Stuckenberg, a little-known ethicist at Wittenberg College; and Graham Taylor, a social activist who founded the first department of Christian Sociology, at Chicago Theological Seminary.

These pioneers of social ethical analysis studied social conditions with a Christian view toward what might be done about them. They shared Richard Ely's concern that the emerging discipline of sociology needed to be informed by the ethical conscience of progressive religion. They updated the liberal third way between authoritarian orthodoxy and secular disbelief. In the social gospel the world became the subject of redemption. If there was such a thing as social structure, salvation had to have a social dimension.

Peabody was an apostle of this theme and the originator of social ethics. His father was a prominent Boston Unitarian pastor; thus Peabody grew up knowing Harvard professors, whom he found to be a rather stuffy, insular bunch, and who didn't improve after he enrolled at Harvard. As far as Peabody could tell, Harvard professors prized their detachment from the world as a virtue. They bored their students with deadly recitations, took no interest in anything besides themselves and their texts, and barely acknowledged that a school must have students.[1]

Proceeding to the Divinity School, Peabody found it equally depressing. He later described his three years of divinity training as "a disheartening experience of uninspiring study and retarded thought." In theory Harvard Divinity School was nondenominational, not Unitarian, but, in reality, a fuddy-duddy brand of Unitarian orthodoxy prevailed. Historical criticism was practiced sparingly, philosophical idealism was spurned, classroom lectures seemed purposely dull, and theology and ethics were taught as subjects of "doctrinal desiccation." Reaching for the strongest way of conveying a bad memory, Peabody recalled: "The fresh breeze of modern thought rarely penetrated the lecture-rooms . . . I cannot remember attaining in seven years of Harvard classrooms anything that could be fairly described as an idea."[2]

That was a bit hyperbolic, but it conveys the feeling that launched Peabody into social ethics. As a graduate student in Germany, browsing in a bookshop in 1872, he was struck with an idea. Perusing a book by Otto Pfleiderer, it occurred to Peabody that a religious philosophy might be validated by its history. Instead of beginning with an a priori doctrine or tradition, one might derive a religious outlook from an inductive study of human nature and ethical activity. That would rescue religion from provincialism—defending it through an inductive study of its historical development.[3]

Peabody expected to preach and write about such things as a pastor, not an academic. Following his father's footsteps, he was called to a flagship Unitarian parish in Cambridge. But Peabody suffered from persistent illness, and after six years he concluded that ministry was too strenuous for him. Sadly he resigned himself to a lower, less important, less demanding vocation: teaching at Harvard Divinity School. There he found an unsuspected calling, at the take-off of the social gospel movement.[4]

The social gospel happened for a confluence of reasons that impacted one another. It was fed by the wellsprings of eighteenth-century Enlightenment humanism, the nineteenth-century Home Missions movement, and the activism of the evangelical and liberal anti-slavery movements. It took root as a response to the corruption of the Gilded Age and the rise of industrial society, goaded by writers such as Edward Bellamy, Stephen Colwell, Richard Ely, and Henry Demarest Lloyd. It took inspiration from the Christian Socialist movement in England. It rode on the back of a rising sociological consciousness and literature.[5]

Above all, the social gospel was a response to a burgeoning labor movement. Union leaders blasted the churches for doing nothing for poor and working-class people. Liberal Christian leaders realized it was pointless to defend Christianity if the churches took an indefensible attitude on this issue. In the public square Josiah Strong and George Herron reached huge audiences, the former with a conservative version of social salvation, the latter with a radical socialist one. In the academy, social ethics was conceived as a successor to moral philosophy.[6]

Nearly every American college put moral philosophy at the center of its required curriculum. In most cases it was a vaguely religious course consisting of four parts. It expounded the method of a given philosophy, offered a theory of human nature and its drives, developed a general ethical system, and applied moral principles to institutional and social concerns. This course, usually taught by a clergyman college president, was remarkably uniform in American schools, because it rested on a dominant philosophy: Scottish commonsense realism.[7]

The commonsense philosophers taught that the fundamental categories of reason and the fundamental principles of morals are self-evident intuitions. Self-consciousness contains principles such as substance, extension, mass, causality, and the moral sense that are prior to experience. Thomas Reid stressed that these principles cannot be denied without self-contradiction, for nobody seriously denies the reality of causality or an external world. The very ideas of rationality and the moral sense are inherent in the process of reasoning: "They make up what is called *the common sense of mankind*; and, what is manifestly contrary to any of those first principles, is what we call *absurd.* "[8]

Commonsense realism offered a broad moral philosophy that was not owned exclusively by any theological or ideological party. It provided a basis for conceiving ethics as an independent science, and it had a long run in American education. But the schoolmaster ethos of moral philosophy was a liability in the Gilded Age. Universities changed to accommodate the needs of an industrial society and the increasing prestige of science, both of which made moral philosophy seem quaint. The founders of social ethics perceived that the climate had changed. They still believed that knowledge had little worth if virtue decreased. But to save the good parts of the old moral philosophy, social ethics had to speak the language of scientific induction. They also contended that the new ethics had to be more Christian than the old one.

Moral philosophy was about nurturing moral values and serving the public good of the Republic, vaguely in the name of religion. Social ethics was about recovering the kingdom faith of Jesus through historical criticism and social analysis. In 1877 Union Seminary took a step toward social ethics, establishing a course in Christian ethics taught by George Prentiss. The idea that Christian ethics might be taught more or less on its own was gaining traction.[9]

From the beginning social ethics had a twofold task: to learn scientifically what *is* and to advocate ethically what *should be*. The crucial thing was to hold together the *is* and the *ought*. To change American society, the social sciences and Christian ethics had to be fused together, mobilizing the churches to effect progressive social change. Peabody's first name for it was "practical ethics." That was a parallel to "Applied Christianity," which is what the social gospel was called for thirty years. Peabody kept tinkering with the name, changing the title of his course many times. For a while he called it "Ethical Theories and Moral Reform," while the students called it "Peabo's Drainage, Drunkenness, and Divorce." Finally, after twenty years of name changes, Peabody's friend and colleague William James said to him, "Why not call it 'Social Ethics'?" That settled the name of this field, but the basic idea of Peabody's method was clear to him from the beginning.[10]

He approached ethics inductively as the study of social movements addressing major social problems. Temperance and divorce were high on the list; so were the labor movement, philanthropy, and Indian resettlement policy. Peabody taught that the principles of social ethics must be derived from the study of social problems and the movements to correct them.[11]

His method had three steps: observation, generalization, and correlation. The first step was to generate data; the second was to assemble and analyze it; the third was to discern the underlying moral unity in nature. Somewhere between the second and third steps, he taught, science passed into philosophy. The hard part was the third step work of drawing ethical principles from the data. All social issues and events were interrelated. Thus the hardest work of the social ethicist was to grasp the underlying unity of the whole, including its ethical character and principles.[12]

Certainly his students found that the hardest part. Peabody required them to study a philanthropic or reform organization and write a term paper that followed the social ethical method. Most of the papers remained stuck in step 1. Only rarely did a student develop a constructive ethical argument from the study and analysis of a social organization.

But social ethics, whenever it took a social scientific bent, adopted some variation of Peabody's approach. Today that approach remains one of the main options in the field. Social ethics could not have become a field without claiming a clear method. Yet this fact is loaded with irony, for the field's greatest figures paid little attention to disciplinary or methodological concerns. The three towering figures in the U.S. tradition are Walter Rauschenbusch, Reinhold Niebuhr, and Martin Luther King Jr. But Rauschenbusch and King did not teach social ethics, and Niebuhr took little interest in disciplinary or methodological issues.

Niebuhr did not worry about the disciplinary standing or boundaries of his field, and he did not share Peabody's fixation with social scientific validation. He ended up in social ethics because that was the place where liberal seminaries took up current social problems. That was what he cared about, the struggle for justice and a decent world order. John Bennett was fond of saying that Niebuhr's consuming question was always, "What should the U.S. government's policy be on this or that issue?"[13]

To the extent that Niebuhr had a method, it was the dispositional one of determining the meaning of justice in the interaction of Christian love and concrete situation. For Niebuhr, justice was an application of the law of love to the sociopolitical sphere, and love was the motivating energy of the struggle for justice, which was regulated by the middle axioms of freedom, equality, and order (or balance of power). Always he stressed the necessity of viewing society and the world order as theaters of perpetual struggles for power among competing interests. In both cases, the meaning of justice could not be taken directly from the middle axioms. It was determined only in the interaction of love and situation, through the mediation of the principles of freedom, equality, and order.

A good deal of social ethics has been Niebuhrian in the sense of being essentially political, activist, and pragmatic. That didn't start with Niebuhr, because in this respect Niebuhr simply assumed the activist orientation of the social gospel. Rauschenbusch had no field; he started with the German Department and ended up, by accident, in church history. Niebuhr had no field either, except for the social ethical space that he inherited from the social gospel. And so the major social ethicists have not been the ones that worried about the social scientific standing of their field.

But some very able thinkers have been caretakers of the discipline that Peabody founded. At Union Seminary, for more than twenty years, it was Harry Ward, who was a stickler for ethical method. Ward taught his students to ask three questions, around which he organized his courses: What are the facts? What do they mean? What should be done? That was a stripped-down version of Peabody's method. Ward stressed that social ethics was about holding together theory and practice, and he based class discussions on student field research. In the early and mid-1930s he had more doctoral students than Niebuhr, and they were known to be blunt about the difference between the two. Ward was more radical and plainspoken, they explained; Ward focused on specific problems, while Niebuhr's students majored in Niebuhr. For over a decade Ward was described as Rauschenbusch's successor, the major social gospeler of his generation. But Ward was fatally smitten with communism, and by the time he retired in 1941 he had destroyed his reputation in the field and in the civil liberties groups that he served, both of which erased him from their collective memory.[14]

After Ward departed, John Bennett assumed the task of building up a method and a field. Bennett wrote judicious essays about Niebuhr's relationship to the social gospel, and he developed the ethical theory of "middle axioms" that Niebuhr subsequently adopted. Middle axioms covered the middle ground between principles and specific policies. General statements of principle about peace or justice had little use, and Bennett judged that it was perilous for Christian ethicists to advocate specific policies or get bogged down in policy details. The place for social ethics was the middle ground. Middle axioms stated the general direction that social policies should take, drawing on Christian principles and empirical evidence. It was unfortunate that Bennett and J. H. Oldham called them "axioms," because they were not logical deductions from a fixed premise. But Bennett's books were models of social ethics as a middle-ground enterprise.[15]

Other schools of thought produced competing social ethical methods. John Ryan and John Courtney Murray developed Roman Catholic models of social ethics that blended policy arguments with Thomist philosophy. Walter Muelder did something similar with Personalist philosophy. An important figure in the building of social ethics as a discipline, Muelder developed a theory of the social mind as the total content of objective spirit. Closer to Peabody's idea, the University of Chicago Divinity School for four generations integrated social scientific research with ethical reasoning. It featured a strongly naturalistic philosophy and usually expounded William James's concept of the relational flow of experience. Shailer Mathews, Henry Nelson Wieman, James Luther Adams, Bernard Meland, and Alvin Pitcher taught their students to search for moral norms within the variegated life of society. Wieman had something like Peabody's idea of an underlying moral unity in nature. Otherwise the Chicago School tended to settle for discerning the hidden moral and religious basis of what Meland called "America's spiritual culture."[16]

I could spend the rest of this lecture unpacking the preceding paragraph and adding further examples: social ethics as liberationist, womanist, or feminist praxis; social ethics as communitarian narrative, biblical application, confessional discipline, postmodern carnival, and so on. But social ethics has more important business than its method, and after all this setting up, I want to focus on something more important. Economic justice is always a major subject; militarization and imperialism have become transcendent subjects; ecology, justice for women, and justice for gay, lesbian, bisexual, and transgendered persons are enormously important. But with time for only one subject, I will say a word about how my field has dealt with America's original sin of racism and white supremacism.

Up from Slavery: The Race Problem in the Social Question

Here my field has not done so well. The social gospel movement was good at helping to build colleges and universities for blacks, an achievement that should not be slighted. It was difficult work that sometimes required moral courage. But the movement as a whole rarely spoke up for the dignity and rights of African Americans, and most forms of Christian social ethics that succeeded the social gospel did not give high priority to racial justice either.

In the social gospel generation, to begin with the worst group, there were Northern and Southern social gospelers who preached an outright racist ideology without apology. Southerner Thomas Dixon Jr. was a best-selling hatemonger on the theme that blacks were biologically inferior and a drag on American society. Southerner Edgar Gardner Murphy offered a more cultural and high-minded case for racist supremacism; and Northern social gospeler Charles H. Parkhurst was equally dreadful on this subject. This group contended that Anglo-Saxons were superior to *all* races, but their chief concern in this area was to put down black people.[17]

Closer to the mainstream of the Northern social gospel, Josiah Strong and Lyman Abbott were right-leaning cultural chauvinists who pressed strongly for black assimilation to an Anglo-Saxon ideal. Abbott was the chief player in making Booker T. Washington famous. Another mainstream group, the left-leaning assimilationists, also lionized Washington and the vocational path to progress, but with a stronger recognition of the rights of blacks; they included Joseph Cook, Quincey Ewing, William Channing Gannett, Jenkin Lloyd Jones, Henry Demarest Lloyd, and William Hayes Ward. There was also a stream of spiritual descendants of the abolitionists who strongly defended the dignity and rights of African Americans. They included Herbert Seeley Bigelow, Algernon Crapsey, Harlan Paul Douglass, Newell Dwight Hillis, and Charles Spahr. But there were never enough of them, and they had little influence.[18]

In 1910 nearly 90 percent of American blacks still lived in the South. Most white social gospel leaders had little acquaintance with African Americans; they felt awkward about addressing a problem that was remote from their experience; and only the bravest of them publicly repudiated the prevalent American assumption of black inferiority. Many liberals believed deeply in the redeemer mission of their nation, which usually led to the belief that Anglo-Saxons were the leaders and saviors of the world. Moreover, evolutionary science was supposedly on their side; Darwinism was said to be a secular explanation of the Anglo-Saxon mission to civilize the world.

Few white Christian leaders publicly questioned the Supreme Court's 1896 *Plessy v. Ferguson* ruling that "separate but equal" segregation was consistent with the Fourteenth Amendment's guarantee of equal protection under the law. Some of them fought against the restriction of black suffrage, but most social gospelers focused solely on education through the programs of the American Missionary Society, and for some that meant vocational education only. Peabody, for example, gave many years of service to the Hampton Institute. He was committed to vocational up-lift, but regarding justice for blacks, he spoke for glacial slowness.[19]

That was the line of the *Outlook* magazine and its editor, Lyman Abbott, who co-authored and serialized *Up from Slavery* by Booker T. Washington. W. E. B. Du Bois criticized Washington for selling out the right of blacks to equal standing before the law and higher education; Abbott replied that Du Bois was ashamed of his race. In Abbott's telling, Du Bois made the white man the standard, but Washington looked for a standard in the ideals of his own race. Du Bois sought social equality for blacks, but Washington was too self-respecting for that. Du Bois tried to push his race to a higher place, but Washington sought to make the race stronger.[20]

Peabody never put it that stridently, but he was on Abbott's side of the argument. He was willing to offend his white audiences when they denied that blacks were educable, or when they fantasized about colonizing African Americans in a "Negro state" (Texas was the usual candidate). He could speak with feeling about the humanity of blacks, but always with a whiff of white supremacy and a stream of stereotypes.[21]

There were a few white social gospelers that converted from the patronizing view to the justice perspective. Washington Gladden was a left-leaning assimilationist for most of his career, but after he met Du Bois and read *The Souls of Black Folk*, he changed his position. The later Gladden told his white audiences that it was wrong to sell out the rights of blacks; he invited black ministers to preach in his pulpit; and he defended President Theodore Roosevelt for having lunch with Washington in the White House, an event that caused a furious national outcry that went on for months. Gladden caught some of the reaction, receiving hundreds of hateful, infuriated letters; he later recalled that it frightened him to realize what blacks were up against in his beloved country.

In the early 1900s a black tradition of the social gospel took root, led by Reverdy Ransom, Ida B. Wells-Barnett, Monroe Work, and Richard R. Wright Jr. Some of these figures had considerable dealings with white social gospelers, especially Ransom and Wright, and Ransom was active in the Federal Council of Churches. But these relationships were not reciprocal. Even Ransom was not treated as an equal counterpart in the development of social Christianity. The black social gospel tradition developed as a subordinated discourse, because U.S. American Protestantism was as segregated as U.S. American society.

The greatest social gospeler is a symbol of this story. In his early pastoral career in New York, Walter Rauschenbusch took a principled stand against racism and immigration restrictions. But in 1895, two years before he joined the faculty of Rochester Seminary, he wrote an anonymous fund-raising letter for the seminary's German Department that played on the racial fears of potential German Department donors: "Are the whites of this continent so sure of their possession against the blacks of the South and the seething yellow flocks beyond the Pacific that they need no reinforcement of men of their own blood while yet it is time?" America needed more German immigrants while yet it was time, Rauschenbusch urged. Two years later he wrote another letter, now as a member of the seminary faculty, and in 1902 Rauschenbusch stood before a commencement assembly and said the same thing, with an added twist. Essentially he argued that Germans were first cousins of the Anglo-Saxons, they helped to build modern democracy, and thus they deserved to be included in Manifest Destiny. It was short-sighted to give Anglo-Saxons exclusive credit for civilization. Rauschenbusch explained that modern democratic civilization was created by a single Teutonic racial stock consisting of Anglo-Saxons, Germans, and their American offspring. But the civilizational achievements of the race were imperiled by "alien strains" arriving from places like France, Spain, the Slavic lands, Bohemia, Poland, and the Russian Jewish territories.[22]

That was a frightening spectacle to the conscience of American liberal Protestantism, a man known for his tender heart and passion for justice. On the subject of black Americans, Rauschenbusch said nothing for many years. He realized that he knew very little on this subject, he knew only a few African Americans personally, and he had no moral authority in speaking about racial justice. More important, what he did know was too depressing to mix into his books and articles on the forward march of the kingdom. Rauschenbusch waited until his last years to break his silence. In *Christianizing the Social Order* (1912) he finally managed to say that the spirit of Jesus "smites race pride and prejudice in the face in the name of humanity." In his last book, *A Theology for the Social Gospel* (1917), he described racial lynching as the ultimate example of evil as a social inheritance. These statements are the kinds of things you might expect to read in Rauschenbusch, yet they came from nowhere, raising a new subject. In 1914 he explained why it took him so long to write even a sentence or two: "For years, the problem of the two races in the South has seemed to me so tragic, so insoluble, that I have never yet ventured to discuss it in public."[23]

To the black social gospelers, that was an existentially plausible reaction, since they understood the difficulty of sustaining hope in a seemingly hopeless situation. They dealt with it every day in ministering to people who had actually suffered the tragedy and sometimes been defeated by it. But for Ransom and other black ministers the response of mute hopelessness was an ethical impossibility. If Christianity had any social ethical meaning in the U.S. American context, it had to begin with the evils of white supremacism and hatred that oppressed black Americans.

I spent the past summer tracking down the writings of Reverdy Ransom, most of which are hard to attain. That he is forgotten is incredible. Ransom was a theological liberal, a socialist, a black nationalist, and, in his later career, an AME [African Methodist Episcopal Church] bishop. He was a liberationist and Afrocentrist before these terms had currency. His rhetorical eloquence was stunning. Often he observed that American blacks got nothing from Christian America despite being faithful Christians and loyal Americans. American blacks wanted to believe they would gain equal rights if they went to church, got an education, and learned a trade: "But their disillusionment is almost complete, since they find that Christ has not been able to break the American color line. If Jesus wept over Jerusalem, he should have for America an ocean of tears."[24]

Du Bois wrote that Ransom's powerful speeches "erected a monument in the history of African Methodism, the U.S., and the world" that would last "through time and eternity."[25] On the contrary, he was almost completely forgotten. After Martin Luther King Jr. had come and gone, a few scholars sought to account for the black social gospel tradition that influenced him. Benjamin Mays, Mordecai Johnson, and Howard Thurman were remembered. But unlike them, Ransom had no connection to King, and Mays and Thurman had more clout with the white Protestant establishment. The activist organizations to which Ransom gave himself either folded or let him down. The Socialist Party self-destructed in the 1920s and was culturally alien to him. He quit the Afro-American Council after it opted for Bookerism. The reincarnations of the old anti-slavery organizations faded away. The Niagara Movement was too radical to be pragmatic and too pragmatic for radicals like William Monroe Trotter; thus it dissolved. The NAACP grew out of the Niagara Movement, but it took a secular path. Then Ransom became a bishop, where the grinding tasks of ecclesiastical administration wore him down. He wanted to work in large interracial organizations that built a cooperative commonwealth for all people. But there weren't any for him to join, and Ransom opted for survival work.

Our distinguished colleague James Cone, in many of his writings and lectures, has challenged white theologians to interrogate the white supremacism of their field, their history, and their writings.[26] How could it be that five thousand American blacks were lynched while white theologians said almost nothing about it? How was it possible for the Federal Council of Churches to issue a Social Creed of the Churches in 1908 and never mention racial injustice? How can it be that after nearly four decades of black liberation theology, the field of theology is nowhere near that of U.S. American history in interrogating its racist past and present?

Many of us grew up believing that racism is essentially a problem of racial bias, a prejudice to be overcome. But the race problem in the U.S. is something deeper and more structural than mere bias; it is the culture of white supremacism, a gaping evil in the culture of whiteness. In the 1950s and 1960s, when Reinhold Niebuhr made remarkably optimistic statements about America's progress toward racial equality, there *were* significant gains to celebrate.[27] The Civil Rights Act was enacted three months before the presidential election of 1964, a year later the Voting Rights Act was enacted, and affirmative action programs were adopted.

But the reaction against these gains was volatile, helping to drive American politics to the right. Political campaigns became coded with racist images of black criminals and welfare queens. Liberals were redefined as guilty-types that coddled criminals, imposed reversely racist affirmative discrimination, and taxed working people to pay for welfare programs. Xenophobic slurs against Latin American immigrants were added to this winning formula, while regressive tax policies set off the economic equivalent of tectonic plate movements—massive increases in economic inequality. Today 1 percent of the population holds one-third of the wealth; the top 10 percent holds two-thirds of the wealth; prisons are stuffed with people of color; and an incredible military budget crowds out social investments for human and ecological needs.

For eighteen years I taught at a liberal arts college that I love dearly and which was very much like most of the others. We struggled to attract black and Asian students and faculty, did even worse attracting Latino/a students and faculty, and had particular problems retaining African American faculty. Some of us took part in anti-racism workshops, confessed our racism, and thought, "Ok, now we're getting somewhere." But nothing really changed, even if entire departments went to the workshops. One year we lost 80 percent of our African American faculty. Why was this happening?

It was tempting to point the finger at colleagues who pined for the white male monoculture of the past and refused to go to the workshops. But the college made a strong commitment to multiculturalism, the opposition decreased through retirements, and we *still* lost black colleagues. On their way out they said things like, "This place is so white, I can't breathe here." Finally our group of workshop veterans began to interrogate the culture of whiteness. It helped that a new scholarly literature in this area was beginning to emerge. I read most of it and learned a great deal, although I didn't like the pretentious style in which some of it was written. More important to me was a departing colleague who talked with me at length on his way out. It turned out that the critique of white supremacism was more slippery, puzzling, and uncomfortable than the anti-bias approach, but also more productive.

Wherever white people are dominant, white culture is transparent to them. It is hard to see because it is everything that is not specifically African American culture, Native American culture, Mexican culture, and so on. To be more precise, it is hard for whites to see because white supremacy makes white culture normative. At its extreme, white supremacy is about bigots wearing sheets and burning crosses. But more broadly and normally it is something that bestows privilege on every white person in this society, some more than others. White supremacy is a structure of power based on privilege that presumes to define what is normal. If you live in this society without being constantly reminded of your race, and don't have to worry about representing your race, and can worry about racism without being viewed as self-interested, and don't have to worry about being targeted by police for your race, you are a beneficiary of white supremacism. Its privileges are your daily bread and environment. Today the shape of this inheritance is complicated immensely by the immigration of Asians, Latino/as and others from every part of the world into the U.S. Some of them move right into white privilege; some struggle to get a piece of it; some have no chance of getting any; all are affected by the ravages of America's original sin. White supremacism is deeply entrenched in our society, reinforced by powerful self-interested institutions, and widely denied, if not invisible to its deniers.

I know very well how any talk about white privilege goes down at the lower end of the white economic spectrum. Where I grew up, the middle-class families on television seemed to live in a foreign country, and there was no consciousness whatsoever of possessing any cultural privileges, aside from the necessity of putting down people of color. My father was taught that he was inferior for being of mixed race, a lesson that scarred him and affected his children. After I climbed into the middle class through education and marriage, I learned that the reality of white privilege is widely denied there, too. Even in ecumenical churches and activist organizations it is very difficult to talk about.

Long before I joined a church, I worked in social justice organizations that struggled to achieve even token diversity: "We're so inclusive and we want to be more diverse: Why don't they join us?" It took me years of asking that question before I realized that to become more diverse, we had to privilege the issues of people of color. And that began by building bonds of trust across racial lines. Most activist organizations and religious communities are not willing to do it. Usually there is an established agenda and ethos that militates against anything stronger than weak gestures toward diversity.

But there are significant exceptions, here and there, across the country. The Industrial Areas Foundation network has done it for fifty years. Groups dealing with environmental racism have done it. The Gamaliel network is another important example. In Gamaliel organizations, representatives from different faith communities build bonds of trust and community for an entire year *before* they decide what issues they are going to work on. This approach is highly intentional and pragmatic, and it brings racially diverse white religious communities into sustained coalitional work with black and Hispanic communities to address local problems. Along the way, culturally privileged Christians come to see marginalization and exclusion that they did not see previously.

When people ask me why I came to Union, I always point to its long-time advocacy of social justice, above all, its commitment to dismantling racism. Union has a special place and mission in theological education. When you think of black liberation theology, feminist social ethics, and womanist theology and social ethics, no seminary comes close to the significance of this one, because of the brilliant work of James Cone, James Washington, Cornel West, Beverly Harrison, Delores Williams, Emilie Townes, and many others. Year after year Union attracts the most remarkable students that I know—reflective, perceptive, sometimes contentious types with a passion for social justice. Working with them and faculty colleagues, I want to learn better what it means to be an agent of social transformation.

This has been the kind of lecture that my beloved companion used to warn me against. My wife Brenda Biggs was a Presbyterian pastor, and a pistol: irreverent, wisecracking, extroverted despite her struggle with depression, wondrously loving, a consummate pastor with a knack for getting people to talk about *the issue* in their lives. She fought cancer ferociously for ten years, and in twenty years of marriage she never stopped reminding me that I was not her type. "You know," she would say, "you're not my type. I never went for the shy, nice boys. I always went for bad boys. And jocks—I couldn't stand those guys. So how in God's name did I end up with a nice boy jock?"

Always I replied, "I just got lucky. I caught you on the rebound from one of your bad boys." Seven years ago, she left this instruction: "You know, there's going to be a huge crowd at my funeral. Could you give them this message? 'In lieu of flowers, please vote for Democrats.'"

Throughout our marriage we worked together on sermons, sometimes at the dinner table, though our daughter, Sara, eventually put a stop to the latter practice. When mine got too intellectual Brenda ripped them apart. Today's lecture featured the other proclivity of mine that she tried to correct. I know with utter certainty what she would have said about it: "Gary, do you always have to explore the backstory? 1880 was so long ago. Can't you just begin where it gets interesting?"

I agree that the most important issues are the ones that cause suffering today. On the road that's what I speak about, and I expect that most of my writing at Union will focus on current issues. Social ethics probably does not need the kind of disciplinary self-consciousness and scrutiny that are second nature to theology and Christian history. It is valuable even as a mere catchall for the discussion of urgent social questions.

Yet upon moving here I immediately took up a big, reflective, disciplinary project. That decision reflects my belief that a field should have an account of its past and doctoral students should know the history of their field. And it reflects my gratitude and amazement at being here. On this day thirty years ago I enrolled at Union Seminary and moved into McGiffert Hall. By then I had read the works of John Bennett. At Union I met Roger Shinn. Years later, after Larry Rasmussen became the Niebuhr professor, he became a treasured friend to me. But now I cannot say the names, "John Bennett, Roger Shinn, and Larry Rasmussen," without choking with embarrassment, because somehow I have been asked to succeed them as the Niebuhr professor. How could Union choose me to carry on the social-ethical legacy of these wonderful teachers and scholars? Never would I have presumed to apply for such an honor. I count it all as grace. For the privilege of joining this distinguished faculty and seminary community, I am ineffably grateful. Blessings and thanks to all of you.

NOTES

Introduction

1. Mary Daly, *Beyond God the Father: Toward a Philosophy of Women's Liberation* (Boston: Beacon, 1973).

2. James H. Cone, *Black Theology and Black Power* (New York: Harper & Row, 1969); Cone, *A Black Theology of Liberation*, 2d ed. (Maryknoll, N.Y.: Orbis Books, 1986 [1970]).

3. Daly, *Beyond God the Father*, 98–131.

4. Mary Daly, *Gyn/Ecology: The Metaethics of Radical Feminism* (Boston: Beacon, 1978), "absolutely," 28–29, "prevailing," 39; Daly, *Pure Lust: Elemental Feminist Philosophy* (Boston: Beacon, 1984); Daly, "Original Re-Introduction," in *Beyond God the Father: Toward a Philosophy of Women's Liberation*, 2nd ed. (Boston: Beacon, 1985), quote xi–xii.

5. Daly, "Original Re-Introduction," quote xviii; see Mary Daly, *Outercourse: The Bedazzling Voyage* (San Francisco: HarperCollins, 1992).

1. Society as the Subject of Redemption

This chapter adapts material from Gary Dorrien, "Social Salvation: The Social Gospel as Theology and Economics," in *The Social Gospel Today,* ed. Christopher H. Evans (Louisville: Westminster John Knox Press, 2001), 101–113; and Dorrien, *The Making of American Liberal Theology: Idealism, Realism, and Modernity* (Louisville: Westminster John Knox Press, 2003), 73–128.

1. See Josiah Strong, *Our Country, Its Possible Future and Its Present Crisis* (New York: Baker & Taylor, 1891 [1886]); George Herron, *The New Redemption: A Call to the Church to Reconstruct Society According to the Gospel of Christ* (New York: T. Y. Crowell, 1893); Herron, *The Christian Society* (Chicago: Fleming H. Revell, 1894); Herron, *The Christian State: A Political Vision of Christ* (New York: T. Y. Crowell, 1895); Herron, *The Larger Christ* (Chicago: T. Y. Fleming H. Revell, 1891); Harry F. Ward, *The New Social Order: Principles and Programs* (New York: Macmillan, 1920); Ward, *Our Economic Morality and the Ethic of Jesus* (New York: Macmillan, 1929); Ward, *The Soviet Spirit* (New York: International, 1944); Charles H. Hopkins, *The Rise of the Social Gospel in American Protestantism, 1865–1915* (New Haven, Conn.: Yale University Press, 1940); James Dombrowski, *The Early Days of Christian Socialism in America* (New York: Columbia University Press, 1936; Paul A. Carter, *The Decline and Revival of the Social Gospel* (Ithaca, N.Y.: Cornell University Press, 1954).

2. See Reinhold Niebuhr, *Moral Man and Immoral Society: A Study in Ethics and Politics* (New York: Scribner's, 1932); Reverdy C. Ransom, *The Spirit of Freedom and Justice: Orations and Speeches* (Nashville, Tenn.: AME Sunday School Union, 1926); Ransom, *Making the Gospel Plain: The Writings of Bishop Reverdy C. Ransom,* ed. Anthony B. Pinn (Harrisburg, Pa.: Trinity, 1999).

3. See Washington Gladden, *Being a Christian: What It Means and How to Begin* (Boston: Congregational Publishing Society, 1876); Gladden, *The Christian Way: Whither It Leads and How to Go On* (New York: Dodd, Mead, 1877); Henry F. May, *Protestant Churches and Industrial America* (New York: Harper & Brothers, 1949), 254; Dorn, *Washington Gladden,* 200–201; Strong, *Our Country,* 138–139; Richard T. Ely, *Ground Under Our Feet: An Autobiography* (New York: Macmillan, 1938), 140–143.

4. Washington Gladden, *Applied Christianity: Moral Aspects of Social Questions* (Boston: Houghton, Mifflin, 1889), 8–32; see Gladden, *Recollections* (Boston: Houghton Mifflin, 1909), 300–304.

5. See William Green, *Modern Trade Unionism* (Washington, D.C.: American Federation of Labor, 1925); *Almanac of American History,* ed. Arthur M. Schlesinger Jr. (New York: Barnes & Noble, 1993), 359–361.

6. Richard T. Ely, *The Labor Movement in America* (New York: Thomas Y. Crowell, 1886); Ely, *Social Aspects of Christianity and Other Essays* (New York: Thomas Y. Crowell, 1889), quote 27; Washington Gladden, *Working People and Their Employers* (New York: Funk and Wagnalls, 1894), 44–45; "industrial system" quote in Gladden, *Applied Christianity,* 32–33.

7. Gladden, *Applied Christianity,* 34–35. See Richard T. Ely, ed., *A History of Cooperation in America* (Baltimore, Md.: Johns Hopkins University Press, 1888); Nicholas Paine Gilman, *Profit Sharing between Employer and Employee: A Study in the Evolution of the Wages System* (London: Macmillan, 1890); Gladden's

thinking on profit sharing was strongly influenced by Sedley Taylor, *Profit-Sharing between Labor and Capital: Six Essays* (New York: Humboldt, 1886).

8. Gladden, *Applied Christianity,* 53–101, quotes 98, 100.

9. Washington Gladden, *Tools and the Man: Property and Industry under the Christian Law* (Boston: Houghton, Mifflin, 1893), quotes 214, 124; discussion of cooperative ownership, 190–203.

10. Ibid., 130, 271.

11. Ibid., 264–265; closing quote in Washington Gladden, *Christianity and Socialism* (New York: Eaton & Mains, 1905), 141.

12. Gladden, *Christianity and Socialism,* 102–138, right to property statement, 92; Washington Gladden, *Social Facts and Forces* (New York: G. P. Putnam's, 1897), 80–86; Gladden, *Recollections,* 308–309; Gladden, *Tools and the Man,* 294–302, quotes 299, 300.

13. Washington Gladden, *The Labor Question* (Boston: Pilgrim, 1911), 3–55, 98–110, quote 55; Gladden, *Recollections,* 306–308; Gladden, *Social Facts and Forces,* 81–82; unidentified "vindictive opposition" quote in *Recollections,* 305; see John L. Shover, "Washington Gladden and the Labor Question," *Ohio Historical Quarterly* 68 (October 1959): 344–345.

14. Gladden, *Tools and the Man,* 1–2.

15. Ibid., 3–4, 6; see Washington Gladden, *Social Salvation* (Boston: Houghton, Mifflin, 1902), 1–31; Gladden, *Burning Questions of the Life That Now Is, and of That Which Is to Come* (London: James Clarke, 1890), 223–248; Gladden, *The Church and the Kingdom* (New York: Fleming H. Revell, 1894).

16. Shailer Mathews, "The Social Teaching of Paul, I: The Social Content of Early Messianism," *The Biblical World* 19 (1902): 34–46; "II: The Social Content of Messianism in New Testament Times," 113–121; "III: The Apocalyptic Messianism of the Pharisees," 178–189; Mathews, "The Gospel and the Modern Man," *Christendom* 1 (1903), 300–302, 352–353, 399–401, 446–449, 489–491, 537–539; Mathews, *The Messianic Hope in the New Testament* (Chicago: University of Chicago Press, 1905); Gladden's conversation with Carl S. Patton quoted in *First Church News: The Gladden Centennial* 6 (February 1936), 6–7.

17. Lyman Abbott, *The Twentieth Century Crusade* (New York: Macmillan, 1918), 62; Shailer Mathews, *Patriotism and Religion* (New York: Macmillan, 1918), 4; Ray H. Abrams, *Preachers Present Arms* (New York: Round Table, 1933), 54–55; Dorn, *Washington Gladden,* 429; see Thomas J. Knock, *To End All Wars: Woodrow Wilson and the Quest for a New World Order* (Princeton, N.J.: Princeton University Press, 1992), 108–122; Ronald Schaffer, *America in the Great War: The Rise of the Welfare State* (New York: Oxford University Press, 1991), xiv–xvii.

18. "All that is needed" text in Washington Gladden, "Loyalty," reprinted in Gladden, *The Interpreter* (Boston: Pilgrim, 1918), 81–96, quote 96; "this war"

in Gladden, "Making the World Safe for Democracy," sermon (April 29, 1917), Gladden Papers, Ohio State University.

19. Walter Rauschenbusch, *Christianity and the Social Crisis* (New York: Macmillan, 1907), 400–401.

20. Jacob Henry Dorn, *Washington Gladden: Prophet of the Social Gospel* (Columbus: Ohio University Press, 1967), 431.

21. Washington Gladden, "A New Heart for the Nation," in Gladden, *The Interpreter*, 131–147, quotes 145.

22. Walter Rauschenbusch, "The Kingdom of God," 1913 Cleveland YMCA Lecture, in *The Social Gospel in America*, ed. Robert T. Handy (New York: Oxford University Press, 1966), quote 267. Rauschenbusch continued to work on *Revolutionary Christianity* in the early 1890s, but he never finished it. Parts of it were later published under the title *The Righteousness of the Kingdom*, ed. Max Stackhouse (Nashville, Tenn.: Abingdon, 1968).

23. Rauschenbusch, *Christianity and the Social Crisis*, quotes 195, 204, 205, 271; see *Fabian Essays in Socialism*, ed. G. Bernard Shaw (New York: Doubleday, 1967 [1889]); G. D. H. Cole, *Guild Socialism Restated* (London: L. Parsons, 1920).

24. Rauschenbusch, *Christianity and the Social Crisis*, quote 341.

25. Ibid., quotes 400, 401.

26. Ibid., quotes 401, 410–411.

27. Ibid., 420, 421.

28. See Washington Gladden, *Applied Christianity: Moral Aspects of Social Questions* (Boston: Houghton, Mifflin, 1889); Josiah Strong, *Our Country, Its Possible Future and Its Present Crisis* (Cambridge, Mass.: Harvard University Press, 1963 [1886; rev. ed. 1891]); George D. Herron, *The Larger Christ* (Chicago: Fleming H. Revell, 1891); Shailer Mathews, *The Social Teaching of Jesus: An Essay in Christian Sociology* (New York: Macmillan, 1897); Francis Greenwood Peabody, *Jesus Christ and the Social Question* (New York: Macmillan, 1900).

29. "If the church" in Rauschenbusch, *Christianity and the Social Crisis*, 339; see George Herron, *The Christian State* (New York: T. Y. Crowell, 1895); Herron, *Woodrow Wilson and the World's Peace* (New York: Kennerley, 1917); Herron, *Germanism and the American Crusade* (New York: Kennerley, 1918); Herron, *The Defeat in the Victory* (London: Palmer, 1921).

30. Rauschenbusch, *Christianizing the Social Order* (New York: Macmillan, 1912), quote vii.

31. Ibid., quotes viii, 9.

32. Ibid., 48–60, quotes 49, 58, 56. Rauschenbusch singled out I. M. Haldemann, a New York minister and prominent premillennial fundamentalist, who condemned *Christianity and the Social Crisis* as sub-Christian; see I. M. Haldemann, *Professor Rauschenbusch's "Christianity and the Social Crisis"* (New

York: Charles C. Cook, n.d.), booklet. Haldemann was pastor of First Baptist Church in New York City; his pamphlets were widely distributed.

33. Rauschenbusch, *Christianizing the Social Order,* quotes 85, 89–90.

34. Ibid., quotes 90, 121.

35. Ibid., 123–125.

36. Ibid., 124–125, quotes 125.

37. Ibid., 125–130, quote 125.

38. Ibid., 130–138, quotes 131, 135. Janet Fishburn's early work claimed that Rauschenbusch opposed female suffrage and that he "abhorred feminism because it was potentially destructive of family and society." See Janet Forsythe Fishburn, *The Fatherhood of God and the Victorian Family: The Social Gospel in America* (Philadelphia: Fortress, 1981), 124. Martin E. Marty, among others, repeated Fishburn's claims; see Martin E. Marty, *Modern American Religion,* Vol. 1, *The Irony of It All, 1893–1919* (Chicago: University of Chicago Press, 1986), 292. Fishburn's excellent recent work is more careful and discriminating on this subject. She allows that Rauschenbusch supported the movement for women's rights, while emphasizing that he championed the late-Victorian ideal of the mother-nurtured family. See Fishburn, "Walter Rauschenbusch and 'The Women Movement': A Gender Analysis," unpublished paper delivered at the 1999 Social Gospel Conference, Colgate Rochester Divinity School/Crozer Theological Seminary, March 18, 1999.

39. Rauschenbusch, *Christianity and the Social Crisis,* quotes 279, 276; see Walter Rauschenbusch, "Some Moral Aspects of the 'Woman Movement,'" *Biblical World* 42 (October 1913): 195–198; Walter Rauschenbusch, "What about the Woman?" Box 20, Rauschenbusch Family Papers; Peter Gabriel Filene, *Him Her Self: Sex Roles in Modern America* (New York: Harcourt Brace Jovanovich, 1974), 23–29; Fishburn, *The Fatherhood of God and the Victorian Family,* 120–127; Fishburn, "Walter Rauschenbusch and 'The Women Movement': A Gender Analysis"; Susan Curtis, *A Consuming Faith: The Social Gospel and Modern American Culture* (Baltimore, Md.: Johns Hopkins University Press, 1991), 107–108, 112.

40. Rauschenbusch, *Christianizing the Social Order,* 137–155, quotes 141, 152–153.

41. Ibid., quote 156.

42. See Daniel Bell, *The Cultural Contradictions of Capitalism* (New York: Basic Books, 1976).

43. Rauschenbusch, *Christianizing the Social Order,* 311–323, quotes 317.

44. Ibid., quotes 311, 313, 314.

45. Ibid., 341–343, 352–356, quotes 343, 353.

46. Ibid., quote 361.

47. John Stuart Mill, *Principles of Political Economy,* 2 vols. (New York: Appleton, 1884), 2:357–359; Rauschenbusch, *Christianizing the Social Order,*

356–371; Walter Rauschenbusch, "Christian Socialism," in *A Dictionary of Religion and Ethics*, ed. Shailer Mathews and Gerald Birney Smith (New York: Macmillan, 1923), 90–91.

48. Rauschenbusch, *Christianizing the Social Order,* quotes 369, 437.

49. Ibid., quotes 367–368, 329.

50. Walter Rauschenbusch to Francis G. Peabody, 14 December 1912, Box 26, Rauschenbusch Family Collection.

51. Rauschenbusch, *Christianizing the Social Order,* 458–466, quotes 433, 464–465.

52. On the post-Rauschenbusch social gospel, see Gary Dorrien, *Social Ethics in the Making: Interpreting an American Tradition* (Oxford: Wiley-Blackwell, 2009), 109–225.

2. Reinhold Niebuhr, Karl Barth, and the Crises of War and Capitalism

This chapter adapts material from Gary Dorrien, "The Golden Years of Welfare Capitalism: Twilight of the Giants," in *The Twentieth Century: A Theological Overview*, ed. Gregory Baum (Maryknoll, NY: Orbis Books, 1999), 91–103; and Dorrien, *Soul in Society: The Making and Renewal of Social Christianity* (Minneapolis: Fortress Press, 1995), 91–161.

1. See Karl Barth, *The Epistle to the Romans*, 6th ed., trans. Edwyn C. Hoskyns (London: Oxford University Press, 1975 [1933]); Gary Dorrien, *The Barthian Revolt in Modern Theology: Theology Without Weapons* (Louisville, Ky.: Westminster John Knox Press, 2000), 47–80; Paul Tillich, "Basic Principles of Religious Socialism" (1923), and "Religious Socialism" (1930), reprinted in Tillich, *Political Expectation*, trans. James Luther Adams and Victor Nuovo (New York: Harper & Row, 1971), 40–57, 58–88; Tillich, *The Socialist Decision* (1932), trans. Franklin Sherman (New York: Harper & Row, 1977); Emil Brunner, *The Divine Imperative* (1932), trans. Olive Wyon (Philadelphia: Westminster, 1947), 423; Niebuhr, "The Blindness of Liberalism," *Radical Religion* 1 (fall 1936): 4; Niebuhr, "Roosevelt's Merry-Go-Round," *Radical Religion* 3 (spring 1938): 4; Niebuhr, "New Deal Medicine," *Radical Religion* 4 (spring 1939): 1–2.

2. Niebuhr, "Catastrophe or Social Control?" *Harper's* 165 (June 1932), 118.

3. Niebuhr, *Moral Man and Immoral Society: A Study in Ethics and Politics* (New York: Scribner's, 1932).

4. Ibid., quotes xx, 144.

5. Ibid., 256.

6. Niebuhr, "Dr. Niebuhr's Position," *Christian Century* 50 (January 18, 1933), quote 91–92; see Theodore C. Hume, "Prophet of Disillusion," *Christian Century* 50 (January 4, 1933), 18–19; Norman Thomas, review of *Moral Man and Immoral Society*, by Reinhold Niebuhr, *The World Tomorrow* 15 (December 14,

1932), 565, 567; John Haynes Holmes, review of ibid., *Herald Tribune Books* (January 8, 1933), 13; John Haynes Holmes, "Reinhold Niebuhr's Philosophy of Despair," *Herald Tribune Books* (March 18, 1934), 7; Niebuhr, "Ten Years That Shook My World," *Christian Century* 56 (April 26, 1939), 546; Niebuhr, "After Capitalism—What?" *The World Tomorrow* (March 1, 1933), 204.

7. Niebuhr, *Reflections on the End of an Era* (New York: Scribner's, 1934), 24.

8. Ibid., 27–28.

9. Niebuhr, "After Capitalism—What?" 203; Niebuhr, *Reflections on the End of an Era*, 30; see Niebuhr, "Is Religion Counter-Revolutionary?" *Radical Religion* 1 (fall 1935): 14–20.

10. Niebuhr, "Why I Leave the F.O.R.," *Christian Century* 51 (January 3, 1934); reprinted in Niebuhr, *Love and Justice: Selections from the Shorter Writings of Reinhold Niebuhr*, ed. D. B. Robertson (Louisville: Westminster John Knox, 1992 [1957]), 254–259.

11. Niebuhr, *An Interpretation of Christian Ethics* (New York: Harper & Row, 1963 [1935]), 23.

12. Ibid., 106–107, 116.

13. Ibid., 114–115.

14. Ibid., 116; see Niebuhr, "Religion and Marxism," *Modern Monthly* 8 (February 1935): 714.

15. Niebuhr, "The Blindness of Liberalism, *Radical Religion* 1 (fall 1936): 4.

16. Ibid., "the inevitable" 4; Niebuhr, "The Idea of Progress and Socialism," *Radical Religion* 1 (spring 1936): "tolerable" and "socialism is" 28. Niebuhr's "tolerable equilibrium" phrase appeared frequently in his writings, as in Niebuhr, "Ten Years That Shook My World," 545.

17. Niebuhr, "The Idea of Progress and Socialism," 28.

18. Niebuhr, "The Creed of Modern Christian Socialists," *Radical Religion* 3 (spring 1938): 16.

19. Ibid., 16; see Niebuhr, "The Idea of Progress and Socialism," 28.

20. See Arthur M. Schlesinger Jr., "Reinhold Niebuhr's Role in Political Thought," in *Reinhbld Niebuhr: His Religious, Social, and Political Thought*, ed. Charles W. Kegley and Robert W. Bretall (New York: Macmillan, 1956).

21. Niebuhr, "New Deal Medicine," *Radical Religion* 4 (spring 1939): 1–2.

22. Niebuhr, "Roosevelt's Merry-Go-Round," *Radical Religion* 3 (spring 1938): 4; Schlesinger, "Reinhold Niebuhr's Role in Political Thought," 142.

23. Niebuhr, "The Socialist Campaign," *Christianity and Society* 5 (summer 1940): 4.

24. Niebuhr, "Crisis in Washington," *Radical Religion* 4 (spring 1939): 9; Niebuhr, "Taxation and the Defense Economy," *Christianity and Society* 6 (fall 1941): 5; Niebuhr, "Better Government Than We Deserve," *Christianity and Society* 7 (spring 1942): 10; Niebuhr, postscript to A. T. Mollegen, "The Common

Convictions of the Fellowship of Socialist Christians: A Suggested Statement as the Basis for Discussion," *Christianity and Society* 8 (spring 1943): 28; see Niebuhr, "Brief Comments," *Radical Religion* 3 (winter 1937): 7; Niebuhr, "Brief Comments," *Radical Religion* (spring 1938): 7; Niebuhr, "The London Times and the Crisis," *Radical Religion* 4 (winter 1938–39): 32; Niebuhr, "Willkie and Roosevelt," *Christianity and Society* 5 (fall 1940): 5.

25. Niebuhr, *The Children of Light and the Children of Darkness: A Vindication of Democracy and a Critique of Its Traditional Defense* (New York: Scribner's, 1944), xi.

26. Ibid., 113–114; see Niebuhr, "The Creed of Modern Christian Socialists," *Radical Religion* 3 (spring 1938): 16.

27. Niebuhr, "Plutocracy and World Responsibilities," *Christianity and Society* 14 (fall 1949): 7–8; see Niebuhr, "Frontier Fellowship," *Christianity and Society* 13 (fall 1948): 4; Niebuhr, "The Organization of the Liberal Movement," *Christianity and Society* 12 (spring 1947): 8–10.

28. Niebuhr et al., "Christian Action Statement of Purpose," *Christianity and Crisis* 11 (October 1, 1951), 126.

29. Niebuhr, "The Anomaly of European Socialism," *Yale Review* 42 (December 1952): 166–167.

30. Niebuhr, *The Irony of American History* (New York: Scribner's, 1952), 101.

31. Niebuhr, *Pious and Secular America* (New York: Scribner's, 1958), 76.

32. Niebuhr, "Uneasy Peace or Catastrophe," *Christianity and Crisis* 18 (April 28, 1958), 54–55; see Niebuhr, *The Structure of Nations and Empires: A Study of Recurring Patterns and Problems of the Political Order in Relation to the Unique Problems of the Nuclear Age* (New York: Scribner's, 1959), 282–283. For his early cold war thinking, see Niebuhr, *Christian Realism and Political Problems* (New York: Scribner's, 1953), 33–42; Niebuhr, "Communism and the Protestant Clergy," *Look* 17 (November 17, 1953), 37–38; Niebuhr, "The Peril of Complacency in Our Nation," *Christianity and Crisis* 14 (February 8, 1954), 1.

33. See Arthur M. Schlesinger Jr., *The Vital Center: The Politics of Freedom* (Boston: Houghton Mifflin, 1949); see John C. Bennett, *Social Salvation: A Religious Approach to the Problems of Social Change* (New York: Scribner's, 1935), 133; Bennett, *Christian Realism* (New York: Scribner's, 1952); Emil Brunner, *Justice and the Social Order*, trans. Mary Hottinger (New York: Harper & Brothers, 1945), 175–183.

34. Karl Barth, "Amsterdamer Fragen und Antwortem," *Theologische Existenz heute* 15 (1949): 3–4. An edited version of this speech featuring a somewhat problematic translation by the staff of the World Council of Churches was published under the title, "No Christian Marshall Plan," in *Christian Century* 65 (December 8, 1948), 1330–1333.

35. Barth, "Amsterdamer Fragen und Antwortem," 4–7.

36. Niebuhr, "Barth—Apostle of the Absolute," *Christian Century* 45 (December 13, 1928), 1523–1524; Reinhold Niebuhr to John C. Bennett, June 10 and July 20, 1930, cited in Richard Wightman Fox, *Reinhold Niebuhr: A Biography* (Ithaca, N.Y.: Cornell University Press, 1996), 123.

37. See Karl Barth, "Continental vs. Anglo-Saxon Theology: A Preliminary Reply to Reinhold Niebuhr," *Christian Century* 66 (February 16, 1949), 201; see Gary Dorrien, *Soul in Society: The Making and Renewal of Social Christianity* (Minneapolis: Fortress, 1995), 84–161, 308–310, 343–350.

38. Niebuhr, "We Are Men and Not God," *Christian Century* 65 (October 27, 1948), 1138–1140.

39. See Karl Barth, "The Christian Community in the Midst of Political Change" (1948), reprinted in Barth, *Against the Stream: Shorter Post-War Writings, 1946–52*, trans. Stanley Godman and E. M. Delacour (London: SCM, 1954), 51–105.

40. See Karl Barth, "Karl Barth's Reply," reprinted in Barth, *Against the Stream*, 114–115; Emil Brunner, "An Open Letter to Karl Barth," reprinted in ibid., 106–113; Niebuhr, "An Answer to Karl Barth," *Christian Century* 66 (February 23, 1949), 234.

41. See Niebuhr, *Christian Realism and Political Problems*, 37–42; Niebuhr, *The Irony of American History*, 128–129.

42. Barth, "Karl Barth's Reply," 116–118.

43. Karl Barth, "How My Mind Has Changed" (1958), reprinted in Barth, *How I Changed My Mind* (Richmond: John Knox, 1966), 66. See Barth, "The Church between East and West" (1949), reprinted in Barth, *Against the Stream*, 127–146.

44. Karl Barth, "Karl Barth's Own Words: Excerpts from the Swiss theologian's letter to an East German pastor," trans. RoseMarie Oswald Barth, *Christian Century* 76 (March 25, 1959), 353–355. On Barth's theme regarding communism as a product of modern Western history, see also "How My Mind Has Changed" (1958), 63–65.

45. Ibid., 354–355.

46. Niebuhr, "Barth's East German Letter," *Christian Century* 76 (February 11, 1959), 167–168.

47. Niebuhr, "Coherence, Incoherence, and Christian Faith," *Journal of Religion* 31 (July 1951): 162; Niebuhr, "Reply to Interpretation and Criticism," in Kegley and Bretall, *Reinhold Niebuhr: His Religious, Social, and Political Thought*, 441–442; see Daniel D. Williams, "Niebuhr and Liberalism," in ibid., 196.

48. Niebuhr, "The Quality of Our Lives," *Christian Century* 77 (May 11, 1960), quotes 568.

49. Patrick Granfield, Interview with Reinhold Niebuhr, in *Theologians at Work* (New York: Macmillan, 1967), 55.

50. See Niebuhr, "The Peace Offensive," *Christianity and Crisis* 25 (January 24, 1966), 301; Niebuhr, "Escalation Objective," *New York Times*, March 14, 1967; Niebuhr, Foreword to *Martin Luther King Jr., John C. Bennett, Henry Steele Commager, Abraham Heschel Speak on the War in Vietnam* (New York: Clergy and Laymen Concerned About Vietnam, 1967), 3; Fox, *Reinhold Niebuhr*, 285.

51. Niebuhr, "Toward New Intra-Christian Endeavors," *Christian Century* 86 (December 31, 1969), 1662–1663.

3. The Niebuhrian Legacy

This chapter adapts material from Gary Dorrien, *The Making of American Liberal Theology: Idealism, Realism, and Modernity* (Louisville: Westminster John Knox Press, 2003), 435–483.

1. Elisabeth Sifton, *The Serenity Prayer: Faith and Politics in Times of Peace and War* (New York: W. W. Norton, 2003), quotes 316, 145, 317.

2. Ibid., quotes 334, 321.

3. Elisabeth Sifton later clarified to me that she was referring to most church leaders and some theologians, not all, since Niebuhr's best friends included church leaders (Will Scarlett) and theologians (John Bennett).

4. Alan Geyer, roundtable symposium on "Christian Realism: Retrospect and Prospect," *Christianity and Crisis* 28 (August 5, 1968), 178.

5. David Brooks, "Obama, Gospel and Verse," *New York Times*, April 26, 2007, A25; see Niebuhr, *An Interpretation of Christian Ethics* (New York: Harper & Brothers, 1935); Niebuhr, *The Nature and Destiny of Man: A Christian Interpretation*, 1 volume ed. (New York: Scribner's, 1949); Niebuhr, *The Self and the Dramas of History* (New York: Scribner's 1955).

6. See Theodore C. Hume, "Prophet of Disillusion," *Christian Century* 50 (January 4, 1933), 18–19; Norman Thomas, review of *Moral Man and Immoral Society*, by Reinhold Niebuhr, *The World Tomorrow* 15 (December 14, 1932), 565, 567; John Haynes Holmes, review of ibid., *Herald Tribune Books* (January 8, 1933), 13; John Haynes Holmes, "Reinhold Niebuhr's Philosophy of Despair," *Herald Tribune Books* (March 18, 1934), 7.

7. H. Richard Niebuhr, "The Grace of Doing Nothing," *Christian Century* 49 (March 23, 1932), 379; Reinhold Niebuhr, "Must We Do Nothing?" *Christian Century* 49 (March 30, 1932), 416–417; H. Richard Niebuhr, "The Only Way into the Kingdom of God," *Christian Century* 49 (April 6, 1932), 447; see [Reinhold Niebuhr] "The League and Japan," *World Tomorrow* 15 (March 1932), 4; *Remembering Reinhold Niebuhr: Letters of Reinhold and Ursula M. Niebuhr*, ed. Ursula M. Niebuhr (San Francisco: HarperSanFrancisco, 1991); H. Richard Niebuhr, *The Social Sources of Denominationalism* (New York: Henry Holt, 1929);

H. Richard Niebuhr, *The Kingdom of God in America* (New York: Harper & Row, 1937).

8. H. Richard Niebuhr to Reinhold Niebuhr, n.d. [mid-January 1933], Reinhold Niebuhr Papers, Library of Congress, Washington, D.C.; cited in Richard W. Fox, *Reinhold Niebuhr: A Biography*, 2nd ed. (Ithaca, N.Y.: Cornell University Press, 1996 [1985]), 144–145.

9. Ibid.; see Fox, *Reinhold Niebuhr*, 145–146.

10. Niebuhr, "Ten Years That Shook My World," *Christian Century* 56 (April 26, 1939), quote 546; Niebuhr, *Reflections on the End of an Era* (New York: Scribner's, 1934), 279–296.

11. Niebuhr, "Reply to Interpretation and Criticism," in *Reinhold Niebuhr: His Religious, Social, and Political Thought*, ed. Charles W. Kegley and Robert W. Bretall (New York: Macmillan, 1956), 431–451; Niebuhr, "Intellectual Autobiography," in ibid., 3–23, quotes 3.

12. See Niebuhr, *The Nature and Destiny of Man: A Christian Interpretation*, 2:15–126; Niebuhr, *Beyond Tragedy: Essays on the Christian Interpretation of History* (New York: Scribner's, 1951); Langdon Gilkey, *On Niebuhr: A Theological Study* (Chicago: University of Chicago Press, 2001), 16–28.

13. Robert L. Calhoun, review of *The Nature and Destiny of Man*, vol. 1, by Reinhold Niebuhr, *Journal of Religion* 21 (October 1941): 473–480, quotes 475, 477.

14. Niebuhr, *The Nature and Destiny of Man*, 1:201.

15. Valerie Saiving Goldstein, "The Human Situation: A Feminine View," *Journal of Religion* 40 (April 1960): 100–112, quotes 100, 101.

16. "A Conversation with Valerie Saiving," *Journal of Feminist Studies in Religion* 4 (fall 1988): 99–115; Carol P. Christ and Judith Plaskow, eds., *Womanspirit Rising: A Feminist Reader in Religion*, 2nd ed. (San Francisco: HarperSanFrancisco, 1992 [1979]), 25–42.

17. Niebuhr, *The Children of Light and the Children of Darkness* (New York: Scribner's, 1944), 76–77.

18. Ibid., 78.

19. Niebuhr, "Brief Comments," *Radical Religion* 3 (winter 1937): quote 7; Niebuhr, "Brief Notes," *Radical Religion* 3 (spring 1938): quote 7; Niebuhr, "European Impressions," *Radical Religion* 2 (fall 1937): 31–33; Niebuhr, *Moral Man and Immoral Society: A Study in Ethics and Politics* (New York: Scribner's, 1932); Niebuhr, *Christianity and Power Politics* (New York: Scribner's, 1940).

20. Niebhr, *The Nature and Destiny of Man*, 1:25.

21. Niebuhr, "An Open Letter," *Christianity and Society* 5 (summer 1940): 30–33; Niebuhr, *Christianity and Power Politics* (New York: Scribner's, 1940); Charles Clayton Morrison, *The Christian and the War* (Chicago: Willett, Clark, 1942); [Morrison], "No Third Term!" *Christian Century* 57 (October 16, 1940), 1273; [Morrison], "Defending Democracy," *Christian Century* 57 (June 5, 1940):

quote 841; Niebuhr, "To Prevent the Triumph of an Intolerable Tyranny," *Christian Century* 57 (December 18, 1940), quotes 1580.

22. Niebuhr, "To Prevent the Triumph of an Intolerable Tyranny," quotes 1580; see Niebuhr, "Editorial Notes, *Christianity and Society* 5 (spring 1940): 10.

23. Niebuhr, *Christianity and Power Politics*, 44, 68.

24. Reinhold Niebuhr, "Notes," *Christianity and Society* 5 (fall 1940), "if Hitler" 12–13; Niebuhr, *Christianity and Power Politics*, "the fact" 91.

25. Niebuhr, "Editorial Notes," *Christianity and Society* 7 (winter 1941–42): 9.

26. Niebuhr, *The Irony of American History* (New York: Scribner's 1952), quotes 74, 42; Niebuhr, *The Structure of Nations and Empires* (New York: Scribner's, 1959), quote 295; see Niebuhr and Alan Heimert, *A Nation So Conceived: Reflections on the History of America from Its Early Visions to Its Present Power* (New York: Scribner's, 1963), 123–155.

27. Niebuhr, *The Children of Light and the Children of Darkness: A Vindication of Democracy and a Critique of its Traditional Defense* (New York: Scribner's, 1944).

28. Niebuhr, "The Peril of Complacency in Our Nation," *Christianity and Crisis* 14 (February 8, 1954), 1; see Niebuhr, *Christian Realism and Political Problems* (New York: Scribner's, 1953), 42; Niebuhr, "Communism and the Protestant Clergy," *Look* 17 (17 November 1953), 37.

29. Niebuhr, *The Irony of American History* (New York: Scribner's, 1952), 128; "X" [George F. Kennan], "The Sources of Soviet Conduct," *Foreign Affairs* 25 (July 1947): 579–580.

30. Niebuhr, "The Peace Offensive," *Christianity and Crisis* 25 (24 January 1966), "we are making" 301; Niebuhr, "Escalation Objective," *New York Times*, March 14, 1967; Niebuhr, Foreword to *Martin Luther King, Jr., John C. Bennett, Henry Steele Commager and Abraham Heschel Speak on the War in Vietnam* (New York: Clergy and Laymen Concerned About Vietnam, 1967), 3.

31. Richard Wightman Fox, *Reinhold Niebuhr: A Biography* (New York: Pantheon Books, 1985), "for the first" 285; Ronald H. Stone, "An Interview with Reinhold Niebuhr," *Christianity and Crisis* 29 (17 March 1969), "any simple" 48–49; Reinhold Niebuhr, "Toward New Intra-Christian Endeavors," *Christian Century* 86 (31 December 1969), "perhaps there is" 1662–1663.

32. Rubem A. Alves, "Christian Realism: Ideology of the Establishment," *Christianity and Crisis* 33 (September 17, 1973), 176; Cornel West, "Christian Realism as Religious Insights and Europeanist Ideology: Niebuhr and the Third World," in West, *Prophetic Fragments: Illuminations of the Crisis in American Religion and Culture* (Grand Rapids, Mich.: Eerdmans, 1988), 144–152, quotes 148, 152.

33. See Gary Dorrien, *The Neoconservative Mind: Politics, Culture, and the War of Ideology* (Philadelphia: Temple University Press, 1993), 1–18.

34. Michael Novak, "Needing Niebuhr Again," *Commentary* 54 (September 1972): 52–61, quote 52; see Novak, "Reinhold Niebuhr: Model for Neoconservatives," *Christian Century* 103 (January 22, 1986), 69–71; Novak, *The Spirit of Democratic Capitalism* (New York: American Enterprise Institute/Simon & Schuster, 1982), 332; James Nuechterlein, "The Feminization of the American Left," *Commentary* 84 (November 1987): 43–47.

35. Paul Ramsey, "Farewell to Christian Realism" (1966), in Ramsey, *The Just War: Force and Political Responsibility*, repr. (Lanham, Md.: University Press of America, 1983 [1968]), 487–488.

36. Novak, "Needing Niebuhr Again," 54, 57.

37. John C. Bennett, interview with author, January 2, 1993, "the only thing"; John C. Bennett, letter to author, December 10, 1992, "I think"; see Gary Dorrien, *Soul in Society: The Making and Renewal of Social Christianity* (Minneapolis: Fortress, 1995), 206.

38. Niebuhr, "The Quality of Our Lives," *Christian Century* 77 (May 11, 1960), 568; Patrick Granfield, *Theologians at Work* (New York: Macmillan, 1967), 55.

39. Niebuhr, "Roosevelt's Merry-Go-Round," *Radical Religion* 3 (spring 1938): 4; Niebuhr, "New Deal Medicine," *Radical Religion* 4 (spring 1939): 1–2.

40. Herbert Croly, *The Promise of American Life* (1909) (Boston: Northeastern University Press, 1989); Henry Churchill King, *The Moral and Religious Challenge of Our Times* (New York: Macmillan, 1911); Richard T. Ely, *Ground under Our Feet* (New York: Macmillan, 1938); Robert LaFollette, *LaFollette's Autobiography: A Personal Narrative of Political Experiences* (1911) (Madison: University of Wisconsin Press, 1960).

41. Harold R. Landon, ed., *Reinhold Niebuhr: A Prophetic Voice in Our Time*, 1961 colloquium discussion (Greenwich, Conn: Seabury, 1962), Bennett citations 88, 92–93.

42. See Niebuhr, "The Confession of a Tired Radical," *Christian Century* 45 (August 30, 1928), reprinted in *Love and Justice: Selections from the Shorter Writings of Reinhold Niebuhr*, ed. D. B. Robertson (Philadelphia: Westminster, 1957), 120–124; Niebuhr, "The Sin of Racial Prejudice," *The Messenger* 13 (February 3, 1948), 6, reprinted in *A Reinhold Niebuhr Reader: Selected Essays, Articles, and Book Reviews*, ed. Charles C. Brown (Philadelphia: Trinity Press International, 1992), 70–71; Niebuhr, "Christian Faith and the Race Problem," *Christianity and Society* (spring 1945); Niebuhr, "The Race Problem," *Christianity and Society* (summer 1942), reprinted in *Love and Justice*, 125–129, 129–132.

43. Richard John Neuhaus, Introduction to Wolfhart Pannenberg, *Theology and the Kingdom of God* (Philadelphia: Westminster, 1969), 31–32; Neuhaus, discussion in *Reinhold Niebuhr Today*, ed. Richard John Neuhaus (Grand Rapids, Mich.: Eerdmans, 1989), 108.

44. See Niebuhr, "The Problem of a Protestant Social Ethic," *Union Seminary Quarterly Review* 15 (November 1959): 1–11; Niebuhr, "Justice and Love," *Christianity and Society* (fall 1950), reprinted in Niebuhr, *Love and Justice*, 27–29; Niebuhr, "Reply to Interpretation and Criticism," 434–436; Niebuhr, *Faith and History: A Comparison of Christian and Modern Views of History* (New York: Scribner's, 1949), 171–195; Niebuhr, *The Nature and Destiny of Man*, 2:246–269.

45. Niebuhr, *An Interpretation of Christian Ethics*, 60.

4. Ironic Complexity

This chapter is adapted from Gary Dorrien, "Niebuhr and Graham: Modernity, Complexity, White Supremacism, Justice, Ambiguity," in *The Legacy of Billy Graham*, ed. Michael G. Long (Louisville: Westminster John Knox Press, 2008), 141–159.

1. Niebuhr, "A Theologian Says Evangelist Is Oversimplifying the Issues of Life," *Life* (July 1, 1957), 92.

2. Niebuhr, "Literalism, Individualism, and Billy Graham," *Christian Century* (May 23, 1956), 64, reprinted in Niebuhr, *Essays in Applied Christianity*, ed. D. B. Robertson (New York: Meridian Books, 1959), 123–131, quote 127.

3. Ibid., quote 128.

4. Niebuhr, "Literalism, Individualism, and Billy Graham," "though a Southerner, he has been" 128; Reinhold Niebuhr, "Proposal to Billy Graham," *Christian Century* (August 8, 1956), reprinted in Niebuhr, *Love and Justice*, ed. D. B. Robertson (Philadelphia: Westminster, 1957), "though a Southerner, he is 'enlightened'" 155.

5. Niebuhr, "Proposal to Billy Graham," "the Negro neighbor" 155; Niebuhr, "Literalism, Individualism, and Billy Graham," "the serious perplexities" 128.

6. See Niebuhr, *An Interpretation of Christian Ethics* (New York: Harper and Brothers, 1935); Niebuhr, *The Nature and Destiny of Man*, 2 vols. (New York: Scribner's, 1941, 1943).

7. Henry Van Dusen, "Billy Graham," *Christian Century* (April 2, 1956), 40; Niebuhr, "Proposal to Billy Graham," "Billy will bring" 156.

8. Niebuhr, "The Billy Graham Campaign," *Messenger* (June 4, 1957), quote 5; Niebuhr "Graham Sermon in Garden on TV," *New York Times*, June 2, 1957, 38; Billy Graham, *Just As I Am: The Autobiography of Billy Graham* (San Francisco: HarperSanFrancisco, 1997), 301; Richard Wightman Fox, *Reinhold Niebuhr: A Biography* (Ithaca, N.Y.: Cornell University Press, 1996), 266. Wayne Cowan, a student at Union in the late 1950s and subsequent editor of *Christianity and Crisis*, told me of Van Dusen's lounge reaction; author's conversation with Wayne Cowan, February 23, 2009.

9. Billy Graham, *Just As I Am*, 135.

10. Ibid., 136–140, quote 139; Graham, *The Journey: How to Live by Faith in an Uncertain World* (Carmel, N.Y.: Guideposts, 2006), 108–109; Graham, *How to Be Born Again*, in Graham, *The Collected Works of Billy Graham*, 1 volume ed. (New York: Inspirational, 1993), 188.

11. Niebuhr, *An Interpretation of Christian Ethics*, 2.

12. Niebuhr, "Literalism, Individualism, and Billy Graham," 130.

13. Ibid.

14. Ibid., 131.

15. Niebuhr, "Proposal to Billy Graham," 156.

16. Ibid., 156, 158.

17. Carl F. H. Henry, *The Uneasy Conscience of Modern Fundamentalism* (Grand Rapids, Mich.: Eerdmans, 1947), 18–19, 29–30.

18. Ibid., 29.

19. Ibid., 29–34, 52–57, quote 54.

20. See Gary Dorrien, *The Remaking of Evangelical Theology* (Louisville, Ky.: Westminster John Knox, 1998), 49–123; George M. Marsden, *Reforming Fundamentalism: Fuller Seminary and the New Evangelicalism* (Grand Rapids, Mich.: Eerdmans, 1987); Daniel P. Fuller, *Give the Wind a Mighty Voice: The Story of Charles E. Fuller* (Waco, Tex.: Word Books, 1972), 189–227; Wilbur Smith, *The Atomic Age and the Word of God* (Boston: W. A. Wilde, 1948); Smith, *World Crises and the Prophetic Scriptures* (Chicago: Moody, 1951).

21. John Pollock, *Billy Graham: Evangelist to the World* (San Francisco: Harper & Row, 1979), 157; Graham, *Just As I Am*, "I had" 425; Graham, "Why Don't Churches Practice Brotherhood?" *Reader's Digest* (August 1960), "If there were" 55.

22. Marshall Frady, *Billy Graham: A Parable of American Righteousness* (Boston: Little, Brown, 1979), 67–69; Graham, *Just As I Am*, 425–426; Graham, "Why Don't Churches Practice Brotherhood?" "Even after" 55.

23. Graham, *Just As I Am*, 426; Michael G. Long, *Billy Graham and the Beloved Community* (New York: Palgrave Macmillan, 2006), 80–83, quote 83.

24. See Long, *Billy Graham and the Beloved Community*, 83–101; William Martin, *A Prophet with Honor: The Billy Graham Story* (New York: William Morrow, 1991), 255–267; Jerry Beryl Hopkins, "Billy Graham and the Race Problem, 1949–1969," Ph.D. dissertation, University of Kentucky, 1986.

25. Graham, *Just As I Am*, 426. In the recollection of Howard Jones, King made this statement at a planning meeting for the 1957 New York crusade; see Martin, *A Prophet with Honor*, 235.

26. Long, *Billy Graham and the Beloved Community*, 99–107, quotes 105, 102.

27. Taylor Branch, *Parting the Waters: America in the King Years, 1954–63* (New York: Simon & Schuster, 1988), 227–228.

28. Billy Graham to President Dwight D. Eisenhower, March 27, 1956, and Graham to Eisenhower, June 4, 1956, cited in Long, *Billy Graham and the Beloved Community*, 112; on the Selma campaign, see ibid., 113; and Hopkins, "Billy Graham and the Race Problem," 41–42.

29. Martin Luther King Jr., "Letter from a Birmingham Jail" (1963), *A Testament of Hope: The Essential Writings and Speeches of Martin Luther King, Jr.*, ed. James W. Washington (San Francisco: HarperSanFrancisco, 1986), 289–302; see John Oliver, "A Failure of Evangelical Conscience," *Post-American* (May 1975), 26–30; Donald W. Dayton, *Discovering an Evangelical Heritage* (New York: Harper & Row, 1976), 2–3. The eight white ministers had published an open letter in January urging King to wait for decisions in the local and federal courts.

30. Long, *Billy Graham and the Beloved Community*, 114.

31. Ibid., 125, 121; Billy Graham, "No Solution to Race Problem 'at the Point of Bayonets,'" *U.S. News and World Report* (April 25, 1960), 94–95.

32. Niebuhr, "The Confession of a Tired Radical," *Christian Century* 45 (August 30, 1928), reprinted in Niebuhr, *Love and Justice*, 120–124; Niebuhr, "The Sin of Racial Prejudice," *The Messenger* 13 (February 3, 1948), 6–7, reprinted in *A Reinhold Niebuhr Reader: Selected Essays, Articles, and Book Reviews*, ed. Charles C. Brown (Philadelphia: Trinity Press International, 1992), 70–71.

33. Reinhold Niebuhr to Adlai Stevenson, February 28, 1956, Reinhold Niebuhr Papers, Library of Congress, Washington, D.C.; Niebuhr to Felix Frankfurter, February 8, 1957, reprinted in *Remembering Reinhold Niebuhr: Letters of Reinhold and Ursula M. Niebuhr*, ed. Ursula M. Niebuhr (New York: HarperCollins, 1991), "more harm" 311; Niebuhr, "A Theologian's Comments on the Negro in America," *Reporter* (November 29, 1956), "slow erosion" 24; Carol Polsgrove, *Divided Minds: Intellectuals and the Civil Rights Movement* (New York: W. W. Norton, 2001), 42–48.

34. See Niebuhr, "The Sin of Racial Prejudice," 70–71; Niebuhr, "Christian Faith and the Race Problem," *Christianity and Society* (spring 1945); and Niebuhr, "The Race Problem," *Christianity and Society* (summer 1942), reprinted in Niebuhr, *Love and Justice*, 125–129, 129–132.

35. Niebuhr, *Pious and Secular America* (New York: Scribner's, 1958), 76.

36. See Peter J. Boyer, "The Big Tent: Billy Graham, Franklin Graham, and the Transformation of American Evangelicalism," *New Yorker* (22 August 2005), 42–55.

37. See David Rausch, "Chosen People: Christian Views of Judaism Are Changing," *Christianity Today* (7 October 1988); CT News, *Christianity Today* (18 November 1977), 57; David Blewett, "What the Protestant Churches Are Saying about Jews and Judaism," lecture at University of St. Thomas, Center for Jewish-Christian Learning, April 11, 1994, www.nclci.org/Articles/art-blewett (accessed July 5, 2007).

5. Norman Thomas and the Dilemma of American Socialism

This chapter adapts material from Gary Dorrien, *The Democratic Socialist Vision* (Totowa, N.J.: Rowman and Littlefield, 1986), 48–77.

1. See W. A. Swanberg, *Norman Thomas: The Last Idealist* (New York: Scribner's, 1976); Murray B. Seidler, *Norman Thomas: Respectable Rebel* (Syracuse, N.Y.: Syracuse University Press, 1961); Harry Fleischman, *Norman Thomas: A Biography* (New York: W. W. Norton, 1964); Bernard Johnpoll, *Pacifist's Progress: Norman Thomas and the Decline of American Socialism* (Chicago: Quadrangle Books, 1970).

2. Seidler, *Norman Thomas: Respectable Rebel*, "it is this" 21; Johnpoll, *Pacifist's Progress*, "How can we" and "Do you really" 22–23.

3. See Morris Hillquit, *Socialism in Theory and Practice* (New York: Macmillan 1909); Hillquit, *Socialism Summed Up* (New York: H. K. Ely, 1910).

4. See W. E. Walling et. al., *Socialists and the War* (New York: Holt, 1915); Walling et al., *The Socialism of Today* (New York: Holt, 1916); V. F. Calverton, "Eugene Debs and American Radicalism," *Common Sense* (July 1933), 10–13; Charles Leinenweber, "The American Socialist Party and 'New' Immigrants," *Science and Society* 32 (winter 1968): 1–25; Sally M. Miller, "Socialist Party Decline and World War I," *Science and Society* 34 (winter 1971): 398–411; Leonard B. Rosenberg, "The 'Failure' of the Socialist Party of America," *Review of Politics* 31 (July 1969): 329–352.

5. See W. E. Walling et al., *Socialists and the War* (New York: Holt, 1915); Walling et al., *The Socialism of Today* (New York: Holt, 1916); V. F. Calverton, "Eugene Debs and American Radicalism," *Common Sense* (July 1933): 10–13; Charles Leinenweber, "The American Socialist Party and 'New' Immigrants," *Science and Society* 32 (winter 1968): 1–25; Sally M. Miller, "Socialist Party Decline and World War I," *Science and Society* 34 (winter 1971): 398–411; Leonard B. Rosenberg, "The 'Failure' of the Socialist Party of America," *Review of Politics* 31 (July 1969): 329–352; Thomas, *As I See It*, quotes 141.

6. Thomas, *As I See It*, quotes 150, 152.

7. Ibid., quotes 171, 167.

8. Ibid., quote 166.

9. Fleischman, *Norman Thomas: A Biography*, 140; Arthur M. Schlesinger Jr., *The Age of Roosevelt: The Politics of Upheaval* (Boston: Houghton Mifflin, 1960), 176–180, quote 180.

10. Niebuhr, *Reflections on the End of an Era* (New York: Scribner's, 1934), 17–30; Niebuhr, "After Capitalism—What?" *The World Tomorrow* 16 (March 1, 1933), 203–204; Norman Thomas, *The Choice Before Us: Mankind at the Crossroads* (New York: Macmillan, 1934), 83–127, quote 89.

11. Thomas, *The Choice Before Us*, 174–175.

12. Ibid., 63–82.

13. Ibid., 78–82, quote 81.

14. Eugene Lyons, *Assignment in Utopia* (New York: Harcourt, Brace, 1937); Fleischman, *Norman Thomas: A Biography*, 184; Mikhail Heller and Aleksandr Nekrich, *Utopia in Power*, trans. Phyllis B. Carlos (New York: Summit Books, 1986), 277–315.

15. Norman Thomas, *A Socialist's Faith* (New York: W. W. Norton, 1951), 311; Fleischman, *Norman Thomas: A Biography*, 179.

16. Norman Thomas, *We Have a Future* (Princeton, N.J.: Princeton University Press, 1941), 42–43, 124.

17. Swanberg, *Norman Thomas: The Last Idealist*, quote 258.

18. Thomas, *A Socialist's Faith*, 46; see Swanberg, *Norman Thomas: The Last Idealist*, 282; Fleischman, *Norman Thomas: A Biography*, 206–207.

19. Johnpoll, *Pacifist's Progress*, Thomas quote 237.

20. Winston Churchill, *The Second World War: Triumph and Tragedy* (Boston: Houghton Mifflin, 1953), 400–401.

21. Fleischman, *Norman Thomas: A Biography*, "a war" 213–214; Thomas, *A Socialist's Faith*, 67.

22. Daniel Yergin, *Shattered Peace: The Origins of the Cold War and the National Security State* (Boston: Houghton Mifflin, 1977), Thomas quote 285; Swanberg, *Norman Thomas: The Last Idealist*, 304.

23. Johnpoll, *Pacifist's Progress*, Thomas quote 256.

24. Thomas, *A Socialist's Faith*, vii–x, quote 37.

25. Ibid., quote 47.

26. Ibid., quote 3; Johnpoll, *Pacifist's Progress*; Dwight Steward, *Mr. Socialism* (Secaucus, N.J.: Lyle Stuart, 1974).

27. Thomas, *The Choice Before Us*, 219–221.

28. Thomas, *We Have a Future*, 150–158.

29. Thomas, *A Socialist's Faith*, quote 191; Norman Thomas, *Socialism Reexamined* (New York: W. W. Norton, 1963), 137–143.

30. Thomas, *A Socialist's Faith*, 320.

31. Norman Thomas, *The Prerequisites for Peace* (New York: W. W. Norton, 1959).

32. Ibid., 57–59.

33. Johnpoll, *Pacifist's Progress*, 280–282; Swanberg, *Norman Thomas: The Last Idealist*, 477–480; see Peter Coleman, *The Liberal Conspiracy: The Congress for Cultural Freedom and the Struggle for the Mind of Postwar Europe* (New York: Free Press, 1989).

34. Swanberg, *Norman Thomas: The Last Idealist*, 449–451.

35. Norman Thomas, "Reflections on Religion," unpublished essay written in Bermuda, 1955.

36. Thomas, *As I See It*, quotes 157, 163–164.

37. Thomas, "Reflections on Religion," 10.

38. Fleischman, *Norman Thomas: A Biography*, "there is" 294–295; Swanberg, *Norman Thomas: The Last Idealist*, "I cannot" 380.

39. Schlesinger, *The Age of Roosevelt*, 179–180.

40. Murray Kempton, *Part of Our Time: Some Ruins and Monuments of the Thirties* (New York: Simon & Schuster, 1955), 324; Irving Howe, *A Margin of Hope: An Intellectual Autobiography* (New York: Harcourt Brace Jovanovich, 1982), 304.

6. Michael Harrington and the "Left Wing of the Possible"

This chapter adapts material from Gary Dorrien, "The Other American," *Christian Century* (October 11, 2000); and Dorrien, *The Democratic Socialist Vision* (Totowa, N.J.: Rowman and Littlefield, 1986), 98–135.

1. See Maurice Isserman, *The Other American: The Life of Michael Harrington* (New York: PublicAffairs, 2000).

2. Michael Harrington, *Fragments of the Century* (New York: Saturday Review Press, 1973), 1; Harrington, *The Other America: Poverty in the United States* (New York: Macmillan, 1993 [1962]), v; Marion Magid, "The Man Who Discovered Poverty," *New York Herald Tribune Magazine* (27 December 1964), 9; "Once Known for Her Own Record, Now She Is Michael's Mother," *St. Louis Post-Dispatch* (January 20, 1971), quote cited in Isserman, *The Other American*, 9–14, quote 12.

3. Harrington, *Fragments of the Century*, 71–77, quote 1.

4. Ibid., quote 66; Michael Harrington, *The Long-Distance Runner: An Autobiography* (New York: Henry Holt, 1988), 1; Isserman, *The Other American*, 54–55.

5. Harrington, *Fragments of the Century*, quotes 76, 77.

6. Ibid., quotes 145, 147.

7. John Kenneth Galbraith, *The Affluent Society* (Boston: Houghton Mifflin, 1958); see Arthur Schlesinger Jr., "The Challenge of Abundance," *The Reporter* (3 May 1956), 8–11.

8. Michael Harrington, "Our Fifty Million Poor," *Commentary* 28 (July 195:), 19–27; Harrington, "Slums, Old and New," *Commentary* (August 1960), 118–124; Oscar Lewis, *Five Families: Mexican Case Studies in the Culture of Poverty* (New York: Basic Books, 1959); Isserman, *The Other American*, 175–220.

9. Michael Harrington, "Notes on the Left," *New Leader* 44 (May 22, 1961), quote 17; see Harrington, "The Economics of Racism," *Commonweal* 74 (July 7, 1961), 367–370.

10. Harrington, *The Other America*, quote 191.

11. Here, as elsewhere in this chapter, I am drawing from memories of statements I heard Harrington say numerous times.

12. Michael Harrington, *Socialism* (New York: Saturday Review Press, 1972), quote 211; Harrington's *Village Voice* articles of this period are reprinted in Harrington, *Taking Sides: The Education of a Militant Mind* (New York: Holt, Rinehart and Winston, 1985), 101–136.

13. Max Shachtman et al., "Statement on Vietnam," *Hammer & Tongs* (October 9, 1970), 8; Michael Harrington, "The Vietnam Moratorium," *New America* (October 25, 1969), 2; Harrington, "Getting Out of Vietnam," *Dissent* 17 (January–February 1970), 6–7.

14. Alan Wolfe, review of *The Other American: The Life of Michael Harrington*, by Maurice Isserman, *The New Republic* (April 3, 2000), 34–37; see Robert A. Gorman, *Michael Harrington: Speaking American* (New York: Routledge, 1995).

15. Harrington, *Socialism*, 29–108; Michael Harrington, *The Twilight of Capitalism* (New York: Simon & Schuster, 1976), quote 5.

16. Harrington, *Socialism*, 36–45; Karl Marx and Frederick Engels, *The Communist Manifesto* (1848), reprinted in *Karl Marx: Selected Writings*, ed. David McLellan (Oxford: Oxford University Press, 1977), 221–247.

17. Marx and Engels, *The Communist Manifesto*, 246; Harrington, *Socialism*, 45–49, quote 49; see Karl Marx, "Address to the Communist League," *Karl Marx: Selected Writings*, 277–285; Marx, "Speech to the Central Committee of the Communist League," *Karl Marx: Selected Writings*, 298–299.

18. Harrington, *Socialism*, 50.

19. Ibid., 50–52; Sidney Hook, *Towards the Understanding of Karl Marx: A Revolutionary Interpretation* (New York: John Day, 1933).

20. Karl Marx to Joseph Weydemeyer, March 5, 1852, in *Karl Marx: Selected Writings*, 341.

21. Karl Marx and Frederick Engels, *The German Ideology* (1844), in *Karl Marx: Selected Writings*, 159–191, quote 169; Marx, "On Bakunin's *State and Anarchy*," (1874), in *Karl Marx: Selected Writings*, 562–563.

22. Harrington, *The Twilight of Capitalism*, quotes 183, 42; Karl Marx, Preface to *A Critique of Political Economy*, in *Karl Marx: Selected Writings*, 388–391; Marx, *Grundrisse*, in *Karl Marx: Selected Writings*, 345–387.

23. Marx and Engels, *The Communist Manifesto*, 222.

24. See Bruno Rizzi, *The Bureaucratization of the World*, trans. Adam Westoby, repr. (New York: Free Press, 1985 [1939]); Max Nomad, *Rebels and Renegades*, repr. (Freeeport, N.Y.: Books for Libraries Press, 1968 [1932]); Nomad, *Apostles of Revolution*, repr. (New York: Collier Books, 1961 [1939]).

25. Max Shachtman, untitled essay written in 1940, reprinted in Shachtman, *Bureaucratic Revolution: The Rise of the Stalinist State* (New York: Ronald, 1962); also reprinted under the title "Stalinism: A New Social Order," in *Essential Works of Socialism*, ed. Irving Howe (New Haven, Conn.: Yale University Press, 1976), 526–546; see Leon Trotsky, "Socialism in a Separate Country?" Ap-

pendix 2; Trotsky, *The History of the Russian Revolution*, trans. Max Eastman, repr. (New York: Monad, 1980 [1932]), 378–418; Leon Trotsky, "A Letter to Max Shachtman"; Trotsky, *In Defense of Marxism: Against the Petty-Bourgeois Opposition* (New York: Merit, 1965), 37–41.

26. See Julius Jacobson, "The Two Deaths of Max Shachtman," *New Politics* 10 (winter 1973), 96–99; Tom Kahn, "Max Shachtman: His Ideals and His Movement," *New America* 10 (16 November 1972), 5; Irving Howe, *A Margin of Hope: An Intellectual Autobiography* (New York: Harcourt Brace Jovanovich, 1982), 40–55; Harrington, *Fragments of the Century*, 67–75; Maurice Isserman, *If I Had a Hammer . . . The Death of the Old Left and the Birth of the New Left* (New York: Basic Books, 1987), 37–75.

27. Harrington, *Decade of Decision: The Crisis of the American System* (New York: Simon & Schuster, 1980); Harrington, *The Next Left: The History of a Future* (New York: Henry Holt, 1986); Harrington, *Socialism: Past and Future* (New York: Arcade, 1989).

28. Michael Harrington, "Harrington Replies," *The Nation* (June 14, 1986), 3.

29. Michael Harrington, "Is Capitalism Still Viable?" *Journal of Business Ethics* 1 (Dordrecht, Holland, and Boston: D. Reidel, 1982), quote 283.

30. Harrington, *Socialism: Past and Future*, 277, 278.

31. Michael Harrington, *The Politics at God's Funeral: The Spiritual Crisis of Western Civilization* (New York: Holt, Rinehart and Winston, 1983).

7. Christian Socialism as Tradition and Problem

This chapter adapts material from Gary Dorrien, "Beyond State and Market: Christianity and the Future of Economic Democracy," *Cross Currents* (summer 1995): 184–204.

1. See Washington Gladden, *Applied Christianity: Moral Aspects of Social Questions* (Boston: Houghton Mifflin, 1886); Francis G. Peabody, *Jesus Christ and the Social Question* (New York: Macmillan, 1900); John A. Ryan, *A Better Economic Order* (New York: Harper & Brothers, 1935); Justin Wroe Nixon, *The Moral Crisis in Christianity* (New York: Harper & Brothers, 1931); Nixon, *Protestantism's Hour of Decision* (Philadelphia: Judson, 1940); Dores Robinson Sharpe, *Walter Rauschenbusch* (New York: Macmillan, 1942); Benjamin E. Mays, ed., *A Rauschenbusch Reader: The Kingdom of God and the Social Gospel* (New York: Harper & Brothers, 1957); George Herron, *The New Redemption: A Call to the Church to Reconstruct Society According to the Gospel of Christ* (New York: T. Y. Crowell, 1893); Herron, *The Christian State: A Political Vision of Christ* (New York: T. Y. Crowell, 1895); Vida D. Scudder, "Christianity in the Socialist State," *Hibbert Journal* 8 (April 1910): 562–581; Scudder, *Socialism and Character* (Boston: Houghton Mifflin, 1912).

2. Federal Council of the Churches of Christ in America, "The Social Creed of the Churches," *Report of the First Meeting of the Federal Council, Philadelphia, 1908* (New York: Revell, 1909), 238–239; Harry F. Ward, ed., *The Social Creed of the Churches* (New York: Eaton & Mains, 1912).

3. Walter Rauschenbusch, *Christianity and the Social Crisis* (New York: Hodder & Stoughton/Macmillan, 1907); Rauschenbusch, *Christianizing the Social Order* (New York: Macmillan, 1912).

4. Emil Brunner, *The Divine Imperative*, trans. Olive Wyon (Philadelphia: Westminster, 1947 [1932]), 423.

5. William Temple, *The Hope of a New World* (New York: Macmillan, 1941), 54–59; Temple, *Christianity and the Social Order* (Middlesex: Penguin Books, 1942), 77–96, quotes 96.

6. Federal Council of the Churches of Christ in America, *Quadrennial Report,* 1932; Reinhold Niebuhr, "Roosevelt's Merry-Go-Round," *Radical Religion* 3 (spring 1938): 4; Niebuhr, "New Deal Medicine," *Radical Religion* 4 (spring 1939): 1–2.

7. Jürgen Moltmann, *On Human Dignity: Political Theology and Ethics,* trans. M. Douglas Meeks (Philadelphia: Fortress, 1984), 174; Gustavo Gutierrez, *The Power of the Poor in History: Selected Writings,* trans. Robert R. Barr (Maryknoll, N.Y.: Orbis Books, 1983), 45.

8. José Mîguez Bonino, "For Life and Against Death: A Theology That Takes Sides," in *Theologians in Transition,* ed. James M. Wall (New York: Crossroad, 1981), 176.

9. Cornel West, "Harrington's Socialist Vision," *Christianity & Crisis* (12 December 1983), 484–485; West, *Prophetic Fragments* (Grand Rapids, Mich.: Eerdmans, 1988), 134–135; Rosemary R. Ruether, *Sexism and God-Talk: Toward a Feminist Theology* (Boston: Beacon, 1983), 232–233.

10. See Gregory Baum, *The Social Imperative: Essays on the Critical Issues That Confront the Christian Churches* (New York: Paulist, 1979); Harvey Cox, *Religion in the Secular City: Toward a Postmodern Theology,* (New York: Simon & Schuster, 1984); Robert McAfee Brown, *Theology in a New Key: Responding to Liberation Themes,* (Philadelphia: Westminster, 1978); Beverly W. Harrison, *Making the Connections: Essays in Feminist Social Ethics,* (Boston: Beacon, 1985); Arthur McGovern, *Marxism: An American Christian Perspective,* (Maryknoll, N.Y.: Orbis Books, 1980); Dorothee Solle, *Beyond Mere Dialogue: On Being Christian and Socialist* (Detroit: Christians for Socialism in the United States, 1978); Franklin I. Gamwell, "Democracy, Capitalism, and Economic Growth," in W. Widick Schroeder and Franklin I. Gamwell, *Economic Life: Process Interpretations and Critical Responses* (Chicago: Center for the Scientific Study of Religion, 1988), 223–250; J. Philip Wogaman, "Socialism's Obituary is Premature," *The Christian Century,* 107 (May 30/June 6, 1990), 570–572.

11. See David Hollenbach, *Justice, Peace, and Human Rights: American Catholic Ethics in a Pluralistic Context*, (New York: Crossroad, 1988); Letty M. Russell, *Human Liberation in a Feminist Perspective—A Theology*, (Philadelphia: Westminster, 1974); Larry Rasmussen, *Moral Fragments and Moral Community: A Proposal for Church in Society*, (Minneapolis: Augsburg Fortress, 1993); Douglas Sturm, *Community and Alienation: Essays on Process Thought and Public Life* (Notre Dame: University of Notre Dame, 1988); Warren R. Copeland, *Economic Justice: The Social Ethics of U.S. Economic Policy* (Nashville, Tenn.: Abingdon, 1988).

12. See Harry F. Ward, *In Place of Profit: Social Incentives in the Soviet Union* (New York: Scribner's, 1933); Ward, *The Soviet Spirit* (New York: International, 1944); Ward, *The Story of American-Soviet Relations, 1917–1959* (New York: National Council of American-Soviet Relations, 1959); Hewlett Johnson, *Christians and Communism* (London: Putnam, 1956); Gilbert C. Binyon, *The Christian Socialist Movement in England*, (London: S.P.C.K., 1931); Maurice B. Reckitt, *Maurice to Temple: A Century of the Social Movement in the Church of England* (London: Faber and Faber, 1947); Paul Tillich, *The Socialist Decision* (New York: Harper & Row, 1977), 160; Tillich, "Basic Principles of Religious Socialism," reprinted in Tillich, *Political Expectation*, ed. James Luther Adams, Victor Nuovo, and Hannah Tillich (New York: Harper & Row, 1971), 78–82.

13. Robert Benne, review of Gary Dorrien, *Reconstructing the Common Good, The Christian Century* 108 (February 27, 1991), 239–240.

14. Max L. Stackhouse and Dennis P. McCann, "Public Theology after the Collapse of Socialism: A Postcommunist Manifesto," *The Christian Century* 108 (January 16, 1991), 1:44–47.

15. Michael Novak, "Father of Neoconservatives: Reinhold Niebuhr," *National Review* (May 11, 1992), 39–42.

16. See Michael Novak, *The Spirit of Democratic Capitalism* (New York: American Enterprise Institute/Simon & Schuster, 1982); Peter L. Berger, *The Capitalist Revolution: Fifty Propositions about Prosperity, Equality and Liberty* (New York: Basic Books, 1986); Richard J. Neuhaus, *Doing Well and Doing Good: The Challenge to the Christian Capitalist* (New York: Doubleday, 1992).

17. Gutierrez, *The Power of the Poor in History*, 37–38, 45–46.

18. Temple, *Christianity and the Social Order*, 101.

19. See Reinhold Niebuhr, *The Children of Light and the Children of Darkness* (New York: Scribner's, 1944).

8. Breaking the Oligarchy

This chapter adapts material from Gary Dorrien, "Financial Collapse: Lessons from the Social Gospel," *Christian Century* (December 30, 2008), 28–30; Dorrien, "A Case for Economic Democracy," *Tikkun* (May/June 2009), 34–37, 75–76; and Dorrien, "Beyond State and Market: Christianity and the Future of Economic Democracy," *Cross Currents* (Summer 1995), 184–204.

1. For my first use of the "two ideal types" model, which drew upon Robert Dahl, *A Preface to Economic Democracy* (Berkeley: University of California Press, 1985), 163, see Gary Dorrien, *Reconstructing the Common Good* (Maryknoll: Orbis Books, 1990), 3.

2. See Michael J. Sandel, *Democracy's Discontent: America in Search of a Public Philosophy* (Cambridge, Mass.: Harvard University Press, 1996), 3–24; Arthur M. Schlesinger Jr., *The Cycles of American History* (Boston: Houghton Mifflin, 1986), 23–48; Howard Zinn, *A People's History of the United States, 1492—Present* (New York: HarperCollins, 1995).

3. Alan Greenspan, *The Age of Turbulence: Adventures in a New World* (New York: Penguin, 2008), 186; Linda J. Bilmes and Joseph E. Stiglitz, "The $10 Trillion Hangover: Paying the Price for Eight Years of Bush," *Harper's* (January 2009), 31–35; Edmund L. Andrews, "Bush Officials Urge Swift Action on Rescue Powers," *New York Times* (September 11, 2008), "perilously close" A1.

4. Karl Marx and Frederick Engels, *The Communist Manifesto*, in *Karl Marx: Selected Writings*, ed. David McLellan (Oxford: Oxford University Press, 1977), 221–247, quote 224; Thomas L. Friedman, *The World Is Flat: A Brief History of the Twenty-First Century* (New York: Farrar, Straus and Giroux, 2005).

5. Thomas L. Friedman, *The Lexus and the Olive Tree: Understanding Globalization* (New York: Anchor Books, 2000), quotes 104, 106; see Friedman, "The Great Unraveling," *New York Times* (December 17, 2008), A39.

6. Mickey Kaus, *The End of Equality* (New York: Basic Books, 1992), 25–57; Kaus, "For a New Equality," *New Republic* 202 (May 7, 1990), 21. For Kaus's running commentary on political issues and trends, see kausfiles.com, on www.slate.com.

7. Kaus, *The End of Equality*, 58–77; Robert Reich, *The Work of Nations* (New York: Knopf, 1991).

8. Kaus, "For a New Equality," 21; expanded revision in Kaus, *The End of Equality*, 58–77, quote 65.

9. See Michael Walzer, *Spheres of Justice: A Defense of Pluralism and Equality* (New York: Basic Books, 1983); Kaus, "For a New Equality," 25–26.

10. R. H. Tawney, *Equality* (London: Allen & Unwin, 1931), 87.

11. Kaus, "The End of Equality?" 25; see Larry L. Rasmussen, *Moral Fragments and Moral Community: A Proposal for Church in Society* (Minneapolis: Fortress Press, 1993), 11; Tom Weisskopf, "Spreading the Wealth," *Tikkun* (January/February 2009), 87–88.

12. See Eamonn Fingleton, *Unsustainable: How Economic Dogma Is Destroying American Prosperity* (New York: Nation Books, 2003); Doug Henwood, *After the New Economy* (New York: New Press, 2005); Barry Bluestone and Ben-

nett Harrison, *The Deindustrialization of America: Plant Closings, Community Abandonment, and the Dismantling of Basic Industry* (New York: Basic Books, 1982); Michael J. Piore and Charles F. Sabel, *The Second Industrial Divide: Possibilities for Prosperity* (New York: Basic Books, 1984); Shoshana Zuboff, *In the Age of the Smart Machine: The Future of Work and Power* (New York: Basic Books, 1988).

13. David Jolly, "Worldwide, A Bad Year Only Got Worse," *New York Times* (January 2, 2009), B1, 5; Greenspan, *The Age of Turbulence*, 351; see Peter S. Goodman and Gretchen Morgenson, "Saying Yes to Anyone, WaMu Built Empire on Shaky Loans," *New York Times* (December 28, 2008), A1, 22; Sherle R. Schwenninger, "Redoing Globalization," *The Nation* (January 12/19, 2009), 30–32.

14. See Padma Desai, *Financial Crisis, Contagion and Containment* (Princeton, N.J.: Princeton University Press, 2003); Jagdish Bhagwati, *The Wind of the Hundred Days: How Washington Mismanaged Globalization* (Cambridge, Mass.: MIT Press, 2001); Bhagwati, *In Defense of Globalization* (New York: Oxford University Press, 2004), 199–207; Joseph Stiglitz, *Globalization and Its Discontents* (New York: W. W. Norton, 2003), 89–132.

15. Greenspan, *The Age of Turbulence*, 366–373; Peter Coy, "Are Derivatives Dangerous?" *Business Week* (March 31, 2003), www.businessweek.com (accessed December 1, 2008); see R. Batra, *Greenspan's Fraud: How Two Decades of His Policies Have Undermined the Global Economy* (New York: Palgrave Macmillan), 2005; Gary Dorsch, "Weapons of Financial Mass Destruction," Financial Sense University, October 8, 2008, wwwfinancialsense.com (accessed October 30, 2008); "A Nuclear Winter?" *The Economist* (September 18, 2008), 12.

16. Alan Greenspan, "Testimony of Dr. Alan Greenspan," Committee of Government Oversight and Reform, October 23, 2008, oversight.house.gov/documents (accessed January 2, 2009); Edmund L. Andrews, "Greenspan Concedes Error on Regulation," *New York Times* (October 23, 2008), B1; Joe Nocera, "Risk Mismanagement: Were the Measures Used to Evaluate Wall Street Trades Flawed?" *New York Times Magazine* (January 4, 2009), 26–33, 46, 50–51; Nassim Nicholas Taleb, *The Black Swan: The Impact of the Highly Improbable* (New York: Barnes and Noble, 2007); see Peter L. Bernstein, *Against the Gods: The Remarkable Story of Risk* (New York: Wiley, 1998).

17. See Thomas Zambito and Greg B. Smith, "Feds Say Bernard Mafoff's $50 Billion Ponzi Scheme Was Worst Ever," *Daily News* (December 13, 2001), 2; Thomas L. Friedman, "The Great Unraveling," *New York Times* (December 17, 2008), A39; Michael Lewis and David Einhorn, "The End of the Financial World as We Know It," *New York Times* (January 4, 2009), 9–10.

18. Hilary Rosenberg, "Compromising Positions," *CFO Magazine* (September 1, 2003) (accessed December 4, 2008); Bill Gross, "Looking for Contagion in All

the Wrong Places," *Investment Outlook* (July 2007), www.pimco.com (accessed December 4, 2008); Andrew Leonard, "How the World Works: The Sub-Slime That Ate Wall Street," Salon.com (June 27, 2007), www.salon.com (accessed December 4, 2008); William Greider, "Waiting for 'The Big One,'" *The Nation* (August 23, 2007), TheNation.com (accessed March 20, 2009); Greider, "A Globalization Offensive," *The Nation* (January 11, 2007), TheNation.com (accessed March 20, 2009); Joe Nocera, "How India Avoided a Crisis," *New York Times* (December 20, 2008), B1, 8.

19. Warren Buffett, Berkshire Hathaway Annual Report, 2002, reprinted in "Warren Buffett on Derivatives," www.fintools.com (accessed October 30, 2008), quotes 1–2; "Buffett Warns on Investment 'Time Bomb,'" BBC News, March 4, 2003, http://news.bbc.co (accessed October 30, 2008); Gretchen Morgenson, "Arcane Market Is Next to Face Big Credit Test," *New York Times* (February 17, 2008); Helen Simon, "Are Derivatives Financial 'Weapons of Mass Destruction'?" Investopedia: A Forbes Digital Company, www.investopedia.com (accessed October 30, 2008).

20. "Bailed-Out Banks," CNN Money.com, n.d. (accessed June 9, 2009); Rick Newman, "The Best and Worst Bailed-Out Banks," U.S. News & World Report. com, June 9, 2009 (accessed June 9, 2009).

21. See Joe Nocera and Edmund L. Andrews, "Running a Step Behind as a Crisis Raged," *New York Times* (October 23, 2008), A1, 20; Edmund L. Andrews, "U.S. Plans $800 Billion in Lending to Ease Crisis," *New York Times* (November 26, 2008), A1, 20; Lewis and Einhorn, "The End of the Financial World as We Know It," 9–10; Michael J. de la Merced, "Buffett to Offer Details on Derivatives," *New York Times* (November 25, 2008), B1, 7; Eric Dash, Louise Story, and Andrew Ross Sorkin, "Bank of America to Receive $20 Billion More," *New York Times* (January 16, 2009), B1, 6.

22. Edmund L. Andrews and Eric Dash, "Deeper Hole for Bankers: Need Keeps Growing for Funds in Bailout," *New York Times* (January 14, 2009), A1, 22; Eric Lipton and Ron Nixon, "A Bank with Its Own Woes Lends Only a Trickle of Bailout," *New York Times* (January 14, 2009), A1, 24; "David M. Herszenhorn, "Senate Releases Second Portion of Bailout Fund," *New York Times* (January 16, 2009), A1, 16.

23. "U.S. Bank Failures Total 31," *The Australian* (May 3, 2009), WorldNews. com, wn.com/view, cited June 5, 2009; "U.S. Bank Failures in Four Months Reach 32," *MercoPress*, May 3, 2009, en.mercopress.com, cited June 5, 2009; Zachary A. Goldfarb, "Fannie Loses $23 Billion, Prompting Even Bigger Bailout," *Washington Post* (May 9, 2009), A12.

24. Edmund L. Andrews, Eric Dash, and Graham Bowley, "Toxic Asset Plan Foresees Big Subsidies for Investors," *New York Times* (March 21, 2009), A1, B4.

25. See Nelson D. Schwartz, "Tight Credit Seen as Corpora
Due," *New York Times* (March 16, 2010), A1, 3; Floyd Norris,
ing Seals a Deal," *New York Times* (April 23, 2010), B1, 4; Dav..
horn, "Bid to Shrink Big Banks Falls Short," *New York Times* (May 7, 20..
B1, 5.

26. Simon Johnson, "The Quiet Coup: How Bankers Took Power, and How
They're Impeding Recovery," *The Atlantic* (May 2009), 46–56.

27. Ibid., 55–56. See also Simon Johnson and James Kwak, *Thirteen Bankers:
The Wall Street Takeover and the Next Financial Meltdown* (New York: Pantheon Books, 2010).

28. See William E. Leuchtenburg, *Franklin D. Roosevelt and the New Deal,
1932–1940* (New York: Harper & Row, 1963), 32–59, 240–274; Arthur M.
Schlesinger Jr., *The Age of Roosevelt: The Coming of the New Deal*, American
Heritage Library ed. (Boston: Houghton Mifflin, 1988 [1958]), 1–23; Schlesinger,
The Age of Roosevelt: The Politics of Upheaval, American Heritage Library ed.
(Boston: Houghton Mifflin, 1988 [1960]); Alan Brinkley, *The End of Reform:
New Deal Liberalism in Recession and War* (New York: Vintage Books, 1995),
15–30; David M. Kennedy, *Freedom from Fear: The American People in Depres-
sion and War, 1929–1935* (Oxford: Oxford University Press, 1999); Adam Co-
hen, *Nothing to Fear: FDR's Inner Circle and the Hundred Days That Created
Modern America* (New York: Penguin, 2009).

29. See Kevin Phillips, *The Politics of Rich and Poor: Wealth and the American
Electorate in the Reagan Aftermath* (New York: Random House, 1990), 76–79;
Donald L. Barlett and James B. Steele, *America: What Went Wrong?* (Kansas
City: Andrews and McMeel, 1992), 4–7; Frederick R. Strobel, *Upward Dreams,
Downward Mobility: The Economic Decline of the American Middle Class* (Lan-
ham, Md.: Rowman & Littlefield, 1993), 91–102.

30. Greenspan wrote in 2007: "It took until 1999 for Glass-Steagall to be
repealed by the Gramm–Leach–Bliley Act. Fortunately Gramm–Leach–Bliley,
which restored sorely needed flexibility to the financial industries, is no aberration. Awareness of the detrimental effects of excessive regulation and the need for
economic adaptability has advanced substantially in recent years. We dare not go
back" (*The Age of Turbulence*, 376).

31. Louis Uchitelle, "Economists Warm to Government Spending but Debate Its
Form," *New York Times* (January 7, 2009), Auerbach quote B1; Thomas L. Fried-
man, "Radical in the White House," *New York Times* (January 21, 2009), A31; see
Herszenhorn, "Senate Releases Second Portion of Bailout Fund," A1, 16; Edmund L.
Andrews, "Bank Crisis Deepens," *New York Times* (January 21, 2009), B1, 4.

32. Kaus, *The End of Equality*, 13–14.

33. See Joseph A. Schumpeter, *Capitalism, Socialism, and Democracy*, 3rd ed.
(New York: Harper & Brothers, 1950 [1942]), 131–163, 415–425.

9. Rethinking and Renewing Economic Democracy

This chapter is adapted from Gary Dorrien, "A Case for Economic Democracy," *Tikkun* (May/June 2009), 34–37, 75–76; Dorrien, "Financial Collapse: Lessons from the Social Gospel," *Christian Century* (December 30, 2008), 28–30; and Dorrien, "Beyond State and Market: Christianity and the Future of Economic Democracy," *Cross Currents* (summer 1995), 184–204.

1. Oskar Lange and F. M. Taylor, *On the Economic Theory of Socialism*, 2nd ed. (New York: McGraw Hill, 1964 [1931]).

2. See H. Thomas and Chris Logan, *Mondragon: An Economic Analysis* (London: Allen and Unwin, 1982); William Foote Whyte and Kathleen King Whyte, *Making Mondragon: The Growth and Dynamics of the Worker Cooperative Complex* (Ithaca, N.Y.: ILR, 1988); K. Bradley and A. Gelb, *Co-operation at Work: The Mondragon Experience* (London: Heinemann Educational Books, 1983); R. Oakeshott, *The Case for Workers' Co-ops* (London: Routledge and Kegan Paul, 1978); Terry Mollner, *Mondragon: A Third Way* (Shutesbury, Mass.: Trusteeship Institute, 1984); Fred Fruendlich, "The Mondragon Cooperative Corporation," Conference on "Shared Capitalism: Mapping the Research Agenda," National Board of Economic Research, Washington, D.C., May 22, 1998; Karen Thomas and John Logue, "Mondragon Today: What Can We Learn?" (Kent, Ohio: Ohio Employee Ownership Center Pamphlet, 2002).

3. Len Krimerman and Frank Lindenfeld, "Contemporary Workplace Democracy in the United States: Taking Stock of an Emerging Movement," *Socialism and Democracy*, 11 (September 1990), quote 117; see Joyce Rothschild and J. Allen Whitt, *The Cooperative Workplace: Potentials and Dilemmas of Organizational Democracy and Participation* (Cambridge: Cambridge University Press, 1989).

4. See Greg Niemann, *Big Brown: The Untold Story of UPS"* (New York: Wiley, 2007); Friedman, *The World Is Flat*, 167–175.

5. See John Logue and Jacquelyn Yates, *The Real World of Employee Ownership* (Ithaca, N.Y.: Cornell University Press, 2001); John Logue, Richard Glass, Wendy Patton, Alex Teodosio, and Karen Thomas, *Participatory Employee Ownership: How It Works* (Kent, Ohio: Worker Ownership Institute, 1998); Charles Varano, *Forced Choices: Class, Community and Worker Ownership* (Albany: State University of New York Press, 1999); Diana Tillman and Karen Thomas, "It's a Give and Take Thing: An Employee Owner's Story," pamphlet (Kent, Ohio: Ohio Employee Ownership Center, 2002); John Logue and Daniel Bell, "Western Experience with Building High Performance Company Networks," *Journal of Employee Ownership Law and Finance* (winter 2000): 1–11; ICA Group, "Frequently Asked Questions about Employee Ownership," www.ica-group.org (accessed November 23, 2007).

6. See Severyn T. Bruyn, *A Future for the American Economy: The Social Market* (Stanford: Stanford University Press, 1991); Bruyn, *The Field of Social Investment* (Cambridge: Cambridge University Press, 1987).

7. See Herman E. Daly, *Steady-State Economics*, 2nd ed. (Washington, D.C.: Island Press, 1991); Daly and John B. Cobb Jr., *For the Common Good: Redirecting the Economy Toward Community, the Environment, and a Sustainable Future* (Boston: Beacon, 1989); Len Krimerman and Frank Lindenfeld, *When Workers Decide: Workplace Democracy Takes Root in America* (Philadelphia: New Society, 1991); Eileen McCarthy and Corey Rosen, *Employee Ownership in the Grocery Industry* (Oakland, Calif.: National Center for Employee Ownership, May 1987); Corey Rosen, Katherine Klein, and Karen Young, *Employee Ownership in America: The Equity Solution* (Lexington, Mass.: Lexington Books, 1986); Michael Quarrey, Joseph Raphael Blasi, and Corey Rosen, *Taking Stock: Employee Ownership at Work* (Cambridge, Mass.: Ballinger, 1986); Joseph R. Blasi, *Employee Ownership: Revolution or Ripoff?* (New York: Harper Business, 1988), 189–219; Thomas H. Naylor, "Redefining Corporate Motivation, Swedish Style," *Christian Century*, 107 (May 30/June 6, 1990), 566–570.

8. See Ota Sik, *For a Humane Economic Democracy*, trans. Fred Eidlin and William Graf (New York: Praeger, 1985); Ann Arbor Democratic Socialists of America, "Toward a Cooperative Commonwealth," pamphlet (Ann Arbor, Mich.: Ann Arbor DSA, 1983). Sik proposes that worker-owned capital could be owned collectively and that all workers could become members of internal democratically managed "assets management" and "enterprise management" associations.

9. See Peter Abell and N. Mahoney, *Small Scale Industrial Co-operatives in Developing Countries* (Oxford: Oxford University Press, 1988); Joanne Barkan and Robert Heilbroner, "From Sweden to Socialism? An Exchange," in *Why Market Socialism? Voices from Dissent*, ed. Frank Roosevelt and David Belkin (Armonk, N.Y.: M. E. Sharpe, 1994), 175–180; Frank Cunningham, *Democratic Theory and Socialism* (Cambridge: Cambridge University Press, 1987); Robert Dahl, *A Preface to Economic Democracy* (Berkeley: University of California Press, 1985); Saul Estrin and P. Holmes, *French Planning in Theory and Practice* (London: George Allen and Unwin, 1983); Estrin and David Winter, "Planning in a Market Socialist Economy," in Julian Le Grand and Saul Estrin, eds., *Market Socialism* (Oxford: Oxford University Press, 1989), 100–138; Estrin and Julian Le Grand, "Market Socialism," in *Market Socialism*, 1–24; David Miller, *Market, State and Community: Theoretical Foundations of Market Socialism* (Oxford: Clarendon, 1990); Miller and Estrin, "A Case for Market Socialism: What Does It Mean? Why Should We Favor It?" in *Why Market Socialism?* 225–240; Alec Nove, *Socialism, Economics, and Development* (London: Allen & Unwin, 1986); John Roemer, "Market Socialism, a Blueprint: How Such an Economy Might Work," in *Why Market Socialism?* Radoslav Selucky, *Marxism, Socialism and Freedom*

(Oxford: Oxford University Press, 1989); Thomas E. Weisskopf, "Challenges to Market Socialism: A Response to Critics," in *Why Market Socialism?* 297–318.

10. David Schweickart, "What to Do When the Bailout Fails," *Tikkun* (May/June 2009), 30–33, 72–75, quote 31.

11. Ibid., quote 33.

12. Ibid., 72–73; David Schweickart, *Capitalism or Worker Control?* (New York: Praeger, 1980), 106–113.

13. Schweickart, *Capitalism or Worker Control?* 93–95; Schweickart, "What to Do When the Bailout Fails," 74.

14. Schweickart, *Capitalism or Worker Control?* 81–90; Schweickart, "What to Do When the Bailout Fails," 74.

15. Rudolf Meidner, "A Swedish Union Proposal for Collective Capital Sharing," in Nancy Lieber, ed., *Eurosocialism and America: Political Economy for the 1980s* (Philadelphia: Temple University Press, 1982); Meidner, *Employee Investment Funds: An Approach to Collective Capital Formation* (London: George Allen & Unwin, 1978); Jonas Pontusson, "Radicalization and Retreat in Swedish Social Democracy," *New Left Review* 165 (September/October 1987), 5–33.

16. Jonas Pontusson, *The Limits of Social Democracy: Investment Politics in Sweden* (Ithaca, N.Y.: Cornell University Press, 1992), 237; see Pontusson, *Public Pension Funds and the Politics of Capital Formation in Sweden* (Stockholm: Swedish Center for Working Life, 1984); Pontusson, *Swedish Social Democracy and British Labour: Essays on the Nature and Conditions of Social Democratic Hegemony* (Ithaca, N.Y.: Cornell University Press, 1988); Gosta Esping-Andersen, *Politics Against Markets: The Social Democratic Road to Power* (Princeton, N.J.: Princeton University Press, 1985).

17. See Saul Estrin, "Workers' Co-operatives: Their Merits and Their Limitations," in Estrin and Le Grand, *Market Socialism*, 190; Belkin, "Vision Long, Sights Narrow," 8–10; Belkin and Joanne Barkan, "Reply to Roemer's 'Market Socialism,'" *Dissent* 38 (fall 1991): 569–572; John Roemer, *Free to Lose: An Introduction to Marxist Economic Philosophy* (Cambridge, Mass.: Harvard University Press, 1988).

18. Roberto M. Unger, *Democracy Realized: The Progressive Alternative* (New York: Verso, 1998), 22–27; see Unger, *Politics: A Work in Constructive Social Theory* (Cambridge: Cambridge University Press, 1987), 87–120; Unger and Cornel West, *The Future of American Progressivism* (Boston: Beacon, 1998); Ivan Petrella, *The Future of Liberation Theology: An Argument and Manifesto* (London: SCM, 2006).

19. See Richard Norman, *Free and Equal: A Philosophical Examination of Political Values* (Oxford: Oxford University Press, 1987); John Baker, *Arguing for Equality* (London: Verso, 1987); G. A. Cohen, "Are Freedom and Equality Compatible?" in *Alternatives to Capitalism*, ed. Jon Elster and Karl Ove Moene

(Cambridge: Cambridge University Press, 1989), 113–126; Irving Howe, "Socialism and Liberalism: Articles of Conciliation?" *Dissent* 24 (winter 1977): 22–35.

10. *The Neoconservative Phenomenon*

This chapter adapts material from Gary Dorrien, *The Neoconservative Mind: Politics, Culture and the War of Ideology* (Philadelphia: Temple University Press, 1993); and Dorrien, *Imperial Designs: Neoconservatism and the New Pax Americana* (New York: Routledge, 2004).

1. See Social Democrats, USA, "For the Record: The Report of Social Democrats, USA on the Resignation of Michael Harrington and His Attempt to Split the American Socialist Movement," undated [1973] and unpublished paper; Maurice Isserman, *If I Had a Hammer: The Death of the Old Left and the Birth of the New Left* (New York: Basic Books, 1987), 57–75; Lewis A. Coser and Irving Howe, eds., *The New Conservatives: A Critique from the Left* (New York: New American Library, 1977).

2. See Michael Harrington, *Fragments of the Century* (New York: Saturday Review Press, 1973), 132–165, 195–225; Harrington, *Toward a Democratic Left: A Radical Program for a New Majority* (New York: Macmillan, 1968).

3. See Irving Kristol, "'Civil Liberties': 1952—A Study in Confusion," *Commentary* 13 (March 1952), 233–236; Kristol, "Liberty and the Communists," *Partisan Review* 19 (July/August 1952), 493–496; Kristol, "Facing the Facts in Vietnam," *New Leader* 46 (September 30, 1963), 7–8; Kristol, "The Poverty of Equality," *New Leader* 48 (March 1, 1965), 15–16.

4. Michael Harrington, *The Other America: Poverty in the United States* (New York: Macmillan, 1962); "sloppy thinking" quote in Walter Goodman, "Irving Kristol: Patron Saint of the New Right," *New York Times Magazine*, December 6, 1981, "sloppy thinking" 202; Daniel Bell and Irving Kristol, "What Is the Public Interest?" *The Public Interest* 1 (fall 1965), "middle aged" 4; Irving Kristol, *Neoconservatism: The Autobiography of an Idea* (New York: Free Press, 1995), "conservatism in" 31.

5. See Terry A. Cooney, *The Rise of the New York Intellectuals: Partisan Review and Its Circle, 1934–1945* (Madison: University of Wisconsin Press, 1986); Alan M. Wald, *The New York Intellectuals: The Rise and Decline of the Anti-Stalinist Left from the 1930s to the 1980s* (Chapel Hill: University of North Carolina Press, 1987); Richard H. Pells, *The Liberal Mind in a Conservative Age: American Intellectuals in the 1940s and 1950s* (New York: Harper & Row, 1985); William Barrett, *The Truants: Adventures among the Intellectuals* (New York: Anchor, 1982); William Phillips, *A Partisan View: Five Decades of the Literary Life* (New York: Stein and Day, 1983); Alexander Bloom, *Prodigal Sons: The New York Intellectuals and Their World* (New York: Oxford University

Press, 1986); Neil Jumonville, *Critical Crossings: The New York Intellectuals in Postwar America* (Berkeley: University of California Press, 1991).

6. Nathan Glazer, "Housing Problems and Housing Policies," *The Public Interest* 7 (spring 1967), 21–51; Aaron Wildavsky, "The Political Economy of Efficiency," *The Public Interest* 8 (summer 1967), 30–48; James Q. Wilson, "The Urban Unease: Community vs. City," *The Public Interest* 12 (summer 1968), 25–39; Daniel P. Moynihan, "A Crisis of Confidence," *The Public Interest* 7 (spring 1967), 3–10; John H. Bunzel, "Black Studies at San Francisco State," *The Public Interest* 13 (fall 1968), 22–38.

7. Kristol, *Neoconservatism*, 31.

8. See Gary Dorrien, *The Neoconservative Mind: Politics, Culture and the War of Ideology* (Philadelphia: Temple University Press, 1993), 137–150.

9. See Norman Podhoretz, "Reflections on Earth Day," *Commentary* 49 (June 1970), 26; Norman Podhoretz, *Breaking Ranks: A Political Memoir* (New York: Harper & Row, 1979).

10. Samuel McCracken, "Quackery in the Classroom," *Commentary* 52 (October 1971); Dorothy Rabinowitz, "The Activist Cleric," *Commentary* 50 (September 1970); Midge Decter, "The Liberated Woman," *Commentary* 50 (October 1970); Jeane Kirkpatrick, "The Revolt of the Masses," *Commentary* 55 (February 1973); Michael Novak, "Needing Niebuhr Again," *Commentary* 54 (September 1972); Podhoretz, *Breaking Ranks*, 307.

11. Sidney Blumenthal, *The Rise of the Counter-Establishment: From Conservative Ideology to Political Power* (New York: Harper & Row, 1988), quote 154; see Norman Podhoretz, "What the Voters Sensed," *Commentary* 55, no. 1 (January 1973), 6.

12. See Norman Podhoretz, "Making the World Safe for Communism," *Commentary* 61 (April 1976), 33–41; Richard Pipes, "Why The Soviet Union Thinks It Could Fight and Win a Nuclear War," *Commentary* 64 (July 1977), 24–34.

13. Daniel Graham, interview with R. K. Bennett, "U.S.–Soviet Military Balance: Who's Ahead," *Reader's Digest* 109 (September 1976), 79–83; Anne Hessing Cahn, "Team B: The Trillion Dollar Experiment, Part One," *Bulletin of the Atomic Scientists* (1993), www.thebulletin.org/issues/1993, 1–4, CPD quotes 4; Richard Pipes, "Soviet Global Strategy," *Commentary* 69 (April 1980); Lawrence Freedman, "The CIA and the Soviet Threat: The Politicization of Estimates, 1966–1977," *Intelligence and National Security* 12 (January 1977), 122–142.

14. Team B, "Soviet Strategic Objectives, An Alternative View: Intelligence Community Experiment in Competitive Analysis," CIA Classified Document, December 1976, unclassified in 1992, National Archives and Records Administration, quotes 9, 10–11.

15. Ibid., 11–15, quotes 14, 15.

16. Ibid., quotes 26, 27.

17. Ibid., quotes 44, 45, 46.

18. David Binder, "New CIA Estimate Finds Soviets Seek Superiority in Arms," *New York Times*, (December 26, 1976; Cahn, "Team B: The Trillion Dollar Experiment, Part One," 4; see John Prados, "Team B: The Trillion Dollar Experiment, Part Two," *Bulletin of the Atomic Scientists* (1993); Anne Hessing Cahn, *Killing Détente: The Right Attacks the CIA* (College Station, Pa.: Penn State Press, 1998); Lawrence Freedman, "The CIA and the Soviet Threat: The Politicization of Estimates, 1966–1977," *Intelligence and National Security* 12 (January 1977), 122–142; Robert C. Reich, "Re-examining the Team A–Team B Exercise," *International Journal of Intelligence and Counterintelligence* 3 (fall 1989): 387–403. The first story on Team B was leaked to the *Boston Globe*'s William Beecher and published on October 20, 1976.

19. See Edward Luttwak, "Why We Need More 'Waste, Fraud, and Mismanagement' in the Pentagon," *Commentary* 73 (February 1982); Luttwak, "A New Arms Race?" *Commentary* 70 (September 1980); Walter Laqueur, "Reagan and the Russians," *Commentary* 73 (January 1982); Laqueur, "What We Know about the Soviet Union," *Commentary* 75 (February 1983); Laqueur, "Glasnost and Its Limits," *Commentary* 86 (July 1988); Robert Jastrow, "Why Strategic Superiority Matters," *Commentary* 75 (March 1983); Patrick Glynn, "Why an American Arms Build-up Is Morally Necessary," *Commentary* 77 (February 1984); Angelo Codevilla, "Is There Still a Soviet Threat?" *Commentary* 86 (November 1988).

20. Pipes, "Why the Soviet Union Thinks It Can Fight and Win a Nuclear War," 24–26.

21. Ibid., 26–31.

22. Ibid., 30–34.

23. See Richard Pipes, "How to Cope with the Soviet Threat," *Commentary* 78 (August 1984); Pipes, "Team B: The Reality Behind the Myth," *Commentary* 82 (October 1986); Edward Luttwak, "How to Think about Nuclear War," *Commentary* 74 (August 1982); Robert Jastrow, "The War Against 'Star Wars,'" *Commentary* 78 (December 1984); Angelo Codevilla, "How SDI Is Being Undone from Within," *Commentary* 81 (May 1986); Eugene V. Rostow, "Why the Soviets Want an Arms Control Agreement, and Why They Want It Now," *Commentary* 83 (February 1987); Patrick Glynn, "Reagan's Rush to Disarm," *Commentary* 85 (March 1988).

24. Norman Podhoretz, "The Culture of Appeasement," *Harper's* 255 (October 1977), 29–32; see Podhoretz, *The Present Danger: Do We Have the Will to Reverse the Decline of American Power?* (New York: Simon & Schuster, 1980).

25. David Stockman, *The Triumph of Politics: How the Reagan Revolution Failed* (New York: Harper & Row, 1986), 108–109.

26. Michael Massing, "Trotsky's Orphans: From Bolshevism to Reaganism," *New Republic* 196 (June 22, 1987), 18–22.

27. See Norman Podhoretz, "The Future Danger," *Commentary* 71 (April 1981), 35.

28. See Podhoretz, *The Present Danger*, 96–101.

29. Podhoretz, "The Culture of Appeasement," quote 31; Podhoretz, "Making the World Safe for Communism," 38–39; Jean-Francois Revel, "Can the Democracies Survive?" *Commentary* 77 (June 1984).

30. Norman Podhoretz, "The Reagan Road to Détente," *Foreign Affairs* 63 (1985), 463–464.

31. Norman Podhoretz, "Reagan's Forbidden Truths," *New York Post*, October 29, 1985; Podhoretz, "How Reagan Succeeds as a Carter Clone," *New York Post*, October 7, 1986; see Podhoretz, "Nixon, The Ghost of Détente Past," *New York Post*, November 5, 1985; Podhoretz, "Reagan—The Crippled Hawk," *New York Post*, June 25, 1985; Podhoretz, "The Madness of Arms Control, *New York Post*, October 1, 1985.

32. Podhoretz, "How Reagan Succeeds as a Carter Clone"; Podhoretz, "Reagan: A Case of Mistaken Identity," *New York Post*, August 6, 1985; Podhoretz, "What If Reagan Were President?" *New York Post*, April 29, 1986.

33. Norman Podhoretz, "The Courage of Reagan's Convictions," *New York Post*, June 3, 1986; Podhoretz, "Gorbachev's Salami Tactics," *New York Post*, October 20, 1987; see Podhoretz, "Moscow's Double Missile Trap," *New York Post*, September 22, 1987; Podhoretz, "What the Soviets Really Want," *New York Post*, November 19, 1985; Podhoretz, "The Danger Is Greater Than Ever," *New York Post*, December 1, 1987; Podhoretz, "Reagan's Reverse Rollback," *New York Post*, November 10, 1987; Podhoretz, "The Myth of Our Military Buildup," *New York Post*, September 30, 1986; Podhoretz, "Propping Up the Soviet Empire," *New York Post*, July 15, 1986; Podhoretz, "From Containment to Appeasement," *New York Post*, June 18, 1985; Podhoretz, "Peace, Peace, When There Is No Peace," *New York Post*, February 16, 1988; Podhoretz, "Reagan Was Right the First Time," *New York Post*, June 7, 1988; Author's interview with Norman Podhoretz, June 12, 1990; Podhoretz, "Gorbachev Wins One for Lenin," *New York Post*, December 13, 1988.

34. Talbott, *Deadly Gambits: The Reagan Administration and the Stalemate in Nuclear Arms Control* (New York: Knopf, 1984), 56–70; Laurence I. Barrett, *Gambling with History: Ronald Reagan in the White House* (New York: Doubleday, 1983), 310–316; Frances FitzGerald, *Way Out There in the Blue: Reagan, Star Wars and the End of the Cold War* (New York: Simon & Schuster, 2000), 174–179; Strobe Talbott, *Master of the Game: Paul Nitze and the Nuclear Peace* (New York: Knopf, 1988); Caspar W. Weinberger, *Fighting for Peace: Seven Critical Years in the Pentagon* (New York: Warner Books, 1990), 331–352; George Shultz, *Turmoil and Triumph: My Years as Secretary of State* (New York: Scribner's, 1993), 887–900, 995–1015.

35. Ronald Brownstein and Nina Easton, *Reagan's Ruling Class* (New York: Penguin Books, 1983), "not in our interests" 500; FitzGerald, *Way Out There in*

the Blue, 175–176; Talbott, *Deadly Gambits*, "it has become" 18; Barrett, *Gambling with History*, 310–316.

36. Lou Cannon, *President Reagan: The Role of a Lifetime* (New York: Public Affairs, 1991), "kept dying" 258; FitzGerald, *Way Out There in the Blue*, "cold war" 467.

37. FitzGerald, *Way Out There in the Blue*, Safire and Will quotes 467; Gannon, *President Reagan: The Role of a Lifetime*, Perle quote 266; Weinberger, *Fighting for Peace*, 340.

38. Norman Podhoretz, "Gorbachev Wins One for Lenin," *New York Post*, December 13, 1988; see Podhoretz, "Munich and Gorbachev: The Lesson Is Still Valid," *New York Post*, October 4, 1988; Podhoretz, "Now for the Left-Wing Dictators," *New York Post*, March 4, 1986; Podhoretz, "Peace, Peace, When There Is No Peace"; Charles Krauthammer, "No, the Cold War Isn't Really Over," *Time* (5 September 1988), 83–84.

39. Podhoretz, "The Present Danger," 37; Podhoretz, "Gorbachev Wins One for Lenin," quote.

40. Author's interview with Norman Podhoretz, June 12, 1990.

41 Irving Kristol, "The Map of the World Has Changed," *Wall Street Journal*, January 3, 1990; Kristol, "Defining Our National Interest," *The National Interest* 21 (fall 1990): 23–24; Jeane J. Kirkpatrick, "A Normal Country in a Normal Time," *The National Interest* 21 (fall 1990): 44–45.

42. See Joshua Muravchik, *Exporting Democracy: Fulfilling America's Destiny* (Washington, D.C.: American Enterprise Institute, 1991); Ben J. Wattenberg, *The First Universal Nation: Leading Indicators and Ideas about the Surge of America in the 1990s* (New York: Free Press, 1991); Charles Krauthammer, "Universal Dominion: Toward a Unipolar World," *The National Interest* 18 (winter 1989): 47–49; Krauthammer, "The Unipolar Moment," *Foreign Affairs* 70, no. 1 (1991): 23–33.

43. Fred Barnes, "They're Back! Neocons for Clinton," *New Republic* 207 (August 3, 1992), 12–14.

44. Russell Kirk, *The Neoconservatives: An Endangered Species*, The Heritage Lectures, no. 178 (Washington, D.C.: Heritage Foundation, 1988), 8.

45. Ibid., 2–9; Stephen J. Tonsor, "Why I Too Am Not a Neoconservative," *National Review* 38, no. 11 (June 20, 1986), 55.

46. Clyde Wilson, "The Conservative Identity," *Intercollegiate Review* 21, no. 3 (spring 1986): 66. See Jeffrey Hart, "Gang Warfare in Chicago," *National Review* 38, no. 10 (June 6, 1986), 32; Ernest Van Den Haag, "The War between Paleos and Neos," *National Review* 41, no. 3 (February 24, 1989), 21–23.

47. David Frum, "The Conservative Bully Boy," *American Spectator* 24 (July 1991), Buchanan and Fleming quotes 12; Robert Moynihan, "Thunder on the Right," *Thirty Days* (September 1989), Gottfried quote 68; see Paul Gottfried and Thomas Fleming, *The Conservative Movement* (Boston: Twayne, 1988), 73.

48. Russell Kirk, interview with author, October 19, 1989.

49. Richard John Neuhaus, "Democratic Conservatism," *First Things* 1 (March 1990), 65; Podhoretz, interview with author, June 12, 1990.

50. Thomas Fleming, "The Closing of the Conservative Mind," *Chronicles* 13, no. 9 (September 1989): 12; Moynihan, "Thunder on the Right," Podhoretz quote 69–70.

51. Tonsor, "Why I Too Am Not a Neoconservative," 55.

52. See Nathan Glazer, *Affirmative Discrimination: Ethnic Inequality and Public Policy* (New York: Basic Books, 1975); Edward C. Banfield, *The Unheavenly City Revisited* (Boston: Little, Brown, 1974); Dinesh D'Souza, *Illiberal Education: The Politics of Race and Sex on Campus* (New York: Free Press, 1991); Norman Podhoretz, "The Disaster of Women's Lib," *New York Post*, August 18, 1987; Midge Decter, "The Liberated Woman," 44; Decter, "For the Family: Millions of Americans Have Been Engaging in Child Sacrifice," *Policy Review* 27 (winter 1984): 44–45; Ruth R. Wisse, "Living with Women's Lib," *Commentary* 86 (August 1988), 45; Carol Ianonne, "The Feminist Confusion," in *Second Thoughts: Former Radicals Look Back at the Sixties*, ed. Peter Collier and David Horowitz (Lanham, Md.: Madison Books, 1989), 150–153.

53. Blumenthal, *The Rise of the Counter-Establishment*, Kristol quote 154.

54. Norman Podhoretz, "Making the World Safe for Communism," *Commentary* 61 (April 1976), 37–41; Richard Pipes, "Why the Soviet Union Thinks It Could Fight and Win a Nuclear War," *Commentary* 64 (July 1977), 24–34; Jean-Francois Revel, *How Democracies Perish* (New York: Harper & Row, 1985).

55. Leslie H. Gelb, "Who Won the Cold War?" *New York Times*, August 20, 1992, Ogarkov quote; see Daniel Deudney and G. John Ikenberry, "Who Won the Cold War?" *Foreign Policy* 87 (summer 1992), 123–138; Benjamin M. Friedman, *Day of Reckoning: The Consequences of American Economic Policy* (New York: Vintage Books, 1989).

56. Irving Kristol, *Neoconservatism: The Autobiography of an Idea* (New York: Free Press, 1995), 40; Norman Podhoretz, "Neoconservatism: A Eulogy," *Commentary* 101 (March 1996), 19–27; see Michael Rust, "The Sunset Years of the Neocons," *Insight* (December 13, 1993), 16–20.

11. *Imperial Designs*

The first half of this chapter adapts material from Gary Dorrien, *Imperial Designs: Neoconservatism and the New Pax Americana* (New York: Routledge, 2004).

1. Charles Krauthammer, "Universal Dominion: Toward a Unipolar World," *National Interest* 18 (winter 1989): quote 48–49; see Krauthammer, "When to Intervene," *New Republic* 192 (May 6, 1985), 10–11; Krauthammer, "The Reagan Doctrine," *Time* 125 (April 1, 1985), 54–55; Krauthammer, "The Poverty of

Realism," *New Republic* 194 (February 17, 1986), 15–16; Krauthammer, "Divided Superpower," *New Republic* 195 (December 22, 1986), 16; Krauthammer, "After the Cold War Is Won," *Time* (November 7, 1988), 33–34.

2. Charles Krauthammer, "Can America Stand Alone?" *Time* (October 22, 1990), 96; Krauthammer, "The Unipolar Moment," *Foreign Affairs* 70 (1991): 25–33; Krauthammer, "How the War Can Change America," *Time* (January 28, 1991), 100; Krauthammer, "Must America Slay All the Dragons?" *Time* (March 4, 1991), 88; Krauthammer, "On Getting It Wrong," *Time* (April 15, 1991), 70.

3. Author's interview with Norman Podhoretz, June 12, 1990; author's interviews with Michael Novak, March 20, 1990 and June 19, 1992; Ben J. Wattenberg, *The First Universal Nation: Leading Indicators and Ideas about the Surge of America in the 1990s* (New York: Free Press, 1991), 20.

4. Ben J. Wattenberg, "Neo-Manifest Destinarianism," *National Interest* 21 (fall 1990), "American taxpayers" 51, "only Americans" 52, "a unipolar" 54.

5. Joshua Muravchik, *Exporting Democracy: Fulfilling America's Destiny* (Washington, D.C.: American Enterprise Institute, 1991), quote 227; Wattenberg, *The First Universal Nation*, quote 96; see Muravchik, "Exporting Democracy in the Arab World," in *Democracy in the Middle East: Defining the Challenge*, ed. Yehudah Mirsky and Matt Ahrens (Washington, D.C.: Washington Institute for Near East Policy, 1993), 1–9.

6. Author's interview with Peter L. Berger, September 26, 1990; Jeane J. Kirkpatrick, "A Normal Country in a Normal Time," *National Interest* 21 (fall 1990): 44; Irving Kristol, "Tongue-Tied in Washington," *Wall Street Journal*, April 15, 1991.

7. Department of Defense, "Defense Planning Guidance" (February 18, 1992); excerpts published in the *New York Times*, March 8, 1992, and the *Washington Post*, March 11, 1992; see Patrick E. Tyler, "U.S. Strategy Plan Calls for Insuring No Rivals Develop," *New York Times*, March 8, 1992, A1.

8. See Patrick E. Tyler, "Senior U.S. Officials Assail Lone-Superpower Policy," *New York Times*, March 11, 1992, A6; Barton Gellman, "Keeping the U.S. First; Pentagon Would Preclude a Rival Superpower," *Washington Post*, March 11, 1992; Gellman, "Aim of Defense Plan Supported by Bush," *Washington Post*, March 12, 1992; Paul Wolfowitz, "Historical Memory: Setting History Straight," *Current* 423 (June 2000): 19; Charles Krauthammer, "What's Wrong with the Pentagon Paper?" *Washington Post*, March 13, 1992, A25; Patrick E. Tyler, "Pentagon Drops Goal of Blocking New Superpowers," *New York Times*, May 24, 1992, 1A; James Mann, *Rise of the Vulcans: The History of Bush's War Cabinet* (New York: Viking, 2004), 212–213.

9. Project for the New American Century, *Rebuilding America's Defenses: Strategy, Forces and Resources for a New Century* (Washington, D.C.: Project for the New American Century, 2000), iv, 6.

10. Robert Kagan and William Kristol, "No Defense," *Weekly Standard*, July 23, 2001, 11–13.

11. Richard A. Clarke, *Against All Enemies: Inside America's War on Terror* (New York: Free Press, 2004), 30–33.

12. Ron Suskind, *The Price of Loyalty: George W. Bush, the White House, and the Education of Paul O'Neill* (New York: Simon & Schuster, 2004), 70–75, 82–86, quote 85.

13. George W. Bush, "Confronting Iraq Threat 'Is Crucial to Winning the War on Terror,'" Transcript, *New York Times*, October 8, 2002, A12; "President's State of the Union Message to Congress and the Nation," Transcript, *New York Times*, January 29, 2003, A12; Seymour M. Hersh, "Who Lied to Whom?" *New Yorker* (March 31, 2003), 41–43, IAEA quote 42; Ackerman and John Judis, "The First Casualty: The Selling of the Iraq War," *New Republic* 228 (June 30, 2003), 17–24; Douglas Jehl, "Iraq Arms Critic Reacts to Report on Wife," *New York Times*, August 8, 2003, A8; Nancy Gibbs and Michael Ware, "Chasing a Mirage," *Time* 162 (October 6, 2003), 38–42; Michael Duffy and James Carney, "A Question of Trust," *Time* 162 (July 21, 2003), 22–26; Condoleezza Rice, "Why We Know Iraq Is Lying," *New York Times*, January 23, 2003; Fred Barnes, "The Phony Scandal," *Weekly Standard* 8 (28 July 2003), 21–23; Interim Report of the Iraq Survey Group, www.cia.gov/cia/public-affairs/ speeches/2003/david-kay.

14. David Rennie, "Powell Threw Out 'Over the Top' Claims on Iraq Arms," *Daily Telegraph*, June 2, 2003, "bullshit" quotes, NA; "Powell's Address, Presenting 'Deeply Troubling' Evidence on Iraq," Transcript, *New York Times*, February 6, 2003, A18, quote; Julia Preston, "Powell to Charge Iraq Is Shifting Its Illegal Arms to Foil Inspectors," *New York Times*, February 5, 2003, A1; Steven R. Weisman, "Powell, in U.N. Speech, Presents Case to Show Iraq Has Not Disarmed," *New York Times*, February 6, 2003, A1; Richard Wolffe and Daniel Klaidman, "Judging the Evidence," *Newsweek* (17 February 2003), 28–33; Charles J. Hanley, "Powell's Case for Iraq War Looks a Lot Thinner Now," *Morning Call*, August 10, 2003, A8; Judith Miller and William J. Broad, "Some Analysts of Iraq Trailers Reject Germ Use," *New York Times*, June 7, 2003, A1; Ackerman and Judis, "The First Casualty," 23–24; Editorial, "The Bioweapons Enigma," *New York Times*, June 1, 2003, A12; James Dao and Thom Shanker, "Powell Defends Information He Used to Justify Iraq War," *New York Times*, May 31, 2003, A6; "In Their Own Words: The Security Council," Transcript, *New York Times*, February 6, 2003, A21; Ian Fisher, "Hussein Aide Denounces Powell's Case as Full of Baseless 'Stunts,'" *New York Times*, February 6, 2003, A22; Editorial, "Reviewing the Intelligence on Iraq," *New York Times*, May 26, 2003, A14. The Powell quotes about his original text were relayed to *U.S. News and World Report* by a senior official.

15. Hanley, "Powell's Case for Iraq War Looks a Lot Thinner Now," A8; Ackerman and Judis, "The First Casualty," 24; Interim Report of the Iraq Survey Group, www.cia.gov/cia/public-affairs/speeches/2003/david-kay; Douglas Jehl

and David E. Sanger, "Powell's Case, a Year Later: Gaps in Picture of Iraq Arms," *New York Times*, February 1, 2004, A1.

16. Ackerman and Judis, "The First Casualty," 16; James Risen and Douglas Jehl, "Expert Said to Tell Legislators He Was Pressed to Distort Some Evidence," *New York Times*, June 25, 2003, A11; James Risen, "Iraq Arms Report Now the Subject of a C.I.A. Review," *New York Times*, June 4, 2003, A1.

17. Robert Dreyfuss, "More Missing Intelligence," *The Nation* 277 (July 7, 2003), 4; Ackerman and Foer, "The Radical: What Dick Cheney Really Believes," "unique intelligence" 21; Seymour M. Hersh, "Selective Intelligence: Donald Rumsfeld Has His Own Special Sources. Are They Reliable?" *New Yorker* (12 May 2003), 44–51; Bryan G. Whitman, Deputy Assistant Secretary of Defense for Public Affairs, to *The Nation* 277 (August 18/25, 2003), 2; David Wurmser, *Tyranny's Ally: America's Failure to Defeat Saddam Hussein* (Washington, D.C.: AEI, 1999), quote xxii.

18. Nicholas D. Kristof, "Cloaks and Daggers," *New York Times*, June 6, 2003, A33; closing quote in Rennie, "Powell Threw Out 'Over the Top' Claims on Iraq Arms," NA.

19. William Rivers Pitt, with Scott Ritter, *War on Iraq: What Team Bush Doesn't Want You to Know* (New York: Context Books, 2002), 33; Bill Keller, "The Sunshine Warrior," *New York Times Magazine*, September 22, 2002, Wolfowitz quote 50; see Scott Ritter, *Frontier Justice: Weapons of Mass Destruction and the Bushwhacking of America* (New York: Context Books, 2003).

20. See Angelo Codevilla, "Victory: What It Will Take to Win," *Claremont Review of Books* (November 2001); Frank Gaffney, "The Path to Victory," *Claremont Review of Books*, Special Issue Symposium (fall 2002): 10; Norman Podhoretz, "The Path to Victory," *Claremont Review of Books* (fall 2002): 11–12; Michael Ledeen, *The War Against the Terror Masters: Why It Happened; Where We Are Now; How We'll Win* (New York: St. Martin's, 2002).

21. Norman Podhoretz, "In Praise of the Bush Doctrine," *Commentary* 114 (September 2002), 19–28, quote 28.

22. Wesley K. Clark, *Winning Modern Wars: Iraq, Terrorism, and the American Empire* (New York: Public Affairs, 2003), 120, 130; Will Dana, "Is Wesley Clark the One?" interview with Wesley Clark, *Rolling Stone* (September 2003), 45–47, quote 46.

23. William Kristol, "The End of the Beginning," *Weekly Standard* 8, May 12, 2003, 9.

24. Inaugural issue of *American Conservative* (summer 2002), cited in Patrick J. Buchanan, *Where the Right Went Wrong: How Neoconservatives Subverted the Reagan Revolution and Hijacked the Bush Presidency* (New York: St. Martin's Griffin, 2005), 29.

25. Buchanan, *Where the Right Went Wrong*, quotes 31, 58–59.

26. Owen Harries, "The Perils of Hegemony," *American Conservative*, June 21, 2004, reprinted in *The Right War? The Conservative Debate on Iraq*, ed. Gary Rosen (New York: Cambridge University Press, 2005), 73–86, quote 82; Andrew J. Bacevich, "A Time for Reckoning: Ten Lessons to Take Away from Iraq," *American Conservative*, July 19, 2004, reprinted in ibid., 96–101; James Kurth, "Iraq: Losing the American Way," *American Conservative*, March 15, 2004, reprinted in ibid., 36–48, quote 47; see Bacevich, "The Real World War IV," *Wilson Quarterly* (winter 2005): 36–61.

27. Buchanan, *Where the Right Went Wrong: How Neoconservatives Subverted the Reagan Revolution and Hijacked the Bush Presidency*, "some horrible" 15.

28. George F. Will, "Time for Bush to See the Realities of Iraq," *Washington Post*, May 4, 2004, reprinted in *The Right War? The Conservative Debate on Iraq*, 67–69, quote 69; Robert F. Ellsworth and Dimitri K. Simes, "Realism's Shining Morality: The Post-Election Trajectory of U.S. Foreign Policy," *National Interest* 78 (winter 2004/2005): 5–10, quotes 10; Fouad Ajami, "Iraq May Survive, but the Dream Is Dead," *New York Times*, May 26, 2004, reprinted in *The Right War? The Conservative Debate on Iraq*, 70–72, quote 70; see Ajami, "Best Intentions: Why We Went, What We've Found," *New Republic* 230 (28 June 2004), 17–19.

29. Joseph R. Biden Jr., "Fires Next Time: Is the Vietnam Syndrome Back?" *New Republic* 230 (June 28, 2004), 14–16, quotes 15; see Peter Beinart, "Partisan Review," ibid., 6; Leon Wieseltier, "What Remains: Disillusion and Its Limits," ibid., 12–14.

30. Jonathan Chait, "Dove Tale: Defending the War," *New Republic* 233 (September 12, 2005), 10–13, quotes 10.

31. Norman Podhoretz, "World War IV: How It Started, What It Means, and Why We Have to Win," *Commentary* 118 (September 2004), reprinted in *The Right War? The Conservative Debate on Iraq*, 102–169, quote 156; this essay adapted from Podhoretz, "How to Win World War IV," *Commentary* 113 (February 2002); Podhoretz, "The Return of the Jackal Bins," *Commentary* 113 (April 2002); Podhoretz, "In Praise of the Bush Doctrine," *Commentary* 114 (September 2002); and Podhoretz, "Israel Isn't the Issue," *Wall Street Journal* (20 September 2001).

32. Podhoretz, "World War IV," 157–169, "as a passionate" 164; Podhoretz, "The War Against World War IV," *Commentary* 119 (February 2005), "amazing" 87; see Podhoretz, "In Praise of the Bush Doctrine," 19–28; Podhoretz, "The Path to Victory," *Claremont Review of Books* (fall 2002), 11–12.

33. Joshua Muravchik, "Iraq and the Conservatives," *Commentary* 120 (October 2005), 50–54, quotes 51, 53, 54.

34. Charles Krauthammer, *Democratic Realism: An American Foreign Policy for a Unipolar World* (Washington, D.C.: AEI, 2004).

35. Francis Fukuyama, "The End of History?" *National Interest* 16 (summer 1989): 3–18; Charles Krauthammer, "Universal Dominion: Toward a Unipolar

World," *National Interest* 18 (winter 1989/1990); Krauthammer, "The Unipolar Moment," *Foreign Affairs* 70 (1991).

36. Francis Fukuyama, "The Neoconservative Moment," *National Interest* 77 (summer 2004): 57–68, quotes 58.

37. Ibid., 58–61, quote 60.

38. Ibid., quotes 61.

39. Ibid., 62.

40. Ibid., quote 66.

41. Ibid., 66–68; David Kirkpatrick, "War Heats Up in the Neoconservative Fold," *New York Times*, August 22, 2004; see Francis Fukuyama, "Invasion of the Isolationists," *New York Times*, August 31, 2005, A19.

42. Charles Krauthammer, "In Defense of Democratic Realism," *National Interest* 77 (fall 2004): 15–25, quote 20.

43. David Frum and Richard Perle, *An End to Evil: How to Win the War on Terror* (New York: Random House, 2003), 98–145.

44. Ruel Marc Gerecht, "The Struggle for the Middle East: Iraq, Iran, and the Path to Democracy," *Weekly Standard* 10 (January 3 and 10, 2005), 22–29, quotes 27; see Gerecht, "What Hath Ju-Ju Wrought! In the Middle East, the Democratic Genie is Out of the Bottle," *Weekly Standard* 10 (14 March 2005), 22–25.

12. Militaristic Illusions

This chapter is the text of a lecture given at Allegheny College on March 12, 2008.

1. John F. Burns and Alisa J. Rubin, "U.S. Arming Sunnis in Iraq to Battle Old Qaeda Allies," *New York Times*, June 11, 2007, A1, 6.

2. Ali al-Fadhily and Dahr Jamail, "Iraq: A Nail in Maliki Government's Coffin?" Inter Press Service, August 3, 2007, http://ipsnews.net (accessed August 27, 2007); Burns and Rubin, "U.S. Arming Sunnis in Iraq to Battle Old Qaeda Allies," quote A6.

3. Jay Bookman, "We Are Fighting for an Iraq That the Iraqis Have Rejected," *Atlanta Journal-Constitution* (August 27, 2007), Odierno citation, www.ajc.com/opinion (accessed August 27, 2007); Damien Cave, "Iraqis Are Failing to Meet Benchmarks Set by U.S.," *New York Times*, June 13, 2007, A1, quote 10.

4. Mark Mazzetti, "U.S. Intelligence Offers Grim View of Iraqi Leaders," *New York Times*, August 24, 2007, A1, Mullen quote A8; see National Intelligence Council, "National Intelligence Estimate: Prospects for Iraq's Stability; Some Security Progress but Political Reconciliation Elusive," August 23, 2007, www.dni.gov/press (accessed August 27, 2007); James Glanz, "Iraqi Prime Minister Says 2 U.S. Senators Need to 'Start Making Sense Again,'" *New York Times*, August 27, 2007.

5. Steven Lee Myers, "Bush Cites Nuclear Risk of Leaving Iraq," *New York Times*, August 29, 2007, Bush quote, in speech to the American Legion annual convention, A12.

6. Seymour Hersh, "The Iran Plans," *New Yorker* (April 17, 2006).

7. Joseph E. Stiglitz and Linda Bilmes, *The Three Trillion Dollar War* (New York: W. W. Norton, 2008); see Linda Bilmes, "The Trillion-Dollar War," *New York Times*, August 20, 2005, A13; Linda Bilmes and Joseph Stiglitz, *Milken Institute Review* update of Bilmes study, October 2006, cited in Nicholas D. Kristof, "Iraq and Your Wallet," *New York Times*, October 24, 2006, A29; see "Iraq War Cost Estimator," AEI-Brookings Joint Center, http://aei-brookings.org/iraqcosts (accessed October 25, 2006); Megan Scully, "Pentagon Budget Request Swells to $419.3 Billion, but Procurement Falls," *The Hill* (October 17, 2006), www.hillnews .com/thehill (accessed October 18, 2006); Jim Lobe, "Groups Urge Overhaul of Pentagon Budget," www.antiwar.com (May 4, 2006) (accessed October 18, 2006).

8. Robert A. Pape, *Dying to Win: The Strategic Logic of Suicide Terrorism* (New York: Random House, 2005).

9. Fareed Zakaria, "Beyond Bush: What the World Needs Is an Open, Confident America," *Newsweek* (June 11, 2007), 22–29, quote 24.

10. Buddhika Jayamaha, Wesley D. Smith, Jeremy Roebuck, Omar Mora, Edward Sandmeier, Yance T. Gray, and Jeremy A. Murphy, "The War as We Saw It," *New York Times*, August 19, 2007, WK-11. Murphy was shot in the head but survived, just before this article was published; two others were subsequently killed in Iraq.

13. Empire in Denial

This chapter is drawn from a lecture at Union Theological Seminary on April 29, 2009, and adapts material from Gary Dorrien, "Grand Illusion: Costs of War and Empire," *Christian Century* (December 26, 2006), 26–29; and Dorrien, *Imperial Designs: Neoconservatism and the New Pax Americana* (New York: Routledge, 2004).

1. John Quincy Adams, "Address of 4 July 1821," in *John Quincy Adams and American Continental Empire: Letters, Papers and Speeches*, ed. Walter LaFeber (Chicago: Quadrangle Books, 1965), 42–46, quote 45.

2. Albert J. Beveridge, *The Meaning of the Times and Other Speeches* (Indianapolis: Bobbs-Merrill, 1908), quotes 143, 131, 57.

3. Lyman Abbott, *The Rights of Man: A Study in Twentieth Century Problems* (Boston: Houghton, Mifflin, 1901), 274.

4. Washington Gladden, "The Issues of the War," *The Outlook*, July 16, 1898, 673–675.

5. Washington Gladden, "The Signing of the Treaty," sermon, December 18, 1898, Washington Gladden Papers, Archives/Library Division, Ohio Historical

Society, Columbus, Ohio; see Gladden, "The Problem of the Philippines," sermon, September 3, 1899, Gladden Papers; Gladden, "The People of the Philippines," sermon, September 10, 1899, Gladden Papers; Gladden, "Good News from the Wide World," sermon, December 27, 1908, Gladden Papers.

6. Edmund Morris, *The Rise of Theodore Roosevelt* (New York: Modern Library, 2001), 747–773; Wilson address in Montclair, N.J., January 28, 1904, cited in Thomas J. Knock, *To End All Wars: Woodrow Wilson and the Quest for a New World Order* (New York: Oxford University Press, 1992), 10–11.

7. Reinhold Niebuhr, "Editorial Notes," *Christianity and Society* 7 (winter 1941–42): 9; Niebuhr, *The Structure of Nations and Empires* (New York: Scribner's, 1959), quote 295; Niebuhr and Alan Heimert, *A Nation So Conceived: Reflections on the History of America from Its Early Visions to Its Present Power* (New York: Scribner's, 1963), 123–155.

8. Editorial, "The Liberal Power," *New Republic* 228 (March 3, 2003), 7. See John B. Judis, "History Lesson: What Woodrow Wilson Can Teach Today's Imperialists," *New Republic* 228 (June 2, 2003), 19–23.

9. Joseph E. Stiglitz and Linda Bilmes, *The Three Trillion Dollar War* (New York: W. W. Norton, 2008); Linda Bilmes, "The Trillion-Dollar War," *New York Times*, August 20, 2005, A13; Brookings Institution, Saban Center for Middle East Policy, "Iraq Index," November 20, 2009; brookingsinstitution.org, accessed November 20, 2009.

10. Office of the Secretary of Defense, "National Defense Budget Estimates for the FY 2007 Budget (Green Book)," and "Financial Summary Tables Fiscal Year 2007," www.dod.mil/comptroller/defbudget/fy2007 (accessed October 20, 2006); Office of Management and Budget, "Department of Defense," www.whitehouse .govomb/budget/fy2007 (accessed October 20, 2006); Jim Garamone, "President Signs 2007 Defense Authorization Act," American Forces Information Service (October 17, 2006), www.defenselink.mil/News (accessed October 18, 2006); Associated Press, "Senate Approves Pentagon Budget," (September 29, 2006), www.military .com/News (accessed October 18, 2006); Renae Merle, "Pentagon Budget 'a Great Surprise,'" *Washington Post*, February 10, 2006, www.washingtonpost.com (accessed October 18, 2006); U.S. Department of Defense, "DoD Releases F: cal 2010 Budget Proposal," www.defenselink, mil/releases, May 7, 2009; access d November 20, 2009; Jim Wolf, "Pentagon Budget Must Rise to Fund Current Plans," Reuters, www.reuters.com, November 19, 2009; accessed November 20, 2009.

11. Peter Spiegel, "Army Warns Rumsfeld It's Billions Short," *Los Angeles Times*, September 25, 2006, www.latimes.com/news/nationworld (accessed October 18, 2006).

12. See Robert D. Kaplan, *Imperial Grunts: The American Military on the Ground* (New York: Random House, 2005); David Rieff, "The Cowboy Culture: The False Friends of the American Military," *New Republic* 233 (10 October

2005), 23–27; Max Boot, "The New American Way of War," *Foreign Affairs* 82 (July/August 2003): 41–58.

13. Thom Shanker and Eric Schmitt, "Rumsfeld Seeks Leaner Army, and a Full Term," *New York Times*, May 11, 2005, A1, A15; Tim Weiner, "Drive to Build High-Tech Army Hits Cost Snags," *New York Times*, March 28, 2005, A1, A10.

14. U.S. Army, "Future Combat Systems News," www.army.mil/fcs (accessed October 17, 2005); Charles A. Cartwright and Dennis A. Muilenburg, "Future Combat Systems: An Overview," 1–3, Army quote 1, www.army.mil/fcs/articles/index (accessed October 17, 2005); GlobalSecurity.org, "Future Combat Systems: Background," 1–3, quote 2, www.globalsecurity.org/military/systems (accessed October 17, 2005).

15. Noah Shachtman, ed., "Pentagon Budget Goes Black," Center for Strategic and Budgetary Assessments," (April 14, 2005), www.defensetech.org (accessed October 18, 2006); Robert D. Kaplan, "Supremacy by Stealth," *Atlantic Monthly* 292 (July–August 2003), 66–83.

16. Marc Kaufman, "Bush Sets Defense as Space Priority," *Washington Post*, October 18, 2006, A01, www.washingtonpost.com (accessed October 19, 2006); see "President Bush Delivers Remarks on U.S. Space Policy," *NASA Facts* (National Aeronautics and Space Administration, Washington, D.C.), January 14, 2004.

17. Center for Defense Information, "Space Weapons Could Emerge from Pentagon Budget," (March 7, 2006), www.cdi.org/program/document (accessed October 17, 2006).

18. Joint Chiefs of Staff, U.S. Department of Defense, Army General Henry H. Shelton, chairman, *Joint Vision 2020* (May 30, 2000), www.dtic.mil/jv2020 (accessed April 17, 2006); Bill Murray, "The Joint Chiefs Take Aim at IT," *GCN* (June 5, 2000), www.gcn.com/print (accessed October 19, 2006); "USSPACACE-COM Vision for 2020," www.fas.org/spp/military (accessed October 19, 2006); see U.S. Department of Defense, *Report of the Quadrennial Defense Review* (Washington, D.C.: U.S. Department of Defense, Government Printing Office," 1997); U.S. Department of Defense, *Report of the Quadrennial Defense Review* (Washington, DC: U.S. Department of Defense, Government Printing Office," 2001); Andrew Bacevich, *American Empire: The Realities and Consequences of U.S. Diplomacy* (Cambridge, Mass.: Harvard University Press, 2003); Rahul Mahajan, *Full Spectrum Dominance: U.S. Power in Iraq and Beyond* (New York: Seven Stories, 2003); Ellen M. Wood, *Empire of Capital* (London: Verso, 2003).

19. "Pope Warns Against War," *AmericanCatholic.org* (15 January 2003), 1–3, www.americancatholic.org/News/JustWar/Iraq/papalstatemen (accessed September 15, 2003).

20. Editorial, "Healing the Wounds of the Iraqi War," *Civilta Cattolica* (May 17, 2003), 5, 7–8.

21. Central Committee of the World Council of Churches, "Statement on Iraq," (September 2, 2003); U.S. Global Ministries Office of the World Council of

Churches, "Churches for Middle East Peace Letter to President Bush," February 4, 2003, www.globalministries.org/meeme020403 (accessed September 15, 2003); United Church of Christ Collegium of Officers, "Statement of United Church of Christ Leaders Opposing U.S. War Against Iraq," September 13, 2002, www.ucc .org/justice/iraq.htm; "An Interview with Bishop Frank Griswold," "SoundVision. com," www.soundvision.com/info/peace/bishop.asp (accessed September 15, 2003).

22. Benjamin R. Barber, *Fear's Empire: War, Terrorism, and Democracy* (New York: W. W. Norton, 2003); see Barber, *Jihad vs. McWorld: Terrorism's Challenge to Democracy* (New York: Ballantine Books, 2001).

23. See Michael Ignatieff, "Why Are We in Iraq? (And Liberia? And Afghanistan?)" *New York Times Magazine*, September 7, 2003, 38–43, 71–72, 85.

24. Michael Ignatieff, "The Burden," *New York Times Magazine*, 5 January 2003, 22–27, 50–54, "is more than being" 24; Ignatieff, "Why Are We in Iraq?" "without" 85.

25. Ignatieff, "Why Are We in Iraq?" 85.

26. See Madeleine K. Albright, "United Nations," *Foreign Policy* (September/ October 2003), 16–24; David Rieff, "Goodbye, New World Order," *Mother Jones* 28 (July–August 2003), 37–41.

27. Edmund Morris, *Theodore Rex* (New York: Modern Library, 2002), quotes 97, 229; John B. Judis, "History Lesson: What Woodrow Wilson Can Teach Today's Imperialists," *New Republic* 228 (June 2, 2003), 19–23; Max Boot, *The Savage Wars of Peace: Small Wars and the Rise of American Power* (New York: Basic Books, 2002), 99–128. This section is indebted to Judis's analysis.

28. Knock, *To End All Wars*, 26–28, quote 28; Kenrick A. Clements, "Woodrow Wilson's Mexican Policy, 1913–1915," *Diplomatic History* 4 (spring 1980): 116–119; Robert E. Quirk, *An Affair of Honor* (Lexington: University of Kentucky Press, 1962).

29. Woodrow Wilson, "An Appeal for a Statement of War Aims," December 18, 1916, *The Papers of Woodrow Wilson* ed. Arthur S. Link, 69 vols. (Princeton, N.J.: Princeton University Press, 1980), 40:273–276; Wilson, "An Address to the Senate," January 22, 1917, 40:533–539, quote 536.

30. Woodrow Wilson, "An Address to a Joint Session of Congress," April 2, 1917, *The Papers of Woodrow Wilson*, 41:519–527; Randolph S. Bourne, *War and the Intellectual: Collected Essays, 1915–1919*, ed. Carl Resek (New York: Harper & Row Torchbooks, 1964), 57; Knock, *To End All Wars*, 147.

31. Woodrow Wilson, "An Address to a Joint Session of Congress," January 8, 1918, *The Papers of Woodrow Wilson*, 45:534–539.

32. Wilson, "An Address to the Senate," quote 536; Wilson, "An Address to a Joint Session of Congress," January 8, 1918, 537–539.

33. Albright, "United Nations," quote 22.

34. President George W. Bush, National Security Strategy of 2002, http://www .mtholyoke.edu/acad/intrel/bush/doctrine.htm (accessed July 30, 2009).

35. Michael Hardt and Antonio Negri, *Empire* (Cambridge, Mass.: Harvard University Press, 2000); Hardt and Negri, *Multitude: War and Democracy in the Age of Empire* (New York: Penguin Books, 2004).

36. See Paul Hirst and Grahame Thompson, *Globalization in Question*, 2nd ed. (Oxford: Polity, 1999); David Held, *Democracy and the Global Order* (Stanford, Calif.: Stanford University Press, 1995); Mary Kaldor, *Global Civil Society: An Answer to War* (Cambridge: Polity, 2003).

37. See Patrick J. Buchanan, *Where the Right Went Wrong* (New York: Thomas Dunne Books, 2005); Samuel P. Huntington, *The Clash of Civilizations and the Remaking of World Order* (New York: Touchstone, 1996).

38. Hardt and Negri, *Multitude*, quote 306.

39. Ibid., 221–222.

14. The Feminist Difference

This chapter is adapted from Gary Dorrien, *The Making of American Liberal Theology: Crisis, Irony, and Postmodernity* (Louisville: Westminster John Knox, 2006), 179–189.

1. Rosemary Radford Ruether, *Disputed Questions: On Being a Christian* (Nashville: Abingdon, 1982), 17–29, "a sense of" 21; Ruether, *Women and Redemption: A Theological History* (Minneapolis: Fortress, 1998), "ghettoized" 221; Ruether, "Beginnings: An Intellectual Autobiography," in *Journeys: The Impact of Personal Experience on Religious Thought*, ed. Gregory Baum (New York: Paulist, 1975), 34–56.

2. Ruether, *Disputed Questions*, quote 29; Ruether, "Beginnings," 36–38; Ruether, "Robert Palmer: First the God, Then the Dance," *Christian Century* 107 (February 7–14, 1990), 125–126.

3. Ruether, *Disputed Questions*, quote 76; Ruether, *Women and Redemption*, 222; Ruether, "Beginnings," 43–46; Ruether, *Gregory of Nazianzus: Rhetor and Philosopher* (London: Oxford University Press, 1969).

4. Ruether, *Disputed Questions*, "one lived" 82.

5. Rosemary Radford Ruether, *The Church Against Itself: An Inquiry into the Conditions of Historical Existence for the Eschatological Community* (New York: Herder and Herder, 1967), quote 235; Ruether, "A Question of Dignity, A Question of Freedom," in *What Modern Catholics Think about Birth Control*, ed. William Birmingham (New York: New American Library, 1964), 233–240.

6. Rosalind Hinton, "A Legacy of Inclusion: An Interview with Rosemary Radford Ruether," *Cross Currents* 52 (spring 2002): 28–37, "every time" 30; see Ruether, *The Church Against Itself*; Ruether, "A Question of Dignity, A Question of Freedom," 233–240; Ruether, *The Radical Kingdom: The Western Experience of Messianic Hope* (New York: Paulist, 1970); Ruether and Eugene Bianchi, *From*

Machismo to Mutuality: Essays on Sexism (New York: Paulist, 1975); Ruether, ed., *Religion and Sexism: Images of Women in the Jewish and Christian Religious Traditions* (New York: Simon & Schuster, 1973).

7. Reuther, *Womanspirit Rising: A Feminist Reader in Religion*, quote 21; Ruether, "Motherearth and the Megamachine: A Theology of Liberation in a Feminine, Somatic and Ecological Perspective," *Christianity & Crisis* 31 (April 12, 1972), 267–273, reprinted in Ruether, *Womanspirit Rising*, 43–52, and Ruether, *Liberation Theology: Human Hope Confronts Christian History and American Power* (New York: Paulist, 1972), 115–126.

8. Ruether, "Motherearth and the Megamachine," in *Liberation Theology*, 118–121, quote 119–120.

9. Ibid., quotes 121, 122.

10. Ibid., quotes 124.

11. Ruether, *Disputed Questions*, "never to" and "as a feminist" 53; Ruether, "Beginnings," "these scholars" 52.

12. Ruether, *Disputed Questions*, 53–54; Ruether, *New Woman, New Earth: Sexist Ideologies and Human Liberation* (New York: Seabury, 1975), 89–133; Ruether, *Faith and Fratricide: The Theological Roots of Anti-Semitism* (New York: Seabury, 1974).

13. Ruether, *Sexism and God-Talk: Toward a Feminist Theology*, 2nd ed. (Boston: Beacon, 1993 [1983]), 12–46, quotes 18, 24.

14. Ibid., 22–33, quote 32.

15. This section adapts material from Gary Dorrien, *Soul in Society: The Making and Renewal of Social Christianity* (Minneapolis: Fortress, 1995), 262–271.

16. Ruether, *Sexism and God-Talk*, quotes 229–230; on Daly's gynocentric dualism, see Ruether, *Gaia & God: An Ecofeminist Theology of Earth Healing* (San Francisco: HarperCollins, 1992), 147–148.

17. Ruether, *Sexism and God-Talk*, quotes 231.

18. Ruether, *Women-Church: Theology and Practice of Feminist Liturgical Communities* (San Francisco: Harper & Row, 1985), 52; Zillah R. Eisenstein, *The Radical Future of Liberal Feminism* (New York: Longman, 1981); Ruether, *Sexism and God-Talk*, 216–222.

19. Ruether, *Sexism and God-Talk*, 222.

20. Ibid., 228.

21. Ibid., 223–234; Ruether, *New Woman, New Earth*, 162–214.

22. Ruether, *Sexism and God-Talk*, 23–31, 116–138; quotes 24, 137, 138; Ruether, *To Change the World: Christology and Cultural Criticism* (New York: Crossroad, 1981), 45–56; Ruether, "Feminist Theology and Spirituality," in *Christian Feminism: Visions of a New Humanity*, ed. Judith L. Weidman (New York: Harper & Row, 1984), 15–16.

23. Ruether, *Gaia & God*, 246; this section adapts material from Dorrien, *Soul in Society*, 314–316.

24. Ruether, *Gaia & God*, 247–249.

25. Ibid., 252–253.

26. Ruether, *Women and Redemption*, "God is not" 223; Hinton, "A Legacy of Inclusion," "legitimize" 30; see Rosemary Radford Ruether and Herman Ruether, *The Wrath of Jonah: The Crisis of Religious Nationalism in the Israeli-Palestinian Conflict* (San Francisco: Harper & Row, 1989); Ruether and Marc H. Ellis, eds., *Beyond Occupation: American Jewish, Christian, and Palestinian Voices for Peace* (Boston: Beacon, 1990); Ruether and James A. Rudin, "A Bumpy, Treacherous Road: The Middle East Accord," *Christian Century* 110 (September 22–29, 1993), 884–886; Ruether, "Christian Zionism Is a Heresy," *Journal of Theology for Southern Africa* 69 (December 1989): 60–64; Ruether, "The Women of Palestine: Steadfastness and Self-help in the Occupied Territories," *Christianity & Crisis* 47 (December 14, 1987), 434–438.

27. Russell, Ross, Ellis, Gebara, and Hinton made their remarks at a conference honoring Ruether at Garrett-Evangelical Theological Seminary on April 3–4, 2002; Letty M. Russell, "Wise Woman Bearing Gifts," *Cross Currents* 53 (spring 2003): 116–120, quotes 116, 118; Susan A. Ross, "Teaching Feminist Theology to College Students: The Influence of Rosemary Radford Ruether," ibid., 111–115, quotes 115; Marc H. Ellis, "At the End of an Era: A Meditation on Ecumenism, Exile, and Gratitude," ibid., 104–110; Ivone Gebara, "Ecofeminism: A Latin American Perspective," ibid., 93–103, quote 103; Hinton "Contextualizing Rosemary," ibid., 86–92; Hinton, "A Legacy of Inclusion," 31.

28. Mary McClintock Fulkerson, "Contesting the Gendered Subject: A Feminist Account of the *Imago Dei,*" *Horizons in Feminist Theology: Identity, Tradition, and Norms*, ed. Rebecca S. Chopp and Sheila Greeve Davaney (Minneapolis: Fortress, 1997), 107–109, "a kind of" 109; Fulkerson, *Changing the Subject: Women's Discourses and Feminist Theology* (Minneapolis: Fortress, 1994), 53–58, "in a realm" 55; Ellen T. Armour, "Questioning 'Woman' in Feminist/Womanist Theology: Irigaray, Ruether, and Daly," in *Transfigurations: Theology and the French Feminists*, ed. C. W. Maggie Kim, Susan M. St. Ville, and Susan M. Simonaitis (Minneapolis: Fortress, 1993), 150–156; Delores S. Williams, "The Color of Feminism," *Christianity & Crisis* 45 (April 29, 1985), 164–165, quote 164; Ruether, "Feminist Theology in the Academy," *Christianity & Crisis* 45 (March 4, 1985), 57–62; Williams, "The Color of Feminism: or Speaking the Black Woman's Tongue," *Journal of Religious Thought* 43 (spring/summer 1986): 42–58; Daphne Hampson, *Theology and Feminism* (Oxford: Basil Blackwell, 1990), 27–29, quote 29; Sheila Greeve Davaney, "Continuing the Story, but Departing the Text: A Historicist Interpretation of Feminist Norms in Theology," in *Horizons in Feminist Theology: Identity, Tradition, and Norms*, 201; Kwok Pui-lan, *Postcolonial Imagination & Feminist Theology* (Louisville: Westminster John Knox, 2005), 147.

29. Elisabeth Schüssler Fiorenza, *In Memory of Her: A Feminist Theological Reconstruction of Christian Origins* (New York: Crossroad, 1983), 17–18; see

Fulkerson, *Changing the Subject: Women's Discourses and Feminist Theology*, 34–40; Hampson, *Theology and Feminism*, 32–38.

30. Schüssler Fiorenza, *In Memory of Her*, 19; see Schüssler Fiorenza, *Discipleship of Equals: A Critical Feminist Ekklesia-logy of Liberation* (New York: Crossroad, 1993), 53–79; Schüssler Fiorenza, *Bread Not Stone: The Challenge of Feminist Biblical Interpretation* (Boston: Beacon, 1984).

31. Hinton, "A Legacy of Inclusion," 32.

32. Ibid., 32–33.

33. Ibid., 32; author's conversation with Rosemary Ruether, February 18, 2005, Pilgrim Place, Claremont, California.

15. Pragmatic Postmodern Prophecy

This chapter is adapted from Gary Dorrien, *Social Ethics in the Making: Interpreting an American Tradition* (London: Wiley-Blackwell, 2008).

1. Cornel West, "On My Intellectual Vocation," interview with George Yancy, in West, *The Cornel West Reader* (New York: Basic *Civitas* Books, 1999), 19–20.

2. Author's conversation with Cornel West and Michael Harrington, May 27, 1988.

3. West, "On My Intellectual Vocation," "high-powered" and "I've always" 21; Cornel West, "The Making of an American Radical Democrat of African Descent," introduction to West, *The Ethical Dimensions of Marxist Thought* (New York: Monthly Review Press, 1991), reprinted in West, *The Cornel West Reader*, 3–18, "Owing to" 5.

4. See West, *The Ethical Dimensions of Marxist Thought*; West, *The Cornel West Reader*, 9–10.

5. West, "On My Intellectual Vocation," "you know" 22; West, "The Making of an American Radical Democrat of African Descent," "I decided" 11.

6. I was a member of the National Board of DSOC and DSA.

7. West, "Harrington's Socialist Vision," *Christianity & Crisis* (December 12, 1983), 484; reprinted in West, *Prophetic Fragments: Illuminations of the Crisis in American Religion and Culture* (Grand Rapids, Mich.: Eerdmans; Trenton, N.J.: Africa World Press, 1988), 25–29.

8. West, *Prophesy Deliverance! An Afro-American Revolutionary Christianity* (Philadelphia: Westminster, 1982), 134–137; see West, "Black Theology and Marxist Thought," in *Black Theology: A Documentary History, 1966–1979*, ed. Gayraud S. Wilmore and James H. Cone (Maryknoll, N.Y.: Orbis Books, 1979), 552–567.

9. West, *Prophesy Deliverance!* 137; on Marxist councilism, see Serge Bricianer, *Pannekoik and the Workers' Councils* (St. Louis: Telos, 1978); Stanley Aronow-

itz, *The Crisis in Historical Materialism: Class, Politics, and Culture in Marxist Theory* (New York: Praeger, 1981); Rosa Luxemburg, *Selected Political Writings of Rosa Luxemburg*, ed. Dick Howard (New York: Monthly Review Press, 1971).

10. See Gary Dorrien, *The Democratic Socialist Vision* (Totowa, N.J.: Rowman & Littlefield, 1986), 129–130; Dorrien, *Reconstructing the Common Good: Theology and the Social Order* (Maryknoll, N.Y.: Orbis Books, 1990), 162–164.

11. Dorrien, *Reconstructing the Common Good*, 164.

12. West, "Alasdair MacIntyre, Liberalism, and Socialism: A Christian Perspective," in *Christianity and Capitalism: Perspectives on Religion, Liberalism, and the Economy*, ed. Bruce Grelle and David A. Krueger (Chicago: Center for the Scientific Study of Religion, 1985), reprinted in West, *Prophetic Fragments*, quote 134–135; see Alec Nove, *The Economics of Feasible Socialism* (London: George Allen & Unwin, 1983); Wlodzimierz Brus, *The Economics and Politics of Socialism* (London: Routledge & Kegan Paul, 1973); Branko Horvat, *The Political Economy of Socialism: A Marxist Social Theory* (Armonk, N.Y.: M.E. Sharpe, 1982).

13. West, "Critical Theory and Christian Faith," *Witness* (January 1986), reprinted in West, *Prophetic Fragments*, quote 122; see Michael Harrington, "Is Capitalism Still Viable?" *Journal of Business Ethics* 1 (1982): 283–284; Harrington, "Corporate Collectivism: A System of Social Injustice," in *Contemporary Readings in Social and Political Ethics*, ed. Garry Brodsky, John Troyer, and David Vance (Buffalo: Prometheus Books, 1984), 245.

14. West, "Michael Harrington, Socialist," *Nation* (January 8/15, 1990), reprinted in West, *Beyond Eurocentrism and Multiculturalism: Prophetic Thought in Postmodern Times* (Monroe, Me.: Common Courage, 1993), 181–188, quotes 183, 184.

15. West, "Toward a Socialist Theory of Racism," Institute for Democratic Socialism, (1985), reprinted in West, *Prophetic Fragments*, 97–108; see Ray Ginger, *The Bending Cross: A Biography of Eugene Victor Debs* (New Brunswick, N.J.: Rutgers University Press, 1949), 259–261; Nick Salvatore, *Eugene V. Debs: Citizen and Socialist* (Urbana: University of Illinois Press, 1982), 225–230.

16. West, "Toward a Socialist Theory of Racism," 98–99, Stalin quote 98; see Marcus Garvey, "Address at Newport News, October 25, 1919," *Negro World* (November 1, 1919), reprinted in *The Marcus Garvey and Universal Negro Improvement Association Papers*, ed. Robert A. Hill (Berkeley: University of California Press, 1983), 1:112–120; Harry Haywood, *Negro Liberation* (New York: International, 1948); James Forman, *Self-Determination and the African-American People* (Seattle, Wash.: Open Hand, 1981).

17. West, "Toward a Socialist Theory of Racism," 99–101; see Oliver C. Cox, *Caste, Class and Race* (Garden City, N.Y.: Doubleday, 1948.

18. West, "Toward a Socialist Theory of Racism," 107–108.

19. Ibid., 108; see West, "Beyond Eurocentrism and Multiculturalism," in West, *Prophetic Thought in Postmodern Times*, 3–30.

20. West, "We Socialists," *Crossroads* (July/August 1991), reprinted in West, *Prophetic Reflections: Notes on Race and Power in America* (Monroe, Me.: Common Courage, 1993), 239–244, "I've got to be" and "We need" 243; West, "Toward a Socialist Theory of Racism," "yet a democratic" 108.

21. West, "The Making of an American Radical Democrat of African Descent," quotes 7.

22. Cornel West, "Martin Luther King, Jr: Prophetic Christian as Organic Intellectual," address delivered at a King symposium at the U.S. Capital, October 1986, reprinted in West, *Prophetic Fragments*, 3–12, quotes 11.

23. Ibid., 11–12.

24. West, *The American Evasion of Philosophy: A Genealogy of Pragmatism* (Madison: University of Wisconsin Press, 1989), 42–111, 194–210, 226–239, quotes 233.

25. Ibid., quotes, 233, 235; see West, *Keeping Faith: Philosophy and Race in America* (New York: Routledge, 1993), 89–105.

26. West, *Keeping Faith*, 67–85, quotes 67, 72.

27. Ibid., quotes 73, xv, xvii.

28. Cornel West, *Race Matters* (Boston: Beacon, 1993; paperback edition, New York: Vintage Books, 1994), quotes 9, 10.

29. Ibid., quotes 12, 23.

30. Ibid., quotes 24, 27.

31. Ibid., quotes 54.

32. Ibid., quotes 56, 58.

33. Ibid., 57–66, quote 66; see Adolph Reed Jr., *The Jesse Jackson Phenomenon: The Crisis of Purpose in Afro-American Politics* (New Haven, Conn.: Yale University Press, 1986); Reed, "What Are the Drums Saying, Booker? The Current Crisis of the Black Intellectual," *Village Voice* 40, April 11, 1995, 31–36; Reed, "Dangerous Dreams: Black Boomers Wax Nostalgic for the Days of Jim Crow," *Village Voice* 41, April 16, 1996, 24–29.

34. West, *Race Matters*, quotes 69, 70.

35. Jack E. White, "Philosopher with a Mission," *Time* (June 7, 1993), 60–62, quote 60; other quotes cited from book jackets.

36. See West and Michael Lerner, *Jews and Blacks: Let the Healing Begin* (New York: Putnam, 1995); West and Henry Louis Gates Jr., *The Future of the Race* (New York: Knopf, 1996); West, *Restoring Hope: Conversations on the Future of Black America*, ed. Kelvin S. Sealey (Boston: Beacon, 1997); West and Sylvia Ann Hewlett, *The War Against Parents: What We Can Do for America's Beleaguered Moms and Dads* (Boston: Houghton Mifflin, 1998); West and Gates, *The African-American Century: How Black Americans Have Shaped Our Country* (New York: Free Press, 2000).

37. African United Front, "Open Letter to Cornel West and the Other Uncle Toms" (1993), www.blacksandjews.com/Open_LetterAUF (accessed March 24, 2007); White, "Philosopher with a Mission," quotes 61–62.

38. Randal Jelks, review of *Race Matters*, by Cornel West, *Christian Century* 110 (June 30/July 7, 1993), 684–685; Delores S. Williams, review of ibid., *Theology Today* 51 (April 1994), 158–162.

39. Leon Wieseltier, "All and Nothing at All: The Unreal World of Cornel West," *New Republic* 212 (March 6, 1995), 31–36, quotes 31, 32; White, "Philosopher with a Mission," 62.

40. David Horowitz, "Cornel West: No Light in His Attic," salon.com (October 11, 1999), 1–6, quotes 2–3, www.frontpagemag.com/Articles (accessed March 23, 2007).

41. West, "Reconstructing the American Left: The Challenge of Jesse Jackson," *Social Text* 11 (1984): 3–19, "despicable" 14; West, *Race Matters*, "underdog" 112; West and Lerner, *Jews and Blacks*, Lerner quote 191, West quote 212; see Garth Kasimu Baker-Fletcher, ed., *Black Religion after the Million Man March* (Maryknoll, N.Y.: Orbis Books, 1998).

42. Nick De Genova, "Gangster Rap and Nihilism in Black America: Some Questions of Life and Death," *Social Text* 43 (1995): 89–132, quote 95; Eric Lott, *The Disappearing Intellectual* (New York: Basic Books, 2006), 114–115.

43. Floyd W. Hayes III, "Cornel West and Afro-Nihilism: A Reconsideration," in *Cornel West: A Critical Reader*, ed. George Yancy (Oxford: Blackwell, 2001), 245–260, quote 248; Lewis R. Gordon, "The Unacknowledged Fourth Tradition: An Essay on Nihilism, Decadence, and the Black Intellectual Tradition in the Existential Pragmatic Thought of Cornel West," in ibid., 38–58; Peniel E. Joseph, "'It's Dark and Hell is Hot': Cornel West, the Crisis of African-American Intellectuals and the Cultural Politics of Race," 295–311, quotes 298, 299; Clevis Headley, "Cornel West on Prophesy, Pragmatism, and Philosophy: A Critical Evaluation of Prophetic Pragmatism," in ibid., 59–82; Charles W. Mills, "Prophetic Pragmatism as Political Philosophy," in ibid., 192–223.

44. Headley, "Cornel West on Prophesy, Pragmatism, and Philosophy," in ibid., 59–82, quotes 66, 70; Iris M. Young, "Cornel West on Gender and Family: Some Admiring and Critical Comments," in ibid., 179–191.

45. John P. Pittman, "'Radical Historicism,' Antiphilosophy, and Marxism," in ibid., 224–244; George Yancy, "Religion and the Mirror of God: Historicism, Truth, and Religious Pluralism," in ibid., 115–135; Nada Elia, "Cornel West's Representations of the Intellectual: But Some of Us Are Brave?" in ibid., 35–345; Lucius Turner Outlaw Jr., "On Cornel West on W. E. B. Du Bois," in ibid., 261–279.

46. West, "Afterword: Philosophy and the Funk of Life," in ibid., 349–350, 356, quotes 358.

47. Ibid., 350, quotes 359.

48. Ibid., 351–355, quotes 351, 352, 353.

49. Ibid., 361, quote 356.

50. Ibid., quotes 350, 360.

51. West, *Democracy Matters: Winning the Fight Against Imperialism* (New York: Penguin Press, 2004), 193; Cornel West, *Brother West: Living and Loving Out Loud, A Memoir* (New York: Smiley Books, 2009), 216–221.

52. Ibid., "upholding" 198; Ross Douthat, "Let Us Now Praise Cornel West," *Harvard Crimson* (January 11, 2002), 1; Fareed Zakaria, "The Education of a President," *Newsweek* (January 14, 2002), http://fareedzakaria.com (accessed March 24, 2007); Editorial, "The Pragmatist," *New Republic* (April 19, 2002), http://www.tnr.com/doc (accessed March 24, 2007).

53. West, *Democracy Matters*, 196, 197; Sam Tanenhaus, "The Ivy League's Angry Star," *Vanity Fair* (June 2002), 201–203, 218–223; Lynne Duke, "Moving Target," *Washington Post*, August 11 2002, F1, F43.

54. West, *Democracy Matters*, 198, 199.

55. Ibid., 2, 3.

56. Ibid., quotes 8.

57. Ibid., quotes 27.

58. Ibid., 28, 29.

59. Ibid., quotes 33, 35.

60. Ibid., 41.

61. Ibid., 60.

62. *Village Voice* and *Seattle Times* statements published as jacket endorsements for the paperback edition of *Democracy Matters* (Penguin Books, 2004); Cheryl Sanders, review of *Democracy Matters: Winning the Fight Against Imperialism*, by Cornel West, *Christian Century* 122 (July 12, 2005), 36; Hamid Khanbhai, review of ibid., *Daily Princetonian*, November 4, 2004; Daniel Levine, review of ibid., *America* 191 (November 8, 2004), www.americamagazine.org (accessed April 4, 2007); Mark Bauerlein, review of ibid., *New Criterion* (December 29, 2004), 32.

63. See West, *Race Matters*, "shabby" 61; Salim Muwakkil, "Cornel West: Public Intellectual," *In These Times* (November 4, 2004), www.inthesetimes.com (accessed April 4, 2007); West, *Brother West*, quote 202; Michael Eric Dyson, *Making Malcolm: The Myth and Meaning of Malcolm X* (New York: Oxford University Press, 1995); Dyson, *Race Rules: Navigating the Color Line* (New York: Vintage Books, 1996).

64. West, *Democracy Matters*, quote 199.

16. As Purple to Lavender

This chapter is adapted from Gary Dorrien, *Social Ethics in the Making: Interpreting an American Tradition* (Oxford: Wiley-Blackwell, 2008).

1. Alice Walker, *In Search of Our Mothers' Gardens: Womanist Prose* (New York: Harcourt, Brace, 1983).

2. Katie Geneva Cannon, "Exposing My Home Point of View," in *Hard Times Cotton Mill Girls: Personal Histories of Womanhood and Poverty in the South* (Ithaca, N.Y.: ILR,1986), 26–39, reprinted in Cannon, *Katie's Cannon: Womanism and the Soul of the Black Community* (New York: Continuum, 1995), 162–170, quote 167.

3. Sara Lawrence-Lightfoot, *I've Known Rivers: Lives of Loss and Liberation* (Reading, Mass.: Addison-Wesley, 1994), quotes 18, 34, 54.

4. Ibid., quotes 54, 59.

5. Ibid., quotes 61, 62, 65.

6. Ibid., quote 90.

7. Ibid., quotes 102, 103.

8. Ibid., quote 104.

9. Ibid., quotes 105, 106, 107.

10. Katie G. Cannon, *Katie's Canon: Womanism and the Soul of the Black Community* (New York: Continuum, 2002), quote 23; Cannon, "Resources for a Constructive Christian Ethic for Black Women with Special Attention to the Life and Work of Zora Neale Hurston," Ph.D. dissertation, Union Theological Seminary, 1983.

11. Walker, *In Search of Our Mothers' Gardens*, xi–xii.

12. Cannon, *Katie's Canon*, quote 23; see Alice Walker, *The Color Purple* (New York: Washington Square Press, 1982).

13. Katie G. Cannon, *Black Womanist Ethics* (Atlanta, Ga.: Scholars, 1988), 2.

14. Ibid., 3–4.

15. Ibid., 6.

16. Zora Neale Hurston, "How It Feels to Be Colored Me," *World Tomorrow* (May 1928), 17; Cannon, *Black Feminist Ethics*, 11.

17. Mary Burgher, "Images of Self and Race in the Autobiographies of Black Women," in *Sturdy Black Bridges*, ed. Roseann Bell et al. (New York: Anchor Books, 1979), 113; Cannon, *Black Feminist Ethics*, 17; see Zora Neale Hurston, *Dust Tracks on a Road* (Philadelphia: Lippincott, 1942); Hurston, *Moses, Man of the Mountain* (Philadelphia: Lippincott, 1939); Hurston, *Mules and Men* (Philadelphia: Lippincott, 1935); Hurston, *Seraph on the Sewanee* (New York: Scribner's, 1948); Hurston, *Their Eyes Were Watching God* (Philadelphia: Lippincott, 1938).

18. Alice Walker, Foreword to Robert Hemenway, *Zora Neale Hurston: A Literary Biography* (Urbana: University of Illinois Press, 1977), xvii; Hurston, *Their Eyes Were Watching God*, quote 119; Cannon, *Black Feminist Ethics*, 103–105; see Katie G. Cannon, "Unctuousness as Virtue: According to the Life of Zora Neale Hurston," *Zora Neale Hurston Forum* (fall 1987): 38–48, reprinted in Cannon, *Katie's Canon*, 91–100.

19. Cannon, *Black Womanist Ethics*, 145.

20. Katie G. Cannon, "Resources for a Constructive Ethic: The Life and Work of Zora Neale Hurston," *Journal of Feminist Studies in Religion* 1 (1984): 37–51, reprinted in Cannon, *Katie's Canon*, 77–90, quote 90.

21. Katie G. Cannon, "Hitting a Straight Lick with a Crooked Stick: The Womanist Dilemma in the Development of a Black Liberation Ethic," *Annual of the Society of Christian Ethics* (1987), 165–177, reprinted in Cannon, *Katie's Canon*, 122–128, quotes 122, 123.

22. Ibid., quote 123.

23. Ibid., quote 126.

24. Katie G. Cannon, "Metalogues and Dialogues: Teaching the Womanist Idea," *Journal of Feminist Studies in Religion* 8 (fall 1992): 125–130, reprinted in Cannon, *Katie's Canon*, 136–143, quote 137; see Emilie M. Townes, ed., *A Troubling in My Soul: Womanist Perspectives on Evil and Suffering* (Maryknoll, N.Y.: Orbis Books, 1993).

25. Cheryl J. Sanders et al., "Roundtable Discussion: Christian Ethics and Theology in Womanist Perspective," *Journal of Feminist Studies in Religion* 5 (1989): 83–112, quote 111; Katie G. Cannon, "Appropriation and Reciprocity in the Doing of Womanist Ethics," *Annual of the Society of Christian Ethics* (1993), 189–196, reprinted in Cannon, *Katie's Canon*, 129–135.

26. Cannon, "Appropriation and Reciprocity in the Doing of Womanist Ethics," quotes 131.

27. Ibid., "rugged endurance" 135; Katie G. Cannon, "Structured Academic Amnesia: *As If This True Womanist Story Never Happened,*" in *Deeper Shades of Purple: Womanism in Religion and Society*, ed. Stacey M. Floyd-Thomas (New York: New York University Press, 2006), 19–27, "from 1983" 22, "experience our" 23.

28. Stacey M. Floyd-Thomas, *Mining the Motherlode: Methods in Womanist Ethics* (Cleveland, Ohio: Pilgrim, 2006), quotes 171, 3–4; see Jacquelyn Grant, *White Women's Christ and Black Women's Jesus* (Atlanta, Ga.: Scholars, 1989); Emilie M. Townes, *Womanist Ethics and the Cultural Production of Evil* (New York: Palgrave Macmillan, 2006); Delores S. Williams, *Sisters in the Wilderness: The Challenge of Womanist God-Talk* (Maryknoll, N.Y.: Orbis Books, 1993); Marcia Y. Riggs, *Awake, Arise, and Act: A Womanist Call for Black Liberation* (Cleveland, Ohio: Pilgrim, 1993).

29. Melanie L. Harrris, "Womanist Humanism: A Deeper Look," *Cross Currents* 57 (fall 2007), quote 396; Harris, "Alice Walker's Ethics: An Analysis of Alice Walker's Non-Fiction Work as a Resource for Womanist Ethics," Ph.D. dissertation, Union Theological Seminary, 2006; Monica Coleman, "Roundtable Discussion: Must I Be Womanist?" *Journal of Feminist Studies in Religion* 22 (spring 2006): 86.

30. Coleman, "Roundtable Discussion: Must I Be Womanist?" 95–96.

31. Traci C. West, "Is a Womanist a Black Feminist? Making the Distinctions and Defying Them: A Black Feminist Response," in *Deeper Shades of Purple*, quotes 293, 294–295, 292; see bell hooks, *Yearning: Race, Gender, and Cultural Politics* (Boston: South End, 1990); Traci C. West, *Disruptive Christian Ethics: When Racism and Women's Lives Matter* (Louisville: Westminster John Knox, 2006).

32. Katie G. Cannon, "Response," *Journal of Feminist Studies in Religion* 22 (2006): 96–98; see Cannon, "Sexing Black Women: Liberation from the Prisonhouse of Anatomical Authority," in *Loving the Body: Black Religious Studies and the Erotic*, ed. Anthony B. Pinn and Dwight N. Hopkins (New York: Palgrave, 2004), 11–30.

33. Cannon, "Response," 97–98.

17. Religious Pluralism as a Justice Issue

Keynote Address, Council of Centers on Jewish-Christian Relations, Sacred Heart University, Fairfield, Conn., December 7, 2008. This lecture adapts material from Gary Dorrien, *The Making of American Liberal Theology: Crisis, Irony, and Postmodernity, 1950–2005* (Louisville: Westminster John Knox, 2006), 397–411; and Dorrien, *Soul in Society: The Making and Renewal of Social Christianity* (Minneapolis: Fortress, 1995), 221–232.

1. Gregory Baum, "Personal Experiences and Styles of Thought," in *Journeys: The Impact of Personal Experience on Religious Thought*, ed. Gregory Baum (New York: Paulist, 1975), 5–33, quote 6; Gregory Baum to author, September 11, 2005.

2. Gregory Baum, "Afterword," in *Faith That Transforms: Essays in Honor of Gregory Baum*, ed. Mary Jo Leedy, N.D.S., and Mary Ann Hinsdale, I.H.M. (New York: Paulist, 1987), 135–136; Baum, "A Response to Haight, Hutchinson, Simpson, and Rotstein," *Toronto Journal of Theology* 3 (fall 1987): 203–208; Baum to author, September 11, 2005.

3. Gregory Baum, *Man Becoming: God in Secular Experience* (New York: Herder and Herder, 1970), quote ix.

4. Gregory Baum, *Is the New Testament Anti-Semitic? A Re-Examination of the New Testament*, rev. ed. (Glen Rock, N.J.: Paulist, 1965 [1961]), 14–15; Baum, "Personal Experience and Styles of Thought," quote 13.

5. Baum, *Is the New Testament Anti-Semitic?* 15; Baum, "Personal Experience and Styles of Thought," quote 13; Jules Isaac, *Jesus and Israel*, trans. Sally Gran (New York: Holt, Rinehart and Winston, 1971); see Isaac, *Has Anti-Semitism Roots in Christianity?* trans. Dorothy Parker and James Parkes (New York: National Council of Christians and Jews, 1961).

6. Baum devoted a separate chapter to each gospel and the Acts of the Apostles, and a four-part, 121-page chapter to Paul.

7. Baum, *Is the New Testament Anti-Semitic?* 17, 21.

8. Ibid., 32–33.

9. Baum, *Man Becoming*, ix.

10. See Karl Rahner, *Geist in Welt: Zur Metaphysik der endlichen Erkenntnis bei Thomas von Aquin*, 2nd ed. (revised by Johannes B. Metz, München: Kösel-Verlag, 1957 [1940]; English ed., *Spirit in the World*, trans. William Dych, S.J., New York: Herder and Herder, 1968).

11. Gregory Baum, *That They May Be One: A Study of Papal Doctrine (Leo XIII–Pius XII)*, (Westminster, Md.: Newman, 1958), 33–76, 117–119.

12. Gregory Baum, *Progress and Perspectives: The Catholic Quest for Christian Unity* (New York: Sheed and Ward, 1962), 182–190.

13. See Rudolf Otto, *The Idea of the Holy*, trans. John W. Harvey (London: Oxford University Press, 1928); Otto, *Naturalism and Religion*, trans. J. Arthur and Margaret Thomson (New York: G. P. Putnam's, n.d); Wilhelm Bousset, *What Is Religion?* trans. F. B. Low (New York: G. P. Putnam's, 1907).

14. See Theodore Parker, *A Discourse on Matters Pertaining to Religion* (New York: G. P. Putnam's, 1877); Gary Dorrien, *The Making of American Liberal Theology: Imagining Progressive Religion, 1805–1900* (Louisville: Westminster John Knox, 2001).

15. Borden Parker Bowne, "The Christian Revelation," *Zion's Herald* 74 (June 10, 1896), reprinted in Bowne, *Studies in Christianity* (Boston: Houghton Mifflin, 1919), quote 19.

16. See Gary Dorrien, *The Making of American Liberal Theology: Idealism, Realism, and Modernity, 1900–1950* (Louisville: Westminster John Knox, 2003), 21–150.

17. See Borden Parker Bowne, *Theory of Thought and Knowledge* (New York: Harper & Brothers, 1897); Bowne, *Metaphysics* (New York: Harper & Brothers, 1898); Bowne, *Theism* (New York: American Book Company, 1902); Bowne, *Personalism* (Boston: Houghton, Mifflin 1908), Bowne, *The Essence of Religion* (Boston: Houghton, Mifflin, 1910); Edgar S. Brightman, *A Philosophy of Religion* (New York: Prentice Hall, 1940); Brightman, *The Problem of God* (New York: Abingdon, 1930); Albert C. Knudson, *The Philosophy of Personalism: A Study in the Metaphysics of Religion* (New York: Abingdon, 1927); Knudson, *The Doctrine of God* (New York: Abingdon-Cokesbury, 1930); Walter G. Muelder, *Foundations of the Responsible Society* (New York: Abingdon, 1959); L. Harold DeWolf, *A Theology of the Living Church* (New York: Harper & Brothers, 1953); Martin Luther King Jr., "A Comparison of the Conceptions of God in the Thinking of Paul Tillich and Henry Nelson Wieman," Ph.D. dissertation, Boston University, 1955, reprinted in Clayborne Carson, ed., *The Papers of Martin Luther King Jr.* (Berkeley: University of California Press, 1994), 2:339–544; King, *Stride Toward Freedom: The Montgomery Story* (New York: Harper & Brothers, 1958).

18. Harry Emerson Fosdick, *As I See Religion* (New York: Grosset & Dunlap, 1932); Fosdick, *The Power to See It Through* (New York: Harper & Brothers, 1935); Fosdick, *Christianity and Progress* (New York: Fleming H. Revell, 1922).

19. Reinhold Niebuhr, *An Interpretation of Christian Ethics* (New York: Harper & Brothers, 1935), quote 105; see Niebuhr, *Moral Man and Immoral Society: A Study in Ethics and Politics* (New York: Scribner's, 1932); Niebuhr, *Reflections on the End of an Era* (New York: Scribner's, 1934).

20. William James, *A Pluralistic Universe* (New York: Longmans, Green, 1909); Horace Kallen, *Cultural Pluralism and the American Idea* (Philadelphia: University of Pennsylvania Press, 1956).

21. Editorial, "Pluralism—National Menace," *Christian Century* 68 (June 13, 1951), 701–703; see Martin E. Marty, *The One and the Many: America's Struggle for the Common Good* (Cambridge, Mass.: Harvard University Press, 1997), 80–81.

22. See Charles Clayton Morrison, *The Social Gospel and the Christian Cultus* (New York: Harper & Brothers, 1933).

23. Charles Clayton Morrison, *Can Protestantism Win America?* (New York: Harper & Brothers, 1948).

24. Ibid., quotes 4, 86–87.

25. Ibid., quote 87.

26. Ibid., 177–178.

27. John Courtney Murray, "Dr. Morrison and the First Amendment," *America* 78 (March 6, 1948), 627–629; Murray, "Dr. Morrison and the First Amendment, II," *America* 78 (March 20, 1948), 683–686; Morrison, *Can Protestantism Win America?* 87–97.

28. John Courtney Murray, *We Hold These Truths: Catholic Reflections on the American Proposition* (New York: Sheed and Ward, 1960); quotes 41, 43.; see Murray, "The Problem of Pluralism in America," *Thought* 24 (summer 1954): 165–208; reprinted in *Catholicism in American Culture* (New Rochelle, N.Y.: College of New Rochelle, 1955), 13–38; short version reprinted in *Commonweal* 60 (August 1954), 463–468; a less pro-American version, titled "Church, State, and Religious Liberty," appeared in *The Catholic Mind* 57 (May–June 1959), 201–215; Murrary, *We Hold These Truths*, chaps 1, 2; Murray, S.J., "The Catholic Position: A Reply," *American Mercury* 69 (September 1949), 274–283; Murray, "Natural Law and the Public Consensus," in *Natural Law and Modern Society*, ed. John Cogley (Cleveland: World, 1963), 62–63.

29. Murray, *We Hold These Truths*, 48–49.

30. Ibid., 54.

31. Baum, *Progress and Perspectives*, 191–192.

32. See Maurice Blondel, *L'Action: Essai d'une critique de la vie et d'une science de la pratique*, repr. (Paris: F. Alcan, 1937 [1893]); Blondel, *The Letter on Apologetics, and History and Dogma* (London: Harvill, 1964); Joseph Maréchal, *Le point de départ de la métaphysique*, 2nd ed., 5 vols. (Bruxelles: L'Edition universelle; Paris: Descleé de Brouwer, 1944–1949); Karl Rahner, *Geist in Welt*; Rahner, *Schriften Zur Theologie*, 9 vols. (Einsiedeln: Benziger Verlag, 1959–

1970). Baum cited this work and, as it became available, the English edition. Karl Rahner, "Christianity and the Non-Christian Religions," *Theological Investigations*, 23 vols. (London: Darton, Longman & Todd, 1966), 5:121–131; *Lumen Gentium*: Dogmatic Constitution on the Church, November 21, 1964, *Vatican Council II: Vol. 1, The Conciliar and Postconciliar Documents*, 350–358.

33. Gregory Baum, "The Church Needs a Theology of Conflict," *U.S. Catholic* 34 (December 1968): 18–20; Baum, "The New Ecclesiology," *Commonweal* 91 (October 31, 1969), 123–128; Baum, "Personal Experiences and Styles of Thought," 28; Rebecca McKenna, "The Transformative Mission of the Church in the Thought of Gregory Baum," *Theological Studies* 59 (December 1998): 608–635; see Gregory Baum, *Religion and Alienation: A Theological Reading of Sociology* (New York: Paulist, 1975); Baum, "Personal Testimony to Sociology," *The Ecumenist* 8 (1969), 1–4; Baum, *The Social Imperative* (New York: Paulist, 1979); Baum, *Catholics and Canadian Socialism: Political Thoughts in the Thirties and Forties* (New York: Paulist, 1980); Baum, *The Priority of Labor: A Commentary on "Laborem exercens," Encyclical Letter of Pope John Paul II* (New York: Paulist, 1982); Baum, with Duncan Cameron, *Ethics and Economics: Canada's Catholic Bishops on the Economic Crisis* (Toronto: James Lorimer, 1984); Baum, *Theology and Society* (New York: Paulist, 1987); Baum, coeditor with Robert Ellsberg, *The Logic of Solidarity: Commentaries on Pope John Paul II's Encyclical on Social Concern* (Maryknoll, N.Y.: Orbis Books, 1989); Baum, *Essays in Critical Theology* (Kansas City, Mo.: Sheed and Ward, 1994); Baum, ed., *The Twentieth Century: A Theological Overview* (Maryknoll, N.Y.: Orbis Books, 1999).

34. Gregory Baum, Introduction to Rosemary Radford Ruether, *Faith and Fratricide: The Theological Roots of Anti-Semitism* (New York: Seabury, 1974), 5–6.

35. Ibid., 7.

36. Ruether, *Faith and Fratricide*, 64–116, 226–261; Baum, introduction to *Faith and Fratricide*, quotes 12–13.

18. The Obama Phenomenon and Presidency

The sections of this chapter are reprinted from, respectively, "Hope or Hype?" *Christian Century*, May 20, 2007; "Yes We Can . . . Change the Subject?" Public Broadcasting System, *Religion and Ethics Newsweekly: One Nation*, August 26, 2008; "Visible Man Rising," Public Broadcasting System, *Religion and Ethics Newsweekly: One Nation*, September 2, 2008; "Impulsive Distractions," Public Broadcasting System, *Religion and Ethics Newsweekly: One Nation*, September 3, 2008; "Back to the Subject," Public Broadcasting System, *Religion and Ethics Newsweekly: One Nation*, September 9, 2008; "Taking Social Investment Seriously," Public Broadcasting System, *Religion and Ethics Newsweekly: One Nation*, September 12, 2008, and "Taking Social Investment Seriously," *Tikkun Online*, December 17, 2008; and "Health-care Fix: The Role of a Public Option," *Christian Century*, July 14, 2009.

1. See Colin L. Powell, *My American Journey* (New York: Ballantine, 1995).

2. Barack Obama, *The Audacity of Hope: Thoughts on Reclaiming the American Dream* (New York: Crown, 2006), 18.

3. Ibid., 19.

4. Ibid., quote 120.

5. See Barack Obama, *Dreams from My Father: A Story of Race and Inheritance*, 2nd ed. (New York: Random House, 2007 [1995]).

6. Obama, *The Audacity of Hope: Thoughts on Reclaiming the American Dream*, 208.

7. Ibid., quote 294.

8. Ibid., quotes 38, 240.

9. Joe Klein, "The Fresh Face," *Time* (October 15, 2006).

10. Obama, *The Audacity of Hope*, 247.

11. Ibid., 247.

12. Ibid., 248.

13. Barack Obama, "Out of Many, One," Keynote Speech, Democratic National Convention, Boston, Mass., July 27, 2004, http://usliberals.about.com (accessed January 20, 2008).

14. Obama, *The Audacity of Hope*, 214.

15. Ibid., 223–224.

16. Ibid., 247.

17. Shelby Steele, *A Bound Man: Why We Are Excited About Obama and Why He Can't Win* (New York: Free Press, 2008).

19. Social Ethics in the Making

This is an abridged version of my Reinhold Niebuhr Inaugural Lecture at Union Theological Seminary on January 30, 2007.

1. See Francis Greenwood Peabody, *Jesus Christ and the Social Question* (New York: Macmillan, 1900); William Jewett Tucker, *My Generation: An Autobiographical Interpretation* (Boston: Houghton Mifflin, 1919); J. H. W. Stuckenberg, *Christian Sociology* (London: R. D. Dickinson, 1881); Graham Taylor, *Religion in Social Action* (New York: Dodd, Mead, 1913); Taylor, *Pioneering on Social Frontiers* (Chicago: University of Chicago Press, 1930); Peabody, *A Little Boy in Little Boston: Reminiscences of Childhood* (Cambridge: n.p., 1935), 17–19; Peabody, *Harvard in the Sixties: A Boy's Eye View* (Cambridge: n.p., 1935), 19–20; William Jewett Tucker, *My Generation: An Autobiographical Interpretation* (Bos-

ton: Houghton Mifflin, 1919); J. H. W. Stuckenberg, *Christian Sociology* (London: R. D. Dickinson, 1881); Graham Taylor, *Religion in Social Action* (New York: Dodd, Mead, 1913); Taylor, *Pioneering on Social Frontiers* (Chicago: University of Chicago Press, 1930).

2. Francis Greenwood Peabody, *Reminiscences of Present-Day Saints* (Boston: Houghton Mifflin, 1927), quotes 65, 66.

3. Ibid., 67–68.

4. Ibid., 114–117; see Sidney E. Ahlstrom, "The Middle Period (1840–80)," in *The Harvard Divinity School: Its Place in Harvard University and in American Culture*, ed. George Huntston Williams (Boston: Beacon, 1954), 78–116; Robert S. Morison, "The First Half Century of the Divinity School," *Addresses Delivered at the Observance of the 100th Anniversary of the Establishment of the Harvard Divinity School* (Cambridge, Mass.: Harvard University Press, 1917), 14–15.

5. See Edward Bellamy, *Looking Backward, 2000–1887*, 2nd ed. (Cambridge, Mass.: Harvard University Press, 1967 [1888]); Stephen Colwell, *New themes for the Protestant clergy: creeds without charity, theology without humanity, Protestantism without Christianity; with notes on the literature of charity, population, pauperism, political economy, and Protestantism* (Philadelphia: Lippincott, Grambo, 1851); Henry Demarest Lloyd, *Wealth against Commonwealth* (New York: Harper & Brothers, 1894).

6. See Josiah Strong, *Our Country, Its Possible Future and Its Present Crisis*, rev. ed. (New York: Baker & Taylor, 1891 [1886]).

7. See Gladys Bryson, "The Emergence of the Social Sciences from Moral Philosophy," *International Journal of Ethics* 42 (April 1932): 304–307; Bryson, "Sociology Considered as Moral Philosophy," *Sociological Review* 24 (January 1932): 26–36; Bryson, "The Comparable Interests of the Old Moral Philosophy and the Modern Social Sciences," *Social Forces* 11 (October 1932): 19–27.

8. Thomas Reid, *An Inquiry into the Human Mind, on the principles of Common Sense*, 3rd ed. (Dublin: R. Marchbank, 1779); abridged edition reprinted in Reid, *Inquiry and Essays*, ed. Ronald E. Beanblossom and Keith Lehrer (Indianapolis: Hackett, 1983), quote 118; Adam Ferguson, *Principles of Moral and Political Science* (Edinburgh: A. Strahan & T. Cadell, 1792); Frances Hutcheson, *A System of Moral Philosophy in Three Books*, 2 vols. (Glasgow: R. & A. Foulis, 1755); Richard Price, *A Review of the Principal Questions and Difficulties in Morals*, 2nd ed. (London: T. Cadell, 1769); see Reid, "Essay Five: Of Morals," in *Essays on the Intellectual Powers of Man* (1785), reprinted in Reid, *Inquiry and Essays*, 351–368; see D. O. Thomas, *The Honest Mind: The Thought and Work of Richard Price* (Oxford: Oxford University Press, 1977); see Roger L. Emerson, "Science and Moral Philosophy in the Scottish Enlightenment," in *Studies in the Philosophy of the Scottish Enlightenment*, ed. M. A. Stewart (Oxford: Clarendon, 1990), 32–38; Mark A. Noll, "Common Sense Traditions and American Evangelical Thought," *American Quarterly* 37 (1985): 216–238; Daniel Walker

Howe, *The Unitarian Conscience: Harvard Moral Philosophy, 1805–1861* (Cambridge, Mass.: Harvard University Press, 1970).

9. George L. Prentiss, *The Bright Side of Life: Glimpses of It Through Fourscore Years*, 2 vols. (Asbury Park, N.J.: Press of M., W., & C. Pennypacker, 1901), 2:395; cited in James Dombrowski, *The Early Days of Christian Socialism in America* (New York: Columbia University Press, 1936), 61–62.

10. David B. Potts, "Social Ethics at Harvard, 1881–1931: A Study in Academic Activism," in *Social Sciences at Harvard, 1860–1920: From Inculcation to the Open Mind*, ed. Paul Buck (Cambridge, Mass.: Harvard University Press, 1965), 94–96, "Peabo's" 95; Peabody, *Reminiscences of Present-Day Saints*, "why not" and "drainage" 136–137; Grace Cumming Long, "The Ethics of Francis Greenwood Peabody: A Century of Christian Social Ethics," *Journal of Religious Ethics* 18 (spring 1990): 56.

11. Francis Greenwood Peabody, review of *The Theory of Morals* by Paul Janet, *Science* 3 (March 21, 1884), 360–362; Peabody, "The Philosophy of the Social Questions," *Andover Review* 8 (December 1887): 561–573, 565–566; Peabody, "Social Reforms as Subjects of University Study," *Independent* 40 (January 14, 1886), 5–6.

12. Francis Greenwood Peabody, *The Approach to the Social Question* (New York: Macmillan, 1909), 34–35.

13. Remarks by Bennett in 1961 colloquium discussion, *Reinhold Niebuhr: A Prophetic Voice in Our Time*, ed. Harold R. Landon (Greenwich, Conn: Seabury, 1962), 88, 92–93.

14. Eugene P. Link, *Labor-Religion Prophet: The Times and Life of Harry F. Ward*, (Boulder, Colo.: Westview, 1984), 234; see Aimee Isgrig Horton, *The Highlander Folk School: A History of Its Major Programs, 1932–1961* (Brooklyn, N.Y.: Carlson, 1989); Frank T. Adams, *James A. Dombrowski: An American Heretic, 1897–1983* (Knoxville: University of Tennessee Press, 1992).

15. John C. Bennett, *Christian Ethics and Social Policy* (New York: Scribner's, 1946).

16. See John A. Ryan, *Distributive Justice: The Right and Wrong of our Present Distribution of Wealth* (New York: Macmillan, 1925); John Courtney Murray, S.J., *We Hold These Truths: Catholic Reflections on the American Proposition* (Kansas City, Mo.: Sheed and Ward, 1960); Walter G. Muelder, *The Ethical Edge of Christian Theology: Forty Years of Communitarian Personalism* (New York: Edwin Mellen, 1983); Henry Nelson Wieman, *The Source of Human Good* (Carbondale: Southern Illinois University Press, 1946); Bernard E. Meland, *America's Spiritual Culture* (New York: Harper & Brothers, 1948).

17. See Edgar Gardner Murphy, *Problems of the Present South: A Discussion of the Educational, Industrial, and Political Issues in the Southern States* (New York: Macmillan, 1904); Murphy, *The Basis of Ascendancy: A Discussion of*

Certain Principles of Public Policy Involved in the Development of the Southern States (New York: Longmans, Green, 1908); Thomas Dixon Jr., *The Clansman: An Historical Romance of the Ku Klux Klan* (New York: Doubleday, Page, 1905); Dixon, *Leopard's Spots: A Romance of the White Man's Burden, 1865–1900* (New York: Doubleday, Page, 1902); Dixon, *The Sins of the Father: A Romance of the South* (New York: D. Appleton, 1912).

18. See Ralph E. Luker, *The Social Gospel in Black and White: American Racial Reform, 1885–1912* (Chapel Hill: University of North Carolina Press, 1991); Ronald C. White Jr., *Liberty and Justice for All: Racial Reform and the Social Gospel (1877–1925)* (New York: Harper & Row, 1990); David M. Reimers, *White Protestantism and the Negro* (New York: Oxford University Press, 1965).

19. See Francis Greenwood Peabody, *Education for Life: The Story of Hampton Institute* (Garden City, N.Y.: Doubleday, Page, 1918), quotes xii, xiii; Peabody, "If Lincoln Came to Hampton," *Southern Workman* 51 (April 1922): 162.

20. Editorial, "Two Typical Leaders," *The Outlook* 74 (May 23, 1903), 214–216; see Booker T. Washington, *Up from Slavery, an Autobiography* (New York: Doubleday, Page, 1901); W. E. B. Du Bois, *The Souls of Black Folk* (Chicago: A. C. McClurg, 1903), 53–54; Luker, *The Social Gospel in Black and White*, 214–216.

21. Peabody, *Education for Life*, 321.

22. Walter Rauschenbusch (unsigned), "What Shall We Do with the Germans" (pamphlet, 1895), quote; Walter Rauschenbusch (unsigned), "The German Seminary in Rochester" (pamphlet, 1897), Box 47, Rauschenbusch Family Collection; Walter Rauschenbusch, "The Contribution of Germany to the National Life of America," Commencement address, Fiftieth Anniversary of the Rochester Theological Seminary German Department, Box 92, Rauschenbusch Family Collection, quoted in *Rochester Democrat and Chronicle*, May 8, 1902.

23. Walter Rauschenbusch, *Christianizing the Social Order* (New York: Macmillan, 1912), 60; Rauschenbusch, *A Theology for the Social Gospel* (New York: Macmillan, 1917), 79; Rauschenbusch, "The Belated Races and the Social Problems," *Methodist Review* 40 (April 1914): 258.

24. Reverdy C. Ransom, "The Negro, The Hope or the Despair of Christianity," Address to the World Fellowship of Faiths, Second Parliament of Religions, Chicago, Ill., 1933, published in Ransom, *The Negro: The Hope or the Despair of Christianity* (Boston: Ruth Hill, 1935), quote 5.

25. W. E. B. Du Bois, "A Tribute to Reverdy Cassius Ransom," *A.M.E. Church Review* (April–June 1959): 1; reprinted in Anthony B. Pinn, ed., *Making the Gospel Plain: The Writings of Bishop Reverdy C. Ransom* (Harrisburg, Pa.: Trinity, 1999), xvii–xix.

26. See James H. Cone, *Risks of Faith: The Emergence of Black Theology of Liberation, 1968–1998* (Boston: Beacon, 1999), 130–137; Cone, "Looking

Backward, Going Forward: Black Theology as Public Theology," in *Black Faith and Public Talk: Critical Essays on James H. Cone's Black Theology and Black Power*, ed. Dwight N. Hopkins (Maryknoll, N.Y.: Orbis Books, 1999), 246–259; Cone, "Theology's Great Sin: Silence in the Face of White Supremacy," *Union Seminary Quarterly Review* 55 (2001): 1–14.

27. Reinhold Niebuhr, *Pious and Secular America* (New York: Scribner's, 1958), 76.

INDEX

Coffin, Henry Sloane, 52, 56–57
Cohen, Eliot, 217
cold war ideology: American imperialism and, 262–63; Barthianism
and, 42–43; neoconservatives and,
193–213; Niebuhr's influence on,
39–40, 45, 47, 58–65; Podhoretz on,
232; Thomas and, 102–3
Coleman, Monica, 347
collective security ideology: historical
context for, 277–82; liberal internationalism and, 271–77; terrorism
and, 252
Collegium of Officers of the United
Church of Christ (USA), 270
Collier's magazine, 100
Colombia, U.S. invasion of, 260
colonialism, American imperialism and,
259–61, 269
Color Purple, The (Walker), 340–41
Colwell, Stephen, 396
Commentary magazine, xvii, 117, 187,
189, 191–92, 196–97, 200, 210
Commission for the Study of Automation, 190
Committee for a Sane Nuclear Policy,
88, 106–7
Committee on the Present Danger
(CPD), 193, 197, 199
Commodities Future Trading Commis-
sion, 159
Commodity Futures Modernization Act,
153
Commonweal magazine, 116
communism: American imperialism and,
262–63; Barth and Niebuhr's debate
over, 42–44; Christian socialism and,
137–39, 141–42; democratic globalism and, 214–15; Harrington's views
on, 113–17, 120–25; labor unions
and, 94–95; neoconservatives and,
191–93, 198–202, 205–6, 213, 232;
Niebuhr's view of, 39–40, 47, 54–65;
Thomas and, 95–98, 104–10; U.S.
Socialist Party and, 90
Communist Labor Party, 90
Communist Manifesto (Marx and Engels), 123, 127
community, neoliberal politics of, 147–48

community finance corporations, 173
community land trusts, 173
community of nations: American exceptionalism and, 259–85; foreign policy
and ideology of, 258
commutative justice, defined, x–xi
Cone, James, xviii, 48, 306, 314, 322,
405, 407
Confederation of Swedish Trade Unions,
180
Conference for Progressive Political Action (CPPA), 91
Congress for Cultural Freedom, 106–7
conservatism: Middle East policy and,
228–32; neoconservatives and, 187–
90, 206–10; Old Right conservatism,
283–85; realism on foreign policy
and, 251–58; West and, 323–26
consumption, economic democracy and,
176–79
Cook, Joseph, 401
Cooke, Willie P., 305
cooperative ownership: democratic
realism and public bank theory
and, 179–84; economic democracy
and, 169–75; liberal theology and,
361–66; social gospel movement and,
8–11
Copeland, M. Shawn, 344
Copeland, Warren, 137
Corey, Lewis, 57
Cornel West Reader, The, 323, 328
Cort, John C., xvi
Cosby, Bill, 379
Costen, James, 338
councilist Marxism, West's study of,
307–10
Council of Constantinople, 291
Counts, George, 57
Cox, Harvey, xvi, 137
Cox, Oliver, 311–12, 320
Crapsey, Algernon, 401
credit-default swaps, economic crash
and, 153–55
crisis theology, emergence of, 29
Critique of Political Economy (Marx),
126–27
Croce, Arlene, 192
Croly, Herbert, 62